D1065508

A Reference Guide
to Historical Fiction
for Children
and Young Adults

A Reference Guide
to Historical Fiction
for Children
and Young Adults

LYNDA G. ADAMSON

GREENWOOD PRESS

NEW YORK · WESTPORT, CONNECTICUT · LONDON

Library of Congress Cataloging-in-Publication Data

Adamson, Lynda G.
  A reference guide to historical fiction for children and young adults.

  Bibliography: p.
  Includes index.
    1. Children's stories—Bibliography.   2. Young adult
fiction—Bibliography.   3. Historical fiction—
Bibliography.   4. Bibliography—Best books—Children's
stories.   5. Bibliography—Best books—Young adult
fiction.   6. Bibliography—Best books—Historical
fiction.   I. Title.
Z1037.A267   1987 [PN1009.A1]   016.80883'81   87-7533
ISBN 0-313-25002-2 (lib. bdg. : alk. paper)

British Library Cataloguing in Publication Data is available.

Library of Congress Catalog Card Number: 87-7533
ISBN: 0-313-25002-2

First published in 1987

Greenwood Press, Inc.
88 Post Road West, Westport, Connecticut 06881

Printed in the United States of America

The paper used in this book complies with the
Permanent Paper Standard issued by the National
Information Standards Organization (Z39.48-1984).

10 9 8 7 6 5 4 3 2 1

To Frank, Frank III, and Gregory

Contents

Preface   ix

Introduction   xiii

The Guide   **1**

APPENDIX A. Setting Dates and Locales   367

APPENDIX B. Age Level of Readability   379

APPENDIX C. Bibliography on Writing Historical Novels: Works by Authors Included in the Guide   391

APPENDIX D. Secondary Bibliography on Writers and Historical Novels Included in the Guide   393

Index   395

Preface

When adults need assistance selecting books for children and young adults about such topics as the American Civil War or Romans in Britain, all too many will be unaware of available books on the subject in either academic history or historical fiction. A major purpose of this work is to alleviate this situation by providing reference to appropriate historical fiction since it conveys ideas in a particularly meaningful way, with description of content and indication of setting date and locale, as well as reading and interest levels. With such information at hand, adults will be able to assemble a basic list of books on a subject for children and young adults that will yield both a history lesson and a worthwhile reading experience. Since the works selected are of recognized merit, historically accurate, and for the most part, well written, this volume is not simply an index. It is a guide. Although the guide makes no pretense of insightful literary criticism, the descriptions include analysis of style and themes along with evaluative comments.

Historical fiction recreates a particular historical period with or without historical figures as incidental characters. It is generally written about a time period in which the author has not lived or no more recently than one generation before its composition. For example, fiction written in 1987 must be set, at the latest, in 1967, for it to be considered historical. Fiction written in 1930 but set in 1925 does not fulfill this criterion for legitimate historical fiction.

Historical facts also provide the basis for novels employing time shifts or other ''supernatural'' occurrences. Since a fiction, according to Jill Paton Walsh, is something ''not known to be true,''[1] a fantasy is a fiction relying on something not known to occur in the logical world. Whether a work becomes labeled fiction or fantasy depends on this difference. Within these narrow confines, one must define a plot propelled by a psychological world as fantasy. If a novel, however, projects accurate history as a basis for plot progression, it belongs in this guide under the designation of historical fantasy.

Creators of historical fiction must be historians as well as writers. Writers and academic historians generally have the same information available, which they must form into a readable entity. Each researches the same family Bible, the court record, the diary, and the letter. One chooses a chronological factual report, while the other chooses to weave the facts into a narration. Readers must always remember that even the academic historian selects and reshuffles the facts to fit a unique and personal thesis. Thus, the history text has the same origin as the historical novel; the difference lies in the instrumentation. Some children and young adults find history books informative and entertaining. But too many others find them dry and irrelevant. Historical fiction provides protagonists with whom to identify, family life and social mores for comparison, and quite often a mystery plot to hold interest.

Historical fiction is valuable aesthetically and educationally. Read prior to or simultaneously with a history text, it can provide a base for historical study of an era. Since it allows historical periods to live through people of all social and economic classes, history teachers should strongly consider supplementing their basic texts with historical fiction. Other teachers should consider assigning historical fiction because it exhibits the qualities expected in good literature and has the added advantage of factual information presented aesthetically. Parents should encourage their children to read historical fiction for all of these reasons, in addition to the concept that it fosters comparison among the present condition and various conditions in the past that reveal that although social mores may change, human universals do not. It also establishes the sense that the reader belongs in a continuum rather than being isolated in the present. Plutarch said, ''I am all that has been, and is, and shall be.'' Children and young adults reading historical fiction often discover the same about themselves.

The scope of this guide extends to novels written since 1940 by authors who have either won an award or been honored or commended for at least one work of historical fiction for children and young adults. Novels written before 1940, including many award winners, are excluded because the plot development is often contrived and the characters stereotyped.

The historical novel for children and young adults evolved during and after World War II and began to fulfill its potential in the early 1950s. Short stories, unless published individually, are excluded, as is writing in genres other than historical fantasy and fiction. Another criterion is that the novels be generally available in libraries within the United States, although some of the novels are not currently in print. Novels unavailable in the U.S. Library of Congress have been excluded.

The major entries in this guide are arranged alphabetically according to the author's last name. Titles of works and protagonists, as well as historical personages, places, and relevant terms that clarify certain historical aspects of some of the novels, appear as short entries within the same alphabetical progression, with brief definitions and cross-references to the author entries as relevant. An asterisk signifies the presence of an entry.

Each author entry includes all of the writer's generally available historical novels. It opens with a section entitled ''Bibliography and Background,'' which

includes an alphabetical bibliography of the works discussed and brief biographical comments, including awards and pertinent information shared with the author
of this guide by the writer about particular historical periods of interest and his
or her creative processes. In the main body of the author entry, "Works,"
appears a short synopsis of each novel. Usually the discussion proceeds chronologically according to date of setting, although other patterns are employed
when more effective. Within the "Works" section, each title discussed appears
first in boldface type for easy spotting. A final paragraph comments briefly on
overall "Style and Themes." Since the included authors are recognized for
excellence, evaluative comments comparing novels of unequal quality have been
inserted when appropriate.

Four appendixes follow the main guide. Appendix A classifies works included
in the guide according to date of setting and locale. Appendix B lists works
according to age level of readability established by the Fry Readability Graph.[2]
Interest level noted in parentheses after each title is based on findings of reading
interest studies and on Lawrence Kohlberg's stages of moral development.[3]
Appendix C is a bibliography of works by authors of historical fiction about
writing historical novels. Appendix D is a secondary bibliography of writing
about the authors and novels included in the guide.

The guide may be used in several ways. One may search for a book title,
author, protagonist, time period, or readability level. For a book about the
Crusades for a twelve-year-old reader, two search strategies are suggested. For
the first, check the historical topic "Crusades" in the guide. Listed after the
brief definition are titles of books in which the Crusades play an important role,
and their authors. To find which of these books has a suitable reading and interest
level, consult Appendix B for reading level of twelve. A second method would
be to identify possible titles under the heading "The Crusades and the East,
1100–1299" in Appendix A. Included in this list are books in which the Crusades
is a setting but may or may not affect the action of the plot. After choosing
potential titles, check Appendix B to find titles listed at a readability level of
twelve. One book that fits is *Perilous Pilgrimage* by Henry Treece. The researcher
should then turn to the author entry, in this case, "Treece," and read the synopsis
of *Perilous Pilgrimage*. Further information about Treece can be gleaned from
the two other sections of his entry, "Bibliography and Background" and "Style
and Themes," as well as from synopses of his other books.

During my preparation of this guide, most of the authors discussed responded
to my questions about their reasons for writing historical fiction, their interest
in a particular time period, and their writing habits, with exciting and, sometimes,
inspirational answers. I thank them for their time and effort. Susan Roth, librarian
at Prince George's Community College, Largo, Maryland, helped me find books
and obtain borrowing privileges from the Library of Congress without which I
would have been unable to complete this guide in this lifetime. My editors at
Greenwood Press, Marilyn Brownstein, Beverly Miller, and John Donohue, have
offered thoughtful comments to clarify content and format in the guide. I thank

my friend and colleague William A. Fry for his support and encouragement throughout the project. I also thank my husband, Frank, for his willingness to read and reread the manuscript, editing and commenting throughout the process. Without his humor, neither of us could have coped. Most of all, I thank God for giving me the energy to finish, and to help me understand, in William Faulkner's words, that "the past is not dead; it is not even past."

NOTES

1. Jill Paton Walsh, "History is Fiction," *Horn Book* (February 1972): 22.

2. Edward Fry, "Fry's Readability Graph: Clarifications, Validity, and Extension," *Journal of Reading* (December 1977): 249.

3. In William Damon, *Social and Personality Development* (New York: W. W. Norton, 1983). See also Carol Gilligan, *In a Different Voice* (Cambridge, Mass.: Harvard University Press, 1982).

___ Introduction _____

The historical novel as a literary genre evolved and rose to heights of popularity in the early nineteenth century with the novels of Sir Walter Scott in England, as well as with authors in other countries, such as Alessandro Manzoni in Italy. In his essay *On the Historical Novel,* Manzoni discussed the difficulties of creating a work of art that incorporates both fact and fiction. He identified the form of historical fiction as concrete narrative utilizing dialogue with precise dates, places, and events. The content, he asserted, included customs and art, as well as social and economic class distinctions. Moreover, he traced the development of the historical novel back to the genre of the classical epic. Nearly one hundred years later, George Lukacs made the same conclusion although he had not read Manzoni. Manzoni, however, prophesied the demise of the historical novel; Lukacs did not.

Lukacs (1963) assesses Scott's novels by generalizing about values of historical fiction that relate directly to the values in historical fiction, as a genre, for children and young adults. The main character must be an ordinary figure because only the everyday life of people—"the joys and sorrows, crises and confusions"— can portray the broad "being of an age." When the reader sees the "personal destinies of a number of human beings coincide and interweave within the determining context of an historical crisis . . . , the historical crisis is never abstract, the split of the nation into warring parties always runs through the centre of the closest human relationships" (p. 41).

Lukacs begins to evaluate the genre itself by generalizing:

What matters therefore in the historical novel is not the re-telling of great historical events, but the poetic awakening of the people who figured in those events. What matters is that we should reexperience the social and human motives which led men to think, feel and act just as they did in historical reality. And it is a law of literary portrayal which first appears paradoxical, but then quite obvious, that in order to bring out these social and human motives of behavior, the outwardly insignificant events, the smaller (from without) relationships are better suited than the great monumental dramas of world history. (p. 42)

This exact literary portrayal of the historical has led some academic historicans to dismiss the validity of fictional accounts of fact. But Lukacs posits that the historical novel *"demonstrates* by *artistic* means that historical circumstances and characters existed in precisely such and such a way" (p. 43). Moreover, it allows an artistic *"connection* between the spontaneous reaction of the masses and the historical consciousness of the leading personalities" (p. 44). However, language theorists have bested Lukacs in defense of the genre. According to Sandra Bermann in her introduction to Manzoni's *On the Historical Novel,* the structuralist Roland Barthes believes that "facts" have nothing more than a linguistic existence and that historical " 'science, the narrative of past events, does not differ from imaginary narrative' " (p. 50). Barthes sees the historical discourse as referring to an exterior (past), but one can never reach that exterior outside of the discourse itself. Thus, fact and fiction, having the same reference, do not differ. Bermann "make[s] moot all problems particular to the genre, ethical no less than aesthetic," of historical fiction when she comments that deconstructionist theorists further destroy perceived differences between history and invention by considering them within "a single rhetorical plane" (p. 51). Whether one accepts the structuralist and deconstructionist theories of language and linguistics or continues to perceive a dichotomy between form and content, the creative literary artist alone can elicit an emotional reaction from the reader.

Of the "literary" genres, only the novel requires literacy. The novel anticipates a solitary reader reacting to its gestalt of words or, in Louise Rosenblatt's (1978) terms, transacting with its text. A text must "evoke" a response from a reader before it can come "alive." Then it exists in the "reality" of the reader's mind. Obviously, a novel must be aesthetically strong enough to hook the reader's psyche, to speak to the unconscious and subconscious dreams and fantasies. Children and young adults, like all other readers, will transact with texts that evoke responses from them. Aesthetic historical fiction with its added dimension can, perhaps, evoke even stronger responses than contemporary fiction. Feuchtwanger (1978) commented, "it is truly remarkable how art enhances the human capacity for lived experience. Genuine historical writing helps the reader to live his own experiences and compels him to recognize himself anew" (p. 144). Jung (1969) also felt that history could provide unexpected insights into individual psychological concerns.

Whether historical fiction or historical fantasy, those novels in which the authors use dreams, what Campbell (1968) calls "personalized myth" (p. 19) or ritual patterns, have depth of theme and meaning not present in those without them. Jung says, "The man who thinks he can live without myth, or outside it, is an exception. He is like one uprooted, having no true link either with the past, or with the ancestral life which continues within him" (p. 5). Of qualities necessary in an aesthetic text, language—imagery and metaphor—remains of utmost importance. Since language must also have contextual substance, narrative parallels the significance of language. However, the language and the narrative must unify with character and thematic development to create a gestalt before the reader can evoke the intangible poem pulsing inside the text.

Goodrich (1961) thinks that the need for the aesthetic closely relates to the need for the ritualistic. She sees myths as the backbone of a culture, imbedded in the collective memory and the common property of every human. Thus aesthetic texts transacting with the reader can transmit a culture's values. Modern characters who progress through the rituals of the monomyth, as Joseph Campbell defines it, give depth of meaning to texts. Such characters can evoke strong responses from readers because the characters move to what Campbell calls the "causal zones of the psyche where the difficulties really reside [where they] clarify the difficulties, eradicate them and break through to the undistorted, direct experience and assimulation of archetypal images" (p. 19). The text can often reassure a young reader's contemporary view of self and others by showing how humans have handled themselves throughout their daily lives and how they have handled separation from their groups, endured ordeals of initiation, and returned to become valued members of their societies throughout the process of history.

Historical writing, often set during times of tribal or national difficulties, perhaps more than any other literary genre places characters in situations where they must make specific choices to accept or reject responsibilities imposed upon them. When characters react according to unspoken but humanly perceived sets of myths and rituals, the reader can gain insight from both their failures and successes. Campbell believes that a "restriction of consciousness" (p. 121) causes a person to be unable to cope with a situation. Conversely, every success must rely on an expansion of consciousness. Worthwhile historical writing not only relays accurate historical background by incorporating known facts and rituals but also presents heroes and heroines who expand their consciousness by completing the sequence of rituals in the monomyth.

The best fiction surpasses interesting narrative by having something extra that catches the reader's imagination. The reader must sense that the writer has not provided all the answers—in fact, may not even have stated all of the questions. Lukacs believes that the hero of a historical fiction must be a "personality complete" psychologically "in order to fulfil [sic] his historic mission in the crisis" (p. 38) of the novel. In this perception of character, the historical novel for children and young adults differs from that for adult readers. A closer examination of some of the patterns in the best historical novels for children and young adults in this guide reveals the mythological formula of the hero and heroine facing perils and obstacles during their quests for happiness and good fortune.

The first step in the monomyth, the protagonist's initial separation from the tribe or family, sometimes occurs not by choice but by circumstance. Outcasts, orphans, the disabled, and the abused automatically confront separation. Several protagonists must endure either exile from or ostracism within their communities. War uproots Maadah in *Madatan,* Aquila in *The Lantern Bearers,* and Yuki in

Journey to Topaz, while it isolates Patty in *Summer of My German Soldier.* Undeserved disgrace faces Alan in *Mohawk Valley* and Margaret in *Time of Trial.* Government decree removes Bright Morning from her home in *Sing Down the Moon.*

Although only one protagonist faces severe physical abuse—Willy in *Good Night, Mr. Tom*—several have endured lifetime disabilities. Drem *(Warrior Scarlet)* hides his withered hand. Coll *(The Stronghold),* Lovel *(The Witch's Brat),* and Alfred Daneleg *(The Namesake)* limp. Jesse *(A Donkey for the King)* remains mute, and Adam *(Manwolf)* copes with beastly features. Other characters develop disabilites after the age of ten and handle them less gracefully—Johnny in *Johnny Tremain,* Marcus in *The Eagle of the Ninth,* and Robin in *The Door in the Wall.*

Because a major accomplishment during adolescence is independence from parental control, the protagonist as orphan permeates all genres of literature for children and young adults. Some of the orphans on the threshold of their individual quests include Ranofer *(The Golden Goblet),* Daniel *(The Bronze Bow),* Randal *(Knight's Fee),* Muno *(The Sign of the Chrysanthemum),* John *(Lost John),* Adam and Gilly *(The 13th Member),* Kit *(The Witch of Blackbird Pond),* Sarah *(Sarah Bishop),* Peter *(The Sentinels),* Willie *(The Snowbird),* and Christina *(Flambards).* Many of the remaining protagonists, although having lost only one parent, are psychological orphans because the living parent exerts little, if any, influence.

Slavery or imprisonment separates others. Mara *(Mara, Daughter of the Nile),* Silvester *(The Dancing Bear),* and Juan *(I, Juan de Pareja)* recall no life outside slavery. Phaedrus, a gladiator in *The Mark of the Horse Lord,* Jestyn *(Blood Feud),* and Jessie *(The Slave Dancer)* relish life before enslavement. Esteban in *The King's Fifth* remembers freedom from within his jail cell.

A final category of hero or heroine whom circumstance has separated from society is the artist. Although physically situated within a group, the artist remains psychologically distinct. The artist or scientist dedicates his or her being, according to Campbell, not to morals of the time but to art: "He is the hero of the way of thought—singlehearted, courageous, and full of faith that the truth, as he finds it, shall make us free" (p. 24). The protagonist dedicated to art still faces initiation, but a unique comprehension of consciousness places him or her closer to the quest threshold. Of the artists, Lubrin *(Sun Horse, Moon Horse),* Stephen *(One is One),* and Juan *(I, Juan de Pareja)* prefer drawing pictures and painting. Geoffrey in *The Great House* longs to become an architect. Adam *(Adam of the Road)* and Jack *(Trumpets of the West)* are musicians. Jiro *(The Master Puppeteer)* creates puppet movements. Bridie in *A Sound of Chariots* loses herself in the wonder of words.

Not separated by circumstance, many protagonists must make a conscious choice to abandon their childhood security. The Vikings who leave the North do so willingly. Other men (and Deborah in *I'm Deborah Sampson*) march toward war with expectations of excitement and glory. Beth in *The Wind Eye* sails from home to Lindisfarne, and Idrum in *A Candle at Dusk* expectantly departs home to study elsewhere. Julian in the Scott O'Dell trilogy *(The Captive, The Feathered Serpent,* and *The Amethyst Ring)* travels excitedly to the New World, and Meribah leaves the security of home for the western frontier in *Beyond the Divide.* Although they stay at home, Shad in *Shadrach's Crossing* and Jethro in *Across Five Aprils* make decisions contrary to or without parental guidance. Many of the characters in Barbara Willard's Mantlemass books psychologically separate from their families.

As protagonists begin their individual quests, they stand at the threshold of adventure. Campbell notes that either an old crone or a wise man, usually unrelated to the protagonist, waits nearby to help them choose the correct paths as they cross the threshold. In these novels, the exceptions occur when an older person does not appear. Such an omission causes the protagonist to begin a chaotic journey that must be reversed in order to prevent a tragic end. Because Friedrich, in *Friedrich,* has no one to retrieve him from Hitler's chaos, he cannot survive.

The second ritual in the monomyth, initiation, occurs as the protagonist faces psychological ordeals. Obvious initiation rites occur in some Native American tribes where the male must make a solitary search for his "medicine" or spirit in the desert. After he experiences his vision, he returns to the tribe and functions as an adult member. In British tribes, boys ended a six or seven years' stay in a Boys' House by single-handedly killing a wolf. Those who failed showed their inability to protect others and were cast out from the tribal family. These rituals symbolize the basic needs of the culture, to sacrifice fears in order to protect.

Protagonists endure various types of journeys of which the most symbolic is the sea journey. Included among those who cross the sea, and who return ready for adult responsibilities, are Jim *(The 290),* Tom *(The Hawk that Dare Not Fly by Day),* Harry *(The Hawk),* Penitence *(Campion Towers),* Kit *(The Witch of Blackbird Pond),* Alan *(Mohawk Valley),* and Erik *(Chase Me, Catch Nobody!).* Those who journey across vast expanses of land on their quests include Jacob *(They Had a Horse),* Jack *(Trumpets in the West),* Sarah *(Sarah Bishop),* Deborah *(I'm Deborah Sampson),* Theo *(Tulku),* and Meriba *(Beyond the Divide).*

On the way to initiation and "at-one-ment" (atonement) with the mythological father-mother, women and men, as god and goddess or tempter and temptress, can either help or hinder protagonists. Protagonists in historical fiction most often encounter the tempter-temptress or trickster who tries to inhibit their development. Sarah *(Sarah Bishop)* and Takiko *(Of Nightingales That Weep)* meet the tempter as does Mara *(Mara, Daughter of the Nile).* Phaedrus *(The Mark of the Horse Lord),* Silvester *(The Dancing Bear),* and Muna *(The Sign of the Chrysanthemum)* are examples of protagonists who encounter a temptress. Only a few seem to gain help from a benevolent figure—a god or goddess. Those who do include Idrun *(A Candle at Dusk),* Brus and Jan *(Black Fox of Lorne),* and Havelock *(Havelock the Dane).*

The goal of the hero or heroine, to achieve "at-one-ment" with the father-mother figure, serves as a prerequisite union for earning what Campbell calls the ultimate boon, that of the bridal bed, or returning to the childhood society worthy of respect. Overt reunifications with the biological father occur in *Manwolf, The Lark and the Laurel, Son of Columbus, The Devil in Vienna,* and *Fathom Five.* Reunification with the biological mother occurs in *North to Freedom* and *Jacob Have I Loved.* However, in two novels, *Good Night, Mr. Tom* and *Beyond the Divide,* the mother creates chaos by not fulfilling her nurturing role. In both of these novels, either the biological or the surrogate father reveals his feminine side by assuming her place.

Some protagonists, without biological parents or whose biological parents have not fulfilled their own responsibilities, often unify with a psychological father-mother in order to reach maturity. Many times the protagonist internalizes this ''parent'' as a method of reconciliation with and acceptance of self. Sometimes the deceased father becomes symbolically reunited when the protagonist searches for knowledge about the parent: Marcus *(The Eagle of the Ninth),* Havelock *(Havelock the Dane),* Jim *(Moccasin Trail),* Willie *(The Snowbird),* Bridie *(A Sound of Chariots),* and Lena *(Words by Heart).* Other times, the Christ spirit becomes this psychological parent. Parent as Christ-spirit surfaces in such novels as *Sun Horse, Moon Horse, A Donkey for the King, The Bronze Bow, The Rider and His Horse, The Sea Stranger* and *The Fire Brother, The Wind Eye, The Witch's Brat, The Road to Damietta, One is One,* and *Beyond the Weir Bridge.*

In literature for children, most protagonists, appropriately, never achieve the ''ultimate boon.'' Some novels for young adults, especially those about warriors—Viking through contemporary—even exclude women characters. Thus the male may complete the difficult task—pulling the sword from the stone—but not reinsert it in the marital ring—Guinevere. In other books for young adults, however, some protagonists mature and marry. Sara Louise *(Jacob Have I Loved),* Mara *(Mara, Daughter of the Nile),* Aster *(Crossing to Salamis),* Coll *(The Stronghold),* Aquila *(The Lantern Bearers),* Silvester *(The Dancing Bear),* Havelock *(Havelock the Dane),* Jestyn *(Blood Feud),* Takiko *(Of Nightingales That Weep),* Constance *(Constance),* Thomas *(Beyond the Weir Bridge),* Mall *(A Parcel of Patterns),* Anna *(Children of the Book),* Deborah *(I'm Deborah Sampson),* Kitty *(The Far-off Land),* Anna *(Anna),* Bright Morning *(Sing Down the Moon),* Pedro *(Komantcia),* and characters in Willard's Mantlemass books all marry. Others such as Kit in *The Witch of Blackbird Pond,* Rosemary in *The Tamarack Tree,* Jeff in *Rifles for Watie,* and Stephen in *The Rebel,* become betrothed at the conclusion of the novels in which they appear.

For the third and final step of the monomyth, protagonists must return to the society from which they separated. Those who choose not to return must exist in a psychological limbo. Geist in *What Happened in Hamelin* refuses physical return and seems less mature for shirking his responsibility. Daniel in *The Bronze Bow* wanders in the ''wilderness'' until acknowledging his need. Takiko *(Of Nightingales That Weep)* refuses to return when asked and bears the guilt for her mother's death. When she eventually accepts her responsibility, she must readjust her superficial and misdirected values. Characters exiled, such as Silvester in *The Dancing Bear,* cannot return in the physical sense; they must psychologically accept a new place, with its attending responsibility. Some protagonists return as warriors, some as civic leaders, some as parents. Others return to lift the quality of life within their communities. Of these, the most obvious is the healer who returns to serve. Lovel *(The Witch's Brat),* Casilda *(Casilda of the Rising Moon),* Justin *(The Silver Branch),* and Sara Louise *(Jacob Have I Loved)* share their medicinal skills to improve the lives of others.

Thus protagonists, after separating either physically or psychologically from their homes, surviving their initiations, and returning from their quests, complete the ritualistic patterns of maturation. As Campbell comments, "The hero, therefore, is the man or woman who has been able to battle past his personal and local historical limitations to the generally valid, normally human forms" (p. 20). Such protagonists, especially in historical fiction, permit readers to experience a sense of closure in the aesthetic text and a hope of success in their own lives. Such protagonists can often evoke responses in readers that linger long after the text has returned to its shelf.

REFERENCES

Campbell, Joseph. *The Hero with a Thousand Faces.* Princeton: Princeton University Press, 1968.

Feuchtwanger, Lion. *The House of Desdemona: The Laurels and Limitations of the Historical Novel.* Translated by Harold A. Bisilius. Detroit: Wayne State University Press, 1978.

Goodrich, Norma Lorre. *Medieval Myths.* New York: New American Library, 1961.

Jung, Karl. *Symbols of Transformation.* Translated by R.F.C. Hull. Princeton: Princeton University Press, 1969.

Lukacs, George. *The Historical Novel.* Translated by Hannah and Stanley Mitchell. Boston: Beacon Press, 1963.

Manzoni, Alessandro. *On the Historical Novel.* Translated by Sandra Bermann. Lincoln: University of Nebraska Press, 1983.

Rosenblatt, Louise. *The Reader, the Text, the Poem: The Transactional Theory of the Literary Work.* Carbondale: Southern Illinois University Press, 1978.

The Guide

_A_

ABOLITIONIST. In the nineteenth century in the United States, a person who worked to terminate slavery acquired this label. Anti-slavery actions in other countries can also be categorized as "abolitionist" movements. See _Thee Hannah!_ by Marguerite *de Angeli; _To Ravensrigg_ by Hester *Burton; _The Sentinels_ by Peter *Carter; and _The Taken Girl_ by Elizabeth Gray *Vining.

ACROSS FIVE APRILS. _See_ Hunt, Irene.

ADAM. Eleven, English protagonist of _Adam of the Road_. _See_ Vining, Elizabeth Gray.

ADAM. Young American protagonist in _Adam and the Golden Cock_. _See_ Dalgliesh, Alice.

ADAM AND DANUSHA. Polish protagonists, son and mother, of _Manwolf_. _See_ Skurzynski, Gloria.

ADAM AND THE GOLDEN COCK. _See_ Dalgliesh, Alice.

ADAM LAWRIE. Sixteen, Scottish orphan, protagonist of _The 13th Member_. _See_ Hunter, Mollie.

ADAM OF THE ROAD. _See_ Vining, Elizabeth Gray.

ADAM QUARTERMAYNE. Eleven, English protagonist of _Adam of the Road_. _See_ Vining, Elizabeth Gray.

ALAN CAREY. English young adult in America, protagonist of _Mohawk Valley_. _See_ Welch, Ronald.

ALAN DRAYTON. Sixteen, English protagonist who goes to *Varna, in *Shadow of the Hawk*. *See* Trease, Geoffrey.

ALAN MACRAE. Thirteen, Scottish protagonist in *The Royal Dirk*. *See* Beatty, John and Patricia.

ALEC MACLEOD. Fourteen, Scot in America in *Who Comes to King's Mountain?* *See* Beatty, John and Patricia.

ALEUTS. These natives of the Aleutian Islands and the western portion of the Alaskan peninsula appeared as early as 2000 B.C. Similar in appearance to Siberians, they are great hunters who use kayaks to gather sea otters, whales, sea lions, seals, and walrus. *See* O'Dell, Scott, *Island of the Blue Dolphins*.

ALEXIS. Sixteen, Greek protagonist in *Web of Traitors*. *See* Trease, Geoffrey.

ALEXIS. Young Russian protagonist in *The Wild Children*. *See* Holman, Felice.

ALFRED TIMBERLEG (DANELEG). Ten, English protagonist in *The Namesake*. *See* Hodges, C. Walter.

ALFRED OF WESSEX (849–899). In 871, he succeeded his brother Aethelred as king of Wessex. He defeated the second invasion of the Danes led by Guthrum (*Guthorm) in Wiltshire in 878 and captured London in 886. After receiving the submission of the *Angles and *Saxons, he became the sovereign of all England not under Danish rule. See *The Marsh King* and *The Namesake* by C. Walter *Hodges, and *Escape to King Alfred* by Geoffrey *Trease.

ALGONKIN. This diversified group of Indian tribes throughout the United States has a common linguistic link. Indian leaders speaking variants of Algonquian, such as King Philip, Powhatan, Tecumseh, and Pontiac played prominent roles in American colonial history. Algonquian Indians were the first to meet members of the *Hudson's Bay Company. These tribes taught white settlers how to use the birch bark canoe, how to hunt buffalo, the importance of maize, the taste of maple syrup, and much else. See *Viking's Sunset* by Henry *Treece and *Red Pawns* by Leonard *Wibberley.

ALIKO. Muslim protagonist who grows from fifteen into adulthood in *Storm over the Caucasus*. *See* Bartos-Höppner, B.

ALISON STEWART. Canadian of Scottish and *Haida descent who matures from nine to sixteen as the protagonist in *Forbidden Frontier*. *See* Harris, Christie.

ALL SAINTS' DAY. Originally this was a Celtic festival welcoming the New Year, called Samhain (Sambain), held on November 1. Bonfires were lit to represent the waxing and waning sun, and worshippers danced around the fires in attempts to acquire power from the sun and to ensure fertility. Household fires were rekindled from these public fires. Table places were set for deceased family members on this date in preparation for the yearly visit. Strangers were most welcome on the eve of Samhain because they represented good fortune for the household. In medieval England, the festival was called All Hallows. Currently, this festival, still observed on November 1, commemorates all the saints of the church, known and unknown. The eve of the festival is called Halloween. For Samhain, see *Warrior Scarlet* and *Knight's Fee* by Rosemary *Sutcliff; for All Saint's, see *The 13th Member* by Mollie *Hunter; *The Perilous Gard* by Elizabeth Marie *Pope; and *The Red Towers of Granada* by Geoffrey *Trease.

ALLECTUS (d. 296). After murdering Marcus Aurelius *Carausius in 293, he succeeded as self-proclaimed emperor of Britain and ruled for three years. *See* Sutcliff, Rosemary, *The Silver Branch*.

ALMEDINGEN, E. M. (1898–1971). Russian/British.

BIBLIOGRAPHY AND BACKGROUND

Anna. Illustrated by Robert Micklewright. London: Oxford, 1972; New York: Farrar, Straus & Giroux, 1972. *A Candle at Dusk*. Illustrated by Doreen Roberts. London: Oxford 1969; New York: Farrar, Straus & Giroux, 1969. *The Crimson Oak*. Illustrated by Kate Mellor. London: Methuen, 1981. *Katia*. Illustrated by Victor Ambrus. New York: Farrar, Straus & Giroux, 1967; *Little Katia*. London: Oxford, 1966. *Young Mark: The Story of a Venture*. Illustrated by Victor Ambrus. London: Oxford, 1976; New York: Farrar, Straus & Giroux, 1968.

Accolades such as the *Atlantic Review* prize and the *Book World* Festival Award, as well as the honor of being a Fellow of the Royal Society of Literature, rewarded Almedingen before her death. Stories related to her about her family in Russia became the background for several of her novels.

WORKS

All of Almedingen's protagonists, whether in the eighth or eighteenth century, learn that human life, no matter what social class, has value. Each finds that concern for others improves the quality of life for everyone. Peter in *The Crimson Oak* has the pleasure of helping his village. In *A Candle at Dusk,* Idrun believes that God has allowed him to survive a *Saracen attack in order to save a valuable manuscript for future readers. The upper-class protagonists in the books Almedingen bases on members of her family learn to help the peasants living on their lands. Katia in *Katia* grows to understand why a servant shot himself when she realizes that serfs have no control over their destinies. The kind, God-loving Anna in *Anna* fulfills her life by sheltering her servants (and children) in the countryside. Mark in *Young Mark* finds that he must accept the responsibility for God's gift of a beautiful singing voice because his songs serve others.

Almedingen uses omniscient point of view in two books, neither based on Almedingen family members but both having twelve-year-old protagonists. The first, **A Candle at Dusk**, is set in Frankland (France), the only book set outside Russia. The protagonist, Idrun, in 731, wants only to study with Dom Defensor at Ligugé Abbey near *Tours. His father, Gunto, disapproves, especially since the new prior, Dom Simeon, has begun claiming lands from families long faithful to the abbey. Fortunately, Dom Defensor finds that Dom Simeon, with his lust for money, has forged documents making the claims. He reports the offense, and Dom Simeon's misuse of power unseats him to swineherd. On Gunto's land, Idrun kills a wild boar as it charges one of the freeborn servants. For Idrun's bravery, Gunto promises him whatever he wants, and Idrun chooses to study at Ligugé. Gunto, relieved to find that his land belongs to him and not the abbey, happily agrees. While Idrun studies, his betrothed, Judith, lives with his parents, trying to learn women's duties. She, however, prefers running barefooted and collecting herbs in the fields to sewing. When Idrun returns for holiday, he enjoys and approves of her independence. Peacefulness, however, suddenly ends when news reaches the steading in 732 that the Saracens have crossed the *Pyrenees. Although the family and the lands survive, the Saracens destroy the abbey. Idrun returns to the ruins and finds only one of Dom Defensor's books, fortunately the most valuable. Idrun sees the purpose in his life as being copier of this collection of sayings anthologized and beautifully illustrated by Dom Defensor. In this book, Almedingen presents a balanced look at both the good and bad in a religious community and in the rest of society.

The setting shifts in **The Crimson Oak** to Russia during 1739 when Peter saves a woman from a bear. She has no money, so she gives Peter a twig from his favorite oak in appreciation for her life and tells him that someday she will repay him. She then reveals herself as the exiled Princess *Elizabeth (Petrovna). When Peter arrives home after his feat, he finds that unscrupulous collectors have taken extra taxes for the Empress *Anna's whims. When his father decides to go to Moscow to petition their unfairness, he takes Peter. There Peter meets a scribe, Egor, and asks him to write Empress Anna saying that he wants to learn his letters. Upon Peter's return to the village, the Secret Chancery arrests him, accusing him of an act of treason, a peasant wanting to learn to read. But he does learn, ironically, when an old man teaches him while both are incarcerated in a Moscow dungeon. After Elizabeth regains the throne, Master Ilya, Peter's friend, rescues him from prison and restores him to health. Master Ilya writes to Elizabeth about Peter, and when she comes to Moscow, she offers him a job as well as all of the items he wants his family and village neighbors to have. Thus the crimson oak, through its symbolic twig, fulfills its destiny— giving Peter the warmth and freedom with which he has always associated it.

For the three novels based on her family, Almedingen chooses a first-person narrator. Mark, Anna, and Katia relate their experiences as young people. In

Young Mark, the great-great grandfather of Almedingen, Mark Poltoratzky, leaves his home in the *Ukraine in 1742 to walk to *St. Petersburg where he plans to sing for the Hetman, Tsarina Elizabeth's supposed husband. He endures many hardships and enjoys innumerable kindnesses on his journey to meet the Hetman. He sings at fairs, stays in huts with priests, breaks his leg, escapes from a monastery where monks had decided he would become a novitiate, meets a Ukrainian woman in Moscow who keeps him, suffers at the hands of highwaymen en route to St. Petersburg, works briefly as a cook in St. Petersburg, and in desperation, steals breakfast from a baker, only to have it stolen from him in turn. Horrid tales of the Hetman's harshness circulate, but the man who befriends Mark at his lowest moment, after his breakfast is stolen in the Tsarina Meadow, happens to be the Hetman. (Artistically, such a coincidence would be contrived; it is, however, a true encounter.) The Hetman listens to Mark sing and introduces him to the Tsarina. Mark serves the Tsarina throughout his life, receiving her material blessings in return for his talents. Thus he reaches and retains his youthful goals by utilizing his God-given gifts.

Anna presents the story of Almedingen's great-grandmother in an episodic plot that shows her growth from five to sixteen. While very young, Anna and her older brother, Yasha, the only two survivors from six children, have a very close relationship. Yasha eventually travels in Europe for two years, returns to Moscow, and reveals that he will marry a British woman and live in England. Anna's disappointed father gives him money and unhappily severs family ties. Left at home, Anna, an exceptionally intelligent girl who knows several languages well, worries when Aunt Xenia accuses her of being an infidel, but a priest reassures Anna that she is not. As Anna grows, religious rituals are very important, and she loves the celebrations, especially Easter in the Russian church. These experiences help her to understand that God and Mother Russia are central to her being. When she is fifteen, a Dimitry Markovich visits and brings a tuber (a potato) that he thinks might interest her father, a corn merchant. First afraid to cook or eat this potato, the servants soon discover its merits. As Dimitry continues to visit, Anna gains respect for and interest in him and welcomes his marriage proposal. Thus, she marries a man whom she has chosen, highly unusual in the Russia of 1786. Although Czarina Catherine (*Catherine II of Russia) raises the family to nobility for their great collection of rare and valuable foreign books, Anna still chooses to marry in her local church, a place that has had magic for her through the years. According to the epilogue, Anna never changes her values of simplicity and goodness.

A third family story is that of Almedingen's great-aunt in **Katia**. At five, after her mother's death, Katia leaves her father and brothers to live with Cousin Sophie, the woman her mother chose to keep her. The story covers the major events during the six years 1836–42, including Cousin Sophie's death and Katia's return to her father and new stepmother. As a member of the Russian nobility, Katia learns French, German, and English as well as most other subjects. Cousin Sophie teaches Katia that the servants cannot respond negatively to masters;

therefore, Katia must treat them with kindness. Katia plays with other children in the huge gardens and parks attached to the summer homes, with days marked by the meals that highlight the adults' lives. When Katia returns to her father at age twelve, highwaymen chase her coach, a common occurrence in Russia. When the coach driver escapes them, he proves himself unexpectedly honest since most coach drivers served as criminal accomplices. At home, her step-mother's acceptance surprises Katia. Soon, however, she leaves again. Like all other intelligent daughters of nobility, she must attend boarding school in Moscow.

STYLE AND THEMES

Almedingen makes many vibrantly stylistic choices. In *Young Mark,* she uses *enameled* as a synonym for *painted,* but its use three separate times indicates a lack of editing. Her ability to create light and beauty with her metaphors, however, overshadows editing slips. Such phrases as "fragile lace of gossamer," "stumpy [snow-covered] firs . . . suggested so many brides veiled in silver," and "the edges of the track . . . had music in them" brighten everyday scenes. Mark metaphorically remembers the pleasures of his childhood home, recalling vivid images: "Nothing could prevent the outer world from walking right into the house and filling it with several fragrances—mint and other herbs, sunflowers, seeds, apples, pears, mushrooms, and so often the cloying breath of watermelon's raspberry colored flesh." Alliteration permeates descriptions like that of Katia's schoolmistress's dog: "he sleeps, snarls, and smells." Almedingen's clean, stylistic attributes, as well as the symbols of faithfulness, love, and strength in Peter's oak tree and Mark's cherry and silver birch trees, attach to her themes in a cohesive wholeness.

ALVARADO, PEDRO (1485–1541). After helping *Cortés conquer Mexico from 1519 to 1521, he began governing Mexico City in 1520. He led an expedition to Guatemala and served as its governor from 1527 to 1529. Later he went to look for the Seven Cities of *Cibola. *See* Baker, Betty, *A Stranger and Afraid.*

ALYS DE RENNEVILLE. Ten, English protagonist who travels to Scotland in *Ransom for a Knight. See* Picard, Barbara.

AMANDA. Thirteen, American, protagonist of *O the Red Rose Tree. See* Beatty, Patricia.

AMBROSIUS. Various authors view Ambrosius differently. According to Nennius, he was a fatherless child who revealed to the British legendary king *Vortigern why the fortress Vortigern was building to hold back the *Saxons disintegrated each night. Geoffrey of Monmouth combines Ambrosius and Merlin with the explanation that Ambrosius's father was a spirit. *See* Sutcliff, Rosemary, *The Lantern Bearers*.

AMELIA BROMFIELD-BROWN. Thirteen, English girl in California, protagonist of *The Queen's Own Grove*. *See* Beatty, Patricia.

AMERICAN CIVIL WAR. This war, a conflict lasting from 1861 to 1865, was between the U.S. federal government and eleven southern states which asserted their right to secede from the Union. See *Wait for Me, Watch for Me, Eula Bee, Blue Stars Watching,* and *Turn Homeward, Hannalee* by Patricia *Beatty; *Caddie Woodlawn* by Carol Ryrie *Brink; *The Tamarack Tree* by Patricia *Clapp; *Orphans in the Wind* by Erik *Haugaard; *Zoar Blue* by Janet *Hickman; *Across Five Aprils* by Irene *Hunt; *Tancy* by Belinda *Hurmence; *Rifles for Watie* by Harold *Keith; *The 290* by Scott *O'Dell; *The Perilous Road* by William O. *Steele; and *The Wound of Peter Wayne* by Leonard *Wibberley.

AMERICAN REVOLUTION. The British colonies along the Atlantic seaboard separated themselves from England and began this war, also called the American War of Independence, with a skirmish in Lexington, Massachusetts, on April 19, 1775. It ended when General *Cornwallis of Britain surrendered at Yorktown on October 19, 1781. See *Who Comes to King's Mountain?* by John and Patricia *Beatty; *The Far-off Land* and *The Tree of Freedom* by Rebecca *Caudill; *I'm Deborah Sampson* by Patricia *Clapp; *My Brother Sam Is Dead* and *War Comes to Willy Freeman* by Christopher and James *Collier; *Adam and the Golden Cock* by Alice *Dalgliesh; *Johnny Tremain* by Esther *Forbes; *The Cow Neck Rebels* by James *Forman; *The Valley of the Shadow* by Janet *Hickman; *The Sherwood Ring* by Elizabeth Marie *Pope; and *Peter Treegate's Musket, Peter Treegate's War, Sea Captain from Salem*, and *Treegate's Raiders* by Leonard *Wibberley.

THE AMETHYST RING. See O'Dell, Scott.

AMISH. This conservative body of Mennonites, characterized particularly by its dress and nonconformed way of life, exists mainly in Lancaster County, Pennsylvania; Holmes County, Ohio; and Lagrange and Elkhart counties, Indiana. Its members do not use electricity, motorized vehicles, or telephones. Persons who do not adhere to the laws of the group are shunned by all other members, including family. See *Beyond the Divide* by Kathryn *Lasky and *Skippack School* by Marguerite *de Angeli.

AND ONE WAS A WOODEN INDIAN. See Baker, Betty.

ANDREW TALBOT. Twelve, English protagonist in *I Will Adventure*. *See* Vining, Elizabeth Gray.

ANDROS, SIR EDMUND (1637–1714). As British colonial governor of the Dominion of New England, including the New England colonies, New York, and New Jersey, in 1686, he interfered with colonists' rights and customs. They revolted and imprisoned him. When he was tried in England, he was not charged. He returned to govern Virginia in 1692 and Maryland in 1693. *See* Haugaard, Erik, *Cromwell's Boy*.

ANDY CLARK. Nine, American, protagonist of *The Buffalo Knife*. *See* Steele, William O.

ANGLE. This Germanic tribe came from an area, probably Schleswig on the European continent, to invade England in the fifth century. See *The Marsh King* and *The Namesake* by C. Walter *Hodges, and *The Fire Brother* and *The Sea-Stranger* by Kevin *Crossley-Holland.

ANGLO. *See* Angle.

ANN KATHERINE SCOTT. Thirteen, American protagonist in *Bonanza Girl*. *See* Beatty, Patricia.

ANNA. Young Russian protagonist who grows from five to sixteen in *Anna*. *See* Almedingen, E. M.

ANNA. *See* Almedingen, E. M.

ANNA AND CALEB. Young American protagonists in *Sarah Plain and Tall*. *See* MacLachlan, Patricia.

ANNA IVANOVA (1693–1740). Being the daughter of Ivan V and niece of Peter the Great allowed her succession to empress of Russia. During her repressive regime, she abolished rights and made certain that her successor would be her great-nephew, *Ivan VI. *See* Almedingen, E. M., *The Crimson Oak*.

ANNA VOGEL. Seventeen, Austrian, with *Janissary recruit Timur, sixteen, and the Polish Stefan Zabruski, protagonists in *Children of the Book*. *See* Carter, Peter.

ANNE RICHMOND. Fifteen, English protagonist in *The Innocent Wayfaring*. *See* Chute, Marchette.

ANTHONY, SUSAN B. (1820–1906). Her active participation as a reformer in the temperance, abolition, and woman's suffrage movements led her to form, with Elizabeth Cady *Stanton, the National Woman Suffrage Association in 1869. *See* Beatty, Patricia, *Hail Columbia*.

ANTHONY GREY. Fourteen, British bond servant in America, captured protagonist in *Pirate Royal*. *See* Beatty, John and Patricia.

APACHE. This term denotes six culturally related Native American tribes in southwestern North America. The family lives with the wife's relatives, with children belonging to the clan of the mother. Tribes in this group are the Western Apache, the Chiricahua, the Mescalero, the Jicarilla, the Lipan, and the Kiowa Apache. See *And One Was a Wooden Indian* by Betty *Baker; *By Crumbs, It's Mine!* by Patricia *Beatty; *Komantcia* by Harold *Keith; and *Sing Down the Moon* by Scott *O'Dell.

AQUAE SULIS. Roman name for *Bath, England. *See* Sutcliff, Rosemary, *The Lantern Bearers*.

AQUILA. Young adult Roman protagonist remaining in Britain in *The Lantern Bearers*. *See* Sutcliff, Rosemary.

ARIK-BUKA. Mongolian young adult protagonist in *Sons of the Steppe*. *See* Baumann, Hans.

THE ARMOURER'S HOUSE. *See* Sutcliff, Rosemary.

ARMSTRONG, WILLIAM (1914–   ). American.

BIBLIOGRAPHY AND BACKGROUND
  Sounder. Illustrated by James Barkley. New York: Harper & Row, 1969.
  Armstrong has amassed many awards for *Sounder*, among them the Newbery Award, the Lewis Carroll Shelf Award, the Mark Twain Award, and the Nene Award. He became interested in the setting after years of study and a lifetime of looking at the world around him. To create *Sounder*, he wrote the manuscript only once, longhand in pencil.

WORK
  According to Armstrong's note at the beginning of **Sounder**, one night he heard from a scholarly old black man stories of two dogs—the faithful dog of Ulysses, Argus, who waited for his master's return, and the faithful dog, Sounder, who also waited for his master's return. Armstrong chose to tell his version of Sounder from the limited omniscient view of Sounder's master's son. The story relates a family's struggle when the father, trying to feed his starving family during the *Depression, steals a ham from a white man and serves at hard labor for the crime while "six crops of persimmons and wild grapes [ripen]." During this period, the mother sells shelled walnuts, and the boy works in the fields. Since the eight-mile walk to school is too long, the boy has to delay learning to read the wonderful stories from the Bible that keep away the loneliness when his mother tells them so beautifully. On the day the men arrest his father, they

also shoot the booming-voiced Sounder as he tries to defend his master. Sounder disappears for months; when he returns, his mutilation and three-legged walk shock the family. And he can only whine. When the father returns years later, his mutilation from a dynamite blast also shocks the family. At his master's return, however, Sounder's voice booms one last time. Like Ulysses, the master determines that he must return home to die; like Argus, Sounder waits faithfully. Yet Sounder, with his visible external wounds, becomes more than Argus. Sounder symbolizes the internal emotional and psychological pain of the father (and to a lesser extent, the boy) who has only tried to protect his family in a vicious world of whites who call him "boy" and who squeeze dirty fingers through the carefully carried gift cake looking for hacksaws. The family survives through the mother's faith that God directs their lives and that the weak become strong because they are morally right. Like Telemachus, Ulysses's Son, the boy's encounter with the teacher during his searches for his father allows him to learn how to read the Bible stories, thereby giving credence to his mother's faith.

STYLE AND THEME

Armstrong emphasizes the mythically timeless quality of *Sounder* with vivid imagery and strong subject-verb sentences. By refusing to identify the human characters with proper names, he allows them to become Everyone who has faced injustice—but especially those who have endured irrational prejudice. After the arrest of the father, Armstrong defines the boy's pain and confusion using parallel construction by beginning six short sentences with "Maybe." About Sounder, the mother comments, "He is only dying," syntax indicating that, to her, life offers much worse pain than death. Armstrong chooses figurative language that clarifies the rural setting: the "road . . . lay like a thread dropped on a patchwork quilt. Stalkland, fallow fields, and brushland, all appeared to be sewn together by wide fencerow stitches of trees." The biblical allusions underscore the basic religious faith needed to cope with harsh reality. Therefore, the form and content in Armstrong's *Sounder* clearly complement one another.

ARNOLD, BENEDICT (1741–1801). After repulsing the British in various battles, including Mohawk Valley in 1777, he was court-martialed in 1779 for financial irregularities during his Philadelphia command but only reprimanded. He began corresponding with the British after taking command at West Point and arranged to surrender West Point to them, but his plot was detected. Working for the British, he led raids in Virginia and Connecticut. He went to England in 1781, where he spent the rest of his life, disgraced and poor. See *My Brother Sam Is Dead* by Christopher and James *Collier and *Treegate's Raiders* by Leonard *Wibberley.

ARNOLD WESTERWOORT. Fourteen, Dutch protagonist in *War without Friends. See* Hartman, Evert.

ASHANTI [ASANTE]. This group of people lives in Ghana, with the extended family serving as its basic social organization. Its descent is matrilineal, with the mode of succession to traditional offices varying in specific families. The kingdom was created with much upheaval throughout the seventeenth and eighteenth centuries. See *The Sentinels* by Peter *Carter and *The Secret of the Hawk* by Leonard *Wibberley.

ASSISI, ST. FRANCIS OF (1181?–1226). Founder of the Franciscan order, he dedicated himself to poverty and religion in 1205 and began to preach in 1208. He founded Poor Clares, a religious order for women, in 1212. He led movements to reform the church before he retired to a mountain retreat. Pope Gregory IX canonized him in 1228. *See* O'Dell, Scott, *The Road to Damietta*.

ASTER. Fourteen, Greek female protagonist in *Crossing to Salamis*. *See* Paton Walsh, Jill.

AT THE SEVEN STARS. *See* Beatty, John and Patricia.

ATAHUALPA (c. 1502–1533). As the last *Inca king of Peru, he disputed the succession with his brother after their father's death by deposing him. *Pizarro arrested him in 1532 when he refused to become a Christian. Later he was executed for the probable murder of his brother. *See* O'Dell, Scott, *The Amethyst Ring*.

ATHELNEY. *Alfred of England led his attack from this spot in the Somerset Marshes against *Guthorm in 878. *See* Hodges, C. Walter, *The Marsh King*.

ATTAR. Young Neanderthal hunter in *Attar of the Ice Valley*. *See* Wibberley, Leonard.

ATTAR OF THE ICE VALLEY. *See* Wibberley, Leonard.

ATTRIBATES [ATTREBATES]. This British tribe, which flourished around 100 B.C., lived near the River Thames to the west of London, although its influence probably went south at least to Atrebatum, now called Silchester. *See* Sutcliff, Rosemary, *Sun Horse, Moon Horse*.

AVERY, GILLIAN (1926–   ). British.

BIBLIOGRAPHY AND BACKGROUND

A Likely Lad. Illustrated by Faith Jaques. London: Collins, 1971; New York: Holt, Rinehart & Winston, 1971.

Although an editor and the author of many novels, Gillian Avery wrote only one work that fits the definition of historical fiction. *A Likely Lad* won *The

Guardian Award in 1972. Avery's own childhood, dominated by the capricious authority of adults, influenced her choice of a late nineteenth-century Victorian setting, a time when parents practiced such authority and children accepted it. Avery says about her research, "I feel I have read enough Victorian fiction (both for adults and for children) to be able to move around in the period easily."

WORK

Six-year-old Willy Overs, the protagonist in **A Likely Lad**, runs away from home in 1895. Bored, he sneaks out the back gate and wanders to the park. Caught picking the daffodils by the gardener, he asserts that his father contributes to the park's upkeep and that he, Willy, has a right to be there. When Willy's father hears of this response, he decides that Willy is "a likely lad" who will be successful in life. The second time Willy runs away, when he is twelve, his father has the opposite reaction. Mr. Overs thinks that Willy's future is doomed because Willy seems to care only about himself. Willy, however, is merely trying to escape his father's decision for him to stop school at thirteen and get a job "working up the ladder" in the Northern Star Insurance Company. Willy loves school, and his teacher believes that he can win a scholarship to a university. A parallel plot presents the competition between the Overs family and Mrs. Overs's sister's family, the Sowters. Each first Sunday of the month, at tea, the Sowters try to demonstrate their superiority. They expect to inherit Aunt Maggie's money since Aunt Maggie has disowned Mrs. Overs. Fourteen years before, when Mrs. Overs married Mr. Overs, whom Aunt Maggie considered unworthy, Aunt Maggie went to bed and stayed there. In turn, Mr. Overs ridicules nobility. A lord Willy meets while "run away" compliments him on his ability to write letters and encourages him to further his education. Then when Aunt Maggie's dogs eat all her money and no one inherits it, Mr. Overs, happy that the Sowters have gained nothing, agrees that Willy should become a scholar.

STYLE AND THEME

The story starts slowly, but as Willy begins to assert himself, it becomes more interesting. All the family members except Willy want only to succeed materially. To them, attending church on Sunday morning is merely a preliminary to the day's highlight of eating crusty potatoes with a joint of beef at the noon meal. Willy exhibits no religious values, but he helps the old lady with whom he stays when he has "run away," and he understands the value of education. Avery allows Willy to refuse his family's myopic view as well as its Victorian discipline and, ironically for that reason, become "a likely lad."

AVI (1937–   ). American.

BIBLIOGRAPHY AND BACKGROUND

Captain Grey. New York: Pantheon, 1977. *Emily Upham's Revenge*. New York: Pantheon, 1978. *Encounter at Easton*. New York: Pantheon, 1980. *The*

Fighting Ground. New York: Lippincott, 1984. *Night Journeys*. New York: Pantheon, 1979. *Shadrach's Crossing*. New York: Pantheon, 1983.

Avi won the first Scott O'Dell Award for Historical Fiction with *The Fighting Ground*. He has also received other accolades for his works. Avi continues his profession as a college librarian while writing as much as possible.

WORKS

Avi's novels, all set on the East Coast of the United States, have young protagonists with friends who are orphaned or emotionally or physically separated from parents. By the ends of the stories, the overt conflicts of money and power give way to the more important inner conflicts as the protagonists realize that the adults they respect and trust have betrayed them. In the last novels, the action projects from the injustice faced by many bond servants transported from England in the eighteenth century. Two others present the disillusionment that war creates. And two novels underscore the moments when a child realizes that parents have lost their integrity.

Parents who compromise values appear in both *Shadrach's Crossing* and **Emily Upham's Revenge**. Emily at seven travels from Boston to North Brookfield by train when her mother sends her to live with her banker uncle after her father disappears on a search for money. When her uncle does not meet her at the station, Emily meets the youth, Seth Marple, who invites her to stay at his hideout in the woods nearby. To get money for Emily's return to Boston, Seth decides that Emily should rob her uncle's bank. When they sneak inside the bank, they find someone else robbing it. Seth recognizes the robber as Emily's father, having seen her photograph of him, but refuses to tell Emily, who hides in terror under the desk. They escape. Later Seth takes the money from Emily's father when he finds him sleeping in the woods. Seth shifts it to Emily's uncle's black box, a portable safe, and Emily, not knowing to whom it belongs, takes it to Boston. She tells her parents that she burned the money, but in Boston, she spends it all on charities. Other than a little girl believing money causes evil, the story has little substance.

On the other hand, **Shadrach's Crossing** has good foreshadowing and mystery. In 1932 during *Prohibition and the *Depression, Shadrach Faherty's parents obey the wealthy Mr. Kinlow's demand that all inhabitants of Lucker's Island extinguish their lights when the smugglers come with loads of liquor. At first Mr. Kinlow pays his helpers large sums of money, but the amount dwindles until he pays them almost nothing, threatening to reveal them as accomplices if they quit. Shadrach disobeys his parents by watching the transaction one night. When Kinlow discovers him and takes him home, Kinlow threatens Shad's parents. Distraught and hurt by their acquiescence, twelve-year-old Shad decides to challenge Kinlow's bullying by catching and reporting him to the authorities. He confides his plan to Mr. Sheraton, a government man who visits the island several times a week. When a stranger, Mr. Nevill, comes to the island in a yacht requesting repair for his boat, Shad's father thinks the motor looks tampered with instead of broken. Shad assumes that Mr. Nevill works with Kinlow, but on the night when Shad catches Kinlow, he discovers that Nevill works for the U.S. Coast Guard and that Sheraton is Kinlow's accomplice. After an escape ordeal, Shad, exhausted, returns to his parents, and realizes that he has crossed into the murky world of adulthood.

Two novels frame the *American Revolution. *Captain Grey* occurs after the war, but **The Fighting Ground** occurs toward the beginning on April 3, 1778. The book shows Jonathan at various times on that day, from 9:30 A.M. when he hears tavern bells calling to arms until 2:45 P.M., and on through the night to 9:30 A.M., April 4. Without parental permission, he uses the tavern keeper's gun and joins a group planning to fight *Hessians supposedly marching toward Rocktown. After the fighting begins and he sees his father's friend lying dead on the ground, he runs. But three Hessians find him, and although he cannot speak German, he knows that they have captured him. Wandering in a sudden storm, they reach a deserted farmhouse, where a cow moos in distress. When the Hessians allow Jonathan to milk the cow, he finds a young boy hiding in the barn and the child's dead parents lying in the field. Jonathan thinks the Hessians have killed the couple. He escapes while they sleep and reunites with the group with which he had fought. Their talk tells him that these men, not the Hessians, killed the parents because they were *Tories. The corporal makes Jonathan lead the group to the Hessians, where Jonathan watches in surprise as the men coldly shoot the Hessians. He reaches home around 9:30 A.M., nearly twenty-four hours after he so much wanted to fight, knowing that he had endured enough intense fear, shame, and hate to want to remain home—and alive. As the only person identified by name in the story, Jonathan seems to be the only one horrified by war's devastation.

A traitor to both America and England during the Revolution reveals himself in **Captain Grey**. In 1783, Kevin Cartwright, his sister, Cathleen, and his father leave Philadelphia for southern New Jersey. While resting on their journey, a group of men led by Captain Grey surround them. When Mr. Cartwright strongly reacts to the mention of governments, Grey stabs and kills him. Cathleen runs away, and Kevin faints. Afterward, Grey shows Kevin two graves, convincing him that Cathleen, his one companion while his Irish father fought for the Americans against the despised English for seven years, is also dead. Grey takes Kevin to his ''nation'' and starves him into submission. The men then train Kevin on a coastal island in basic warfare survival so that he can take part in their raids on lone ships coming up the Atlantic coast. On his first raid, Kevin sees the men kill an unsuspecting crew and sink the ship with men remaining in the hold. Grey tells Kevin that he does such cruel things because he enjoys them while nations do likewise under the guise of glory to God and mankind. By quietly acquiescing, Kevin soon earns Grey's trust. Kevin begins to understand that Grey's humanity had died with his wife and son and that Grey expects Kevin to replace them in his life. While roaming the island, Kevin finds a cave and his sister hiding in it. A schooner returning to avenge one of Grey's raids helps their escape plan. As Kevin and Cathleen leave the island to return to Philadelphia, Kevin notes that the unhappy Grey is not among the dead lined up on shore and has thus escaped capture.

The escape of two bond servants from their master in 1767 begins the action in **Night Journeys**. The four parts of the novel ("Morgan's Rock," "The River," "The Promise," and "The Roads of Night") seem to signify the stages of the decision that orphaned Peter York must make at age twelve whether to help two runaways. At first he gleefully joins the searchers sixteen miles north of Trenton across the river in Pennsylvania in hopes of winning the reward money for their capture. But when he finds that a young girl whom he has befriended during the search is one of the runaways, he begins to weigh the harsh reasons for the girl's being bound and whether those who sold her are justified. The *Quaker with whom he lives, Mr. Shinn, gives him no guidance. This at first infuriates Peter, but after Peter makes his decision to guide the young pair to freedom, Mr. Shinn thanks him for having the strength to do what Mr. Shinn in his role as justice of the peace could not.

As a continuation of *Night Journeys*, **Encounter at Easton** tells what happened to Elizabeth Mawes and Robert Linnly, the two runaways. A series of first-person narratives presents the action. The two main narrators are Nathaniel Hill, the man hired by John Tolivar to find his ward, Elizabeth, and Robert Linnly, the bond servant who escaped with her. Nathaniel Hill calls himself a gentleman, but his actions belie these words; he is lawless. Elizabeth suffers from a gunshot wound in her arm, and Robert endeavors to help her. As each narrative develops the story, the reader finds that Mad Moll, a woman living alone in a forest cave, sees the two trying to ford the river to Delaware and tries to save Elizabeth. Robert meets Hill at the ferry, and when Hill offers to hire him for work in Easton, Robert trusts him. But when the innkeeper reveals to Robert that Hill comes from Trenton, Robert realizes that Hill is the man he should fear. Robert searches in Hill's saddlebags where he finds papers about Elizabeth that verify his fear. Hill follows Robert to Moll's and finds Elizabeth. Moll, however, has maddened over the years because neither her family nor the family of her intended has acknowledged her since a soldier raped her decades before. She decides that Elizabeth is her daughter and tries to heal her wound. When Hill tries to capture Elizabeth, and Elizabeth is killed in the ensuing scuffle, Moll loses all sense of reality. But Robert's fortune improves because the innkeeper purchases him from Tolivar. Neither Elizabeth nor Robert had committed crimes other than being poor and hungry. Trying to satisfy those elementary needs doomed them to lives of bondage.

STYLE AND THEMES

The novels, generally well written, present dilemmas that realistically motivate the protagonists. The figurative language, although sparse, is effective. In *Encounter at Easton*, Robert notes that the tall trees "made me think of long, golden fingers, the fingers of God." Several coincidences, such as a pigeon relaying messages in *Captain Grey,* mar some of the concepts. Although lacking real depth, Avi's controlling themes are clear. These young protagonists, unencumbered by economic responsibility, refuse to equivocate, and they keep their integrity, unlike the adults in their lives who no longer view right and wrong as absolute.

_B_

BACK HOME. *See* Magorian, Michelle.

THE BAD BELL OF SAN SALVADOR. *See* Beatty, Patricia.

BAEDECKER. The German Karl Baedecker began publishing his travel guides in 1829 with a guide about Coblenz. Other handbooks followed in German, French, and English, for many countries. They have been reprinted and revised and are currently available. *See* Rees, David, *The Exeter Blitz*.

BAKER, BETTY (1928–   ). American.

BIBLIOGRAPHY AND BACKGROUND

And One Was a Wooden Indian. New York: Macmillan, 1970. *The Blood of the Brave.* New York: Harper, 1966. *Do Not Annoy the Indians.* Illustrated by Harold Goodwin. New York: Macmillan, 1968; London: Collier Macmillan, 1968. *The Dunderhead War.* New York: Harper, 1967. *The Great Desert Race.* New York: Macmillan, 1980. *Killer-of-Death.* Illustrated by John Kaufmann. New York: Harper, 1963. *The Night Spider Case.* New York: Macmillan, 1984 *The Spirit Is Willing.* New York: Macmillan, 1974. *A Stranger and Afraid.* New York: Macmillan, 1972; London: Collier Macmillan, 1972. *Walk the World's Rim.* New York: Harper, 1965.

Betty Baker's historical fiction has won such honors as the Western Heritage Award and the Spur Award of the Western Writers of America. Her books focus on either the sixteenth or nineteenth centuries in America's development, with the West and Midwest serving as setting for all but one. Befitting the settings, most of the protagonists are male, over twelve years old, and brave, but the few female protagonists lack no daring. All the stories naturally develop through first-person, limited omniscient, or omniscient point of views, which Baker uses equally well. Baker presents characters from different ethnic origins—Spanish, Native American, black, and Caucasian—which displays her grasp of varied cultural perspectives.

WORKS

Her three earliest novels chronologically present both the Spanish conqueror and the Native American conquered. The first, **The Blood of the Brave**, takes place in 1518. From Castile, Spain, Juan comes to Cuba with his father and joins Cortez's (*Cortés) expedition to Mexico as a priest's translator. In *Tabasco, the Spanish trade horses for twenty slaves, including Doña Marina, who knows Spanish. As the group travels toward *Montezuma, it passes temples smeared with blood indicating human sacrifice. The men meet Montezuma and honor him, but word soon arrives that natives have raided *Vera Cruz, a city Cortez has already claimed; in retaliation, Cortez imprisons Montezuma. As Montezuma's translator, Juan learns that Montezuma offers the blood sacrifices because he believes that the sun will not rise in the morning unless it receives the liquid of life. Montezuma also fears that Cortez's arrival fulfills *Quetzalcoatl's prophecy of returning in the year of *One Reed, and unlike Montezuma, Quetzalcoatl did not sanction blood sacrifice. Since Cortez's men also do not practice blood sacrifice, Montezuma believes that Quetzalcoatl's other prophecy—that at his return, people will embrace a new religion—has come true. Hence Montezuma declares allegiance to the Spanish king, *Charles I, and Cortez. Although the people at first rise against Cortez, he returns the following year and triumphs. Juan and his father begin their own farm, but other men destroy the temples and build Christian churches with their stones, some still covered in blood. Juan realizes that all life builds upon the past.

In 1527, another group sails from Cuba and lands in Florida. The first sentence of **Walk the World's Rim** declares that of 600 men, only four survive. One is the black slave *Esteban who encourages the young Indian Chakoh, hungry enough to leave his home, to accompany the men to Mexico. Visiting first the Land of the Buffalo Indians and then the agrarian Pimas, they hear about the legendary wealth in the seven cities of *Cibola. When they reach Mexico, the leaders petition for an expedition to this land. While waiting to hear the results of the petition, Chakoh becomes separated from Esteban and stays in a monastery near the palace, learning about the priests whom he perceives to be medicine men, and waits for Esteban's promised visit. One day the old Cortez comes to the palace and commands Chakoh to feed his horse. In the viceroy's stables, Chakoh finally finds Esteban, who as a slave has not been free to visit. In Chakoh's culture, slaves are cowards. Chakoh loses respect for Esteban until Esteban explains that his parents sold him in order to have money to feed their other children. Chakoh realizes quickly that Esteban has never lied to him and that his character remains unchanged. In preparation for *Coronado's expedition to Cibola, the two are chosen to lead a preliminary group. At the Cibulan pueblo, Cibulans capture Esteban and then release him, only to shoot him in the back. Also wounded, Chakoh returns to Mexico, desolate without the hope of seeing Esteban. His adventure ends when he decides that, despite the lack of food, his past home is more desirable than loneliness.

Another pueblo tribe, the Cicuyens, appears in **A Stranger and Afraid**. As an adolescent captured by the Cicuyens, Sopete longs to return home to his *Wichita family in 1540. But he refuses to leave his younger brother, Zabe, even though Zabe loves his foster mother. A white stranger, *Alvarado, comes to hunt buffalo. Later Coronado comes, destroys the pueblos, and marches the people to Sopete's homeland in search of gold about which a Pawnee captive, Kima, has bragged. Coronado finds no gold and eventually kills Kima for his lies. Sopete remains with his father and by Indian custom, never mentions either Sopete's mother who died during Sopete's capture, or Zabe, who deserted them to remain with the Cicuyens. Sopete's intense desire to protect his brother almost costs his life, but he learns to accept that his brother has the right to make his own choices.

In two mid-nineteenth-century novels, Baker's protagonists, as members of The People, also present an ethnic perspective. *And One Was a Wooden Indian* shows their attitudes toward whites and **Killer-of-Death** set in 1850, reveals reactions to other tribal members. An uncle dreams before his nephew's birth that although the child will never lead the tribe, he will save the leader. In this way, the protagonist, Killer-of-Death, obtains his name. At age twelve, however, he inadvertently offends the shaman's son, Gian-nah-tah. Their rivalry follows him through such tribal rituals as eating the raw heart of his first deer, drowning ducks for food, and living alone in the wild for fourteen days before his three raids in preparation for becoming a tribal warrior. During this time, Gian-nah-tah tries to kill him and, during a later raid, tries again. When Killer-of-Death returns to camp, he finds that the shaman's son has falsely accused him of being a coward. As they prepare to fight over the loss of honor, Mexicans ambush the tribe and kill almost everyone. Isolated from the fight and facing real danger, the petty arguments no longer matter, so Killer-of-Death and Gian-nah-tah help the survivors, including the leader, hide in a cave. Thus, Killer-of-Death fulfills his name while he and the shaman's son become brothers in their loss and grief.

An experience between two boys of The People and the ''white-eyes'' establishes the plot of **And One Was a Wooden Indian**. Around 1860, Hatilshay and Turtlehead of The People encounter a ''white-eyes'' working on the Butterland Express. Hatilshay's poor eyesight causes him not to see the railroad worker until another man shoots at him and misses. Turtlehead falls, and the worker takes Turtlehead to his camp to fix his wounds. In the camp, Turtlehead sees a wooden statue, thinks it a ''spirit-carving,'' and believes the man has captured his spirit. When they return home, Turtlehead demands that the shaman, his uncle, go with them to retrieve his spirit. When they find the statute, the shaman realizes that it is only a wooden carving of a *Hopi Indian, not even an *Apache. In order to placate Turtlehead, the shaman drowns the carving. The shaman understands about Hatilshay's poor eyesight, but Turtlehead's constant search for signs and visions lets him misinterpret Hatilshay's disability by thinking he has powers like a witch. The Shaman believes that Giver-of-Life, with reasons for everything, is helping Hatilshay to develop his spiritual inner vision.

The abstracts of Native American cultures make the story difficult to follow at times, but the action shows these abstracts as well as any other book trying to explain the extremes between the Native American and the white European ways of perceiving life. Native Americans achieve inner peace by becoming an integral part of their environment.

Two other books set in the mid-nineteenth century present the West from a white point of view. *The Dunderhead War* explores the difficulty of a German immigrant; characters in **Do Not Annoy the Indians** interact with the Native Americans. The Barnes family travels to join their father in Arizona's third largest city where he is station manager for the Butterfield Overland Main. The *Yuma Indians's monosyllabic responses when first encountered in Arizona make the Indians seem unintelligent to the Barnes family. Several experiences teach them otherwise. Before they even see Mr. Barnes, Mrs. Barnes gets a fever and has to remain in Fort Yuma for several weeks. When the children arrive alone at the station, they find that their father has left to pan for gold. Jeff and Sally begin to help the man looking after the station, but sibling squabbling occurs as they plan how to feed stage passengers quickly enough to keep the mail on time. They also want to give their Indian friend Tebarro a stagecoach ride. The alien stagecoach intrigues the Indians, and they need to conquer its power. Because Jeff and Sally cannot immediately negotiate the ride, Tebarro steals the stage one night while the driver remains inside the station eating dinner. The Indians want Jeff and Sally's younger brother, Benjie, in return for the stage because they think his temper tantrums show his supernatural power. After Jeff demonstrates that Benjie cannot evoke the Yuma spirits, he retrieves the stage and prepares for further business. Jeff's discovery that the Yuma Indians' knowledge of the environment far surpasses his allows him to appreciate their abilities.

The Dunderhead War shows Uncle Fritz's ability to keep order even in the summer heat of *Santa Fe during the 1846 *Mexican-American War. The action begins in Independence, Missouri, with the arrival from Germany of Uncle Fritz, Quince Heffendorf's mother's "little brother." Fritz's help loading goods in Mr. Heffendorf's store wagon shows Quince that Uncle Fritz expects order above everything else. Fritz asks about the police when Quince's friends shoot their guns in the air. Quince responds that his friends have freedom, but Uncle Fritz notes that it is freedom for "dunderheads and donkeys." Fritz earns the town's irritation, so Fritz and Quince join a wagon train heading to Santa Fe. During the journey, people call Fritz "Ein-Zwei" ("one-two") for his methods of hooking up his oxen team each day. Eventually his sense of order prevails because he helps the group guard against sheep stealing, and he feeds the army by trading with the Indians. Quince and Fritz decide to join the army, where Quince helps his friends suffering from the disloyalty of Rufus, a home-town boy. Before they had even left Independence, Rufus had stolen gunpowder from Mr. Heffendorf's store for the Mexicans. After the Americans win, the Independence contingency returns. Uncle Fritz, Mr. Heffendorf, and others start talking about the West Coast and the proposed settlement of New Helvetia. The men assure

Quince that he can continue studying law there because that area will also need lawyers. The first-person narrative allows Quince to reveal his uncle's situations with a warm humor and to show his gradual approval of Uncle Fritz's efficiency.

Three novels give insight about summer boredom in the later nineteenth and early twentieth centuries. Females race cars in *The Great Desert Race*. A "strong man" thrills New Yorkers in *The Night Spider Case*. And spiritualism enthralls bored teenaged girls in **The Spirit Is Willing**. To entertain themselves in their slowly dying desert mining town during the summer heat of 1885, Carrie and Portia have a seance in Carrie's kitchen. When something moves against Portia's leg while she is invoking the spirits, they consider their seance a success. Soon after, a saloon keeper wanting to compete against cockfights on the opposite side of the street buys a mummy to display, and the girls want to see it. Although ladies are not supposed to enter saloons, Carrie and Portia sneak inside, and the mummy grabs Portia. The town, titillated by news of spiritualism, becomes convinced that Portia can contact spirits of the dead. Many citizens pay to watch a test of Portia's ability. Frank, a young man attractive to Portia, releases fleas inside an inverted bowl over a scale, and the fleas cause the scale to move as Portia requests information from the netherworld about mine closings, an important economic concern to the townspeople. Soon after, Carrie's younger brothers reveal that they had originally touched Portia's leg and that Frank had finagled the test. Portia moves to San Francisco, but Carrie tries another seance, hoping to find a missing cat. The willingness of the people to believe such foolish claims indicates that bored people can believe almost anything.

In **The Night Spider Case**, Lambert Grew unwillingly becomes involved with Frances and her collection of spider webs during the summer of 1890. New York propriety expects Lambert's widowed mother not to take boarders, but she needs the money to support the family. While he sweeps the stoop in front of their Washington Square home, he pretends to Frances, a school friend, that he is trying to solve a mystery. She offers to help, and their investigations lead them to men digging a tunnel underneath a neighboring house. When the children follow, they find the men's gambling chips near an adjoining tunnel, an old passage known to their parents as Beach's subway. Sandor, the Strong Man performing in the neighborhood, saves the children from the tunnel diggers, and his presence delights a young adult female boarder. Sandor's main achievement, however, is ridding the parks of men who charge people for sitting in chairs. Like the other novels in this grouping, this story seems implausible and coincidental.

In a race from San Julio to Phoenix between a steam car called an ABCO and an electric car, two young women drive the ABCO in **The Great Desert Race** of 1908. Trudy, daughter of the newspaper editor, and Alberta, daughter of the ABCO salesman, become the basis of a bet. Trudy's father does not believe that anyone can successfully drive the ABCO; Alberta's father says that even she can drive it. And she does. Throughout the adventure, Trudy's mother worries about their being ladies. But the girls win the race, and Trudy decides to accept an offer to advertise ABCO cars in the East.

STYLE AND THEMES

Baker's straightforward style relies little on figurative language; she prefers to utilize imagery. Of the novels, the most successful are the earlier ones, both in Baker's career and chronologically. In them she makes valuable contributions to the understanding of ethnic cultures, especially Native Americans. Baker contrasts the depth of Native American spirit to the superficiality of many whites who went west to satisfy material interests with little or no concern for what they destroyed on their way.

BAR MITZVAH. This ritual commemorates the religious coming of age for a Jewish boy on his thirteenth birthday. *Bar mitzvah* means "son of" or "one responsible for the commandments." See *The Murderer* by Felice *Holman and *Friedrich* by Hans *Richter.

BARBARA AND GEOFFREY. Young English protagonists in *The Great House*. *See* Harnett, Cynthia.

BARBARA HOFF. American orphan living with German Separatists in Ohio as protagonist in *Zoar Blue*. *See* Hickman, Janet.

THE BARON'S HOSTAGE. *See* Trease, Geoffrey.

THE BARQUE OF BROTHERS. *See* Baumann, Hans.

BARTOS-HÖPPNER, B. (1923–   ). German.

BIBLIOGRAPHY AND BACKGROUND

The Cossacks. Illustrated by Victor Ambrus. Trans. Stella Humphries. London: Oxford, 1972. *Hunters of Siberia*. Trans. Anthea Bell. New York: Henry Z. Walck, 1969. *Save the Khan*. Illustrated by Victor Ambrus. Trans. Stella Humphries. New York: Henry Z. Walck, 1964; London: Oxford, 1963. *Storm over the Caucasus*. Trans. Anthea Bell. New York: Henry Z. Walck, 1968; London: Brockhampton Press, 1967.

Bartos-Höppner has been internationally acclaimed for her historical fiction. Her books, set in the eastern Soviet Union, show cultural developments from the late sixteenth through the twentieth centuries. The omniscient point of view permits readers to understand the motivations not only of the male protagonists but also of the antagonist and other characters. By witnessing both sides of altercations, readers can gain insight into behavior enigmatic to the Western mind.

WORKS

The same character, Mitya, appears in *The Cossacks* and *Save the Khan*. In **The Cossacks**, the action begins when *Yermak Timofeyevich visits his childhood home in 1579. His friend's daughter, Irina, overhears Yermak reveal his identity as chieftain of the *Cossacks, an outlaw band of Christians fighting to avenge *Ivan IV's deeds. As a child, Yermak had watched Ivan's soldiers strangle his parents. Irina rushes to tell Mitya, her friend who longs to leave the village, about Yermak. Mitya asks Yermak if he can join the Cossacks. After questioning, Yermak decides to accept him. Mitya follows Yermak into the depths of Russia and into Siberia to conquer lands for the czar. During this five-year maturation process, Mitya not only learns to kill humans, but he also learns to heal them. When Mitya realizes that soldiers need treatments after battles, he transports herbs and medicines for the Cossacks. The futility and horror of war, however, overcomes him when Yermak drowns. Mitya returns home to marry Irina and become a doctor. The lively dialogue allows explicit statements of theme, such as Yermak's comment that "every man has his path mapped out for him by Destiny and he must follow it whether he will or no," and "all we can do is to search our own hearts and act in good faith." The novel does not glorify the Cossack's life; it presents a realistic picture of its dangers and difficulties.

In another exciting novel set in 1598, **Save the Khan**, as Mitya is riding across the steppes from Sarai after visiting Gulai Khan, he stops at a shepherd's tent for the night. The shepherd says he is Daritai, Gulai Khan's son, the man the ailing Khan wants to see before he dies. Through flashback, Daritai tells Mitya his story. His mother, Daukai, died trying to save Daritai from a wolf during a hunt. His father, Gulai Khan, never wanted to see Daritai again. But eight years later, when Daritai's grandfather died, Gulai accepted Daritai's return. Gulai began to admire Daritai's qualities. During his ten years in Sarai, Daritai overcame his loneliness by becoming blood brothers with *Kuchum Khan's son Amanak and enjoying his daughter's company. Daritai helped Kuchum's people fight the White Russians whose guns destroyed them. After much devastation, Gulai Khan demands that Daritai kill the old, blind Kuchum Khan to stop the fighting. Since Kuchum has loved him like a son, Daritai refuses. He withdraws from society to become a shepherd. Daritai has always hated his father's materialistic values, symbolized by his often-fingered red jade necklace and his empty boasts of fighting the infidel Russians. Although still feeling bitter, Daritai finally accepts Mitya's suggestion that he think more kindly of his father, a lonely, remorseful old man, and alleviate some of his guilt before his death. Thus Mitya, the protagonist in *The Cossacks,* becomes the catalyst in *Save the Khan.*

Storm over the Caucasus is separated into Book I, which establishes the setting in 1834, and Book II, which begins five years later and covers events until 1870. Throughout, *Imam Shamyl tries to protect his Believers, the Moslems, from the Unbelievers, the Russians trying to conquer the *Caucasus. The protagonist, Aliko, meets the imam when taking a message to him. Aliko continues to serve him in the name of Allah for over twenty years. Aliko rapidly becomes best friends with the imam's son, Jamalludin. Soon after, the imam has to send Jamalludin to the Russians as a hostage but is unable to capture a valuable exchange for fourteen years. Jamalludin's experience shows him that the Russians are not unbelievers as his father proclaims. After the Russians capture Aliko's bride, Aliko does not see her until Jamalludin contacts the Russians and asks for her return. Jamalludin finds that he cannot fight against the Russians who have become his friends, and someone in the imam's army shoots him as a traitor. Throughout, Rachman, Aliko's old servant, tries to protect him as he had tried to protect Aliko's father and grandfather before they died in other wars defending the Caucasus. Aliko escapes death, but he has to move his wife, young son, and Rachman out of the mountains into Armenia to start a new life. Bartos-Höppner explicitly states the theme that every human must make individual decisions in life; "every man is alone in battle." And all humans must support their beliefs regardless of the consequences.

Hunters of Siberia, shows how hunters survive. In 1910, Nikolai Karalkan sees his family's way of life change when the forestry commissioner, Kyrill, arrives in his village. As the best hunter and fisherman, Nikolai's father, Ibrahim, dislikes having to guide Kyrill through the area settlements. On their travels, they see traps, some forgotten but still killing, as well as the blatant murder of elk herds. Slowly a friendship develops between the two men. Kyrill reveals that he used to love hunting but that his old serf convinced him to care for the animals instead. Ibrahim explains to Kyrill that he is exiled in Siberia because he was blamed for killing a cousin who was actually struck by lightning. Kyrill appreciates Ibrahim's refusal to slaughter game, and eventually Ibrahim understands that the new laws the commissioner brings, which prohibit hunting of females and young, will keep the animals from becoming extinct. In addition, he agrees when the commissioner bans unnecessary tree cutting, startled that villagers cut down the tall trees for nuts and leave the wood to rot rather than pick up the nuts from the ground. When the bears whom the peasants call "Mihail Ivanovich" appear, the two men, Nikolai, and the commissioner's daughter, Kyra, go hunting for them. Nikolai describes Ibrahim as an honest man who rarely drinks and rarely attends church. Nikolai indicates that the way one acts, not what one says, shows one's character. The story ends with the greatest Christian festival time in Russia, an Easter service. Nikolai and Kyra attend and share the traditional words, "Christ is risen," with each other. Thus they, the hunter Nikolai, and the city girl, Kyra, verify the importance of acceptance and understanding of others with different backgrounds.

STYLE AND THEMES

Bartos-Höppner's style complements the tapestry of thought in these novels. Her mastery of metaphor and personification shines with such clauses as "the wind sang eerily through the rushes and the tall thick spears blew in their faces and slapped against their shoulders and arms." Within the weave of her words,

the reader runs across the windswept steppes, suffers in the freezing snow, and
luxuriates in the love of a loyal friend.

BAUMANN, HANS (1914–   ). German.

BIBLIOGRAPHY AND BACKGROUND

The Barque of Brothers: A Tale of the Days of Henry the Navigator. Illustrated
by Ulrik Schramm. Trans. I. and F. McHugh. New York: Henry Z. Walck,
1958. *I Marched with Hannibal*. Illustrated by Ulrik Schramm. Trans. K. Potts.
London: Oxford, 1972. *Son of Columbus*. Trans. I. and F. McHugh. London:
Oxford, 1957. *Sons of the Steppe: The Story of How the Conqueror Genghis
Khan Was Overcome*. Trans. I. and F. McHugh. New York: Henry Z. Walck,
1957.

Baumann has been recognized as an important author with an international
reputation. He has numerous titles in translation.

WORKS

Baumann's four historical novels present a common theme: men convinced
of their personal invincibility and importance wage wars that needlessly destroy
human life. The almost tedious accounts of battle marches, battles, and battle
regroupings emphasize the desires of the four men to reshape the world according
to their own individual plans: Hannibal in the second century B.C., Genghis
Khan in the thirteenth, Henry the Navigator in the beginning of the fifteenth
century, and Christopher Columbus at the end of that century.

An old man tells his story in **I Marched with Hannibal** to two young teenagers
while sitting in the ruins of *Saguntum. When *Hannibal had destroyed the
town, the old man was twelve years old. He was left as dead, but Hannibal's
elephant, Suru, and its driver saved him. The boy became one of the thousands
in Hannibal's train of mercenaries, horses, and elephants traversing the Alps to
fight the Romans. Even after Hannibal lost 17,000 mercenaries and 2,000 horsemen in nine days crossing the Alps, his soldiers remained loyal because Hannibal
seemed to care for each individually. Much of the story relates the habits of
elephants, including Suru. The boy blames Hannibal for Suru's death, and after
Suru dies, the boy renames himself Suru. Roman soldiers later capture him and
sell him in Rome as the last remnant of Hannibal's elephants. Also traveling
with Hannibal is his Greek secretary, Silenos, who records Hannibal's campaigns
and conquests. Silenos befriends Suru, teaches him to read, appreciates nature's
beauty with him, and helps him endure the difficulties of survival. After his
flashback ends, Suru tells the children, whose family still digs for treasures
supposedly buried in the town, that Hannibal took everything of material value
but that pure water, the source of life itself, remains.

The prologue of **Sons of the Steppe** introduces Kublai and Arik-Buka, grand-
sons of *Genghis Khan. Arik storms into China to subdue Kublai, but Kublai's
men capture him instead. Together after many years, the brothers recall their
pledge made as young boys to stay together. That recollection leads them to

investigate the time during which Kublai's perception of life began to differ from
that of Arik. Their story recounts how their guardian, an old blind man, prepared
them to meet the Khan by telling them how Temuchin, called Genghis Khan,
gained his power. Temuchin followed the Mongol belief that clan is more important than individual and even killed his brother when he would not obey. His
fearlessness drew men to him, and he formed an army. After he had subdued
all others with aspirations of ruling the Mongols, he declared himself Genghis
Khan, lord of the Mongols. With his men, Genghis Khan invaded China. There
he became interested in Eastern wisdom. When he returned to the steppes, he
brought Yeliu, a believer in the stars, to advise him. Since Yeliu advocated
peace and contemplation, the followers of the Khan, who wanted only war and
action, viewed him as a traitor. Yeliu's insight, however, fascinates Kublai, and
Kublai becomes, at the Khan's request, his pupil. Arik, however, condemns
Yeliu as an evil force and leaves them. Yeliu tells Kublai that one day he will
rule with clemency for his subjects. By the time Yeliu dies, Kublai understands
much of the old man's wisdom, and the Khan expects Kublai to advise him.
Succession eventually passes to Kublai who goes into China to rule. Kublai
brings compassion and harmony to the Chinese by feeding the poor and housing
the wretched. In addition, he creates gardens and buildings of beauty like ones
he had seen the Khan destroy in the land of the shah. He tries to make amends
for the 40 million Chinese whom Genghis Khan's army killed during his quest
for power. As an adult, Arik, still controlled by Mongol beliefs, again fails to
unite with Kublai; Arik can interpret Kublai's loving acceptance only as
weakness.

The Barque of Brothers also tells of war's senseless destruction. Orphans
Tinoco and Aires leave their Portuguese village with their old friend Manuel's
guitar to join the navy of the Infante Henrique, *Henry the Navigator. As they
prepare to fight, they meet the captured young black Lopo who never speaks
until he hears Aires play his guitar. They and others disagree with Henrique in
his attempt to add Tangier to the already conquered Ceuta in Morocco. Later
the brothers sail to the Ivory Coast. When the man who finances Henrique's
fleet decides to bring "black ivory" from Africa, the men on *The Barque of the
Brothers* separate from the fleet. However, drums announcing the atrocious
captures of the natives spread down the coast ahead of the ship, and most of the
crew die from poisoned arrows. With Tinoco and the captain dead, the fourteen-
year-old Aires sails back to Portugal through a hurricane. By chance, he lands
during a fog in the harbor of his native village. He returns the guitar, pierced
with a poisoned arrow, to Manuel but realizes that he prefers to return to Africa
with Lopo rather than remain in his village. In this novel as well as the others,
Baumann balances the horror of war with the need of humans to see beauty in
life and to share it with someone else.

By 1502, King Ferdinand and Queen Isabella had driven the Moors from
Spain, and Christopher Columbus wanted to return to the New World. Columbus's son, Fernan, thirteen, in **Son of Columbus** lives with monks in the *Sar-

acen-built fortress *La Rabida. While Fernan looks over the treasures left with him by his father, a man rushes in the room and begins to tell Fernan that his selfish and cowardly father has stolen the man's claim to being the first to see the New World. Then the man frees a bag of snakes, which Fernan rapidly kills with the sword given him by Yehudi, a young boy he had once tried to protect. Fernan decides he needs to find what his father is really like, although the Padre, Father Juan *Perez, tells him that he will hear different stories from each person with whom he speaks. Fernan leaves school, secures a job as page for Queen Isabel, and in the palace makes friends with the silent Indian Tahaka. The two decide to voyage with Columbus's father on his fourth Atlantic crossing. Difficulties arise, and the ship becomes unfit to return to Spain. Columbus's enemies try to incite the local people so that they will not give food to either him or his men. Knowing that an eclipse will come on February 29, 1504, Columbus gains food for his loyal men by telling the people that their god is angry and will cover the moon. His ploy works, and before the people discover that Columbus has duped them, a captain who likes Columbus retrieves him and his men and takes them to Spain. The omniscient point of view throttles the suspense and creates dramatic irony since the reader always knows what Fernan's enemies think. The reader, however, realizes, as does Fernan, that many complex desires motivate Columbus but that people who have power and fear its loss continue trying to control others.

STYLE AND THEMES

Baumann's careful structure controls all of his novels. In *I Marched with Hannibal* and *Sons of the Steppe,* Baumann uses a frame. In the first chapter, an adult decides to tell a story about his youth. In *The Barque of Brothers,* Baumann uses a more subtle structure: a village adult, Manuel, influences one of two orphans to join his brother in sailing with explorers. Manuel gives his guitar to Aires as a token, which the boy returns at the end of his adventure. In *Son of Columbus,* the son goes on a voyage with his father in order to get to know him. In all the books, power destroys, but at least one character understands and desires beauty above all other qualities.

BAWDEN, NINA (1925–   ). British.

BIBLIOGRAPHY AND BACKGROUND

Carrie's War. Philadelphia: Lippincott, 1973; London: Gollancz, 1973. *The Peppermint Pig.* Illustrated by Alexy Pendle. Philadelphia: Lippincott, 1975; London: Gollancz, 1975.

Bawden, an accomplished author writing in several different genres, has been honored numerous times. In 1976, she won *The Guardian* Award and the *Yorkshire Post Award for The Peppermint Pig,* based on a family story about a pig her mother owned around the turn of the century. To research this novel, Bawden "visited elderly aunts, uncles, listened to stories, visited graveyards, looked at parish records, etc., in Lwaffhern, Norfolk, where the story is set." *Carrie's*

War, cited for the Carnegie Award, comes from Bawden's experience of being evacuated to Wales in World War II. Bawden spent her "school terms in a mining valley and holidays in a farm house rather like Druid's Bottom." Thus her subject matter intimately reflects her own life.

WORKS

The action of **The Peppermint Pig** begins in 1901 when Poll's father, James, takes the blame for a robbery he did not commit so that the real thief's father would not know about his son. He loses his job, decides to go to the United States to work with his brother, and sends his wife and three children to two aunts living in Norfolk to wait for his summons. Aunt Sarah supports the family until Poll's mother resumes her career as seamstress. Many women in town remember the abilities she exhibited before her marriage. The family buys a tiny runt pig for a shilling from the milkman and names him Johnnie. Since he stays clean and follows them around, they think he is a special pig. The mother comments, however, that pigs are a poor person's investment, thereby foreshadowing Johnnie's demise. During the following year, Theo, eleven, begins to grow physically; Poll catches and recovers from smallpox while a best friend's little brother dies from it; the community celebrates the king's coronation; and Poll meets her wandering grandfather. Poll's mother finally slaughters the pig, an action that symbolizes the harshness of maturation, taking responsibility, and shattered fantasies. Bawden captures the pain of growing up, of recognizing and coping with fear, and of learning that indecision and uncertainty comprise much of life.

The format of **Carrie's War** differs from *The Peppermint Pig.* The first and last chapters, set thirty years after the rest, are from the point of view of Carrie's oldest son. The inside of the frame flashes back to Carrie as an eleven- and twelve-year-old evacuee from London living in a Welsh town in 1939. She and her brother live with Samuel Evans, a niggardly man, and his weak sister, Louise. Mr. Evans's wealthy sister, Mrs. Gotobed, with whom he no longer communicates, lives in Druid's Bottom. Carrie and Nick go to visit Druid's Bottom at Christmas to get a goose from Hepzibah, Mrs. Gotobed's helper. Carrie discovers that Alfred Sandwich, a boy she had met on the train to Wales, also lives there. All three children become friends with Johnny, Mrs. Gotobed's cousin who cannot speak clearly. Hepzibah tells them that a legend about Druid's Bottom reveals that bad luck will come to the house when the skull of an African slave leaves the premises. The one previous removal caused all the windows and mirrors to crack overnight. They soon forget the story, and Carrie visits Hepzibah often because of the love and warmth she generates. After Mrs. Gotobed dies and Mr. Evans gives Hepzibah and Johnny notice to leave, Carrie throws the skull into the supposedly bottomless Horse Pond. The next morning she and Nick, on the train going to Glasgow to reunite with their mother, see the house on fire. Unable to contact Alfred or Hepzibah, she lives with the fear that she has done something terrible. Not until her return thirty years later, as a widow with her own children, does Carrie find out that no one was harmed in the fire. A rather unexpected twist to the theme of this novel is that children can sometimes help parents overcome fears. That aspect will please young readers; Carrie's fears will remind adults how incidents of childhood can continue to control their lives long after others have forgotten them.

STYLE AND THEMES

Bawden's deft abilities with language appear in metaphors such as the "day was a pale lemon streak over the rooftops." Her solid writing in this genre allows her to explore psychological themes of depth and import.

BEATTY, JOHN (1922–1975) and PATRICIA (1922–   ). Americans.

BIBLIOGRAPHY AND BACKGROUND

At the Seven Stars. Illustrated by Douglas Gorsline. New York: Macmillan, 1963; London: Chatto and Windus, 1966. *Campion Towers.* New York: Macmillan, 1965; London: Chatto and Windus, 1967. *A Donkey for the King.* Illustrated by Ann Siberell. New York: Macmillan, 1966. *Holdfast.* New York: Morrow, 1972. *King's Knight's Pawn.* New York: Morrow, 1971. *Master Rosalind.* New York: Morrow, 1974. *Pirate Royal.* New York: Macmillan, 1969; London: Collier Macmillan, 1969. *The Queen's Wizard.* New York: Macmillan, 1967. *The Royal Dirk.* Illustrated by Franz Altschuler. New York: Morrow, 1966. *Who Comes to King's Mountain?* New York: Morrow, 1975. *Witch Dog.* Illustrated by Franz Altschuler. New York: Morrow, 1968.

The Beattys, husband and wife, won several awards, especially in California, for their collaborated novels. In these books, the expertise of John as Professor of English History and of Patricia in Americana united to allow characters to have realistic experiences on both sides of the Atlantic Ocean. The eleven novels by the Beattys present four historical time frames: the Romans in Israel, the Elizabethan era, the Puritan period, and the end of the British rule in the American colonies.

WORKS

In the one novel set in Roman times, **A Donkey for the King,** the protagonist, a mute twelve-year-old orphan, Jesse Ben Abdiel, loves animals and teaches Belshazzar, a donkey abused by his circus owner, how to dance. When the owner sells the aging and ailing donkey, Jesse leaves the circus group to find it. For twelve days during which a star shines so brightly that people cannot sleep, he looks until he sees three men riding white camels enter a barn where the couple who bought Belshazzar sits next to a baby. Jesse steals Belshazzar whose improved health he credits to a possible tonic. But when Belshazzar's health deteriorates, Jesse returns him to the couple. Jesse decides to follow Belshazzar though his disinterest disheartens the boy. The couple invites Jesse to travel with them in a caravan going toward Egypt with both Romans and Jews to escape Herod's hated decree to kill all male children. He repays their hospitality by playing his shepherd pipes. In Ashkelon, Jesse and Belshazzar thwart a man's attempt to kill the couple's child. With pictures and acting, Jesse shows the servant what happened, and she tells Jesse that people think the child is the Messiah. Jesse's own father in his last words had noted that Jesse would know the Messiah; therefore, Jesse believes. The couple gives Belshazzar to Jesse as they board the ship for Egypt, telling him that Belshazzar really belongs to him. Jesse returns to Jerusalem and his dreams of being a scribe and a pipe player. As an outcast, an unwilling orphan left to survive as he can, Jesse finds love from this family and the donkey, and he returns it.

The second time period represented in the Beatty novels is the late Elizabethan period, with *Master Rosalind* set in 1595, *The Queen's Wizard* in 1599, and *Holdfast* in 1600. In **Master Rosalind**, Rosalind, at twelve, dressed as a boy, journeys to see Dr. Hornsby in Oxford to borrow a valuable book for her grandfather. As she returns, a person pretending to be an "Abraham Man" (crazy man) tries to steal the book. He kidnaps her and makes her become a thief in London. When she shows no talent for "nipping," Moll, her keeper, frees her, but instead of returning home, Rosalind, entranced with the players she had seen in Oxford, spends nearly a year with *Shakespeare's actors helping them and as "boy" to Master Pope. Her adventures during the year include Ben *Jonson's rescuing her from a murderer. Not until Robert *Cecil imprisons her within the Tower walls does she discover that Fenchurch, an unknown cousin, wants her dead so that he can inherit the recently deceased baron of Broome's property in her place. She also learns that the rogues who originally kidnapped her are actually spying on the earl of *Essex for Cecil and *Elizabeth I. Her year ends when people discover her carefully disguised sex. With her newly acquired wealth, she returns home to her scholar grandfather without ignominy.

In 1599, when the recently orphaned Nicholas Quill and his brother, Peter (thought to be "moonstruck"), go to Dr. Griffin at Mortlake in **The Queen's Wizard**, Nicholas is only eleven. Although as an astrologer, Dr. Griffin cannot cure Peter, he allows Peter to stay when he finds that Peter is a "scryer," one who sees the future. Peter foretells the earl of Essex's ambition and death which cements his credibility with Dr. Griffin's noble customers. Nicholas becomes Dr. Griffin's messenger. One questioner, Queen Elizabeth, decides that Nicholas must learn to read and write. Dr. Griffin teaches Nick, a rapid learner, and takes him as an apprentice. Nick learns about the stars which the limited omniscient point of view shows have always fascinated him. Gunpowder given Dr. Griffin by the queen before her death to help protect him from the superstitious Mortlake villagers eventually brings him blame in the gunpowder plot to overthrow King James. A search, however, revealing that Guy *Fawkes did not take his gunpowder absolves Dr. Griffin. Through his study of astrology, Dr. Griffin tries to help people. His constant questioning helps Nick to find goals for his adult life.

A third novel set in the time of Elizabeth is **Holdfast**, the story of Catriona Burke, the Irish lady of Kilrain captured by an English soldier and taken with her Irish wolf dog, Manus, to England in 1600. Since Manus allows only women to control him, Catriona frees him as they disembark in England in hopes that he can escape being killed. A gypsy girl finds him and sells him. Catriona becomes the queen's ward, and Latimer takes Catriona into his home in order to collect the rents from her father's English lands and marry her to his eldest son when she is fourteen. The tempestuous Catriona hears stories about a wolf dog baiting bears at the Paris Garden in London. On May Day, she dances so well for Elizabeth I that she wins a chance to see the dog. The dog is Manus, as Catriona suspects. When she confronts the queen with her plight, Elizabeth frees her. Personifying the dog mars the plausibility of the book and makes it historical fantasy, and the plot based on getting girl and dog together stretches thin; but the story gives an interesting look at customs late in the reign of Elizabeth I, including the dissoluteness of Southwark, the Globe Theater's location.

A third general time period—immediately before, during, and after the *English Civil War—incorporates the settings of *Witch Dog, King's Knight's Pawn, Campion Towers,* and *Pirate Royal.* In **Witch Dog,** the protagonist again prefers a dog to humans. *Rupert, a Bohemian prince imprisoned in 1638 at *Linz, receives a dog from the English earl of Arundel. A second gift is the orphaned Hugh, who becomes Rupert's serving boy while in prison. As nephew of King *Charles I and a known soldier, Rupert gains freedom and a chance to fight when his dog, Boye, and his brother, Maurice, help him lead *Cavalier forces against the *Roundheads. Hugh follows Rupert to England but hates Boye because Rupert obviously prefers his dog to him. Boye's repeated successes of helping Rupert when in trouble and his white coat make Boye seem almost supernatural. Hugh even sells Boye to a Roundhead, expecting him to kill the dog, but the man instead displays Boye in a cage as Rupert's "witch dog." A little girl sees Boye in his cage, steals the key, and frees him. When Boye is loose in Oxford, Rupert finds him. Although Hugh continues his attempts to kill Boye, Boye does not die until the Battle at *Marston Moor outside of *York where *Cromwell defeats Rupert. Although Rupert prefers the dog to Hugh, he shows his loyalty by retaining Hugh rather than abandoning him.

A second English Civil War novel, **King's Knight's Pawn**, seems fraught with coincidence when the protagonist, Christopher Barstow, considered a changeling by his family, runs away, arrives in London on the day of Charles I's beheading, and has a Cavalier sympathizer, Captain Peter Dell, immediately befriend him. Dell even accompanies Kit to Ireland to see Kit's godfather, Aston, who waits to avenge the king against Cromwell. Kit enjoys Dell's joviality, but when war begins and the king's army sits at *Drogheda, Kit finds that Dell is actually Cromwell's spy. Thus, the apparent coincidence disappears. The Irish hatred of the English, probably begun when an English king forced them to become Protestant, shows clearly when the Catholic boy Conn, in service to Aston, hisses vile comments at the Protestant English Kit immediately after his arrival. During the annihilation at Drogheda, however, Kit kills Dell and saves Conn, who has become his best friend. Kit learns from his relationships and his

games of chess that without boldness, one has almost no chance for victory—
or survival.

A third Civil War story begins in Salem colony where Penitence Hervey
receives a letter in 1651 from her deceased mother's relatives in England requesting her to sail before her grandmother dies to receive the Killingtree inheritance in **Campion Towers**. A man who visits Penitence on her arrival in
*Bristol, England, gives her information about her family and asks her to help
him reveal their papist tendencies. When Penitence attends the funeral of her
grandmother, she sees that they are actually Anglican, and she has been fooled.
She supports Cromwell and rides to him with the news that *Charles Stuart,
whom he is about to fight at Worcester, will be hiding in the family home,
Campion Towers, after the battle. But Penitence, captured by the Cavaliers,
talks with Charles Stuart and realizes that she sympathizes more with him. She
warns the family of her Cromwell encounter and decides to help Charles escape
in disguise. She falls in love with one of Charles's supporters, her distant cousin
Julian Killingtree, who remains an outlaw in England as long as Cromwell rules.
When Julian promises to come to Salem, Penitence gives him and Charles her
inherited jewels to help their cause and returns to Salem to wait for Julian.
Penitence realizes that people easily dupe the uninformed and that only maturity
helps one to beware.

The action in **Pirate Royal** begins after the *Stuarts regain the throne. Falsely
accused of stealing silver by his master, the protagonist, Anthony Grey, faces
deportment as a bond servant to the Massachusetts Bay Colony. In 1667, Anthony
spends seventy days crossing the Atlantic in a three-masted merchantman ship.
A good master recognizes his intelligence and honesty and makes him his clerk
until a pirate kidnaps the prospering Anthony and takes him to *Port Royal.
There Captain Dawkins gives Anthony to Harry *Morgan, a man whom the
English Crown has given rights to plunder Spanish ships. After Anthony raids
with Harry for several years, British soldiers arrest them for fighting against the
Spanish once too often. They go to England, but instead of imprisonment in the
Tower, Harry is knighted, and Anthony's stories of battle entertain the duke of
Albemarle. Anthony returns to Bristol to see his mother but realizes his true
home is now with Morgan in Port Royal. He finds that his seemingly horrible
misfortune has led him to a life that he loves and wants.

The three novels set in the eighteenth century finds roots in the 1746 Battle
of *Culloden when the British beat the Scots. In *The Royal Dirk,* Alan helps
Bonnie Prince Charlie (*Charles Edward) escape from Scotland. A second novel,
At the Seven Stars, finds Richard newly in England from the colonies trying to
help the Stuarts regain the throne from the *Hanoverians around 1752. And
finally, in *Who Comes to King's Mountain?* Alec MacLeod fights against the
British in the *American Revolution in retaliation for the loss.

In **The Royal Dirk,** thirteen-year-old Alan Macrae helps Bonnie Prince Charlie, son of the exiled King James of Scotland, escape from the British duke of
*Cumberland after the Battle of Culloden defeat in the Scottish highlands. Then

Alan marches in the name of his dead brother, Rory, toward Edinburgh with nineteen other prisoners from the decimated glen. Hearing that Alan knows about the prince's escape, an unknown woman frees Alan from the Castle Tolbooth. Jessie and her highwayman husband, Captain Pride, take Alan to England. In London, an enemy murders the couple, and Alan unexpectedly finds work at the home of an Italian master-at-arms known for his expert swordplay. Alan watches the master spar with David *Garrick, the famous actor, as well as a Frenchman, André Desaix, who when unconscious cries Gaelic, not French. When Desaix shows Alan a dirk matching the one given Alan by the prince, Alan finally believes Desaix's story that he, a Scot, has come to England to kill the duke of Cumberland. At the races, Alan stops a man planning to kill André, thereby saving the duke's life. Instead of prison, Alan receives safe passage back to Scotland. By risking himself for others, Alan eventually regains his beloved home.

As an orphan in the American colonies, in **At the Seven Stars,** Richard Larkin at fifteen leaves the Pennsylvania Colony for London where he expects to live with his uncle. However, his uncle dies in prison soon after Richard arrives. Samuel *Johnson befriends him as he stands outside *St. Paul's with Abby, a little girl foisted on him by a passing woman, and tells him that Jeremy Belcher at the Seven Stars may have work for him. At the inn, Richard inadvertently sees a man murdered while he serves a group of men planning to overthrow the Hanoverian king, *George, for the Stuarts. He escapes from them and takes Abby to Chiswick where they live with William *Hogarth, known to help foundlings. Some of the men in the group find Richard, accuse him of the murder, and take him to France to see the Stuart prince. A traitor within the group, however, reports to the Hanoverians, and they thwart the Stuart Elibank plot. For his help, Richard receives money which pays for passage to the colonies for him, Abby, and Betsy, another foundling working in the Hogarth home. The explicit theme that one must "do well by oneself" applies to Richard as he learns survival for himself and others without families.

In **Who Comes to King's Mountain?,** Alec Macleod's grandmother, known as "fey" because of her ability to predict the future, and his grandfather, branded by the English as a traitor at the Battle of Culloden, Scotland, in 1746, remain rebels while his father claims for King George. Alec's father demands that the fourteen-year-old ride for the British with neighbor Jamie, and after Jamie hangs Alec's grandfather, Alec sees the British leader Tarleton kill Jamie over cards merely for Jamie's horse. Alec coerces a little girl to wash her pokeberry-stained hands in the rum that Tarleton and his men are drinking. They wretch for three days, which gives many rebels time to hide from them. The British colonel, *Ferguson, does not believe that Alec's father is a *Loyalist, so he almost kills him and demands that Alec join his troop. Alec escapes to join the rebel Colonel *Marion, known as the Swamp Fox, and becomes his spy. Ferguson's men capture Alec, and he has to fight for the British at King's Mountain. Alec's refusal to shoot entices a red coat to bayonet his left hand, and the rebel mountaineers think him a traitor. His grandmother's prescience of Alec's trouble leads her to the battle site where she convinces the condemners that Alec supports Marion and the colonies. The loyalty garnered by the Stuarts in the Culloden defeat has far-reaching and unexpected consequences. People with strong ideals will die for them. Alec watches his family suffer, split by values and beliefs, but the strong convictions and loyalty of his grandparents gain them respect through life and after death.

STYLE AND THEMES

The Beattys write with intense imagery but little figurative language. A metaphor, however, in *A Donkey for the King* captures the hot desert setting as the "afternoon drained itself slowly away." The characters often ask rhetorical questions to help themselves solve problems and perhaps, to prod the reader to consider alternative ideas. The device works in most instances. Thematically, the protagonists succeed by using their intelligence to follow their personal ideals. For *Campion Towers,* the Beattys researched which words were used during the 1640s and purged their book of words not yet evolved. Their syntax, however, remains contemporary, with little attempt to remind readers of the time period. The results of the Beattys' writing are readable, exciting adventures in historically accurate settings.

BEATTY, PATRICIA (1922–). American.

BIBLIOGRAPHY AND BACKGROUND

The Bad Bell of San Salvador. New York: Morrow, 1973. *Billy Bedamned, Long Gone By*. New York: Morrow, 1977. *Blue Stars Watching*. New York: Morrow, 1969. *Bonanza Girl*. Illustrated by Liz Dauber. New York: Morrow, 1962. *By Crumbs, It's Mine!* New York: Morrow, 1976. *Eight Mules from Monterey*. New York: Morrow, 1982. *Hail Columbia*. Illustrated by Liz Dauber. New York: Morrow, 1970. *How Many Miles to Sundown*. New York: Morrow, 1974. *Jonathan Down Under*. New York: Morrow, 1982. *Just Some Weeds from the Wilderness*. New York: Morrow, 1978. *Lacy Makes a Match*. New York: Morrow, 1979. *A Long Way to Whiskey Creek*. New York: Morrow, 1971. *Me, California Perkins*. Illustrated by Liz Dauber. New York: Morrow, 1968. *Melinda Takes a Hand*. New York: Morrow, 1983. *The Nickel-Plated Beauty*. Illustrated by Liz Dauber. New York: Morrow, 1964. *O the Red Rose Tree*. Illustrated by Liz Dauber. New York: Morrow, 1972. *The Queen's Own Grove*. Illustrated by Liz Dauber. New York: Morrow, 1966. *Red Rock over the River*. New York: Morrow, 1973. *Something to Shout About*. New York: Morrow, 1976. *That's One Ornery Orphan*. New York: Morrow, 1980. *Turn Homeward, Hannalee*. New York: Morrow, 1984. *Wait for Me, Watch for Me, Eula Bee*. New York: Morrow, 1978.

Beatty's various awards have come from such groups as the Western Writers and the Society of Children's Book Writers. In addition, she received the Southern California Council on Children's and Young People's Literature award for a distinguished body of work in 1974 when fewer than half of her novels had been published. Beatty says that "anybody can have a drug experience—but who can 'live' in eighteenth century America except through a book? I find much about the past more colorful and interesting than I do about today." Since she considers "boy-meets-girl" books set in urban or suburban areas boring, she tries to avoid simple plot lines. Such thoughts have propelled Beatty, who wrote first with her husband, Dr. John Beatty, to continue recreating historical Americana. She researches her ideas for months in public and university libraries using microfilmed newspapers. She saves newspaper pieces and collects old catalogs and source books. Since she writes in spurts, she generally revises only once, usually as a result of editorial conferences. Using this procedure, Beatty has written over twenty books set in the western area of North America during the nineteenth century.

WORKS

In Beatty's novels, each protagonist is thirteen, and all but five are female. A female protagonist narrates fourteen of the novels in first person, but Beatty uses limited omniscient point of view to tell the stories of the male protagonists. Several general patterns allow a closer examination of the novels.

Of five novels with male protagonists, only one presents a Native American viewpoint. **The Bad Bell of San Salvador**, set in 1842, introduces the young *Comanche, Spotted Wild Horse, captured by Mexicans for stealing their horses and renamed Jacinto. Jacinto's refusal to worship the Catholic god and his recalcitrance leads his master to send him from *Santa Fe to Gamboa's ranch where he will work and fight invading *Utes. Jacinto looks forward to stealing one of Gamboa's horses and returning to his tribe with an enemy Ute's scalp. Gamboa suspects Jacinto and keeps him busy doing what Jacinto considers "women's work." He thinks only weak men farm, and he hates building adobe houses. He soon makes friends with Teodoro and convinces him to sneak out at night to catch and tame two wild horses. The Utes ruin his plan to escape by raiding, and Jacinto fails to stop Gamboa's son, El Chino, from fatally pursuing them. Thus El Chino returns, his body preserved in snow. After moving in with the priest, Tio Carlos, Jacinto helps him create a church bell with scrap metal weighing nearly a ton. When finished, the bell sounds raspy, and villagers blame the unbeliever, Jacinto. But when Jacinto soon hears a flood rushing down the Santa Ana River, he rings the bell and saves the town. In appreciation, Gamboa offers Jacinto freedom to rejoin his tribe, but Jacinto decides that he will leave only after he helps rebuild the destroyed adobe houses.

In **Jonathan Down Under**, Jonathan Cole accompanies his gold-crazed father, Charlie, to Australia after digging in California for two years. As *Brother Jonathans, they arrive in 1851 and pay for a small claim where they begin panning. Soon Jonathan develops sandy blight, and to keep from going blind, he stays inside for several months while having his eyes scraped daily. When he recovers, he discovers that his father's interim partner has disappeared with their gold. Then the mine roof collapses and crushes Charlie's chest, killing him. Jonathan gets a job with Molly Quinn, a woman who blatantly stole a petticoat during the potato famine knowing that the British would transport her from Ireland but that they would also feed her. When an Irish trooper blackmails and inadvertently kills her, two other Irish former convicts befriend Johnny. Aborigines dig a deep pit, and Johnny helps the two men gather gold from the bottom. Knowing that he has never acquired gold fever like his father and pleased with his help and his pleasant disposition, they send him back to America. Jonathan survives by his willingness to work.

Also an orphan, Parker Quiney has the distinctly distasteful task of retrieving his brother Jess's body in **A Long Way to Whiskey Creek** during 1879. He invites Nate, another "leppie" (orphan), to go with him and his dog, J.E.B. Stuart, on the 400–mile-journey to Ruination. Throughout the trip, the two argue about the *Confederates and the *Yankees. Nate wants to teach Parker to read, but Parker insists that being a horse breaker does not require reading skills. Their adventures include escaping from a preacher who thinks they belong in an orphans' home, having to dive for petroleum to add to a "professor's" elixir, riding in the center of a steer stampede during a storm, and scaring a *Comanche. Tonkawa, known as Mr. Bailey, offers to exhume Jess's body in repayment for previous crimes and twenty years' imprisonment. He also accompanies the boys home and requests that Nate teach Parker and him to read. When Tonkawa leaves, he makes Parker promise to attend school and wishes Nate success with the family that has offered him a home.

Three novels present viewpoints on the *American Civil War from different areas of the country. In one of the novels, set in 1861, the war serves as backdrop. In **Wait for Me, Watch for Me, Eula Bee,** of the seven Collier family members only three-year-old Eula Bee and her brother, Lewtie, remain after two have left Texas to fight for the Confederates and Comanches have killed the rest. After Lewtie's capture, a Comanche woman who speaks English tells him that his bravery kept him alive. He shows further bravery by rescuing his master from a rushing buffalo herd. This feat gains him the privilege of herding horses, a freedom he uses to escape. He finds Mr. Cabal, a neighbor he distrusts but also the father of two other captured children, in the autumn, and they plan to search in the spring when good weather arrives. When they find the children, Yankee soldiers choose the same time to stampede the Comanche-Kiowa camp, killing both Mr. Cabal and his son. Lewtie goes to *Santa Fe to Mr. Cabal's brother whose commanchero (whites trading ammunition to Indians) sons take him to the summer trading spot. Since Lewtie does not find Eula Bee, he returns to the Indian camp. He locates Small Buffalo's tent and avenges the killing of his family by slitting it open, stealing Small Buffalo's scalp lock (his symbol of honor), and grabbing Eula Bee. Eula Bee, however, shows no recognition and screams for her Indian mother. Her attachment reveals that white children captured by Indians generally received much love and care. After several months,

Eula Bee overcomes her shock and calls Lewtie by name. Lewtie shows his bravery throughout and risks his life several times to reunite his remaining family.

An unusual view of the American Civil War appears in **Blue Stars Watching.** Although the action begins on the East Coast, it shifts to San Francisco and reveals the effects of enterprises outside the war zone. The protagonist, Will Kinmont, finds the hired hand, Rab, murdered in the barn and sees a black man running away. His father tells him that the farm has been an *Underground Railway station and that Confederates have killed Rab. In 1861, Will's parents send him and his seven-year-old sister, Eugenia, on ship via Panama to an aunt and uncle living in San Francisco. On their arrival in port, runners board the ship trying to coerce passengers to particular inns and restaurants—nineteenth-century marketing. The lack of news in San Francisco frustrates Will, but a job at the newspaper *Alta California* lets him know when his father's Maryland unit fights. Mr. Fortune, Will's Delaware school teacher turned secret service man, appears and with Will's help, under the code name ''Blue Stars,'' exposes Will's relatives as supporting the Confederates. His aunt stuffs gold into dolls and passes the dolls to members of the ''Chivalry for *Emmaline*.'' The exposure stops *Emmaline,* a schooner and would-be pirateer, from delivering the money to Confederates. The story illustrates the division of values in families during civil war.

The last book set in the American Civil War, **Turn Homeward, Hannalee,** shows the Yankees' arrival in Roswell, Georgia, during 1864, where they gather all of the mill workers, including Hannalee Reed and her brother Jem, accuse them of treason, and ship them to Indiana. Mrs. Reed, expecting another child, has to watch her younger children leave after seeing her older son, Davey, depart with the Confederates, as well as her husband return in a brown box, dead from a fever. The Indiana couple who hires Hannalee treats her like a slave. She escapes by climbing out a window, stealing boys' garments from a clothes line, and pretending to be a ''Hannibal'' Reed. She ferries across the Ohio to find her brother Davey's fiancée, Rosellen, but after working with her for a few weeks, realizes that Rosellen will probably remain in Indiana. Hannalee finds Jem, and they take a train to Nashville using Hannalee's mill wages. The last long leg of their journey deposits them in the middle of a battle with its horrors of war. A peddler rescues them and transports them within twenty miles of home. There they find their mother and the new baby, Paulina, with little food and no heat. Davey soon returns, missing one arm. The war almost destroys them, but Hannalee's intelligence and determination help reunite those remaining.

Two novels involve several members of a family unseparated by outside forces. In **Billy Bedamned, Long Gone By,** while the father stays home, Merle Tucker's mother drives Merle, her brother, and grandmother from Pasadena to New Orleans in 1929 with a stop at the family home in MacRae, Texas. Two great uncles entertain the family with tall tales and family history. Much dialogue among the family members never allows Merle to understand which stories are true.

A more satisfying family novel is **The Queen's Own Grove**. When Amelia Bromfield-Brown's father suffers a lung hemorrhage, the doctor advises him to move his wife, children, and mother-in-law Thorup from England to Canada in 1887. With Canada's weather no better than England's, they move again and find a comfortable climate in Riverside, California. There they buy an orange grove, which they rename the Queen's Own Grove. Grandmother Thorup unexpectedly encounters Hesketh Thorup, her brother-in-law who has lived in California since his brother, her late husband, demanded that he leave England after marrying an unacceptable Irish woman. Shocked, she refuses to speak to him. Bill Lee, the Chinese servant, helps the family overcome several cultural differences. First, he helps the three children enjoy Halloween by pretending to be spirits for their neighbors, the Appelbooms. Then he suggests that the children invite Hesketh Thorup's family to tea in order to meet the two young Thorups. Having to face Hesketh as well as his family in her own home, Grandmother begins to accept the American Thorups. When a fire destroys their Grove home, Mr. Mercer, a man infatuated with Grandmother, loans the family his empty house. Mr. Mercer's generosity also softens Grandmother's attitude toward him. Hesketh helps them by going to Australia to find a treatment for white scale found on the oranges, while Amelia's father learns to distinguish frozen oranges from good ones by their weight. Supporting each other, the family copes with problems encountered in a new physical and social environment.

In another category of novels, the young female protagonists tell stories of strong, older women who achieve their goals. In **Something to Shout About**, Hope Foster moves with her family from Oregon to Idaho Territory during 1875 to operate the Whole Shebang Store. The new schoolteacher arrives and finds that the schoolhouse is a former chicken coop. The mayor, however, wants a jail and a town hall before any other buildings. Dr. Marah, a woman masquerading as a man and boarding with the Fosters, encourages the women to collect money in the town's thirty-eight saloons for a school house. They raise almost all of the money, but one saloon owner, Mr. O'Hare, has them arrested for sitting on his property. Dr. Marah convinces a female lawyer and a female reporter to come to Ottenberg to aid the women. An editorial comment states the explicit feminist theme: "apparently there were choices other than being a schoolteacher." When a man shoots O'Hare, Dr. Marah, as the only physician, treats him and sends him for specialized care elsewhere. After O'Hare leaves, Dr. Marah reveals her identity, explaining her demand for complete privacy and her strong support of the town's women. The relationship between the child Hope and the adult Dr. Marah seems somewhat unrealistic.

In **Me, California Perkins**, Callie tells about her mother, who during 1882, furious at being moved to a silver mine area in Mojaveville, California, desires to leave. Her husband, Gideon, refuses, so she stays, living in the whiskey bottle and mortar house (cooler in 110 degree heat) built by Hiram, her husband's brother, but making Gideon move into the men's hotel. Throughout the year that they remain apart, several things happen to unite the town. Cornish miners from England and several others contract *La grippe,* a disease that kills twenty but starts people caring for each other. Female schoolteachers marry members of the school board within weeks of coming to town. A flash flood almost kills the children, Wyatt Earp visits, and Grandpa strikes a silver vein that makes him wealthy. Mrs. Perkins and the spinster Jennieveva who runs a boardinghouse together mastermind the town's elections without even having a vote. Mrs. Perkins notes that during Callie's life, women will probably begin voting and serve on school boards themselves. But while they cannot, to get what they want, they must gently manipulate the men who can. When Mama finally agrees to see Pa, she convinces him to leave Mojaveville with the family so that Callie can go to high school and become a teacher.

In 1884 in **Bonanza Girl**, Ann Katherine Scott accompanies her widowed mother and brother, Jemmy, to Idaho Territory. They meet Helga Storkersen who convinces Mrs. Scott to open a tent restaurant instead of teaching school. With the help of the unusually named O'Neil O'Neil and Jemmy's mule, Timothy Clover, they succeed. When O'Neil discovers a silver mine, they move the restaurant, and the rest of the town, to the claim area. A nasty man, Farr, tries to kill O'Neil and Jemmy and gain the claim as repayment for their demanding that he not beat his mules. An avalanche, however, conveniently kills him before he can succeed. The women go into saloons to collect money for a church. Then they hire a preacher so that Helga can marry O'Neil, and Mrs. Scott can marry Luke Gordon, one of the more couth citizens of the new town of Wallace.

Widowed Aunt Columbia in **Hail Columbia** comes from Philadelphia with her two children to spend 1893 in her brother Captain Baines' Astoria, Washington, home. Having heard nothing other than Christmas greetings from her in nineteen years, Louisa's father expects a spinster over forty. Columbia, however, an Oberlin College graduate, uses her maiden name and makes no secret of her role as a suffragette who corresponds with Susan B. *Anthony and Elizabeth Cady *Stanton. Captain Baines stops speaking to her. Columbia, not deterred by his rudeness, decides to help the town by befriending the Finnish immigrants and acknowledging their contribution of meter from the Finnish *Kalevala* to Longfellow's *Hiawatha.* She understands Chinese customs and successfully teaches English to the Chinese workers. Finally, in her role as temperance worker, she decides to clean Swill Town, the row of bars whose owners shanghai men to become sailors. To complete the task, she succeeds in getting the wealthy Captain Baines nominated and elected mayor. Columbia's achievements impress the captain, and he begins speaking to her. Content that he will stop the illegal politics, Columbia decides to return to Philadelphia; at her departure, the captain hires four cannons to fire a twenty-one gun salute. Louisa sees Columbia act on her beliefs that people can do anything if they try hard. Columbia also believes, as stated in the explicit theme, that "every lie a maiden tells destroys a leaf of her beauty."

Another widow appears in **Eight Mules from Monterey**. Fayette Ashmore's mother graduates from library school in 1916, and Fayette helps her secure a job taking books requested by five women into the mountains of Monterey to Big Tree Junction. A mule driver and his eight mules loaded with supplies and books ride the family into the hills. On the way, Mrs. Ashmore loans books to residents, which she plans to retrieve on her return. Before they ride very far, the first mule driver almost chops off his foot with an ax. A second mule driver carries them through the almost pathless woods. Several unusual adventures on the way include conducting a funeral service for a man's wife and children dead from typhoid. In Big Tree Junction, they find that the five women desperate for books are only two; they have forged three other names in hopes of getting a library. When Mrs. Ashmore establishes the library there, she knows that she has learned enough to be independent and will not have to marry her deceased husband's law partner upon returning to Monterey. The realistic interaction allows Mrs. Ashmore to be discouraged during her rough trip. She nearly turns back several times, but her perseverance rewards her with newly gained self-confidence.

In a final grouping of novels, all but two of the thirteen-year-old female protagonists tell of accomplishing feats thought impossible by adults. None of the protagonists is memorable, but customs of the latter nineteenth century reveal the pioneer spirit. Beatty fulfills her intent of showing heroines in positive roles, but the didacticism sacrifices literary integrity. The two books with limited omniscient point of view are the two in which the protagonist does not achieve an unusual feat.

In the first, the protagonist merely survives. When Hallie Lee Baker's grandfather dies in 1889, she has to enter the Texas orphan asylum run by Miz Hopkins with all the other "leppies" in **That's One Ornery Orphan**. Hallie tries to adjust to three "pickers" (foster parents) but fails. The first, the preacher Spiller, uses Hallie as a heathen to baptize and as a hired girl but sends her back when she refuses immersion. The second, Doc Wiley, wants someone to help with patients' children, and Hallie does well until she mixes twins during diapering. On a third try with Miz Hopkins's sister, an actress, Hallie hires a horse to appear in a play, but it stops on stage instead of running rapidly across it. On her return to the asylum, she finally goes with the German Mr. Farber whom she has avoided because she disdains "sodbusters" (farmers). She finds that he and his wife raise horses and have a baby, the two things Hallie loves most. Orphans have difficult lives, and the limited choices require strong character to survive.

In the second novel with limited omniscient point of view, the protagonist, Beulah Land, accompanies her brother and his friend across New Mexico and Arizona in 1881 searching for Sundown, the last place the friend's father was known to have visited. The three in **How Many Miles to Sundown** have adventures that include traveling briefly with a small circus; meeting the famous Major Gordon, who says that "single blessedness is a lot better than misery in double harness"; and sharing a campfire with an outlaw similar to Billy the Kid.

The narrator notes that "what Beulah Land did, she tried to do well." Such comments give Beulah more individuality than the other young protagonists.

Brief comments about the feats and the customs in the other seven novels will suffice. Lucinda Lavina Howard helps her aunt make tonic to sell against her husband's wishes in **Just Some Weeds from the Wilderness**. Although Oregon in 1874 encouraged female education, it would not allow women to enter banks. Lucinda also helps sell the tonic while playing matchmaker for an older couple.

In Washington Territory, twelve years later, Hester calls herself "the one with the good head on her shoulders." In **The Nickel-Plated Beauty**, she unites her siblings to earn money to purchase a stove for their mother. They dig clams, pick berries, and gather oysters. Hester also works at her aunt's hotel. In 1886, women did not like cuspidors, wore rice powder on their faces, and bled red flannel for rouge. The family's total harmony is at times implausible, but perhaps being both poor and proud keeps them from feuding. The theme that people working together can accomplish much more than alone is clear.

The same theme appears in another novel set in Washington. In **O The Red Rose Tree**, four girls led by Amanda find red material of six different colors for an eighty-year-old woman wanting to make an originally designed quilt. Finding different shades of red in 1893 without money to buy cloth is an almost impossible challenge. The girls, however, use their ingenuity, luck, and some guile to help the lonely Mrs. Hankinson. A chest protector, flotsam, doll dress, union suit, gift dress material, and a petticoat contribute to the seven roses of the pattern. When the girls have to finish the quilt for the ailing old woman, she states the explicit theme: "It's not so much what you *get* done, it's *how* you did it."

In the same year but in California, Lacy, after her foster mother's death, becomes exhausted from cooking, cleaning, washing, and schooling. When an older brother elopes, she decides to find wives for the remaining two in **Lacy Makes a Match**. After trying tactics such as taking names of lovesick women from a magazine, *The Barbershop Patron's Friend and Manly Companion,* and writing letters in one brother's name, her matchmaking attempts finally succeed when a magician comes to Coyote Mountain, California, and his unmarried female helper stays. On a trip to San Francisco in 1893, in addition to her awe of seven-story buildings, the electric lights in the Palace Hotel's Palm Court, trolleys, telephones, and dental laughing gas, she searches old newspapers and finds that her real family was part of a group of Irish settlers massacred by an outlaw gang. Lacy illustrates that with initiative, one can accomplish many feats.

In **Melinda Takes a Hand**, Melinda reunites her sister, Sarah Jane, and Sarah Jane's fiancée after a misunderstanding. In Chicago at the 1893 World's Columbia Exposition, Sarah Jane fell in love with Edgar Everette Potter III next to the prune sculpture of a knight and horse. Later, in Colorado to meet Edgar's parents, Sarah Jane receives her first letter from him. He writes that she is the "loneliest" woman he has ever met, and she breaks the engagement. The two sisters stay in town, with Sarah Jane housekeeping for Judge Garway and Melinda retrieving the judge's often-straying Great Dane. Melinda learns that her Jewish friend, Esther, wants to be a rabbi, and to help the family find a *minyan* for religious services, Melinda tries to advertise at the train station. Other unusual townspeople include the two remittance men (paid to remain abroad) from England who are having a family castle shipped piece by piece to them from London. Melinda finally writes to Edgar about the "lonely"; he comes immediately to explain that he had written in his terrible handwriting "lovely." Melinda uses her creativity to make things happen.

Two novels are set in Arizona Territory. In **Red Rock over the River**, Dorcas befriends Hattie when she comes to Fort Yuma. The girls attend school in 1881, and as part of their "good works," they go to the local prison to write letters for tubercular prisoners. Hattie steals a hot air balloon from a traveling circus after rushing one of the prisoners into it. Dorcas unwittingly becomes a passenger and during the flight finds that the dying prisoner is Hattie's half-brother whom she does not want to die in prison. He dies in the air from lack of oxygen, and when the balloon crashes, Yuma Indians rescue the girls. Hattie escapes in the Colorado River, and Dorcas returns home to the dusty fort.

A last book, **By Crumbs, It's Mine**! shows Damaris Boyd, known as a female "terror on two feet" or "don't give up the ship Boyd," in 1882. As the family travels west, a man on the train gambles with her father and wins. When Damaris accuses him of cheating her father, the man gives her a traveling hotel, an unusual cardboard building that could be erected anywhere one needed a hotel. As soon as they leave the train, news of gold lures Mr. Boyd away from the family, but Damaris and her Aunt Willa set up the hotel and rent the rooms. Ten months spent working at the hotel, as well as matchmaking and thwarting the dime-novel-reading local tomboy, keeps Damaris busy. When she finally notices her mother's weakening health, she asks an *Apache helper to take her on the five-day journey to a gold camp to retrieve her father. During the action, Damaris notes Apache marriage customs, reads a guidebook called *The Ladies Indispensable Assistant, Being a Companion for the Sister, Mother, and Wife,* and serves both Chinese and Irish railway builders. Aunt Willa explicitly states the theme that "ladies don't have to sit back and accept just everything that comes along in life."

STYLE AND THEMES

The adventures in Beatty's novels entertain, but on the whole, they give only short-lived satisfaction. Most lack the depth of theme or the individuality of character to remain long in the reader's memory. Diction serves as one of the strongest points in the novels. In *Wait for Me, Watch for Me, Eula Bee,* Lewtie notes that "arithmetic . . . didn't slip and slide around the danged way spelling words did." And in *How Many Miles to Sundown,* the especially appropriate diction filled with figurative language captures the flavor of the area and the times. Beulah and her brother "knuckle scratch" (fight) and watch out for "sin busters" (preachers) or "sodbusters" (farmers). Beulah feels "like a wart on a big pickle'' when she sees pictures of the Alps and thinks that the circus bicy-clienne ''was handsome as a heifer knee-deep in red clover.'' Figurative language in other novels includes describing the surf during a storm that ''looked like water boiling in a pot on the stove.'' In another spot, a schooner ''leaped'' from the sea. Beatty interweaves definitions of unusual words, such as *masher* and *remittance man*, into the diction. In books where the characters have education, she uses more allusions, some more than once, like *The Last of the Mohicans;* Rosinante, Don Quixote's horse; and *The Three Musketeers*. Perhaps the im-balance in the novels comes from the paucity of older males who hold strong but reasonable convictions about values. However, the adventures give twentieth-century readers a sense of nineteenth-century life in the uncultivated areas of the American Southwest.

BELTANE. Signifying the Celtic name for *May Day, this ceremony involves the lighting of bonfires, beltane fires, which could have represented the druidical worship of the sun god. Jumping over the fires successfully also promised fertility for humans as well as animals. Beltane fires were still kindled as late as the eighteenth century in Scotland. See *The 13th Member* by Mollie *Hunter and *Warrior Scarlet* and *Knight's Fee* by Rosemary *Sutcliff.

BEN BUCK. American who matures from nine to fifteen as protagonist in *The Bloody Country*. *See* Collier, Christopher and James.

BEN PENDRILL. Fourteen, orphan, English protagonist who lives with William *Blake in *The Gates of Paradise*. *See* Carter, Peter.

BENDY. Young English protagonist in *The Load of Unicorn*. *See* Harnett, Cynthia.

BENT IS THE BOW. *See* Trease, Geoffrey.

BEOTHUK. The members of this Indian tribe, living in Newfoundland, were hunters and canoemen. Their habit of rubbing red ochre over their bodies might be the origin of the term *red* for Native American. The last-known Beothuk died in 1829. *See* Treece, Henry, *Viking's Sunset*.

BERIC. British orphan in Rome who returns to Britain, protagonist of *Outcast*. *See* Sutcliff, Rosemary.

BERSERKER. A fierce Norse warrior, this man fought in battle with frenzied violence and fury, perhaps loving the fight for its own sake. See *Viking's Dawn, The Road to Miklagard, Viking's Sunset,* and *Splintered Sword* by Henry *Treece.

BERT BREEN'S BARN. *See* Edmonds, Walter.

THE BEST BAD THING. *See* Uchida, Yoshiko.

BETH, MICHAEL, and SALLY. Young English protagonists in *The Wind Eye*. *See* Westall, Robert.

BEULAH LAND QUINEY. Thirteen, American, protagonist of *How Many Miles to Sundown? See* Beatty, Patricia.

BEYOND THE DIVIDE. *See* Lasky, Katherine.

BEYOND THE WEIR BRIDGE. *See* Burton, Hester.

BILDUNGSROMAN. A novel of education in which the protagonist progresses toward maturity. See *Johnny Tremain* by Esther *Forbes; *Across Five Aprils* by Irene *Hunt; and *One Is One* by Barbara *Picard.

BILL. Pseudonym of English protagonist, fifteen, returned to London after evacuation in *Fireweed*. *See* Paton Walsh, Jill.

BILLY BEDAMNED, LONG GONE BY. *See* Beatty, Patricia.

BJORN AND FRYTHA. Young protagonists who mature in Britain in *The Shield Ring*. *See* Sutcliff, Rosemary.

THE BLACK FOX OF LORNE. *See* de Angeli, Marguerite.

BLACK JACK. *See* Garfield, Leon.

THE BLACK LAMP. *See* Carter, Peter.

BLACK SHIRTS. This designates members of fascist party organizations wearing a black shirt as part of the uniform. *See* Zei, Aliki, *Wildcat under Glass*.

BLAKE, WILLIAM (1757–1827). As an engraver, this English poet used the new process of printing from etched copper plates for his own poems and then hand illustrated and colored them. Many of his writings explored mystical and metaphysical concepts. *See* Carter, Peter, *The Gates of Paradise*.

BLITZ. The night bombing of Britain by the Germans in World War II during the winter of 1940–41 became known as the blitz. See *In Spite of All Terror* by Hester *Burton; *Fireweed* by Jill *Paton Walsh; and *The Exeter Blitz* by David *Rees.

BLOOD FEUD. A continuing series of killings and counterkillings among members of two consanguinal groups becomes a blood feud when the counterkillings are not accepted as right and proper in a society that settles its wrongs by this "due process." See *Blood Feud* by Rosemary *Sutcliff and *John Treegate's Musket* and *Peter Treegate's War* by Leonard *Wibberley.

BLOOD FEUD. See Sutcliff, Rosemary.

THE BLOOD OF THE BRAVE. See Baker, Betty.

THE BLOODY COUNTRY. See Collier, Christopher and James.

BLOS, JOAN (1928–   ). American.

BIBLIOGRAPHY AND BACKGROUND
Brothers of the Heart: A Story of the Old Northwest, 1837–38. New York: Scribner's, 1985. *A Gathering of Days: A New England Girl's Journal, 1830–32.* New York: Scribner's, 1979.

The years of history represented by a New England house built in 1827 and the similarity of the lives of its occupants with the present intrigued Blos and became the basis for her first book, *A Gathering of Days,* which won the Newbery and the American Book awards in 1980. She turned to mysteries of the Midwest for *Brothers of the Heart.* She believes that the characters' stories incorporate the essence of her work, with the historical parts being of interest but important only in their relationship to the characters. She researches sites, some covered with new housing projects where she must imagine the land in its virgin state; museums, where old shoes often give her insight about the people of the time; and libraries. Using these primary resources, she adds secondary sources where necessary until all the parts of the work fit together. The writing begins on yellow pad with pencil, followed by typing and returning to hand correction. She makes three to four drafts with innumerable simultaneous revisions, working best in the early morning.

WORKS
In **A Gathering of Days: A New England Girl's Journal, 1830–32,** Catherine Cabot Hall, intelligent and artistic, records events beginning with her fourteenth year in a journal, a time during which she undergoes several major rites of passage. Blos frames the story within two letters that Catherine writes to her great-granddaughter in 1899. With the first letter, Catherine sends the diary to her for her fourteenth birthday; in the second, she responds to her great-grand-daughter's questions. Catherine reveals in her first letter that she has endured the various changes in her life and, in the second, what happened to some of her friends. In the diary she tells the rest. With her mother dead, Catherine helps her father raise the young Matty and keeps the house until her father, in Boston to trade furs, brooms, and maple syrup, meets a woman with a teenaged son

and marries her within three weeks. Later Catherine finds a message in her lost lesson book from a runaway slave who hides in the woods, and she leaves one of her mother's dozen quilts for him. Her best friend, Cassie, dies in the late summer from a chill caught while swimming after berry picking. One of her friends leaves to work in a *Lowell, Massachusetts, factory to help support her family. And a couple living in Exeter asks her to help them raise their child. That she copes so well is either a tribute to her attending church twice each Sunday or learning her lessons full of moral sayings. The quiet dignity of language captured in her diary entries also indicates emotional stability and an ability to cope with these changing circumstances.

In **Brothers of the Heart: A Story of the Old Northwest, 1837–38**, Blos chooses the same decade as *A Gathering of Days* but changes the setting. Shem, a cripple, travels with his family to Millfield, Michigan, where he lives all of his life except for the one year detailed in the story. A frame introduces and ends the story that Shem tells during his fiftieth wedding anniversary celebration. In essence, the family goes to Michigan expecting to find a lovely town but actually finding that their house stands on a piece of undeveloped land. Shem can find work only with Mr. Ellsworth and his daughter, Margaret. After other disappointments, Shem leaves home for Detroit, where his excellent clerical work at the docks leads the boss to ask him to keep records on a Canadian fur expedition. In the Canadian winter, when he cannot walk through the deep snow, the men have to leave him, promising to return. After many days, Shem realizes that he will not see them again. An old Indian woman, Mary Goodhue, left to die by her tribe, follows wolf prints to his hut. She teaches Shem arts of healing and survival, including how to walk on snowshoes. While Mary teaches him confidence, initiating him to life, his family flounders. His mother pines for him, his father contracts and recovers from ague, and his sister, Sophy, comes from her beloved school in Massachusetts where she went after working in Lowell. In Millfield, however, Sophy meets John and decides to marry him. She sacrifices those things she likes back East for his more important love. In Canada, Mary dies. Shem buries Mary and understands that she prized him as much as she did her husband who died as the result of a foolish quarrel. She saw the two as brothers in their similar goodness, honesty, and perseverance. Shem uses the language she taught him to buy a canoe, and he paddles back to Detroit and then travels on to Millfield. The narrator notes the fairy tale motif of the silly boy and the wise old woman. Shem's life resembles that of the third son, physically marked, who goes away and finds his goodness through the help of a fairy godmother. In the mythic sense, he separates from the home, is initiated, and returns the hero. Traders who knew of Mary Goodhue and her secrecy are surprised to find that she had befriended Shem. His story, innocently told, ironically brings him unexpected respect. No longer noticing his disability, Margaret decides Shem will be a worthy husband.

STYLE AND THEMES

The authentic diction with which Catherine writes and converses places *A Gathering of Days* clearly in its time. Blos uses shorter sentences to emphasize and longer, complex sentences with commas to separate phrases in explanations. Catherine wants to please her father and says, "I shall assay such tasks and virtues as may sustain his comfort and increase his pride." About other incidences, she says, "These be the thoughts" and "Still must my capitals be improved." Catherine records riddles and jokes she hears and notes a story, "Old Man of the Sea" ("The Fisherman and His Wife"), told by her father. To add realism, she crosses out and revises words in the diary. The complex characters appear real—the father who has had to bury his young wife and infant son when Catherine was ten and the new wife/mother who carefully tries to find her place in the unfamiliar home. Catherine's friends awaken slowly to the attentions of the opposite sex but stay within the mores of their society. Blos has skillfully incorporated some of the customs of the time such as "breaking out" (going outside after a big snowfall), hacking frozen soup with an axe, saving pewter bowls for guests, Fourth of July all-day celebrations, and family memories associated with cloth pieces sewn into quilts. Although the runaway slave motif fits into the plot, it seems somewhat contrived for Catherine to have to face this situation during a year already jammed with events. But that does not detract from the theme that something worth doing is worth doing well and that a life unchanging becomes stagnant.

In *Brothers of the Heart,* moments of beauty appear in Blos's imagery such as the "sky . . . rumbled and iridescent . . . looked like [the] inside of a shell . . . lavender tone suffused with pinks and golds." She experiments with point of view, shifting from first person to omniscient and back. In addition, she attempts to recreate the syntax of the 1830s with an excessive use of *it* where the antecedent is often ambiguous. These factors make the novel sometimes difficult to follow. Another unusual stylistic device includes the use of one word *Shem* as a title to introduce a following paragraph with information about him. The letters and historical information interspersed throughout the text sometimes disrupt the flow of story and suspense, and whether the rhetorical questions are effective is debatable. Some of the research could have been integrated into the plot since reports function as documentation for the story rather than advancing the action. In this novel, Blos continues her strong storytelling, but here, unlike *A Gathering of Days,* the style often intrudes on content instead of enhancing it.

BLUE STARS WATCHING. See Beatty, Patricia.

THE BOMBARD. See *Ride to Danger* by Henry *Treece.

BONANZA GIRL. See Beatty, Patricia.

BONAPARTE, NAPOLEON. *See* *Napoleon I.

BONNIE DUNDEE. See Sutcliff, Rosemary.

BONNIE PRINCE CHARLIE. *See* *Charles Edward.

BOSTOCK AND HARRIS. Thirteen, English protagonists in *The Night of the Comet* and *The Strange Affair of Adelaide Harris. See* Garfield, Leon.

BOSTOCK AND HARRIS; OR, THE NIGHT OF THE COMET. See *The Night of the Comet* by Leon *Garfield.

BOUDICCA (d. 60 A.D.). After her husband, *Prasutagus, king of the *Iceni, died, the Romans took her fortune and annexed her kingdom. She raised a rebellion among the British tribes, and they burned towns and army camps, including London. Her force massacred around 70,000, including the Ninth Legion, until the provincial Roman governor, *Suetonius Paulinus, defeated her. She probably died from taking poison after the loss. See *Song for a Dark Queen* by Rosemary *Sutcliff and *War Dog, The Queen's Brooch,* and *The Centurion* by Henry *Treece.

BOWMAN OF CRÉCY. See Welch, Ronald.

BOWS AGAINST THE BARONS. See Trease, Geoffrey.

BOXER REBELLION. In China, in 1900, a secret society attempted to drive foreigners from the country by violence and to force Chinese Christians to renounce their religion. *See* Dickinson, Peter, *The Dancing Bear*.

THE BOY AND THE MONKEY. See Garfield, Leon.

BOY YANCEY. Eleven, female black American protagonist in *A Girl Called Boy*. *See* Hurmence, Belinda.

BOYE. Dog who is main focus in *Witch Dog*. *See* Beatty, John and Patricia.

BOYS' HOUSE. When British tribal boys reached the age of nine, they began their warrior training in the Boys' House. There they spent seven years learning the skills they needed to help their families survive, including killing a wolf singlehandedly. See *Warrior Scarlet* and *The Eagle of the Ninth* by Rosemary *Sutcliff.

A BOY'S WILL. See Haugaard, Erik.

BRIDIE MCSHANE. Scottish protagonist who grows from nine in *A Sound of Chariots* and who matures from fifteen into a young adult in *Hold On to Love*. *See* Hunter, Mollie.

BRIGANTES. This northern British tribe inhabited the country from the Humber estuary on the east and the Mersey to the west on northward to the Antoine wall. Their chief town was Isurium (Aldborough) and, later, *Eburacum (*York). The Romans first defeated them during Claudius's reign c. 50 A.D., but they were not subdued until c. 155 when Antoninus Pius ruled. See *The Silver Branch* by Rosemary *Sutcliff and *The Centurion* by Henry *Treece.

BRIGHT MORNING. Fourteen, Navaho, protagonist of *Sing Down the Moon*. *See* O'Dell, Scott.

BRINK, CAROL RYRIE (1895–1981). American.

BIBLIOGRAPHY AND BACKGROUND

Caddie Woodlawn: A Frontier Story. Illustrated by Kate Seredy. New York: Macmillan, 1935; London: Collier Macmillan, 1963. *Lad with a Whistle*. Illustrated by Robert Ball. New York: Macmillan, 1941. *Louly*. Illustrated by Ingrid Fetz. New York: Macmillan, 1974.

Brink received the Newbery Medal in 1936 for *Caddie Woodlawn* and the University of Minnesota Kerlan Award for her body of work in 1978. Of her writing in various genres, three novels classify as historical fiction.

WORKS

The least successful of these, **Louly**, relates the adventures of Louly, her friends, and her sister and her brother in Idaho during the summer of 1908 while her parents visit family back East. With friends Chrys and Cordy, the girls present plays, camp outside in the back yard, cook, and ride a pony cart during the Fourth of July parade. The girls become angry with fourteen-year-old Louly when she joins Eddie Wendell and his family to picnic on the Fourth. Eddie suggests that Louly enter a recitation contest in another town later in the summer; she does, and she wins. Unafraid to be dramatic, Louly delights the audience. After watching her, Chrys decides not to be embarrassed by her poems and not to hide her own creativity, which is revealed through the omniscient point of view. The unimaginative style and the episodic plot offer no excitement. In addition, the relationship between the girls and the adults seems unrealistic.

A more interesting novel, set in Edinburgh in 1810, is **Lad with a Whistle**. A dying man, Kirkness, attracted by Rob McFarlane's honest looks, names him guardian for his two grandchildren. As a fifteen-year-old orphan who plays whistle and drums, Rod neither understands what he is to do nor why he has been chosen, but he senses that he has to protect the children from "wolves." The wolves reveal themselves as the servants who have been selling all of the Kirkness valuables for their own profit. Rob's sleuthing allows him to find the reportedly dead father's Spanish address and write to him. Meanwhile, a man arrives whom the servants announce as the children's father. Having seen John Kirkness's portrait hanging in the gallery, Rob knows that the man is an impostor. Fortunately, Rob's bagpiping friend, Tammas, knows enough wandering men whom he meets at Walter *Scott's so that they can identify the usurper as the son of a servant, Mrs. Minnocle. Coincidentally, on the day they accuse the criminals, John Kirkness arrives home, and Rob relinquishes his duty. The dialect gives a sense of place, and the plot is intriguing.

Although **Caddie Woodlawn** takes place in 1864, the *American Civil War is hardly acknowledged. Caddie's father has paid someone to fight for him, and the family lives in Wisconsin, unaffected by the war. Caddie has spent her childhood until age eleven playing with her brothers outdoors. She can plow but not quilt. She swims nude in the river, looks after her friend Indian John's dog while he hunts, races her uncle to the river for a silver dollar, and participates in Saturday morning spelling bees. When a rumor starts that Indians plan to massacre, Caddie overhears men saying that the whites should attack first. Caddie rushes to tell Indian John, and he reassures her father that the Indians will not fight. A cowardly white man, however, sends his Indian wife back to her people. In school, Caddie shows compassion for her brother Tom's first love, but at home, she plays tricks on their prissy Boston cousin, Annabelle. Caddie's punishment helps her realize that Annabelle has suffered enough and that maybe the things she can do, including quilting, are worth learning. The surprise of the summer comes when Caddie's father, very poor in England as a child because his father was disowned for marrying a shoemaker's daughter, receives a letter saying he can inherit the huge estate and become Lord Woodlawn if he becomes a British citizen. Each member of the family votes, and they decide to remain American.

STYLE AND THEMES

Feminists and others may find the double standards exhibited in *Caddie Woodlawn* distasteful, but readers must remember that Brink illustrates the standards of 1864. These books will certainly remind readers how much social standards have changed. The adventures in the three novels are interesting, but each relies too much on coincidence as a method of advancing plot.

BRISTOL. Always a commercial city, this town at the confluence of the Avon and Frome rivers in England has always been an important port. It played a large part in the prosperous African slave trade which the *Quakers vigorously opposed. See *Campion Towers* by John and Patricia *Beatty; *To Ravensrigg* by Hester *Burton; *Jack Holborn* by Leon *Garfield; and *The Overland Launch* by C. Walter *Hodges.

BRONZE AGE. This term refers to the third phase in human material development after the Paleolithic (Old Stone) Age and the Neolithic (New Stone) Age. Beginning probably around 7000 B.C. with the use of copper, it ended with the advent of iron sometime after 1000 B.C. *See* Sutcliff, Rosemary, *Warrior Scarlet*.

THE BRONZE BOW. See Speare, Elizabeth.

THE BRONZE SWORD. See *The Centurion* by Henry *Treece.

BROTHER DUSTY-FEET. See Sutcliff, Rosemary.

BROTHER JONATHAN. British soldiers originally applied this term to American patriots during the *American Revolution, but the meaning broadened to apply to the people or government of the United States, or simply, an American. *See* Beatty, Patricia, *Jonathan Down Under*.

BROTHERS OF THE HEART. See Blos, Joan.

BRUCE CAMERON. Sixteen, American, protagonist of *Cow Neck Rebels. See* Forman, James.

BRUS AND JAN. Thirteen, twin Viking protagonists in *Black Fox of Lorne. See* de Angeli, Marguerite.

THE BUFFALO KNIFE. See Steele, William O.

BURBAGE, RICHARD (1567–1619). He played chief parts in *Shakespeare's plays at The Theatre, which he helped move from Shoreditch to Bankside, and the *Globe Theatre, which he helped establish as a summer playhouse. *See* Trease, Geoffrey, *Cue for Treason*.

BURGOYNE, JOHN (1722–1792). He commanded the British expedition from Canada into the American colonies in the *American Revolution during 1776 where he captured Ticonderoga but was forced to surrender to Gates at *Saratoga during which he agreed to leave the colonies via Boston, never to return. *See* Wibberley, Leonard, *Sea Captain from Salem*.

BURTON, HESTER (1913–   ). British.

BIBLIOGRAPHY AND BACKGROUND
   Beyond the Weir Bridge. Illustrated by Victor Ambrus. New York: Crowell, 1970; as *Thomas*. London: Oxford, 1969. *Castors Away!* Illustrated by Victor Ambrus. London: Oxford, 1962; Cleveland: World, 1963. *The Henchmans at Home*. Illustrated by Victor Ambrus. London: Oxford, 1970; New York: Crowell, 1972. *In Spite of All Terror*. Illustrated by Victor Ambrus. London: Oxford, 1968; New York: World, 1969. *Kate Ryder*. Illustrated by Victor Ambrus. New York: Crowell, 1975; as *Kate Rider*. London: Oxford, 1974. *No Beat of Drum*. Illustrated by Victor Ambrus. London: Oxford, 1966; Cleveland: World, 1967.

The Rebel. Illustrated by Victor Ambrus. London: Oxford, 1971; New York: Crowell, 1972. *Riders of the Storm*. Illustrated by Victor Ambrus. London: Oxford, 1972; New York: Crowell, 1973. *Through the Fire*. Illustrated by Gareth Floyd. London: Hamish Hamilton, 1969. *Time of Trial*. Illustrated by Victor Ambrus. London: Oxford, 1963; Cleveland: World, 1964. *To Ravensrigg*. Illustrated by Victor Ambrus. London: Oxford, 1976; New York: Crowell, 1977.

Among Burton's honors are two prestigious awards, the Carnegie Medal in 1964 for *Time of Trial* and the *Boston Globe–Horn Book* Award in 1971 for *Beyond the Weir Bridge*. Her own life has greatly influenced her subjects and settings. A childhood spent in East Anglia (England) led to many scenes in *Castors Away!, Time of Trial,* and *The Henchmans at Home*. After writing a contemporary story about a flood, Burton wanted to write another ''in which children are thrown into great danger and help themselves and others by their own courage and resourcefulness.'' Her belief that modern children ''are too well protected by loving parents, teachers, and policeman—and the law'' led her to choose the years of the Napoleonic Wars (1793–1815) for the next two books. These years reflected those of World War II when ''England was fighting for her life—alone—against an all-powerful European tyrant. I understood exactly how Englishmen must have felt in that earlier period of great national danger.'' *In Spite of All Terror* takes place in her own village during 1940 and has been translated into German. Her stories usually emerge ''from a true historical event, such as a riot *(No Beat of Drum, Time of Trial)* a fire *(Through the Fire)* a plague *(Thomas),* a siege *(Kate Rider).*'' Research may take six months while she visits the place, studies the fashions and popular songs of the period, and examines street maps, street cries, letters, and diaries. She utilizes the Bodleian Library to which, as an Oxford graduate, she has access. She revises only at the suggestion of her editor.

WORKS

An overview of the novels reveals several similarities. All of the books use either omniscient or limited omniscient point of view, with the story mainly confined to the protagonist's perspective. No protagonist has both parents at home. Those not orphaned live either with widowed fathers or mothers. The novels fall into several broad categories. Some take place during wars; others expose religious persecution; and several explore the difficult processes necessary to change social conditions.

One novel fits none of these groupings. **The Henchmans at Home** reveals life in a physician's family, the Henchmans, during the class-conscious society of *Victoria's reign in the 1890s. The children, Rob, Ellen, and William, present episodes occurring over a period of eleven years. Rob at seven, furious at his mother for inviting an unwanted guest to his birthday, steals a boat, and rows away. At twelve, Ellen loses some of her innocence when she tries to visit her friend Etty during a holiday and discovers that the girl's working-class mother has rejected Etty and her newly-born child. William at nineteen, home from

Cambridge, unwillingly accompanies his physician father on rounds. Their conversation and his father's ability to cope with an unexpected situation changes his concept of his father and his rural medical practice. A final episode reveals Ellen at twenty-one appreciating the kindness of the young doctor who has recently come to town while he recognizes her artistic talents. As the children become more physically and emotionally mature, the dialogue syntax becomes more complex. A young Rob grows up to become a young man seriously preparing for an Australian expedition. William, embarrassed by his family as a young adolescent, decides to become partners with his father after traveling abroad. These adolescents confirm their needs to be recognized as positive contributors to the family's life. Their parents react to them realistically and lovingly. As the children mature, they become more understanding of their parents as well as the layered society in which they must function. The motif of gradual maturation controls the unusually enjoyable episodic plot.

Of the two novels exploring religious persecution against the peace-loving English *Quakers, one, *Through the Fire,* will appeal to young readers. The other, **Beyond the Weir Bridge**, clearly communicates the complex problems of people whose beliefs deviate from mainstream expectations. With a background of *Parliament rule under *Cromwell, Burton uses a weir bridge to frame her story—its significance in 1651 and then in 1667 after both the *plague and the *Great Fire of London. Two characters, Richard and Richenda, interact with a third, Thomas. When they first meet, each dares the other to cross the rickety bridge. Thomas appears physically weak, but his kindness and innocent joy at the abilities of the other two endears him to them. Thomas and Richard cement their friendship at school, but Thomas's drunken *Royalist father cannot afford to send Thomas to Oxford while Richard goes and squanders his opportunity. Dismissed from Oxford, Richard goes to London where his inquisitiveness about natural phenomena gains him a position helping a physician. Meanwhile, Richenda and her family, while traveling to meet a prospective bridegroom, meet Margaret Fell, a *Quaker. Her peace of mind converts the family, and their joy satisfies some of Thomas's inquisitiveness about the spiritual world. Although these Quakers support their government, they refuse to swear allegiance to it. Their belief in peace causes them religious persecution, each going to prison at least once. As a child, Thomas worried about a God who blessed both prophets and witches, but as an adult, he believes anyone, even Turks, should be free to choose how to worship God. After Thomas and Richenda become Quakers, Richard refuses to see them. When Thomas and Richenda inevitably marry, they revive Thomas's estate, neglected by his father. But Thomas believes that God calls him to London to help during the plague. He leaves, finds Richard, and aids him with the sick. Richenda, expecting their child, follows Thomas. Shocked by the city's state, she sees Thomas during the week before his death. The once-brash Richard carefully reestablishes his friendship with Richenda and her son. She realizes during the Great Fire that a person's value can be measured only by the number of other persons helped, and she knows that Richard needs her.

Thus they return to the weir bridge, having psychologically crossed it many times, but no longer needing to prove bravery. Burton makes this important period in English history come alive.

Another brief look at Quaker persecution occurs in **Through the Fire**. Rachel and Will Elmy accompany their father into London to help Quakers held in prison during 1666. When the *Great Fire sweeps through the City, Rachel and Will save men left to burn in prison, including their father, who was arrested at a Quaker meeting. The two children climb through a prison window, retrieve the key from the empty guard house, and unlock the door. Afterward, rumors circulate that either the foreigners or the Quakers believed to be plotting against King *Charles II had started the fire. The family leaves London, taking survivors with them to their home.

Three novels depict how war changes people's lives: *Kate Ryder, Castors Away!* and *In Spite of All Terror*. **Kate Ryder** reveals the Ryder family's mixed loyalties during the *English Civil War. At twelve in 1646, Kate misses her brother Ralph who has gone to sea, and she feels rejected helping siblings Adam and Priscilla on the farm while their father fights against King *Charles I. Her mother leaves to nurse her feverish husband, and by the time they return, the neighbors have helped the children bring in the harvest. More important, Adam declares his love for Tamsun, an orphan with no money for a dowry. He also declares his support for the king in opposition to his father. Tamsun's uncle opposes the marriage because of Adam's political beliefs, so Adam and Tamsun run away. Kate's feeling of rejection worsens when her father finds a husband for Priscilla. Trying to help Adam and Tamsun, Kate arrives at the beginning of the eleven-week Colchester siege and has to stay for its duration. She realizes then that Tamsun's life revolves around Adam and Abel, their baby. But Adam dies. Tamsun's return to the farm with Abel helps the family find solace in the loss. During the four years that Kate grows into womanhood, she realizes that Ralph had gone to sea because he, the second son, had no inheritance, and therefore, no choice. Her childhood insecurities about being ugly fade when her father begins to search for a husband for her. Kate's mixed emotions accurately reflect the pains of adolescence.

In **Castors Away**! family members eventually fight in the *Napoleonic wars. As a prelude, in 1805, twelve-year-old Nell Henchman expresses her hostility toward being a girl sewing while her twin brother, Tom, and sixteen-year-old brother, Edmund, fish. With their widowed father, they go to Aunt Susan's for vacation. After a storm, four-year-old Martin finds a man washed ashore, and Mr. Henchman feels warmth around the man's heart. After he spends two hours of massaging and inflating the man with a bellows, James Bubb revives. His army colleagues had left him aboard a wrecked ship because he was drunk. However, the family likes him, and he helps them harvest. Soldiers arrest Bubb and sentence him to a flogging; Edmund helps him escape. Word arrives from Uncle Simon, captain of the *Pericles,* for Ben, his hired man, and Tom to join the ship before Lord *Nelson's navy begins assault on the French. The children contrive for James to replace Ben who has a broken wrist. After Tom leaves, Edmund goes to London to learn surgery with his father's friend, Dr. Coke. Nell hates home, but she stays and studies with Monsieur Armand, an exile whose family died in the *French Revolution. Tom fights in the Battle of *Trafalgar with Nelson in charge and sees Uncle Simon lose two fingers. On the return voyage after the victory, Uncle Simon dies of gangrene, and Tom loses his spirit. In an afterword about the characters as adults, Martin has become a professor of Semitic languages who does not remember what "Castors Away!" means, so Tom, an old man, tells Martin's children that it means "to shove the boat away." Nell marries one of Edmund's doctor friends who is happy to be marrying an intelligent female. Although appealing, the afterword adds nothing to the action.

World War II triggers the action of **In Spite of All Terror**. At fifteen, Liz Hawtin recalls the unhappy experience of living with her unpleasant Aunt Ag and Uncle Herb after the death of her parents and welcomes the news in 1940 that the government will evacuate her school to a village. The beauty of tiny Chiddingford stuns her, but the cold response of Mrs. Burton, her hostess, dampens her pleasure. Mrs. Burton would have preferred a male evacuee, but she soon adjusts to Liz. Liz's love of learning attracts the Oxford don father, the army general grandfather, the loving grandmother, the artistic son Ben with talents unappreciated by the family, and the son Simon who wants to join the army but whom the family expects to attend Cambridge. The war, however, overcomes them all. Simon joins the army anyway, and Ben helps his ill grandfather rescue soldiers from *Dunkirk on the small family boat. Liz waits inside the calm of a Ramsgate church fearing for their safety and Simon's. The grandfather dies in the shelling, while Ben, burned with petrol, falls into the water. Someone rescues Ben, but they have to wait for news of Simon, fighting behind French lines. Liz's cousin Rose writes that she is pregnant and that her mother, Aunt Ag, has denied her a home. Ben and Liz go to bombed London, find her in the horrible destruction, and bring her back. Their spirits rise when reports say Simon is only "missing," Ben joins the air force, and fear decreases as the routine of life away from the front continues. Even Rose regains some of her happiness as she prepares for the birth of her child in this beautiful and sheltered place. Liz blossoms in this atmosphere of sharing which she has missed so much since her parents' deaths.

A final category of Burton's novels discloses the difficulties and dangers of enacting social reforms. Working-class men fear both navy press gangs, who will grab them off the streets, and machines, which can do their jobs. Women remain their father's property until marriage. Slave trade flourishes. And the poor live in collapsing tenements.

To Ravensrigg reveals England's slave trade in a time, 1786, when slavery had already been outlawed. Discontent with her bird-cage life living with her aunt, fourteen-year-old Emmie Hesket equates a cat's life with freedom. She helps Cato, a Negro slave, escape from a posse by giving him her aunt's clothes to wear and thus becomes an *abolitionist. Her aunt, shocked at Emmie's "un-Christian" attitude, makes her leave when her sea captain father returns from a voyage. Emmie persuades him to take her on his next trip. The ship sinks off the English coast, and Emmie is the lone survivor. Her father's dying words are for her to go to Ravensrigg and tell its owners that she is Mary's daughter. Robert Fenton's family rescues her and helps her search for Ravensrigg while simultaneously working to abolish the slave trade. A visiting Quaker, James Kendall, and Fenton's son take Emmie to Ravensrigg via *Bristol, where a slaver spots and almost captures them as they exit the city. At Ravensrigg, Emmie finds her grandmother whom she has never known. Her grandmother tells Emmie that her mother had loved a sea captain, but they had lied to Mary that he was killed on a voyage. Mary had then married the first man who proposed, Captain Bradmore. After Bradmore beat her and when Hesket returned unharmed, Mary ran away with him. Emmie is Bradmore's daughter, not Hesket's, and their shared physical defect of one-jointed little fingers verifies the fact. James realizes that her slave-trader father had recognized her in Bristol and would again pursue them. In order to escape Bradmore's assertion of owning Emmie, James and Emmie marry immediately. The father's recognition after so long seems coincidental, but the carefully constructed plot is intriguing.

At the same time that some men merely oppose the slave trade, others like Stephen in **The Rebel** openly defy allegiance to the nobility. Stephen's hostilities in 1788 almost jeopardize the futures of his siblings, Josh and Catherine. His intelligence, however, convinces his uncles to send him to Oxford on the remainder of the children's inheritance. Josh, a farmer at heart, has gone to sea to earn money by bringing back items to sell in England, and Catherine remains with her uncles and aunt to face a dull, unfulfilling life. At Oxford, Stephen befriends another who also believes that peasants cannot be free under a monarch. They go twice to France, where, on the second trip, the Commune of the *French Revolution imprisons Stephen for "inciting riot." Nearly killed, mad from fever and malnourishment, he returns to England. Catherine and his former schoolmaster, Tristram, nurse him back to physical health; for mental and spiritual renewal, he turns to Tristram's friend Joel in his *Manchester school for the poor. Stephen faces the doubts of all other young perceptive persons, but he must answer them alone. The schoolmaster, although sixteen years older, finds a kindred soul in the gentle Catherine, and she responds by marrying him.

Riders of the Storm, a sequel to *The Rebel,* begins in 1793 with Stephen in Manchester helping Joel at his school for workers' children. Stephen's loneliness fades when Ben Winter, owner of the school and the mill, welcomes him into his home. Stephen falls in love with Lucy Winter, also a teacher at the school. With England at war with France, people consider any Briton daring to question Parliament as seditious. Like Stephen, Ben Winter believes parliamentary reform is necessary. After his newspaper article on reform, mobs try to destroy his home while Stephen, Joel, and his servants attempt to scare them away. After becoming drunk in a pub and declaring his doubts about the government, Stephen is arrested and held in solitary confinement. He eventually escapes and tells the family that Mr. Bulstead, the magistrate, believes that they are all revolutionaries and wants to destroy them. Later, when Ben, Joel, and Stephen stand trial for sedition, the dull-witted Dan betrays them. Taverner, a treacherous man who knew about Stephen's French experiences, sent Dan to work for Ben in an attempt to still his reform hopes. The best lawyer available to argue their case exposes Dan's lies. All their money spent on the defense, they move to the country where they realize that with the water power, they can rebuild the mill and restart the school. Stephen's immoderation almost destroys their crusade for improving working-class conditions. The setbacks and accusations are exactly what one would expect proponents of ideas unpopular to an upper economic class to suffer.

Reform has not arrived ten years later when, in **Time of Trial**, the Pargeter family suffers for their beliefs. Margaret's London bookseller father, a friend of Tom *Paine, hates to see money wasted on war with France that could help those needing homes and jobs. After a building down the street collapses and kills people, Pargeter writes a tract, *New Jerusalem,* citing ways and reasons for reform. Convicted for seditiousness, he receives six months in prison. Mobs burn the shop in which Margaret has so lovingly helped, and the fire destroys his printing press. The anatomy student staying with the family, Robert, asks his father to give Margaret and Mrs. Neech, the housekeeper, a place to stay near the Ipswich prison at Herringsby. On the Essex coast, the two observe the army's attempt to stop smuggling, a secret and dangerous way of life for the men and their families. One of the soldiers stationed there is John, Margaret's brother, who left home to buy a commission when he could not face the ignominy of his father's prison sentence. They reconcile, and John immediately goes to visit his father. Robert's parents ignore Margaret's presence, and Robert's father accuses her of trying to marry Robert for his money, but she marries Robert anyway with only her father's blessing. When the two visit Margaret's father in prison before returning to London, he explains his new project—writing a book on how to teach reading. He plans to teach unfortunate children to read so that he can put his beliefs into action. Margaret supports her father throughout his ordeal. Her thoughts about Robert's parents epitomize those of all lovers who have wished that the beloved's intolerant and selfish parents would disappear. In London, however, Margaret and Robert can satisfy their needs to help others.

A final novel, **No Beat of Drum**, shows that conditions of the working class worsen with the return of the armies from France. The gentry seems to think that the workers are worthwhile only for fighting its wars. In 1829, Joe Hinton's childhood friend, Mary, jumps on a horse, which runs away with her and destroys itself. As an orphan unable to pay for the horse, Mary is transported to *Van Dieman's Land for seven years. Soon after, Joe's twenty-year-old brother, Dick, joins the "higglers," men living as outlaws by poaching. Starvation threatens the whole class of threshers because the new threshing machines are replacing them on gentry farms. Group uprisings destroy some of the machines, and outlaws start fires. Joe organizes the men to ask the owners for higher wages, but he is caught near one of the fires and transported to Van Dieman's Land for seven years; Dick gets transported for life. Joe shows spiritual resources while sailing to Van Dieman's Land, and his faith continues after he arrives. He herds a drunkard's sheep and improves the flock. He locates Dick, but Dick escapes from his masters, and they shoot him. A settler, Major Rendell, admires Joe's abilities and becomes Joe's master. While going to Rendell's home, Joe helps save a woman and child from a bush fire. The woman is Mary, who loses her husband in the fire. Mary inherits his land, and after three years, Rendell frees Joe, and he and Mary work on her land and bring Joe's mother and sister to be with them. Unfortunately, Mary and Joe's encounter is too coincidental. An unusual device, however, that Burton uses in this novel are editorial comments that create dramatic irony. The reader sometimes knows events or character traits not revealed to Joe.

STYLE AND THEMES

Burton repeatedly displays her mastery of language, of story, and of theme. Her strong imagery brings smells of sea coal or fish and eels to the reader. It allows one to understand Richard's wonder in *Beyond the Weir Bridge:* "His nose sniffed the sweet scent of hay and the dry, sharp prickle of harvest dust, while he puzzled hard that a tiny mote or speck snuffed up one's nostrils should make the whole of one's body explode in a sneeze." In *Kate Ryder*, her figurative language reveals Kate's view of a "cobweb morning [where] long scarves of mist lay over the river." It underscores theme in *Beyond the Weir Bridge:* "And, with a single magic touch on Time's wheel, they were back again where they had been before." Burton uses sentence fragments to emphasize thoughts and ideas. Her dialogue slips into appropriate dialect when characters leave London. Her realistic characters function within the parameters of their time in history, not achieving more than would be possible in their time. Best, her themes explore the painful, the poignant, and the powerful needs of human beings as they search to find their true selves.

THE BUTTY BOY. See *The Huffler* by Jill *Paton Walsh.

BY CRUMBS, IT'S MINE! *See* Beatty, Patricia.

BYZANTIUM. *See* *Istanbul.

C

CADDIE WOODLAWN. Eleven, American, protagonist of *Caddie Woodlawn*. *See* Brink, Carol Ryrie.

CADDIE WOODLAWN. *See* Brink, Carol Ryrie.

CADIZ. Located in southern Spain on an inlet of the Atlantic Ocean, it was the headquarters of the Spanish treasure fleets in the fifteenth century when it became the wealthiest port of Western Europe. See *I Will Adventure* by Elizabeth Gray *Vining and *The King's Beard* by Leonard *Wibberley.

CADWALADER (d. 1172). A Welsh prince, he conquered several towns. Owain expelled him from Wales, and he returned with an army of Irish Danes but made peace before battle. Henry II restored his lands in 1157. *See* Treece, Henry, *Ride into Danger*.

CADWAN. British harper who tells the story of *Boudicca in *Song for a Dark Queen*. *See* Sutcliff, Rosemary.

CAESAREA. This ancient seaport, originally built 25–13 B.C., lies on the coast of Palestine, the site of the modern village of Qisarya, in northern Israel. *See* Haugaard, Erik, *The Rider and his Horse*.

CAJE AMES. Eleven, American protagonist in *Winter Danger*. *See* Steele, William O.

CALAIS. A seaport on the strait of Dover, this town includes in its history the story of the six burghers who surrendered themselves to save the sieged townspeople from starvation in 1346. The town remained English until reversion to France in 1558. See *Thunder in the Sky* by K. M. *Peyton and *Ride into Danger* by Henry *Treece.

CALEDONIA. The Romans called north Britain, the area beyond the isthmus of the Clyde and Forth rivers, by this name. It is also the name of a tribe in Inverness-shire. See *The Mark of the Horse Lord* by Rosemary *Sutcliff and *Message to Hadrian* by Geoffrey *Trease.

CALICO BUSH. See Field, Rachel.

CALICO CAPTIVE. See Speare, Elizabeth George.

CALLIE PERKINS. Thirteen, American, protagonist in *Me, California Perkins. See* Beatty, Patricia.

CALVERT, PATRICIA (1931–   ). American.

BIBLIOGRAPHY AND BACKGROUND
    Hadder MacColl. New York: Scribner's, 1985. *The Snowbird*. New York: Scribner's, 1980.
    The Snowbird was named Best Book for Young Adults by the American Library Association and received awards from the Friends of American Writers and the Society of Midland Authors. The novel is set in an area where Calvert grew up, left, and returned. For *Hadder MacColl,* Calvert recounts events in Scotland two centuries earlier. The protagonists in both novels, fourteen-year-old females with a love for horses, tell their first-person stories.

WORKS
    In **Hadder MacColl** during 1745, the protagonist, Hadder MacColl, has the same love of the Highlands and of clan traditions as her father. She is strong and proud, willing to use guile and perseverance to have her way. Looking forward to her brother Leofwin's return from his studies in Edinburgh, Hadder becomes disappointed when he brings David Forbes, son of his philosophy teacher and brother of Elizabeth, his intended. However, Leofwin brings Hadder a beautiful horse, Sionnach. Leofwin tells Hadder that studying Socrates has led him to examine his own philosophy, as well as the clans' tradition of quick retribution for all wrongs. When they go deer hunting in order to have meat for the *shieling* (summer cattle grazing), Leofwin refuses to kill a mountain lion that threatens the dogs. Irritated by Leofwin's hesitation, Hadder proudly shoots and brings it home for her father's praises. Leofwin explains that he hates to see this almost extinct animal lose its freedom. When Hadder gazes at Leofwin dead on *Culloden field after fighting in vain to restore the *Jacobites to the throne of Scotland, she realizes that the mountain lion symbolizes his own life, extinct and never free to pursue his desire of living in the New World. She knows that she must go for him. Her father soon follows Leofwin in death, with leg amputated after a fall from his horse and sadness over the loss of his son whom he had commanded to fight at Culloden. Hadder takes Glenisha, her maid,

to Edinburgh, and the Forbes family helps them go to America. On board ship, they open Elizabeth Forbes's farewell gift, a portrait she had painted of Leofwin.

In **The Snowbird**, Willanna Bannerman (Willie) describes her reaction to life after the death of her parents in a fire set by someone trying to destroy the evidence that her reporter father had found in an investigation. Willie takes her brother TJ (Thomas Jefferson) from Tennessee to the Dakota Territory by train to live on a farm with their uncle and aunt. Just as they arrive, the mare foals a silvery filly whom they call Snowbird because birds flying during snow supposedly bring good luck. Willie loves Snowbird and the farm, but her uncle, more musician than farmer, loses his crops. After a baby's birth and death, Aunt Belle eventually leaves, her wanderlust spirit unable to resist the unknown. Willie wants to write and asks Miss Pratt, her teacher, to help. Miss Pratt gives her books but goes on vacation to San Francisco and decides to remain there. Willie feels that as soon as she loves someone, the person leaves. When the Finnish immigrant Urho, who evokes her first feelings of sexuality, asks her to marry him, Willie realizes that having children and growing crops will limit her. She refuses. Aunt Belle had accused Willie of being a free spirit like herself, and Willie finally realizes that her aunt understood her as no one else had.

STYLE AND THEMES

Several phrases from the novels show their thoughtful creation. In *Hadder MacColl,* Calvert unobtrusively explains the pronunciation of *Leofwin* by noting that the sound is "softer than the sigh of a Highland wind through the trees: luff-win, luff-win." She comments that "mac" before Coll means sons and daughters of Coll. Her figurative language depicts the scenery: "tiny islands . . . float like green gems from a princess's necklace on the blue-gray waters of the sea next to the coast of Scotland." Calvert lets Hadder disclose the mythic hardness of the clans by telling that a newborn babe would be dipped in a loch, held up, and turned three times by a fire. The form also fits content in *The Snowbird.* The imagery is distinctive in phrases such as "griddlecakes, fringed at their edges with brown lace." Similes reflect the locale when Willie says that her uncle "hugged him to me tighter than a tick hugs a hound," and she describes the landscape: "tattered scraps of mist were snagged like ladies veils in the branches." The novels, tightly written, exhibit unusual depth of feeling through the realistic protagonists facing emotionally painful situations in their lives.

CAMERON, ELEANOR (1912–   ). Canadian-American.

BIBLIOGRAPHY AND BACKGROUND

The Court of the Stone Children. New York: Dutton, 1973.

The Court of the Stone Children won the American Book Award in 1974. (Cameron's other novels have also won several awards.) Although the novel cannot be considered accurate historical fantasy, its content best evokes the sense of past for which all historical fiction novelists should strive. At the beginning of the novel, Cameron quotes William Faulkner: "The past is not dead; it is not even past." By fusing the past and present in *The Court of the Stone Children,* Cameron avers that the past *is* the present. About her work, Cameron notes that she researched the novel

to discover what Napoleon did with the art treasures of the countries he conquered and as well to get the whole atmosphere of the time in France to discover what might have happened to a man like Antoine de Lombre who fiercely opposed Napoleon's tyranny, and what might have been the feelings of a wife expected to accompany her husband to Napoleon's court when she loathed the mood of it, the gossip and backbiting, and so loved the quiet of her own home and rambles in the countryside with her small daughter.

Other influences include Cameron's reading in art history and biography, her love of art museums, and "the fact that I, myself, have always been one to have the Museum Feeling. That sense that the past is close, is all around us." She says that the book "began growing in my mind, but wasn't written until several years later, because I always let novels grow slowly in my mind, while working on those that had started to come close earlier." She adds that the book is "wholly imagined, though of course it couldn't have been written if there were no Napoleon; or at least a different powerful man in some other country would have changed the whole mood and atmosphere of the book. There'd have been no French Museum. Oh, without doubt, no book."

WORK
In **The Court of the Stone Children**, new acquaintances laugh at Nina when she says she plans to become a museum curator because she has a Museum Feeling. She finds solace in San Francisco's French Museum, a place that greets people with a Chagall painting, *Time Is a River without Banks*. In the museum, Nina meets Dominique, a figure in a Chrystostome painting from *Napoleon's era. Dominique tells Nina that she dreamed about Nina when still a girl in France and knows that Nina can help her solve the mystery behind her father's arrest and subsequent assassination by Napoleon's men. Dominique is certain that her father was not guilty as accused of murdering his servant, a man he considered a friend. When Nina finds Odile's diary left on a museum bench, Dominique translates it for her, and Nina realizes that Odile was in love with Kot, Dominique's widowed father. She guesses that Odile's father, Chrystostome, painted Odile and Kot together when they announced their engagement but that Kot's immediate death led Odile's father to paint over the male figure with the likeness of the man Odile later married. When they find the painting and have it examined, Nina proves to be correct.

STYLE AND THEME
The beauty of Cameron's imagery and figurative language permeates the novel. The "tops of trees beginning to bend and whisper" tower above a girl, Maury, who is "impervious as a crocodile." The "mushrooms with their little hats of earth" complement Mrs. Henry, who is "trim as a plump bird in her bright cherry red." Cameron states another explicit theme in addition to the general

theme of past and present fused when she notes that "a moment of touching is the difference between complete, hopeless despair and being able to endure." Also Odile quotes Kot in a diary as expounding that "if a man believes something is wrong, immoral, he must speak." The integration of the psychological and the logical creates a timelessness achieved in few pieces of literature.

CAMPION TOWERS. *See* Beatty, John and Patricia.

A CANDLE AT DUSK. See Almedingen, E. M.

CANDLEMAS. The church festival celebrated on February 2 commemorates the occasion when the Virgin Mary went to Jerusalem to be purified for forty days after the birth of her son, Jesus, and to present him as her first-born to God, in accordance with Jewish law. By the fifth century, the custom of keeping the festival with lighted candles gave it this name. *See* Hunter, Mollie, *The 13th Member*.

CAPTAIN AHAB. In Herman Melville's *Moby Dick,* this complex, one-legged character spent the later part of his life trying to conquer the white whale, Moby Dick. *See* O'Dell, Scott, *The Dark Canoe*.

CAPTAIN GREY. See Avi.

CAPTAIN OF DRAGOONS. See Welch, Ronald.

THE CAPTIVE. See O'Dell, Scott.

CARAUSIAS, MARCUS AURELIUS (d. 293). As a Roman general serving Emperor Maximian, he fought rebelling Gauls in 286. As commander of a fleet at Boulogne, fighting Frankish and *Saxon pirates, he took much plunder. In 286, he decided to declare himself emperor in Britain, defeating Maximian's fleet in 289. He was eventually murdered by one of his ministers, *Allectus. *See* Sutcliff, Rosemary, *The Silver Branch*.

CARIBOO TRAIL. See Harris, Christie.

CARLOTA. Sixteen, Mexican protagonist in *Carlota. See* O'Dell, Scott.

CARLOTA. See O'Dell, Scott.

CARNAC. A village in northwest France, Carnac is best known for the long avenues of menhirs, or standing stones, which date from the late Neolithic Age. Passage graves and other configurations of stone can also be found in the area. Dating the stones becomes difficult because they were erected at different times. *See* Treece, Henry, *Perilous Pilgrimage*.

CARNIVAL. This celebration of merrymaking and festivity takes place in many Roman Catholic countries in the last days and hours of the pre-Lenten season. *See* Dalgliesh, Alice, *The Little Angel*.

CARRIE. Young black American protagonist in *Who Is Carrie? See* Collier, Christopher and James.

CARRIE WILLOW. At twelve, and as a mother, English protagonist in *Carrie's War*. *See* Bawden, Nina.

CARRIE AND PORTIA. Fourteen, American protagonists in *The Spirit Is Willing*. *See* Baker, Betty.

CARRIE'S WAR. See Bawden, Nina.

CARTER, PETER (1929–   ). British.

BIBLIOGRAPHY AND BACKGROUND
   The Black Lamp. Illustrated by David Harris. Nashville, Tenn: T. Nelson, 1973; London: Oxford, 1973. *Children of the Book*. London: Oxford, 1982. *The Gates of Paradise*. Illustrated by Fermin Rocker. London: Oxford, 1974. *Madatan*. Illustrated by Victor Ambrus. London: Oxford, 1974. *The Sentinels*. New York and London: Oxford, 1980.
   Peter Carter's books have been acknowledged with many awards. *The Gates of Paradise* was cited by *The Guardian* Award in 1974. In 1982, *The Sentinels* won *The Guardian* Award and the Premio di Lettaratura of Italy. *The Observer* Award and the German Leseratten Award went to *Children of the Book* in 1983. Different interests have led Carter to his various books. He says, "The sight of the new mosque in Regent's Park, London, led me to think about the resurgence of Islam and to my writing *Children of the Book*. The interest in Black Studies led me to writing *Sentinels*—showing the hardship of the *anti*-slave patrol of the Royal Navy. The collapse of the textile industry in England made me want to say something about industrial change in *The Black Lamp*. I wrote *The Gates of Paradise* because I admire Blake and 'stiff-necked' people generally." He sees historical fiction as a "way of using history as a kind of perspective against which we can view the present" and that the "emotional truth" controls the rest of the work. He uses as much contemporary material as possible, like diaries and newspapers, to complement his wide knowledge of history. He prefers to write evenings after spending lunchtime working on ideas and afternoons climbing in the Derbyshire hills.

WORKS

In **Madatan**, set around 790, the Norsemen raid Madaah's village, kill his people, and capture him. At sea, Olaf, the owner of the ship, hits Madaah and then dies the next night. The men think that Madaah bewitched Olaf, and in order to survive, Madaah allows them to believe. His quickness to learn their language seems to convince them of his wizardry. While wintering in the Orkneys with them, Madaah recommends raiding England the following summer. Soon after the raid begins, the ship wrecks, and Madaah swims to shore; someone finds him and takes him to a monastery. An inhabitant who speaks Celtic learns Madaah's background. Again Madaah shows great language facility by learning to speak and read their language. Within a year, he begins to enjoy scholarly pursuits. His abbot sends him to *Lindisfarne. He arrives in 793 just as more Norsemen burn it to the ground. He moves to *York, where he helps the abbot Ealdred in the library, enjoying the beautiful manuscripts. Soon, however, the abbot sends him to the home of Lord Cedric to keep accounts. Unfortunately, Madaah had previously met Lord Cedric's son, Oswald, and immediately disliked him. Their second encounter leads to a hostility that results in the death of a man and his son whom Madaah is trying to help. When Madaah eventually battles Oswald face to face in the York chapel, someone enters through a trap door to help Madaah, and Oswald kills the intruder. Seeing that Oswald has killed Ealdred so distresses Madaah that he kills Oswald and then respectfully burns Ealdred's body among his manuscripts in the cellar. He continues to lose his faith when he realizes that most of the church leaders are mainly concerned with achieving power. To escape Lord Cedric's vengeance, Madaah becomes an outlaw. But Lord Cedric's man finds him, tortures him, and leaves him to die. A stranger, Colum, finds him on the rocks near the sea and nurses him to health. He convinces Madaah that the two were meant to confess their sins to each other and to understand that they had already served their penance. Madaah returns to his former village, retrieves his old sword, and reports to the longships. In the last chapter, the point of view shifts to Colum. When Colum tells Madaah that he saved him because he saw Christ in his mutilated face, Madaah begins to regain some of his lost faith.

In 1682, in **Children of the Book**, the Turks break their treaty with the Austrians and attack Vienna. The point of view shifts among three teenaged characters: one Polish, one Austrian, and one Turk. During the time that the Austrian, Anna, awaits the announced arrival of the Turks in Vienna, she becomes betrothed to Kaspar, one of the soldiers designated to fight. Timur, the Turk, at sixteen, accompanies the *Janissary leader Vasif on the long march to Vienna and helps him during the summer siege of 1683. The third character, Stefan Zabruski, arrives from Crakow, Poland, on September 12, 1683, to aid the Austrians. On his journey, he and his father stay with friends, and Stefan falls in love with and asks Vera, their daughter, to marry him. But outside the walls of Vienna that September, Timur shoots off Stefan's head, and Stefan's father skewers Timur's ribs. Inside the walls, Anna starves with the rest of the

Viennese but survives to marry Kaspar. The vivid characterizations of the protagonists and the lesser characters create a powerful story exploring the motivations behind the Moslem invasion as well as the Christian defense. Since each
group calls the other infidel, and moral human beings form each group, what is
right becomes ambiguous. Carter portrays the concept that individual desire for
power and ambition can destroy anyone.

In 1796, in **The Gates of Paradise**, Ben Pendrill escapes his dreary life
making candles and finds himself in the yard of William and Sophy *Blake,
who offer him clothing and food. Ben has difficulty understanding William and
his conversations with his brother, Robert, who has been dead for ten years.
But when Ben wants to learn William's trade of engraving, William willingly
teaches him. Then William brings Grale, a man who has accused him of sedition
during the *French Revolution, to the house. Grale's smell and evil intentions
revolt Ben, but William contends that no human can see into another's heart,
and therefore, should not judge him. What Ben finds is that William and Sophy
are kind and generous with what little they have during a time in England when
the government, reeling from the revolution in France, suspects almost every
British citizen of plotting against it. When Sophy decides to apprentice Ben to
Mr. Fox, she helps Ben realize that he must have a trade that he can practice
daily in order to become independent. Ben makes his own journey from in-
noncence to experience by discovering and reading some of William's poems
and by observing William's devout belief that God is in all humans and that
each person must deal with God individually.

Daniel Cregg, in **The Black Lamp**, tells his experience as a seventeen-year-
old weaver's son before and during the weavers' march in 1819 on *Manchester
where they wanted to assert their needs peacefully. New machines had replaced
many of them, and they had to work in the mills if they had jobs at all. When
the offensive mill owner, Mr. Cranley, offers Daniel a job, his father makes
him take it because he thinks that Daniel should learn to be an engineer. But
the motivation behind Cranley's offer is his recognition of Mr. Cregg as a member
of the group named Black Lamp which had destroyed the new weaving machines
nineteen years before. Cranley believes that personable conversation with Daniel
will lead Daniel eventually to acknowledge his father's participation. But Mr.
Cregg investigates Cranley and finds that he has previously been jailed for forgery
and other misdeeds. As Cranley verbally prods Daniel, he mentions the Stafford
gaol (jail) were Cranley was once incarcerated, and Cranley fires him. When
Mr. Cregg and his fellow workers march the thirteen miles to Manchester, the
police cavalry charges them—wounding, killing, and arresting. One of Mr.
Cregg's Black Lamp friends saves Daniel, and another rescues Mr. Cregg. When
Daniel steals back to his village, he finds that Cranley has kidnapped his ten-
year-old sister, Emmie, and put her to work in the mill. Bloom, a compassionate
mill engineer, lets Daniel into the locked and guarded mill to rescue Emmie.
When the dog barks at a rat as Daniel runs across the yard with Emmie, Cranley
sees them. Simultaneously, Briggs, a man crazed by the death of his wife in

Manchester, slashes the mill wheel. As Cranley rushes toward Daniel, the dam breaks, and both Cranley and Briggs fall into the swirling water. Six years later, Daniel remembers the frightening time. Although working in a forge and barely surviving poverty, he is glad that he no longer has to fight for his rights.

In **The Sentinels**, during 1840, omniscient point of view reveals the condition of persons at three different locales before their ships meet off the coast of Africa. The story focuses mainly on the experiences of John Spencer, a fifteen-year-old British orphan who becomes a gentleman volunteer on an anti-slave ("legal" *abolitionist) patrol ship, the *Sentinel*, under the captaincy of Murray, an honest and religious man. In Africa, men from the *Dahomey tribe capture Lyapo, a *Yoruba, as he hunts near his village, and after marching him through the jungles, sell him at the slave market. Across the Atlantic, the *Phantom* moves from Baltimore to Havana under Captain Kimber; then it sails to Africa to load slaves, a cargo promising a 150 percent profit to the *Phantom* owners. Other less significant but revealing points of view include those of a lord in Parliament, who thinks that the British should leave the slavers alone, and his emissary, a nephew Brooke, who tries to wield power on the *Sentinel*. The principals meet when the *Sentinel* spots *Phantom*, with its load of slaves including Lyapo, and pursues it. After a fight, a retreat, another fight, and a search, the *Sentinel* claims *Phantom* as her prize. With the *Phantom*'s crew locked in the hold, John, a rapid learner, becomes *Phantom*'s captain. The French ship *San Felipe* arrives and attacks *Phantom*, but the *Sentinel*'s men defend it after John hands the freed Lyapo a sword to fight the enemy trying to board. Before *San Felipe* leaves in defeat, it gouges a hole in *Phantom*'s side, which permits the imprisoned Kimber to escape and shoot the men from the *Sentinel* crew. John and Lyapo almost drown but find a boat and eventually wash up on the African coast. While stranded for months, they learn each other's language and learn to respect each other's abilities. The Royal Navy finally rescues them and welcomes them back to the *Sentinel*. Lyapo decides to remain in Africa instead of going to England with John. An epilogue reveals that three years later, after the *Tories have defeated the *Whigs, Murray has lost his ship and Brooke has gained one. John becomes a respected navy man. Carter balances Lyapo's terrible loneliness and horrifying experiences with humor and hope, as well as much valuable information about the Royal Navy's nineteenth-century customs.

STYLE AND THEMES

The form of each of Carter's tightly written novels complements the content. In *The Sentinels*, he develops the many short interior monologues with fragments verbalizing the thought processes of the characters. His figurative language emphasizes theme and setting. A nautical metaphor from *The Sentinels* illustrates: "John an apt pupil, enjoying mathematics and navigation, catching up on Fearnley, overtaking Scott, and leaving Potts in his wake." In the same novel, Carter describes Brooke's uncle using alliteration: "a noble lord, full of port and pheasant, rising to address his fellow peers." Personification heightens the sense in

Madatan: "the wind cried along the wall, and poked cold fingers through its holes." Throughout the novels, Carter uses dreams as a method of unraveling plot and foreshadowing. They also clarify theme, especially the pervading theme that lust for power and wealth destroys. In a clear but subtle undercurrent, Carter confirms in all his novels that only strong spiritual conviction can create the psychological contentment for which all humans search.

CASILDA. Thirteen, Moor in Spain, protagonist of *Casilda of the Rising Moon.* *See* de Treviño, Elizabeth.

CASILDA OF THE RISING MOON. *See* de Treviño, Elizabeth.

CASSIA YOUNG. Chinese protagonist of eight who matures into a young woman in *The Serpent's Children. See* Yep, Lawrence.

CASSIE LOGAN. At eight, female black American protagonist in *Song of the Trees,* at nine in *Roll of Thunder, Hear My Cry,* and ten in *Let the Circle Be Unbroken. See* Taylor, Mildred.

CASTORS AWAY! *See* Burton, Hester.

CATHERINE II OF RUSSIA (1729–1796). Called Catherine the Great, she became empress in 1762. Married to Peter, the nephew of the empress *Elizabeth, she deposed him soon after his accession with the help of her paramour, Grigory Orlov. Although serfdom and misery increased during her reign, she extended the frontiers of her empire with large conquests. She also secularized the property of the clergy. *See* Almedingen, E. M., *Anna.*

CATHERINE CABOT HALL. Fourteen, protagonist in *A Gathering of Days: A New England Girl's Journey 1830–32. See* Blos, Joan.

CATRIONA BURKE. Irish, protagonist of *Holdfast. See* Beatty, John and Patricia.

CATUVELLAUNI. This British tribe was at the height of its influence when the Romans invaded Britain. Its members lived in the general area northwest of London south of the River Avon. *See* Treece, Henry, *War Dog.*

CAUCASUS. This range of mountains extends for 750 miles from Anapa on the Black Sea in the Soviet Union to the western shores of the Caspian Sea. *See* Bartos-Höppner, B., *Storm over the Caucasus.*

CAUDILL, REBECCA (1899–   ). American.

BIBLIOGRAPHY AND BACKGROUND
The Far-off Land. Illustrated by Brinton Turkle. New York: Viking, 1964.
Tree of Freedom. Illustrated by Dorothy Bayley. New York: Viking, 1949.

For her novels, Caudill has received several commendations. The Newbery and the *New York Herald Tribune* honored *Tree of Freedom.* The Friends of the American Writers awarded *The Far-off Land* in 1964. Caudill sets both stories in 1780 and tells them using a limited omniscient point of view to present the teenaged female protagonists who leave North Carolina with their families. The *American Revolution, however, concerns the pioneer characters only because the British have paid Indians to massacre them. As the characters journey and resettle, they want only to survive the Indians.

WORKS
In **Tree of Freedom**, Stephanie Venable's father wants to escape the Carolina colony's taxes, so the family moves to Kentucky to a new claim. Mr. Venable allows each child to choose one favorite item to take. He tells Noel, Steph's brother, however, that he cannot bring his impractical dulcimer. Mrs. Venable, with her French heritage and love of music, intervenes, and Noel brings the dulcimer. Steph decides to take an apple seed from a tree her great-grandmother transported from France. When they arrive at the claim, she plants it and names it her "Tree of Freedom," to symbolize the freedom to be what and where one wants in a free land. A stranger comes and tells them that someone from England has already claimed their spot, but a neighbor, Tilly Balance, who brings them berries, throws a slithering snake at the lying man. Others come to build on neighboring claims. One day when Stephanie and Noel go to the nearby *Harrod's Fort, Noel sees Colonel *Clark, brother of Lewis's companion. He decides to join Clark in fighting Indians whom the British have bribed to kill Kentucky's people. Noel believes that he will be keeping the British out of the back door of America. After the war, when Noel's illiterate father cannot read his own deed, Noel decides to go to Williamsburg to study law in order to protect others like his father. He suggests that Steph come with him to continue her own learning. Caudill emphasizes that unless one has knowledge, one's freedom can be threatened, even in the wilderness.

At the same time Steph's family resettles in Kentucky, Ketty in **The Far-off Land** resettles with her brother, Anson, in French Lick, Indiana. The story begins when Anson reappears in Salem, North Carolina, after fourteen years. Ketty informs him that of their family of seven, they are the only two living, the others having died mainly of fevers. As she leaves to join Anson and his family, one of the Moravians with whom she has been living tells her to remember that the greatest gift she can give to anyone will be to "be present" to that person when needed. Ketty tries to remember this advice as she meets all of the people traveling together, especially Anson's wife, who resents her as someone else needing food. On the journey, Ketty helps the children gather bark for paper and char sticks for pens and teaches them to read. Since Ketty cannot deny her Moravian upbringing, which espouses that all humans are equal, she refuses to believe that all red men are bad, so when she discovers a sick Indian on a river bank, she helps him. Her kindness most likely keeps the group from being ambushed at a point farther along the river where Indians earlier had destroyed several other boats. She soon falls in love with George, a moral man raised in the wilderness. Illness, fighting, and misfortunes reduce the group's members, but most finally reach French Lick. Ketty and George marry and adopt a child orphaned on the journey. The astonishing difficulties the many pioneers faced who traveled this same route indicate that they were brave people.

STYLE AND THEMES

Caudill's depth of theme makes each novel worth reading. In both, her biblical allusions enlarge the concepts. The appropriate use of dialect and diction keeps the stories focused in 1780. Moreover, Caudill's integration of imagery, figurative language, symbols, and theme are obvious when she says in *Tree of Freedom*, "A tender green shoot of knowing how to read was breaking through the dark brown dullness that was her mind, and making its way to the light."

CAVALIERS. The enemies of the *Royalists in the *English Civil War also pejoratively called them "cavaliers" after the brutal and papist Spanish *cavalieros* ("troopers"). See *Witch Dog, King's Knight's Pawn,* and *Campion Towers* by John and Patricia *Beatty.

CAXTON, WILLIAM (c. 1422–1491). After learning printing in Cologne, he returned to England and established the first English press at Westminster in 1476. He printed his own translations, as well as such texts as Mallory's *Morte d'Arthur* in 1485. See *Caxton's Challenge* and *The Writing on the Hearth* by Cynthia *Harnett.

CAXTON'S CHALLENGE. See Harnett, Cynthia.

CECIL, ROBERT (1563–1612). He succeeded his father, William, as *Elizabeth I's adviser. As her secretary of state, he secured the succession to the throne for James VI of Scotland as *James I of England. He also led Elizabeth's secret service. See *Master Rosalind* by John and Patricia *Beatty and *Cue for Treason* by Geoffrey *Trease.

CECILY JOLLAND. Sixteen, English co-protagonist with Lewis Mallory, seventeen, in *The Lark and the Laurel. See* Willard, Barbara.

CEDD (d. 664). Educated at *Lindisfarne, he christianized East *Saxons while founding and heading a monastery at Lastingham, Yorkshire. See *The Fire-Brother* and *The Sea Stranger* by Kevin *Crossley-Holland.

CENTURION. In the ancient Roman army, the commander of a *centuria,* the sixtieth part of a legion (seventy men), was called a centurion. Of plebian origin, usually promoted from the ranks to his position, he was most often considered a noncommissioned officer. Senior centurions resembled modern company commanders. See *The Centurion* by Henry *Treece and *The Eagle of the Ninth* and *Frontier Wolf* by Rosemary *Sutcliff.

THE CENTURION. *See* Treece, Henry.

CEREMONY OF INNOCENCE. *See* Forman, James.

CHAD RABUN. Eleven, American, protagonist of *Flaming Arrows.* *See* Steele, William O.

CHAKOH. Fourteen, Native American protagonist in *Walk the World's Rim.* *See* Baker, Betty.

A CHANCE CHILD. *See* Paton Walsh, Jill.

CHARLES I OF ENGLAND (1600–1649). After enraging British commoners by disbanding Parliament and fighting many expensive battles, he declared war on the *Parliamentarians at Nottingham in 1642. After losing at Naseby in 1645, he was eventually condemned to death and beheaded at Whitehall. See *Witch Dog* and *King's Knight's Pawn* by John and Patricia *Beatty; *Kate Ryder* by Hester *Burton; and *For the King* by Ronald *Welch.

CHARLES I OF SPAIN (1500–1558). Son of Philip I of Castile and grandson of Ferdinand and Isabella, he served as king from 1516 to 1556 and as Holy Roman emperor from 1519 to 1556. In addition to accomplishments on the European continent, he extended New World possessions with conquests of Mexico by *Cortés and of Peru by *Pizarro. Before his death, he abdicated and retired to a monastery. See *Blood of the Brave* by Betty *Baker and *The Amethyst Ring* by Scott *O'Dell.

CHARLES II OF ENGLAND (1630–1685). After trying to save the life of his father, *Charles I, he made promises that allowed his restoration to king in 1660. He was forced to drive Catholics from office and to consent to the marriage of his niece Princess Mary to *William of Orange. He died with no legitimate heir. See *Campion Towers* by John and Patricia *Beatty; *Through the Fire* by Hester *Burton; and *Cromwell's Boy* and *A Messenger for Parliament* by Erik *Haugaard.

CHARLES CAREY. Young adult, English, protagonist of *Captain of Dragoons.* *See* Welch, Ronald.

CHARLES EDWARD (1720–1788). His nicknames include the Young Pretender, the Young Chevalier, and Bonnie Prince Charlie. As grandson of James II and son of James Edward, the Old Pretender, he succeeded as head of the *Jacobites. He landed in Scotland from France in 1745, garnered an army from the clans, and led an uprising known as the Forty-Five, which gained control of Edinburgh and claim to the name James VIII. He briefly invaded England but was thoroughly defeated at *Culloden by the Duke of *Cumberland on April 16, 1746. His wanderings through Europe to gain support for *Stuart restoration were unfulfilled. He settled in Italy. See *The Royal Dirk* by John and Patricia *Beatty; *The Lothian Run* by Mollie *Hunter; and *The Young Pretenders* by Barbara *Picard.

CHARLIE SAMPSON. Young English protagonist returned from France in *The Drummer Boy*. *See* Garfield, Leon.

CHAS. Fourteen, English protagonist in *The Machine Gunners* who matures to sixteen as protagonist in *Fathom Five*. *See* Westall, Robert.

CHASE ME, CATCH NOBODY! *See* Haugaard, Erik.

CHEROKEE. An important U.S. tribe of Iroquoian lineage, its members were originally located in Tennessee and North and South Carolina. The Cherokee towns were either "red" (war) or "white" (peace). Those in the red towns answered to a supreme war chief; those in the white towns answered to a supreme peace chief of the tribe. The white towns were places of sanctuary. See *The Life and Death of Yellow Bird* by James *Forman; *Rifles for Watie* by Harold *Keith; and *Wayah of the Real People, The Man with the Silver Eyes, Winter Danger, Flaming Arrows, Trail through Danger,* and *The Lone Hunt* by William O. *Steele.

CHILDREN OF THE BOOK. *See* Carter, Peter.

THE CHILDREN'S CRUSADE. See *Perilous Pilgrimage* by Henry *Treece.

THE CHOCOLATE BOY. *See* Trease, Geoffrey.

CHRIS BABSON. Eleven, American, protagonist of *The Perilous Road*. *See* Steele, William O.

CHRIS CAREY. Young adult, English, protagonist of *Captain of Foot*. *See* Welch, Ronald.

CHRISTEL GOTH. Eight, Austrian, protagonist of *Fly Away Home*. *See* Nostlinger, Christine.

CHRISTINA RUSSELL. English protagonist of twelve in *Flambards* who grows to twenty-two through *The Edge of the Cloud, Flambards in Summer,* and *Flambards Divided. See* Peyton, K. M.

CHRISTOPHER BARSTOW. Young English protagonist in *King's Knight's Pawn. See* Beatty, John and Patricia.

CHUTE, MARCHETTE (1909–   ). American.

BIBLIOGRAPHY AND BACKGROUND

The Innocent Wayfaring. Illustrated by the author. New York: Scribner, 1943; London: Phoenix House, 1956. *The Wonderful Winter*. Illustrated by Grace Golden. New York: Dutton, 1954; London: Phoenix House, 1956.

A scholar of English literature, Marchette Chute has been honored with such awards as the Women's National Book Association Constance Lindsay Skinner Award. She is also a member of the American Academy. *The Innocent Wayfaring* and *The Wonderful Winter* demonstrate her research skills.

WORKS

In **The Innocent Wayfaring** set during the time of Chaucer (around 1380), Anne Richmond, fifteen, runs away from the convent where her parents have sent her to learn household duties. She takes the pet monkey Agatha with her. When Anne encounters a local fair, she decides to make Agatha do tricks to earn money for their travel, but instead, Anne loses her. She finds Agatha wrapped around the neck of Nicholas Ware. She accuses him of stealing Agatha, but the judge finds her guilty of false accusation. To help Anne escape the jail sentence, Nick grabs her, and they run away. Together they walk to London, stopping for visits with Nick's friends and talking about their hatred of marriage. Suddenly they realize that they care for each other, so they return to Anne's home where her parents have been worried for the four days she has been gone. Each episode of the novel centers on a visit: they stop, eat, talk, and leave for the next episode. With no sustaining suspense and the incredibility of a young girl walking around England in the fourteenth century, the book is unconvincing.

Another protagonist runs away in **The Wonderful Winter**. In 1596, Sir Robert Wakefield decides that he must escape from the three aunts who control his life. He visits several places with his dog, Ruff, and finds that he must go to London for a job since men in small towns do not hire outsiders. In London, when a man tries to steal Ruff, Robin runs inside a theater. His new life begins in the properties' room where John Heminges discovers him asleep. He takes Robin home, and Robin begins working for the family while Mr. Heminges's apprentice, Sandy, helps more at the *Globe Theater. Robin enjoys the experience of living with such a loving family. When Robin saves Heminges's daughter Seena from drowning, Heminges lets him also work in the theater. Robin's first role is to dance in *Romeo and Juliet,* a new play by *Shakespeare. Robin loves the theater and wants to stay, but when the season is over, Heminges tells him that the players expect to lose the building. He offers to find him an apprentice job at another theater, but Robin reveals his background and decides that his love of animals and nature calls him back to his native Suffolk. After buying presents and having dinner with Shakespeare at the Mermaid during which time Michael Drayton, an English poet, stops by to visit, Robin leaves. At home, the aunts welcome him and accept him as the new master of the house. Although this story relates an informative view of the Globe Theater personages, Robin's character hardly has time to develop from one who runs away to one who would assert himself so readily to three hostile aunts.

STYLE AND THEMES

Chute's sentence cadence catches a sense of the language. From the top of *St. Paul's, the Thames looks "like a ribbon of silk." Before Robin leaves his aunts, he sits at dinner with them and exhibits his sense of humor by thinking, "it seemed probable that time had ceased altogether and that some form of eternity had taken its place." Although Chute's writing is a pleasure to read, the protagonists' implausibilities preclude any concerns about them as characters.

CIBOLA [CIBULA], SEVEN CITIES OF. The search for this fabled wealthy land began in Arizona in 1536 when de Vaca arrived to explore the unknown north. It continued when others, including *Coronado, left Mexico in 1540 and traveled throughout an area as far north as Nebraska. *See* Baker, Betty, *Walk the World's Rim.*

CIVIL WAR. *See* *American Civil War.

CLAPP, PATRICIA (1912–). American.

BIBLIOGRAPHY AND BACKGROUND

Constance: A Story of Early Plymouth. New York: Lothrup, Lee, & Shepard, 1968. *I'm Deborah Sampson: A Soldier in the War of the Revolution.* New York: Lothrup, Lee, & Shepard, 1977. *The Tamarack Tree: A Novel of the Siege of Vicksburg.* New York: Lothrup, Lee, & Shepard, 1986. *Witches' Children: A Story of Salem.* New York: Lothrup, Lee, & Shepard, 1982.

Patricia Clapp's books have been selected as an American Book Award Finalist in 1969, placed on the American Library Association Best Books for Young Adults list in 1982, and honored by the Jefferson Cup Committee of the Virginia Library Association in 1983. Clapp was cited as a Notable New Jersey Author in 1983. Family genealogy led Clapp to the *Mayflower*-Plymouth story via "years living in Massachusetts, trips to London and Leyden, and Plimoth Plantation reconstruction." Since she finds people "fascinating," she conceives her heroine first, which immediately establishes her dates and settings. For research, she says, "I read and read and read. And go on reading." Her extensive travels allow her to visualize places. If she has time, she may write for two or three hours, but she writes for pleasure—hence deadlines are self-imposed. The innumerable revisions come as she writes, again before the final typing, and finally after editorial suggestions. She says, "I never planned on becoming a writer, and no one is more surprised than I at how much fun it is!"

WORKS

Clapp's heroines tell their first-person stories, three of them using flashbacks. Constance in **Constance**, however, tells her story in journal form. In 1620, she arrives in America on the *Mayflower* with her father, Stephen Hopkins, and stepmother, Elizabeth. The females wait aboard ship while men, including her father, Will Bradford, and Myles *Standish, decide where they will locate. Many contract scurvy before the buildings can be erected. Soon the Commons House is available for the sick, and Elizabeth goes ashore to nurse them. Although Constance's father recovers, her young sister, Demaris, and fifty-one others do not. An Indian, Samoset, befriends them, and Constance gives him a gold bracelet for his daughter. In return the daughter makes Constance a pair of moccasins and occasionally comes to visit. They learn to communicate without a common language. Among the events that Constance recounts are her friend Priscilla's endeavors to get John Alden (instead of Myles Standish) to ask her to marry him, of the Indian *Massasoit being invited to the thanksgiving dinner and unexpectedly bringing ninety others with him, and of their hunger through the winter. Another civic problem is how to expel two vile families. The Plymouth church's clergyman handles the situation so fairly that he attracts many un-churched citizens, including Constance's father, to his services. As important to Constance, however, are her feelings of unattractiveness at fifteen giving way to her rising sexual awareness and a coquettishness difficult to control. She invites both Stephen Deane and Nicholas Snow to court her. Not until after Stephen asks her to marry him does she realize that she actually loves Nicholas. The novel breathes life into the dreary story of Plymouth. These characters are ancestors one can cherish.

Witches' Children tells a less attractive story of America's beginnings. Mary Warren, in 1692 a girl bound to John and Elizabeth Proctor, often has freedom to visit friends. At the Parris family home, she listens to Tituba, the Barbados woman, read tarot cards and palms. Tituba refuses to reveal what she "sees" for Abigail, an eleven-year-old who yearns for excitement. Eventually ten girls gather in the afternoons and begin seeing visions. After Abigail rushes into a tavern and starts screaming, the girls begin blaming witches for "possessing" them. To identify the unknown witches, Tituba says that feeding a dog a baked cake of rye mixed with urine will make the dog growl at any witch. After the test, the dog growls at Tituba and two others often chastised by the townspeople, Goody Good and Mistress Osburne. Villagers scorn all three for various reasons; hence they are willing to think them witches. The girls in their visions accuse more and more people as witches, including John and Elizabeth Proctor, whom Mary knows are innocent. When named a witch herself after separating from the group, Mary realizes that if she admits being a witch, the questioners believe her but they will not believe her if she denies the charge. The continuing accusations indicate the children's enjoyment of having a chance to be the center of attention and having control over adults. After numerous hangings, including John Proctor, those accused and jailed begin to disappear; the keepers leave the gates open and look away. Mary knows that she has aided evil, and fifteen years later, she is still remorseful about the destructive accusations made in the name of God.

In a flashback, Deborah at age sixty recalls her youth in **I'm Deborah Sampson**. In 1765, Deborah's mother could not support her, so Deborah was eventually bound to the Thomas family for eight years. The ten Thomas sons accept Deborah as part of their family. Deborah especially cares for Robbie and falls in love with him when she is fifteen. The same summer, Robbie goes to fight in the *American Revolution after word comes that the British have killed his oldest brother, Nat. The sexual fires that awaken in Deborah and in Robbie surprise them both, but with their parting, they look forward to his return and their marriage. After five years, the British kill Robbie, and Deborah decides to fight in his place. She enlists and finds keeping her sex secret a constant struggle. She relieves herself after midnight, is fortunate to have light periods, and keeps her breasts bound. So that doctors will not expose her, she extracts bullets in her thigh and shoulder with a knife. Finally she contracts a fever, but the doctor who examines her and discovers she is female honors her request to return her to the regiment. Not until the war ends does she reveal her sex. After the war, friends reintroduce her to Ben, who had once brought the Thomases news of Nat. She and Ben laugh about her difficulties, and they eventually marry. When forty-two, Deborah goes on tour, dressed in a regimental uniform, to tell about her Revolutionary War experience. Deborah overcomes her anguish by putting her beliefs into action.

In **The Tamarack Tree**, Rosemary Monical Staford Leigh records her experiences in 1863 during the siege of Vicksburg, Mississippi, beginning with her arrival from London in 1859 at age fourteen. She shifts from the present to the past and back as she tells about her mother's death and living with her brother, Derry, who calls her Tad, while he works as an aide for their lawyer uncle in Vicksburg. She recalls the visit of Vicksburg neighbors, Mary Byrd and her mother, on her day of arrival and meeting Jeffrey Howard, a Harvard student soon to become a Union (*Yankee) soldier, on her sixteenth birthday. Jeff contrives to send her handpainted cards on each subsequent birthday until he reappears in her life July 4, 1863, the day Vicksburg surrenders. During the siege, Rosemary, Mary Byrd, and Derry help *Confederate soldiers in the makeshift hospitals. Helpless, they also watch them starve. Rosemary cannot understand the concept of owning another human being, and when she finds that the free blacks who help her family as well as her brother and her uncle are part of the *Underground Railway, she approves. However, she also likes Mary Byrd and her cousin Ben very much, and they own slaves and a plantation. When Mary Byrd finds out about the tunnel under the house where the Leighs stay and that Derry has helped slaves escape, she ends their relationship. Ben, afraid and starved, dies in Derry's bed on the night of July 4. After *Grant's victory, Jeff reappears, and Rosemary agrees to marry him after the war. At the end of July, Derry decides to return to London for medical school, and before they leave, Rosemary visits Mary Byrd. Mary Byrd's father has explained to her that masters often abused their slaves, something she never realized, and that the old way has ended. Rosemary reports Mary Byrd's acceptance of the new way to Derry, and the two marry before leaving for London where Rosemary will wait for Jeff.

STYLE AND THEMES

Deborah, Constance, and Rosemary supply humor to their own tense situations, but *Witches' Children* lacks anything humorous. The comparison of settings in these well-written novels lends credence to the truism that idleness is the devil's workshop. People trying to survive must balance their own tense situations with laughter, or they will never be psychologically capable of continuing life.

CLARK, GEORGE ROGERS (1752–1818). He led frontiersmen in Kentucky against Indian raids in 1776–77 and helped save the Illinois and Kentucky region for the colonies. From 1779 to 1783, he fought to hold this territory from the British and the Indians. *See* Caudill, Rebecca, *Tree of Freedom*.

CLAVERHOUSE, JOHN GRAHAM OF. Scot devotedly followed by the protagonist in *Bonnie Dundee*. *See* Sutcliff, Rosemary.

A COLD WIND BLOWING. *See* Willard, Barbara.

COLIN LOCKWOOD. Fifteen, English protagonist in *The Exeter Blitz*. *See* Rees, David.

COLL. Eighteen, orphan and disabled, Scottish protagonist in *The Stronghold*. *See* Hunter, Mollie.

COLLIER, CHRISTOPHER (1930–   ) and JAMES (1928–   ). Americans.

BIBLIOGRAPHY AND BACKGROUND

The Bloody Country. New York: Four Winds Press, 1976. *Jump Ship to Freedom*. New York: Dell/Delacorte, 1981. *My Brother Sam Is Dead*. New York: Four Winds Press, 1974. *War Comes to Willy Freeman*. New York: Delacorte, 1983. *Who Is Carrie?* New York: Dell/Delacorte, 1984. *The Winter Hero*. New York: Four Winds Press, 1978.

The collaboration between Christopher and James Collier has won such accolades as the Newbery Honor, a National Book Award nominee, the Jane Addams Peace Prize Honor, the American Library Association Notable Books list, and other awards from the National Council of Social Studies and the

National Council of the Teachers of English. Christopher Collier is an academic historian specializing in the American Revolution and the Early National Period. He is also Connecticut State Historian. While teaching junior high school, he realized that "students would learn better and remember more if they had exciting treatments of important historical themes and concepts." Christopher Collier establishes the themes and story lines for the novels and presents his brother, James Lincoln Collier, with descriptions of episodes, including all necessary research information. James writes the drafts, and Christopher edits until both are satisfied.

WORKS

The young teenaged protagonists in the Collier novels use first-person point of view to tell their *American Revolutionary period stories from 1775 to 1787. With an overall motif concerning the pursuit of individual freedom, three books present the concerns of both slaves and free blacks. Another depicts the loss of freedom during war, and two more reveal problems of survival for white colonists.

In the epilogue to **My Brother Sam Is Dead**, the protagonist, Timmy Meeker, wonders fifty years after the Revolution if the same goals could have been attained without war. The horrors of war begin revealing themselves to Timmy in 1775 when his brother, Sam, leaves Yale in defiance of their father to join Captain Benedict *Arnold's rebels. Timmy wonders who is right: the *Tories or the rebels. He knows his father and his friends are Tories, but he sees the British kill his ten-year-old friend. On a trip to trade cattle for rum and tavern supplies, cattle thieves capture his father, who later dies of cholera on a British prison ship. Throughout the war, prices rise, and people starve. Sam returns briefly and tells Timmy and his mother to kill their cattle and freeze the beef under snow to keep soldiers from taking it. They keep postponing the task until one night they hear people taking the cattle. Sam runs to rescue, but the cattle thieves capture and blame him. Because General Putnam had decreed death for theft, he ignores the evidence that Sam was defending his family and executes him as an example to other men. Thus Timmy experiences the deaths of a friend, his father, and his brother in situations unrelated to the actual fighting. In this novel, almost everything bad that could happen to Timmy does. The epilogue adds hope that others could survive such terrors. However, so many bad experiences happen to Timmy that the story seems contrived.

A better balance of positive and negative events controls the three novels with black protagonists. In **War Comes to Willy Freeman**, Willy, thirteen, accompanies her father to Fort Griswold, Connecticut. Cut off by a British advance and unable to leave the fort, she watches a British soldier gore her father to death. By joining the militia, Willy's father obtained freedom for his family, but he had not expected to sacrifice his life for it. By the time Willy reaches home, the British have captured her mother and disappeared. Wearing masculine milking clothes, Willy begins her odyssey to find her mother. In New York City, she inquires at Sam Fraunces's Tavern, and Mr. Fraunces hires her. During her free time, she searches the canvas towns of the city, where she eventually finds that her mother has gone to her sister in Stratford, Connecticut. Willy follows though her aunt's master, Captain Ivers, will probably claim her as his slave. Captain Ivers allows Willy's mother to lie ill and die in his house, and he does try to claim Willy. But Willy receives help in fighting him in court, and she wins. She comments in her realistically illiterate dialect that a man would give a woman orders, and a white would give a black orders, and the old would give the young orders; therefore, she as a young black female would get orders from everyone. She thinks, "When you was a woman you was half a slave, anyway. You had to get married [to] support yourself." That a young black girl in this time period would have questioned her situation as much as Willy does is doubtful. Willy's lack of an intellectual background makes one wonder where she got her ideas and feminist views. The book does not say.

Three years after Willy searches New York for her mother, Carrie watches the newly inaugurated president, George Washington, arrive at New York's waterfront in **Who Is Carrie**? She is immediately kidnapped but escapes from the ship by yelling for *Daniel Arabus and Mr. Fraunces, people she knows who happen to be passing. Captain Ivers, the kidnapper, declares that Fraunces, Carrie's employer, does not own Carrie and that he, Ivers, will get her back. When Ivers comes to the tavern with papers, Carrie hides. Fraunces, asked to be Washington's steward, takes Carrie with him to the president's home, where she works until she decides she will go to Philadelphia to be with *Willy Freeman. When she asks Dan, also Fraunces's employee, for help, he realizes that she is ill. As Dan accompanies her back to the tavern, Ivers recognizes her, but Dan says that she works for Washington. Ivers asks Washington, and he remembers her as the person hidden in the clock at one of his dinner parties. He commands her to stay bedridden, a disappointment for Ivers. Finally Fraunces admits to Carrie that Dan's father, Jack, brought her to the tavern with papers that he gave to Mr. Johnson, a lawyer, but that he does not know her origin. They reconstruct that when Willy's mother had come to New York, she had brought a baby about whom Ivers did not know. Carrie now knows that she is that baby, which makes her Willy's sister and, best, free. The novel displays some of the terrors blacks faced when masters tried to claim them even if they were free.

Two years later during 1787 in **Jump Ship to Freedom**, Daniel Arabus retrieves his father's money earned as a soldier that his master, Ivers, took from his mother. Captain Ivers accuses Daniel of stealing and takes him to the West Indies to sell him. But Daniel jumps ship after a terrible storm drowns his white friend and blows much of the cargo overboard. However, he has to leave the soldier's notes hidden on board. Soon the wounded ship returns to port, and, helped by the same Sam Fraunces who helped his aunt Willy (actually cousin Willy according to *War Comes to Willy Freeman),* Daniel tries to escape from Captain Ivers and Big Tom, a black who hates for other blacks to have white friends. Daniel retrieves the soldier's notes and remembers that his father, Jack, took Captain Ivers to court to establish that Captain Ivers had given him freedom when Jack fought in place of Ivers during the Revolution. In addition, his father had helped General Washington cross a river. When Daniel accompanies the *Quaker Fatherscreft to Philadelphia, he meets General Washington and takes a message concerning slavery to William Samuel Johnson. An encounter with Alexander *Hamilton reveals Hamilton to be nasty and prejudiced. Although Daniel knows the agreement to have slaves will unite the North and South, he also knows that he will have to return to Captain Ivers. Several years later, when the government finally supports the soldier's notes kept for him by Mr. Johnson, he buys his and his mother's freedom. Daniel's unusual experiences and relationships give insight about government policies during the Constitutional period.

Two novels disclose the difficulties of survival for settlers during the late eighteenth century. In **The Bloody Country**, after Ben Buck's father establishes a mill in the Wyoming Valley near Wilkes-Barre, the British and Indians unite to rampage the area, killing and scalping. On the day that the Indians scalp Ben's mother and brother-in-law, his sister Annie gives birth to Isaac. Ben's father decides to stay at his own mill in a fertile land rather than return to the stone-filled upper Connecticut area to work for others. However, the new government rules in 1782 that the Wyomming Valley belongs to the Pennamites rather than Connecticut and a man named Patterson comes to drive out the Connecticut farmers. He arrests men by claiming that he must honor prior Pennamite claims. He also says that slaves unregistered in Pennsylvania are freed. Since Mr. Buck had never registered Joe Mountain, almost a member of the Buck family, Joe is free. The excessive snow in 1784 causes spring floods, which destroy homes, livestock, and crops. Ben's father decides to rebuild his wrecked mill, but Patterson arrives to arrest him as soon as he finishes. Wanting to stay, Mr. Buck hides in mountain caves while Ben, his sister, and his nephew join 500 others returning to Connecticut. Having run away during the floods, Joe Mountain comes to tell Ben that the government has accused Patterson of illegally regaining the land. When Ben sees Joe in the woods, he realizes that a person must be able to choose before feeling human. Then he accepts his father's decision to stay. He takes Annie and little Isaac to Connecticut, settles them with an uncle, and returns to his father and the freedom of the mill in Wilkes-Barre. Ben's initial inability to understand that his father and Joe need freedom shows a realistic reaction for an adolescent having never been bound to another human.

The Winter Hero shows the attempt to survive by soldiers returning home from the Revolutionary War. Taxes began to increase, and people had to borrow money for necessities. Justin Conkey lives with his sister, Molly McCullough, and her husband, Peter, when Sheriff Porter comes to claim their oxen as payment for a debt owed Major Mattoon. Peter and Justin ask their neighbor, *Shays, for advice about the problem. He suggests that Justin work for Mattoon to pay off the debt and at the same time, spy on Mattoon's and his friends' reaction to the rebellion planned by the poor and led by Shays. The men in debt unite by physically barring court doors on the day they expect the circuit judges to hear cases. Without court, the judges could not give the wealthy permission to take property in place of money. These poor men had no legal recourse because they could not afford the high fees of the lawyers. Justin discovers that Mattoon has a list of the culprits, including Peter and Shays. When the men rebel, the government fires guns at them. Shays flees, but Peter is imprisoned and sentenced to hang. He stands with the noose around his neck before he is reprieved. Justin had wanted to be a hero during the rebellion, but the only time he does not run is when he tries to save Peter. For what he thinks is an inconsequential action, others call him a hero. After the fighting ends, Justin discovers his two friends suffocated in a potato hole by the newly fallen snow. He realizes that war is a series of inglorious events. A didactic afterword comments that federal government control of the states stops such rebellions and keeps state laws from being preferential. Thus strong state government representation becomes even more necessary. The historical setting and action of this novel show that the Revolutionary War did not solve all the colonies' problems. How men gained freedom from their own governments is as absorbing.

STYLE AND THEMES
    Since the Colliers profess to didacticism in their novels, they have successfully fulfilled their intent. The stories, however, could exhibit more literary merit if the characters were not so forced to take stands about difficult moral concerns.

COLUMBUS SAILS. *See* Hodges, C. Walter.

COMANCHE. The ancestors of the Comanches probably inhabited the Yellowstone River country in the seventeenth century. They moved south and are first reported in New Mexico in 1705. They early possessed numerous horses and developed the pattern of equestrian nomadism that became characteristic of Plains Indians in the eighteenth and nineteenth centuries. The Comanche social organization lacks integrating tribal ceremonies, government, lineage, clans, and military societies. They did not hunt buffalo and went as far south as Durango, Mexico, searching for booty and captives. Not until June 1875 did the Comanches cease their war against the U.S. government. See *The Bad Bell of San Salvadore* and *Wait for Me, Watch for Me, Eula Bee* by Patricia *Beatty, and *Rifles for Watie* by Harold *Keith.

CONFEDERATES. Persons who supported the Confederate States of America, the confederation of eleven states that seceded from the United States in 1860–61, and soldiers who fought for these states, gained this name. See *A Long Way to Whiskey Creek, Wait for Me, Watch for Me, Eula Bee, Blue Stars Watching,* and *Turn Homeward, Hannalee* by Patricia *Beatty; *The Tamarack Tree* by Patricia *Clapp; *Orphans in the Wind* by Erik *Haugaard; *Across Five Aprils* by Irene *Hunt; *Rifles for Watie* by Harold *Keith; and *The 290* by Scott *O'Dell.

THE CONFIDENCE MAN. See Garfield, Leon.

CONNAL ROSS. Fifteen, Scottish, protagonist of *A Pistol in Greenyards. See* Hunter, Mollie.

THE CONQUERED. See Mitchison, Naomi.

CONSTANCE HOPKINS. English protagonist transported to the colonies who matures from fifteen to twenty in *Constance. See* Clapp, Patricia.

CONSTANCE. See Clapp, Patricia.

CONSTANTINE I (d. 337). Known as the Great, he was crowned caesar by his father at *Eburacum, Britain, in 306, as one of six claimants to the throne of the *Roman Empire. After several battles, he became sole emperor in the West in 312 and probably became Christian at that time. He called the Council of Nicaea in 325 where the Nicene Creed was adopted. In 330, he renamed Byzantium as Constantinople (*Istanbul). *See* Sutcliff, Rosemary, *The Silver Branch*.

CONSTANTINOPLE. *See* *Istanbul.

CONTINENTAL DIVIDE. A stretch of high ground serves as a divide from which each side of the river systems of a continent flow in opposite directions. In the United States, the crests of the Rocky Mountains form the Continental or Great Divide. *See* Lasky, Kathryn, *Beyond the Divide*.

COPPERHEAD. This term was applied during the *American Civil War to those in the North who felt that conquering the Confederacy was impossible. They opposed the war policy of the president and of Congress and wanted to declare peace. The term was probably first used in 1861 by the *New York Tribune*. *See* Hunt, Irene, *Across Five Aprils*.

CÓRDOBA. A city in southern Spain, Córdoba became the capital of Moorish Spain in 756 and was not recaptured until 1236 by Ferdinand III of Castile. *See* Trease, Geoffrey, *The Red Towers of Granada*.

CORNWALLIS, CHARLES (1738–1805). A major general for the British in the *American Revolution, he defeated Horatio Gates at Camden and Nathanel Greene at Guilford Court House before he was besieged at Yorktown and forced to surrender on October 19, 1781. *See* Wibberley, Leonard, *Treegate's Raiders*.

CORONADO, FRANCIS VASQUEZ DE (c. 1510–1554). He left Spain to explore Mexico in 1535. In 1540, he commanded an expedition searching for the reportedly incredibly rich seven cities of *Cibola. After he found the Zuni pueblos, he began looking also for the supposedly wealthy Grand Quivara. His search ended in what is now Kansas at the *Wichita Indian village. See *A Stranger and Afraid* and *Walk the World's Rim* by Betty *Baker.

CORPUS CHRISTI DAY. This festival in the Western Christian church honors the Real Presence of Christ in the Eucharist on the Thursday after Trinity Sunday, also called Whitsunday, the first Sunday after Pentecost. *See* Picard, Barbara, *Ransom for a Knight*.

CORTÉS [CORTEZ], HERNANDO (1485–1547). A Spanish explorer, he sailed to the New World with Diego Velasquez and took an expedition to the mainland. He defeated and made an alliance with the Tlaxcalans and in 1519 entered the Aztec capital Tenochtitlán, now Mexico City, where he held *Montezuma hostage. He left on a short expedition and returned to find the Aztecs in revolt. At Montezuma's death in 1520, he led the Spaniards and allies out of the city. He captured Mexico City and later found lower California. See *Blood of the Brave* and *Walk the World's Rim* by Betty *Baker, and *The Feathered Serpent* and *The Amethyst Ring* by Scott *O'Dell.

COSSACK. The Turkic word *kazak* means "free man," or "adventurer" or "rebel." Fugitives from the central Asian Turkic states preferring a nomadic life in the steppes north of the Black Sea instead of serfdom in the Middle Ages first acquired this designation. Later the term was used in much the same way to designate peasants escaping from Poland and servitude. Eventually Cossacks began to protect borders of both Poland and Russia. They gained certain privileges by promising to give twenty years of military service in return. See *The Cossacks* by B. *Bartos-Höppner; *The Trumpeter of Krakow* by Eric *Kelly; and *Kevin O'Connor and the Light Brigade* by Leonard *Wibberley.

THE COSSACKS. See Bartos-Höppner, B.

THE COURAGE OF SARAH NOBLE. See Dalgliesh, Alice.

THE COW NECK REBELS. See Forman, James.

CRAZY HORSE (1842?–1877). As a Native American chief of the Oglala tribe of the *Sioux, he helped defeat General George Crook at Rosebud Creek on June 17, 1876, and was a leader in the Battle of Little Big Horn when *Custer was killed on June 25. He surrendered in 1877 and was killed while resisting imprisonment. *See* Forman, James, *The Life and Death of Yellow Bird*.

CRÉCY. This battle was fought on August 26, 1346, by an army under the leadership of *Edward III of England. Leading one of the divisions was *Edward, the Black Prince. The combination of dismounted men-at-arms with archers defeated the French and led to their further disarray at *Calais. See *Ride into Danger* by Henry *Treece and *Bowman of Crécy* by Ronald *Welch.

CREEP AND CHRISTOPHER. Young English protagonists in *A Chance Child*. *See* Paton Walsh, Jill.

CRIMEAN WAR. Fought in 1854–56 in the Crimean peninsula between Russia and the allies Great Britain, France, and Turkey, this war arose from a series of misunderstandings over conflicts of interest. Russia realized from its defeat the need to modernize, and the isolation of Austria brought about the eventual unification of Italy and Germany. See *A Pistol in Greenyards* by Mollie *Hunter and *Nicholas Carey* by Ronald *Welch.

THE CRIMSON OAK. *See* Almedingen, E. M.

CROMWELL, OLIVER (1599–1658). He became known as a Puritan and enemy of the established church. He and his Ironsides regiment helped to defeat *Charles I for the *Parliamentarians. He eventually led the British government after overcoming Scotland and Ireland, although he refused the title of king. See *Witch Dog, King's Knight's Pawn,* and *Campion Towers* by John and Patricia *Beatty; *Beyond the Weir Bridge* by Hester *Burton; and *Cromwell's Boy* and *A Messenger for Parliament* by Erik *Haugaard.

CROMWELL'S BOY. *See* Haugaard, Erik.

CROOKLEG. Protagonist from the British Isles in *The Dream-Time*. *See* Treece, Henry.

CROSSING TO SALAMIS. *See* Paton Walsh, Jill.

CROSSLEY-HOLLAND, KEVIN (1941–   ). British.

BIBLIOGRAPHY AND BACKGROUND

   The Fire-Brother. London: Heinemann, 1974; New York: Seabury Press, 1975. *Havelock the Dane*. New York: Dutton, 1965. *The Sea Stranger*. London: Heinemann, 1973; New York: Seabury Press, 1973.

   Crossley-Holland "fell in love with the *Anglo-*Saxon world" at Oxford because of the "moods and the music of Old English poetry." He says, "I like the earthy common-sensicality *[sic]* of the Anglo-Saxons, I like their grittiness and backs-to-the-wall heroism, their streak of nostalgia, their natural piety, their love of the sea." Since he feels that people should be aware of their background, he notes that "the Anglo-Saxons were the people who gave to us our legal system, our coinage and, more importantly, our language and the way our land looks. When they came to England the whole place was more or less deserted and afforested; by 1066, ninety per cent of the villages one sees in England today already existed.'' To recreate such times, he revises a text many times because ''every word and piece of punctuation and, indeed, silence counts.'' Three of Crossley-Holland's works can be considered historical fiction. Two take place in the seventh century and another around the tenth.

WORKS

In **The Sea Stranger**, one day in 655, Wulf searches for a crab near his private place overlooking the sea and sees a boat. A man, *Cedd, comes ashore and asks for King Aethelhere. Wulf tells him that Rendlesham, the king's castle, lies farther along the shore, but Cedd delays his journey to talk with Wulf. Cedd wants the king to give him land to build a church and to give him permission to spread news about Christ. Wulf becomes interested in this message of hope and is disappointed when Cedd leaves the next morning. Cedd, however, gives Wulf a spoon engraved with ''SAULUS'' and promises to return in the spring to explain the spoon's story and to bring its mate, but Wulf feels lonely without Cedd. During the winter, King Aethelhere dies in battle. Wulf and his brother, Oswald, go to the king's burial grounds to see the people gather with valuable items to bury in a ship in his honor. Wulf sees a match to his spoon, and a man explains that the second spoon is the ''PAULUS,'' which represents the man Saul who had a vision of God and changed his name to Paul. When Cedd returns, he tells him that the new king, Aethelwald, has given him Wulf's favorite piece of land for the church. When Cedd asks Wulf to join him in the monastery, Wulf agrees to be baptized and join Cedd at Ythancestir (Bradwellon-Sea, Essex). Wulf needs a 'father' to replace his dead one, and Cedd, with his message of love through Christ, reasonably replaces him.

A sequel to *The Sea Stranger* is **The Fire-Brother**, set after the church with its surrounding monastery becomes self-sufficient. A bad corn crop causes local people to think that they should be making sacrifices to the old god, Freya, rather than to the new one. When Wulf's family becomes hostile toward the new god, Oswald burns the monastery buildings and flees. Cedd tells Wulf that the most difficult but important thing for him to do as a boy of twelve is to find Oswald and ask him to return. Although Oswald has destroyed years of work, he needs to know that Christians practice love, not retaliation. Wulf searches for Oswald in the forest, tells him the news, and leaves knowing that Oswald believes him.

In **Havelock the Dane**, Crossley-Holland has recreated the historical fantasy of Havelock, almost killed by the man who stole his kingship, and Grim, the man who saved him by taking him to England. When Lord Godard commands Grim to kill the ten-year-old Havelock, a supernatural halo enveloping the sleeping Havelock reveals that he is the dead King Birkabeyn's son. Grim and his family sail with Havelock to Grimsley, where Havelock lives as a family member. At twenty-eight, Havelock leaves and finds work as the cook's porter in Godric's castle. Godric had imprisoned Goldborough, daughter of Aethelwold, and taken her crown. Havelock wins a long stone throw, and Godric decides to punish

Goldborough by making her marry a "strong" peasant. After Goldborough and Havelock marry, she is surprised by his compassion, and they soon begin to love each other. Goldborough does not realize until she too sees the light around a sleeping Havelock that her husband is actually a king. The two return to Denmark and with Havelock's father's friends gain a bloodless victory over the shocked Godard. Havelock and Goldborough live the rest of their lives ruling alternate years in Denmark and England. The story seems coincidental and implausible, more legend than history, but the underlying theme of honesty and helping others makes it worthwhile.

STYLE AND THEMES

Among his stylistic devices, Crossley-Holland uses rhetorical questions along with his imagery. Alliteration augments figurative phrases such as "the weird shadows of flickering flames danced on the walls." Crossley-Holland's novels help establish the importance of love as the best way to overcome the ills of existence. The love of Christ permeates human relationships and helps people accomplish more than they could alone.

CROW. A Siouan-speaking Plains Indian tribe, the Crow moved westward from the upper Missouri River in the eighteenth century. By 1740, they were established middlemen in the trading of horses, bows, shirts, and featherwork to village Indians in return for guns and metal goods, which they carried to the Shoshone in Idaho. Their lives revolved around buffalo and horses. The matrilineal descent allowed paternal relatives respect, but conversation between son-in-law and parent-in-law was taboo. Brothers and sisters avoided speech and bodily contact. The search for a supernatural guardian who adopted the Crow's "child" was basic to religious belief and practice. Visions were induced by tormenting the body, and mementos of the experience were gathered in "medicine" bundles, which were then associated with the sun dance, medicine arrows, and tobacco. Before one could be recognized as a chief, he had to take a weapon from an enemy, strike an enemy with a coupstick, take a horse tethered within an enemy camp, and lead a war party without loss of life. War exploits were announced on every religious and social occasion. *See* McGraw, Eloise, *Moccasin Trail.*

THE CROWN OF VIOLET. See *Web of Traitors* by Geoffrey *Trease.

CRUSADES. The term from the Spanish *cruzada* ("marked with the cross") generally refers to any war sanctioned by the papacy that is directed toward anyone declared to be an enemy of Christ. The nine crusades began in 1095 and continued until the mid-fifteenth century for the purpose of recovering the Holy Sepulchre at Jerusalem from the Muslims. See *The Road to Damietta* by Scott *O'Dell; *Lost John* by Barbara *Picard; *Bows against the Barons* by Geoffrey

*Trease; *Perilous Pilgrimage* by Henry *Treece; and *Knight Crusader* by Ronald *Welch.

CRYSTAL NIGHT. On November, 9, 1938, after a Polish Jewish boy assassinated a junior German embassy official in Paris, the *Nazi groups of the SA *(Sturmabteilung)*, the SS *(Schutzstaffel)*, the Hitler Youth, and the gestapo *(Geheime Staatspolizei)* plundered Jewish homes and shops throughout Germany. More than 30,000 Jews were arrested, with many sent to concentration camps. Over 600 synagogues were burned and desecrated. The general German populace neither participated nor sympathized with these Nazi acts. See *The Survivor* and *The Traitors* by James *Forman.

CUE FOR TREASON. See Trease, Geoffrey.

CULLODEN, BATTLE OF. On April 16, 1746, the hope of the house of *Stuart to regain the English throne in the person of *Charles Edward, the Young Pretender, was destroyed by the duke of *Cumberland. Nearly one thousand *Jacobite Highlanders were killed and as many taken prisoner; only fifty British lost their lives. See *At the Seven Stars, Who Comes to King's Mountain?* and *The Royal Dirk* by John and Patricia *Beatty; *Hadder MacColl* by Patricia *Calvert; *The Cow Neck Rebels* by James *Forman; and *Peter Treegate's Musket* by Leonard *Wibberley.

CUMBERLAND, DUKE OF (1721–1765). As William Augustus, he was the third son of *George II and Queen Caroline. He commanded the British forces that quelled the *Jacobite rebellion headed by Prince *Charles Edward at *Culloden in 1746. He suppressed the Jacobites so severely that he earned the name "the Butcher." See *The Royal Dirk* and *At the Seven Stars* by John and Patricia *Beatty, and *A Pistol in Greenyards* by Mollie *Hunter.

CUSTER, GEORGE (1839–1876). He served the U.S. Army through the *American Civil War, becoming a general at twenty-three. He was especially effective against Robert E. *Lee at Richmond. He earned more fame for leading his troops into battle against the *Sioux in the South Dakota Black Hills where he and all his command were killed in the Battle of Little Big Horn. *See* Forman, James, *The Life and Death of Yellow Bird.*

CUTHBERTUS (635?–687). As a monk, he became the prior at *Lindisfarne in 664 following the reform of the Celtic church to the Roman ways. After retiring to a cell on Inner Farne in 676, he had to become bishop of Hexham and of Lindisfarne but again retired to his cell in 687. His body was believed to work miracles and was transferred to *Durham Cathedral in approximately 999. *See* Westall, Robert, *The Wind Eye*.

CYMBELINE [CUNOBELINUS] (d. c. 42). He was king or chief of the *Catuvellauni tribe and achieved strong influence over the other tribes. *Suetonius described him as "Britannorum rex." *See* Treece, Henry, *War Dog*.

_D

DAHOMEY. This African tribe became slave traders in the eighteenth century by conquering smaller states on the slave coast. *See* Carter, Peter, *The Sentinels*.

DAG. Eight, orphaned Dane, protagonist of *The Untold Tale*. *See* Haugaard, Erik.

DAI. Eleven, American protagonist named Dailey in *Fiddlestrings*. *See* de Angeli, Marguerite.

DALGLIESH, ALICE (1893–1979). West Indian-American.

BIBLIOGRAPHY AND BACKGROUND
   Adam and the Golden Cock. Illustrated by Leonard Weisgard. New York: Scribner, 1959. *The Courage of Sarah Noble*. Ilustrated by Leonard Weisgard. New York: Scribner, 1954; London: Hamish Hamilton, 1970. *The Little Angel*. New York: Scribner, 1943.
   As an editor at Scribner's for twenty-six years, Alice Dalgliesh must be considered an important force in children's literature. *The Courage of Sarah Noble* was honored by the Newbery in 1955. In her three historical fiction novels written since 1940 for younger readers, Dalgliesh uses omniscient point of view.

WORKS
   In **The Courage of Sarah Noble**, Sarah accompanies her father from Connecticut to Massachusetts when she is eight years old in 1707. She helps her father while he builds a new house for the family. When children from a nearby Indian family start coming to watch Sarah read the Bible aloud in front of the new cabin, Sarah and her father make friends with them. Sarah's father leaves her with Tall John's family while he returns for his wife and his other children. Sarah learns their Indian customs and feels comfortable with them. But Sarah is still happy to see her own mother who does not believe that the Indians could be as good to her daughter as she is. This story does not distinguish among

Native American tribes. Also, Sarah's mother shows little regard for the Indian family as individuals deserving appreciation for protecting her daughter. Because of these stereotypes, the book no longer has merit.

Adam in **Adam and the Golden Cock** also helps an adult. He keeps sheep in Newtown, Connecticut, during 1781. The French soldiers under *Rochambeau's leadership approach the town while Adam is working, and he cannot resist leaving to see the soldiers. Although his father has told him not to speak to his friend Paul because Paul's father is a *Tory, Adam asks Paul to look after the sheep for him. As soon as Adam reaches the center of town, he realizes that he has betrayed the trust of the old shepherd, who had told him not to leave the sheep with anyone else, so he rushes back before the soldiers arrive. He finds soldiers camped where the sheep are grazing. Adam begins talking to Pierre, the only one who can speak English. Pierre tells Adam that even children might be spies so the army pays for all food. When Adam sees Paul picking strawberries, he fears he is a spy, but Pierre assures him that Paul is not. A year later, when the French return, Paul asks Adam to go with him to see Pierre. Adam tells the golden cock weather vane atop the church that he wants to be friends with Paul again. Although the frustrations of friends having to separate during war because of parental differences is realistic and the information about French troop behavior during the *American Revolution is instructional, Adam is more a stereotype than a believable character.

Maria Luiza, in **The Little Angel**, set in Brazil during 1819, as the only girl in a family of five, wants a sister. She prays to Santo Antonio and eventually her sister, Maria de Gloria, is born on the same day as the daughter of Brazil's king, Dom *Pedro. During the time between Maria de Gloria's birth and age six, Dom Pedro frees Brazil from Portugal's control. The story's action resumes with Maria Luiza at fifteen when her father makes arrangements for her marriage. She refuses his choice because the man is old, bald, and cruel to the cat. In fact, he scares the cat away, and Maria de Gloria gets lost trying to find it. A handsome young man kindly helps her return home. He meets Maria Luiza, and from their reactions, the reader assumes the two will marry. This episodic narrative exposes that wealthy young girls in early nineteenth-century Brazil were raised to sew, pray, and marry. Although Carnival events and the close relationship of the two girls with Father Sebastian are realistic, that the six-year-old Maria de Gloria would think of her rescuer as a potential mate for her sister lacks credibility. The mother's chastising attitude toward her slaves shows her to be as egotistical as her daughters.

STYLE AND THEMES

The most successful aspects of *The Little Angel* are the descriptions of flowers and scenery. None of these books has endured the test of time. Read in the present day, they are unconvincing and superficial, with no stylistic aspects worth noting.

DALRIADA. People from this group migrated in the sixth century from the Ulster kingdom of Dalriada in Antrim to Scotland. *See* Sutcliff, Rosemary, *The Mark of the Horse Lord.*

DAMARIS BOYD. Thirteen, American, protagonist of *By Crumbs, It's Mine!* *See* Beatty, Patricia.

THE DANCING BEAR. *See* Dickinson, Peter.

DANIEL ARABUS. Fourteen, Black American protagonist in *Jump Ship to Freedom* and minor character in *War Comes to Willy Freeman* and *Who Is Carrie? See* Collier, Christopher and James.

DANIEL BAR JAMIN. Eighteen, Galilean protagonist in *The Bronze Bow.* *See* Speare, Elizabeth George.

DANIEL BARATZ. Sixteen, Polish Jew who reaches Palestine in *My Enemy, My Brother. See* Forman, James.

DANIEL CREGG. Seventeen, British, protagonist in *The Black Lamp. See* Carter, Peter.

DARITAI. Siberian young adult protagonist in *Save the Khan. See* Bartos-Höppner, B.

THE DARK CANOE. *See* O'Dell, Scott.

THE DAUGHTER OF SAN SATURNINO. See *Carlota* by Scott *O'Dell.

DAVID. Fourteen, Jewish protagonist in *The Rider and His Horse. See* Haugaard, Erik.

DAVID. Twelve, Danish, protagonist of *North to Freedom. See* Holm, Anne.

DAVID HOPKINS. Sixteen, American protagonist in Russia in *White Nights of St. Petersburg. See* Trease, Geoffrey.

DAVID MARLAIS. Fifteen, English protagonist in *Ride to Danger. See* Treece, Henry.

DAVID ULLMAN. Dutch Jew who matures from sixteen to twenty in *The Survivor. See* Forman, James.

DAWN WIND. See Sutcliff, Rosemary.

DEADMEN'S CAVE. See Wibberley, Leonard.

DE ANGELI, MARGUERITE (1889–   ). American.

BIBLIOGRAPHY AND BACKGROUND

Black Fox of Lorne. New York: Doubleday, 1956; Kingswood, Surrey: World's Work, 1959. *The Door in the Wall.* New York: Doubleday, 1949; Kingswood, Surrey: World's Work, 1959. *Fiddlestrings.* New York: Doubleday, 1974. *The Lion in the Box.* New York: Doubleday, 1975. *Skippack School.* New York: Doubleday, 1939. *Thee, Hannah!* New York: Doubleday, 1940. *Whistle for the Crossing.* New York: Doubleday, 1977.

Among the awards garnered by Marguerite de Angeli are the Newbery Medal in 1950 for *The Door in the Wall* and a Newbery honor for *Black Fox of Lorne* in 1957. She received the Regina Medal in 1981. De Angeli uses either omniscient or limited omniscient point of view in telling the stories of her male and female protagonists. She writes comfortably about several different time periods.

WORKS

Black Fox of Lorne takes place in 950. In it, Harald Redbeard warns his twin sons, Brus and Jan, that if anything should happen to one of them, the other should hide and watch, waiting for the right moment to help. When they are thirteen, they and their father shipwreck on the Scottish coast. The local chief, Gavin the Black Fox, kills Harald's men at a betrothal feast and captures Jan. Then someone kills Harald in his hiding place. Brus watches Jan from the woods as he marches in custody to Gavin's castle and trades places with him. Separately they see that Gavin wears Harald's brooch. With this certain knowledge that Gavin killed their father, each vows to avenge his death. Jan vows, however, in front of a shepherd and his wife who have become Christians and believe that the way of peace is better. After hearing their stories, Jan wonders why Christ's brothers did not avenge his death, but as he hears more about him, he begins to understand. Jan becomes surprised at his more positive attitude when he eventually begins to view his tiny *Thor's hammer as a cross. When the boys discover that Gavin plans to betray King Malcolm of Scotland as well as King Ethelred of England in order to gain more land, one of Gavin's servants rushes with Jan to warn Malcolm at Edin's Boro. Inside Edin's Boro, Jan discovers his mother, safe from one of the other two ships thought lost during the storm on the journey from Denmark. He finds that the Christian queen has influenced her too, and when he later tells his brother, Brus also becomes more receptive to Christianity. Thus the boys, who grew up learning the Norse ways of poetry, law, draughts (checkers), chess, and animal care, begin to learn the ways of Christianity in their new land. For the adult male Vikings to accept the concept of Christ and peace must have been quite difficult, but the young protagonists and their mother probably would have had less problem accepting the idea after all their troubles. The stories about Christianity, however, are not integrated with the plot's action as well as they could be. The intriguing idea of twins shifting places with each other is more successfully entwined. In fact, a picture of Thor's hammer inserted into the text signifies the shift in viewpoint from one son to the other. De Angeli gives them different talents, and sometimes one of them cannot fulfill a request for something that the other can do very well.

The Door in the Wall shows that in 1325, during the reign of *Edward III, Christianity is the only acceptable religion in England. Robin, ten, ill and unable to walk, finds protection at a monastery. Expecting Robin to become Sir Peter's page, his father left for war against the Scots while his mother went to serve the ailing queen as lady-in-waiting. But Robin's sudden illness keeps him from traveling, and his unpleasant attitude alienates the woman delivering his food. Fortunately, Brother Luke rescues him and takes him to St. Mark's hospice. During Robin's long, boring days of recovery, Brother Luke teaches him how to carve, read, write, play music, and swim to strengthen his arms. When Sir Peter finds Robin and learns of his disability, he asks Brother Luke to bring him to his home. On the journey, they escape robbery by climbing out an inn window when Robin overhears thieves planning. After Robin and Brother Luke reach the castle, the Welsh attack. Robin saves Sir Peter and his household by swimming across the river in the fog to get help. He tells John-go-in-the-Wynd, the minstrel, to inform Hugh *Fitzhugh, Sir Peter's ally. Fitzhugh's aid helps defeat the Welsh, but Robin gets credit for contacting him. When Robin's parents finally appear after Christmas, King Edward knights Robin for his bravery. Throughout the story, Brother Luke keeps encouraging Robin. He tells Robin that all walls have doors and that each person has to find his own door in each wall. This strong theme of learning how to use life's advantages rather than being overcome by life's adversities permeates the novel.

Although well written, none of de Angeli's other novels has the depth of theme exhibited in the first two. Of three novels set in Pennsylvania, **Skippack School** takes place around 1700. Eli comes to America with his family from Germany trying to escape religious persecution as a Mennonite (*Amish). He becomes a student of Master Christopher at Skippack School. Eli prefers wood carving to school, but to his surprise, Master Christopher never uses a rod to punish him for either forgetting lessons or breaking a window with a ball. His parents, however, make him pay for the window by selling the bench he had recently carved for his mother. When left alone while his mother helps a sick neighbor, Eli cooks, milks, and looks after his baby brother. Master Christopher asks Eli to go with him to Germantown, another surprise. Attempting to show his appreciation for the trip, when they return, Eli carves and paints a book cover for his written account about the interesting printer's and bookbinder's shops. Eli grows with every experience, which de Angeli signifies by a maxim with which she begins each chapter. Finally Eli can read the Bible, "a lamp unto my feet." When Master Christopher gives Eli a painting, he feels proud of his accomplishments.

Both of the remaining Pennsylvania stories occur in the mid-nineteenth century. **Thee Hannah!** shows Hannah's frustration as a *Quaker in 1850, not being permitted to wear pretty dresses as her friend, Cecily, does. Hannah must wear an ugly old bonnet. In secret, Hannah wears Cecily's brightly colored sash, but she dirties it and has to buy her a new one with her meager allowance. "Old Spotty" (the devil) continues to plague Hannah as she does one wrong thing after another. But when a runaway slave tells Hannah that her bonnet revealed her as an *abolitionist prepared to help the slave escape North through the *Underground Railway, Hannah realizes that the Quaker bonnet is a symbol, and she becomes proud of it. Each chapter begins with a rhyme about the people whom Hannah sees throughout the year: the town crier; the mussel, shad, pepperpot, and peach sellers; the whitewash man; and the umbrella mender.

In **Whistle for the Crossing**, Eddie's father takes a job managing the new Main Line railway between Pittsburgh and Philadelphia. Eddie rides on the first run of the line in 1852. On the first trip lasting three days, the passengers have to stop for lunch and to spend the night. They can see Indians who still inhabit some of the area. Eddie sees a little girl who first thinks her father has sold her when he pays the conductor for her trip to visit family. When Eddie settles in Pittsburgh, his new home, people at his school know that his father runs the railway, which gains him immediate popularity.

In **Fiddlestrings**, Dai(ley), eleven, and his family move to Atlantic City, where his father begins work as the entertainment manager of the new Steel Pier in 1898. His father hires John Philip Sousa. He also arranges for Dai to play his violin with Victor Herbert's orchestra one night. However, Dai, instead of practicing violin, prefers to sail toy boats he has made and to play with his dog. A fight causes Dai to have to pay for a broken violin bridge. He also hurts his hand and loses his position as concertmeister for the first performance of the student orchestra in his new music school. The episodic plot leads Dai to realize that he must take responsibility for his actions in order to be accepted by others.

At seven, Lili wants a doll for the Christmas of 1901 in **The Lion in the Box** but knows that her widowed mother cannot afford it. The family lives in New York, and her mother supports her four daughters and a son by cleaning Madison Avenue offices at night. For Christmas, the children make paper decorations for a tree given to them. On Christmas Eve, however, a man delivers a box and says it has a lion inside. The next day, they open the box and find wonderful gifts for everyone sent by a woman whom their mother had met. Lili gets her wish, a beautiful Chinese doll. The family's fellowship would have kept them content even without the box, but the gifts make the day special.

STYLE AND THEMES

De Angeli's style is always appropriate. In *The Door in the Wall,* she uses unobtrusive syntax shifts to indicate time period. As an example, Brother Luke tells Robin, "Fear not for the manner of our going to St. Mark's." In the same book, she exhibits her concise structure and vivid imagery with "hunger sauced [the cold pasty] better than the finest cook could have done." In the other books, dialogue and dialect reflect place and time. The books set in America, appropriate for younger readers, tend to be episodic. Their lack of strong, rising action makes them less satisfying although the writing remains consistent.

DEAR FRED. *See* Peyton, K. M.

DEBORAH SAMPSON. American who matures from ten to twenty, protagonist of *I'm Deborah Sampson*. *See* Clapp, Patricia.

DELAWARE. These Algonquian-speaking Indians occupied an area along the Atlantic coast from Cape Henlopen, Delaware, to western Long Island in New York, probably arriving around 1000. They called themselves the *Leni Lenape* or *Lenape,* "the people." They were friendly with William Penn, but as whites encroached on their lands and treated them "as women," they moved farther west. After mistreatment, they decided to strike back. They defeated the English general Edward Braddock in the *French and Indian War. After supporting the Americans in the *American Revolution, they shifted to British allegiance because of the invasion of their Ohio hunting grounds. See *Valley of the Shadow* by Janet *Hickman and *Red Pawns* by Leonard *Wibberley.

DELK ROGERS. Sixteen, American protagonist in *Tomahawk Border*. *See* Steele, William O.

DEMEAS. Young Greek male protagonist in *The Walls of Athens*. *See* Paton Walsh, Jill.

DEPRESSION. The general term *depression* refers to a major downswing in the business cycle of an economy. Specifically, after the stock market crash in October 1929, the worst depression in industrialized nations during the first half of the twentieth century occurred. See *Shadrach's Crossing* by *Avi; *The Murderer* by Felice *Holman; *No Promises in the Wind* by Irene *Hunt; *Far from Home* by Ouida *Sebestyen; and *Song of the Trees, Let the Circle Be Unbroken,* and *Roll of Thunder, Hear My Cry* by Mildred *Taylor.

DERRY LARKINS. Thirteen, English protagonist in *The Overland Launch*. *See* Hodges, C. Walter.

DE TREVIÑO, ELIZABETH (1904–   ). American.
BIBLIOGRAPHY AND BACKGROUND
   Casilda of the Rising Moon: A Tale of Magic and of Faith, of Knights and a Saint in Medieval Spain. New York: Farrar, Straus & Giroux, 1967; London:

Gollancz, 1968. *I, Juan de Pareja*. New York: Farrar, Straus & Giroux, 1965; London: Gollancz, 1966. *Nacar, The White Deer*. Illustrated by Enrico Arno. New York: Farrar, Straus & Giroux, 1963; Kingswood, Surrey: World's Work, 1964. *Turi's Poppa*. New York: Farrar, Straus & Giroux, 1968; as *Turi's Papa*. London: Gollancz, 1969.

Elizabeth de Treviño notes that the love of history and "the significance of certain specific events or personages in the past inspired me to devise fiction around these events, or personages." *I, Juan de Pareja* won the Newbery for de Treviño in 1966, and *Turi's Poppa* received the *Boston Globe–Horn Book* award in 1968. For each of her novels, she generally researches nearly a year. She says, "For *I, Juan de Pareja* I went to Spain and visited every painting of Velasquez, and of Juan de Pareja, and read in Spanish." After such thorough preparation, one thoughtful revision usually completes the work. In all the books, regardless of setting, de Treviño creates humane protagonists with warmth, showing both a love of and a faith in the goodness of others.

WORKS

De Treviño's last novel chronologically, **Turi's Poppa**, occurs after World War II. When eight-year-old Turi's mother dies in Budapest, his father earns so little money as a violin maker that they struggle to exist. A letter from the Violin Institute in Cremona, Italy, where his father was once a student, arrives asking him to be the first non-Italian director. No Italian qualified for the post survived the war. He accepts. They walk for weeks toward Cremona, having to cross borders secretly since they lack the required identification papers. They work odd jobs and often stop to pray in churches along the way. When they finally arrive in Cremona, without papers, they have to prove their identity. Turi's Poppa authenticates himself as Istvan Hubay by making a violin that pleases a violinist who has come to the institute to play its Stradivari. Their new life begins, and Poppa promises to make Turi his own three-quarter violin. Although not actually war refugees, Turi and his father could not have survived in Budapest. Turi's faith in his father's talent and wit keeps them walking toward their goal.

Casilda of the Rising Moon, set in 1046, relates the virtues of Casilda, a Moorish princess who converts to Christianity and becomes a revered saint. Her psychic ability to look into the future predicts that her brother, Prince Ahmed, will become a Moslem holy man, that her sister, Princess Zoraida, will marry a Christian prince, and that her father will soon die of his afflictions. The story contrasts the three strands of faith—Christianity, Judaism, and Islam—in medieval Spain. Casilda's father, Alamun, Moorish king of *Toledo, has pledged undying friendship to the Christian king of Castile, Fernando, because Fernando asked for his friendship in battle instead of killing him. Then Ben Haddaj, Ahmed's friend, comes to visit and falls in love with Casilda, though Zoraida pursues him. Intrigued by the faith of his Judaic ancestors, Ben Haddaj slowly begins to reject Islam. Casilda, who secretly feeds the prisoners in the dungeon of her father's castle, hears about the selflessness of Jesus and realizes that she must follow him as a Christian and serve others rather than marry. She goes to Castile to release Christian prisoners while Ben Haddaj goes to sea, where he dies in a storm. The inclusion of miraculous occurrences such as the bread turning to roses when Casilda's father discovers her inside the prison and her ability to untie the Cid's bonds with fire from her fingertips makes the story become historical fantasy. But the view of Spain and its three religions coexisting in the eleventh century, as well as the fine writing, creates an absorbing story.

Nacar the White Deer is another slightly supernatural story, historical fantasy. In 1630, Nacar, a white deer with pink eyes and hooves like pearl, arrives in Acapulco on his way to becoming a gift for the king of Spain. The king's Mexican viceroy realizes that the journey has weakened the deer, and it needs care. Someone suggests that a young boy who herds animals and knows about herbs could best rejuvenate Nacar. The child, Lalo, mute since enemies burned his mother, comes to Nacar and nurses him back to health before taking him to winter in the mountains. When a snake bites Nacar and an Indian boy shoots him, Lalo's knowledge of healing herbs and plants saves the deer. Lalo keeps Nacar safe until the voyage, accompanies him to Spain, and meets the king. Not until he hears the king declare that everyone can join him for a hunt with a reward going to the one who kills Nacar does Lalo's voice return. He cries out against the king's cruelty. The king recognizes the miracle and instead gives Lalo an inheritance. The book vacillates between fantasy and realism when Lalo credits various emotions to the deer based on the deer's actions.

A superb novel by any standard is **I, Juan de Pareja**, the story of Diego *Velasquez's slave. In her foreword, de Treviño notes that Arabs, Hebrews, and even Greeks, with their democratic ideals, had slaves, and the white Spanish slaves of which Juan's father was one were part of this heinous tradition. Don Diego Rodríguez de Silva y Velasquez inherits Juan de Pareja in the seventeenth century from a Seville relative who taught Juan to write. Using flashback, Juan tells his story as the son of a white man and a black woman and his sadness at leaving Seville but also his relief at escaping the *plague brought by foreign ships. In Madrid, he mixes paints and learns Velasquez's art by watching his every move. Juan sees that Velasquez "paint[s], in every case, a soul impris-oned" regardless of the way the person looks. He hears Velasquez say, "Art should be Truth; and Truth unadorned, unsentimentalized, is Beauty." Velasquez asserts that light is of the utmost importance, more than either the paint or the canvas. Since Spanish law forbids slaves to practice the arts, Juan furtively succumbs to his longings and secretly practices painting during his free moments. He even sells the only remaining memento of his mother, an earring, to pay for canvas and brushes. Juan continues to serve both Velasquez and God. When Juan attends church, he feels "like a person who comes home where love awaits him." He speaks of one experience: "I knelt a long time, for I had much to offer up to God, and I placed before him countless thoughts, so that he might winnow them like a thresher, leaving me the wheat and blowing the chaff with the breath of his Mercy.'' Juan watches Velasquez entertain Peter Paul Rubens, the Flemish painter, during a court visit in 1628 and becomes aware that unlike Spanish painters, Rubens uses nude models. Juan sees Velasquez design the area in which the Infanta Maria Teresa marries King Louis XIV of France by proxy. Juan also goes with Velasquez to Italy in 1649 to collect art work for the king and to paint portraits of the pope and Italian nobles. Juan admires Velasquez's apprentice, Bartolomé Murillo, who paints saints and angels because he sees Christ in every human. Not until the age of forty does Juan reveal to Velasquez (and the king simultaneously) his artistic accomplishments. To avoid any repercussions, Velasquez immediately frees him. De Treviño notes in the afterword that although she cannot verify any details of a relationship between Velasquez and Juan, she knows that Velasquez had a black slave whom he freed. Her clues of character come from Velasquez's one painting of Juan and his one self-portrait found in *Las Meninas* (The Ladies-in-Waiting). Dispelling the stereotypical hot-tempered Spaniard, de Treviño visualizes Velasquez as ''coolly dispassionate.'' This riveting story reveals the human need for friendship and love. Velasquez soothes *Philip IV by refusing to paint lies; Juan soothes Velasquez by accommodating his painting needs; and God soothes Juan.

STYLE AND THEMES

Elizabeth de Treviño is a superb stylist, choosing appropriate sentence structure and diction for each novel. Parallelism in *Casilda of the Rising Moon* illustrates her mastery. She compares Alamun to his beloved Berber wife, mother of Casilda—''golden as he was swarthy, gentle as he was strong, compassionate as he was merciless, a singing nightingale, as he was a predatory hawk.'' Alliteration complements consonance in a phrase describing the moon as a ''round shining silver disc.'' In *I, Juan de Pareja,* de Treviño uses short sentences for emphasis in the midst of long, complex clauses. Figurative language broadens concept in such phrases as ''hands, fluttering over the silks like two dark birds''; light in Italy glowing ''like firelight''; king's ''hair like yellow embroidery silk''; and dancers ''like watching the courtship of two beautiful birds or wild forest creatures.'' In the clause, ''space is the medicine for eyes that have always to look at things too closely,'' one can see metaphor but also diction that sets the novel. Alliteration brings attention to one of the explicit themes: ''Time is a great traitor who teaches us to accept loss.'' Thus de Treviño balances form and concept to create insightful, compassionate stories communicating humanity as well as history.

DEVEREUX, ROBERT (1566–1601). As the earl of Essex, he became a favorite of *Elizabeth I of England. When he offended her, he was deprived of his offices. Others convinced him to form a plot to remove the queen's counselors, but he failed. He was prosecuted for treason and executed. See *Master Rosalind* and *The Queen's Wizard* by John and Patricia *Beatty and *I Will Adventure* by Elizabeth Gray *Vining.

THE DEVIL IN VIENNA. See Orgel, Doris.

DEVIL-IN-THE-FOG. See Garfield, Leon.

THE DEVIL ON THE ROAD. See Westall, Robert.

DICK ARLINGTON. Fourteen, English protagonist in *The Silken Secret. See* Trease, Geoffrey.

DICK STOCKTON. Fourteen, English protagonist who goes to Rhodes and Constantinople (*Istanbul) in *The Seas of Morning. See* Trease, Geoffrey.

DICKINSON, PETER (1927–   ). British.

BIBLIOGRAPHY AND BACKGROUND

The Dancing Bear. Illustrated by David Smee. London: Gollancz, 1972; Boston: Little, Brown, 1973. *Tulku*. London: Gollancz, 1979; New York: Dutton, 1979.

Peter Dickinson's writing in other genres has won *The Guardian* Award and the Carnegie Medal. *Tulku* won a Whitbread Award in 1979 and a second Carnegie Medal in 1980. Both of Dickinson's historical fiction novels were precipitated by his children's desires expressed on long car journeys for ''a new story with a battle in it.'' He believes that battles fare better in historical settings; thus his memories of *Justinian in Byzantium (*Istanbul) and the *Boxer Rebellion in China established the locations. The story of Tulku, however, lost its battle in revision after further research. Dickinson prefers to write the book first and then to ''do the research to see what I've got wrong.'' He believes that writing is a ''serious procedure'' and that imagination is the ''prime excitement, both for writer and reader, and if you're on form you will imagine true. Even when you know the truth, you still have to imagine to make it live.''

WORKS

The Dancing Bear begins in 558 with the Kutrigur Hun invasion of the Emperor Justinian's Byzantium. On the eve of the invasion, the Celsus household enjoys one of its favorite forms of entertainment, a religious debate. The *Monophysites, who believe that Jesus had one nature, argue with the *Orthodox, who believe that Jesus had two natures, as the Son and the Father. The next day, the Huns ransack the dwelling. Silvester, a slave born on the same day as Lady Ariadne (Addie), the daughter, tries to protect her as well as the dancing bear, Bubba, also with the same birth date. However, the Huns find Addie and take her hostage. Silvester, the household priest, Holy John, and bear escape outside the city walls. They travel north to find Addie, as well as the Huns, whom Holy John plans to convert. Holy John's religious discussions propel the action and justify everything as God's choice. Although he seems to enter epileptic trances, he shows much knowledge and common sense during their journey. Along the way, they find a dying Hun, Urrguk. The blue beads dangling from his turban show that he belongs in the Khan's household. Silvester knows healing arts so he revives Urrguk and carries him north. Holy John talks to everyone he meets and finds that Silvester has been placed on the wanted lists by Addie's uncle, which means that whoever finds him will gain a reward. Since Silvester and Bubba have to walk hidden from the road, their journey becomes more difficult. Various ruses allow them to reach the Hun camp, where they are initially welcomed. Bubba, however, smells the Hun who struck him in Byzantium and kills him. The ensuing argument about honor reveals that Addie is in the camp. The Huns consider the bear to be both totemic and a lucky charm; thus they decide that the Hun who harmed Bubba deserved to die. The Khan takes Silvester, Holy John, and Addie as his wards. When a warring tribe ambushes the camp, Addie and Silvester escape with Bubba. They go to live on an outpost with a Roman who earlier had wanted Silvester to stay with him instead of search for Addie. They both stay after the Roman dies because Silvester cannot return to Byzantium and because Addie does not want to become a slave to the man to whom she has been betrothed. No one in Byzantium will understand what either has endured. The theme that social status does not make a humane person as well as the appealing characters make this an enticing story.

Tulku begins in a Chinese Christian settlement lovingly established by thirteen-year-old Theodore Tewker's father. When Mr. Tewker sends a messenger to tell Theo to flee, he does, although he feels like a traitor. But his flight saves him as the camp's only survivor in the Boxers' purge of foreigners. He encounters Mrs. Jones who visits the charred settlement and returns to verify his father's death. Mrs. Jones suggests that Theo travel with her and Lung, her guide. Theo expresses distrust of her blasphemous language which she offers to curtail in return for his translating abilities. Mrs. Jones reveals that, as a plant collector, she has traveled the world drawing and collecting exotic plants. Since the Boxers have closed all other ways out of China, they head toward Tibet, one of the places to which Mrs. Jones has not yet traveled. At their last stop in China, they meet a man who also draws pictures of plants. Mrs. Jones recognizes that he can capture the inward nature of the plant, while she can draw only the outward appearance. Charmed with her, he gives her a map of Tibet which he has drawn. During the journey, Mrs. Jones relates her story that the family of a very wealthy man, also a collector of exotic plants, paid her to leave England because her love affair with him was unacceptable. Mrs. Jones, Lung, and Theo finally reach Tibet after being twice ambushed by disloyal porters. In Tibet, a lama takes them to Dong Pe monastery, first thinking that Theo is the reincarnation of one of the former religious leaders, Tulku. He decides instead that Theo is the Guide for which he has been looking and that Tulku is Lung's unborn child, which Mrs. Jones carries. The lama's teachings about reincarnation and the spirit answer many of Mrs. Jones's questions; she decides to remain in Tibet to bear Tulku, though the birth of her first child almost killed her. Lung returns to China, and Theo goes to England, taking the unique Tibetan lily to Mrs. Jones's former lover and the father of her first child. Although the novel is set during 1900, the sequences in Tibet are timeless. Theo spiritually matures in this moving story from being very pious and moralistic to a person who nonjudgmentally accepts the beauty of happiness and the acts that create happiness.

STYLE AND THEMES

Dickinson uses literary devices with authority. Imagery as well as alliteration and consonance appear in phrases like "sweep of grassland . . . silvering toward brown . . . to the lion colored hills" and "heart of heat" in *The Dancing Bear*. He metaphorically presents a wasted life as "wine, long before it was ready to drink, had been poured out of the bottle, wasted, and the bottle tossed into a river to float with the current." Alliteration emphasizes personification in *Tulku* with "uncaring clouds" and solid description in the simile "sharp as a green lemon." The lurking dark of the Chinese forests contrasts with the soaring beauty of the Tibetan mountains. Another device successfully employed in the beginning of *The Dancing Bear* is the cliffhanger in such clauses as, "But Silvester's world ended in another fashion." Dickinson also uses dreams to foreshadow several segments. Throughout both novels, the unwritten customs and mythological beliefs of the people propel their actions, and one of the important realizations is that with enough money, one can buy material things but neither happiness nor inner peace.

DICKON. Sixteen, English protagonist in *Bows against the Barons*. *See* Trease, Geoffrey.

THE DOLPHIN CROSSING. See Paton Walsh, Jill.

DO NOT ANNOY THE INDIANS. See Baker, Betty.

A DONKEY FOR THE KING. See Beatty, John and Patricia.

THE DOOR IN THE WALL. See de Angeli, Marguerite.

DORCAS FOX. Thirteen, American, protagonist of *Red Rock over the River*. *See* Beatty, Patricia.

THE DRAGONFLY YEARS. See *Hold on to Love* by Mollie *Hunter.

DRAGONWINGS. See Yep, Lawrence.

DRAGOON. A dragoon was originally a mounted soldier trained to fight on foot only. The name comes from the soldier's musket, called a "dragon." Eventually the dragoon of the eighteenth and nineteenth centuries learned to improve his horsemanship to the calvary standard. *See* Welch, Ronald, *Captain of Dragoons*.

THE DRAWBRIDGE GATE. See *The Sign of the Green Falcon* by Cynthia *Harnett.

THE DREAM-TIME. *See* Treece, Henry.

DREM. Young Bronze Age protagonist of the British Isles in *Warrior Scarlet*. *See* Sutcliff, Rosemary.

DROGHEDA. A fortified town in Ireland, the *Royalist troops in the *English Civil War were billeted there when *Cromwell on September 10–11, 1649, massacred them. *See* Beatty, John and Patricia, *King's Knight's Pawn*.

DRUCUS POLLIO. Roman adult living in Britain, protagonist of *The Centurion*. *See* Treece, Henry.

DRUID. As a religious leader in druidism for the Celts of ancient Gaul and the British Isles, the druids left no written information about their beliefs or practices. The word in Old Irish seems to mean ''he who knows.'' See *The Stronghold* by Mollie *Hunter; *Warrior Scarlet* and *Outcast* by Rosemary *Sutcliff; and *Perilous Pilgrimage* by Henry *Treece.

THE DRUMMER BOY. *See* Garfield, Leon.

THE DUNDERHEAD WAR. *See* Baker, Betty.

DUNKIRK [DUNKERQUE]. The British Army evacuated from this town on the French coast before the Germans arrived in World War II. Every small craft possible was recruited, and between May 26 and June 3, 1940, 198,000 British troops and 140,000 Allied troops were rescued. See *In Spite of All Terror* by Hester *Burton and *The Dolphin Crossing* by Jill *Paton Walsh.

DURHAM CATHEDRAL. This church in Durham, England, houses the remains of St. *Cuthbertus and the Venerable Bede, an *Anglo *Saxon scholar, historian, and theologian. It was begun in 1093 in the *Norman style, characterized by massive construction with round arches over recessed doors and carvings, and has had additions and renovations since that time. *See* Westall, Robert, *The Wind Eye*.

THE DUTCH ARE COMING. *See* Trease, Geoffrey.

_E_

THE EAGLE OF THE NINTH. *See* Sutcliff, Rosemary.

EARTHQUAKE OF SAN FRANCISCO. On April 18, 1906, a violent earthquake hit this California city. It and a fire following demolished most of the central district. Hundreds were killed or injured, while thousands of homeless residents camped on the dunes west of the city. *See* Yep, Lawrence, *Dragonwings*.

EBURACUM. Latin name for *York, England.

EDDIE MOORE. Young American protagonist in *Whistle for the Crossing*. *See* de Angeli, Marguerite.

THE EDGE OF THE CLOUD. *See* Peyton, K. M.

EDMONDS, WALTER D. (1903–   ). American.

BIBLIOGRAPHY AND BACKGROUND
   Bert Breen's Barn. Boston: Little, Brown, 1975. *The Matchlock Gun*. Illustrated by Paul Lantz. New York: Dodd, Mead, 1941. *They Had a Horse*. Illustrated by Douglas Gorsline. New York: Dodd, Mead, 1962. *Wilderness Clearing*. Illustrated by John de Martelly. New York: Dodd, Mead, 1945.
   Edmonds has won awards over a span of years beginning with the Newbery Medal in 1942 for *The Matchlock Gun* and continuing through the National Book Award and the Christopher Medal in 1976 for *Bert Breen's Barn*. He notes, "I am a story teller," but "I found from the reviews [of my first book] that it was a historical novel." He took no notes in preparation for writing until his third novel when he had become conscious of being a "historical novelist," but that novel was also the last one for which he kept notes. For authenticity in the rest of his books, he has either corresponded with persons who could inform him or

read background information and other fiction. He says, ''the main force behind my writing is to tell a story in a reasonably convincing way.''

WORKS

Edmonds tells a convincing story in **They Had a Horse**. In 1714, seventeen-year-old Jacob Borst wants a horse to help him farm his wheat and run a mill so his wife, Elizabeth, will not have to travel twenty miles to buy flour for them. When Elizabeth returns from a trip for flour, she tells Jacob about a horse she saw for sale. Jacob decides to ask his Palatine Settlement neighbors to share in buying the horse for each to use one day a week. Jacob has to give the man offering the most money his chair with a back, the only one in the area, in return for the investment. Although Elizabeth regrets losing the chair, she understands Jacob's desire for the horse and agrees. When the men go to buy the horse, the seller has already sold it, but he offers them an old mare for one-fourth the price. Unlike the other men, Jacob sees that the mare is in foal, and he accepts the offer. The mare nearly dies of exhaustion on the arduous journey home but soon delivers a healthy colt. Jacob, elated at his wise purchase, hears about another birth when Elizabeth tells him they are expecting their first child. Jacob's desire for a son underscores his need for help with his farming and milling, and his ability to lead the older men in his community lends a positive tone to the story.

Two stories illustrate the American settlers' problems with Indians. In **The Matchlock Gun**, young Edward Van Alstyne has to help his mother defend their home from Indians in 1757. His father has to help other men defend the area, leaving his family at home alone. After his departure, Edward's mother takes the children for a walk up a nearby hill. She sees smoke and realizes that Indians have broken through the local defense. Back inside their house, she shows ten-year-old Edward how to shoot the huge Spanish matchlock gun, twice as long as he is tall. She goes outside to watch for the Indians, and when they arrive, she yells an agreed-upon signal for Edward to fire. He shoots the gun from the window and kills two men who have already thrown their tomahawks at his mother. While the house burns, the family can rescue only the gun. When Edward's father returns, he sees that Edward has killed more enemies than all the men together.

In 1777, Maggie Gordon and her father, in **Wilderness Clearing**, reluctantly prepare to leave their farm in Jerseyfield (later Ohio) because the Indians are collecting white scalps to receive British awards of money, a musket, and a copper kettle. While Maggie and Mr. Gordon harvest the wheat, he has a stroke, and Dick Mount, a sixteen-year-old neighbor in love with Maggie, comes to help. Before they depart, their trapper friend, Adam, comes to visit and kills an Indian he hears outside. When neighbors come to warn Mr. Gordon about the dangers, one kisses Maggie outside in the dark. She never identifies him, but her own sexual response surprises her. Soon after, Dick's parents go into town, leaving the children home alone, and two Indians kill two of the children. Dick and one brother escape to warn Maggie and her father. The four flee in the

Gordon cart and eventually reach safety, although one of the horses goes lame and they encounter a band of men looting and burning the area. The social taboo of Maggie loving Dick who is a few months younger than she shows that some aspects of adolescence seem to stay the same.

Bert Breen's Barn, set in 1910, combines history and mystery. In part I, a brief account of Bert Breen's life in Boonville reveals the genesis of his barn and how, as the land became infertile, people like Tom Dolan's mother's family, the Hannaberrys, moved into abandoned houses and lived in them until they disintegrated. Tom's father left when Tom was two, but at thirteen years old, twenty years after Bert dies, Tom decides that he wants to move Bert Breen's barn onto his family's property as shelter for cows he wants to raise. A neighbor, old Birdy Morris, an original builder of the barn, advises him how to tear it down and reconstruct it. They visit the widow Breen to arrange for purchase; she reads Tom's future in her cards and says that he will become wealthy. Tom begins work at the feed mill and starts saving money to buy the barn. When Widow Breen dies, the shiftless Flancher brothers destroy her house and dig up the yard looking for Bert's money, known to be hidden since he never trusted banks. Tom plans to buy the deserted place and the barn for the cost of taxes, but a rich New Yorker, Armond, buys it first. Tom offers Armond money for the barn, and Armond accepts it. After tearing down the barn's walls and hearing that no one has found Breen's money, Tom realizes that the barn floor's unusual construction hides it. He and his mother go to retrieve it one night. The foreshadowing of the widow telling Tom's future relieves suspense because the reader knows that he will get the money without being hurt by the Flanchers who have threatened him, torn up the Breen house, and followed him back to the barn site that night. Tom deposits the money in the bank, gives some to Birdy, and begins to improve his family's fortunes.

STYLE AND THEMES

Although all the novels have an unexpected twist in plot, Edmonds's storytelling reaches a high level in *Bert Breen's Barn*. The carefully structured plot intrigues throughout. He uses an informal style in the novel, inserting "you" to address the reader. His diction and dialogue enhance the authenticity with such words as *vamoose, damn,* and the repulsive but appropriate *snot*. In *Wilderness Clearing,* his description of setting— "the house stood a short gunshot from the road"—is especially fitting. Edmonds's unusual treatment of situations continually entertains.

EDMUND MEDLEY. Fifteen, English character important in *Harrow and Harvest*. *See* Willard, Barbara.

EDWARD I (1239–1307). He was the eldest son of Henry III and married *Eleanor of Castile. Before becoming king, he kept his detractors silent by supporting barons in their insistence upon reform by cooperating with Simon de

Montfort in 1258 although he eventually killed Montfort at Evesham in 1265. He joined the Eighth *Crusade in 1270. He became king in 1272 and enacted a parliament representing the three estates. Then he banished 16,000 Jews from England in 1290 on charges of extortionate usury. After many battles against Scotland during his reign, he died while returning to Scotland in expectation of crushing Robert Bruce. See *The Baron's Hostage* and *The Red Towers of Granada* by Geoffrey *Trease.

EDWARD II (1284–1327). Born in Caernarvon, Wales, he was the first to bear the title Prince of Wales. He led an army to Stirling in Scotland, the only fortress not occupied by Robert Bruce, but Bruce beat him at Bannockburn in 1314. He married the French Isabella, daughter of Philip IV, in 1308. She formed a criminal connection with Roger Mortimer, her paramour and Edward II's enemy, which forced Edward to flee from England. Baronial exiles captured him and forced him to resign the throne in 1327 before they murdered him.

EDWARD III (1312–1377). The oldest son of *Edward II, he became king when his mother and Roger Mortimer deposed his father. Eventually he executed Mortimer and claimed the French throne through the right of his mother, Isabella. He fought in France, first winning and then losing Aquitaine. He introduced Flemish weavers into England. See *The Door in the Wall* by Marguerite *de Angeli; *Ride to Danger* by Henry *Treece; and *Bowman of Crécy* by Ronald *Welch.

EDWARD, THE BLACK PRINCE (1330–1376). The eldest son of *Edward III, he died of a mortal disease contracted in Spain before he could succeed to the throne of England. He was the prince of Wales and fought at *Crécy and *Calais. He caused a revolt in his southern France holdings by requiring hearth taxes to obtain needed funds for five consecutive years. *See* Treece, Henry, *Ride to Danger*.

EDWARD VAN ALSTYNE. Ten, American, protagonist of *The Matchlock Gun*. *See* Edmonds, Walter.

EIGHT MULES FROM MONTEREY. *See* Beatty, Patricia.

THE ELDEST SON. *See* Willard, Barbara.

ELEANOR OF CASTILE (1246–1290). The wife of *Edward I of England, she accompanied him on a *crusade from 1270 to 1273.

ELEAZAR BEN YA'IR (d.73). As a *Zealot, he supported his cousin who claimed messiah status. After the cousin was slain, he fled to *Masada, on the shores of the Dead Sea, and eventually committed suicide when the Romans took the fortress in 73 A.D. *See* Haugaard, Erik, *The Rider and His Horse*.

ELI. Young German protagonist living in Pennsylvania of *Skippack School. See* de Angeli, Marguerite.

ELIZABETH I OF ENGLAND (1533–1603). The only child of *Henry VIII and Anne Boleyn, she succeeded to the throne in 1558 after being imprisoned in both the Tower and Woodstock. She increased her persecution of Roman Catholics after discovering the Babbington plot in 1586 and finally signed *Mary, queen of Scots's death warrant. She defeated the Spanish and as ''Good Queen Bess'' helped England emerge as a world power. See *Master Rosalind* and *The Queen's Wizard* by John and Patricia *Beatty, *Stars of Fortune* by Cynthia *Harnett; *The Spanish Letters* by Mollie *Hunter; *The Perilous Gard* by Elizabeth Marie *Pope; *The Queen Elizabeth Story* by Rosemary *Sutcliff; *Cue for Treason* by Geoffrey *Trease, *The Hawk* by Ronald *Welch; and *The King's Beard* by Leonard *Wibberley.

ELIZABETH PETROVNA (1709–1762). As the younger daughter of Peter the Great and *Catherine I of Russia, she gained the throne by overthrowing the government of Ivan VI. She reinstituted the senate and freed Russia from German dominance. She established the University of Moscow in 1755 and the Academy of Fine Arts at *St. Petersburg in 1758. See *The Crimson Oak* and *Young Mark* by E. M. *Almedingen.

EMILY AND TOBY. Fifteen and sixteen, respectively, English orphans and protagonists in *The Maplin Bird. See* Peyton, K. M.

EMILY UPHAM. Seven, American, protagonist of *Emily Upham's Revenge. See* Avi.

EMILY UPHAM'S REVENGE. *See* Avi.

EMMIE HESKET. Fourteen, English protagonist in *To Ravensrigg. See* Burton, Hester.

THE EMPEROR'S WINDING SHEET. *See* Paton Walsh, Jill.

ENCOUNTER AT EASTON. *See* Avi.

ENGLISH CIVIL WAR. Also called the Great Rebellion, between the years of 1642 and 1651, supporters of *Charles I fought the *Parliamentarians. The first phase began in 1642 and ended with Charles I a prisoner of the Parliament in January 1647. The second phase, begun with the Scottish engagement of December 1647, ended with Charles I's execution in January 1649. The third part of the civil war saw the Scots rising in 1650 on behalf of *Charles II but being defeated at Worcester in September 1651. See *Witch Dog, King's Knight's*

Pawn, and *Campion Towers* by John and Patricia *Beatty; *Kate Ryder* by Hester *Burton; *A Messenger for Parliament* and *Cromwell's Boy* by Erik *Haugaard; *Simon* by Rosemary *Sutcliff; *For the King* by Ronald *Welch; and *Harrow and Harvest* by Barbara *Willard.

ERASMUS, DESIDERIUS (1466?–1536). A Dutch humanist and scholar, he traveled widely and became a great friend of Sir Thomas More in England. He also taught Greek at Cambridge. *See* Trease, Geoffrey, *Shadow of the Hawk.*

ERIK HANSEN. Fourteen, Danish protagonist who visits Germany in *Chase Me, Catch Nobody! See* Haugaard, Erik.

ESAU. The brother of *Jacob in the Bible, he gave up his birthright as eldest son of Isaac. *See* Paterson, Katherine, *Jacob Have I Loved.*

ESCAPE FROM FRANCE. See Trease, Geoffrey.

ESCAPE FROM WARSAW. See Serrailler, Ian, *The Silver Sword.*

ESCAPE TO KING ALFRED. See Trease, Geoffrey.

ESSEX, EARL OF. *See* Robert *Devereux.

ESTEBAN. This man, a slave, came to the New World and shipwrecked on Galveston Bay with Cabeza de Vaca. They wandered for eight years and eventually reached northern Mexico. Viceroy Antonio de Mendoza sent him to serve as guide for Fray Marcos de Niza as he tried to find the legendary Seven Golden Cities of *Cibola beginning in 1539. *See* Baker, Betty, *Walk the World's Rim.*

ESTEBAN DE SANDOVAI. Seventeen, Spanish, protagonist of *The King's Fifth. See* O'Dell, Scott.

EXETER BLITZ. See Rees, David.

EXETER CATHEDRAL. This cathedral in Exeter, England, was begun c. 1300 in the curvilinear style. See *The Exeter Blitz* by David *Rees and *Trumpets in the West* by Geoffrey *Trease.

_F_

FAIRY FOLK. Fairies are common in British folklore, and various theories have been posited as to their origin and attributes. They were thieves who were often detected robbing stalls at fairs and markets. One of their most dreaded habits was stealing a human baby and substituting a child of their own so that it might benefit from human milk. Of different physical sizes, they were organized in clans with their own kings, queens, and armies living in subterranean palaces reached through caves or through gates magically opening in hillsides. _See_ Pope, Elizabeth Marie, _The Perilous Gard_.

FANTI. This group of people who live along the south coast of Ghana formed their strong confederacy in the nineteenth century. As an _asafo_ organization, they base political allegiance, succession, and inheritance on a matrilineal descent, but membership and succession to offices is patrilineal, unlike the *Ashanti. _See_ Wibberley, Leonard, _The Secret of the Hawk_.

FAR FROM HOME. _See_ Sebestyen, Ouida.

THE FAR FRONTIER. _See_ Steele, William O.

THE FAR-OFF LAND. _See_ Caudill, Rebecca.

FATHOM FIVE. _See_ Westall, Robert.

FAWKES, GUY (1570–1606). Roman Catholic repression led him to conspire against them by planning to blow up the Houses of Parliament on November 4–5, 1605. For this ill-fated Gunpowder plot, he was tried, convicted, and executed after revealing under torture the names of his cohorts. _See_ Beatty, John and Patricia, _The Queen's Wizard_.

FAYETTE ASHMORE. Thirteen, American protagonist in *Eight Mules from Monterey. See* Beatty, Patricia.

THE FEATHERED SERPENT. See O'Dell, Scott.

FERGUSON, PATRICK (1744–1780). The inventor of the first breech-loading rifle, he served in the British Army in America and was killed at the Battle of King's Mountain. See *Who Comes to King's Mountain?* by John and Patricia *Beatty and *Treegate's Raiders* by Leonard *Wibberley.

FERNAN. Thirteen, Spanish, protagonist of *Son of Columbus. See* Baumann, Hans.

FIDDLESTRINGS. See de Angeli, Marguerite.

FIELD, RACHEL (1894–1942). American.

BIBLIOGRAPHY AND BACKGROUND
   Calico Bush. Illustrated by Allen Lewis. New York: Macmillan, 1931; London: Collier Macmillan, 1966.
   Rachel Field won awards for writing in several genres. In 1932, she was honored by the Newbery for *Calico Bush*.

WORK
   In **Calico Bush**, in 1740, Marguerite Ledoux sails from France to America. She and her grandmother disembark in Marblehead, Massachusetts, and her grandmother's sudden death leaves her alone. At twelve, she becomes bound out to Joel Sargent's family. The Sargents decide to resettle north, and on their sea journey, a storm almost capsizes their boat, but Marguerite saves the sheep. When they sail into the harbor bordering their plot of land, they spot the burned ruins of their house. Neighbors tell them that Indians have long considered the Sargent plot sacred and have sabotaged all settlers on that land. The Sargents decide to stay even though an added incentive to the Indians will be that the French are paying Indians for English scalps. The generally kind family often chastises Marguerite's Frenchness during the *French and Indian War. Maggie, as the family calls Marguerite, meets Hepsa Jordon, an old woman of Scottish descent who tells her about herbs and the calico bush, a low-growing plant bearing pinkish flowers. Field divides the book into four sections, one for each season. The family arrives in summer. In fall they have a roof raising, and Maggie thwarts a bear on the edge of the clearing by throwing a bucket of water on him. When Maggie searches for witch hazel with the children, she finds a cave with an evil smell and inside it a buckle close to a shank of human hair. She senses that in this place, the Indians burn their sacred fires. She does not tell even Caleb, the Sargent family member closest to her age, about her discovery. In winter, all attend a "shelling" bee, and Maggie finds the hidden red

ear of corn signifying the next to be married. Since she knows that Ira, Joel's brother, is in love with a neighbor, Abby, and is rival to Hepsa's nephew Ethan, Maggie slips the ear to Ira so that he can claim finding it. The family does not celebrate Christmas, and Maggie, fighting depression, goes outside the house for a private celebration. She sings "Noel," and an Indian hidden in the trees repeats the word and responds to her with a French phrase. She gives him the only gift she has, her Uncle Pierre's button. Back inside with the family, she does not tell. As winter continues, the baby Debbie, after saying *Maggie* as her first word, falls into the fire and burns herself so badly that even Maggie's and Caleb's rough walk across the ice to get Hepsa does not save her. In spring, the Indians come. Since Joel is incapacitated with a broken leg, and the other males are away, Maggie saves the family by feeding the Indians and staging a Maypole dance for their entertainment. When Joel offers her freedom to go to a convent in Quebec, she decides to remain with the family though she misses practicing her religion. Marguerite, a mature twelve-year-old, seems credible because in her short life she has endured the pain of major separations.

STYLE AND THEME

Field carefully integrates fact and fiction so that the story develops naturally, with Hepsa's Scottish wisdom comforting the lonely Marguerite, no longer allowed to be either French or Catholic, by teaching her about plants and people. One contemporary concern is that the specific Indian tribe remains unidentified. However, the settlers themselves probably made few distinctions. The tone of gentleness in this desolate setting, emphasized by Field's word choice, and the omniscient point of view also allow a glimpse of the adolescent Abby, courted by two desirable young men. As an amalgam of Indian customs, herbal cure, and human courage, the story engrosses the reader.

THE FIGHTING GROUND. See Avi.

THE FIRE-BROTHER. See Crossley-Holland, Kevin.

FIREWEED. See Paton Walsh, Jill.

FITZ-. A male with this prefix to his name was the bastard son. The name "Fitzwilliam" indicates that the holder is a bastard son of William. See *The Door in the Wall* by Marguerite *de Angeli; *Lost John* by Barbara *Picard; and *The Lark and the Laurel* by Barbara *Willard.

FLAMBARDS. See Peyton, K. M.

FLAMBARDS DIVIDED. See Peyton, K. M.

FLAMBARDS IN SUMMER. See Peyton, K. M.

FLAMING ARROWS. See Steele, William O.

FLAN TAYLOR. Ten, American protagonist in *Wilderness Journey. See* Steele, William O.

FLEISCHMAN, PAUL (1952–   ). American.

BIBLIOGRAPHY AND BACKGROUND
   Path of the Pale Horse. New York: Harper & Row, 1983.
   Paul Fleischman was honored by the Newbery for a collection of historical
fiction short stories in 1983. Although short stories fall outside the scope of this
guide, he has written one historical fiction novel.

WORK
   Path of the Pale Horse begins in 1793 when Uzziah Botkin contacts fourteen-
year-old Lep (Asclepius) Nye's family for the first time in twenty years. Mr.
Botkin had once given Lep's father money to rebuild his burned silversmith's
shop and had received silver throughout the years until Mr. Nye's death during
the *American Revolution. Mr. Botkin wants Lep to help him in Philadelphia
for three months with a new money-making endeavor, but Lep cannot because
he is apprenticed to Dr. Peale. Instead, Lep's sister Clara, fifteen, decides to
go. When several weeks pass with no word from Clara, Mrs. Nye worries. Dr.
Peale takes Lep with him to Philadelphia to buy medicines and look for Clara.
The *yellow fever has emptied the streets, but Dr. Peale finds his druggist. While
he buys, a gunshot scares the horse. It runs away with Lep, and Lep cannot find
his way back to the shop. He remembers the address of a Mr. Tweakfield whose
driver he had helped when a horse threw him. Mr. Tweakfield welcomes him,
but the obsequious servants make him uncomfortable. In his subsequent searches
for both Dr. Peale and Clara, Lep discovers that Clara has moved, but he finds
Uzziah Botkin's twenty-year-old grave and realizes that the man with Clara is
an impostor. When Lep finds Clara selling copper rings covered with tar, supposedly to fight the fever, he discloses Botkin's scam. While Lep plans Clara's
rescue, he finds Dr. Peale and reveals that Mr. Tweakfield's servants are robbing
their master. Unfortunately, he cannot save Mr. Tweakfield from the fever.
Distressed with his failure, Lep realizes that medicine is not as advanced as he
had thought, and he pledges himself to find more answers.

STYLE AND THEME
   Fleischman's description of Lep reveals his appropriate use of syntax, figurative language, and imagery: "thin as a wick, and wanted dipping in wax."
The many allusions to Greek personages give the story depth, but the puzzle
pieces of the mystery plot do not quite fit together. Regardless, the story presents
an unusual view from a physician's perspective during a major epidemic.

A FLIGHT OF SWANS. See Willard, Barbara.

FLY AWAY HOME. See Nostlinger, Christine.

FOLLOW MY BLACK PLUME. See Trease, Geoffrey.

FOOTSTEPS. *See* Garfield, Leon.

FOR THE KING. *See* Welch, Ronald.

FORBES, ESTHER (1891–1967). American.

BIBLIOGRAPHY AND BACKGROUND
Johnny Tremain. Illustrated by Lynd Ward. Boston: Houghton Mifflin, 1943.
For the one historical fiction novel, *Johnny Tremain,* that Esther Forbes wrote for young adults, she received the Newbery Medal in 1944. Using information from biographical research on Paul Revere, she created Johnny and his world.

WORK
In the **Bildungsroman* **Johnny Tremain,** the orphaned Johnny matures from an arrogant apprentice silversmith of fourteen into a *Whig messenger of sixteen aware that adults may choose to do things, in James *Otis's words, so " 'that a man can stand up.' " In 1774, after Johnny's dying mother apprentices him to old Mr. Lapham, Johnny's artistry quickly appears, and he begins bullying his less talented peers. When Johnny decides to work on Sunday, against the law, to complete a prized order from John *Hancock, an older apprentice's prank causes Johnny to burn his hand so badly that he can no longer work. Johnny's pride leads to his destruction according to Mr. Lapham's Bible in Proverbs 16:18. Unable to find work, Johnny approaches Mr. Lyte, a wealthy merchant, to reveal their kinship through a silver cup Johnny's mother had given Johnny. Mr. Lyte accuses him of stealing, but Priscilla Lapham had seen the cup before the date Mr. Lyte said it was stolen. Johnny decides to sell the cup to Mr. Lyte for food money, but Mr. Lyte blackmails him and keeps the cup. Johnny's friend Rab at the *Observer* press hires him to deliver papers, and the patriotically motivated Rab becomes Johnny's mentor and helps him discover his beliefs as the *American Revolution begins. Johnny learns quickly about the *Tories and the *Whigs. "In only a few weeks he changed from knowing little enough about the political excitement, and caring less, to being an ardent Whig." Finally as the Tory Mr. Lyte escapes to London, his daughter, Lavinia, reveals to Johnny that she has verified that they are indeed related, that his wild and beautiful mother had run off to France where he was born. After Johnny's father died, his mother had returned to Boston but never contacted the family.

STYLE AND THEME
Forbes opens the story by observing actions of the awakening animals, followed by the personification, "Boston slowly opened its eyes, stretched, and woke." In the harbor, the ships sit "content as cows waiting to be milked," but later, during the embargo, "the ships were lying like dead birds along the wharves." One of the British brigades becomes a "scarlet dragon" as the "thousands of separate feet merged into one gigantic pair." The character development of Johnny, Lavinia Lyte, and Rab vacillates. Johnny matures while recovering

from his burns, alone in the Lapham's birth and death room. He remembers that "in a way he had died in that room; at least something had happened and the bright little silversmith's apprentice was no more. . . . now he was somebody else." Lavinia's disdainful treatment of others makes her decision to investigate Johnny's birth seem implausible. Forbes's writing style and her incorporation of historical personages within the story make Revere's honesty and kindness, Hancock's generosity, Adams's taste for war, and Otis's wavering mental abilities come alive. The occupying British socialize with the Bostonians in times of peace but become enemies when the war starts. Forbes's vivid use of imagery and figurative language allows her to present a Whig approach to the Revolutionary war emphasizing the equality of all humans.

FORBIDDEN FRONTIER. *See* Harris, Christie.

FORMAN, JAMES (1932–   ). American.

BIBLIOGRAPHY AND BACKGROUND

   Ceremony of Innocence. New York: Hawthorn, 1970. *The Cow Neck Rebels*. New York: Farrar, Straus & Giroux, 1969. *Horses of Anger*. New York: Farrar, Straus & Giroux, 1967. *The Life and Death of Yellow Bird*. New York: Farrar, Straus & Giroux, 1973. *My Enemy, My Brother*. New York: Hawthorn, 1969. *Ring the Judas Bell*. New York: Farrar, Straus & Giroux, 1965. *The Skies of Crete*. New York: Farrar, Straus & Giroux, 1963. *So Ends This Day*. New York: Farrar, Straus & Giroux, 1970. *The Survivor*. New York: Farrar, Straus & Giroux, 1976. *The Traitors*. New York: Farrar, Straus & Giroux, 1968.

   James Forman won the Lewis Carroll Shelf award for *Ceremony of Innocence*. The older adolescent and young adult protagonists in this book, as well as others, make important contributions to an understanding of attitudes before, during, and after World War II. Still other protagonists provide valuable insights about the *American Revolution, the *American Civil War, and the conflict at Wounded Knee. Forman's novels adamantly advocate the importance of freedom.

WORKS

   Forman's books set in the United States are his only novels about the eighteenth and nineteenth centuries. The earliest setting, the American Revolution, appears in **The Cow Neck Rebels**. The protagonist, Bruce, a sixteen-year-old boy living on Long Island and long in love with Rachel, a young woman the narrator compares to Joan of Arc, recognizes that his older brother, Malcolm, will soon assert his right to marry her. Their lives change, however, with the beginning of the Revolutionary War in 1775. Bruce's grandfather, Rob Roy Cameron, hates the British because they destroyed the Scots at *Culloden in 1746; he, therefore, supports the *Patriots. He hates Rachel's father, a Campbell *Loyalist whom Rob Roy thinks betrayed the Scots at Culloden. Bruce's father asserts that he wants no part in any war and that his faith remains with the "imagine-nation." But to protect his family, he has to sail to Jamaica; he has been selling wheat to the British in Boston simply because they paid him the highest price. Before the Patriot soldiers go to battle, they tar and feather Rachel's father, and she hides in the Cameron house against Rob Roy's wishes. Of the three Cameron males who fight, only Bruce returns. Malcolm dies from a saber wound in his side, and no news comes of Rob Roy. Eventually, Rob Roy reappears, rescued by the *Tory slave Billy, whose master lives in the area. After the rebel defeat, Rachel's father roars back from battle to claim the Cameron lands. The Cameron men sail away to escape him, and on the water, Bruce realizes that he can help recapture freedom by sailing into shore at night to burn Tory wheat fields. The novel reveals the complexity of people's loyalties and how unexpected events often motivate them.

The Cameron family reappears in **So Ends This Day**. In 1846, the grandson of Bruce Cameron, Guy Cameron, flashes back to the story of his father's last whaling voyage. Guy first recalls the story his father told him about his intended duel with Captain Coffin, a former admirer of his mother and a despicable slaver. Captain Cameron's gun would not fire, but he kept trying to shoot after Coffin's errant shot until Coffin became so cowardly that he ran away. Guy's mother appeared from among the trees with a "rose" growing on her breast, blood from a gunshot wound. Captain Cameron, blamed for her death, leaves town aboard the whaling ship *Icarus* with Guy and his sister, Bonnie. Captain Cameron searches for Coffin's ship, *Black Joke,* which had sailed several days before. Bonnie thrives on sea life, enjoying the motley crew, but Guy never quite accepts it. They spot the *Black Joke* off the African coast, land, and find Coffin, wounded by the natives. Cameron humanely rescues him, and Coffin shows his appreciation by gradually coercing Cameron to resume opium smoking. Cameron returns a crew member Tapu to Tahiti, and Bonnie stays and marries him. Assured that the opium controls Cameron, Coffin convinces the crew that slaves, not whales, will bring them money. They return to Africa and load blacks, including a former member of the crew, Scipio, earlier abandoned by Coffin. Guy and Scipio plan a mutiny, and when Guy discovers and destroys the opium, Captain Cameron helps them. Off the coast of Barbados, Guy finally kills Coffin. Guy, Captain Cameron, and Scipio escape, with Guy returning home while Captain Cameron and Scipio go west to investigate the gold rumors. The unusual threads of plot make this an appealing novel.

The Life and Death of Yellow Bird presents a distinctive view of the white man's treatment of Native Americans. The blond Yellow Bird relates that his *Cherokee mother, in 1876, showed him the dead General *Custer on the battleground at Little Bighorn and said that Custer was his father. Custer once chose her as his guide and then left her expecting a child. Yellow Bird feels no relationship to Custer and distrusts all white men. When his mother dies, the *Sioux *Crazy Horse finds him and takes him to his own father, Worm. With Worm, Yellow Bird feels secure. Yellow Bird's continued visions show both he and Worm that he will be a shaman. After another defeat and Crazy Horse's death, the tribe joins *Sitting Bull in Canada. When Worm dies, they return to

Wounded Knee to bury him next to Crazy Horse. Afterward, Buffalo Bill takes several Cherokee braves on tour with him, including Yellow Bird. In London, when Bill realizes that Yellow Bird is Custer's son, he offers to make Yellow Bird a star, which will earn him more money. Yellow Bird refuses. He returns to his people to become their shaman. Soon after, the father of the only woman he loves sells her to a white man for liquor, and the man kills her. Yellow Bird devotes himself to The People until 1891 when he dies at Wounded Knee with Sitting Bull and many others. In this book, Forman's style reflects the Native American's fusion of reality with dream by emphasizing abstracts. Certainly Yellow Bird's point of view makes the reader wonder what whites proved by their merciless attacks on the almost helpless Indians.

Seven of Forman's novels explore aspects of World War II. Two of them concern Greece, and five uncover attitudes of the various factions in and around Germany. Crete became one of Hitler's targets in 1941. In **The Skies of Crete**, Penelope looks out her window on May 20 and sees lightning. She soon realizes that the clear sky reflects flames from bombs rather than a storm. In a flashback, Penelope reveals that she never expected the war to touch their happy lives other than the arrival of her Greek-Scot cousin Alexis. His fear of birds swooping overhead and horror of the donkey whose face looks like a gas mask staring in the kitchen window surprises her. Alexis hates war and disagrees with his grand-father Markos, who boasts of his role in clearing the Turks from Crete. But the war comes, and the family has to leave their home. They flee through mountains to the southern coast. After hiding for several days, the women escape to Al-exandria, Egypt, on an open boat. The novel emphasizes that Penelope's idyllic view of her island starkly contrasts to the reality of hostile factions competing for Crete.

The Greek underground soldiers of *The Skies of Crete* surface in 1917 in **Ring the Judas Bell**. Nicholas Lanaras, a shepherd, expects to be a priest like his father. One night, he searches for a lost sheep, Ajax, and finds members of a rebel group of Andartes devouring it. He reports the theft to the recently arrived Greek soldiers staying in the chapel, and to Nicholos's horror, they kill all but one, Nicholos's friend Stavro, whom he is able to save. But Stavro's father breaks into the chapel and kills Stavro for deserting the family. When the village men leave to hunt foraging wolves, the Andartes come and destroy the village. They march the children away to camps, mining the trails behind them. Eventually Nicholos and his sister, Angela, who had once spied for her Andarte boyfriend, escape from the Yugoslavian camp with twenty other children. They march through bitter cold and deep snow trying to return to Greece. When they ask for help, they discover that the seemingly kind couple is trying to trap them. Angela kills the woman and takes food, but she unwittingly leaves the compass that has led them through the whitened mountains. Nicholos's faith returns, and he senses that God will guide them. Angela has no faith and returns to the Andartes whom Nicholos has seen patroling the area. Nicholos takes charge and walks the remaining eleven children across thinning ice into the hands of the

Greek army. At home in Serifos, Nicholos finds his passivist father changed and ready to fight. But after his ordeal, Nicholos knows that the most important thing is to raise the chapel bell, fallen in the Andarte raid. He and the eleven children raise the bell believed to be forged with one of the thirty coins for which Judas Iscariot sold Christ. The novel reveals a frightening view of Greek violence after horrors of war had supposedly ended.

Historically, **The Traitors** gives the earliest view of World War II in Germany. In the prologue, Forman enters the small town of Ravenskirch at the end of World War I in 1918; the epilogue returns to the town twenty years after the end of World War II. In between, Paul Eichhorn, a foundling adopted by the Lutheran minister, reveals his attitude toward Hitler's war which completely contrasts with that of his brother Kurt. When Kurt, sixteen, asks Paul at thirteen to accompany him to the Nuremberg rally of Hitler Youth in October 1938, Paul naively asks his Jewish friend Noah to go with him. Noah's parents gently decline the invitation. Not until after *Crystal Night on November 9, 1938, does Paul realize how much the *Nazis hate the Jews and that Kurt perpetrates this hate. Paul and one of Kurt's girlfriends repeatedly risk their lives to help Noah and his family. After thinking Noah dead, Paul unexpectedly finds him hiding in the family's summer home. Paul and his father hide Noah in the church tower. Kurt joins the army and returns from fighting several times, each time with a different wound but with the same chorus that Paul is a coward. The townspeople against Hitler secretly plan to help the Allies capture the town. Paul, his father, Noah, and three others save the town by crawling through the sewers to sever Nazi explosives planted to destroy the bridge when the Americans appear. After the Americans arrive, Kurt admits that he is the coward, having deliberately wounded himself in hope of escaping death. In the epilogue, Paul returns to Ravenskirch and thinks of Kurt's postcards from South America. That so many non-Jewish Germans risked their lives for freedom from Hitler's tyranny reveals that the Germans themselves were a great force in Hitler's defeat.

A second novel set in Germany, **Ceremony of Innocence**, begins when the Gestapo takes Hans and Sophie Scholl from a university building to a waiting car in 1943. The remainder of the book takes place in a Munich prison where Hans at twenty-four undergoes interrogation for treason against the state. Hans's flashbacks tell the story of his writing and distributing pamphlets condemning Hitler, the activities leading to his death sentence. He remembers childhood acquaintances like Otto, leader of the local Youth for Hitler group. He thinks of Franz, a weak, unattractive boy whom he protected from Otto but whom he disliked. He remembers that he psychologically first joined the resistance when Otto destroyed a flag that Sophie, Hans's sister, had made. Then he recalls the incident at Oktoberfest in 1938 uniting him with two other medical students, Alex and Christl, and led to their pamphlet publishing. They had tried to save a Jewish boy determined to threaten a group of Youth for Hitler members in retaliation for his parents' arrest the previous day, but a single gunshot had killed him. He recalls Sophie's arrival and involvement in the cause, a Joan of Arc.

Then Hans wonders why the man he had saved on a French battlefield stayed alive until reunited with his wife when he then hemorrhaged to death in the street. He realizes that he lost his faith in God while in Russia and in France and at Oktoberfest. However, he refuses to recant his beliefs in freedom from Hitler even when Franz, graduated to one of Hitler's elite guards, comes to his prison cell, gives him a gun, and offers to whisk him away in a waiting car. Hans knows that his sister Sophie will not condemn his return to life, but he knows that he will lose his "freedom" if he does not face his sentence. The title, an allusion to William Butler Yeats's "The Second Coming," enhances the reader's understanding of the irrational behavior of the Nazis, and any other ruling group, in killing people who fight only with words.

Horses of Anger also alludes to a poem, Stephen Benet's "John Brown's Body." One of the characters, the German soldier Konrad, knew Sophie and Hans Scholl in *Ceremony of Innocence* although the book concerns Konrad's nephew, Hans Amann, who finds Hitler's charismatic voice and eyes exciting. The omniscient story, mainly from Hans's point of view, evolves as Hans, on his fifteenth birthday, April 20, 1944, remembers past birthdays beginning when he was ten in 1939. In 1939, Hans, a new member of the *Jungvolk (Youth for Hitler)*, mentally pledges himself to Hitler when Hitler, celebrating his own birthday, speaks to and rides through the Munich masses. Hans's grandfather warns Hans to live his own life, but too young, Hans does not comprehend the warning. On his next birthday, he goes hunting with Uncle Konrad where killing a partridge disgusts him although the day in the mountains is beautiful. In 1941, on a skiing trip with Konrad, Hans listens to Konrad mourn for his lost Astrid, the Jewess wife he had sent to Holland. Soon after, Konrad transfers to Africa, where he finds himself attacking the German ally, Russia. In 1942, on Hans's birthday, Gretchen, a girl whose family has been killed, arrives. During the summer, Hans falls in love with her, but Konrad returns and sees qualities in Gretchen similar to those in Astrid. In 1943, Hans invites Siegfried, his patriotic friend, for his birthday dinner, and Siegfried complains that the lamb Hans's butcher father serves should be reported to authorities since no one should eat so well. The family suggests he either enjoy the birthday party or leave. Hans faces his present birthday in 1944 waiting for enemy bombers with three of his friends, Siegfried, Ernst, and Heime, in their tower post. The bombers kill all the other young people in the camp. Ernst, covered with burns, dies soon after. Siegfried will not accept defeat and tries to kill Konrad, whose strange dreams of horses have led him to join the underground fight against the Secret Service in Munich. Only Heime's knife in Siegfried's back stops the murder. After the war ends and the Americans arrive, the durable Gretchen explains to Hans that Konrad needs her. Hans's love of books and desire to be a poet, she feels, will help him survive. The device of having Hans review his life on successive birthdays works well to show the changing German attitudes toward Hitler and his policies.

The time period of **The Survivor** also spans World War II. The action begins in August 1939 when the Dutch Jews believe nothing will happen to neutral Holland and ends in 1945 with David Ullman's release from Auschwitz. No one in the Ullman family heeds Uncle Daniel's warning to go to *Palestine, though he has just escaped from Berlin on *Crystal Night, leaving his wife dead in bed. Instead they remain in Amsterdam until the Nazis arrive. Everyone but David's grandfather leaves the family home, but they flee no farther than an abandoned mill near their summer house. As the Nazis search the area, a Catholic priest tries to save them by separately moving each one inside a coffin. He succeeds in transferring the youngest, Rachel, to a cave hideout; Nazis catch the others and transport them first to Westerbork and then to Auschwitz. At Westerbork, David and his twin brother, Saul, find Ruth, their older actress sister who looks Aryan and had been an excellent spy for the Dutch Underground. As a Jewish entertainer at this camp, she has many privileges. At Auschwitz, however, she tries to engineer a revolt and kills a guard; for this brave attempt she dies. David's false papers do not identify him as Saul's twin, which helps them escape the atrocities that the physician Mengele performs on twins. When the war ends, twenty-year-old David, having seen or heard of five family deaths, walks almost the entire way to Amsterdam with Hannah, a girl coming from Vienna whom he meets on the road. At home, David recovers the hidden family valuables, his grandfather's diary recording the action of the book from 1940 to 1942, and a note from his grandfather predicting that David will be the survivor. When he decides that he must try to find Rachel, he goes to the cave and sees her name listed as departed for Palestine. He follows her on the next available boat. Jews outside Germany could not comprehend that Hitler included them in his hatred; this book reveals that blindness.

My Enemy, My Brother begins after World War II ends when Daniel Baratz, at sixteen, hesitatingly accepts his freedom from the Zambrow, Poland, concentration camp. Dan and his one surviving relative, his grandfather Jacob, return to the Warsaw ghetto where Daniel's parents died, retrieve the buried family treasures, and begin a new life utilizing Jacob's watchmaking skills. These skills had saved them from the gas chambers because Jacob's knowledge helped the Germans create mine-triggering mechanisms. They continue to Jacob's home, Gora, and there Daniel meets young people building a way station for Jews marching to Palestine. Their zeal, especially that of the lovely Hanna, intrigues him although he dislikes the militant Gideon. He eventually reaches the Palestinian coast after being rescued from almost certain death along the way and becomes reunited with Hanna and Gideon at the Promise of the Future kibbutz. As a sheepherder with a hillside vigil, he meets an English-speaking Arab sheepherder, Said, and they become friends. When Dan saves Said from drowning in a flash flood, Said asks him to meet his family, though both risk derision from their communities. As the fighting between the two groups escalates, each warns the other of planned attacks, but neither can help. Dan hates fighting, and the one person he kills while on guard duty is Said's father. By 1955, in the epilogue, Said, as a soldier, wonders why the Jews have destroyed his town and his family as the Germans once destroyed them. The ironies are apparent. Also apparent is that people willing to talk to each other in an attempt to understand and resolve their difficulties do not fight.

STYLE AND THEMES

Forman's use of language enhances the content. Throughout the novels, allusions allow deeper understanding of theme. Such references to Yeats, Benet, El Greco, Don Quixote, St. Francis, and Saint George with his dragon accent the meaning. Imagery and metaphor also augment Forman's insights. In *Ceremony of Innocence,* Franz is so pale that he looks "dipped in bleach." Forman comments that Hitler's "voice played on, a full orchestra of sounds without one note of music." In *The Cow Neck Rebels,* Bruce looks at the "porcelain sky" and sees the enemy as "a far-off game involving tiny chess pieces." When Bruce has his tooth pulled, "he was just pain covered with skin." Other phrases from different novels show "orange leaves like raccoon paws" and "threads of rain link[ing] sky to earth." Repeated motifs include strong, independent women willing to sacrifice for freedom and religious leaders less than certain of their roles. Only children seem to retain faith in humanity. In *My Enemy, My Brother,* a guard dies "with the graceless resignation of the last dinosaur accepting extinction." An explicit theme in *Horses of Anger* reveals that "education is the only thing that will never disappoint you." In all the novels, the characters understand themselves and others more fully through their dreams. Thus the psychological coalesces with the logical to produce clear, thematic development. Forman's varied points of view and methods of revealing plot keep each novel unique and intriguing.

FOX, PAULA (1923–   ). American.

BIBLIOGRAPHY AND BACKGROUND

The Slave Dancer. Illustrated by Eros Keith. Scarsdale, N.Y.: Bradbury, 1973; London: Macmillan, 1974.

The Slave Dancer won the Newbery Medal in 1974. Fox has received many other literary awards, including the Hans Christian Andersen Award in 1978.

WORK

In **The Slave Dancer** during 1840, Jessie Bollier, thirteen, finds himself captured by slavers to play his fife for their illegal cargo. Not allowed to let his widowed mother know of his fate, Jessie boards the *Moonlight.* At first, Ben Stout treats Jessie kindly, while another hand, Purvis, yells at him. The captain has interest only in the money for which he can sell the slaves. Others who also value only the money are the black African *cabocieros* who sell their own people. Jessie tells in his first-person narrative that during the journey to Africa and back to New Orleans, he begins to prefer the honest Purvis to the sneaky Stout. He sees that Stout has no regard for humans unless he can use them for his own gain. When Stout realizes that Jessie understands his motives, Stout begins to harass him. Once he throws Jessie's fife into the hold filled with tightly packed slaves. Jessie has to walk over living human bodies to find it. During a storm off the coast of Cuba, Stout and the captain throw slaves overboard so approaching American ships will not arrest them. When the ship wrecks, only Jessie and Ras, one of the blacks, survive. Many years later, after becoming an apothecary in Rhode Island, Jessie still cannot listen to music because he always has visions of the miserable slaves being forced to dance on the ship's deck.

STYLE AND THEME

Fox develops the obvious themes of the horror of slaving and the even greater horror of men selling their own people. By using a young and innocent first-person narrator, she achieves a more powerful tone of disbelief in man's propensity to sacrifice humanity for money. Secondary themes include the power of clothing—that one clothed most likely controls those unclothed—as the slavers controlled the slaves. This tightly constructed novel reveals a sordid era of American history.

FRANCIS AND BELLA RIMPOLE. Scots of fourteen and eleven, respectively, protagonists of *The Young Pretenders*. *See* Picard, Barbara.

FRANCIS WASHINGTON. Young English protagonist in *The Stars of Fortune*. *See* Harnett, Cynthia.

FRANKLIN, BENJAMIN (1706–1790). Remembered as a statesman, scientist, and philosopher, he became an important American spokesman during the time of independence from the British. He invented the lightning rod and bifocal, among other discoveries. His philosophy remains well known from his *Poor Richard's Almanac*. See *Victory at Valmy* by Geoffrey *Trease and *Sea Captain from Salem* by Leonard *Wibberley.

FRENCH AND INDIAN WAR. This was the American counterpart of a worldwide nine years' war waged between 1754 and 1763. At first only Great Britain opposed France, but eventually Hanover, Brunswick, Hesse-Cassel, and Portugal joined Great Britain, with Spain joining France. The war began over the issue as to whether the upper Ohio valley was part of the British empire, open to settlement and trade from inhabitants of Pennsylvania and Virginia, or part of the French empire. Great Britain won, but the American colonists began to question the value of connections with the empire. See *Calico Captive* by Elizabeth *Speare and *Mohawk Valley* by Ronald *Welch.

FRENCH REVOLUTION. This term traditionally denotes the revolutionary movement in France between 1787 and 1799, with its first climax in 1789 at the May 5 meeting of the Estates-General at Versailles. On July 14, the people seized the Bastille, symbol of royal tyranny. On August 26, the National Assembly proclaimed the liberty, equality, and inviolability of property, as well as the right to resist oppression. After the first stage of the war, Louis XVI was tried and condemned; he was executed on January 21, 1793. In 1795, the young *Napoleon Bonaparte rose to power. See *Castors Away!*, *The Rebel*, and *Riders of the Storm* by Hester *Burton; *The Gates of Paradise* by Peter *Carter; *Victory at Valmy* by Geoffrey *Trease; and *Escape from France* by Ronald Welch.

FREYA. In Norse mythology, Freya is goddess of peace and love. See *The Sea Stranger* and *The Fire-Brother* by Kevin *Crossley-Holland.

FRIEDRICH. Young German Jewish male, protagonist of *Friedrich*. See Richter, Hans.

FRIEDRICH. *See* Richter, Hans.

FRISIANS. This people of western Europe, whose name survives, have lived north of the Hague along coastal regions at the mouth of the Rhine. *See* Paton Walsh, Jill, *Hengest's Tale*.

FRITZ ROMBERG. German-American who grows from thirteen into a young adult as protagonist in *The Obstinate Land*. *See* Keith, Harold.

FRONTIER WOLF. *See* Sutcliff, Rosemary.

G

GARFIELD, LEON (1921–   ). British.

BIBLIOGRAPHY AND BACKGROUND

Black Jack. Illustrated by Anthony Maitland. London: Longman, 1968; New York: Pantheon, 1969. *The Boy and the Monkey*. Illustrated by Trevor Ridley. London: Heinemann, 1969; New York: Watts, 1970. *The Confidence Man*. London: Kestrel, 1978; New York: Viking, 1979. *Devil-in-the-Fog*. Illustrated by Antony Maitland. London: Constable, 1966; New York: Pantheon, 1966. *The Drummer Boy*. Illustrated by Antony Maitland. New York: Pantheon, 1969; London: Longman, 1970. *Footsteps*. Illustrated by Antony Maitland. New York: Delacorte, 1980; as *John Diamond*. London: Kestrel, 1980. *Jack Holborn*. Illustrated by Antony Maitland. London: Constable, 1964; New York: Pantheon, 1965. *The Night of the Comet*. Illustrated by Martin Cottam. New York: Delacorte, 1979; as *Bostock and Harris; or, The Night of the Comet*. London: Kestrel, 1979. *Smith*. Illustrated by Antony Maitland. London: Constable and New York: Pantheon, 1967. *The Sound of Coaches*. Illustrated by John Lawrence. London: Kestrel; New York: Viking, 1974. *The Strange Affair of Adelaide Harris*. Illustrated by Fritz Wegner. London: Longman, 1971; New York: Pantheon, 1971.

Leon Garfield has won numerous awards, including *The Guardian* Award in 1967, the Carnegie in 1971, the Whitbread in 1980, and the Federation of Children's Book Groups Award in 1982 for his writing in several genres. He received Carnegie Medal citations for *Black Jack* in 1968 and *The Drummer Boy* in 1970. Since Garfield's historical fiction rarely mentions specific dates, references to famous or infamous people, events, and places help the reader identify a general time frame. The characters, however, function within the parameters of the period, and the tenor of the mid-eighteenth century develops through them.

WORKS

Three of Garfield's novels are more frivolous than the others. In **The Boy and the Monkey**, Garfield personifies the monkey, which places the book in the category of historical fantasy. Around 1740, Tim, eleven, makes his monkey steal from people. When the monkey steals a diamond ring, he returns it to the owner because he is afraid the boy will sell the ring and stay in England. The monkey wants to return to Brazil, his home, and if Tim is convicted of theft and deported to Virginia, the monkey will be halfway there. In court, the judge sets the worth of the diamond at eleven and one-half pence since theft of a shilling (twelve pence) or more would warrant Tim's hanging. Although embarrassed at the low assessment, the owner realizes that the ring should not be worth more than a child's life. When her betrothed agrees, she loves him even more. And the monkey is happy to be going to Virginia.

The second novel, **The Night of the Comet**, presents lovers planning to go to the party on the hill in honor of Pigott's comet on April 6. Cassidy, an Irishman, comes to town searching, as he has in other English towns, for his love, Mary Flatley, and he finds her. Bostock at thirteen loves his friend Harris's sister Mary, who ignores him. Other sets of lovers appear, and everyone gets in some sort of trouble before the evening's festivities conclude.

A third rather complicated but shallow plot is **The Strange Affair of Adelaide Harris**. Harris and Bostock of *The Night of the Comet* reappear as protagonists in this novel. Harris hears his teacher, Mr. Brett, say that ancient Greeks sometimes exposed their babies on mountains, as Laius exposed Oedipus. He decides to leave his seven-week-old sister, Adelaide, in the woods, and Bostock helps him. Tizzy Alexander, while walking in the woods with the school owner's son, Ralph, finds Adelaide. Ralph takes the baby to a neighboring parish church instead of the local one. With Harris's parents frantic over Adelaide's disappearance, Harris and Bostock take a baby from the local church steps to replace Adelaide. Recognizing the substitute, Dr. Harris hires a detective, Mr. Raven, to find his child. Mr. Raven creates strange clues for himself by piecing together the wrong information. Meanwhile Harris and Bostock create plans to rescue Adelaide, now in the poorhouse. Why they do not immediately reveal where she is remains a mystery. After Tizzy and Ralph's illicit walk in the woods, Tizzy's father challenges Ralph to a duel over Tizzy's honor. Mr. Brett loves Tizzy, whom he tutors, and the only intelligent action in the novel occurs when he, as the second for both duelers, tells them to meet at locations three miles apart. Then he leaves with Tizzy for the New World.

Four of the novels have titles naming characters. Two are protagonists, *Smith* and *Jack Holborn*, and two, *Black Jack* and *John Diamond (Footsteps* in the United States), are other characters with whom the protagonists become intricately involved. In **Smith**, Smith is a twelve-year-old pickpocket who witnesses the murder of a man, Field, after he has taken his wallet. He finds a document in the wallet but cannot read it. He tries unsuccessfully to get others to teach him to read because he does not trust anyone he knows to read the document to him. Eventually he guides a blind man home from a pub, and Mr. Mansfield, a magistrate, asks him to stay. Smith agrees when told that Mr. Mansfield's daughter will teach him to read. On the day Smith feels that he can read competently, he greets Miss Mansfield's lawyer suitor, Mr. Billing, at the door. Mr. Billing accuses him of Field's murder and takes him to *Newgate, asking for the document en route. Smith realizes Mr. Billing's evil intent and refuses to tell him that the document is hidden in Mr. Mansfield's study. Later Mr. Billing pretends to help Smith escape from prison but actually tries to trap him. Smith escapes under his sister's skirt. Various coincidences lead Smith and Mr. Mansfield to Field's home where they find the money that Field has so carefully hidden from his degenerate son, the man who actually killed him. With his share of the reward money, Smith buys his sisters a new house, but he elects to remain with Mr. Mansfield.

Jack Holborn, in **Jack Holborn**, tells his first-person adventures after stowing away on the *Charming Molly* in *Bristol at thirteen. Abandoned in the London section of Holborn as a baby, Jack has been living on parish funds until he moves on board. Pirates capture the ship, but the pirate captain gives Jack hope for a better life by telling him that he will reveal Jack's birth if Jack saves him three times. Soon after their conversation, several pirates go ashore and are ambushed. The wounded captain returns to the ship where he stays hidden while recovering. At sea, the ship rescues another pirate, Mr. Trumpet, expelled from his own ship. The *Charming Molly* soon wrecks, and only four survive: the captain; the captain's protector, Mr. Morris; Mr. Trumpet; and Jack. When they see the wreck of Mr. Trumpet's former ship, Mr. Trumpet rushes on board to find the White Lady, a huge diamond. From the treasure, he gives each man a bag of jewels. After they go ashore and wander through the forest, Mr. Trumpet recognizes the captain and calls him Lord Sheringham. To find that the captain leads a double life as an honored judge as well as a lowly pirate shocks Mr. Morris. One day, Lord Sheringham disappears, but Mr. Morris takes Jack and Mr. Trumpet to safety before he dies from a wound. The two eventually find and purchase Lord Sheringham from slave traders. They return him to England, where he is arrested for his evil deeds. What they find, however, is that Sheringham has an identical twin who was the pirate captain. When the lord identifies Mr. Trumpet as a man he once tried for fraud, he is exonerated. Eventually Mr. Trumpet helps Jack locate his mother. At the same time, he gives Jack the jewels that Mr. Morris had "willed" him. The intricacies of the plot enable characters to develop and for their goodness to show through their weaknesses.

The protagonist of **Footsteps** *(John Diamond)* is not John Diamond but William Jones. On the night William's father dies, he gives William his watch and tells him to guard it carefully. He also tells him that he once cheated Alfred Diamond, his partner in the coffee business. William goes to London to apologize to Alfred Diamond. He thinks an explanation will stop the footsteps of his father's ghost, which he hears at night. Using the few clues he has, William searches for a Mr. K'nee and meets Mr. Seed who works for K'nee. Mr. Seed tries to help William although he charges him for everything. William meets Mr. Robinson who tells him that Alfred Diamond is dead but that his son still lives. He promises to introduce the two. While William waits, ruffians chase him in the street, but William had earlier saved one of them, Shot in the Head, from Mr. Seed's wrath, and he helps William escape. As the two hide in Shot in the Head's hovel, William discovers a note with an address inside his father's watch. When he visits the place after attending church with Mr. Seed, he finds K'nee and Alfred Diamond. He learns that Robinson is John Diamond, a man bitterly hostile to both his own and William's father. They all rush to William's home in Hertford when word comes that John has gone there. John has already set the house on fire, but William rescues him. Shot in the Head arrives with William's lost purse and decides to stay. The Dickensian characters lend exciting action and intriguing mystery to this absorbing novel.

The omniscient point of view in **Black Jack** clouds whether Tolly or Black Jack is the protagonist, but the story focuses more on Tolly. In 1749, Black Jack hangs from *Tyburn, but Mrs. Gorgandy, the Tyburn widow, retrieves his body. She supports herself by pretending to be the grieving widow of unclaimed dead men and then selling their bodies to local surgeons. To carry the seven-foot Black Jack, she pays Bartholomew (Tolly) Dorking, age fourteen. She locks Tolly inside her house to wait with the body until her return. But Black Jack motions for Tolly to release the bent silver tube from his throat, thereby thwarting both the gallows and Mrs. Gorgandy. He makes Tolly escape with him through the window. Tolly decides to stay with Black Jack to keep him from harming others, among them Belle Carter, a mad young woman they encounter as men take her to a private Bedlam house. Black Jack robs the coach while Tolly disappears with Belle and the Carmody family, traveling elixir salespeople. They help Belle regain her senses, and when she realizes her identity, they are near her Reigate home. Unfortunately her father has committed suicide, and Black Jack, who has reappeared, encourages her, successfully, to commit herself to the private Bedlam in order to stifle Tolly's love for her. The northern lights soon flash, and the ground shakes like an earthquake, which makes Black Jack think the world is ending. He has a change of heart and rushes to retrieve Belle. Black Jack, Tolly, and Belle then go to London, where Black Jack learns from Mrs. Gorgandy, who sold Belle's father's body, that he was shot in the back, murdered. Belle and Tolly escape to Tolly's uncle's ship and sail to New England with him. The incredible beginning of the novel leads realistically to its incredible ending.

Two novels name professions. The first, **The Drummer Boy**, begins with a present-tense account of Charlie Sampson as he falls in battle and ends in present tense when he sees the reality of life after living in a past-tense dream world where he tries to tell Sophia Lawrence of the brave (although untrue) death of her love, James Digby. Charlie returns to England from France with smugglers and decides to go to London to deliver James Digby's last message to Sophia Lawrence. At the Lawrence home, he finds that Sophia's father, a general, is to be hanged for misleading his men in battle. Charlie falls in love with Sophia and sees her life waning; she envelopes him with her melancholy. Charlie hears Lawrence blame his son-in-law, Maddox, whom he believes to be dead, for his predicament but whom Charlie knows to be alive because he saved him from drowning. Charlie rushes to warn Maddox that the general is coming to kill him. Maddox escapes and in the ensuing snarl, Charlie realizes that Sophia and her father feed on death and that he is lucky to escape them. The Lawrence's maid, Charity, suggests that she accompany Charlie to meet the family from which he had once run.

The second novel naming a profession is **The Confidence Man**. The first and fourth parts present the omniscient point of view, while Hans tells his first-person view in the second and third parts. In this novel, fourteen-year-old Hans Ruppert sees his sister's suitor's head rolling in the street. Catholics in this German town think Protestants have murdered him, and they ruin their shops. A black hussar stranger decides to help the Protestants by offering them places on his land in the New World. When the group gathers for the journey, 416 people from fifty-one families arrive. The group eventually reaches London, destitute, and the hussar disappears. Hans dreams that he is dead, but his ghost keeps reappearing telling him how to rouse the group to act. A London barmaid, Geneva Brown, sees them and begins to bring food. Although she cannot speak German, she and Hans fall in love. One day, she and Hans perform songs and dances in front of a tavern where they meet a man who speaks German. Hans tells of the group's misery as it camps in a nearby church yard, and the man brings his German congregation to help them. The present queen, a German princess from Mecklenberg, evidently convinces the king to give the group passage to South Carolina in the New World around 1765. Geneva Brown decides to accompany Hans. In the New World, after the group resettles, Hans sees the hussar in Charles Town, who has taken a new identity. He admits to Hans that in Germany, Hans's eyes, with their look of complete confidence in him, had kept him with the group longer than he had planned to stay. The coincidence of Hans encountering the hussar in South Carolina mars the plausibility of this plot, but the only way that Hans can feel personally vindicated for being abandoned and having his trust betrayed is with such a meeting.

Two final novels involve actors. **Devil-in-the-Fog** introduces fourteen-year-old George Treet on the day his conjurer father tells him that he is not really his son. Mr. Treet says that George's parents are the wealthy Dexters. At his new home, George finds that Sir John Dexter, his father, is recovering from a gunshot wound inflicted by his brother, Richard. Thinking that Richard is a villain, George tries to decide what to do when Richard summons him from the woods near the house and asks his help for a reconciliation with Sir John. A family employee confuses George further by telling him that the villain is Mr. Treet, not Sir John or Richard. When Sir John tries to kill George on a hunt and someone else kills Sir John, the truth appears that George is actually a Treet. Sir John did not want Richard to inherit the family fortune, and when his fourth male heir died, Sir John buried him quietly and told his lawyer to purchase an heir. Mr. Treet needed the money, and his bargain helped his family. All he had to do was have George pretend to be a Dexter whenever the Stranger, who visited Mr. Treet twice yearly, arrived to tell him the moment had come. Sir John, however, could not cope with George's acting abilities and refused to see him falsely carry the Dexter name. Lady Dexter, however, likes George and from her new London home helps the Treet family.

The first sentence of **The Sound of Coaches** begins like a fairy tale and ends in parody: "once upon a winter's night when the wind blew its guts out." The novel, divided into three parts, traces Sam Chichester's growth from a baby whose mother dies in an inn at his birth into a young actor. "Shouldered" by the coachman, Chichester, who carried his mother to the Red Lion in Dorking, the Chichesters take care of Sam throughout his childhood. Sam's favorite memento of his mother is a pistol, with which he sleeps each night. He becomes an excellent coachman but wrecks The "Flying Cradle" on one of his first journeys alone. He has to leave home because his actions distress his foster father, who has recently been paralyzed from the waist down when a man shot -him for not letting him ride in an already loaded coach. Since Covent Garden had been the intended destination of his mother, Sam goes to London and begins frequenting a tavern where Covent Garden actors meet. An old actor, Dan Coventry, apprentices Sam for thirty pounds, which Dan plans to spend rather than teach Sam to act. On the road, Coventry looks through Sam's possessions trying to find more money and sees a pistol that matches another that he had once used as a stage prop. When Sam discovers the match, he realizes that Coventry is his real father. Having dreamed of a gallant father, he is very disappointed with his heritage. The two continue to act in the troupe, and Coventry begins revealing his acting secrets to Sam. They go to Dorking, and when Sam's surrogate father sees Coventry, he recognizes Coventry as the man who shot him. Coventry leaves because he had not intended to hurt the elder Chichester; his frustration at being unable to rapidly reach Dorking had led him to fire the pistol. Jenny, Sam's London love, follows Sam to Dorking where they marry and produce another Chichester. The novel's last chapter begins as does the first with a young girl aboard a coach hoarding a black chest, but this time, instead of the beginning bringing an end, the end brings a beginning.

STYLE AND THEMES

Leon Garfield reveals his mastery of plot by developing the complex stories with paradox and irony, each utilizing mystery. Some of the novels rely too much on a central coincidence to further the plot, but Garfield's realistic action generally overcomes this flaw. In all the novels, characters dream. Their subconscious and unconscious lives are integrated with the conscious to make them cohesive characters, complex and changing. Garfield's language reveals appropriate dialogue and accurate dialect. He uses unusual personifications such as "Thursday's dawn was grey of face" *(Black Jack)* and a "shocked mackerel saying 'oh' " *(The Confidence Man)*. Garfield's similes enhance his vivid descriptions. In *Footsteps,* the parson "put his hand on my shoulder as if he were going to hit me and was steadying me while he took aim." In *The Night of the*

Comet, the music teacher "in his long green coat . . . looked like a tottery caterpillar waving at the edge of a leaf." "Mrs. Bunnion slept like a stately ship, rising and falling at anchor" in *The Strange Affair of Adelaide Harris.* The street in *The Confidence Man* lies "with bends as sharp as a pauper's elbow." In the same novel, a new palace is "like an enormous gilded blister with a liberal discharge of marble stairways, marble urns, and marble children." In *Jack Holborn,* the alliteration hisses through the river "endlessly slit by the sinful smile of crocodiles." Finally, in *Jack Holborn,* Garfield's carefully understated humor surfaces in describing "a seedy attorney who'd sold his soul so often that he was like a spiritual circulating library." Garfield's stories, set in the eighteenth century, grip readers with their mysteries and keep them reading as the complex plots develop.

GARIBALDI, GIUSEPPE (1807–1882). He was an Italian military leader fighting for the unification of Italy along with *Mazzini. He organized an expedition of 1,000 men whom he called the Redshirts and attacked Sicily in 1860, after which he crossed to the Italian mainland and captured Naples. The union of the Two Sicilies with Sardinia and the proclamation of Victor Emmanuel as king of Italy led to his retirement. Other expeditions against Rome failed. See *Follow My Black Plume* and *A Thousand for Sicily* by Geoffrey *Trease, and *Nicholas Carey* by Ronald *Welch.

GARRETT MCKAY. Eleven, American protagonist in *The Stones. See* Hickman, Janet.

GARRICK, DAVID (1717–1779). As one of the greatest actors in the history of the English stage, he made his reputation as Richard III. He introduced a revolutionary style of acting, natural and interpretative. Samuel *Johnson was his teacher and friend while he continued to act in other *Shakespeare productions, managed the Drury Lane Theater, and wrote twenty plays. *See* Beatty, John and Patricia, *The Royal Dirk.*

THE GATES OF PARADISE. *See* Carter, Peter.

A GATHERING OF DAYS. *See* Blos, Joan.

GAUL. In antiquity, Gaul was the name of the area in Europe south and west of the Rhine, west of the Alps, and north of the Pyrenees, approximately the area of modern France and Belgium. See *The Conquered* by Naomi *Mitchison and *The Silver Branch* by Rosemary *Sutcliff.

THE GAUNTLET. *See* Welch, Ronald.

GEIST. Fourteen, German male protagonist in *What Happened in Hamelin. See* Skurzynski, Gloria.

GEMPEI WARS. From 1180 to 1185, the momentous power struggle between the Japanese clans of Taira (Heike) and Minamoto (Genji) houses inspired many legends. The Minamoto forces decisively defeated the Taira clan at the sea battle of Dannoura. *See* Paterson, Katherine, *Of Nightingales that Weep*.

GENGHIS KHAN [TEMUJIN] (c. 1162–1227). After becoming the leader of a destitute Mongolian clan, he defeated other clan leaders and was proclaimed Genghis Khan, or universal ruler of all the Mongols, in 1206. He established his capital in Karakorum. He personally conquered Peking while his generals subdued what is now Iran, Iraq, and part of Russia. His successor was his son Ogodei; he had another son, Chagatai. *See* Baumann, Hans, *Sons of the Steppe*.

GENJI. See *Gempei Wars.

GEOFFREY AND ALYS DE BEAUREGARD. Young French protagonists in *Perilous Pilgrimage*. *See* Treece, Henry.

GEORGE III OF ENGLAND (1738–1820). He became king of England in 1760, and the policies he supported helped England lose the American colonies. He also blocked attempts to emancipate the Roman Catholics. Later in his life, he lost his mental capabilities, and his son, who later became George IV, acted as his regent. See *At the Seven Stars* by John and Patricia *Beatty and *Sarah Bishop* by Scott *O'Dell.

GEORGE TREET. Fourteen, English protagonist in *Devil-in-the-Fog*. *See* Garfield, Leon.

GETTYSBURG. This town in Pennsylvania was the site of the battle considered to be the turning point of the *American Civil War. It began on July 1, 1863, and lasted three days. Union losses were approximately 23,000; Confederate losses were over 20,000. General George Meade stopped the Condfederates from pushing farther north in this decisive battle. *See* Hickman, Janet, *Zoar Blue*.

THE GHOSTS OF GLENCOE. *See* Hunter, Mollie.

A GIRL CALLED BOY. *See* Hurmence, Belinda.

GLOBE THEATER. This summer playhouse in Bankside, on the south side of the Thames, housed the players who presented works of William *Shakespeare from 1599 until 1613. See *Holdfast* and *Master Rosalind* by John and Patricia *Beatty; *The Wonderful Winter* by Marchette *Chute; and *Cue for Treason* by Geoffrey *Trease.

GODWIN, HAROLD. *See* *Harold II of England.

GOEBBELS, JOSEPH (1897–1945). He led the *Nazi party in Berlin in 1926 and was the master of modern propaganda, which kept the Germans supporting the war effort during World War II. Hitler named him as his successor, but he committed suicide in Hitler's bunker in Berlin. *See* Sommerfelt, Aimée, *Miriam*.

THE GOLDEN GOBLET. *See* McGraw, Eloise.

GOOD NIGHT, MISTER TOM. *See* Magorian, Michelle, *Good Night, Mr. Tom*.

GOOD NIGHT, MR. TOM. *See* Magorian, Michelle.

GRANADA. A city in southern Spain, it houses the most celebrated of all the monuments left by the Moors, the Alhambra. See *Columbus Sails* by C. Walter *Hodges and *The Red Towers of Granada* by Geoffrey *Trease.

GRANT, ULYSSES (1822–1885). The eighteenth president of the United States, Grant served in the *American Civil War where he broke *Confederate control of Mississippi. He took command of all the Union armies and heard *Lee's surrender at Appomattox Court House. *See* Clapp, Patricia, *The Tamarack Tree*.

THE GREAT DESERT RACE. *See* Baker, Betty.

GREAT FIRE OF LONDON. In 1666, the great fire began on September 2 in a wooden house on Pudding Lane and burned for three days. It consumed 13,200 houses, St. Paul's Church, eighty-seven parish churches, six chapels, the guildhall, the royal exchange, the customhouse, many hospitals and libraries, fifty-two companies' halls, three of the city's gates, four stone bridges, and the prisons of *Newgate, the Fleet, and the Poultry and Wood street compters. Six persons died. This fire is credited with the founding of fire insurance. See *Beyond the Weir Bridge* and *Through the Fire* by Hester *Burton, and *Master Cornhill* by Eloise *McGraw.

THE GREAT HOUSE. *See* Harnett, Cynthia.

GREENE, BETTE (1934–). American.
BIBLIOGRAPHY AND BACKGROUND
Morning Is a Long Time Coming. New York: Dial, 1978; London: Hamish Hamilton, 1978. *Summer of My German Soldier*. New York: Dial, 1973; London: Hamish Hamilton, 1974.

Among Bette Greene's awards are National Book Award finalist for *Summer of My German Soldier* in 1974. Although neither of her historical novels is supposedly autobiographical, a childhood in Arkansas with Jewish merchant parents presents a basis for their plot development.

WORKS

The Arkansas summer of 1944 bores Patricia Bergen, twelve, because no one seems to need her and the only person who loves her is Ruth, the Negro maid, in **Summer of My German Soldier**. In her father's store, Patty meets Anton Reiker, a German prisoner of war, and delights in his politeness, as well as his correct English learned from a British mother and a father who attended school in England. Anton subsequently escapes from the prisoner-of-war camp. Patty hides him in the garage attic, but he jeopardizes his freedom when he almost runs outside to protect Patty when her father beats her for talking to a poor boy in the neighborhood. Ruth sees him, understands why Patty has taken extra food, and when they talk, supports Anton's suggestion that he leave. Anton gives Patty a family ring, which she treasures. She cannot help showing it to her father's clerk, who tells an FBI (Federal Bureau of Investigation) agent. When he questions Patty, she admits nothing. After another FBI agent shoots and kills Anton, he finds him wearing Patty's father's shirt. The FBI accuses her. After her trial, she attends reform school for several months. In reform school, Patty dreams of going to Göttingen to meet Mrs. Reiker and talk to her about Anton. Only Ruth comes to visit her. Although Patty is not an orphan, her parents give her neither love nor support. Ruth and Anton make her feel special, so she wants to help them. The first-person point of view allows the reader to sympathize with Patty. Her strong ethical values, received from Ruth, distance her from her parents' material values.

The Patricia Bergen accused of being a *Nazi lover in *Summer of My German Soldier* resurfaces in **Morning Is a Long Time Coming**. Patty continues her first-person account at age eighteen after graduating from high school. In 1950, her grandparents give her money to go to a college where she can meet pleasant Jewish boys, but Patty decides to use the money to go to Paris. Before she leaves, she returns to talk to Ruth, whom she has avoided for several years. She realizes again that Ruth is the one person who understands her. Patty sails on the same ship with novelist Katherine Anne Porter and hears her read poetry. She also experiences a shipboard romance, surprised that someone likes her. In Paris, she meets Roger, a Frenchman who had lived much of his life in Atlanta. They begin an affair. When Patty's unsuspected peptic ulcer explodes, her weeks spent lying in the hospital thinking leave her convinced that she must visit Anton's family in Germany. Once there, she is dismayed to find that his mother has died and that this part of her life will have no satisfactory resolution. She returns to Roger and Paris, accepting that what one dreams of or hopes for does not always materialize.

STYLE AND THEMES

Greene tells her stories in a loosely constructed style that emphasizes the humor rather than the underlying serious themes. The second novel seems less realistic than the first, and it also ends somewhat indeterminately.

GUIDO. Twelve, Italian orphan protagonist in *The Little Fishes*. *See* Haugaard, Erik.

GUILLOTIN, JOSEPH (1738–1814). Although a physician, during the *French Revolution, he defended capital punishment and suggested the use of the beheading machine which was later named after him. *See* Trease, Geoffrey, *Victory at Valmy*.

GUNPOWDER PLOT. *See* Guy *Fawkes.

GUTHORM [GUTHRUM] (d. 890). He led a large Danish invasion of *Anglo- *Saxon England in 878, but *Alfred defeated him and required that he adopt Christianity. Afterward, he reigned peacefully. See *The Marsh King* and *The Namesake* by C. Walter *Hodges and *Escape to King Alfred* by Geoffrey *Trease.

GUY CAMERON. Fifteen, American, grandson of Bruce Cameron in *The Cow Neck Rebels*, protagonist of *So Ends This Day*. *See* Forman, James.

_H_

HADDER MACCOLL. Fourteen, Scottish protagonist in _Hadder MacColl_. _See_ Calvert, Patricia.

HADDER MACCOLL. _See_ Calvert, Patricia.

HADRIAN (76–138). He became Roman emperor in 117 at the death of his cousin *Trajan who had designated him as his successor. He established the Euphrates River as the eastern boundary of the *Roman Empire and traveled throughout all parts of the empire, including Britain in 122. There he ordered the construction of Hadrian's Wall, a large physical barrier crossing Britain from the North Sea to the Irish Sea on the northern border, just north of the comtemporary city of Carlisle. On another tour he visited Athens and became an avid promoter of the Hellenic culture. From 132 to 135, he suppressed a revolt of the Jews. See _The Eagle of the Ninth_ by Rosemary *Sutcliff and _Message to Hadrian_ by Geoffrey *Trease.

HAIDA. This Indian tribe moved to southern Alaska in the eighteenth century. In 1841, 9,000 Haida were reported in census; forty years later, the number had shrunk to 1,700. The tribe, with succession through maternal lineage, was divided into two groups, the Ravens and the Eagles, with marriage between them forbidden. The culture produced unique social organization with carefully executed ceremony. Art has kept the tribe extant; woodworking on boxes and canoes as well as the integration of ''black slate'' into wood on totem poles has brought them much acclaim. See _The Ravens' Cry_ and _Forbidden Frontier_ by Christie *Harris.

HAIL COLUMBIA. _See_ Beatty, Patricia.

HAKON. Viking protagonist in _Hakon of Rogen's Saga_ and character in _A Slave's Tale_. _See_ Haugaard, Erik.

HAKON OF ROGEN'S SAGA. See Haugaard, Erik.

HALLIE LEE BAKER. Orphan of thirteen, American, protagonist of *That's One Ornery Orphan. See* Beatty, Patricia.

HALLOWMAS. *See* *All Saint's Day.

HAMILTON, ALEXANDER (1755–1804). Among his important positions in the newly formed U.S. government, he was a member of the Continental Congresses and the first secretary of the treasury (1789–95). He helped the public credit reach a sound basis, but his opposition to governing policies led to the creation of political parties, with himself emerging as head of the Federalist party. He helped defeat Aaron Burr for president, and Burr eventually mortally wounded him in a duel. *See* Collier, Christopher and James, *Jump Ship to Freedom.*

HANCOCK, JOHN (1737–1793). He was a member of the Continental Congresses from Massachusetts and served as its president from 1775 to 1777. He became the first signer of the Declaration of Independence and the first governor of Massachusetts in 1780. See *Johnny Tremain* by Esther *Forbes and *John Treegate's Musket* by Leonard *Wibberley.

HANNAH. Young Quaker protagonist of America in *Thee, Hannah! See* de Angeli, Marguerite.

HANNALEE REED. Twelve, American southern protagonist in *Turn Homeward, Hannalee. See* Beatty, Patricia.

HANNE HOYGARD. Sixteen, Norwegian, protagonist of *Miriam. See* Sommerfelt, Aimée.

HANNIBAL (247–183 B.C.). After training under his father's command in Spain, where he learned to hate Rome, and then under his brother-in-law before his assassination, he became the chief of the Carthaginian army in 221 B.C. He began the Second Punic War by capturing the Roman city of *Saguntum in Spain in 218. He crossed the Alps, defeating various Gallic and Celtic tribes, and carried the war into Italy. After spending many years trying to conquer Rome, he tried to subdue North Africa. After he was defeated, the Romans accused him of breaking the peace, and when he realized he could no longer escape, he committed suicide. *See* Baumann, Hans, *I Marched with Hannibal.*

HANOVER. This electoral house began in Germany and became a royal family of England when George I gained the English crown in 1714. Other rulers in this line were *George II, III, IV, William IV and *Victoria. See *At the Seven Stars* by John and Patricia *Beatty and *The 13th Member* by Mollie *Hunter.

HANS AMANN. Fifteen, German, protagonist of *Horses of Anger*. See Forman, James.

HANS RUPPERT. Fourteen, German who goes to England and the United States as the protagonist of *The Confidence Man*. See Garfield, Leon.

HANS AND SOPHIE SCHOLL. Hans at twenty-four and Sophie at twenty-one, German protagonists in *Ceremony of Innocence*. See Forman, James.

HANSEATIC LEAGUE. This association of north German towns and groups of German merchants abroad was formed to defend their trading interests. It lasted from the late thirteenth until the end of the fifteenth century, with England according it many privileges. See Trease, Geoffrey, *The Secret Fiord*.

THE HAPPIEST ENDING. See Uchida, Yoshiko.

HARALD. Viking, adult protagonist of *Viking's Dawn*, *The Road to Miklagard*, and *Viking's Sunset*. See Treece, Henry.

HARALD HARDRADA. Viking, adult protagonist in *Swords from the North*, *Man with a Sword*, and *The Last Viking*. See Treece, Henry.

HARALD [HAROLD] HARDRADA (1015–1066). In 1033, he left his Norwegian home to visit the courts of Novgorod, Kiev, and Constantinople (*Istanbul) where he had many adventures in the service of the Byzantine emperor Michael IV. He returned to Russia in 1044 and to Norway in 1045 where he became co-ruler with Magnus I Olafsson and then sole king as Harold III of Norway when Magnus died. He fought the Danes from 1047 to 1062, and when Tostig, the brother of the English king, *Harold II, asked his help in conquering England, he arrived in 1066 but met death at the Battle of Stamford Bridge near *York. See *Swords from the North, Man with a Sword*, and *The Last Viking* by Henry *Treece.

HARNETT, CYNTHIA (1893–1981). British.

BIBLIOGRAPHY AND BACKGROUND

Caxton's Challenge. Cleveland, Ohio: World, 1960; as *The Load of Unicorn*. London: Methuen, 1959. *The Great House*. Minneapolis, Minn.: Lerner, 1984; London: Methuen, 1949; Cleveland, Ohio: World, 1968. *The Merchant's Mark*. Minneapolis, Minn.: Lerner, 1984; as *The Wool-Pack*. London: Methuen, 1951; as *Nicholas and the Wool-Pack*. New York: Putnam, 1953. *The Sign of the Green Falcon*. Minneapolis, Minn.: Lerner, 1985; as *Ring Out the Bow Bells*. London: Methuen, 1953; as *The Drawbridge Gate*. New York: Putnam, 1954. *Stars of Fortune*. Minneapolis, Minn.: Lerner, 1984; London: Methuen, 1956. *The Writing on the Hearth*. Minneapolis, Minn.: Lerner, 1984; New York: Viking, 1973; London: Methuen, 1971.

Cynthia Harnett's many awards include a Carnegie Medal for *The Wool-Pack* in 1951 and a Carnegie citation for *The Load of Unicorn* in 1959. As an artist interested in archaeology but bored by history in school, Harnett began writing novels full of interesting details about life in the past. She said about her influences, ''I had two much older brothers, and when one died the other turned for companionship to his little sister, and so I tagged along everywhere with him, shared all his interests until he married. It was Philip who told me about archaeology, and how, if you learn to recognize coats of arms, you can spot them at unlikely places and put together all sorts of clues about the families.'' In an essay she commented that writing a historical novel is like constructing a puzzle, piece by piece. She illustrates her books with unfamiliar items, which add a visual touch to the work.

WORKS

After reading the four novels Harnett sets in the fifteenth century, one has a sense of life for the gentry from the reign of *Henry V to that of *Henry VII. The earliest date is 1415 in **The Sign of the Green Falcon** when Henry V sits on the throne and Dick Whittington is mayor of London. In the novel, the point of view switches among Nan Sherwood, who must stay home and learn to sew in order to get a husband; her brother Dickon, recently apprenticed to the mercier (cloth merchant) mayor Dick Whittington; and the older brother, Adam, who wants to be an apothecary but must prepare to inherit the family grocer business. Since their parents are dead, they live near the City with their grandfather, where they can hear the particular sound of each church bell as it rings. Their grandfather partially placates Adam by giving him a corner of the huge grocer warehouse in which to collect spices and herbs. One day an alchemist, Salomon Gross, visits Adam and convinces him that his search for an elixir recipe to help humans live longer is close to fruition. He invites Adam to meet with him at the Green Falcon, a tavern in the undesirable Southwark area. After the favorite summer holiday, St. John's Day, Dick faces rites of new apprentices wanting to join the mercer apprentice club. His main adversary, a boy he happened to fight the day before being unexpectedly apprenticed, charges him to go to the Tower Bridge and retrieve the hanging head of a traitor. If he fails, the two will fight with clubs, a custom usually between rival apprentice gangs such as clothiers and grocers rather than within one group. Dickon's careful plans go awry when the head drops in the river and awakens the guard on the bridge. The king's messenger's unanticipated arrival allows Dickon to disappear undetected. On another night, he reaches the city gate too late to return to his lodging and decides to hide in a nearby church where he, like anyone else, will have sanctuary from the law. Two watchmen find him on the church porch near a seditious sign and blame him for posting it. Dickon, however, actually saw men known as *Lollards attach the paper. Whittington believes Dickon's convoluted story because he knows that some of his apprentices are Lollards and that they meet at the Green Falcon. Whittington understands that they were going to use the severed head as a relic with which to incite trouble. Then the family discovers that Gross has been using the unsuspecting Adam as a front for the group, but Adam's skill in medicine proved while ministering to soldiers in France during their victory at Agincourt absolves him. The novel not only reveals interesting aspects of fifteenth-century London but is also an engaging mystery.

The Writing on the Hearth, set in 1439, shows Stephen's concerns ten years after the siege of Orléans against Jeanne d'Arc where his father died defending the earl of Suffolk. His death gained for his family the earl's lifetime protection. After his mother dies, Stephen's scholarly skills enable him to become a scribe in the earl's home, but he still returns to see his friend, old Meg, a woman whom several suspect of witchcraft. On one visit, he meets Roger Bolingbroke, and because of a pentangle etched in the hearth dust, Stephen begins to think that Meg might be guilty as accused. But Gilles the Bowman reminds Stephen that Meg healed his sister, Lys, who was wounded while trying to escape from a forced marriage arranged by their stepfather. Gilles, himself a priest in hiding, posits that good goes deeper than evil. Stephen accompanies the earl to London, where he meets the young mercer apprentice William *Caxton and where the other household scribe dies quickly from *plague caught in forbidden Southwark. When *Henry VI subsequently accuses Bolingbroke of witchcraft, the earl requests that Meg be questioned. Stephen promises to retrieve her. On the way, he decides instead to warn her, but upon arrival at her home, he finds nothing; her home has disappeared into a sinkhole. When Stephen tells the earl and his wife all the things that have happened to him and to his sister since their parents' deaths, they fulfill his life's desire by sending him to Oxford, and they permit Lys to remain in the convent. Stephen learns that one must look beneath appearances before making judgments.

By 1482 in **Caxton's Challenge**, William Caxton has brought the printing press from Germany to London. The protagonist, Bendy, has an older brother, Matthew, who hires scribes to copy books while someone reads them aloud. Bendy overhears Matthew mention *Madelena,* a ship; a load of Unicorn; and ''mucking''; from this, Bendy deduces that Matthew has bought a load of Unicorn a high-quality paper watermarked with the image of a unicorn, to keep someone with a printing press from getting the paper because the press will ruin his business. When Caxton comes to the shop trying to buy Unicorn paper, Bendy realizes that Caxton is the victim. Bendy and one of his friends arrange for Caxton to get the paper, and Caxton takes Bendy as an apprentice. Bendy gives Caxton his beloved partial manuscript of Malory's King Arthur tales and undergoes unexpected experiences trying to locate the remainder for printing. Finally Matthew admits his guilt when his retired father confronts him with the fact that by paying people not to deliver the paper, Matthew has been inadvertently supporting the red rose plan to bring Henry *Tudor from Brittany while Edward IV reigns. Being hanged for treason is much less attractive than letting Caxton have paper. The intrigue, coupled with the threat of the printing press to the hand-copying business, makes this story most interesting.

The Merchant's Mark, set in 1493, shifts to the Cotswold area of England where Nicholas Fetterlock learns his father's wool merchant trade. When the wealthy Lombards from Florence, the money lenders of Europe, come to visit, Nicholas discovers that his father's wool packer, Leach, makes secret deals with them. Instead of sending only the prime wool expected of the Fetterlock name, Leach skims the wool so that bad bags appear on the European market. The process of discovery involves intelligent investigation by Nicholas and Cecily, the eleven-year-old to whom he is betrothed. The sheepherder's son Hal finds Leach's barn key, and inside his barn, they locate the missing wool. Cecily realizes that they can hide feathers in the wool Leach has taken so that when the wool regulators open the bags at the market, they can see that the Fetterlocks are not to blame for the poor quality. When all the pieces of the sham are revealed, the Fetterlocks retain their good name in the international wool market.

In **Stars of Fortune**, Harnett presents a sixteenth-century scenario. Inadvertently Francis Washington, an ancestor of George, saves the princess *Elizabeth (later Elizabeth I) from treason. Francis discovers that his brothers have become involved in a plot to rescue the princess from Woodstock where the Catholic queen *Mary has her kept. Elizabeth, who is intrigued with Doctor Dee's readings of the stars, requests his help with her reading. He predicts that she will become queen, and Francis's brothers and others think that they can hasten her ascension by engineering her escape from England in the company of her uncle, Sir William Parr. Francis tells his friend, Tom, Sir William's nephew, about the plan, and Sir William, sensing intrigue, tortures Tom to find out what he knows. When Tom reveals that the plan calls for Sir William to take Elizabeth with him, Sir William departs immediately. An interesting subplot involves priests, who, to survive, had to become outlaws during *Henry VIII's annihilation of Catholics. Although not as suspenseful as the other stories, this one explores exciting sixteenth-century possibilities.

The journey and subsequent events in **The Great House** occur in 1690. Barbara and Geoffrey's father, an architect, receives a commission to build a large house outside London. Since his wife has recently died of smallpox, he takes the children with him. On the departure day, the treat of morning coffee delights the children, as does the first leg of the journey, by river to Westminster. The ensuing ride through Houndslow Heath where highwaymen patrol unnerves all of them. For the remainder of the journey, they travel on various qualities of highway, totally dependent on the responsibility each parish feels toward road maintenance. When they arrive, the lord employing their father has had to leave unexpectedly, so the father returns to London, and the children stay with the innkeeper's wife. One of the highlights of the stay is a visit from the chapman with his wares, welcomed since the village has no commerce. Geoffrey, who wants to go to Oxford to learn architecture, as did his idol, the great Sir Christopher *Wren, decides that the new house should not replace the old one but be built overlooking the beautiful river view. He and Barbara use his father's plans, left in his care, to block the floor layout of the new house. Barbara fills between the pegs with rocks. Eventually Sir Humphrey's daughter, Elizabeth, becomes friends with Barbara. Barbara secretly tells Elizabeth the plan, and Elizabeth, who keeps no secrets, tells her grandmother, Lady Ainsley. When Sir Humphrey returns with their father, he realizes the sense of the plan and offers to send Geoffrey to Oxford as his pay for the idea while Barbara arranges to live with Elizabeth.

STYLE AND THEMES

One way that Harnett develops plot is by letting young people solve mysteries or have original ideas without threatening the integrity of adults. Because of their different perspectives and their chances to roam in unusual places, the children can sometimes find information unavailable to the adults. This important thematic aspect plus the lively style and engrossing stories make Harnett's novels enlightening reading.

HAROLD II OF ENGLAND (1022–1066). After serving as chief minister of his brother-in-law, Edward the Confessor, he subjugated Wales and secured his own election as king at Edward's death in 1066. He defeated his brother Tostig and *Harald Hardrada at Stamford Bridge (September 25), but *William, duke of Normandy, killed him in the Battle of Hastings (Senlac) on October 14. See *Man with a Sword* and *The Last Viking* by Henry *Treece.

HARRIS, CHRISTIE (1907–   ). Canadian.

BIBLIOGRAPHY AND BACKGROUND

Cariboo Trail. New York and Toronto: Longman, 1957. *Forbidden Frontier*. Illustrated by E. Carey Kenney. New York: Atheneum, 1968; Toronto: McClelland and Stewart, 1968. *Raven's Cry*. Illustrated by Bill Reid. New York: Atheneum, 1965; Toronto: McClelland and Stewart, 1965. *West with the White Chiefs*. Illustrated by Walter Fero. New York: Atheneum, 1965.

Christie Harris has won many awards, including the Canadian Book of the Year in 1967 and 1977, the Pacific Northwest Booksellers Award in 1967, and in 1981, the Canada Council Children's Literature Prize, as well as the Order of Canada. As a small child, Harris lived on a homestead in the central interior of British Columbia. About this experience, she says, "Vivid memories of this time increased my interest in the area and in pioneering generally. My pioneer families in [*Cariboo Trail* and *Forbidden Frontier*] are Irish, like my own family [which] came to the West Coast in 1908." When married, she moved to the Northwest Coast, where she received a commission to write about the native cultures. She usually collects information about a certain time and place for several years. She notes, "I like to spend the entire summer 'on location,' then write the book." She adds, "I write in the mornings, all morning. I usually do one big revision, then quite often, a final polishing rewrite; and I enjoy this."

WORKS

In **Cariboo Trail**, Maeve Hawthorne, twelve, and her family decide to leave Minnesota because of the warring *Sioux and travel west in Canada toward gold in 1862. The men in the group at first are hostile to the two women, but smelling Mrs. Hawthorne's bread causes them to decide that the women will bring good luck. Various adventures occur on the trail, and many of them involve the boy Ian, who befriends Maeve at the beginning of the journey. One of the highlights to Maeve is viewing the Rocky Mountains. When they reach the end of their long trip, they receive news that Sioux have murdered their neighbors who remained in Minnesota. In the novel, the superficial characterization creates unrealistic adult-child relationships, and the omniscient point of view does not reveal conflicts that could deepen the story. That people went to Canada to resettle because of the Sioux, however, lends interest.

During the same time as *Cariboo Trail,* another difficult journey occurs in **West with the White Chiefs**. Louis Battenotte, known as the "Assiniboine" with the bad temper, has been charged with killing a troublesome half-breed, and as of 1863, the *Hudson's Bay Company at Fort Pitt will no longer hire him as an Indian guide. Louis, his son, helps his father get work. Since his father is the best guide in the area, two British nobles, Lord Milton and Dr. Cheadle, and one Irish scholar, O'Byrne, hire him to lead them across the Rockies. He guides them through incredibly rough terrain, though the disgustingly lazy and pompous O'Byrne questions every decision. Louis understands, however, that the calmness of both his mother and Dr. Cheadle helps conquer many of the wilderness difficulties. When they reach Kamloops, Dr. Cheadle takes young Louis into Victoria so that he can see that all white men do not have revolting personalities like O'Byrne. The trip expands Louis's horizons, but returning home by a safer route pleases him more. In the prologue, Harris describes in three short vignettes the different parties who will meet at Fort Pitt, allowing the reader to expect the various behaviors of those men who hire Assiniboine.

Since **Raven's Cry** begins in the year 1775 and ends around 1894, the protagonist is not an individual but an Indian tribe, the *Haida, who live on the southern coast of Alaska. During the eighteenth century, traders buy sea otter skins from the Haida for shirts or trinkets, sell the skins to the Chinese for hundreds of dollars, and return with tea and silks to sell to still other buyers. The traders become exceedingly rich from the Haida skins but treat the Haida like savages. Harris shows that these Indians, with their strong sense of ritual and decorum, are artists, very proud of their heritage and their accomplishments. As the traders continue to belittle the Haida, hostile incidents occur. One Haida takes a shirt in retribution for earlier wrongs, and a trader captain reacts by killing several men in the tribe. When the captain returns, Haida board his ship to capture him, but his sailors kill one hundred more of them. The Haida also encounter smallpox, consumption, and the vile treatment of additional traders during the mid-nineteenth-century gold rush. The Haida shame at these events leads them to be more receptive to white missionaries who understand none of the Haida spiritual life and unjustly accuse them of worshipping idols on their totem poles. In 1884, the chief, always called Edinsa, agrees to baptism, and ten years later when he dies, only 600 Haida remain. Museum interest in the beautiful art of the Haida saves the culture from extinction. Harris covers a lot of information in this history of the Haida, and the passage of many years within one sentence can sometimes confuse the reader, but she overcomes this difficulty surprisingly well.

Forbidden Frontier reveals both the white and the Indian reaction to settlement in the area around the Hudson's Bay Company's Fort Kamloops near the Fraser River during the mid-nineteenth century. In part I, Alison Stewart, half-Haida Indian and half-Scot, begins her story when nine and continues until she becomes sixteen. Her Haida mother, Djaada, teaches her to be proud so that she can return to the Haida tribal home and receive her tribal name with honor. When they finally visit the village, they find that liquor has permeated the dignity of the people, and the potlatch-naming ceremony no longer retains its esteem. (*Raven's Cry* reveals reasons for the Haida demise.) When Djaada returns to the fort, she decides to show that Indians can think for themselves and refuses a smallpox shot. She dies from the disease. The Scottish father of Alison's friend Ross deserts his Indian wife and children, returning to Scotland alone. When Ross tries to protect his half-breed dignity, he suffers, but Alison supports his decisions. In Part II of the book, during 1862, sixteen-year-old Megan Scully arrives with her family at the fort with others clamoring for the Cariboo gold. Having left Minnesota as the Sioux began murdering the whites, Megan views the Indians as savages. When she and Alison meet, Alison explains that the whites' refusal to fulfill treaties caused the waiting Sioux to starve. She thinks that the whites should have anticipated the Sioux retaliation. Megan accuses Ross of a murder he did not commit but realizes her mistake and takes action to correct it before he hangs. After the trauma, the two girls become friends, and their two loves, Ross and Connell, propose marriage to them. The twist on finding the real murderer makes the book more interesting, but long time lapses within Part I stultify the action. Since Part II covers less time, its tighter structure makes it more successful.

STYLE AND THEMES

Harris's figurative language highlights some of the important descriptions. In *Raven's Cry,* "the swells of the Pacific broke on the reefs in a fury at being stopped after thousands of miles of unbroken ocean." Her novels present information about events and societies unavailable in other historical fiction.

HARROD'S FORT. This spot was the first permanent white settlement in Kentucky. *See* Caudill, Rebecca, *Tree of Freedom.*

HARROW AND HARVEST. *See* Willard, Barbara.

HARRY CAREY. English, young adult protagonist in *The Hawk. See* Welch, Ronald.

HARRY MEDLEY. English protagonist who matures from eighteen to thirty in *The Eldest Son. See* Willard, Barbara.

HARTMAN, EVERT (1937–   ). Dutch.

BIBLIOGRAPHY AND BACKGROUND

War without Friends. Trans. Patricia Crampton. New York: Crown, 1982.

In 1980, Evert Hartman received the European Juvenile Book Award for Contemporary Literature. He is recognized internationally for his total contribution to children's literature. Hartman endured the German occupation of Holland during World War II, to him "a period of fear, tension, and hope." He says that the question behind *War without Friends* is "why do people do things like this and how can youth be indoctrinated by wrong beliefs and opinions (i.e. *Nazism)." On the same tack, he wonders "at what age young adults can be held responsible for their own actions and under what conditions and circumstances they can change." For writing his historical fiction, Hartman follows a process of idea, study, and writing. Time spent in libraries, archives, and reading historical documents precedes weekend and evening writing since Hartman teaches. Until he completes the manuscript, "ideas come and disappear."

WORK

In **War without Friends**, as the son of a Dutch Nazi, Arnold Westervoort at fourteen faces ostracism and bullying from his school peers between 1942 and 1945. When Piet Bergman, also a Nazi, comes to his school, the two protect each other, although Piet is unafraid and openly hostile. When peers call Arnold a spy, he understands that his father, who worries only about party advancement and attending meetings, is reporting various people in the community to Nazi authorities. When Arnold finds an underground newspaper in a bag belonging to Marloes, a girl he likes in his class, he takes it home and reads about concentration camps for the first time. His father posits that the camps are greatly needed for retraining. In the summer, men break into his father's office and steal ration coupons. Later Arnold trails Marloes and sees some of the coupons fall from her bag. He promises not to report her, but when her father is captured two weeks later, Arnold cannot convince her that he did not tell. Two boys call Arnold a bastard and knife him. In the hospital in bed next to him is Jeroen. Arnold eventually realizes that the nurses are protecting the completely healthy Jeroen from the Nazis. At Arnold's release, he tells Jeroen he will return to help him escape. Arnold steals his father's gun and takes it to Jeroen in a cookie box. As a reward, Arnold only wants Jeroen to tell Marloes that he helped. When the Allies arrive, Arnold's family rushes to board a train to Germany, but Arnold hides until the train leaves, a final denial of his father's beliefs.

STYLE AND THEME

Hartman's perspective of World War II discloses the universal pain that children have endured because their parents' values were severely distorted. Asserting independence from such parents remains a difficult but necessary task for children who want to retain their decency.

HATILSHAY. Native American protagonist in *One Was a Wooden Indian*. *See* Baker, Betty.

HATSHEPSUT (1503–1482 B.C.). After the death of her father, Thutmose I, she married her half-brother, Thutmose II, but after his death c. 1504, she became regent for his son, *Thutmose III, and proclaimed herself pharaoh. She promoted trade and building, renovating part of Karnak and building new temples. *See* McGraw, Eloise, *Mara, Daughter of the Nile*.

HAUGAARD, ERIK (1923–   ). Danish.

BIBLIOGRAPHY AND BACKGROUND

A Boy's Will. Boston: Houghton Mifflin, 1983. *Chase Me, Catch Nobody!* Boston: Houghton Mifflin, 1980; London: Granada, 1982. *Cromwell's Boy*. Boston: Houghton Mifflin, 1978. *Hakon of Rogen's Saga*. Illustrated by Leo and Diane Dillon. Boston: Houghton Mifflin, 1963; as *Hakon's Saga*. London: Faber, 1964. *Leif the Unlucky*. Boston: Houghton Mifflin, 1982. *The Little Fishes*. Illustrated by Milton Johnson. Boston: Houghton Mifflin, 1967; London: Gollancz, 1968. *A Messenger for Parliament*. Boston: Houghton Mifflin, 1976. *Orphans of the Wind*. Illustrated by Milton Johnson. Boston: Houghton Mifflin, 1966; London: Gollancz, 1967. *The Rider and His Horse*. Illustrated by Leo and Diane Dillon. Boston: Houghton Mifflin, 1968; London: Gollancz, 1969. *The Samurai's Tale*. Boston: Houghton Mifflin, 1984. *A Slave's Tale*. Illustrated by Leo and Diane Dillon. Boston: Houghton Mifflin, 1965; London: Gollancz, 1967. *The Untold Tale*. Illustrated by Leo and Diane Dillon. Boston: Houghton Mifflin, 1971.

Among the international awards that Erik Haugaard has received for his novels are the *Horn Book–Boston Globe* and *New York Herald Tribune* Festival for *The*

Little Fishes. Additionally, he has received the Jane Addams Award and the Danish Cultural Ministries Award. Although Danish, Haugaard attended Black Mountain College in North Carolina where several World War II refugee artists continued their work. A phrase from *The Samurai's Tale* best shows Haugaard's view of writing. The protagonist says, "the way a story is told is as important as the tale itself."

WORKS

For the backgrounds of his novels, Haugaard chooses conflicts that have changed the lives of groups of people: Masada, the story of Christ arriving in the North, the American Revolution and Civil War, the English Civil War, World War II, and others. He demonstrates through his protagonists that humans can survive and keep their integrity intact. Most of Haugaard's young teenaged protagonists (with two exceptions) communicate through the first person. Several tell their stories as flashbacks. A curious comparison among them is that most of the protagonists have succeeded in spite of having coped with ineffectual fathers; to compensate, they choose mentors whom they respect to help them find and keep their values. Almost all the protagonists dream; the dreams are sometimes a method of foreshadowing, or they may be a way of guiding the protagonist toward the answer to a crucial concern. Haugaard inserts comments throughout that explicitly state secondary themes in the novels. For example, in *A Messenger for Parliament,* he notes, "rumors are the steady diet of a soldier."

Chronologically, the first event about which Haugaard writes is the siege of *Masada in 73 A.D. in **The Rider and His Horse**. David, fourteen, is captured by bandits while returning with his wine merchant father from *Caesarea to *Tyre. He escapes when Roman soldiers kill the outlaws. Instead of returning home, David detours to see the destroyed city of Jerusalem. There he visits the wise Simon ben Judas, with whom he decides to stay and study. He befriends Rachel, a woman who also asks for Simon's help. She wants to rescue her brother's children from Masada, but her brother, the Masada leader, *Eleazar Ben Ya'ir, refuses to send them to her. David goes with Rachel to Masada and remains to become Eleazar's scribe. The Romans arrive, and their slaves start building an ingenious ramp. Eleazar recognizes their brilliant plan and comprehends that the only honorable way his people can avoid either slavery or crucifixion is to kill themselves. Before the mass suicide, Eleazar demands that David, Rachel, and the two children hide; their survival will enable them to relate the bravery of Masada's victims to others. The story offers an unusual view of this first-century conflict.

Three novels explore the strife of individual Viking groups fighting for power. Two occur in the tenth century, a third in the fifteenth. Hakon, the motherless son of Olaf the Lame in **Hakon of Rogen's Saga** endures first his father's indifference and then his father's remarriage to a bride taken against her father's will. The woman, Thora Magnusdaughter, treats Hakon as a friend, and she becomes his first love. Soon Thora's father sends someone to kill Olaf, and

Thora returns to her father's house. Hakon's uncle Sigurd declares himself the ruler of Rogen, usurps Hakon's rights, and attempts to kill him. Hakon's supporters plot against and overthrow Sigurd and his supporters. To capture the saga style and advance the abstract concepts of the story, Haugaard incorporates rhyming verses. Figurative language heightens the importance of nature in the Viking environment in personifications—the "winter sea has a deep voice"—and similes—"disasters lurking behind each day like hungry wolves behind trees."

In **A Slave's Tale**, the sequel to *Hakon of Rogen's Saga*, Helga flashes back to the events following Sigurd's ruin. She remembers that she was a slave until Hakon gained power and commanded her to wear her hair long like the free women on the island. She quickly realized then that Hakon's verbal declaration of her freedom would not suffice. To live free, she had to unshackle herself mentally. She begins by defying Hakon's dictum that she remain in Rogen while he and the men take Rark home. Rark, captured on a southern Viking raid, had helped defeat Sigurd. Hakon freed him and promised to sail him home. She stows away on the ship and arrives with them in Frankland around 997. Rark's twelve-year absence and presumed death had led his wife to remarry recently. Thus the new husband, Hugues, had taken ownership of Rark's land and family. The priests negotiate between Rark and Hugues, but Hugues ignores the agreement and murders Rark in his own home. His men simultaneously kill others from Rogen at their camp. Only the four who run from Hugues's hall after Rark's death live to return home. The priests of the new religion give them supplies and tell them how to escape Hugues. Helga recalls this difficult time after she has laid aside the old gods of revenge like Thor and become a believer in the man of peace, Jesus Christ.

Leif the Unlucky hypothesizes about one of the Viking outposts in Greenland about 1406. No reinforcements have arrived from Norway, and internal difficulties continue. Leif, fifteen, hereditary leader of the area, encounters Egil, fifteen, who decides that he wants to rule. Leif's father refuses to acknowledge the threats, remaining interested only in his silver, which ironically will buy nothing on the supply-starved island. Egil's sister, Bera, also refuses to assist her aggressive brother. Egil's followers destroy Leif's father's home and kill him and his servant. Leif and his father's servant's son, Odd, plot to avenge the killing, but the plan brings tragedy when Ingebord, Leif's intended, is inadvertently killed in the fight. When Leif chases Egil across fragile ice, Egil sinks and drowns. Bera refuses to rescue him. Leif's earlier dream indicates that he will marry the enigmatic Bera, best described by the comment: "some people are like the inland ice that covers most of Greenland, they are filled with deep clefts and secret caves." Even so, the future appears bleak for those remaining on the island.

The Samurai's Tale investigates discord in Japan around 1550. As an adult, Taro flashes back to his naming. An enemy who kills his mother and brothers decides that the four-year-old is brave and instead of killing him names him Taro. In this man's house, Taro becomes a friend of the cook. The cook teaches him about his inner spirit, and these values allow Taro to succeed. They also cause him to be horrified when he finds the day after he was commanded to accompany Lord Katusuyori to the temple that Katusuyori's brother, Yoshinobu, had committed hari-kari while Taro waited. Taro realizes that Katusuyori had probably murdered the brother because of his insurrection against the father. As Taro matures, his master, Lord Akiyama, gives him a new name, Murakami Harutomo, and a new distinction, samurai. As Taro serves his master in the palace, he notices a beautiful girl, Aki-hime. Using his servant, Yoichi, as the go-between, he begins sending her poetry. Only when her father is present in the castle does she answer. Their correspondence is interrupted when Taro has to search for reinforcements against Akiyama's enemy. He leaves in disguise but can gather no help from Akiyama's old friends. He sneaks back to the besieged castle to see Aki-hime, but in the village he views the hanging heads of all the castle's samurai. As he gazes at them, his servant, Yoichi, furtively summons him and leads him to Aki-hime, saved by cutting her hair and dressing in rags. They depart, but Taro intimates that his next task will be to avenge his master's death.

In 1600, Sweden and Denmark fought. Peter Gram reveals an episode of this war in **The Untold Tale**. A first-person prologue from an unidentified narrator leads into the omniscient story of Dag, an eight-year-old Dane who becomes involved in the war after his parents starve to death. As Dag walks to get help at the king's castle, Black Lars, a well-known poacher, rescues him. When Black Lars's wife senses Dag's fear, she tells him that Black Lars's act of bringing Dag home was an affirmation of responsibility for him, just as he would care for a lost puppy. Her father arrives at the hideout with the news that the king has offered a lot of silver for Black Lars's capture. Black Lars sends Dag to his cousin, Bodil, at the castle. On the way, Dag meets Peter Gram, a lute player who tells exceedingly exaggerated stories. The two go to Bodil and then follow the soldiers with her and her daughter, Kristen, to find the king. Their experiences along the way reveal Bodil's lust for money, Black Lars's life of being an unloved foundling, Peter Gram's weakness, and Dag's rapid understanding of the ambiguities in the adult world. When the Swedish prince, Gustavus Adolphus, unexpectedly arrives in Christianopolis and massacres those present, Dag dies while saving Kristen. In the epilogue, the narrator exposes himself as Peter Gram, who in 1648 as the king's steward remembers his nineteenth year when he had abandoned the children, irritated with Bodil for destroying his lute.

In two novels, the protagonist helps Oliver *Cromwell in the *English Civil War beginning in 1641. In **A Messenger for Parliament**, Oliver Cutter sits in Boston in 1685 remembering being eleven years old in England during the days of Cromwell. Separated from his drunkard philosopher father while they were trying to become attached to a regiment fighting for Parliament against *Charles II, Oliver joined a band of boys. He and one of the boys, Jack, go to London and work for a man who sends them to Oxford to sell his newspapers. Mr. Waldon thinks his printing press will be more powerful than the cannon, but unfortunately, he embellishes truth with his own perceptions. Once in Oxford, Jack admits that his father is an Oxford clergyman supporting the king. The two boys leave to deliver a letter to Cromwell near Cambridge, Oliver Cutter's home. On the way, highwaymen wound Jack, but Oliver escapes to take the letter to Cambridge and then on to Ely where Cromwell lives. As he travels, he encounters an actor who pronounces that the delivery of a message counts more than the message. He remembers this advice and charms Cromwell so much that Cromwell invites him to stay. As Oliver reminisces, he comments, "It is hard for the young to understand that the world was not created at their birth." He ends this novel by noting that he will tell more of the story at another time.

The rest of Oliver's story appears in **Cromwell's Boy**, the sequel to *A Messenger for Parliament*. Oliver Cutter recalls it during 1686 in Boston as he experiences a loss of freedom under Governor *Andros, a despot for King James. Oliver's service to Cromwell takes him back to London and then to Oxford, where he spies on the court of Charles II. He hears that Master Powell, with whom he stayed at the Unicorn on his first Oxford visit, was the previous spy, now captured. The danger of spying and earning a "hempen neckband" (noose), however, does not deter him. Oliver protects Faith, Powell's daughter, by taking her to Cambridge and leaving her with his friends, the childless blacksmith and his wife. Oliver serves Cromwell with his best talent, his horse-riding ability. This aids him in escaping from Oxford, after the enemy discovers his identity, by stealing a beautiful horse from an Irish lord. Later Cromwell allows him to keep it. Memories of his nighttime ride encourage Oliver in 1686 to ride again into the night to talk to his friends about curtailing James's power in the colonies. Such ruminating also leads Oliver to reflect about "youth, a word to whisper, a time of promises all too rarely kept."

In **A Boy's Will**, a book for younger readers set during the time of British and American fighting in 1779, Patrick hears a British Navy captain tell his grandfather that his ships plan to capture John Paul *Jones as he sails into the smuggler area of Valentia on the southern Irish coast. Having no sympathy for his grandfather, who chastises Patrick's dead mother's Catholic ways, Patrick decides to warn Captain Jones. He takes his grandfather's boat and sails it to Skellig Michael, the almost inaccessible holy place where St. Patrick killed the last snake in Ireland. There he watches for the ships. When Patrick sees the ships, he sails to them and actually collides with one, but his warning saves all five of them. When Jones asks him to sail with him, Patrick responds, "I will."

Jim, an orphan during the *American Civil War, sails away from Bristol in 1863 on a brig, the *Four Winds,* in **Orphans of the Wind**. No one knows until the brig leaves port that it sails for Charleston with guns and powder for the *Confederates. Throughout the voyage, Jim learns much about sailing, and Haugaard deftly interweaves ship terms with plot. As they near the South Carolina coast, Noah, the ship's conscience, decides to burn the cargo instead of allowing it to reach the "slavers." Jim and three friends escape the burning ship on a small leaking boat and after three days reach an island plantation. Their host claims that blacks, the sons of Ham, should work for others. The boys disagree and soon decide that they want to join the Union (*Yankee) Army. To escape notice, they travel with groups of Confederate soldiers whom they expect to lead them to the Union troops. After a battle near Manassas where one of them dies, the rest try to join the Union Army at Bull Run. The induction officer tells Jim he is too young. He then goes to Washington and hears that he can join the crew of an American ship journeying to California. Looking forward to sailing again with the wind to protect him, he understands that he has become an "orphan of the wind."

The frightening *Nazi mania touches fourteen-year-old Erik Hansen in **Chase Me, Catch Nobody**! An admitted snob, he tells the story of his Easter holiday visit to Germany in 1937. On the ferry from Denmark, a man wearing a gray raincoat asks him to take a package across the border. Erik sees the secret police questioning the man on arrival in Hamburg and understands that he will have to deliver the package to the Golden Lamb as the man had requested. On the trip, Erik befriends his avowed anarchist schoolmate, Nikolai Karl Leon Linde. Although the son of Communist parents, Nickolai likens *Lenin's state inside his tomb to a stuffed owl on display in Snow White's glass coffin. When Erik, who wants to be a poet, enters a bookshop and asks for poems of Heinrich Heine, the shopkeeper yells "Jude" at him. That people with such prejudices could look normal shocks Erik. He notes that "brutes should remain brutes and wear the mark of Cain. They had no business playing with their children or waving cheerfully to a busload of boys." Conversations with Nikolai help Erik further comprehend how politics can affect people's lives. Erik delivers the package that contains Danish passports but discovers that students in his group sympathetic with the Germans have identified them in his luggage. He escapes from the group, finds unexpected sanctuary, and agrees to take a half-Jewish girl who calls herself "Nobody" to Denmark. Their rescuer betrays them, but they escape, reach the water, and row a stolen boat to Denmark.

War's destruction of families underlies the action in **The Little Fishes**. In 1943, Guido, twelve, runs away from his aunt's farm to Naples after the death of his mother. When bombing starts, two children, Anna and Mario, ask for Guido's help. With money for food that Guido has saved by begging, they start walking north. At one point, a man forces them to accompany him while he robs people. The children escape the drunken man one night and go to a monastery in Cassino, where many others have gathered. Little Mario dies of a fever, and the other two continue their journey to a cave where they can hide with other refugees. When a woman needs food for her newly born baby, Guido leaves and approaches American soldiers for help. They eventually give Guido food, but the children still have to search for a place to stay.

STYLE AND THEMES

Haugaard's abilities with figurative language, including allusion (biblical title of "the horse and his rider"), hyperbole, simile, and metaphor, couple with vigorous imagery to create sense of story. In *The Untold Tale,* a "weak plank sinks a ship." Hyperbole shows humor in *A Messenger for Parliament,* with Oliver "digging a canal through my porridge." The careful choice of words is illustrated in the alliteratively sibilant "thoughts . . . soft as the southern breeze." The psychologically orphaned and always motherless protagonists in the novels have inner spiritual strength and convictions that keep them alive. The values come from either mothers recently dead or from mentors whom the characters meet. These strengths provide positive and powerful themes for Haugaard's plots.

HAVELOCK. Danish protagonist of ten who matures to adulthood in England of *Havelock the Dane. See* Crossley-Holland, Kevin.

HAVELOCK THE DANE. *See* Crossley-Holland, Kevin.

THE HAWK THAT DARE NOT FLY BY DAY. *See* O'Dell, Scott.

HEIKE. *See* *Gempei Wars.

HELGA. Thirteen, Viking protagonist in *A Slave's Tale* and young character in *Hakon of Rogen's Saga. See* Haugaard, Erik.

HENCHMAN FAMILY. Rob, Ellen, and William, English young people who mature in *The Henchmans at Home. See* Burton, Hester.

THE HENCHMANS AT HOME. *See* Burton, Hester.

HENGEST. Viking protagonist who matures in *Hengest's Tale. See* Paton Walsh, Jill.

HENGEST'S TALE. *See* Paton Walsh, Jill.

HENRY THE NAVIGATOR (1394–1460). As the prince of Portugal, he conquered and became the governor of Ceuta on the northern coast of Africa. Although he made no voyages himself, he established an observatory and school of navigation and directed voyages along the African coast. He improved both the compass and shipbuilding. *See* Baumann, Hans, *The Barque of Brothers.*

HENRY II OF ENGLAND (1133–1189). *Matilda's son was also count of Anjou. The Anjou family badge was a sprig of broom (*Planta genista*) from which their name, Plantagenet, was derived. He married Eleanor of Aquitaine and their sons, *Richard and John, became kings in turn. He created a national coinage system, no longer allowing the barons to issue their own coins. When Thomas á Becket, the man Henry appointed as archbishop of Canterbury, refused to allow Henry to try accused clergy in royal courts, Henry may have ordered four men to murder him on the steps of Canterbury Cathedral. Henry also began the process of trial by jury.

HENRY III OF ENGLAND (1207–1272). After favoring foreigners and living beyond his means, he provoked a rebellion from barons who compelled him to agree with a series of reforms. He refused, and the Barons' War, led by Simon de Montfort, took place in 1264. He was imprisoned, but his son *Edward rescued him by defeating Montfort at Evesham in 1265. Edward then succeeded him. *See* Trease, Geoffrey, *The Baron's Hostage*.

HENRY IV OF ENGLAND (1366–1413). Named Bolingbroke and often called Henry of Lancaster by his comtemporaries, he traveled throughout Europe on his way to the *Crusades. For his coronation, the golden eagle flask holding sacred oil was used for the first time. He founded the Knights of Bath, those who conduct the sovereign after he or she bathes in the City of London before being crowned to Westminster Abbey. He defeated Richard II in 1399 and suppressed Richard's sympathizers, Owen Glendower and Henry Percy (Hotspur) in the battle of Shrewsbury in 1403. His son *Henry V succeeded him. *See* Trease, Geoffrey, *Bent is the Bow*.

HENRY V OF ENGLAND (1387–1422). He won the Battle of Agincourt in France over Charles VI, who had gone mad. He thus won Charles's daughter Catherine in marriage and the promise that he would succeed to the French throne with the Treaty of Troyes in 1420. His son *Henry VI succeeded him. *See* Harnett, Cynthia, *The Sign of the Green Falcon*.

HENRY VI OF ENGLAND (1421–1471). Since Henry's father died when Henry was eight and his grandfather, Charles of France, died two months later, he became king of both England and France. Joan of Arc and others, however, expelled his forces from France, except for *Calais, by 1453. When older, he preferred the company of religious men and formed Eton and King's (Henry's) College at Cambridge for poor boys. His mother, Catherine, married Owen *Tudor and had two sons. He lost his reason as he aged, and the House of *York challenged his rule. This hostility began the Wars of Roses, which lasted from 1455 to 1485. His wife, Margaret, would not reconcile with the Yorkists, but Henry recognized Edward of York as King *Edward IV. He went to the Tower of London, where he was murdered. *See* Harnett, Cynthia, *The Writing on the Hearth*.

HENRY VII OF ENGLAND (1457–1509). First monarch of the house of *Tudor, he lived as an exile in Brittany until he entered England, defeated *Richard III at Bosworth Field on August 22, 1485, and was declared king. He married Elizabeth, daughter of *Edward IV, which united the houses of *Lancaster and *York. He decided that nobles could have servants but no armies.

He named one of his sons Arthur after the character in Mallory's *Morte d'Arthur* recently printed by William *Caxton. His son *Henry VIII succeeded him.

HENRY VIII OF ENGLAND (1491–1547). At eighteen, on becoming king, he married Catherine of Aragon, the widow of his brother, Arthur. He formed various European alliances based on the advice of Cardinal Wolsey. When the pope refused his request for a divorce from Catherine, he blamed Wolsey and appointed Sir Thomas More as chancellor in 1529. Then he married Anne Boleyn, who became the mother of *Elizabeth I. He accused Anne of crimes and beheaded her. Jane Seymour, his next wife, bore him a son, but she soon died. He tried a political liaison by marrying Anne of Cleves but hated her looks and divorced her. Catherine Howard, his next wife, aroused his suspicions, and he beheaded her. Finally he married Catherine Parr, who outlived him. He improved naval defense, unified Wales with England, and placated Ireland. His son Edward VI succeeded him. See *Stars of Fortune* by Cynthia *Harnett; *The Armourer's House* by Rosemary *Sutcliff; and *A Cold Wind Blowing* and *The Eldest Son* by Barbara *Willard.

HERSHY MARKS. Twelve, American Jew, protagonist of *The Murderer*. See Holman, Felice.

HESSIANS. In the *American Revolution, men from the German area of Hesse fought as mercenaries for the British Army and were called Hessians. See *The Fighting Ground* by *Avi; and *Peter Treegate's War* and *Red Pawns* by Leonard *Wibberley.

HESTER. Twelve, American protagonist in *The Nickel-Plated Beauty*. See Beatty, Patricia.

HESTER JEBB. Thirteen, English female protagonist in *Hetty*. See Willard, Barbara.

HETTY. *See* Willard, Barbara.

HICKMAN, JANET (1940–   ). American.

BIBLIOGRAPHY AND BACKGROUND
The Stones. New York: Macmillan, 1976. *The Valley of the Shadow*. New York: Macmillan, 1974. *Zoar Blue*. New York: Macmillan, 1978.

Hickman's awards include the Child Study Association Book of the Year, Florence Roberts Head Award of the Ohioana Library Association, and Selection of the English-Speaking Union for *Zoar Blue*. *The Valley of the Shadow* was a Notable Children's Trade Book in Social Studies. An assignment for an eighth-grade class to write a fictional story based on information in the history book led Hickman to historical fiction. She wrote a story along with her students and sold it. The pleasure in the " 'feel' of writing about/from a different time" piqued her interest. Her visits to places led to further research and finally *The Valley of the Shadow* and *Zoar Blue*. Her preference to write with all source materials close at hand requires taking many notes from noncirculating archive collections. She usually revises as she writes, but she especially enjoys "the final-polish revision when I type up a clean copy to show the editor."

WORKS

A war lurks in the background of each novel. In **The Valley of the Shadow,** set in 1781, the *American Revolution continues. Buckongehelas, a *Delaware Indian, warns the Moravian town leaders where protagonist Tobias lives that the Long Knives (Virginian Indians) fighting with the British will destroy them. Unfortunately, neither their Christian beliefs nor their neutrality saves them from being captured and moved to temporary homes. In desperation, they return to town for food, and there they are scalped. Tobias's nightmare from nights past becomes a reality. Only Tobias, from whose point of view the story unfolds, and his friend Thomas escape alive to tell those waiting about the massacre. But Tobias has youth's resilience and anticipates returning to his beloved school and becoming the man his father wanted him to be. Hickman's control of imagery creates lively descriptive passages about little-known events. At times the movement of the characters is confusing, but a front map helps clarify the locales.

In **Zoar Blue** set in 1862, one sees two diverse worlds: the ordered world of the German Society of Separatists in Zoar, Ohio, and the chaotic world of the American Civil War. The Separatists believed that all humans are equal, with only God exalted; hence everyone, including children, worked for the community at the jobs to which the trustees assigned them. Children worked with adults other than their parents so that they would not be too coddled. Barbara, the protagonist, cares for Rosina, the Keffers' slightly crippled daughter who cannot fulfill the duties normally given to young children. But the young people hear about the war and feel that the closed community denies them excitement and glory. John Keffer, at seventeen, runs away with boys his age to join the fight. Barbara, an orphan, finds a letter from her uncle in Pennsylvania that Rosina had hidden under the steps several months earlier and forgotten. She decides to run away to him in Abbotstown. She finds that he has gone to war, so she stays to help his wife. She soon realizes that chores are always mundane and that she wants to be with those she loves. To help her return to Zoar, her uncle's wife takes her to Gettysburg to find a ride. What they observe there are wounded and dead from the just finished three-day battle. While they help nurse the suffering, Barbara simultaneously searches for John. When she does not find him, a few kind people give her train fare to Zoar. In Zoar, she sees John, who has suffered typhoid and a wounded arm. There she feels safe from the fears of war and warm with Rosina's pleasure at her return. The omniscient point of view allows the reader to observe simultaneous action in Abbotstown, Zoar, and Gettysburg, thus relieving some of the story's suspense. The young people appreciate the value of what they have only after they lose it.

World War II forms the backdrop for **The Stones**. Garrett McKay, a sixth grader whose father is away fighting in the war, must cope with the jibes of the older boys if he wants to be included in their play. He thinks that his father's return will help him, but notification arrives that his father is missing in action. That unhappy situation ironically gains stature for Garrett, but he becomes even lonelier. The hostility toward Germans becomes more acute when the boys with whom Garrett plays start taunting Jack Tramp, a man whose real name, according to Garrett's great Aunt Em, is Adolf Schilling. The boys pretend that Jack's dilapidated house is the Berlin war zone, and they bomb it with mud. Jack's patience ends and he shoots at one of the boys, killing a dog. The boys laugh at Garrett when his family entertains Jack Tramp at dinner, but Garrett begins to feel sorry for the man. When Linnie, Garrett's four-year-old sister, becomes caught at a spot called the Stones during a storm, Jack follows Garrett and helps him rescue her. Jack suffers a heart attack during the process, but he survives. On the same day, the family receives news that the father has been located with only a shoulder wound. When Garrett receives a letter from him, he realizes that his father will not be the same, but he has begun to understand that nothing ever is.

STYLE AND THEMES

Hickman's concise style complements her content. In *Zoar Blue,* "chickens to be fed, breakfast tables to be set, water buckets to be carried, blades to be sharpened, countless things to be done" illustrates her use of parallelism. The figurative language of *The Stones* emphasizes the tenor of World War II when the yard is "trimmed close as a Marine's haircut" and something is "mucky as chocolate pudding." The underlying thematic idea in all the novels is that young people need security and love, and they need it even more during times of national turmoil.

THE HILLS OF VARNA. See *Shadow of the Hawk* by Geoffrey *Trease.

HISPANIOLA. This island of the West Indies, formerly Haiti, is occupied in the west by the Republic of Haiti and in the east by the Dominican Republic. *See* Wibberley, Leonard, *Deadmen's Cave.*

HODGES, C. WALTER (1909–). British.

BIBLIOGRAPHY AND BACKGROUND

Columbus Sails. New York: Coward McCann, 1939; London: Bell, 1939. *The Marsh King.* New York: Coward McCann, 1967; London: Bell, 1967. *The Namesake.* New York: Coward McCann, 1964; London: Bell, 1964. *The Overland Launch.* New York: Coward McCann, 1970; London: Bell, 1969.

For *The Namesake,* C. Walter Hodges received a Carnegie Commendation in 1964. The same year he was selected as the British entry for the Hans Christian Anderson Award. The times about which Hodges has written suggest themselves to him because of their "pictorial attraction" such as sailing ships, the Vikings, *Saxon battlefields, and the *Elizabethan theater. He uses reference books but usually does not choose a time period unless he already knows or feels something about it. He says, "I have everything plotted carefully before I begin (though not so tightly that unplanned events and people have room to enter). I like to feel the *shape* of the book, chapter, para, from the beginning." Each day working is difficult for him until the "writing takes over by itself and does unplanned things." He writes slowly, reworking each page until it looks like "an old bird's nest." Of the four Hodges's novels considered historical fiction, two revolve around King *Alfred of England, a third relates Columbus's voyage, and a fourth reveals an unusual late nineteenth-century accomplishment.

WORKS

In **The Namesake**, Alfred Timberleg or Dane-leg tells his first-person story of serving Alfred of Wessex. As a boy of ten, he dreams that he should take a harness to his namesake, Alfred, brother of the king. Not understanding God's directive but having grown up in a monastery where he learned to trust God's messages, he journeys to meet the twenty-one-year-old Alfred. During this period, Danes ravage the countryside, destroying houses and killing indiscriminately. Soon after Alfred Dane-leg arrives, King Ethelred dies; Alfred becomes king and asks the boy to remain with him. The new king defeats the Danes and exchanges "guests" (hostages) with them. Eventually a horse appears, and the boy knows that the harness belongs to it, and he gives it to the king. During times of great stress, King Alfred is sick with high fever and chills. He takes his followers to Stonehenge, a place thought by many to be inhabited by the devil, but Alfred remarks that the place is Memory to him, a place where he has spent much time in his life. Alfred goes to battle only when he has no other choice, and when his hostage, *Guthorm, resumes fighting, King Alfred has to subdue him. During the conflict, the Danes capture Alfred Dane-leg, thinking he is the king's son, and hold him hostage. Having learned to read and write at the king's suggestion, Alfred writes the king a note to tell him that the Danes are dishonest. King Alfred finally wins the war, bringing the Danes under control. Alfred Dane-leg's love for King Alfred elevates the king's status as a fair, honest man in this interesting story.

A first-person narrator in **The Marsh King** retells the story his grandfather told him about Guthorm's attempt to overthrow King Alfred of Wessex around 878 A.D. Guthorm plots with Edgar's guardian to place Edgar, the only person who has a claim, on the throne. They plan to kill Alfred when he attends Edgar's winter marriage to Edith. Edith overhears the plot and sends Hildis, her maid, to warn King Alfred. Alfred escapes, but his attendants die. Not knowing that Alfred has survived, Guthorm prepares to have Edgar declared king and himself to control Edgar. Alfred, however, establishes himself in the Somerset Marshes where only those who know the paths hidden under water can enter. In the spring, he musters enough men for Guthorm's defeat. As punishment, he makes Guthorm take the name Athelstan and be baptized a Christian. The narrator comments that he was two years old when Athelstan died.

Three first-person narrators tell of their experiences with Columbus in **Columbus Sails**. The first, Father Antonio de la Vega, lives at *La Rabida, a monastery where Columbus meets Father Juan *Perez and sees his maps. Perez speaks for Columbus at court, and Columbus, along with Father Antonio, goes to *Granada for an audience with Isabel and Ferdinand. When Columbus's outrageous demands to become a knight and a viceroy over all the lands he discovers, as well as inherit a tenth of the wealth, irritates the court, Columbus leaves for France. His friends intervene, and Isabel sends a messenger to retrieve him. Armed with supplies and ships, Columbus sets sail on August 3, 1492, with the second narrator, the sailor Miguel Pericas. Pericas tells of his fear that he would never again see land and the subtle mutinies rising on board, as well as Columbus's own disagreements with Martin Pinzon, a merchant seaman sailing the *Pinta*. Miguel writes his story as he waits both for death in the fort of La Navidad and Columbus's return from Spain. When the Indians attack, Miguel notes that he and the others plan to take one of the rowboats left from the wrecked *Santa Maria* to escape the natives. The final narrator, Brother Ignacio, meets Cortez (*Cortés) after he returns with *Montezuma's wealth and *Pizarro who has seen the *Incas, at La Rabida. Brother Ignacio, the Indian named Coatta who returned with Columbus, relates the difficult journey to Spain from the New World. Thus the reader finds three different views of the circumstances surrounding the first voyage of Columbus.

A novel based on another true story is **The Overland Launch**. In 1899, men from Lynmouth, England, unable to launch their lifeboat into the rough seas in one of the worst storms of the century, rescue a distressed ship off the coast of *Bristol by using horses to pull the lifeboat up and down steep cliffs of the shoreline to Portlock. The first chapter establishes the incredible steepness of the roads through which the launch has to pass so that the reader can understand the achievement of the men in their endeavors to rescue sailors in the violent seas. Eighteen horses pull the launch in a train 120 feet long. Among the obstacles that the men overcome during the nine-hour journey are skittish horses, a broken wheel, too narrow paths, trees, a stone wall, and a house corner. The omniscient view reveals the fears and pride of several of the men involved in this unique exercise, including thirteen-year-old Derry Larkins. When Derry likens the fierce storm to Poseidon's pursuit of Ulysses, his memory of his lessons surprises the schoolmaster. In the last chapter, the schoolmaster returns and unexpectedly finds Derry as the local garage owner. Derry's lack of opportunity for further education has spurred him to help his own children succeed. They have grown and decided to study classics at the university. The feat accomplished by the men on that stormy night joins the local lore, and both Derry and the schoolmaster are proud to have been included.

STYLE AND THEMES

Hodges's use of multiple first-person narratives and the omniscient point of view gives the reader more understanding of risks in several situations. In *The Namesake,* the point of view shifts during battle to King Alfred's trusted Frankish friend Gunram and to Esdras, the monk who fights the Danes with intensity. In *The Marsh King,* a similar shift reveals the diverse motives for fighting—some men willing to risk all for power and then Alfred who views fighting (maybe because he already has power) as a way to preserve peace. In *Columbus Sails,* two monks and a sailor tell stories of Columbus's voyage. In *The Overland Launch,* the doubts and fears of the men portaging the boat increase the tension of the underlying endeavor. The strong dialect in the novel also sets it in north Devon. Hodges's imagery reflects an artist's eye when Columbus meets Isabel and Ferdinand in a room filled with the warmth of "subdued light." A further example also illustrates parallelism. In the same novel, anticipated wealth from the voyage includes "elephants . . . whose thick hides are inset with jewels patterned like a carpet . . . tusks are carved in exquisite lace . . . and ears are hung with bells of silver and gold." Although at times wordy, Hodges uses allusions and figurative language. In *The Overland Launch,* the men with cork life jackets look "like a boatload of tough old armoured knights with their lances." Hodges entertains with adventure stories having the clear theme that a life lived with concern for others is the only kind worth living.

HOGARTH, WILLIAM (1867–1764). An English painter and engraver, he secured legislation in 1735 protecting designers from piracy. His pictures were often satirical. *See* Beatty, John and Patricia, *At the Seven Stars.*

HOLD ON TO LOVE. *See* Hunter, Mollie.

HOLDFAST. *See* Beatty, John and Patricia.

HOLM, ANNE (1922–   ). Danish.

BIBLIOGRAPHY AND BACKGROUND

North to Freedom. Trans. L. W. Kingsland. New York: Harcourt, Brace, 1965.

North to Freedom, under the title *David,* won the 1963 Gyldendal Prize for the Best Scandinavian Children's Book. In the United States, it was chosen a 1965 Notable Book by the American Library Association. It also was a Gold Medal Winner in the Boys' Club of America, a Junior Book Award winner, and a Lewis Carroll Shelf Award winner. Holm says, "what motivates my writing is not history, but man's right to live in liberty and act according to his own idea of what is right and wrong. I believe that young people have a right to think of such things too—it should not be reserved for adults.'' Her ideas germinate from one week to a year or two, and she researches at home in an extensive library or asks for help from friends who work in museums or universities. Then she begins to work quickly for fear of having the idea die, writing three to four hours a day without major revisions.

WORK

In **North To Freedom**, twelve-year-old David decides to escape from a war camp in which he has lived almost his entire life when a man tells him to jump over the fence during a thirty-second electricity interruption, grab the bundle from under a nearby tree, go to Salonika (*Thessalonica), get a ship for Italy, and travel north to Denmark. David thinks that the risk of getting shot at the fence is better than having to endure a lifetime in the camp. He escapes safely; not for many weeks does he finally believe that no one has pursued him. During those weeks of fear, he experiences a world he has never known before. His memory of the dead Johannes, a man who taught him languages and about many things, keeps him sane. David knows French, German, Italian, English, Spanish, some Hebrew, and Russian. When he reaches Italy, he sees vivid colors for the first time and realizes what the word *beautiful* means. There he uses the soap provided by the man in the camp to wash away his dirt, literally and figuratively. When he finds an orange sphere, he picks it up and decides to eat it. It does not kill him so he looks for more, not knowing to call it ''orange.'' Hearing people laugh shocks him, and when he sees a baby for the first time, its helplessness horrifies him. He loses the compass from his bundle and utters ''God.'' Surprised, he has no idea who God is, but he thinks that God who helped another David of whom Johannes often spoke might also help him. When David asks an English couple if England has a king, they tell him that a queen sits on the throne. When he sees a huge house, he tries to describe something he hears for the first time: ''If you could turn into a balloon, that sound was what you might feel like . . . as if you had a great space inside you and it was all filled with air, a heavenly air full of sweet voices that made you fly up and up and your heart beat faster and faster . . . not because you were afraid, but because you were . . . happy? Was that what happiness felt like?'' Near this house where he hears the music, he rescues a little girl from a fire. The family asks him to stay, and when he sees that they have books, he does. He requests books written before 1917, which ''they'' would not have controlled. The reader can infer that David must have been in a Soviet camp, although David never says. When he overhears a conversation between the parents wondering about his origin, he leaves. On his travels he often requests God's help and guidance. As he wanders through a field in Switzerland, a woman asks him to model for her painting. When he finds an intriguing photograph, the artist tells him that the woman is a friend in Denmark whose husband and son were captured, and she gives David the friend's address. Later, a man barricades David into a barn in retaliation for his statement to the family that ''everybody has a right to his life and freedom, and anyone who takes them away has lost his own right to be a human being.'' David escapes, finds his way to to the house in Denmark, and announces he is David. The woman responds ''David . . . my son David . . .''.

STYLE AND THEME

The coincidence of David's meeting the artist in Switzerland mars plot development, and Holm uses an unnecessary cliffhanger at the end of a chapter. She says, ''David did not know that the very next day something would happen that he could not tackle alone and he still would not ask for help.'' However, the concept of having a character who has lived in the isolation of a prison for his entire life but has learned enough languages to survive outside its walls is so intriguing that one can ignore these slight problems and unlikely coincidences.

HOLMAN, FELICE (1919–   ). American.

BIBLIOGRAPHY AND BACKGROUND

The Murderer. New York: Scribner's, 1978. *The Wild Children*. New York: Scribner's, 1983.

Felice Holman has won many awards for her writing, including a nomination for the 1986 Mark Twain Award. *The Wild Children* was cited as a Best Book for Young Adults by the American Library Association. For this book, she says her ''initial awareness of the children was after a casual remark of Margaret Mead's during a talk about something entirely different.'' She continues, ''I was fascinated by the heretofore neglected subject of these hoards of children, homeless, criminal, sick, needy, pitiful, who were left untended after the Russian Revolution'' in 1917. She spent two years researching in a California university library, with a student doing further research in Moscow's huge *Lenin Library. She revises several times and stops ''when I know the book by heart or can't stand to read it one more time, whichever comes first.''

WORKS

One morning in Kovrov, Russia, several years after the *Russian Revolution, twelve-year-old Alex, in **The Wild Children** wakes up to find that his family has been removed from their home. He realizes that he has escaped because his room, a small closet, is isolated from the rest of the house. His teacher, Katriana Sokolova, gives him money to go to Moscow to see his uncle and tells Alex that if he decides to leave Russia, he should see her cousin Basil in Leningrad (*St. Petersburg). She admits having considered leaving herself because the Russia that she sees now with all of the shelterless *bezprizoni* (''wild children'') is not the *matusa Rus* (''Mother Russia'') that she has known. Alex departs, surprised that his father, a school administrator, should have been arrested. Unable to find room on the train filled with soldiers, Alex has to walk the hundred miles to Moscow. There he finds that his uncle has also been arrested. He sees a waif steal in a marketplace but refuses to acknowledge the deed to a merchant. Another boy, Peter, asks Alex why he protects the child, and Alex says that he looks hungry. Peter takes him to his hideout where he has gathered children who would otherwise be condemned to the horrible government children's homes. Peter, however, accepts only children who abide by his rules: no syphilis or typhus, no alcohol or cocaine, and no killing for food. Peter carefully apportions the small amount of food after each returns from foraging. As suspicions grow about the children, they move south from Moscow. At one stop, an older child becomes enamored with the money to be gleaned from alcohol and cocaine and betrays the others to the police. While incarcerated in a children's house, one dies from the director's beating. Peter kills the man. Alex takes Peter and ten others to Leningrad by riding a train either on top or below in the dog compartments, where he contacts Basil, who helps them reach Finland. The descriptions of what happens to these children are truly shocking.

The scene changes in **The Murderer** to a dismal time in the United States, the *Depression. In an unusual present-tense, limited-omniscient narrative, Hershy Marks, twelve, questions the quality of his life in Ashlymine, Pennsylvania. As a Jew who attends *cheder* after school to study for his *bar mitzvah, he cannot understand why children of the Polish miners constantly malign him and other merchants' children for killing Christ. He actually likes some of the boys and has a special admiration for Lorsh Jabieski, the talented Polish leader of a local baseball team. When a new rabbi arrives, he explains to Hershy that the Jews have a heritage regardless of the continual prejudice against them and that Romans, as well as Jews, killed Christ. During this time, Hershy's father extends credit at his hardware store to the miners and becomes frustrated when they do not pay. Eventually Mr. Marks has to borrow money from an aunt and uncle. Another unpleasant event during the year is the death of Hershy's friend Lenny. By the end of the year at his bar mitzvah, Hershy realizes that alternatives to living in Ashlymine are available. He learns that discontented people often blame others for their frustrations.

STYLE AND THEMES

Holman's tightly written novels reveal characters who do not overtly understand their circumstances but who learn that survival with dignity requires honest appraisal of what is possible for them to accomplish.

HOPE FOSTER. Thirteen, American protagonist in *Something to Shout About*. *See* Beatty, Patricia.

HOPI. The term *hopi* means "peaceful" and is the name of the most westerly located Pueblo Native American tribe, currently inhabiting a reservation in northeastern Arizona. The Hopi typically live on mesas, with the men sheepherding and farming and the women making baskets and pottery. They are monogamous, self-controlled, and religious. Both sexes begin partaking in tribal ceremonies after six years of age when they are inducted into the kachina cult, a ritual during which masked adults give dolls representing the sacred spirits through whom the Hopis pray to their gods. Although the tribe is matrilineal, the women seldom take active part in the tribal ceremonies. Most widely publicized is the snake dance, which occurs late in August each year. *See* Baker, Betty, *And One Was a Wooden Indian.*

HOPKINS, MATTHEW (d. 1647). He caused scores of people to be tried and hung for witchcraft in Norfolk, Suffolk, Essex, and Huntingdonshire in England. He was known as the ''Witch Finder Generall'' in 1644 and was finally suspected of witchcraft himself, tried, and hung. *See* Westall, Robert, *The Devil on the Road.*

HORSEMEN ON THE HILLS. *See* Trease, Geoffrey.

HORSES OF ANGER. *See* Forman, James.

HOSPITALLERS. *See* Order of Hospital of *St. John of Jerusalem.

HOW MANY MILES TO SUNDOWN. *See* Beatty, Patricia.

HUDSON'S BAY COMPANY. This corporation consisted of ''the Governor and Company of Adventurers of England trading into Hudson's Bay'' in 1670 to seek the northwest passage, occupy the lands adjacent to Hudson Bay, and carry on any commerce in those lands that might prove profitable. Until 1870, when it turned increasingly to retail merchandising, the company found little of value other than the fur trade. See *West with the White Chiefs* and *Forbidden Frontier* by Christie *Harris.

THE HUFFLER. *See* Paton Walsh, Jill.

HUGH. English young adult protagonist in *Bowman of Crécy.* *See* Welch, Ronald.

HUGH COPPLESTONE. Young English orphan, protagonist of *Brother Dusty-feet.* *See* Sutcliff, Rosemary.

HUGH OF AVRANCHES (d. 1101). He contributed sixty ships to *William the Conqueror's invasion of England in 1066 and became the first earl of Chester. In addition to fighting a long war with the Welsh, he became a principal adviser to Henry I. *See* Treece, Henry, *Splintered Sword.*

HUGH AND MEG. English young adult protagonists in *Bent Is the Bow. See* Trease, Geoffrey.

HUNT, IRENE (1907–   ). American.

BIBLIOGRAPHY AND BACKGROUND

Across Five Aprils. Chicago: Follett, 1964; London: Bodley Head, 1965. *No Promises in the Wind*. Chicago: Follett, 1970.

The Newbery honored Irene Hunt in 1965 for *Across Five Aprils*. She has also won awards for her writing in contemporary realistic fiction. Her historical fiction shows characters who survive severe adversities because of their inner strength.

WORKS

Across Five Aprils follows the Creighton family through the five years of the *American Civil War. In April 1861, when Jethro Creighton is nine, the war's influence reaches across southern Illinois, overtaking his brothers and their friends. The omniscient point of view in this *Bildungsroman* reveals the feelings and frustrations of Jethro and of others faced with this sudden change in their lives. Jethro watches two of his brothers, Tom and Bill, always close, physically fight each other when the intellectual Bill decides he must support the Rebels. *Copperheads burn the Creighton barn when Bill joins the *Confederates, though two sons and a cousin fight for the Union. Soon after, one of the town bullies tries to kill Jethro, but Dave Burdow, a strange old man whose son had inadvertently killed Jethro's sister Mary, saves him. The troubles lead Jethro's father, Matt, to a heart attack, and Jethro becomes the main worker on the farm, with only his sister Jenny to help. Her humor as well as the family's steadfast religious faith helps them both prevail. But Jenny longs for the young schoolteacher, Shadrach Yale, also gone to war, and she hurts Jethro, who admires Shad's intelligence, when she refuses to let him read Shad's letter to her. With the death of one son at Shiloh, the capture of another, the wound to Shadrach, and the desertion of Eb, the cousin raised in the household, the family endures all aspects of the war. As each April passes, Jethro continues to have difficulty understanding the reasons for the war, although he reads the newspaper and listens to the adults. He reads about the battles, the vacillation of public opinion concerning the effectiveness of the Union generals and *Lincoln, and the widespread respect for Robert E. *Lee. When Eb deserts, Jethro decides to write Lincoln and ask him what to do. Lincoln's response thrills Jethro, and his solution of offering amnesty to deserters—letting them return to their units without punishment—makes him even happier. When the war ends in 1865, the news of Lincoln's death tempers the excitement. Jethro understands the town newspaper editor's comment to him that peace is two-edged.

A different kind of war appears in **No Promises in the Wind**. In 1932, the *Depression disrupts Josh Grondowski's family when his unemployed father accuses him of demanding too much. Fifteen-year-old Josh tells his first-person story of leaving to find a job playing piano and taking his ten-year-old brother, Joey, and a friend Howie, who plays the banjo, with him. They hop a train, but Howie falls off and dies. The other two, in shock, decide to keep looking for work. A kindly truck driver, Lonnie, takes them to Louisiana and helps Josh get a job playing the piano for a carnival. The two boys survive until the carnival burns; then they go to Omaha to find Lonnie. The sordid events in this segment are further blackened when the boys encounter Charlie, a man who thrives from the Depression. On the trip, Josh becomes angry at Joey and hits him; Joey leaves. Josh rests inside a barn where he nearly dies from a fever, but a couple discovers him, finds Lonnie's name and address, and contacts him. Lonnie rescues Josh and searches for Joey, and after weeks, he finally locates him. Josh falls in love with Janey, Lonnie's niece, which shows him maturing. When he is well, Josh plays piano in a restaurant but realizes from all his troubles that he has been too harsh toward his father and must apologize. When the boys reach Chicago, Josh's father cries, and Josh knows that returning home is right. The ensuing election of Franklin Roosevelt gives the family, as well as the rest of the country, hope for a better future.

STYLE AND THEMES

In both novels, Hunt tells candid stories. She uses few outstanding stylistic devices in *No Promises in the Wind,* but in *Across Five Aprils,* she successfully employs diction, imagery, figurative language, and symbolism to give the novel exceptional depth. She uses the area dialect as a method of showing the characters' levels of education. Jethro's mother, loving but illiterate, responds to Jethro's story about Copernicus's realizing that the earth was not the center of the universe with, "furriners is allus stirrin' up somethin'." The imagery excels in such descriptions as, "That hour was pink with sunrise and swelling redbud and clusters of bloom over the apple orchard across the road." The only questionable construction in the novel occurs when Hunt inserts the contemporary opinion that Shiloh was a very important battle when Jethro's perception of it in 1862 is of a few trees and a church where his brother died. Religion is essential to the Creightons, and some of the figurative language and symbolism reflects its status. At least one allusion refers to Herod's marching soldiers. When Jethro first works in the fields, he sits at the adult table, and Bill offers him the adult drink, coffee. Bill dips a morsel of bread into the coffee and feeds Jethro as if he were serving him the Eucharist. Although not religious in intent, the timelessness of being appears in Hunt's description of the Creighton land by referring to the glacier that once covered that spot of earth. In *Across Five Aprils,* Hunt superbly demonstrates the ability of civil war to split families and friends.

HUNTER, MOLLIE (1922–   ). Scottish.

BIBLIOGRAPHY AND BACKGROUND

The Ghosts of Glencoe. London: Evans, 1966; New York: Funk and Wagnalls, 1969. *Hold On to Love.* New York: Harper & Row, 1983; as *The Dragonfly Years.* London: Hamish Hamilton, 1983. *The Lothian Run.* New York: Funk and Wagnalls, 1970; London: Hamish Hamilton, 1971. *A Pistol in Greenyards.* Illustrated by Elizabeth Grant. London: Evans, 1965; New York: Funk and

Wagnalls, 1968. *A Sound of Chariots*. New York: Harper & Row, 1972; London: Hamish Hamilton, 1973. *The Spanish Letters*. Illustrated by Elizabeth Grant. London: Evans, 1964; New York: Funk and Wagnalls, 1967. *The Stronghold*. New York: Harper & Row, 1974; London: Hamish Hamilton, 1974. *The Third Eye*. New York: Harper & Row, 1973; London: Hamish Hamilton, 1979. *The 13th Member*. New York: Harper & Row, 1971; London: Hamish Hamilton, 1971.

Mollie Hunter has received various awards for her work in several genres. They include the Child Study Association of America award, the Scottish Arts Council Literary Award twice, and the Carnegie Medal in 1975 for *The Stronghold*. Her historical fiction presents male and female protagonists from several points of view. Her stories are convincing, whether set in prehistory or in the twentieth century. What makes them especially perceptive is her practice of using psychological forces as one method of motivating protagonists.

WORKS

Chronologically her first novel is **The Stronghold**. In a preface note, Hunter comments that strongholds were probably built in the Orkney Islands between the first century B.C. and the first century A.D. as lookout towers to thwart Roman slave roundups. Hunter imagines who might have designed these unique towers and decides to let her protagonist, Coll, eighteen, be the architect. He calculates the logistics of a structure that will allow his people to patrol for raiders. When Coll was five, Roman raiders maimed him, killed his father, and captured his mother. Throughout the novel, Coll has flashbacks in which he relives the horrors of that day. He lives with the Boar tribe chief, Nectan, and his wife, Anu, as their foster son. Coll at first cannot convince Nectan that his defense plans will work, but several things happen that force Nectar to test them. First, the *druid Domnall declares his godly power by demanding that the warriors fight all Roman raiders in opposition to Nectan's declaration that the few surviving warriors hide if the Romans appear. The arrival of Taran, a young boy who supposedly escaped from his Roman master, furthers the hostility. Taran and Domnall plot against Nectan, but Coll's brother, Bran, tells Coll. As a novice druid training to become poet, seer, or priest, Bran is not allowed any family ties, but he secretly warns Coll that Taran will try to kill him. Taran wants to marry Cloda, Nectan's oldest daughter, because the tribal line passes through her, and as her husband, he would become chief at Nectan's death. Cloda detests Taran, but assuming himself physically attractive with his yellow bleached hair and himself lucky with his carnelian stone talisman, Taran continues to pursue her. Nectan decides to remind Domnall and Taran that he remains chief. He fights a wild boar, something he must do every seven years to show his ability to lead the tribe. When he wins, Domnall counters that with his spiritual powers, he will take away the life after death from everyone in the tribe who follows Nectan. When Domnall then chooses Fand, Nectan's younger daughter, to be sacrificed to the gods, the rift widens. Coll, however, rescues her from this death. When the several strains of the novel merge at the sacrifice, Coll's stronghold plan saves the lives of all the tribe. The threads of the story weave together into an intricate and satisfying pattern.

From prehistory, Hunter jumps to the sixteenth century. In **The Spanish Letters**, Jamie, at fifteen, helps an English official foil an overthrow of Scotland by thwarting an Edinburgh plot in 1589. An orphan for seven years working as a "caddie" (guide), Jamie takes a job with Macey, who has recently come from London. With the help of a local fencing master, Forbes, he convinces Macey that Edinburgh's several hundred caddies know all the business of Edinburgh. They find that several Edinburgh men killed Macey's friend Norton as Norton began to suspect that the men were bargaining with Philip of Spain to capture Scotland and then England and reestablish Roman Catholicism. Of the plotters, Forbes wants to find Semphill, the man who killed his brother at the Battle of Liége where they had fought together as Scottish mercenaries for the Netherlands against Spain. One of the caddies had been in the battle and knew that Semphill had betrayed his soldiers because he could not get them food. After Semphill's capture, Semphill tells Forbes that he had tried to protect Forbes's daughter from her kidnapper, the evil "man in black," d'Aquirre. Semphill's debt repaid, Macey captures the man carrying letters to the Spanish king and reports to Queen *Elizabeth in London. He returns to Edinburgh in time to save King *James from capture by one of his "trusted" friends. Then Macey offers loyal Jamie a chance to work with him after he learns to read and cipher and fence to perfection. Although lacking thematic depth, the novel's adventure and historical setting are captivating.

The second novel set in Scotland during this time, in 1590, is **The 13th Member.** Adam Lawrie, a lowly bond-servant of sixteen, scurries outside in the middle of a summer night from his Master Seton's house to follow Gilly, another servant, as she hastens toward a strange light. Adam is certain that he sees her encounter the devil. The next day, Gilly works as if nothing has happened, and Adam becomes baffled by the terrible apparition. He decides to confide in Grahame, a scholar whom he trusts and who has taught him to read. Grahame recognizes Adam's description as that of a witches' meeting that would have taken place on July 31, *Lammas Eve, with Gilly probably the thirteenth member of the witches' coven. He is aware of similar meetings taking place at Candlemas, Beltane, and Hallowmas (*All Saints' Day). Grahame urges Adam to help the fifteen-year-old Gilly escape from the witches who will kill her if she reveals their identities. Grahame convinces Adam and Gilly that phosphorus and olive oil create the effect of light surrounding the man with his horse who plays the role of the devil to the witches. Grahame, Adam, and Gilly capture the devil on his way to the meeting where he expects to meet the earl of Bothwell and plot the death of the earl's cousin, James VI. When Adam and Gilly see the devil's face, they realize that he is Grahame's identical twin. Unfortunately, Jardine, a free stable helper for Master Seton, is jealous of Adam. When he sees Adam and Gilly leave that night, he accuses them of witchcraft. But Gilly's and

Adam's separate confessions agree, so Seton takes them to James VI. Concerned that Adam may be telling the truth, James VI decides to investigate the charges. After the witches confess and Gilly is freed at Adam's request, Adam and Gilly walk to England, where they can begin new lives using Adam's intelligence and Gilly's healing abilities. This novel exposes some of the consequences of pagan practices that through the centuries have been part of Great Britain's history.

Robert Stewart in **The Ghosts of Glencoe** desires to be an honorable military representative of his country. Not realizing that his billet in the Macdonald clan's homes in the winter of 1692 is an occupation, he makes friends with the sons and goes hunting with them. By taking their "salt" (eating their food), Robert pledges friendship. On a hunt, he wears the traditional kilt and brogans (shoes with holes in the bottom to let water seep in and out). He realizes that the clothes fulfill their intent extremely well. When Robert saves a man from being killed by a stag, the man pledges Robert as his brother forever (much like Native American honor). A private billeted with Robert, MacEachern, known to be "cursed" with the second sight, tells Robert of a vision of death for the Macdonalds. When the Macdonald women sense the impending slaughter, they lend credence to the comment, "women by nature [are] quicker witted and more suspicious than men." Robert ignores the vision, but the Campbells in the regiment, archenemies of the Macdonalds, fabricate an order to destroy them. The action of one soldier in ripping off Mrs. Macdonald's finger flesh with her rings reveals the brutality of the butchery. Instead of fighting, Robert helps some of the Macdonalds escape. To avoid his own death, he swims a river to reach his aunt's house, and she rushes him north to hide at a Gordon home. After several weeks, soldiers come to find him and tell him that he can rejoin the regiment with full respect because the Campbells, not the king, gave the false command. Thus Robert preserves the honor of father's name and gains his desire: to fight in Flanders with his new gun, a Brown Bess. The carefully developed foreshadowing leads naturally to the inevitable massacre of the Macdonalds.

Although set over one hundred years after *The Spanish Letters,* **The Lothian Run** has a similar plot. In 1736, Sandy Maxwell, sixteen and apprenticed to a lawyer, helps Deryck Gilmour, a special investigator for customs, uncover smugglers organized by a man named St. Clair. Sandy realizes that he likes that job when he uses his wit to escape from smugglers by throwing a sheepskin over himself and disappearing with a flock of sheep. Sandy's knowledge of the smuggling area helps Gilmour locate George Robertson, an escaped smuggler. The plot becomes complicated when the smugglers start taking documents to *Jacobites in France planning to overthrow the *Hanoverians. An Edinburgh mob aids the capture of St. Clair and Robertson when it gathers to hang the reprieved tollbooth keeper, Porteous. Gilmour wants to arrest both Robertson and St. Clair. St. Clair searches Robertson, and Robertson wants Porteous for killing his friend. Therefore, they all meet with the mob. The omniscient point of view discloses that Sandy's self-assurance agrees with an older man's opinion of his worthiness, which makes Gilmour's trust in Sandy more realistic. In this novel, like *The

Spanish Letters, a boy proves to adults that he has surprising capabilities. Even so, the book is exciting in its own right.

Another novel about the Scottish clans, **A Pistol in Greenyards**, presents a story different from *The Ghosts of Glencoe* but like it uses the device of a character's second sight. While on a ship sailing to the Americas, Connal Ross flashes back to the Greenyards incident when the Lowlanders wanted better land for raising sheep in 1854 and evicted the Highlanders. Before any action, Blind John had a vision that Katrina, Connal's sister, had blood on her face and that someone was aiming a gun at Connal. When Connal, fifteen, hears that the sheriff is coming to Greenyards with an eviction notice, he retrieves his grandfather's gun, hidden in the thatch since 1747 when *Cumberland banned weapons for the Highlanders. The sheriff comes, points a gun at Connal's mother, Anne, and in turn, Connal threatens him. After Connal disappears to a cave with other people from the glen in hiding, the sheriff remembers the warning, arrests Anne, and charges her in the Inverness jail with attempted murder. Connal coerces an honest lawyer, Cameron, to defend Anne, and he shrewdly gets the charge reduced, but the judge still sentences Anne to a year in prison and Peter Ross, Connal's brother, to eighteen months. Most of the people who still have any hope for a future sail from Scotland. On board ship before he begins writing, Connal contracts typhus, and a Lowlander doctor, Hamilton, restores his health. Katrina falls in love with the doctor while Connal is writing the story of Greenyards for him. When Connal finishes, he feels that he has dwelt too much on his own life, but Hamilton can understand the fierce loyalty and Christian support that the people of the glen have had for each other. In one case, each family had contributed to the university training of one of the young people wanting to be a doctor. An interesting aspect arises when a reporter cannot get space in the newspaper to tell of the forty men attacking the women and children in Greenyards and taking their homes because the British had just started fighting the Russians in the *Crimea, and that story took most of the space. The story shows that groups without money lack power.

The Third Eye also develops because a character has second sight. On February 14, 1935, as Jinty Morrison sits waiting to be called for questioning about the death of the earl of Ballinford in a village near Edinburgh, she recalls the events of preceding years that have led her to this place. Several people say she is fey or has the second sight or the third eye with an ability to know things otherwise unknown. When Jinty takes a weekend winter job at the earl's house that requires her to check the earl's alcohol intake, she begins to have conversations with him. During the party for his son's twenty-first birthday, Jinty wanders from the crowd, and soon after, the earl stumbles over her. She remembers hearing of the Ballinford doom—the curse that the oldest son had always died before inheriting the title—and begins to understand some of the old earl's behavior and his fears for his only son. At that time she realizes that he plans to escape the curse in the only way possible. She knows that she cannot reveal his strategy, or the citizens will damn him. By the time she undergoes examination, several events have matured her enough to cope with the questions. One sister sneaks out at night to attend the harvest celebration with its corn dolly ritual, which has endured since pagan times, and she becomes unpleasantly involved with "paddies" (Irish workers hired in gangs to pick Scottish potatoes). A little boy Jinty befriends dies, but as a female, she cannot attend the funeral. Her sister unexpectedly marries, the smithy performing the ceremony over an anvil as in centuries past when a priest was unavailable. A niece is born. Another sister departs for London to work, and Jinty discovers that her mother's first pregnancy led to marriage, not vice-versa. Learning so much at thirteen surprises Jinty, but she senses that such secrets had previously been hidden from her. Jinty's ability to understand the outcasts, her little friend as well as the earl, helps them live more happily for at least a little while.

Also in the twentieth century, two final novels follow Bridie McShane from age nine until she decides to marry. **A Sound of Chariots** poignantly relays Bridie's feelings about her father. The limited omniscient flashbacks show the intense relationship that Bridie and her father shared since both loved words and had such a similar perspective of life. When Bridie sees the physical impairment of all the men, including her father, who returned to rural Scotland after World War I, she begins to empathize with their spiritual wounds. Bridie thinks about God a lot and hears her deeply religious mother gently disagree with her father's view of Christ as a revolutionary. Her Irish father vehemently speaks against the sin of poverty at socialist meetings. She becomes overwhelmed by the concept of time and the fear of death, but ordinary things, like the colors gold and green, restore her happiness. Her ability for total recall of speech and the printed word makes her classmates clamor at lunch to hear her wonderfully vivid stories. After her father's death, when she timidly shows some of her poems to her father's friend, he tells her that her themes embody those of Andrew Marvell's phrase, "Time's winged chariot hurrying near" (the allusion in the title). At a community Christmas party, the first social event attended by the family after the father's death, Bridie reveals her disconsolateness. Her stark sorrow disconcerts her audience, but Bridie knows they "were all inside it, linked together and pushing back against the great dark outside . . . linked together to hold off the great world of darkness." Bridie's flashbacks reveal an enormously intelligent child with amazingly abstract thoughts at age seven. But the warm relationship between Bridie and her father, her emptiness at his death, and her love for words and their meanings make the novel absorbing.

Bridie McShane continues to mature while she works as an apprentice in her mother's family's florist business in Edinburgh at age fifteen in **Hold On to Love**. Still wanting to write, she also attends night school. One night in class she has an appendicitis attack, and Peter McKinley, the student whom she has privately admired, calls an ambulance for her. His later visit to the hospital surprises her because they have exchanged very few words. In the hospital, she continues to record her reactions to women around her, including the fat Liz and the dirty but beautiful tinker girl who disappears and is later found dead in an overgrown field. Bridie understands that these women are so bored with their lives that being in the hospital invigorates them. Back in class, Bridie sees a new instructor, and her anger at the former one for not commenting on her poetry before he resigned causes her to insult Peter. A year passes before Bridie meets him again. She secretly attends a dance with one of the lower-class helpers in the shop, and after seeing Peter there, she has to persuade him that she has never before attended one of these unacceptable affairs. Their friendship grows based on a mutual love of ideas and words, with Bridie becoming aware of her sexuality. Peter convinces her that her talent, like Sir Walter Scott, lies in the telling of tales rather than poetry. His comments help her realize that her instructor had been kind not to discuss her immature poetry. Peter forbids her to see other males, but she will not accept his control over her. When Bunty, the shop girl, becomes pregnant by a "keelie" (a young tough) she met at one of the dances, Bridie becomes even more determined not to be dominated by someone else. Peter leaves her in March 1939 and joins the army. In September, Great Britain declares war, and a Jewish customer, Mr. Finkelstein, convinces her to send Peter a token, four lines of a Yeats poem about dreams. She does, and he responds with the next four lines. His return in March 1940 reunites them, and Bridie's grandmother tells her before her death that Bridie should "hold on to love" rather than money. Although not as powerful as *A Sound of Chariots, Hold On to Love* brings a satisfying sense of closure to Bridie's adolescence.

STYLE AND THEMES

Hunter's merging of style and content leads her to employ appropriate literary devices to emphasize specific content. To show Bridie's inner turmoil in *Hold On to Love,* Hunter uses more fragments than in her other novels. Allusions to biblical figures and to literature give depth to the stories. Figurative language expands descriptions like that of the Edinburgh mob in *The Lothian Run,* which was "like a river bursting suddenly from a deep, containing bed to flood across a plain." In *A Sound of Chariots*, striking imagery and rich figurative language reveal phrases such as "feeling summer in a peach" and the "opalescent heart of this sunrise afterglow." In all the novels, either the primary theme or a secondary one involves the use of power. Misuse of power by religious figures such as druids or by government officials destroys society's fragile bindings. People with any kind of power must be honest and have the good of the governed at heart.

HUNTERS OF SIBERIA. See Bartos-Höppner, B.

HURMENCE, BELINDA (1921–   ). American.

BIBLIOGRAPHY AND BACKGROUND

A Girl Called Boy. New York: Clarion, 1982. *Tancy.* New York: Clarion, 1984.

Belinda Hurmence has won several awards for her novels. *A Girl Called Boy* received the Parents' Choice Award. *Tancy* won both the Golden Kite and the American Association of University Women Award in 1984. For her choice of subject matter, Hurmence acknowledges the influence of *Slave Narratives,* a collection of more than two thousand oral histories of slaves.

WORKS

A Girl Called Boy is a historical fantasy time shift in which the protagonist, Boy, an eleven-year-old who prefers to be called by her initials instead of her given name, Blanche Overtha Yancey, crosses a stream and finds herself in 1853. Before her experience, Boy haughtily ignores her father's proud references to their slave heritage. When a man, Ike, and a boy, Isaac, pull her inside a shack and hide her in a tater (potato) hole, she does not understand that they think she is a runaway slave. Not until the next day, Christmas, when they run away to look for their mother and wife, taking her with them, does she begin to comprehend the terrors of pursuit by slave patrols. Because she can read, an illegal activity for slaves, the males think she is LeMont, whom Mrs. Yancey taught to read before he ran away several months previously. An overseer catches Boy and takes her to Mrs. Yancey who welcomes her back, thinking she is LeMont, only slightly changed. Eventually Boy joins Lookup, another runaway hiding in the Yancey slave quarters, and they leave for Freetown, where Boy hopes to find the runaway Overtha about whom she read in a newspaper. When they realize that Boy can write passes for them as if a master had given them permission to be away from home, they feel less threatened. They soon encounter Ike and Isaac. Lookup happens to be the Lucie for whom Ike and Isaac have been searching. Boy recognizes her sneakers by the stream where they stand and tries to get the three to cross with her. They refuse to leave the shelter of the brush, so as they fade away, Boy hands Lucie her ballpoint pen. When she rushes back to the family's picnic, the group says she has been gone only ten minutes. But her unusual experience changes her attitude toward her slave ancestors, and she welcomes her father's comments about them. The vehicle of historical fantasy is one way to lighten the serious content about slaves and their struggles to survive, but the shift from the present into the past in this novel needs more careful execution to permit the suspension of disbelief necessary for fantasy.

In **Tancy**, a traditional historical novel, the omniscient point of view discloses not only what Tancy the slave thinks but also what her owners think near the end of the *American Civil War in 1865. Tancy's master's son, Billy Gaither, taught her to read, and when she is sixteen, she reads in an open ledger that her mother's name was Lulu. Further snooping shows her that Master Gaither sold Lulu to a neighbor. When Miss Puddin, Master Gaither's wife, catches Billy trying to sexually molest Tancy, she tells them that they are brother and sister. Tancy then understands why she and her deceased master had always had such a close relationship. Not having to worry about Billy pleases Tancy because she

is so modest that a man merely seeing her underwear in a pile of clothes embarrasses her. After Billy dies in the war, Tancy decides to search for her mother.
She takes Jemmy, a four-year-old whose mother was sold long before, with her.
Tancy's ability to read and write gains her an office job registering former slaves.
She becomes attached to Jemmy and eventually takes him to the shantytown to
look for his mother. They find both Jemmy's and Tancy's mothers. The realism
of her mother as property owner and persistent rent collector destroys Tancy's
dreams. Tancy leaves her and returns to the lonely Miss Puddin. But having met
her real mother, she feels a need to live near her. More fortunate than most other
freed slaves, Tancy finds security without subjugation.

STYLE AND THEMES

Hurmence's novels present interesting material with intelligent imagery. *Tancy*
is a tightly written, enjoyable novel.

_I_

I, JUAN DE PAREJA. *See* de Treviño, Elizabeth.

I MARCHED WITH HANNIBAL. *See* Baumann, Hans.

I WAS THERE. *See* Richter, Hans.

I WILL ADVENTURE. *See* Vining, Elizabeth Gray.

I'M DEBORAH SAMPSON. *See* Clapp, Patricia.

ICENI. This British tribe occupied what is now Norfolk and Suffolk. When the Iceni king *Prasutagus died in 60 A.D., the Romans annexed the territory, which led his wife, *Boudicca, to revolt. When the Romans finally conquered the tribe, they punished it severely. See *Sun Horse, Moon Horse* and *Song for a Dark Queen* by Rosemary *Sutcliff and *War Dog, The Queen's Brooch,* and *The Centurion* by Henry *Treece.

IDRUN. Twelve, French, protagonist of *A Candle at Dusk*. *See* Almedingen, E. M.

IMAM. In Arabic, this term means ''leader'' in the sense of one whose pattern of life is an example for others. Imam is the name of the head of the Muslim community. *See* Bartos-Höppner, B., *Storm over the Caucasus*.

IN SPITE OF ALL TERROR. *See* Burton, Hester.

INCA. The history of this Andean civilization begins around 1200, but its expansion did not start until 1438 and lasted until the conquest by Francisco *Pizarro in 1532. It extended from the present Colombia-Ecuador border to central Chile, an area of approximately 380,000 square miles. The culture was agricultural, but the welfare state government distributed land and goods according to family size. Thus people had no initiative to improve their lives or to change locales. The emperor, or "Inca," was divine, thought to have descended from the sun. Although he had absolute power, custom kept him from being a tyrant. He most often married his sister but had a large seraglio. Human sacrifice was rare, unlike the Aztec. The culture was so highly organized that Pizarro was able to begin ruling without any retaliation. *See* O'Dell, Scott, *The Amethyst Ring*.

INGE DORNENWALD. Thirteen, Austrian Jewish female, protagonist of *The Devil in Vienna*. *See* Orgel, Doris.

THE INNOCENT WAYFARING. *See* Chute, Marchette.

IRON AGE. Although iron was in use as early as 3000 B.C., it did not begin to replace bronze weapons and utensils until around 1200 B.C. in the Near East and Southeast Europe. It changed the face of Europe and Asia by placing weapons into the hands of the masses. *See* Sutcliff, Rosemary, *Sun Horse, Moon Horse*.

THE IRON LILY. *See* Willard, Barbara.

IROQUOIS. This confederacy or league of North American Indians originally included the Mohawk, Oneida, Onondaga, Cayuga, and Seneca nations. Corn planters, they were partially sedentary, living in long multi-fireside shelters with their matrilineal crests painted on gables, which gave them the so-called long house image. Kinship and locality were the basis for political life, with each community having a ruling council of adult males, as well as peace chiefs who were appointed by women. The Iroquois liked many long meetings. *See* Wibberley, Leonard, *Red Pawns*.

ISLAND OF THE BLUE DOLPHINS. *See* O'Dell, Scott.

ISTANBUL. Known by several names during its history, this city was called Byzantium until 330 A.D. Then *Constantine named it Constantinople, a name it kept until the Turks called it Istanbul in 1930. See *The Dancing Bear* by Peter *Dickinson; *The Emperor's Winding Sheet* by Jill *Paton Walsh; *Blood Feud* by Rosemary *Sutcliff; *The Seas of Morning* by Geoffrey *Trease; and *The Road to Miklagard, Swords from the North*, and *The Last Viking* by Henry *Treece.

IVAN IV (1530–1584). As Ivan the Terrible, he was the first Russian ruler to use the title of czar. He created an inner circle of advisers and terrorized disfavored boyars. He ravaged Novgorod in 1570 but lost several battles against foreign enemies, although he acquired Siberia through the conquest of the *Cossack, *Yermak Timofeyevich. In a fit of anger, he killed his son Ivan in 1581. *See* Bartos-Höppner, B., *The Cossacks*.

— J

JACINTO. Thirteen, *Comanche named Spotted Wild Horse, captured by Mexicans, protagonist of *The Bad Bell of San Salvador*. *See* Beatty, Patricia.

JACK HOLBORN. Fourteen, orphan, English protagonist in *Jack Holborn*. *See* Garfield, Leon.

JACK HOLBORN. *See* Garfield, Leon.

JACK NORWOOD. Fifteen, English, protagonist of *Trumpets in the West*. *See* Trease, Geoffrey.

JACOB. As the brother of *Esau in the Bible, he took Esau's birthright when he accepted his father, Isaac's, blessing as the oldest son. *See* Paterson, Katherine, *Jacob Have I Loved*.

JACOB BORST. Seventeen, American in New York Palatine Settlement, protagonist of *They Had a Horse*. *See* Edmonds, Walter.

JACOB HAVE I LOVED. *See* Paterson, Katherine.

JACOBITE. This name was given to supporters of the exiled *Stuart king James II and his descendants after the revolution of 1688. See *Hadder MacColl* by Patricia *Calvert; *The Lothian Run* by Mollie *Hunter; and *The Young Pretenders* by Barbara *Picard.

JAMES I OF ENGLAND. *See* *James VI of Scotland.

JAMES VI OF SCOTLAND (1566–1625). After ruling Scotland as the son of *Mary, queen of Scots, he became the successor to *Elizabeth I of England. In Scotland, Protestant nobles seized him in the 1582 raid of Ruthven, but he escaped. He curbed the powers of Scottish Roman Catholic nobles by centralizing power in the monarchy. As English king, he asserted the divine right of kings and alienated both the Scots and English with his religious proclamations. His attitude toward Catholics precipitated the Gunpowder Plot (*See* Guy *Fawkes) in 1605, and he spent much money on court life. The King James version of the Bible, which he had scholars prepare by 1611, bears his name. See *The Queen's Wizard* by John and Patricia *Beatty; *Cromwell's Boy* by Erik *Haugaard; *The Spanish Letters* by Mollie *Hunter; and *Bonnie Dundee* by Rosemary *Sutcliff.

JAMIE MORTON. Fifteen, Scottish orphan, protagonist of *The Spanish Letters*. *See* Hunter, Mollie.

JANISSARY [JANIZARY]. *Mehmet II, a Muslim leader, began the Janissary troops in the fourteenth century from the tribute of Christian children and some boy prisoners who were considered slaves of the sultan. First assigned to households, they were trained in the Turkish language and Muslim religion and then transferred to the capital, where they learned military discipline and the arts of war. They were sworn to absolute obedience, abstinence, and celibacy, with all energies devoted to military training. In return, they enjoyed many privileges. These troops were not abolished until 1826. *See* Carter, Peter, *Children of the Book*.

A JAR OF DREAMS. *See* Uchida, Yoshiko.

JEFF AND SALLY BARNES. Young American protagonists of *Do Not Annoy the Indians*. *See* Baker, Betty.

JEFF BUSSEY. Sixteen, American, protagonist of *Rifles for Watie*. *See* Keith, Harold.

JESSE BEN ABDIEL. Twelve, mute Palestinian orphan protagonist in *A Donkey for the King*. *See* Beatty, John and Patricia.

JESSIE BOLLIER. Thirteen, American, protagonist of *The Slave Dancer*. *See* Fox, Paula.

JESTYN. Young adult British protagonist transported to the East in *Blood Feud*. *See* Sutcliff, Rosemary.

JETHRO CREIGHTON. American who matures from nine to fourteen as protagonist in *Across Five Aprils*. *See* Hunt, Irene.

JIHAD. Only religious purposes in Islam justify fighting; jihad refers to holy war for the spread of Islam to unbelievers and enemies of the faith. *See* Paton Walsh, Jill, *The Emperor's Winding Sheet*.

JIM KEATH. Eighteen, American who lived with *Crow Indians, protagonist of *Moccasin Trail*. *See* McGraw, Eloise.

JIM LYNNE. Sixteen, American in England, protagonist of *The 290*. *See* O'Dell, Scott.

JIM POND. Twelve, English protagonist in *Orphans of the Wind*. *See* Haugaard, Erik.

JINTY MORRISON. Fourteen, female Scottish protagonist in *The Third Eye*. *See* Hunter, Mollie.

JIRO. Thirteen, Japanese male protagonist in *The Master Puppeteer*. *See* Paterson, Katherine.

JOE HINTON. Sixteen, English protagonist transported to Australia in *No Beat of Drum*. *See* Burton, Hester.

JOHN. Seventeen, English protagonist in *The Dolphin Crossing*. *See* Paton Walsh, Jill.

JOHN CAREY. Young adult, English, protagonist of *Tank Commander*. *See* Welch, Ronald.

JOHN DIAMOND. See *Footsteps* by Leon *Garfield.

JOHN FITZWILLIAM. Fourteen, English, protagonist of *Lost John*. *See* Picard, Barbara.

JOHN FORRESTER. Sixteen, English protagonist of *The King's Beard*. *See* Wibberley, Leon.

JOHN SPENCER. Fifteen, orphan, English protagonist of *The Sentinels*. *See* Carter, Peter.

JOHN TREEGATE'S MUSKET. *See* Wibberley, Leonard.

JOHN (JACK) WEBSTER. Nineteen, English protagonist in *The Devil on the Road*. *See* Westall, Robert.

JOHNNY TREMAIN. American protagonist who matures from fourteen to sixteen in *Johnny Tremain*. *See* Forbes, Esther.

JOHNNY TREMAIN. See Forbes, Esther.

JOHNSON, SAMUEL (1709–1784). Known as Dr. Johnson, he was an English writer, lexicographer, and critic whose intelligence and wit gained him much that his poverty and ungainly appearance did not. See *At the Seven Stars* by John and Patricia *Beatty and *Victory at Valmy* by Geoffrey *Trease.

JONATHAN. Thirteen, American protagonist in *The Fighting Ground*. *See* Avi.

JONATHAN COLE. Thirteen, American protagonist in Australia of *Jonathan Down Under*. *See* Beatty, Patricia.

JONATHAN DOWN UNDER. See Beatty, Patricia.

JONES, JOHN PAUL (1747–1792). Although born in Scotland and once in the British mercantile navy, he joined the American Navy at the beginning of the *American Revolution. He cruised around the British Isles and with the French organized a naval attack on the British. He supposedly said, ''I have not yet begun to fight!'' before he defeated the British ship *Serapis* in 1779. *See* Haugaard, Erik, *A Boy's Will*.

JONSON, BEN (1572–1637). An English playwright and poet, he wrote many plays. Among his poems is the familiar ''Drink to me only with thine eyes.'' By some, he has been regarded as the first poet laureate of England. *See* Beatty, John and Patricia, *Master Rosalind*.

JOSEPH CHARNETSKI. Fifteen, Polish, protagonist of *The Trumpeter of Krakow*. *See* Kelly, Eric.

JOSH GRONDOWSKI. Fifteen, American, protagonist of *No Promises in the Wind*. *See* Hunt, Irene.

JOSIE. Eleven, English protagonist in *Landslip*. *See* Rees, David.

JOURNEY HOME. See Uchida, Yoshiko.

JOURNEY TO TOPAZ. See Uchida, Yoshiko.

JUAN. Young Spanish protagonist in *The Blood of the Brave*. *See* Baker, Betty.

JUAN DE PAREJA. Spanish adult protagonist in *I, Juan de Pareja*. *See* de Treviño, Elizabeth.

JULIAN ESCOBAR. Spanish young adult protagonist in *The Captive, The Feathered Serpent,* and *The Amethyst Ring. See* O'Dell, Scott.

JUMP SHIP TO FREEDOM. See Collier, Christopher and James.

JUST SOME WEEDS FROM THE WILDERNESS. See Beatty, Patricia.

JUSTIN. Young adult Roman protagonist serving in Britain in *The Silver Branch. See* Sutcliff, Rosemary.

JUSTIN CONKEY. Fourteen, American protagonist in *The Winter Hero. See* Collier, Christopher and James.

JUSTINIAN I (483–565). Known as the Great, he married Theodora in 525 and became emperor at the death of Justin I in 527. His reign was one of the most brilliant of the Eastern Roman Empire (*Roman Empire, Eastern). His able generals helped him make many conquests, with actual occupation of Rome in 536. He built many important forts, public buildings, monasteries, and churches in Ravenna and Constantinople (*Istanbul). He tried to placate the *Monophysites but alienated the Roman church in the process. His law codes form the foundation of law in most of contemporary continental Europe. *See* Dickinson, Peter, *The Dancing Bear.*

JUTES. This Germanic people, like the *Angles and *Saxons, invaded Britain in the fifth century. They have no recorded history on the Continent, but they were probably the Eotens of the Anglo-Saxon poem *Beowulf*, which places them in a feud with the *Frisians and a branch of the Danes with a Danish king taking refuge among them. Their home seems to have been in a Scandinavian area that the Danes later absorbed. *See* Paton Walsh, Jill, *Hengest's Tale.*

K

KARANA. Young woman who survives on a California coastal island in *Island of the Blue Dolphins*. *See* O'Dell, Scott.

KARL KERNER. Fifteen, American protagonist in *The Tempering*. *See* Skurzynski, Gloria.

KATE. Young English protagonist who relates her cousin Harry's story in *The Huffler*. *See* Paton Walsh, Jill.

KATE RIDER. See *Kate Ryder* by Hester *Burton.

KATE RYDER. English protagonist of twelve who matures to sixteen in *Kate Ryder*. *See* Burton, Hester.

KATE RYDER. *See* Burton, Hester.

KATE SUTTON. English young adult protagonist in *The Perilous Gard*. *See* Pope, Elizabeth Marie.

KATIA. Young Russian protagonist who grows from five to eleven in *Katia*. *See* Almedingen, E. M.

KATIA. *See* Almedingen, E. M.

KEITH, HAROLD (1903–). American.

BIBLIOGRAPHY AND BACKGROUND
   Komantcia. New York: Crowell, 1965; London: Oxford, 1966. *The Obstinate Land.* New York: Crowell, 1977. *Rifles for Watie.* New York: Crowell, 1957.
   Rifles for Watie won Harold Keith the Newbery Award in 1958, and *The New York Times* noted *Komantcia* as a Best Book in 1965. Writing in other

genres has gained Keith the Western Heritage Award twice and the Western Writers of America Spur Award. A master's degree in history from the University of Oklahoma, as well as the ability to "reach people (*especially* people) as well as diaries, letters etc." during research, has kept Keith's settings close to Oklahoma. He says, "I avoided other books written about my research field, preferring to contact people, diaries, letters, personal interviews concerning the subject." He reads, becomes interested in a particular background, and then researches heavily, finding "ten times more information than I'm ever able to use." He comments, "Once I get this research, I apply to it the plot formula I learned in the University of Oklahoma Professional Writing School and the story literally jumps out before my eyes." In the early 1930s, Keith traveled in eastern Oklahoma talking to people while researching his thesis, "Clem Rogers and His Influence on Oklahoma History." Not only did he find needed information on Will Roger's father, Clem, but he also found many people who knew about the *American Civil War in Oklahoma and the *Cherokee Indian nation, which led to *Rifles for Watie*.

WORKS

Rifles for Watie begins in Kansas in 1861, where sixteen-year-old Jeff Bussey and his family endure raids from Missouri border ruffians championing slavery. Jeff's father, lame from an accident and unable to fight, decides to allow Jeff to join the Kansas Union volunteers to battle Watie's raiders, a *Confederate group. Jeff marches, hating the food or lack of it, the bugs, and the exhaustion. After more than a year, he enters his first battle at Wilson's Creek, Missouri, and the horror of it shocks him. He and his friend Noah rush to help the wounded. They receive unanticipated medals for bravery but think they have done only what any other humans would do. The main conflict arises between Jeff and his superior officer, Clardy, who detests Jeff's full name, Jefferson Davis Bussey. Later Jeff finds that the real Jefferson Davis had once defeated Clardy for an officer position that Clardy really wanted. To assert his power, Clardy assigns Jeff ambulance duty, where he endures suffering, assisting with amputations, and burying the dead. General Blunt admires Jeff's abilities and asks him to scout across enemy lines. Knowing that he will be brutally murdered if caught, Jeff agrees anyway, feeling that his scouting might help the war end earlier. He and his partner, when captured, tell the enemy that they want to join Watie. In the fourteen months that Jeff serves the Confederates, he conveniently contracts malaria, which keeps him out of battle. When well, he returns to Watie's band and hears that a shipment of repeating rifles should reach them through a federal officer who wants payment in gold. Jeff has to identify the officer before he can return to General Blunt. The officer is Clardy, but Clardy spies Jeff as he leaves. Jeff makes friends with the bloodhound searching for him, a plausible action since Jeff has made friends with every other dog he has met. A subplot involves his encounter with Lucy Washbourne in the Cherokee nation. Circumstances keep them apart, but when the war ends and Jeff returns home, a letter from

Lucy renews his happiness. Jeff seems too perfect for a young man, but given his circumstances, one can accept his reactions. The novel does confirm that neither side in a conflict is entirely innocent or entirely evil. Dilemmas often arise from the conflict of personal convictions.

Komantcia begins after the Civil War, in 1867, when fifteen-year-old Pedro Pavon arrives from Spain at the Rancho de Pavon in Mexico, just outside the raiding perimeter of the *Comanches and *Apaches. Pedro is part gypsy, very wealthy, an accomplished guitarist, and knows five languages. Banished from Spain for protecting his older brother, Roberto, who supposedly attacked the governor of Seville, he resembles outwardly the "average young Spanish aristocrat . . . proud, unintelligent, dreary, possessed of an exalted notion of his own personal dignity and preoccupied with dress, gossip, and love." But inwardly, Pedro has a strong religious faith on which he relies. Soon after Pedro's arrival, Komantcia (*Ute name for Comanches, meaning "enemy") raid the ranch, kill his mother, and capture him and his brother. With this reversal of fortune, Pedro must utilize all of his abilities in order to survive. Creek Water, an important chief without a son, buys him from his sadistic Comanche master. Old Sore, an old man left to die by the tribe to whom Pedro gives food, becomes his teacher in the ways of the Comanche. Pedro, repelled by the filthy life and savage treatment of other humans, adjusts to his situation by realizing that if he learns all that Old Sore teaches him and if the Virgin to whom he prays helps him, he will be able to escape one day. Creek Water tries to marry him to several women, but all disgust him. He falls in love with and wants to marry the half-Cherokee Willow Girl, but he has no horses to buy her from her father. Instead, the wealthy, fat Paunch buys her as his third wife and then beats her. Pedro decides to steal the Tafoya herd, the one thing that Paunch wants and for which many Comanches have died, to trade for the beautiful (and clean) Willow Girl. He and his "blood brother" Coby (whose child he saved from snake bite) successfully steal the horses, and Pedro trades them for Willow Girl. Although Pedro earns complete freedom, he still has not left the tribe by the time Willow Girl enters his tipi. The folkways and natural abilities of the Comanches are absorbing.

In **The Obstinate Land**, thirteen-year-old Fritz Romberg and his German-American family travel from Texas to the Cherokee strip land in northwest Oklahoma to settle in 1893. Known as nesters to the jealous ranchers, the Rombergs and other families try to start new lives. Among the traumas they endure after building their sod houses are trying to grow kafir corn with drought, hail storms, robbery, and malicious destruction by the ranchers. While working in town, Fritz cannot make himself kill calves after their mothers are sold. He teaches the calves to drink from a pail and thereby starts his own herd. For entertainment, the family goes to town for Christmas, staying at the camp house. Other social events include box suppers and ranch dances. When his father dies in a snowstorm, Fritz becomes the supporter of his mother, brother, and sister. Taught about planting during the sharecropping days in Texas, Fritz helps his family and the Pattersons, earning a reputation of being dependable and honest.

The daughter Mattie of a nearby "sooner" family (illegal settlers) knows about medicine, and her ability to cure various ailments keeps them alive. When Fritz is sixteen, he borrows money from the bank and helps sell windmills to ranchers. As he thinks of marriage, he realizes that Mattie will be a better wife for him than the lovely Dobie who can corral horses but is unable to cook, sew, or deal with adversity. Fritz knows a lot and is very industrious for one so young. He never seems to miss what other teenagers might do. He accepts his responsibilities for his family and helps it succeed.

STYLE AND THEMES

Rifles for Watie and *Komantcia* are tightly written, filled with figurative language. *The Obstinate Land* is less successful, especially when the narrator steps outside the story to tell a future event and slips into the passive voice to explain life on the range. In *Rifles for Watie,* the "iron blade of the plow sang joyously," with the Kansas land "like a child, happy and laughing one minute, hateful and contrary the next." Jeff is "hungrier than a woodpecker with a headache." *Komantcia* reveals that the "sinister thornbush looked friendly in its jacket of small green leaves with a scarlet blossom for a boutonniere" and that Indians were "thick as flies on the fruit of a mulberry tree." Keith's lively language and his exciting stories make these two novels attractive.

KELLY, ERIC (1884–1960). American.

BIBLIOGRAPHY AND BACKGROUND

The Trumpeter of Krakow. Illustrated by Angela Pruszynska. New York: Macmillan, 1928; London: Chatto and Windus, 1968.

For *The Trumpeter of Krakow,* Eric Kelly won the Newbery Award in 1929. When asked to do relief work for Polish legions during World War I, Kelly fell in love with Krakow. There he heard about the trumpeter who took a vow to play each hour at the Church of Our Lady Mary until his death. Each time Kelly visited Krakow, he spent many hours in this church.

WORK

The introduction to **The Trumpeter of Krakow** tells the story of the young man who continued to play the trumpet each hour on the hour in the Church of Our Lady Mary in Krakow until *Tartars shot him in 1241. Since that time, anyone playing the same tune, the Heynal, omits the last three notes, which remained for the young man to play when he died. An omniscient narrator appears in the second chapter and begins making comments about future conditions of certain buildings or individuals outside the story. In 1461, Joseph Charnetski, when fifteen, accompanies his parents to Krakow after someone burns their Ukrainian farm; they carry only a pumpkin in their cart. Outside the city gates, an unidentified man stops the cart and tries to buy the pumpkin. Pan Andrew Charnetski, Joseph's father, refuses. Joseph releases the man's horse so that he cannot pursue them. After the family enters the gates, Joseph saves a young girl, Elzbietka, from being attacked by a German shepherd dog. When her uncle, Scholar Kreutz, hears Joseph's story that the family's cousin has been run out of the city and others still search for his relatives, Kreutz offers them shelter. Having once studied music at the university, Pan Andrew secures a job as the night trumpeter. Joseph continues his studies at the famous university near the Street of the Pigeons where they live. Joseph and Elzbietka spend time together listening to the street scholars profess the new learning of Dante and Petrarch in Latin. Scholar Kreutz, an alchemist, becomes influenced by his student Tring, who is possessed by the desire to make gold. Tring hypnotizes Kreutz into helping him, and Elzbietka watches helplessly as her kind uncle becomes more incommunicative and preoccupied. The man who accosted the Charnetskis outside the gates, known throughout the country as Peter of the Button Face and to the *Cossacks as Grozny the Terrible, continues to search for the family. When bribed, Stas, the doorkeeper of the house, reveals that the family lives inside. Peter promises Stas gold for helping him find the treasure that he thinks the family hides, but Kreutz thwarts their attack by throwing balls of fire at the men. Peter ultimately finds the treasure, the Great Crystal of Tarnov; however, Kreutz takes it for himself. Under the crystal's influence, Kreutz almost destroys the city with fire. When Pan Andrew takes the crystal to the king as his family had vowed to do hundreds of years before, Kreutz follows, and having experienced some of its possible evils, grabs it and throws it into the river. The king restores Pan Andrew's wealth, and eventually Joseph and Elzbietka marry.

STYLE AND THEMES

Kelly uses figurative language throughout the novel. One of the narrator's comments about future events concerns the street on which the family lives; the street, known as a dwelling place of scholars, astrologers, and magicians, will later house Copernicus. A secondary theme—that the innocent suffer the most in a war—underlies the primary theme that loyalty and honor always win and that an inherently good person can overcome evil's temptations. Although some of the stylistic devices lack literary merit, the story is fascinating.

KELSEY BOND. Twelve, American, protagonist of *The Year of the Bloody Sevens*. *See* Steele, William O.

KETTY PETRIE. Sixteen, American, protagonist of *The Far-off Land*. *See* Caudill, Rebecca.

KEVIN CARTWRIGHT. Eleven, American, protagonist of *Captain Grey*. *See* Avi.

KEVIN O'CONNOR. Irish, seventeen, protagonist of *Kevin O'Connor and the Light Brigade*. *See* Wibberley, Leonard.

KEVIN O'CONNOR AND THE LIGHT BRIGADE. *See* Wibberley, Leonard.

KILLER-OF-DEATH. Native American protagonist of twelve in *Killer-of-Death*. *See* Baker, Betty.

KILLER-OF-DEATH. *See* Baker, Betty.

THE KING'S BEARD. *See* Wibberley, Leonard.

THE KING'S FIFTH. *See* O'Dell, Scott.

KING'S KNIGHT'S PAWN. *See* Beatty, John and Patricia.

KIT TYLER. English from Barbados to America, protagonist of *The Witch of Blackbird Pond.* *See* Speare, Elizabeth George.

KNIGHT CRUSADER. *See* Welch, Ronald.

KNIGHT'S FEE. *See* Sutcliff, Rosemary.

KOICHI. Twelve, Japanese male in America, protagonist of *Samurai of Gold Hill.* *See* Uchida, Yoshiko.

KOMANTCIA. *See* Keith, Harold.

KUCHUM. (d. 1598) He was head of the *Tartar khanate of Sibir who in 1582 tried to destroy the *Cossacks. The Cossacks won because they carried firearms and occupied the capital, Kashlyk, but Kuchum's people continued to fight from the steppes. In 1584, Kuchum attacked and destroyed a small party of Cossacks led by *Yermak Timofeyevich, who escaped but drowned in the Irtysh River weighed down by a coat of chain mail. The systematic annexation of Siberia began in 1586 after the Cossack forces left the area. *See* Bartos-Höppner, B., *Save the Khan.*

KUKULCÁN. *See* *Quetzalcoatl.

L

LA GRIPPE. An acute infectious respiratory disease caused by a virus known as influenza, its epidemics have sometimes been severe and deadly. *See* Beatty, Patricia, *Me, California Perkins*.

LA RABIDA. At this monastery near Huelva in Spain, Columbus met two men in 1490, the friar-astronomer Antonio de Marchena and the pilot-shipowner Martin Alonso Pinion, who told him of undiscovered lands. Two Rabida friars, Juan *Perez and Marchena, succeeded in having Columbus recalled to court, which eventually led to his expedition to the New World. See *Son of Columbus* by Hans *Baumann and *Columbus Sails* by C. Walter *Hodges.

LACY BINGHAM. Thirteen, adopted, American protagonist in *Lacy Makes a Match*. *See* Beatty, Patricia.

LACY MAKES A MATCH. *See* Beatty, Patricia.

LAD WITH A WHISTLE. *See* Brink, Carol Ryrie.

LAFAYETTE (1757–1834). A Frenchman, he entered the American military service during the *American Revolution in 1777. He became a friend of George Washington and helped defeat *Cornwallis in 1781. When he returned to France, he commanded the force that fired on the mob at the Champ-de-Mars in 1791 but opposed the rise of *Napoleon and took no part in politics. *See* Wibberley, Leonard, *Sea Captain from Salem*.

LAFE BIRDWELL. Eleven, American, protagonist of *Trail through Danger*. *See* Steele, William O.

LAIRD. Eleven, American captured by *Shawnee, protagonist of *Tomahawks and Trouble*. *See* Steele, William O.

LALA. Young Greek female protagonist in *Persian Gold*. *See* Paton Walsh, Jill.

LALO. Young mute Mexican goatherd, protagonist who goes to Spain in *Nacar, the White Deer*. *See* de Treviño, Elizabeth.

LAMBERT GREW. Young American protagonist in *The Night Spider Case*. *See* Baker, Betty.

LAMMAS. This quarter-day in Scotland falls on August 1. In the early English church, it was a harvest festival, when loaves of bread made from the new grain were consecrated, *Lammas* being derived from "loaf-mass." See *The 13th Member* by Mollie *Hunter and *Sun Horse, Moon Horse* by Rosemary *Sutcliff.

LANCASTER. This English royal house was derived from the fourth son of *Edward III, John of Gaunt, who was created the duke of Lancaster after his marriage in 1359 to the daughter and heiress of Henry, the first duke of Lancaster. This branch of the Plantagenet family fought the house of *York after 1399 in the War of Roses flying the red rose emblem. The reigning Lancastrian kings were *Henry IV, V, and VI. *See* Willard, Barbara, *The Lark and the Laurel*.

LANDSLIP. *See* Rees, David.

THE LANTERN BEARERS. *See* Sutcliff, Rosemary.

THE LARK AND THE LAUREL. *See* Willard, Barbara.

LASKY, KATHRYN. American.

BIBLIOGRAPHY AND BACKGROUND
   Beyond the Divide. New York: Macmillan, 1983. *The Night Journey*. Drawings by Trina Schart Hyman. New York: Warne, 1981.
   Kathryn Lasky has won awards in several genres. *Beyond the Divide* has been honored as Best Book for Young Adults, an American Library Association Notable Book, and a National Council of Teachers of English Recommended Book. *The Night Journey* has received the National Jewish Libraries Award and the National Jewish Book Award. Of Lasky's two books, the story of *The Night Journey* "chose" her since much of the information came directly from her aunt, Ann Lasky Smith, who as a young girl left Russia at the turn of the century. *Beyond the Divide* resulted from a sense that the gold rush had consistently been misrepresented to children. Lasky says, "It was a complicated, misunderstood part of our history. I wanted to try, based on my extensive research, to give a more accurate picture of the event and its impact on peoples' characters—spirit—psyches." She spent nearly ten years extensively researching primary sources

and visiting the area in the Sierras where most of the story takes place. She made countless revisions, but her preplanning and outlining allow her to know a book's direction before she starts her process of writing three days a week. Her "tight" manuscripts usually require only "fine tuning" for a finish.

WORKS

In **Beyond the Divide**, Meribah Simon travels west with her father from April to December in 1849. Shunned by the *Amish community in Holly Springs, Pennsylvania, for attending the funeral of a man of whom the community disapproved, her father, Will Simon, leaves his wife and other children. Meribah goes with him, understanding at fourteen that such Amish judgments will continue to confine her as they have her father. On their journey, they join other wagons to form a company. With 7,000 other wagons, they wait to cross the Missouri River at St. Joseph and then plod across the deserts and mountains during the gold rush period. In her group, Meribah becomes friends with Serena from Philadelphia and watches Serena's growing relationship with the British Mr. Wickham. After Serena's mother insults two unsavory members of the group, they catch Serena with Mr. Wickham, drag her away, and rape her. From that time, almost everyone ignores Serena. Meribah, unable to condone people who condemn the victim but not the criminals, refuses to shun her and takes Serena for walks. As the wagon train nears the *Continental Divide, Serena first and then her mother disappear and are found dead. Thus at the divide, Meribah becomes a woman, with adult understanding but also questions and anger—the symbolism behind the title of the story. As they travel, further difficulties rise, and the real characters of the people appear; only one man other than Will can be trusted. Will, however, is soon incapacitated with a cut hand. At Fort Hall, Mrs. Grant, an *Iroquois, teaches Meribah about herbs and medicines and gives them to her to nurse the train members. But she uses all the yarrow, which eases the lung sickness, and the Whitings in the wagon behind, kill themselves, in despair. When the Simons's wagon breaks, the group votes to leave them, and Meribah finds a cave in which to move her father, slowly dying from gangrene. Suddenly a man whom she recognizes as Goodnough, a man she met while buying artist's chalk in St. Joseph, appears in the cave. He adds them to his own train, and when food is low and travel difficult, he sends the train forward, instructing some to return with food. They do not. After Goodnough leaves, Will dies, and Meridah fights starvation by vying with vultures for a doe carcass. Yani (Mill Creek) Indians help her survive. With the Indians, she finds the balance in her life for which she has searched while traveling across the country. The last two chapters shift the point of view from Meribah to Goodnough when he returns and spots her walking with a Yani. He sees a strong young woman who knows what she can do and who has found how "to be." She tells him of her plans to return to the Valley of La Fontenelle where she met Mrs. Grant, the woman who helped her understand that faith and belief in things unseen allow one to be human.

A search for humanity also underlies **The Night Journey**. Thirteen-year-old Rache's grandmother, Sashie, tells of her escape from Russia in 1900, and through the story Rache experiences her family heritage. With Nicholas II's continued murder of Jews in pogroms, the family knows they must leave. A worker in Sashie's father's factory hides the family in a cart under chicken crates and takes them past the local guards. He deposits them in the country, and they walk disguised as *Purim players, one side of their clothes brightly colored but reversible to drab brown. With this disguise and gold hidden in cookies to pay their bribe to cross the border, they leave Russia. They discover later that, in the confusion at the border, the parcel containing the unfilled cookies had been substituted for the package of cookies filled with gold. So not only did the family have its freedom, but also it retained its wealth. The device of having Sashie remember the experience and having her memory become the story itself creates an unusual structure. The telling becomes marred when contemporary vernacular phrases such as "weak-minded boob" infiltrate the nine-year-old Sashie's vocabulary.

STYLE AND THEMES

The style and language choice in *Beyond the Divide* reveal Lasky's writing skill. The imagery and figurative language coalesce in such phrases as the wagons and animals "seemed to ooze in slow undulations across the prairie like a ribbon of molasses, languid but destined" and "once you've cleared granite from wheatfields in New Hampshire, moving through this crowd is like spooning out Indian pudding." When someone says "nothing," it is "as if crockery had shattered when the word was uttered." The social Serena and the Amish Meribah's friendship is "as unlikely as corn and violets growing side by side in a field." Alliteration and assonance complement the view of the prairie which has "a loveliness to an endless wind and an everywhere sky." Allusions to British poetry and comparing the crossing of Missouri to seeking the Golden Fleece add further depth. Meribah's maturation heightens the story's power and meaning.

THE LAST BATTLE. *See* Wibberley, Leonard.

THE LAST OF THE VIKINGS. See *The Last Viking* by Henry *Treece.

THE LAST VIKING. *See* Treece, Henry.

LAURA. English protagonist who matures from thirteen to nineteen in *Dear Fred. See* Peyton, K. M.

LEE, ROBERT E. (1807–1870). After serving in various capacities for the military, he suppressed John Brown's raid at Harpers Ferry, Virginia, in 1859. In 1861, he resigned from the U.S. Army and accepted the command of the Army of Northern Virginia. He was defeated at Antietam (1862) and *Gettysburg

(1863) but repulsed the *Union Army at Richmond (1862), Fredericksburg (1862), and Chancellorsville (1863). He surrendered the *Confederate forces to *Grant at Appomattox Court House in 1865. See *Across Five Aprils* by Irene *Hunt and *The Wound of Peter Wayne* by Leonard *Wibberley.

LEIF MAGNUSSON. Fifteen, Viking protagonist in *Leif the Unlucky*. *See* Haugaard, Erik.

LEIF THE UNLUCKY. *See* Haugaard, Erik.

LENA SILLS. Twelve, female black American protagonist in *Words by Heart*. *See* Sebestyen, Ouida.

LENIN, VLADIMIR ILICH (1870–1924). A Marxist, he assumed control of the Bolsheviks in Russia and took control from Aleksandr Kerensky's provisional government in 1917 after the overthrow of the czar. He denounced World War I as imperialistic and established the dictatorship of the proletariat. He formulated the present official Communist ideology. See *Chase Me, Catch Nobody!* by Erik *Haugaard; *The Wild Children* by Felice *Holman; and *The White Nights of St. Petersburg* by Geoffrey *Trease.

LENINGRAD. *See* *St. Petersburg.

LEOPARD'S PREY. *See* Wibberley, Leonard.

LEP NYE. Fourteen, American, protagonist of *Path of the Pale Horse*. *See* Fleishman, Paul.

LET THE CIRCLE BE UNBROKEN. *See* Taylor, Mildred.

LETTRE DE CACHET. Such a letter generally meant "orders from the king" but had to be countersigned in France. The letters often enforced imprisonment in state fortresses, particularly the Bastille located in Paris. Without a stated release date, prisoners had to rely on the king's pleasure because no legal process existed for appeal. The letters were outlawed by the Constituent Assembly in 1790, two years before the monarchy fell. *See* Trease, Geoffrey, *Victory at Valmy*.

LEWALLEN. Thirteen, American protagonist in *Wait for Me, Watch for Me, Eula Bee*. *See* Beatty, Patricia.

LEWIS MALLORY. Seventeen, English co-protagonist with *Cecily Jolland, sixteen, in *The Lark and the Laurel* and character in *The Miller's Boy*. *See* Willard, Barbara.

THE LIFE AND DEATH OF YELLOW BIRD. *See* Forman, James.

A LIKELY LAD. *See* Avery, Gillian.

LILI. Seven, American protagonist in *The Lion in the Box*. *See* de Angeli, Marguerite.

LILIAS ROWAN MEDLEY. English protagonist who matures from fifteen to mother of *Ursula Medley in *The Iron Lily* and as character in *A Flight of Swans*. *See* Willard, Barbara.

LINCOLN, ABRAHAM (1809–1865). The sixteenth president of the United States, he had little formal schooling and studied law in his few leisure hours. He was elected, after senatorial defeat, president. He issued the Emancipation Proclamation on January 1, 1863, which freed all slaves. Renominated and reelected in 1864, he was shot five days after the end of the *American Civil War and died on April 15, 1865. See *Across Five Aprils* by Irene *Hunt and *The Wound of Peter Wayne* by Leonard *Wibberley.

LINDISFARNE. This holy island lies in the North Sea off the coast of Northumberland, England. Its history began with the arrival of St. Aidan in 635, who made it the site of his church and monastery. The sixth bishop was St. *Cuthbertus (685–687). In 793, the Danes burned the church, and although survivors rebuilt it, they went inland in 875 fearing another invasion. See *Madatan* by Peter *Carter and *The Wind Eye* by Robert *Westall.

LINDUM. The Latin name for Lincoln, England.

LINZ. A provincial Austrian capital, it grew out of the Roman castle of Lentia and became a medieval trading center. *See* Beatty, John and Patricia, *Witch Dog*.

THE LION IN THE BOX. *See* de Angeli, Marguerite.

THE LITTLE ANGEL. *See* Dalgliesh, Alice.

THE LITTLE FISHES. *See* Haugaard, Erik.

LITTLE KATIA. See *Katia* by E. M. *Almedingen.

LIZ HAWTIN. Fifteen, orphaned English protagonist of *In Spite of All Terror*. *See* Burton, Hester.

THE LOAD OF UNICORN. See *Caxton's Challenge* by Cynthia *Harnett.

LOLLARD. In late medieval England, followers of John Wycliffe earned this name, which means "mumbler" or "mutterer." It was applied to groups suspected of combining pious pretensions with heretical beliefs. *See* Harnett, Cynthia, *The Sign of the Green Falcon*.

LONDONIUM. The Latin name for London, England.

THE LONE HUNT. *See* Steele, William O.

A LONG WAY TO WHISKEY CREEK. *See* Beatty, Patricia.

LOST JOHN. *See* Picard, Barbara.

THE LOTHIAN RUN. *See* Hunter, Mollie.

LOUIS BATTENOTTE. Young Canadian protagonist in *West with the White Chiefs*. *See* Harris, Christie.

LOUISA BAINES. American, thirteen, protagonist of *Hail Columbia*. *See* Beatty, Patricia.

LOULY. Fourteen, American protagonist in *Louly*. *See* Brink, Carol Ryrie.

LOULY. *See* Brink, Carol Ryrie.

LOVEL. Young English orphan, protagonist of *The Witch's Brat*. *See* Sutcliff, Rosemary.

LOWELL, MASSACHUSETTS. The site of a "spindle city" or "*Manchester of America," Lowell factories in the nineteenth century were places where girls could work in order to support their families. The girls established schools for themselves and even published literary magazines. See *A Gathering of Days* and *Brothers of the Heart* by Joan *Blos.

LOYALIST. This name was given to colonists who kept their allegiance to Great Britain during the *American Revolution. Approximately one-third of the colonists remained loyal and were nicknamed *Tories. See *Who Comes to King's Mountain?* by John and Patricia *Beatty and *The Cow Neck Rebels* by James *Forman.

LUBRIN. Young *Iceni male who matures into a tribal leader as protagonist in *Sun Horse, Moon Horse*. *See* Sutcliff, Rosemary.

LUCINDA LAVINA HOWARD. Thirteen, American, protagonist of *Just Some Weeds from the Wilderness*. *See* Beatty, Patricia.

LYNMOUTH. A seaside village in Devon, England, it lies on the *Bristol channel. *See* Hodges, C. Walter, *The Overland Launch*.

_M_

MCGRAW, ELOISE (1915–   ). American.

BIBLIOGRAPHY AND BACKGROUND

The Golden Goblet. New York: Coward McCann, 1961; London: Methuen, 1964. _Mara, Daughter of the Nile._ New York: Coward McCann, 1953. _Master Cornhill._ New York: Atheneum, 1973. _Moccasin Trail._ New York: Coward McCann, 1952.

Eloise McGraw has won awards in several genres. _Moccasin Trail_ won a Newbery Honor Award in 1952 and the Lewis Carroll Shelf Award in 1963 in addition to being a Junior Literary Guild Selection. _The Golden Goblet_ was a 1962 Newbery Honor Book, and _Master Cornhill_ was nominated for the William Allen White Award. In 1984, McGraw received the Evelyn Sibley Lampham Award for her body of work. McGraw's longing to return to Oregon childhood summers manifested itself in settings for her first books. About her books set in ancient Egypt, she says, "That's hard to explain except by supposing, like Don Marquis's famous Mehitabel, that in another life I was Cleopatra—only for me it would be Hatshepsut. I took an art history course in college that introduced me to ancient Egypt and fell obsessively in love with its art, its history, everything about it. Wherever I lived for the next dozen years (and we moved around a lot) I went straight to the library, checked out everything on ancient Egypt, and read them all." A visit to Egypt in 1964 "was like coming home, to go down to Luxor." For writing historical fiction, she has relied on a lifetime of research in books and letters to authorities on a specific subject. She thinks that history at first gave her story ideas that contemporary life did not because it seemed "romantic." She even drew a London map and color coded it to the three days of the London fire, finding tiny street names from _Stow's Survey of London_ and recording them. In the past, McGraw outlined thoroughly, but now she records ideas on index cards—white for plot, blue for characters, orange for questions. After a reasonable collection of cards, she begins the writing and the simultaneous revising. She believes that good writing is "meticulous paring and pruning and polishing." A word processor allows her to write three or four pages, print it, revise, and transfer corrections until chapter 6 or 7, when she begins to understand the deeper meaning of the book. The rest of the writing weaves from this "silk thread."

WORKS

Mara, Daughter of the Nile presents Mara, a blue-eyed Egyptian slave girl, during the reign of *Hatshepsut around 1550 B.C. In addition to her non-Egyptian features, seventeen-year-old Mara speaks Babylonian and reads, highly unusual abilities for a slave girl. These traits interest two evil brothers, powerful in the pharaoh's court, to buy her services as a spy on *Thutmose, the brother of Hatshepsut. Simultaneously, she meets Sheftu, a man whose profession she does not know, and he suggests that she spy for Thutmose on the brothers. Believing that she can do both and still survive, she agrees. As the interpreter for the Syrian princess Ianni, chosen by Hatshepsut for Thutmose's wife, Mara easily moves in the court's company. She, however, does not expect to fall in love with Sheftu. After she discovers that Sheftu also fills a powerful position in the court, Mara teases him to ease her discomfort, but this affectation causes Sheftu to suspect her of lying. Yet she never betrays him even when caught. She endures a beating rather than reveal Sheftu's leadership of those trying to take power away from the spendthrift Hatshepsut. Someone else whom Sheftu trusts betrays him. Thutmose and Sheftu's plan succeeds anyway, and it destroys the evil brothers. When Sheftu's experience of taking gold from Thutmose's father's tomb scares him into realizing that one only has one chance to live on earth, he immediately marries Mara. Mara then no longer treats other slaves haughtily. Instead she asks Sheftu to buy a slave who once befriended her in order to give her freedom.

The Golden Goblet takes place in *Thebes around 1400 B.C. where Ranofer lives with his half-brother, Gebu. Gebu, as his father's oldest son, claimed Ranofer's inheritance when their father died even though he had not visited him during Ranofer's twelve years. Ranofer's dreams of being a goldsmith fade when Gebu refuses to pay for an apprenticeship. When Ranofer returns with a few coins earned at his menial job, Gebu takes them or beats him. What Ranofer discovers is that Gebu uses him to transport bits of gold, which the disgusting Ibni, Gebu's friend who washes gold, collects in wineskins. Ranofer asks Heqet, an apprentice, to tell the goldsmith to watch Ibni and catch him for hiding the gold. However, Ibni's release from the goldsmith shop leads Gebu to make Ranofer become his apprentice in his horrible stonemason shop. From his brother's evil friends and his strange midnight meetings, Ranofer decides that Gebu has other sources of gold. The Ancient One, an old man who befriends Ranofer, and Heqet help Ranofer spy, but Ranofer goes alone into Gebu's room and finds a golden goblet. Then he follows Gebu to the Tombs of the Dead. Ranofer realizes that Gebu is robbing the tomb of Queen Tiy's parents. He rushes to inform palace guards, but they do not believe him. When he identifies an object on the north wall of the tomb, the queen knows he tells the truth. Ranofer exposes Gebu's evil and earns for himself the freedom to become a goldsmith. McGraw enhances the setting by inserting several Egyptian words needing no translation.

McGraw sets **Master Cornhill** in London in 1666. Michael returns to London when eleven after being evacuated by his adoptive family during the *plague but finds not one of them has survived. He meets a musician, Tom, who hires him to sell music sheets after Tom sings the songs. Eventually, Michael finds Susanna, a girl he had met on the cart returning to London, near London Bridge working for Mr. Maas, the best mapmaker in London. As the English begin to lose their war with the Dutch, press gangs start picking up males to serve on ships. Michael hides at Susanna's and starts helping Mr. Maas with maps. Tom, disguised as a woman, appears during a storm to say he is safe and will return. But the *Great Fire begins. *St. Paul's burns, including its stone basement, which harbors many treasures. After the fire, Mr. Maas teaches Michael that being an artist takes courage. One has to dare to touch the paper, and he thinks Michael has that ability. Michael realizes that, as Mr. Maas says, he must always look forward, not backward, and be pleased with life. He knows that Tom has helped him symbolically to bridge the insecurity in his personal life just as the London Bridge realistically connects him to the City. This story of the fire includes unusual details about its ferocity.

Moccasin Trail also presents a character separated from his past. At eighteen in 1844, Jim Keath recalls the bear mauling that led him to live six years in the *Crow tribe. Adopted by Red Deer when found unconscious underneath the dead bear, Jim grew to count coup (scalps) and wear the eagle feather. He also had a medicine dream in which he dreamed a phrase, "The Lord is my shepherd"; he recognizes the lines only as some sort of white medicine. When he sees a blond scalp, memories stir, and he decides to leave the Crow. While he hunts beaver with Tom, a trapper acquaintance, friendly Digger Indians find him and deliver a letter from his brother, Jonnie. Since he has forgotten how to read, Jim rides to the nearest settlement. There he coincidentally finds his younger siblings, two brothers, Jonnie and Dan'l, as well as his sister, Sally, trying to reach Willamette Valley in Oregon. They need Jim to sign for their land since both parents have died, and Jim agrees to go with them, although they have difficulty accepting each other's ways. Jim still wears his Crow braids and eagle feather; they expect orderliness and have no feel for the signs of nature. Going through the difficult portage on the Columbia River and establishing a farm out of wilderness confirm Jonnie's and Sally's worth. Jim's ability to track Umpqua Indians who have taken the young Dan'l as a slave makes him acceptable to the settlers. When Jim tells Jonnie about his medicine dream and the words, Jonnie tells him that their mother always comforted them during sickness with the Twenty-third Psalm. Jim realizes that he has found his home, his "still waters and green pastures," and that tracking almost extinct beaver no longer draws him to the wilderness. The concept of a white male having to forget his Indian ways makes this an engrossing novel.

STYLE AND THEMES

McGraw fills her novels with appropriate language, both diction and dialect. Examples from *Mara, Daughter of the Nile* illustrate her mastery. Vivid imagery occurs in the description of the ''rank smell of the river—an odor compounded of fish, mud, water-soaked rope, pitch and crocodiles.'' Humor appears in curses: ''I wish they clothed his corpse.'' And her figurative language personifies ''Nuit'' (night) as it watches people scurry inside. Similes describe a barge ''like a gigantic water bug, twelve oars on each side dipping rhythmically'' and racing chariots from which ''pedestrians scattered like birds frightened from their marshes.'' McGraw presents unique aspects of the time periods about which she writes.

THE MACHINE-GUNNERS. See Westall, Robert.

MACHU PICCHU. This fifteenth-century *Incan city thrived in the Cuzco region of Peru. *See* O'Dell, Scott, *The Amethyst Ring*.

MACLACHLAN, PATRICIA. American.

BIBLIOGRAPHY AND BACKGROUND

Sarah, Plain and Tall. New York: Harper & Row, 1985.

Patricia MacLachlan is an accomplished author in several genres. Among the awards she has received for *Sarah, Plain and Tall* are the Newbery Award, the Scott O'Dell Award, and the Golden Kite Award, all in 1985.

WORK

Sarah, Plain and Tall, Anna's first-person narrative, reveals that Anna, her brother, Caleb, and their father have longed for the mother and wife who died the day after Caleb's birth in the mid-nineteenth century. Caleb asks Anna if his mother sang and wants to know why his father never sings to him as he once did for Anna. Their father tells them he has advertised outside of their Midwest area for a wife, and a Maine woman, Sarah, has responded. Anna and Caleb want to know if she sings. The correspondence between the family and Sarah reveals that Sarah loves animals, the sea, and painting. On her month-long visit, she shows them that she likes fun but can also be serious. When a neighbor visits and says that she misses her former home, Sarah realizes that a person always misses something. Sarah learns to ride the horse, and her decision to drive the wagon into town alone makes the children fear that she is purchasing a train ticket back to Maine. But she returns and produces pencils so that she can add the colors of the sea to her paintings. She informs the children that she will miss them if she does not stay. The children need a woman both tender and independent who can complement their father; Sarah fulfills the needs of all, even her own need to be loved after her brother's marriage. She stays.

STYLE AND THEME

The clear, direct diction reflects Sarah's heritage and nineteenth-century pioneer life. Appropriate figurative language appears in phrases such as "three old aunts who all squawk together like crows at dawn." The cat becomes personified like many other pets. The imagery and alliteration accent the tasks necessary to keep a household in order: "we swept and straightened and carried wood and water." One of the most refreshing aspects of the plot is that the children want Sarah as a stepmother and fear that she will reject them.

MADAAH. Young protagonist from the British Isles who matures to young adulthood in *Madatan*. *See* Carter, Peter.

MADATAN. *See* Carter, Peter.

MAEVE HAWTHORNE. Twelve, Canadian protagonist in *Cariboo Trail*. *See* Harris, Christie.

MAGGIE GORDON. Seventeen, American, protagonist of *Wilderness Clearing*. *See* Edmonds, Walter.

THE MAGIC AMULET. *See* Steele, William O.

MAGORIAN, MICHELLE. British.

BIBLIOGRAPHY AND BACKGROUND

Back Home. New York: Harper & Row, 1985. *Good Night, Mr. Tom*. New York: Harper & Row, 1981; as *Good Night, Mister Tom*. London: Kestrel, 1981.

Michelle Magorian won the International Reading Association Children's Book Award for *Good Night, Mr. Tom* in 1982.

WORKS

Willie Beech, an eight-year-old evacuee from London during 1939, is assigned to Mr. Oakley, a crotchety man who has never recovered from the death of his wife and baby during childbirth forty years before in **Good Night, Mr. Tom.** The omniscient point of view discloses the townspeople's dim view of Mr. Oakley before Willie's arrival and the change when he begins creating a home for the boy. Mr. Oakley calls Willie "Will" and suggests that Will call him Mr. Tom. Mr. Tom discovers bruises all over Will's body and realizes that Will's fanatically religious mother has battered him. Mr. Tom's concern allows Will to blossom as he begins to trust and enjoy activities normal for his age. Will even makes friends with another evacuee, Zach, a Jewish actor's son, who says he has to make friends fast because he never stays long in the same place. After Mr. Tom gives Will paints at Will's first birthday party ever, Will discovers that he is a talented artist. Mr. Tom takes Zach and Will on a holiday to the beach; when they return, Zach goes to London to see his parents. He is later killed in a bombing raid. Will has to cope with his death, and a new man in town helps him. Will's mother summons him back to London where she treats him horribly and even interprets his smiles as a threat to her discipline. A dream urges Mr. Tom to go to London to check on Will, and he finds Will abandoned by his mother and in terrible condition. Another dream leads Mr. Tom, who by now is not legally allowed to see Will, to kidnap him from the hospital and take him back home. This poignant story emphasizes the human need for bonding and that seemingly incompatible people can sometimes allay loneliness in each other.

In 1945, Rusty (Virginia) Dickinson returns to England in **Back Home** after living in America for five years during World War II. Not able to purchase sugar, milk, or curtains and being ridiculed for her accent make her long for the family she left "back home" in America. She and her mother, Peggy, have difficulty understanding each other. Beatie, an older woman living with them in Devon near Totnes, helps them begin to readjust. Peggy determines that Rusty should attend boarding school to prepare for the university. Before the term, when they move in with Mrs. Dickinson, Rusty feels claustrophobic with a grandmother who dislikes her and her four-year-old brother. When their father unexpectedly arrives, released from the army, only his mother can tolerate his dictatorial ways. Rusty hates the school's rigidity and class consciousness and looks forward to her visit with Beatie, the only sane connection she has. But Beatie shocks Rusty by dying even though she had warned Rusty that she might not be home when Rusty arrived in Devon. Rusty runs away from the school, which makes her mother realize that, like Rusty, her own life is no longer what it was. She separates from her husband and takes Rusty and Charlie to the Devon house that Beatie willed to her. Rusty starts attending the local school, so different from the insufferable boarding school. Rusty and Peggy finally accept that the other has a right to be an individual with her own interests—Rusty the artist, and Peggy the car mechanic. The Dickinsons are representative of a schism in Western society after the war. Many women who had found they could survive, even thrive, without authoritarian husbands chose not to return to stultifying circumstances.

STYLE AND THEMES

In *Good Night, Mr. Tom,* Magorian uses appropriate diction and heavy dialect in the dialogue. Although neither novel is tightly constructed, the sound and sense of words complement each other. Alliteration moves the thought forward in such phrases as "her sackful of letters stuffed compactly into a basket." Both novels lend understanding to the unexpected adjustments necessary for evacuees during World War II.

MALL PERCIVAL. Sixteen, English protagonist in *A Parcel of Patterns. See* Paton Walsh, Jill.

MALTA, SOVEREIGN AND MILITARY ORDER OF THE KNIGHTS OF. *See* Order of the Hospital of *St. John of Jerusalem.

MAN WITH A SWORD. See Treece, Henry.

THE MAN WITH THE SILVER EYES. See Steele, William O.

MANCHESTER. Through this city in northwestern England, one of the principal Roman roads, Watling Street, passed north from Chester. The modern city results from the Industrial Revolution and the exploitation of steam power. The first English canal opened here in 1761 to transport coal. In 1789, the first steam engine for spinning cotton was erected here. In St. Peter's Fields, the "massacre" of Peterloo occurred in 1819. The local police killed many men gathering peacefully to protest the machines replacing them in their jobs. See *The Rebel* and *Riders of the Storm* by Hester *Burton and *The Black Lamp* by Peter *Carter.

MANCHU DYNASTY. Manchu warriors invaded China in the seventeenth century and established the Ch'ing dynasty, which lasted from 1644 to 1912 when they were defeated. They engaged in a war with the British known as the Opium Wars in 1839–42. *See* Yep, Lawrence, *The Serpent's Children.*

MANLY TREEGATE. American protagonist, thirteen, in *Leopard's Prey,* eighteen in *Red Pawns*, and twenty-one in *The Last Battle. See* Wibberley, Leonard.

MANWOLF. See Skurzynski, Gloria.

THE MAPLIN BIRD. See Peyton, K. M.

MARA. Seventeen, Egyptian and Babylonian protagonist in *Mara, Daughter of the Nile. See* McGraw, Eloise.

MARA, DAUGHTER OF THE NILE. See McGraw, Eloise.

MARCUS. Young adult Roman protagonist living in Britain in *The Eagle of the Ninth. See* Sutcliff, Rosemary.

MARCUS VOLUSENUS. Roman in Britain, protagonist who grows from seven to seventeen in *The Queen's Brooch. See* Treece, Henry.

MARGARET PARGETER. Seventeen, English protagonist in *Time of Trial. See* Burton, Hester.

MARGUERITE LEDOUX. Twelve, French female in America, protagonist of *Calico Bush*. *See* Field, Rachel.

MARIA LUIZA. Brazilian protagonist who grows from nine to fifteen in *The Little Angel*. *See* Dalgliesh, Alice.

MARION, FRANCIS (1732?–1795). Called "The Swamp Fox," in the *American Revolution, he commanded militia in South Carolina where he harassed British forces with raids and escaped into the swamps and forests. See *Who Comes to King's Mountain?* by John and Patricia *Beatty and *Treegate's Raiders* by Leonard *Wibberley.

MARK APPERLEY. English young adult protagonist of fifteen in *Follow my Black Plume* and of twenty-six in *A Thousand for Sicily*. *See* Trease, Geoffrey.

THE MARK OF THE HORSE LORD. *See* Sutcliff, Rosemary.

MARK POLTORATZKY. Russian young adult protagonist who matures in *Young Mark*. *See* Almedingen, E. M.

THE MARSH KING. *See* Hodges, C. Walter.

MARSTON MOOR, BATTLE OF. Fought on July 2, 1644, seven miles west of *York between 27,000 *Parliamentarians and 17,000 *Royalists, this battle was the first major Royalist defeat in the *English Civil War. *See* Beatty, John and Patricia, *Witch Dog*.

MARTEL, CHARLES. As the leader of the Franks, he defeated the Muslims in 732 at *Tours. *See* Almedingen, E. M., *A Candle at Dusk*.

MARY, QUEEN OF ENGLAND (1516–1558). Often called Bloody Mary, she, as Mary *Tudor, was the daughter of *Henry VIII and Catherine of Aragon who succeeded to the throne at the death of her half-brother, Edward VI, in 1553. She married Philip II of Spain; repealed the laws establishing Protestantism in England and reestablished Roman Catholicism; martyred at least 300 Protestants; and lost *Calais, the last English possession on the Continent. See *Stars of Fortune* by Cynthia *Harnett; *The Perilous Gard* by Elizabeth Marie *Pope; and *The Hawk* by Ronald *Welch.

MARY ALLEN. Ten, English protagonist in *When the Drums Beat*. *See* Trease, Geoffrey.

MARY WARREN. American young adult protagonist in *The Witches' Children*. *See* Clapp, Patricia.

MASADA. Located in the eastern Judaean Desert on the Dead Sea, Masada was the spot where the Jews had their last fight against the Romans in the Jewish revolt of 66–77 A.D. Nine hundred and sixty defenders burned their possessions and took their own lives when they realized their cause was hopeless. *See* Haugaard, Erik, *The Rider and His Horse*.

MASSASOIT (d. 1661). As the chief of the Wampanoags, a Massachusetts tribe, he negotiated peace with the Pilgrims in 1621 and remained friendly with them all of his life. *See* Clapp, Patricia, *Constance*.

MASTER CORNHILL. *See* McGraw, Eloise.

THE MASTER PUPPETEER. *See* Paterson, Katherine.

MASTER ROSALIND. *See* Beatty, John and Patricia.

THE MATCHLOCK GUN. *See* Edmonds, Walter.

MATILDA, QUEEN OF ENGLAND (d. 1083). The wife of *William I, the Conqueror, she was crowned on her arrival in England after serving as regent in Normandy during William's absences. She is associated with the famed Bayeux Tapestry relating the story of 1066. *See* Treece, Henry, *Man with a Sword*.

MATT PULLEN. Fifteen, English protagonist in *Sea Fever*. *See* Peyton, K. M.

MATT HALLOWEL. Twelve, American, protagonist of *The Sign of the Beaver*. *See* Speare, Elizabeth George.

MAY DAY. *See* *Beltane. On May 1, many countries celebrate the beginning of spring. In England, the morris dances may be performed, and some may "sing in the May." In addition, people may dance around Maypoles decorated with flowers and streamers. See *The Armourer's House* and *Knight's Fee* by Rosemary *Sutcliff.

MAZZINI, GIUSEPPE (1805–1872). Almost always associated with the democratic movement in Italy, he was exiled to France in 1831 but returned in 1848 at the outbreak of revolution. Although not always the winner, he remained an uncompromising republican. See *Follow My Black Plume* by Geoffrey *Trease and *Nicholas Carey* by Ronald *Welch.

ME, CALIFORNIA PERKINS. *See* Beatty, Patricia.

MEDLEY PLASHET. English, young adult protagonist in *The Sprig of Broom*. *See* Willard, Barbara.

MEHMET [MEHMED] II (1432–1481). After succeeding his father in 1451 as Muslim leader, he laid siege to Constantinople (*Istanbul) in 1453. He used cannon of unprecedented size to fell the walls and captured the city on May 29, 1453. He converted the Hagia Sophia, an important Byzantine church, into a mosque and renamed the city Istanbul. Then he encouraged Greek and Italian scholars to settle, accumulated a large library, and welcomed the Greek Orthodox and the Jews. He extended his empire by defeating the Turks in 1473. Although he died during an attempted raid of Italy, he is considered the true founder of the Ottoman Empire. *See* Trease, Geoffrey, *The Seas of Morning*.

MELIA. Young Greek protagonist in *Wildcat under Glass*. *See* Zei, Aliki.

MELINDA CARPENTER. Orphan of thirteen, American, protagonist of *Melinda Takes a Hand*. *See* Beatty, Patricia.

MELINDA TAKES A HAND. *See* Beatty, Patricia.

MENDOZA, ANTONIO DE (1490–1552). As the viceroy of New Spain, he brought the first printing press to the New World in 1535. He tried to stop exploitation of the Indians and built schools and churches. He also tried to develop agriculture. He sent *Coronado on an expedition to what is now New Mexico and Colorado. *See* O'Dell, Scott, *The King's Fifth*.

THE MERCHANT'S MARK. *See* Harnett, Cynthia.

MEXICAN-AMERICAN WAR. This war began in April 1846 with skirmishes between Mexican and U.S. troops along the north bank of the Rio Grande. In January 1848, the war ended, with the United States acquiring a vast expanse of territory stretching from the Rio Grande to the Pacific Ocean. *See* Baker, Betty, *The Dunderhead War*.

MERIBAH SIMON. Fourteen, American Amish protagonist in *Beyond the Divide*. *See* Lasky, Kathryn.

MERLE TUCKER. Thirteen, American girl, protagonist in *Billy Bedamned, Long Gone By*. *See* Beatty, Patricia.

MEROMIC. Nineteen, Gallic protagonist in *The Conquered*. *See* Mitchison, Naomi.

MESSAGE TO HADRIAN. *See* Trease, Geoffrey.

A MESSENGER FOR PARLIAMENT. *See* Haugaard, Erik.

MICHAEL CORNWALL. Eleven, orphan, English protagonist in *Master Cornhill*. *See* McGraw, Eloise.

MICHAEL VALLIER OF HARDRAW. Sixteen, English protagonist in *The Baron's Hostage*. *See* Trease, Geoffrey.

THE MILLER'S BOY. *See* Willard, Barbara.

MIRABEAU, MARQUIS OF. *See* Honoré-Gabriel *Riqueti.

MIRIAM WILLARD. American young adult protagonist captured and sent to Montreal in *Calico Captive*. *See* Speare, Elizabeth George.

MIRIAM. *See* Sommerfelt, Aimée.

MIST OVER ATHELNEY. See *Escape to King Alfred* by Geoffrey *Trease.

MITCHISON, NAOMI (1897–). Scottish.

BIBLIOGRAPHY AND BACKGROUND
　　The Conquered. London: Jonathan Cape, 1954.
　　Many of Naomi Mitchison's books have influenced younger historical fiction authors, and for her writing, she has received three honorary university degrees. Mitchison uses information gained in research for adult books when writing books for children. She says, "I enjoy writing for children because one has to do straight writing not playing tricks as with writing for adults." With no set time to write each day, she calls on her knowledge, which she has gained throughout her life, but she knows where to research when she needs to verify details.

WORK
　　In **The Conquered**, the omniscient point of view reveals reactions of participants on both sides in the Gallic wars from 58 to 46 B.C., with the major characters being Meromic, a *Veneti chieftain's son captured at nineteen, and Titus Barrus, a noble and young Roman soldier. The conflict begins when Meromic's tribe captures Roman soldiers trying to buy food. Titus becomes a prisoner in Meromic's home. After the Veneti defeat, Meromic surrenders, and Roman soldiers sell him coincidentally to Titus's grandfather in Rome. When Titus visits, he requests Meromic's services and saves him from death for an infraction of the house rules but does not recognize their former relationship.

Meromic supports Titus and fights with him against his own people, the *Gauls, because of a vow to protect Titus. In Britain, however, Meromic avenges his sister's suicide by killing Gandor, the man who planned to marry her but refused to help the tribe when the Romans first attacked. In the last battles between the Romans and Gauls, Meromic fights against the Romans, knowing that Titus is not in the area. After Meromic's last battle, the Romans chop off his hand. Titus unexpectedly finds him, and they return to Rome, where Meromic eventually dies.

STYLE AND THEME

Although examining opposing viewpoints simultaneously lends interest to the novel and allows dramatic irony, Mitchison relies on several coincidences to advance the action, thereby undermining the plausibility of the plot.

MITYA. Young Russian protagonist in *The Cossacks* and minor character in *Save the Khan*. *See* Bartos-Höppner, B.

MOCCASIN TRAIL. *See* McGraw, Eloise.

MOHAWK VALLEY. *See* Welch, Ronald.

MONOPHYSITES. Christians known as Monophysites teach that the person of Jesus Christ exhibited only one nature instead of two natures, divine and human, as asserted at the Council of Chalcedon in 451. *See* Dickinson, Peter, *The Dancing Bear*.

MONTEZUMA [MOCTEZUMA] II (1466–1520). Chief of the Aztecs, he tried to persuade Cortez (*Cortés) not to come to Mexico City in 1519, but Cortez seized him in Tenochtitlán and held him hostage after the Aztecs rose against the Spanish. He died a few days later. See *The Feathered Serpent* by Scott *O'Dell; *The Blood of the Brave* by Betty *Baker; and *Columbus Sails* by C. Walter *Hodges.

MOON SHADOW. Young Chinese boy in America, protagonist of *Dragonwings*. *See* Yep, Lawrence.

MORGAN, DANIEL (1736–1802). A soldier in the *American Revolution, he helped *Arnold assault Quebec, opposed *Burgoyne at *Saratoga, and commanded troops in North Carolina where he defeated the British at Cowpens in 1781. *See* Wibberley, Leonard, *Peter Treegate's War*.

MORGAN, HARRY (1635–1688). This British buccaneer born in Wales probably seized Jamaica in 1655. Buccaneers chose him as their commander in 1668, and he helped them capture Puerto Principe in Cuba and Portobelo in Panama where he took a large sum from the governor. After the treaty between

Spain and England, the king called him to England to explain his conduct in 1672, but he gained the king's favor and returned to be a Jamaican leader in 1674. See *Pirate Royal* by John and Patricia *Beatty and *Deadmen's Cave* by Leonard *Wibberley.

MORNING IS A LONG TIME COMING. *See* Greene, Bette.

MUNA. Thirteen, Japanese male protagonist who matures to late teens in *The Sign of the Chrysanthemum*. *See* Paterson, Katherine.

THE MURDERER. *See* Holman, Felice.

MY BROTHER SAM IS DEAD. *See* Collier, Christopher and James.

MY ENEMY, MY BROTHER. *See* Forman, James.

_N_

NACAR. *See* de Treviño, Elizabeth.

THE NAMESAKE. *See* Hodges, C. Walter.

NAN, DICKON, AND ADAM SHERWOOD. Teenaged English protagonists in *The Sign of the Green Falcon*. *See* Harnett, Cynthia.

NAPOLEON I (1769–1821). He rose to command after the *French Revolution and won portions of Italy and Egypt before Lord *Nelson destroyed his fleet in the Battle of the Nile in 1798. In 1799, he took control of the French government, and in 1803, he abandoned hopes of an overseas empire by selling Louisiana to the United States. He declared France a hereditary empire in 1804 and had himself crowned emperor. He gained control of Europe but lost at sea when Nelson defeated his navy at *Trafalgar in 1805. Finally, European land forces overcame him in 1814; he abdicated and was exiled to Elba. He reentered Paris on March 20, 1815, and raised new armies. He lost at Waterloo on June 18, 1815, and abdicated again. After surrendering to the British, he spent the remainder of his life on the island of St. Helena. See *Castors Away!* by Hester *Burton; *The Court of the Stone Children* by Eleanor *Cameron; *Victory at Valmy* by Geoffrey *Trease; and *Captain of Foot* by Ronald *Welch.

NATHAN CLEGG. Sixteen, American, protagonist of *The Dark Canoe*. *See* O'Dell, Scott.

NAVAHO. The largest Indian tribe in the United States, the Navaho live in the Southwest, where they have borrowed extensively from the culture of the Pueblo Indians—agriculture, weaving, sand paintings, and ceremonial traits. Their matrilineal descent dictates that newly married couples almost always live near the bride's mother. The mother's brothers take responsibility for the upbringing, marriage, and property of their sister's children. No Navaho may marry a spouse from the clan of either mother or father, but they may choose from sixty clans. The religious system is quite intricate, with important ceremonies that many times have the purpose of curing bodily illness or psychiatric problems. Weaving and silversmithing are important Navaho arts. *See* O'Dell, Scott, *Sing Down the Moon*.

NAZI. Members of the National Socialist German Workers' Party, founded in Germany in 1919 and brought to power by Adolf Hitler, are called this name, a German phonetic shortening of *National-socialist*. See *The Traitors, Ceremony of Innocence, Horses of Anger, The Survivor,* and *My Enemy, My Brother* by James *Forman; *Summer of my German Soldier* by Bette *Greene; *War without Friends* by Evert *Hartman; *Chase Me, Catch Nobody!* by Erik *Haugaard; *Fly away Home* by Christine *Nostlinger; *The Devil in Vienna* by Doris *Orgel; *The Winter When Time Was Frozen* by Els *Pelgrom; *Friedrich* and *I Was There* by Hans *Richter; *The Silver Sword* by Ian *Serrailler; and *Miriam* by Aimée *Sommerfelt.

NED. Twenty, English protagonist in *The Right-Hand Man*. *See* Peyton, K. M.

NEIL CAREY. Young adult, English, protagonist of *For the King*. *See* Welch, Ronald.

NELL HENCHMAN. Twelve, English protagonist in *Castors Away!* *See* Burton, Hester.

NELSON, HORATIO (1758–1805). A British naval officer, he conquered *Napoleon I at the Battle of the Nile in 1798 and won other battles in league with several other countries during the next years. In 1803, he took command of the Mediterranean fleet and after blockading the French for two years, defeated them at *Trafalgar in 1805 by leading the British fleet with his ship *Victory*. Struck by an enemy bullet, he died as victory became his. *See* Burton, Hester, *Castors Away!*

NEWGATE. A prison stood at this site in London from the twelfth century until 1902 when it was demolished. See *Smith* by Leon *Garfield and *The Right-Hand Man* by K. M. *Peyton.

NICHOLAS AND THE WOOL-PACK. See *The Merchant's Mark* by Cynthia *Harnett.

NICHOLAS CAREY. English young adult protagonist in *Nicholas Carey. See* Welch, Ronald.

NICHOLAS CAREY. *See* Welch, Ronald.

NICHOLAS FETTERLOCK. Fourteen, English protagonist in *The Merchant's Mark.* *See* Harnett, Cynthia.

NICHOLAS LANARAS. Fifteen, Greek, protagonist of *Ring the Judas Bell.* *See* Forman, James.

NICHOLAS QUILL. Eleven, orphan, English protagonist in *The Queen's Wizard.* *See* Beatty, John and Patricia.

THE NICKEL-PLATED BEAUTY. *See* Beatty, Patricia.

THE NIGHT JOURNEY. *See* Lasky, Kathryn.

NIGHT JOURNEYS. *See* Avi.

THE NIGHT SPIDER CASE. *See* Baker, Betty.

THE NIGHT OF THE COMET. *See* Garfield, Leon.

NIKOLAI KARALKAN. Thirteen, Russian, protagonist of *Hunters of Siberia.* *See* Bartos-Höppner, B.

NINA. Fifteen, American protagonist in *The Court of the Stone Children.* *See* Cameron, Eleanor.

NO BEAT OF DRUM. *See* Burton, Hester.

NO PROMISES IN THE WIND. *See* Hunt, Irene.

NOORTJE VANDERHOOK. Eleven, Dutch female protagonist in *The Winter When Time Was Frozen.* *See* Pelgrom, Els.

NORMAN. Originally, this term denoted Northmen "Nortmanni," the barbarians who came from Denmark, Norway, and Iceland to make plundering raids on the West in the eighth century. In the form "Normans," it refers to those Vikings who settled in northern Francia, the Frankish kingdom, and to their descendants who founded the duchy of Normandy and sent new expeditions to various places, including the British Isles. *William the Conqueror began Norman rule in England in 1066. See *The Shield Ring* and *Knight's Fee* by Rosemary *Sutcliff.

NORTH TO FREEDOM. See Holm, Anne.

NOSTLINGER, CHRISTINE (1936–   ). Austrian.

BIBLIOGRAPHY AND BACKGROUND

Fly Away Home. Trans. Anthea Bell. New York: Watts, 1975.

Many awards have come to Christine Nostlinger, among them the Freidrich-Bodecker Prize for Children's Literature in 1972 and the German State Children's Book Prize in 1973 for *Fly Away Home*. For her major contribution to international literature, Nostlinger won the Hans Christian Andersen Medal in 1984.

WORK

Christel Goth, eight, in **Fly Away Home**, lives in Vienna during 1945. In her first-person narrative, she sees enemy planes fly into Vienna but refuses to tell her grandmother because the lady in the bomb shelter who spouts "Heil Hitler" scares her more than the planes. Her grandmother intensifies encounters with the woman by openly declaring her hatred of Hitler. When bombs destroy part of their house, Christel, her sister, and her parents go to live in Frau Von Braun's villa outside Vienna. Frau Von Braun's daughter-in-law and her two children live with the family. Since Russians wounded Mr. Goth's leg, he no longer has to fight for the *Nazis, whom the family dislikes even though Mrs. Goth's brother serves the führer in Munich. When the Nazi storm troopers leave Vienna, the family celebrates even though they momentarily expect the Russians. But before the Russians appear, the family hides Mr. Goth's army uniform so that they will not capture him. After their arrival, a Russian soldier saunters into the house and shoots the chandelier. Christel wants to walk on the sparkling glass, but the adults disapprove. Eventually a Russian major decides to stay in the house, and his presence actually protects everyone from the bullying of other soldiers. Christel makes friends with the cook, Cohn, who tells her enticing stories about "his" Leningrad (*St. Petersburg). When Cohn goes to central Vienna to obtain new eyeglasses, Christel hides in the cart so that he will take her to her grandparents' home. Christel finds them alive but notes that her grandmother is less obstinate than she was before the occupation. When the family realizes where Christel has gone, her father retrieves her, at great personal risk. Later, when she says all of the foul words she knows, her father ignores her. She seems to understand that he expects her to become bored with her tirades. When the Russians leave Austria, the family returns to the bombed city to resume their lives.

STYLE AND THEME

Nostlinger's word choice clearly imitates the point of view of her young protagonist. Christel thinks of "snot" and likes to eat the dirt under her fingernails. She exaggerates to friends, which causes them trouble when they believe her. She does not comprehend that the Russians consider the war a deadly serious situation, and her parents' reactions to particular events surprise her. The imagery and figurative language reflect a country at war, especially when the bombs "looked like strings of shining, silvery, beads hanging from each aircraft." Most important, Christel feels secure in the midst of chaos, exemplifying Nostlinger's implicit theme that even in war, families who keep their values of love and support can more easily face the loss of material advantages.

_O_

O THE RED ROSE TREE. _See_ Beatty, Patricia.

THE OBSTINATE LAND. _See_ Keith, Harold.

O'DELL, SCOTT (1898–). American.

BIBLIOGRAPHY AND BACKGROUND

The Amethyst Ring. Boston: Houghton Mifflin, 1983. _The Captive_. Boston: Houghton Mifflin, 1979. _Carlota_. Boston: Houghton Mifflin, 1977; as _The Daughter of Don Saturnino_. London: Oxford, 1979. _The Dark Canoe_. Illustrated by Milton Johnson. Boston: Houghton Mifflin, 1968; London: Longman, 1969. _The Feathered Serpent_. Boston: Houghton Mifflin, 1981. _The Hawk That Dare Not Hunt by Day_. Boston: Houghton Mifflin, 1975. _Island of the Blue Dolphins_. Boston: Houghton Mifflin, 1960; London: Constable, 1961. _The King's Fifth_. Illustrated by Samuel Bryant. Boston: Houghton Mifflin, 1966; London: Constable, 1967. _The Road to Damietta_. Boston: Houghton Mifflin, 1985. _Sarah Bishop_. Boston: Houghton Mifflin, 1980. _Sing Down the Moon_. Boston: Houghton Mifflin, 1970; London: Hamish Hamilton, 1972. _The Treasure of Topo-el-Bampo_. Illustrated by Lynd Ward. Boston: Houghton Mifflin, 1972. _The 290_. Boston: Houghton Mifflin, 1976; London: Oxford, 1977. _Zia_. Illustrated by Ted Lewin. Boston: Houghton Mifflin, 1976; London: Oxford, 1977.

Scott O'Dell has won many major awards throughout his career. _Island of the Blue Dolphins_ received the Newbery Medal in 1961, and three other books—_The King's Fifth_ (1967), _The Black Pearl_ (1968), and _Sing Down the Moon_ (1971)—received Newbery Honor awards. O'Dell has also won the De-Grummond Medal, the Nene Award, the William Allen White Award, the Regina Medal, the Rupert Hughes Award, the German Jugenbuchpreis twice, and the Hans Christian Andersen Medal for his body of work. In 1984, he granted the first Scott O'Dell Award for Historical Fiction, offered for a book published for children and/or young adults set in the New World written in English by a U.S.

citizen and selected by the Advisory Committee of the *Bulletin for the Center of Children's Books*. A desire to let people know how he felt about unregulated hunting led O'Dell to write his first book, *Island of the Blue Dolphins*. He continued writing on topics about which he wanted to know more and about which he wished to "make a statement." His writing habits have changed through the years. Instead of writing all day, currently he writes before noon for approximately six hours. The research on a book takes him about three months, with the composition of the book requiring another six months. He says, "All of my stories are in a certain sense written not for children but for myself, out of a personal need."

WORKS

The first-person narrative (in all but one of O'Dell's historical fictions) impels the reader to empathize with the protagonists' inner journeys, which occur simultaneously with their outward land or sea journeys. The protagonist or someone close to the protagonist in each story interacts with an antagonist whose greed for barter—silver, gold, otter, slaves—harms those involved. Money intermittently tempts some of the protagonists, but they all escape its power by realizing that it enslaves instead of frees. Examining the novels from other aspects will illustrate different motives and themes.

The Treasure of Topo-el-Bampo deviates from O'Dell's general pattern since it is written for younger readers in picture book form, with the protagonists being two burros, Leandro and Tiger. They live in the poorest village in Mexico in the 1770s, Topo-el-Bampo, until the father of a family of twelve sells them to the owner of the richest silver mine in the world. Like the humans who labor in the mine, earning little food or shelter and no pay, the burros work constantly. One day the burro train leaves the mine carrying its largest silver load. But Juan Q, a notorious outlaw, attacks the train. The two burros wander away during the fracas and find themselves on the road to Topo-el-Bampo. They reenter the town, and their bars of silver make it the richest in Mexico. O'Dell avoids blatant personification, but he allows Tiger to wander away from a burro train earlier in the story and follow the road to Topo-el-Bampo. This action makes the burros' eventual return to the town plausible. The mine owner's pleasure with his wealth makes him a relative of characters in O'Dell's "explorer" novels.

A trilogy—*The Captive, The Feathered Serpent,* and *The Amethyst Ring*— addresses the motives of Spanish explorers for coming to the New World. The first chronologically, **The Captive,** presents Julian Escobar, a seminarian, who in 1506 leaves Seville for the New World to save heathen souls on Don Luis's ship, the *Santa Marguerita*. As he watches the ship's crew force native Indians to dig gold and load it and themselves for slavery on the ship, he realizes the real purpose of his inclusion on the journey: bestowing God's blessings on the actions of the crew. Julian watches Don Luis sail the ship into a horrible storm on his way to more gold. When the ship sinks, Julian and Don Luis's black stallion swim to a volcanic island shore. There Julian tries to survive. An island girl, Ceelah, leaves him fire after he fails to keep his coals alive. He eventually convinces her to talk, and she teaches him Mayan, a difficult language. One day, with gunpowder recovered from the ship, he destroys a huge, hideous statue of the goddess of the seven serpents. Having heard the explosion, a dwarf from the City of the Seven Serpents at the island's other end sails into Julian's harbor, sees his long blond hair, and suggests that Julian pose as Kukulcán (*Quetzal-coatl), the god who had left the island over 400 years earlier but whose return the natives have always anticipated. The dwarf, also a Spaniard, tells Julian that he must act the god or the Mayan priests will cut out his heart. Julian acquiesces and sails to the city robed in Kukulcán's feathers while the dwarf ecstatically describes the wealth and power they will gain together. As Julian watches the priests cut hearts from humans in his honor, Kukulcán's power begins to tantalize him, and he loses some of the Christian godliness that led him to throw his share of Don Luis's gold overboard. He begins to think of the possible beauty of the city and becomes a captive, in mind as well as body.

In **The Feathered Serpent**, Julian begins to revive the city from its ruins. The dwarf, Cantu, surprises him with the news that Don Luis has survived the shipwreck and rules Tikan. Knowing Don Luis will attack his city looking for gold, Julian decides to attack first. Tikan's warriors recognize Julian as Kukulcán and immediately submit. Julian returns with a thousand prisoners to help him renovate his city. The priests, however, expect to sacrifice the prisioners in the spring fertility rites. To protect his guise, Julian must allow sacrifice, but he authorizes only fifteen slaves. This meager offering does not bring rain, and when the rains finally come, they do not sustain the crops. The priests' veiled hostility increases Julian's concern about controlling his city efficiently and effectively. He decides to visit Moctezuma (*Montezuma) of Tenochtitlán in Azteca to observe his methods. Soon after Julian's arrival, Moctezuma shows him a picture recently drawn by his coastal spies in which Julian recognizes a Spanish fleet. An unknown explorer, *Cortés, requests to visit Moctezuma. Julian immediately senses that this Cortés will soon invade his own city and find the gold hidden in the salvaged *Santa Marguerita*. When Cortés's entourage arrives in Azteca, Julian spots two of his own subjects—Don Luis and Ceelah, newly named Doña Marina, who has become Cortés's interpreter. How the two met Cortés and left the City of the Seven Serpents remains unexplained. After Moc-tezuma's death, fighting, and further encounters with Cortés, the natives cut out Don Luis's heart. Julian and Cantu escape and return to the City of the Seven Serpents.

In the final book of the trilogy, **The Amethyst Ring**, Julian finds when they return that their people have captured a Spanish ship and a Bishop Pedroza. When the bishop reveals that he brings Cortés a message from King Carlos (*Charles I of Spain), Julian finds a letter in the captured ship condemning him as a traitor for unlawfully keeping the king's fifth of gold. Julian requests that the bishop make him a priest, but the bishop refuses, believing Julian has lost his faith. Julian protests by proclaiming that without holy orders he can do little to bring Christianity to the people. Julian takes the bishop and his amethyst ring to the palace and orders him to watch the human sacrifices that Julian has had to endure. The bishop's defiance continues, so Julian does not intervene when the high priest cuts out the bishop's heart. Instead Julian retrieves the amethyst ring and wears it. In his attempt to save his city from Cortés's attack, Julian sails the islands looking for people to help him fight. What he finds are indolent and nonproductive tribes constantly chewing the coca plant. He realizes that this habit may underlie the decline of his city and of all the Mayans. With no new forces, Julian cannot overcome Cortés. Doña Marina, however, helps him escape. Julian walks north, working at various jobs, always visible because of his bleached hair and white Spanish skin. He finally joins *Pizarro in Panama and views Pizarro's massacres of the Indian followers of *Atahualpa, king of the *Incas in Peru. Before the destruction, Chima, Atahualpa's daughter, charms Julian, and afterward, he searches for her as far as *Machu Picchu. She disdains his interest, and he returns to Spain, where he joins the Brothers of the Poor. In this trilogy, O'Dell clearly illustrates that religious faith often did not deter self-aggrandizement during the Spanish slaughter of the native Indians. Obtaining gold obsessed the Spanish, and saving souls in the name of Christ was an excellent ruse that allowed them to get it.

The most structurally complex of O'Dell's novels and the last with the explorer motif, **The King's Fifth**, presents Esteban de Sandoval as he awaits trial for hoarding the king's fifth, the portion of the spoils captured belonging to the king. The trial begins on September 27, 1541, his seventeenth birthday. O'Dell alternates Esteban's flashbacks to his time in the desert looking for gold and finding it with Captain *Mendoza, Father Francisco, their guide Zia, and other men, between scenes of the trial where Esteban appears before the judges who question him. The flashbacks gradually reveal Esteban's role as the cartographer of the expedition and that he is guilty as charged but also that he did not maliciously cheat the king. When he realized how humans destroy other humans to obtain gold, as the survivor of his group, he threw the collected gold into a desert sinkhole. What becomes apparent when Esteban converses with his jailer, Don Felipe, and with a visitor, Captain Martin, is that they want to know where Esteban hid the gold so that they can find it when the trial ends. They offer to free him from his three-year jail sentence if he will show them the gold's location. Esteban refuses. He knows that he has more freedom inside the cell than those outside whom the gold enslaves.

Greed also controls persons in those novels whose action occurs on board or around a ship. In **The Hawk That Dare Not Hunt By Day**, Tom Barton's Uncle Jack sails a cargo ship, the *Black Pearl,* on which he often carries contraband between London and the Continent. He returns to London from Germany in 1524 with illegal Martin Luther manuscripts. Tom finds that William *Tyndale might buy them. When Tom contacts him, he likes his demeanor so much that he offers Tyndale a passenger berth to Antwerp. When Uncle Jack hears that Tyndale plans to print a translation of the Bible into English and that the cargo profits will become his, he accepts the passenger. Hebert Belsey, a man dis-approving of Luther's ways and interested in making money, applies for work on the *Black Pearl* so that he can tail the three men. Tom endeavors to smuggle Tyndale's Bibles into England and in the process discovers that Belsey's friend Henry Phillips plans to hang Tyndale for his "crime." While trying to warn Tyndale in Antwerp, Tom discovers that Phillips visits Tyndale and that Tyndale trusts him. But Phillips soon betrays Tyndale and sees him hung for his beliefs. After Tyndale's death, Phillips becomes a pitifully poor man who does not receive the gold promised for his treachery.

In the second shipboard novel, **The Dark Canoe**, the greed of a minor char-acter and a dead brother propel the protagonist. Although sixteen-year-old Nathan Clegg does not reveal the date, Nathan's brother Caleb's interest in *Captain Ahab of Melville's *Moby Dick* and other indicators place the story in the later nineteenth century. Because of a crippled leg, Caleb identifies with Captain Ahab. On the ship *Alert* near Baja, California, the two brothers search for a sunken whaler, the *Amy Foster,* lost while Caleb captained it. On this voyage, Nathan's brother Jeremy has been murdered, and no one knows the identity of the assassin. Caleb, stripped of his captain's license, madly searches for the lost *Amy Foster* with little concern for avenging Jeremy's murder. Caleb desperately wants the logbook because he thinks that Jeremy disobeyed his orders about steering the ship. On that voyage, Caleb had contracted a fever, and he cannot be certain that he actually gave the order. However, Caleb had never intimated during his trial that Jeremy might be lying about Caleb's orders. The local Indians help the crew find the *Amy Foster* with its valuable load of ambergris, and Caleb recovers the logbook. When Nathan sees the embalmed Jeremy displayed on an island altar by Indians who worship blond gods, they begin to reconstruct his disappearance. They realize that Jeremy had capsized one night when trying to steal gold from the Indians. When he floated ashore, the Indians thought he was their god returning. At the beginning of the novel, Nathan finds a chest bumping against the *Alert,* which he retrieves. When he finally shows it to Caleb, Caleb recalls Melville's description of Queequeg's coffin, an exact description of the chest. Caleb carefully restores it and regretfully returns it to the sea, but not until Nathan convinces him not to search for the "white whale" but to go home. The structure in this novel is intriguing because the characters create layers of fiction by first being fictions themselves and second by believing still other fictions to be the reality.

A third novel set on shipboard, **The 290**, involves sixteen-year-old Jim Lynne, an American sent to England to be educated, who helps design the *290* in Liverpool in 1862. As this unusually sleek sloop nears completion, Jim's brother Ted, whom he has not seen in six years, appears and requests information about the trial runs of the *290*. Ted has heard that the ship will become a *Confederate raider after being fitted with guns in the Azores. (He also informs the naive Jim that their family money comes from their father's slave trading with his two ships.) Not until the *290* leaves port does Jim know the truth; amid the champagne, a man announces that all who do not want to fight for the South in the *American Civil War should return to shore. Jim decides to remain on board, although he does not believe in slavery. The *290* raids federal ships as it crosses the Atlantic, but Jim's happiest experience is boarding his father's ship, the *Dauphine,* taking it to Port-au-Prince, and freeing prisoners who were to be sold into slavery by his father's partner. When he reboards the *290,* having missed a scheduled Cuban rendezvous while with the *Dauphine*, Captain Semmes punishes him but approves his excuse. While the ship awaits refurbishing in Cherbourg, a federal ship, *Kearsarge,* arrives for battle and defeats the *290*. A yacht owner watching the battle retrieves the survivors and deposits them on English soil, where they cannot be taken prisoners. Unable to resume ship designing with his battle-wounded hand, Jim receives word that his recently dead father has left him an inheritance. He goes to New Orleans not knowing what will happen but knowing that he has grown capable of coping. Jim escapes from the greed controlling his father and brother, and this moral strength aligns him closely to the strong women in the other novels.

Several of O'Dell's novels present strong female protagonists. The wealthy thirteen-year-old Ricca in **The Road to Damietta** falls in love with the young Francis Bernardone when he talks an angered bull into submission. Even as she watches him change from an egocentric fop into the inward-reaching being known as St. Francis of *Assisi, she expects him to renounce God and choose her for his bride. Ricca's Moslem tutor has taught her languages and to copy and illustrate beautiful manuscripts. She writes love letters to Francis using texts from Song of Solomon and Heloise and Abelard. When Ricca accompanies Francis as his translator when he tries to persuade the sultan Malik-al-Kamil outside Damietta to surrender to the Crusaders, the sultan decrees that the final test of Francis's godliness will be Ricca's dance with seven veils. When Francis worries of Ricca's sin, not her sensuality, Ricca realizes that Francis's love will always be for God and not for woman. When they return to the camp of the Fifth *Crusade and present a compromise offered by the sultan, the greedy Cardinal Pelagius rejects it. His distaste for Francis's life of poverty never changes, and he represents those men who call themselves Christians but in no way represent God's way of life. When Francis dies, Ricca realizes that she has lost her dream, but she also thinks of someone other than herself for the first time when she greets a leper at the end of the story. O'Dell begins this story with a leper's appearance; by ending it with a leper, he brings the story full circle.

One might consider King *George's greed to be the major cause of another strong female protagonist's problems during 1776 in **Sarah Bishop**. An English immigrant in a family loyal to Britain, Sarah Bishop sees rebels tar and feather her father. With his death and her mother dead, Sarah leaves the burned homestead to find her brother Chad, enlisted in the rebel army, in New York. During her search, police arrest her for starting a fire from which she was actually escaping. She finds that the British captured Chad and that he became ill and died. At that point, she flees from the British, shears her hair, buys a musket from a ferryboat man, and rapidly walks north. She gets a ride with a Sam Goshen who tries to molest her, but she evades him. When she thinks the British cannot find her, she spies a cave and begins her new life inside it. She discovers how to survive in the wild, and when an Indian couple stops to visit, they help her start making a dugout canoe and give her snowshoes. When she finds Sam Goshen caught in a bear trap, she feels repulsed but obligated to free him and help him recover. On a second visit to the nearest village, Ridgeford, Isaac Morton, the *Quaker storekeeper, recognizes her and reveals that a British notice of her escape had been posted and that he had removed it. He invites her to a Quaker meeting, and when she attends, townspeople call her a witch and blame her for the spring drought and sickness. Fortunately, a mail carrier tells the people that Boston's similar drought has also caused much sickness. She decides that she will remain in her cave.

A third strong woman able to cope with her father's hate of the gringos who have stolen so long from the Mexicans appears in **Carlota**. By loving horses, diving for gold coins, and throwing a lance, Carlota in 1846 helps her father overcome the death of her brother Carlos. She even accompanies him into battle against the gringos. They seriously wound him, and unconscious, Carlota's father does not know that Carlota also brings home a gringo whom she speared during the same encounter. When nearly recovered, his discovery that his money has saved a gringo kills him. Thus at sixteen, Carlota becomes the mistress of the huge ranch. After a difficult year of drought, Carlota asserts her position by returning Rosario, her grandmother's servant boy, to his tribe, the tribe that had killed her brother. That action symbolically severs her ties to the animosities of her forefathers and prepares her to face a future based on her own anti-hate and anti-slavery values.

Also in the mid-nineteenth century, the **Island of the Blue Dolphins'** Karana survives after *Aleuts kill twenty-seven of the forty-two tribal men, including her chieftain father, in order to gain control of the island otter hunting. Karana jumps off the ship, taking the remaining tribal members to the mainland in order to protect her brother, Ramo, who is left when he runs to retrieve one last memento. She and Ramo begin to gather food and try to scatter wild dogs gathering in the tribe's ruins, but soon the pack leader kills Ramo. Karana vows to retaliate by killing this dog, but to be successful, she must first defy the tribal taboo against women making weapons. Since she knows that the teeth of the seal elephant make the best spear points, she prepares to kill one. Two huge bulls help her by fighting to the death over a female. She sharpens one of their teeth and stabs the dog, but the dog does not die. Karana finds him several days later and takes him to her house, where she nurses him. When Rontu (her name for the dog) befriends her, she becomes acutely aware of her loneliness. Over time, she tames other animals, including sea gulls and a wounded otter, and realizes that she will never kill animals because they have alleviated her solitariness. After several years, the Aleuts return. A girl with them finds Karana and spends many afternoons communicating with her. Several years later, a white man's ship arrives and takes her to Father Gonzales at Santa Barbara Mission. There she learns that the ship going to her aid many years before had sunk.

Zia, a sequel to *Island of the Blue Dolphins*, explains how the men knew that Karana existed. When Zia's mother (Karana's sister) died, Zia and her brother, Mando, went to the Santa Barbara Mission, a spot close to the island, in hope of reaching it and rescuing Karana. When Zia is fourteen, she and Mando find an abandoned boat, stock it, and begin the sixty-mile sail to the island. Their inexperience foils them, and they turn toward shore. Men from the *Boston Boy,* a whaling ship, spot them, claim the boat, and enslave them on board. By stealing another boat, they escape and return to the mission. Zia tells Captain Nidever her story, and he promises to bring Karana back with him from his next trip. A subplot reveals the greed of local men who use mission orphans for their endeavors. Zia stays at the mission waiting for Karana, and when Karana arrives, Karana has difficulty with the language, but she and Zia create their own communication. Zia understands that Karana, after living so freely, does not like the mission rules. Karana and her dog move into a cave. Karana sickens and soon dies, probably homesick for her island. Having fulfilled her goal of bringing Karana to civilization, Zia and Karana's dog leave the mission and return to Zia's former home.

A final novel with a strong female protagonist, **Sing Down the Moon**, begins in 1864 when Spanish slavers capture *Navaho sheepherders Bright Morning and Running Bird. The slavers take them south to sell as menial houseworkers. Several weeks later, they escape. As they flee toward their canyon, Tall Boy, the warrior Bright Morning wants to marry, finds them. Simultaneously, the Spaniards spot them and shoot Tall Boy in the arm. Soon after they return to the tribe, the Long Knives (white men) drive the tribal members from their canyon and lead them on a long journey of death and illness to Fort Sumner to live with other exiled Navahos. Although Tall Boy's disabled arm costs his status in the tribe, Bright Morning still marries him. Bright Morning becomes pregnant, and they search the surrounding area for wood with which to build a hut. An *Apache blames them for stealing his wood and starts to throw a rock at them, but Tall Boy spears his arm. The Long Knives imprison Tall Boy, but he escapes. He and Bright Morning leave the tribe and fulfill Bright Morning's desire to return to a small, deserted canyon near their former home. There they find Bright Morning's remaining sheep, which they plan to raise for future income. Hidden by the steep canyon walls, they look forward to their son growing without fear of soldiers destroying his home.

STYLE AND THEMES

Brief examples illustrate O'Dell's mastery of figurative language and imagery. In *Island of the Blue Dolphins*, metaphors create new comparisons. The "sea . . . is a flat stone without any scratches." An Aleut ship becomes "a gull with folded wings." The same ship also looks like a "small shell afloat." In *Topo-*

el-Bampo, a short phrase indicates O'Dell's abilities for using parallelism, alliteration, and imagery. In the town sits a "man who sold sandals and straw hats, candles, charcoal, and cooking pots." Thus O'Dell's style complements his depth of content.

OF NIGHTINGALES THAT WEEP. See Paterson, Katherine.

OLIVER CUTTER. Eleven, English protagonist in *A Messenger for Parliament* and at thirteen as the protagonist in *Cromwell's Boy. See* Haugaard, Erik.

ONE IS ONE. See Picard, Barbara.

ONE REED. Part of the Aztec fifty-two year cycle, this is the year that the man called *Quetzalcoatl prophesized that he would return, and it is the year that *Cortés arrived in Mexico. Many of the Indians, including *Montezuma, thought that he was the returned god-king and gave him a turquoise mask and feather mantle in welcome. This attitude facilitated Cortés's conquest of Mexico. *See* Baker, Betty, *The Blood of the Brave.*

ONEIDA. This tribe was one of the original nations of the *Iroquois group in New York State. In the eighteenth century, the 700 members of this small tribe decided to support the colonists in the *American Revolution. *See* Treece, Henry, *Viking's Sunset.*

ORGEL, DORIS (1929–   ). Austrian-American.

BIBLIOGRAPHY AND BACKGROUND
  The Devil in Vienna. New York: Dial, 1978.
  Doris Orgel has received several awards for *The Devil in Vienna,* including the Child Study Committee Award and the Association of Jewish Libraries Award in 1978. The book is also a Golden Kite Honor Book for 1979. For this novel, Orgel based its fictionalized account on her own experiences in pre–World War II Vienna.

WORK
  The Devil in Vienna begins in February 1938 with Inge Dornenwald celebrating her thirteenth birthday. Her homework assignment on the weekend of her birthday is to write an essay about her best friend. In this first-person composition, she recalls her friendship with Lieselotte Vessely, which began six years previously when Inge bumped into her while running from an old man who offered her American chewing gum and then exposed himself. She mourns Lieselotte's move to Munich and is disappointed at receiving only one letter during the three months' separation. Lieselotte's letter revealed that her father

was a *Nazi storm trooper and that she had to join the Hitler youth movement. When Inge tried to respond, she discovered Lieselotte's home address marked out, so Inge sent her letter to Lieselotte's school. The weekend concludes after Inge's birthday dinner with her grandfather and her mother returning home from a ski trip with a broken leg. Although unhappy with her essay, Inge submits it. Later in the spring, the Austrian leader *Schuschnigg bows to Hitler, and as Inge's grandfather had predicted, nazism becomes legal. Lieselotte's family moves back to Vienna, but the two girls have to meet secretly because Mr. Vessely disapproves of Lieselotte's friendship with a Jewess. Mitzi, the Dornenwald's maid, gives Lieselotte's unmailed letters to Inge, and Inge finds how much Lieselotte missed her while in Munich, wanting to share such events as starting her period and how much she hated the Nazi propaganda. Inge also watches family and friends lose jobs, including her mother, and leave the country, including her grandfather. She does not understand the seriousness of the situation until she notices signs degrading Jews posted everywhere, detects Nazis making Jews demean themselves, and observes her mother's subversive methods of obtaining tickets for the family to leave Austria.

STYLE AND THEME
The novel exposes how Nazis indoctrinated young children and permeated society with propaganda. German words without translation validate the authentic setting. The integration of letters and the essay within the text allows Orgel to reveal the strong friendship of Lieselotte and Inge even though they are often separated. Orgel's vivid description creates credible characters, and her natural flow of dialogue establishes viable relationships between adults and children. That national governments' whims can control friendships between the Catholic and the Jew, murdering one and deifying the other, clearly shows the possibilities of power for fanatics.

ORPHANS OF THE WIND. See Haugaard, Erik.

ORTHODOX. From the early fourth century, the Greek church fathers have used this term to define the true Christian doctrine as opposed to heretical doctrines. The word comes from the Greek meaning "of the right opinion." In the fifth century, the Orthodox had a sizable controversy with the *Monophysites. See Dickinson, Peter, The Dancing Bear.

OTIS, JAMES (1725–1783). Although the British king's advocate general in the American colonies when the royal customs collectors began to search for violations of the Sugar Act of 1773, Otis resigned his office and opposed the searches. He based his opposition on natural law as being superior to acts of Parliament. Along with Samuel Adams and others, he opposed other revenue acts. See Forbes, Esther, Johnny Tremain.

OUTCAST. *See* Sutcliff, Rosemary.

OUTREMER. Crusader states in the East were called outremer. *See* Welch, Ronald, *Knight Crusader*.

THE OVERLAND LAUNCH. *See* Hodges, C. Walter.

OWAIN. Young British orphan, protagonist of *Dawn Wind*. *See* Sutcliff, Rosemary.

_P_

PAINE, THOMAS (1739–1809). After going bankrupt in England, he emigrated to America in 1774 and in 1776 published *Common Sense,* urging a declaration of independence. Back in England in 1787, he defended revolutionary France and tried to organize a revolt of the English against their own monarchy. The English tried him for treason and banished him in 1792. In Paris, he was imprisoned as an Englishman, but an American, James Monroe, claimed him as an American citizen. He published *The Age of Reason* while still in France and returned to America, where he lived in ostracism and poverty. *See* Burton, Hester, *Time of Trial.*

PALESTINE. This name refers to a former land of the eastern Mediterranean comprising parts of modern Israel, Jordan, and Egypt. The name originated with the Philistines, who occupied the area around 1200 B.C. Since Jesus Christ lived and taught there, it is also known as the Holy Land. See *The Survivor* and *My Enemy, My Brother* by James *Forman, and *The Bronze Bow* by Elizabeth George *Speare.

A PARCEL OF PATTERNS. *See* Paton Walsh, Jill.

PARKER QUINEY. Thirteen, orphan, American protagonist in *A Long Way to Whiskey Creek. See* Beatty, Patricia.

PARLIAMENTARIANS. Members of this group supported Parliament instead of *Charles I in the *English Civil War. See *Beyond the Weir Bridge* by Hester *Burton; *Simon* by Rosemary *Sutcliff; *When the Drums Beat* by Geoffrey *Trease; *For the King* by Ronald *Welch; and *Harrow and Harvest* by Barbara *Willard.

PATERSON, KATHERINE (1932–   ). American.

BIBLIOGRAPHY AND BACKGROUND
Jacob Have I Loved. New York: Crowell, 1980; London: Gollancz, 1981. *The Master Puppeteer.* Illustrated by Haru Wells. New York: Crowell, 1975. *Of Nightingales That Weep.* Illustrated by Haru Wells. New York: Crowell, 1974; London: Kestrel, 1976. *Rebels of the Heavenly Kingdom.* New York: Dutton, 1983. *The Sign of the Chrysanthemum.* Illustrated by Peter Landa. New York: Crowell, 1973; London: Kestrel, 1975.

Katherine Paterson won the Newbery Medal in 1981 for *Jacob Have I Loved.* She has received numerous other awards including the National Book Award (1977), Parents' Choice Awards, Child Study Association Books of the Year, American Library Association Notable Books, American Booksellers Pick of the Lists, Library of Congress Books of the Year, Mystery Writers of America Special Award, and the National Council for Social Studies Notable Book. She says about her settings, "I loved the places and the times spoke to my own times. I was a bit homesick for Japan and am fascinated by Japanese history." Her research takes from one to two years and the actual writing and revising another year. She notes, "When I am revising I can work longer days than when I'm writing first drafts, chiefly because I love revising and have to push myself on the first draft." In each of Paterson's superbly written novels, the action includes a startling but carefully foreshadowed and totally plausible occurrence.

WORKS
The *Gempei War (1180–85) between the Genji and Heike clans in Japan propels the characters in **Of Nightingales That Weep**. When Takiko, the protagonist, is eleven, her Heike samurai father dies in battle. Left with little money for a dowry, her mother marries an ugly potter, Goro. Takiko thinks him repulsive but slowly learns that the inner beauty of his pottery resembles the inner beauty of the music she loves to play on the koto. At fifteen, the beautiful Takiko begins serving Princess Aoi, whose blackened front teeth denote her as high born and married. When Takiko sings for the five-year-old emperor, his mother asks her to leave Aoi and serve the emperor. The last command of Princess Aoi is that Takiko deliver a message to her lover, Hideo, one of the enemy Genji. Takiko does and falls in love with him herself. With the emperor in exile, Takiko sees Hideo spying on the family. She starts meeting him, even refusing to return home to look after her pregnant mother when Goro comes for her. When the Heike lose the war, Takiko comes home, only to find her mother and brother dead of plague. She begins working in the fields, and in an accident, her face becomes branded by a hot poker. After many months, Hideo arrives as promised, but Takiko's calloused hands and her scarred face repulse him. She plans to join the convent, but the emperor's mother suggests that she serve the "godly" Goro. At sixteen, Takiko bears him a son. The beautifully inlaid inside lid of an ugly pot symbolizes Goro's uniqueness.

In **The Sign of the Chrysanthemum**, Muna, a thirteen-year-old "no name" a child with an unknown father, goes from his island at his mother's death to the Japanese capital to search for his father. On the ship, he meets Takanobu, who tells Muna to meet him in the city at the Rashomon gate. At the gate, Muna is disappointed to see that Takanobu is a ronin (samurai in disrepute) rather than a strong, clean samurai. Takanobu gets Muna a job at the imperial stables, where he can hear stories about the Genji and the Heike and relate them to Takanobu and his friends. Not realizing that these men plot, Muna begins to embellish the stories, eventually admitting to them that he searches for his father. A fire in the sordid area near the gate almost kills him, but Fukuji, a sword maker, rescues him. Fukuji has no apprentice and will make swords only for men worthy to wear his signature. When Takanobu needs a sword, he reappears and claims that he is Muna's father. Muna steals a sword for him but challenges Tanakobu's assertion and rushes to hide the sword near a temple. In shame, Muna grovels near the Rashomon gate until the Gengi and Heike start fighting. He retrieves the sword and returns it to Fukuji. Fukuji remarks that Muna has decided to accept himself and wonders what adult name he will choose. Muna shows maturity by keeping the name he has, no longer feeling the need for another man's name. After this wise decision, Fukuji offers Muna a position as his apprentice. In this novel, Paterson states a theme implicit in all her novels that pride "will slay us all in the end."

A five-year famine in eighteenth-century Osaka, Japan, forces Jiro to leave his parents to become Yoshida's apprentice in **The Master Puppeteer**. Yoshida's son Kinshi befriends Jiro and teaches him skills of puppeteering. The pervasive hunger that continues upsets the boys, especially when Jiro sees his mother in a band of night rovers outside the Honaza Theater, where the boys work, destroy homes trying to find food. A bandit called Saburo continues to amaze the people by raiding the wealthy for food, which he distributes to the poor. Government rewards for Saburo increase after several especially daring raids. In the theater, Jiro's proficiency improves, but Yoshida continues to chide Kinshi, expecting perfection from his son. Okada, the blind chanter, coaches Jiro, but Jiro discovers that Okada is actually Saburo and that his own father is also a member of the bandits. Soon after, Jiro rushes through a mob after a robbery to find Kinshi. When he finds him, police have already chopped off Kinshi's hand thinking him a thief when he has only been trying to rescue Jiro's mother, Isako. Jiro takes him home and refuses to reveal Saburo's identity, preferring to remain Kinshi's friend.

In **Rebels of the Heavenly Kingdom**, after being kidnapped by Red Eye and purchased by a woman disguised as a man, Wang becomes a member of the rebels during the *Taiping Rebellion of 1850–53 in China. As a lowly woman with ugly, unbound feet, Mei Ling's status in the rebel group baffles Wang, but she has earned her position by freeing Feng, one of the group's leaders, from imperial soldiers. The shifting point of view between Wang and Mei Lin reveals Wang's questions about the group's beliefs and Mei Lin's unwavering faith that the group is right. The rebels had first applied Christian teachings to themselves, but the leaders, beginning to enjoy power, start murdering innocent people in order to control more of the country. Their procedure to keep power includes separating men and women and a prohibition against mourning the dead. Friends report friends, and children betray parents. When Mei Lin receives love notes written in the calligraphy of the one calling himself king, she realizes that the leaders feel they have more rights than the followers. Wang disassociates from the group, and Red Eye recaptures and sells him again. The cook, One Ear, soon realizes that his housemaid is male, but Wang does his work well. He also begins teaching the young Precious Jade to write while she recovers from the painful binding of her feet, which will give her ''golden lilies,'' tiny feet to make her attractive to prospective suitors. One Ear asks Wang to teach him at the same time; however, another maid discovers their lessons, and Wang has to flee. He searches for Mei Lin and rescues her from becoming the king's bride. Mei Lin and Wang escape to his family home where they plant the rice seed hidden by Wang's father several years before. A final chapter written in first-person plural shows the two farmers with their five children, including two girls with unbound feet learning to read on their way to becoming two women whom men will not want as wives. Although the rebels failed to find peace, Mei Lin and Wang together project a promise of the future.

Paterson's one twentieth-century novel, **Jacob Have I Loved**, is Sara Louise Bradshaw's first-person flashback to her adolescence. Wheez (Sara Louise) recalls her life on Rass Island in Maryland's Chesapeake Bay, from the time she is thirteen. Being the strong twin to the beautiful, talented, delicate, and coddled Caroline causes Wheez to feel rejected and unloved. But her grandmother, prattling scripture as she vacillates between the present and the past, notes astutely that Wheez sees herself as *Esau and Caroline as *Jacob. Her grandmother also identifies Wheez's crush on Captain Wallace, a man older than her grandmother. Wheez only feels comfortable crabbing with her father or Call Purnell until Call returns from World War II and announces his engagement to Caroline, who is studying music in New York. Captain Wallace tells Sara Louise that nothing keeps her from leaving the island. After angrily blaming her mother for wasting her life on Rass Island, Sara Louise goes to college where, discouraged from applying to medical school, she becomes a nurse. She chooses to live in a small town, Truitt (her father's name), in the Appalachian mountains, where she meets a Polish widower with three children and marries him. When she helps deliver breech birth twins, one healthy and one sickly, she urges the parents to love the strong one as much as the sickly. The circle turns, and only as an adult can Sara Louise understand her mother's choices.

STYLE AND THEMES

Paterson's depth of theme and superiority of writing skill cannot be overstated. Each book illustrates some type of excess: of religion, power, pride, selfishness, or self-pity. Most of the characters have senses of humor; some tell jokes. In

Rebels of the Heavenly Kingdom, one learns to "sink your teeth into hope and chew on expectation." The appropriateness of diction and language appears throughout all the novels. In *The Sign of the Chrysanthemum,* the manor looks "like a great, lazy cat stretched out for a summer nap," with the thatched huts of the serfs "like a litter of new born kittens." In *Rebels,* the "rice bowls stacked into a pagoda." And in *Of Nightingales That Weep,* Paterson paints a Japanese landscape with "the wisteria, falling in white and violet showers from the trellises." The perceptive and inevitable resolutions in Paterson's stories leave the reader somewhat saddened but completely satisfied.

PATH OF THE PALE HORSE. *See* Fleishman, Paul.

PATON WALSH, JILL (1937–   ). British.

BIBLIOGRAPHY AND BACKGROUND

A Chance Child. London: Macmillan, 1978; New York: Farrar, Straus & Giroux, 1978. *Crossing to Salamis.* Illustrated by Robin Eaton. London: Heinemann, 1977. *The Dolphin Crossing.* New York: St. Martin's, 1967; London: Macmillan, 1967. *The Emperor's Winding Sheet.* New York: Farrar, Straus, & Giroux, 1974; London: Macmillan, 1974. *Fireweed.* New York: Farrar, Straus & Giroux, 1970; London: Macmillan, 1969. *Hengest's Tale.* New York: St Martin's, 1966; London: Macmillan, 1966. *The Huffler.* Illustrated by Juliette Palmer. New York: Farrar, Straus & Giroux, 1975; as *The Butty Boy.* London: Macmillan, 1975. *A Parcel of Patterns.* New York: Farrar, Straus & Giroux, 1984. *Persian Gold.* Illustrated by Robin Eaton. London: Heinemann, 1978. *The Walls of Athens.* Illustrated by Robin Eaton. London: Heinemann, 1977.

Jill Paton Walsh has received for her writing in several genres a Carnegie citation, the *Book World* Festival Award (1970), the Whitbread Award (1974), the *Boston Globe–Horn Book* Award (1976), and an Arts Council Creative Writing Fellowship (1976). She says, "I have a butterfly mind, and I write whatever I am interested in at the time. I have never been motivated to write historical fiction—just fascinated by a place or a story." In all but *A Chance Child* and *The Dolphin Crossing,* Paton Walsh presents the story through a first-person point of view.

WORKS

Three novels—*Crossing to Salamis, The Walls of Athens,* and *Persian Gold*— collected in *The Children of the Fox* (Farrar, Straus & Giroux, 1978) but published separately are part of the Heinemann "Long Ago" series for younger readers. **Crossing to Salamis** tells of Aster's departure from Athens in 497 B.C. with her mother, servant, and friend for *Salamis as the Persians under Xerxes invade the city. As a free female, Aster has stayed inside the walls of her home for almost all her life. From the Salamis encampment, Aster sees a ship leave at night and thinks a traitor has gone to inform the Persians of their location. She cuts her hair like a servant and goes to warn Themistokles, their military leader. He tells her that he has sent the ship to make the Persians think the area is undefended. Falling for the ploy, the Persians come for victory but depart in defeat. Aster's mother, horrified at Aster's short hair, exclaims that no man will marry her. But Aster's brother Nikias and Themistokles come to thank Aster for not telling about the scheme and to offer her a husband.

In **The Walls of Athens**, Demeas regrets that he cannot help rebuild the walls of Athens after the Persian War (479 B.C.). He has to help his father on the farm even though they have no crop; their ruined olive trees will have to be replaced. The new trees will need five years as saplings and then ten more years to mature before producing oil. While looking for the neighbors' sheep and goats in the hills, Demeas sees a lone runner fall. The runner, Lysias asks Demeas to run to Sparta to tell Themistokles, without letting the Spartans hear, that the walls of Athens have been completed. The Spartans have disapproved of a wall, and Themistokles the Athenian spokesman negotiating with the Spartans, has been telling them that Athenians have no time for wall building. Before Demeas returns, a Spartan supporting the Athenians sends Demeas's family olive tree saplings, which gives them personal hope for the future just as Demeas has given Athens public hope by delivering the message.

In the last novel of this group, **Persian Gold**, Lala tells about finding the "criminal," Themistokles, in her and her brother Perdiccas's backyard hideout. Although both Spartans and Athenians have been searching for him, Lala and Perdiccas believe Themistokles's story that he did what he thought would defeat the Persians on sea and could not help that his Spartan friend Pausanias lost the battle on land. Their mother tells Themistokles to hold her baby, and according to the Molossian custom, her husband will have to welcome him in his home or face the gods' reprisals. When her husband, the king of the Molossians, arrives, he demands to know who has revealed the custom. The entire family admits guilt, and the children take Themistokles to the great king of the Persians as he requests. When safe, Themistokles sends Lala a golden collar in gratitude. When it arrives, she begins to boast that her gift has belonged to both an Athenian general and a Persian satrap.

Another novel set in the Middle East, **The Emperor's Winding Sheet**, involves the final fall of the Eastern *Roman Empire to the Turks in 1453. The novel begins with the protagonist, Piers Barber, hiding in an orange tree, fainting, and falling at the feet of a man who is the Emperor Constantine XI. Piers, an English boy, ventured to a ship recently sunk, escaped from Turks who retrieved him from the water, and found his way to Constantine's court. Piers remembers in detail his uncle's hostile face, when he made him sail instead of attend school, but he has no distinct recall of his loving mother, who is dead. Piers becomes Constantine's *vrethiki* ("lucky find") in response to an old man's dream that as long as a person loyal to the emperor stayed with him, the Roman Empire would not fall. The mythic import of the story arises with a comparison of the landscape to England, but in Constantinople (*Istanbul), the green is unexpectedly "cold," not because Piers arrives in winter but because it seems deathly rather than rejuvenating. Since Piers understands no Greek, the emperor's eunuch translates to Latin for him. Furious at having to stay with the emperor, Piers hates his dog-like role, but as he watches the emperor try to defend the city of Constantinople from the Turks outside and from the various religious factions within, he begins to admire him and decides to remain when told he can leave. Before the city falls, an eclipse of the full moon occurs, a hail storm destroys an holy icon, and an unseasonal fog encircles the walls. When the Turks pray toward Mecca five times a day, even during battle, the defenders realize that the Turks see the battle as a *Jihad. The Turks finally win, and Piers flees by swimming to a departing ship. Throughout the novel, Paton continues the dramatic irony by having the reader know immediately what is happening but Piers unsure until Stephanos translates for him, and when Stephanos dies, Piers can only infer from men's actions what they mean. Stephanos reveals an explicit theme in his comment that "men are not judged by the fate God appoints for them, they are judged by the manner in which they meet that fate." The novel presents an enlightening view of the Turks overtaking the Roman Empire and the necessity of human valor during conflict.

Confrontations also flourish in Northern Europe. In **Hengest's Tale**, Hengest flashes back to a story that began around 425 and has caused him misery in later life. As a young boy, Hengest accompanies his father, king of the *Jutes, to visit the *Frisian leader, Hoc. He offers his daughter, Hildeburg, to Finn, son of Hoc's man Folcwald, and the promise to build Finnland in return for help against the Danes. When Hoc and Hengest's father soon die, Hoc's son Hnaef becomes the king. Hneaf has more Danish friends than Jutes and gives them positions rightfully belonging to the Jutes. The unhappy Jutes join Finn and his Jutish bride. After more than a decade, Hnaef and Hengest visit Finn, but after a pleasant stay, Hneaf's men rise against Finn and kill his son Garulf. The Frisians retaliate by killing Hnaef. Hildeburg requests that Hneaf and Garulf burn together on the funeral pyre to show solidity between the groups. But in another outrage at the end of winter, Hengest permits the Danes to influence him, and he kills Finn. A storm during his escape wrecks him on the coast near the hall of Finn's father, Folcwald. Folcwald decides to punish Hengest, not by death but by exile to Britain and service to *Vortigern. Because Vortigern will not share battle spoils with his men, Hengest eventually kills him around 450. Hengest, driven by uncontrolled forces, kills people that he actually likes and lives remorsefully for his deeds.

The protagonist, Mall Percival, in **A Parcel of Patterns** endures circumstances totally outside her control. In her village of Eyam, from September 7, 1665, until after October 1666, 267 people die. When the new parson's wife requests that the new tailor, George Vicars, make her a fancy dress quite unlike any sanctioned during *Parliament rule, he requests patterns from London. The patterns arrive damp, bringing the *plague. When George airs them, he dies. Mall, at sixteen, watches her friends, her parents, and others cope with the illness and try to understand how such misery could be God's will. She also tries to comprehend why one parson says those living should help the sick and why the new parson says they should not. The new parson's wife, not listening to her husband and perhaps, in atonement, continues to visit the sick and help their families until she too dies. Mall's fear that Thomas, her sweetheart from the next village, might catch the disease makes her avoid him throughout the year. She then sends a neighbor to tell him that she is dead. No longer caring if he dies, Tom comes to help those left. He finds Mall, nursing her sick mother. As soon as Mall's mother dies, the parson marries them. But Tom soon dies, and Mall's happiness becomes dust. Eventually Francis, who has loved Mall throughout, asks her to go with him to New England. She finally consents, but the ghosts of those dead haunt her as they walk out of town. Francis convinces her to free herself of the terrors by writing about them. The syntax and diction add to the novel's plausibility. Although plague stories are painful to read, the realism in this one makes it even more moving than most others.

Of two stories set in the nineteenth century, **A Chance Child** is an unusual juxtaposition of past and present, making it historical fantasy. The odd-numbered chapters present the point of view of Creep and the alternate chapters the point of view of Christopher. Although Christopher and his sister, Pauline, live in contemporary times, not until chapter 12 does the reader understand that Creep lives in the 1820s. In the novel's beginning, Creep finds a boat near the Place (a ruined foundry) and floats past dirty towns down one of England's canals. Christopher, who sees Creep float away, searches for him, calling him his lost half-brother who lived under the stairs rejected by his mother because a man not her husband sired him. Christopher, however, finds only the word "Creep" written on a bridge that a man tells him is over 150 years old. Creep helps a boy, Tom, escape from an evil master in the coal mines, and together they join Blackie, an eight-year-old girl, who begins to look after them and the boat. Creep neither eats nor laughs until he sees a man who had beaten his young helper in turn beaten by the helper's mother. Then he becomes "human." Christopher finds the story of Nathaniel Creep in the Parliamentary papers in the library and knows then that his lost brother is real. The unsettling aspect of the story is that Christopher's sister Pauline also knows Creep. Thus he becomes less imaginary than if he existed solely for Christopher. In powerful writing, Paton Walsh depicts a sordid scene of mining conditions in England when child labor was rampant.

In **The Huffler**, also a canal story but set during *Victoria's reign in England, Kate retells her cousin Harry's story of helping two young people take their butty boat (barge) down a canal. Harry dislikes moving to the new house, and she sees a boat with children on the nearby canal. The children, Ned and Bess Jebb, thinking her a servant, tell her they will help her escape her unhappy life. Not until they reach the Jebb home where Mr. Jebb shows Harry a servant's backside does Harry comprehend what a real beating is. When the family returns her to her home, in deference to their wishes, she refuses to reveal their name.

When Harry tells Kate the story in front of Edward, who wants to marry Harry, Edward does not understand that Harry still views herself as a vagabond. Kate knows, unlike Edward, that Harry will never marry him. Although the story is slight, it suggests that one can and should subtly measure another's attitudes before making serious decisions involving that person.

The scene shifts to World War II in two other novels. In **The Dolphin Crossing**, seventeen-year-old John continues school but wants to join in the war effort while his brother works as a conscientious objector and his father captains a merchant ship. When John defends Pat, a London evacuee, from several boys, Pat shows him the hut where he and his pregnant stepmother live. John shows his mother their hovel, and she agrees to offer them the family's stable. A carpentry student, Pat makes all the repairs and surprises his mother with their new home just before the baby's birth. On the same day, Pat and John decide to take John's boat, the *Dolphin,* across to France to help rescue British forces during the German invasion. They spend two days under fire transporting soldiers from *Dunkirk to awaiting ships. They return to England with eight men before running out of gas. John's mother helps the men while John lies unconscious for three days from a wounded arm. When he awakens, Pat has disappeared. John understands that Pat has taken the *Dolphin* and been shot. John's father, back from a voyage, tries to explain that war separates, but knowing and understanding do not reduce John's pain. Paton Walsh deepens the meaning by alluding to the Battle of *Salamis as comparable to World War II.

A second novel set in World War II, **Fireweed**, begins with the phrase, ''Remember? I can still smell it.'' Bill flashes back to 1941 when he is a fifteen-year-old evacuee to Wales who returns to London with money his aunt sends him. He finds her home off-limits, an unexploded bomb having hit it. With nowhere to live, Bill realizes he must stay away from authorities looking for supposedly evacuated young people. He meets Julie in the Aldywich Underground during the air raids of the *blitz. Since both are lonely, they spend all their time together. They do odd jobs during the day and sleep in bomb shelters at night. Julie's parents think that she has gone to Canada, but the ship on which she supposedly sailed sinks. She wants to call her parents, but Bill becomes upset. He had seen his own father home on leave from a distance but had ignored him in order to remain with Julie. She does not call, and although she has money that she was supposed to use in Canada, Bill prefers not to spend more than they must. The two find shelter in the remains of Julie's aunt's house for several days, and then they find Dickie on the sidewalk waiting for a mother who does not come. When Bill leaves early one morning to find milk for the feverish Dickie, he returns to find a caved-in row of houses. When the authorities finally uncover the bodies, both Dickie and Julie have miraculously survived. Bill visits Julie in the hospital but refuses to return after meeting her upper-class family. The novel shows how difficult circumstances can elicit friendliness and small acts of heroism.

STYLE AND THEMES

Each of Paton Walsh's novels exhibits a style and a syntax appropriate to the story. Imagery and figurative language enrich each novel's fabric. In *A Chance Child,* the word choice enhances subject matter in such comments as "reflected walls hung black curtains into the water" and "gray sky oozed a misty rain of fine droplets." In contrast, in *Crossing to Salamis,* "olive trees . . . carpeted the valley floor . . . with a lovely shimmer like silken garments when the wind caressed them"; "stars . . . clustered as thick as buttercups"; and "the sky . . . was radiant, clad in veil upon shimmering veil of golden and ivory silk." Paton Walsh's writing, coupled with the worthwhile themes, enrich the reader's horizons.

PATRICIA BERGEN. American-Jewish female, protagonist of twelve in *Summer of my German Soldier* and of eighteen in *Morning Is a Long Time Coming. See* Greene, Bette.

PATRICK. Thirteen, Irish, protagonist of *A Boy's Will. See* Haugaard, Erik.

PATRIOT. This term identified those colonists who supported independence from England during the *American Revolution. See *The Cow Neck Rebels* by James *Forman and *The Witch of Blackbird Pond* by Elizabeth George *Speare.

PAUL. Fifteen, Roman orphan living in Britain, protagonist of *Message to Hadrian. See* Trease, Geoffrey.

PAUL. Young English protagonist in *A Voice in the Night. See* Trease, Geoffrey.

PAUL EICHHORN. German who matures from thirteen into a young adult, protagonist of *The Traitors. See* Forman, James.

PEACE OF GOD MANLY. Adult American protagonist of *Sea Captain from Salem* and character in *Peter Treegate's War* and *Treegate's Raiders. See* Wibberley, Leonard.

PEDRO, DOM (1798–1834). As second son of John VI of Portugal, he escaped the French by fleeing from Portugal to Brazil where he became regent. He took sides with Brazil against the Portuguese policy and declared independence on September 7, 1822. At first popular as the new emperor, he became more despotic and had to return to Portugal, where he was eventually crowned king. *See* Dalgliesh, Alice, *The Little Angel.*

PEDRO PAVON. Fifteen, Spanish protagonist captured by *Comanches in *Komantcia. See* Keith, Harold.

PEGGY GRAHAME. Seventeen, American protagonist come from Europe in *The Sherwood Ring. See* Pope, Elizabeth.

PELGROM, ELS (1934–   ). Dutch.

BIBLIOGRAPHY AND BACKGROUND
   The Winter When Time Was Frozen. Trans. Maryka and Raphael Rudnik. New York: Morrow, 1980.
   Els Pelgrom won several awards for *The Winter When Time Was Frozen,* including the Batchelder Award in 1980.

WORK
   In **The Winter When Time Was Frozen**, during the harsh winter of 1944–45, Noortje Vanderhook, eleven, and her father, refugees from their town after the Germans defeat the British, wander in the forest and unexpectedly find the Everingen family's Dutch farm. The Everingens and their helper, Henk, welcome them as they have accepted Theo, a resistance leader with tuberculosis. The household increases even more when the Wolthuis family of five also joins them. During the cold winter, the food disappears more rapidly than expected for the number of people, but Henk's and Mrs. Everingen's unusual actions indicate that something unrevealed happens to the food. One night Noortje awakens and hears several people outside. She reaches the barn in time to see a calf born, and the rapidity with which the slimy, still creature becomes lovely shocks her. On the same night, after a man comes to the door asking for Aunt Janna (Mrs. Everingen), Aunt Janna takes Noortje into the woods where a family hides literally underground. Noortje assists her with the birth of a Jewish baby girl, whose brothers sleep in the dugout corner. Several weeks later, Aunt Janna brings Sarah, the baby, to the house because her crying threatens to expose the family's location. But one night when Henk takes food, he finds that the Germans have discovered them anyway. Soon German *Nazi soldiers occupy the house, and Theo hides in the attic. After they leave, a V-1 bomb explodes nearby and knocks out all of the windows. As the Allies arrive, Noortje watches the bombs drop from the airplanes; their beauty coupled with their terror underscores the conflicts in her life. After the war ends and spring arrives, Sissy, Aunt Janna's mongoloid child of seven, dies of diphtheria, and Sarah's uncle arrives for her with the news that the rest of her family died in a concentration camp. After Noortje and Evert, twelve, help Theo escape, Noortje goes to Amsterdam with her father.

STYLE AND THEME
   Pelgrom has created a scene of love and warmth isolated in the middle of hate and chill. The characters in the novel, like ''the winter wheat [that] slept in furrows'' waiting for spring to arrive, watch quietly for their chance to regenerate their lives in peacetime. They gather strength from the love they show each other by making an uncontrollable situation at least tolerable.

PENELOPE METAXAS. Fifteen, Greek, protagonist in *The Skies of Crete*. *See* Forman, James.

PENITENCE HERVEY. Fifteen, American protagonist who goes to England in *Campion Towers*. *See* Beatty, John and Patricia.

THE PEPPERMINT PIG. *See* Bawden, Nina.

PERDITA. Young English protagonist in *The Queen Elizabeth Story*. *See* Sutcliff, Rosemary.

PEREZ, FATHER JUAN. At the monastery of *La Rabida, Columbus met this friar, who aided his attempt to be recalled to the court of Ferdinand and Isabella. See *Son of Columbus* by Hans *Baumann and *Columbus Sails* by C. Walter Hodges.

THE PERILOUS GARD. *See* Pope, Elizabeth.

PERILOUS PILGRIMAGE. *See* Treece, Henry.

THE PERILOUS ROAD. *See* Steele, William O.

PERSIAN GOLD. *See* Paton Walsh, Jill.

PETER. Twelve, Russian protagonist in *The Crimson Oak*. *See* Almedingen, E. M.

PETER BROWNRIGG. Fourteen, English protagonist in *Cue for Treason*. *See* Trease, Geoffrey.

PETER MILLET. Sixteen, English protagonist in *The Secret of the Hawk*. *See* Wibblerley, Leonard.

PETER STAUNTON. Young English protagonist in *The Gauntlet*. *See* Welch, Ronald.

PETER TREEGATE. At eleven, American protagonist of *John Treegate's Musket*, as a young man in *Peter Treegate's War* and *Treegate's Raider*, and as a unifying character in *Leopard's Prey, Red Pawns*, and *The Last Battle*. *See* Wibberley, Leonard.

PETER TREEGATE'S WAR. *See* Wibberley, Leonard.

PETER WAYNE. Seventeen, American southerner, protagonist of *The Wound of Peter Wayne*. *See* Wibberley, Leonard.

PETER YORK. Twelve, American orphan, protagonist in *Night Journeys*. *See* Avi.

PETROS. Nine, Greek protagonist in *Petros' War*. *See* Zei, Aliki.

PETROS' WAR. *See* Zei, Aliki.

PEYTON, K. M. (1929–   ). British.

BIBLIOGRAPHY AND BACKGROUND

Dear Fred. New York: Philomel, 1981; London: Bodley Head, 1981. *The Edge of the Cloud*. Illustrated by Victor Ambrus. New York: World, 1970; London: Oxford, 1969. *Flambards*. Illustrated by Victor Ambrus. Cleveland: World, 1968; London: Oxford, 1967. *Flambards Divided*. New York: Philomel, 1982; London: Oxford, 1981. *Flambards in Summer*. Illustrated by Victor Ambrus. New York: World, 1970; London: Oxford, 1969. *The Maplin Bird*. Illustrated by Victor Ambrus. Cleveland: World, 1965; London: Oxford, 1964. *The Right-Hand Man*. Illustrated by Victor Ambrus. New York: Oxford, 1979; London: Oxford, 1977. *Sea Fever*. Illustrated by Victor Ambrus. Cleveland: World, 1963; as *Windfall*. London: Oxford, 1962. *Thunder in the Sky*. Illustrated by Victor Ambrus. Cleveland: World, 1967; London: Oxford, 1966.

K. M. Peyton won the Carnegie Medal and *The Guardian* Award in 1970 for *The Edge of the Cloud*, part of the Flambards trilogy. She received Carnegie citations for *The Maplin Bird* (1964), *Thunder in the Sky* (1966), and *Flambards* (1967). When Peyton came to live in the area of her book settings, the coast of England, she says, "The history of it fascinated me. The men who used to sail the fishing smacks and Thames barges told me all about it." About her research, she comments, "I read up about the period for a long time—all subjects, not just the one I am studying. I go to the place I am using and walk about, looking at it." She writes slowly and needs "virtually no revisions." She adds, "I write all the time save when I have to shop, clean house, or garden." All of her novels take place in the nineteenth or early twentieth century.

WORKS

The earliest nineteenth-century novel, **The Right-Hand Man**, traces Ned's relationship with Lord Ironminster. The one-armed lord decides to hire Ned, twenty-one, to drive his coach in 1818. Circumstances force Ned to accept the job, and Ironminster tells him to drive his horse team as daringly as Ironminster did before he lost his arm. As part of their growing friendship, Ned, against Lady Ironminster's will, secretly takes the consumptive Ironminster to see his love. Ned also agrees to race the horses and carriage against Ironminster's cousins for an old wager. When an "accident" destroys two of the horses, Ned has to fight a cousin for Ironminster's honor. He wins, and the cousins try to kill him. In self-defense, Ned kills one of them, and authorities imprison him in *Newgate. The family lawyer defends Ned by pretending that he had impregnated one of the maids on the night in question; she promises to testify if Ned will marry her. When Ironminster marries the judge's daughter, his mother's choice, instead of his real love, Ned comprehends that Ironminster has sacrificed his happiness in order to obtain an acquital from the judge for Ned. The omniscient point of view helps reveal the theme that having money does not necessarily cause one to lose all human compassion. Ironminster remains loyal to Ned as long as Ned protects him.

In **The Maplin Bird**, the only remaining portion of sixteen-year-old Toby's inheritance is the sailboat *My Alice*. When his uncle wants to refurbish the boat for his own sons, Toby and his sister, Emily, fifteen, sail it to Southend where they hope a man his father knew can help them find work. The man has drowned, but Toby becomes friends with a boy whose family permits Toby to earn money fishing with them for repairs to *My Alice*. Emily can find no work for five weeks, but her bravery in saving a woman and child thrown overboard from a wrecked ketch induces Mrs. Seymour to hire her to "live in." She works for her and her two children, Selina and Adam, under Mrs. Briggs who complains about Mrs. Seymour's requests for that "new-fangled habit" of afternoon tea in the late 1860s. The omniscient point of view reveals that in his boredom, Adam has begun to smuggle brandy across the Channel in his yacht, the *Maplin Bird*. Selina, also bored, wants to study in London, but the servants cannot understand why anyone would *want* to work. When customs officials arrive to arrest Adam, Emily says he is gone. Adam decides he can trust Toby and asks him to help retrieve the captured yacht. Since Toby needs money, he agrees, not expecting the gunfire or broken leg he receives. Mrs. Seymour brings Toby into her home and allows Selina to nurse him. Selina's surprising ability enables Toby to recover from gangrene and return to work. Toby and Emily then attempt to take Adam to France on *My Alice,* but weather foils their trip, and customs men capture Adam. With Selina in London and Adam in prison, Mrs. Seymour loans Emily and Toby a cottage until they can begin to pay her rent. The excellent sailing sections during the storm create much of the novel's suspense.

The action in **Sea Fever** occurs in the 1870s. Matt Pullen's family still sails the *Fathom,* a smack his grandfather built in 1825. The boat's boom hits Matt's father, Tom, and he drowns wearing a money belt containing a seventy-five pound reward earned for saving a man. Beckett, a man having lived only five years in Marshfield, refuses to help rescue Tom, and others find Tom's body, missing the money belt. Matt then knows that Beckett found the body first. When fishing from the *Fathom,* Matt prevents a yacht, the *Good Fortune,* from running aground, and the owner hires him to crew. The owner's son, Francis Shelley, loves the smacks and fishing, preferring them to his Oxford studies. He and Matt become friends, and he twice helps Matt with the fishing. As the skipper of the *Good Fortune* during a major race, Beckett mistreats Matt. He tries to have Matt killed when he realizes that Matt has overheard his plans to "throw the race." Matt survives, exposes Beckett, and wins race money, which pays for his new boat, *Reward*. When Francis comes to help Matt fish during the winter, they part amiably, knowing they have different interests. From the beginning to the exciting climax, when Matt outwits Beckett, the story holds the reader's full attention.

Although **Dear Fred** ostensibly is the story of Laura as she matures from thirteen to nineteen and marries Tiger, the omniscient point of view reveals the affair between her mother and uncle, as well as her own experience with her cousin, in carefully chosen but quite revealing language. The awakenings of a young girl to sexual pleasure by unexpectedly seeing her mother make love to her Uncle Harry in a field one night makes this book inadvisable for young readers. The underlying story concerns Laura's admiration for Fred Archer, a British jockey in Newmarket during the 1880s. His marriage to someone else disappoints both Laura and her governess. Laura meets Tiger when he arrives and begins to work for Uncle Harry. Although Tiger refuses to reveal his background, Harry begins to love him like a son. They eventually find that Tiger escaped from his family's circus where he once performed on the highwire and where his prescient dreams of racehorse winners won his father money. But Tiger also dreams about unpleasant future events, which he hates. When of legal age, Tiger returns to his father to tell him he will become Uncle Harry's partner and will marry Laura. Several surprising and sad events keep this novel credible.

In **Thunder in the Sky**, Sam and Gil Goodchild continue to work on the barges after their brother Manny enlists in 1914. Their respective skippers also enlist, and new ones come aboard. Sam gets Bunyard, a man reputed to be a terror, but whom Sam finds to be an excellent skipper believing that brute force, not honor, wins wars. Bunyard despises the war and says he prefers his German brother-in-law to many Englishmen he has known. When a Frenchman throws a packet aboard on one of their *Calais runs, Sam suspects Bunyard of being a spy. When confronted, Bunyard shows Sam the brandy that the man continues to give him in payment for a kindness many years past. Sam instead discovers that Gil and his new skipper are spying, and Sam nearly gets killed because of it. Depressed, Sam goes to the battle zone in Bethune outside Boulogne to ask Manny's advice, but Manny has been severely wounded and cannot talk. Sam tells Bunyard who asks to see Gil. During their talk, a *Zeppelin bombs Gil's barge. He rushes to move it so that its munitions cargo will not incinerate the other barges. He succeeds but sacrifices his life. Sam finds that Gil had enlisted, and Sam, at sixteen, pretends to be Gil and goes to war. The carefully constructed story creates strong suspense throughout.

The first of four novels about the Russell family estate, Flambards, **Flambards** follows Christina's life from the age of twelve in 1908 when she goes to live with her Uncle Russell and cousins Mark and Will until she leaves at eighteen. She meets the self-assured Mark, interested, like his father, only in horses, and the sensitive, intelligent Will whose fear of horses incurs his father's disdain. After Will breaks his patella falling off a horse, he purposely walks before it heals because the doctor warns him it will remain stiff if used too soon. Christina loves riding, and Dick, the stable boy, teaches her well. As part of a subplot,

Dick and his sister Violet work as servants until Uncle Russell fires Dick for honoring Christina's request that he not shoot an old horse, and Mark impregnates Violet. Because Christina will not receive her inheritance until twenty-one, she has no money to help Dick or Violet. Will, however, has another life with Mr. Dermot, a pilot. Intrigued by Blériot's flight across the English Channel, they build and test flying machines. Christina watches fearfully as Will flies, and she rides with him in a car going the neck-breaking speed of twenty-seven miles per hour. She realizes when Mark asks her to marry him that she loves Will. When Will's father expels him from the house for crashing a plane into the middle of an important horse race, Christina also leaves Flambards.

The second Flambards book, **The Edge of the Cloud**, begins with Christina and Will appearing in Aunt Grace's kitchen, announcing that they have left Flambards and plan to marry when Will is twenty-one. Will becomes an airplane mechanic, but he is unable to fly because of his stiff leg. Christina, with Aunt Grace's approval, begins working in a hotel near Will's job. When Mr. Dermot kills himself flying, Will inherits his plane. Then Will flies to Switzerland to have his leg repaired. When he returns four months later, completely healed, he forces Christina to overcome her own intense fear of flying to be with him when he begins stunt flying. They, Will's colleague, Sandy, and Sandy's friend, Dorothy, become a foursome. When old Uncle Russell unexpectedly dies, Will and Christina decide to marry. Before the wedding, Sandy and Will fly two planes in a single stunt, and Sandy crashes. Dorothy copes better than Will because she has met Mark and knows he is coming to the wedding. Because Austria declares war, Will joins the air force and leaves soon after the wedding. The story, with its shifting point of view between Will and Christina, shows the subtle humors in their relationship.

In **Flambards in Summer**, Christina returns to Flambards in 1916 as a twenty-one-year-old widow. Mark is missing in Gaza and also considered dead. Christina faces the empty, dilapidated house. Continued illnesses force her to call Dr. Porter, who finds that she is pregnant. With this revelation, she decides to rebuild Flambards using her newly inherited money. With most workers away, she secures a German prisoner of war, Wilhelm, who as a peacetime farmer knows how to grow wheat. When she hears that Violet, Dick's sister and mother of Mark's child Tom (Tizzy), lives in London, Christina visits and offers to pay her 500 hundred pounds for Tom. Violet agrees, and Christina adopts Tizzy. When Tizzy tells her that Uncle Dick lives in London, she asks him to help her rejuvenate Flambards. Dick's arrival, after Isabel's birth, keeps the farm alive. Mark also appears, expecting to be master of Flambards but not having any money to back his claim. When Dorothy visits and Mark decides to marry her, he happily accepts Christina's purchase offer before he returns to the French front. Christina realizes that she loves Dick's stability and decides that with him, she, Isabel, and Tizzy can become a family.

Christina and Dick marry in the beginning of **Flambards Divided**. The other servants and area landowners cannot accept Dick in the role of master, and Dick cannot accept Christina as the boss of Flambards. He detests Mark, who returns uninvited to recover from a severe war wound. After Mark's and Dorothy's marriage, Dorothy refuses to bear children, and she starts an affair with a man in London. When Christina, seven months pregnant, decides to ride her horse, it throws her when Mark's auto frightens it. A few days later, her son is still-born. Dick begins an affair with Clara, the children's nursemaid. Peyton aptly captures Dick's and Christina's love when Christina puns, "We must get electricity." Twice Mark and Dick fist fight in rage, and in the second fight, Mark wins. When Christina goes to the Hunt Ball with Fergus, a friend she met while motor car racing whose face is half-blown off from the war, she sees Mark there and realizes that she loves him. Although the law prohibits a woman from marrying her dead husband's brother, Dorothy introduces Christina to her lover, a member of Parliament, who says that the law will soon change. The writing of this novel becomes pedestrian in some parts such as a "pair of thrushes were singing their heads off." But the last in the Flambards saga solidifies the concept that wealth cannot break social class barriers. The different expectations within each class influence how its members think and act. Although realistic, these characters lead convoluted and often unfulfilled lives completely lacking in spiritual values. They could hardly expect to be other than superficial.

STYLE AND THEMES

Peyton propels the reader with her carefully crafted sense of story. She balances sentiment with humor as illustrated by her translation of a Frenchman's *mercredi* (Wednesday) into "mare cruddy" (*Thunder in the Sky*). Figurative language heightens her descriptions. From *Thunder in the Sky* comes the comment, "He felt his heart plummet like a shot bird." In *Flambards*, "The wet grass, hoof-churned, was a sea beneath the moon, smelling warm and pungent." In *Dear Fred,* one hears a "thudding of hooves . . . nothing like it, save the organ in church with all the stops out." And in *The Edge of the Cloud,* Christina alludes to *La Bohême* when describing her room. Peyton's loving tone in the novels indicates that she cherishes these characters, not only their courage but also their shortcomings.

PHAEDRUS. Young adult Roman gladiator in Britain, protagonist of *The Mark of the Horse Lord*. *See* Sutcliff, Rosemary.

PHAROS ISLAND LIGHTHOUSE. As one of the Seven Wonders of the World, this lighthouse, built by the two Ptolemys, stood 400 feet high on the coast of Alexandria, Egypt. *See* Trease, Geoffrey, *A Ship to Rome*.

PHILIP IV OF SPAIN (1605–1665). During his reign, Spain's fortunes continued to decline, and foreign wars impoverished the country. Portugal gained its independence in 1640. But in spite of the losses, he was a poet and a patron of the arts, with *Velazquez serving as his court painter. *See* de Treviño, Elizabeth, *I, Juan de Pareja*.

PHILIP D'AUBIGNY. Young adult of English descent in Jerusalem, protagonist of *Knight Crusader*. *See* Welch, Ronald.

PICARD, BARBARA LEONIE (1917–   ). British.

BIBLIOGRAPHY AND BACKGROUND

Lost John. Illustrated by Charles Keeping. New York: Criterion, 1963; London: Oxford, 1962. *One Is One*. Illustrated by Victor Ambrus. New York: Holt, Rinehart and Winston, 1966; London: Oxford, 1965. *Ransom for a Knight*. Illustrated by C. Walter Hodges. New York: Henry Z. Walck, 1967; London: Oxford, 1956. *The Young Pretenders*. Illustrated by Victor Ambrus. New York: Criterion, 1966; London: Ward, 1966.

Barbara Picard received Carnegie commendations for *Ransom for a Knight* (1956) and *One Is One* (1965). Picard chose the settings for these books because she is "particularly interested in the Middle Ages." She set *The Young Pretenders* in the eighteenth century because "it seemed to me a good period in which to set a story the theme of which was the irony of double standards of morality in social life." She adds, "I am far more interested in the past than in either the present or the future." After the necessary research using "as much time as is needed," she begins composing, working "with as few breaks as possible, aiming solely to get the story down on paper." On a second draft she checks details and divides paragraphs and chapters. A final revision polishes and prunes.

WORKS

Picard's three novels set in the Middle Ages begin with **Lost John** set around 1190 during the *Crusades of *Richard I. The protagonist, John *Fitzwilliam, fourteen, unwillingly leaves his own land in the hands of his stepfather to avenge his father's death by killing Raoul de Farrar. On the journey to Warwick, a band of men robs him, kills his servant, and takes John to their leader, Sir Ralf, a notorious robber rumored to have killed his wife and stowed his son, Alain, in a monastery. When John ably rides Sir Ralf's inhospitable horse, the impressed Sir Ralf makes John his squire, and they develop a father-son relationship. With Sir Ralf's guidance, John becomes inured to robber victim distress. Alain eventually appears at the hideout, but Sir Ralf denies him his rights because he resembles his mother. Alain's exhibitions of courage, however, keep John jealous of him. When John tells Sir Ralf his real reason for leaving home, Sir Ralf agrees to help him. Soon after, John sees Alain write his name, de Farrar. John knows that Sir Ralf, the man he now loves like a father, is actually Raoul de Farrar. When he confronts Sir Ralf, Sir Ralf suggests that John kill him, but John cannot. Later, John joins Sir Ralf in battling Robert de Wellsfont, and Sir Ralf saves John's life by leaping in front of him to take a sword thrust aimed at John. His father's death avenged, John takes Alain home with him. The vicious killing and robbing demonstrate the lawlessness rampant in England while Richard squeezed money from the people to fight his crusades.

In **Ransom for a Knight**, a messenger arrives in Sussex in 1315 and tells Alys de Renneville that her father and brother have been captured but remain alive in Scotland. The exhausted messenger develops immediate amnesia, and all but ten-year-old Alys think the two lie dead from the Battle of Bannockburn. Alys takes Hugh, a serf, and one of the horses with her, as well as the family jewels to pay the ransom. The main story involves their adventures. In London, a young man and his mother aid them, and they see King *Edward II (Longshanks) and his queen, *Isabella, whom Alys dislikes on sight, arrive at Westminster. Another young man takes them to Oxford. Someone else accompanies them north by Coventry where they see a *Corpus Christi Day morality play and on to *York and other towns toward Glengorman. Near Scotland, where understanding the language becomes difficult, they separate from their guide. Alys almost starves during the winter, but Hugh begs the local witch to feed her with a mare's milk after it foals. Gypsies steal the jewels, but another returns them. They finally reach Glengorman and pay the ransom to a man impressed with Alys's accomplishment. One knows throughout this nearly episodic plot that Alys will succeed, but Picard's descriptions of life in fourteenth century retain one's interest.

One Is One traces Stephen de Beauville's life from the time he is nine in 1318 living with his father, stepmother, and half-brothers and -sisters until 1335 when he returns to Richley monastery. In this poignant story, Stephen has only three friends, each the topic of one part in the book. The first, Amile, is the runt dog whom lonely Stephen learns to love after his half-sisters and -brothers taunt him mercilessly about his fear of dogs. When Stephen's father sends him to the monastery, Stephen has Amile killed rather than subject her to his half-brother Harry's cruelty. At Richley, as punishment for dreaming at lessons, Stephen must help querulous Brother Ernulf with his manuscript drawings. Stephen's sense of beauty, established by his amazement at seeing one day the blood-red sphere of the sun, causes him to love the work. The omniscient point of view creates dramatic irony when Brother Ernulf thinks Stephen's talent will surpass his own. But without praise, Stephen has no confidence, and he flees the monastery to become a knight. Almost starving, he meets his second friend, Pagan, a knight who trains Stephen at jousting and fighting. Their friendship lasts until Pagan loses his head for trying to help the deposed Edward II. As Stephen wanders the countryside in despair, his uncle recognizes him and takes his dead sister's son into his home. His third friend becomes the wayward son, Thomas, of his uncle's friend. When requested to take Thomas as his squire to battle the Scots, Stephen unhappily acquiesces. Stephen punishes Thomas for salting his wine by making him drink it. The fair treatment wins Thomas's devotion to Stephen until Thomas dies from smallpox. Having proved himself a worthy knight, Stephen returns to the monastery to paint for God, the only thing that truly gives him peace.

The only novel set in the eighteenth century, **The Young Pretenders**, describes how two children, Francis Rimpole, fourteen, and his sister Bella, eleven, hide a criminal on their estate for a month in 1746. When they find the man in a deserted cottage, he thrills the two by saying he is a fleeing *Jacobite. They have secretly supported the pretender to the English throne, Bonnie Prince Charlie (*Charles Edward), unlike the rest of their family. They use their wits to heal the man's broken ankle and to obtain extra food. When he admits that he is a criminal named O'Leary and not a Jacobite, they try to make him leave. However, an uncle from *Bristol arrives in need of sailors for his slave ship, and they get O'Leary a job. They keep their promises, even to a criminal. The episodic plot depicting interaction between the classes, although well written, seems implausible.

STYLE AND THEMES

Picard's tight structure complements her word choice. She relies less on diction than on detail and uses figurative language. In *Ransom for a Knight,* the "rounded hills had seemed like a long body stretched in sleep, a huge green giant under a green coverlet." In *One Is One,* she illustrates Stephen's loneliness in phrases like "cloudless sky as dull as unpolished silver" and the "huge grey castle . . . perched like a proud, unyielding eagle on its rocky crag." Of all the novels, the *Bildungsroman, One Is One,* has the most rewarding content.

PIERRE VALAIRE. Sixteen, French protagonist in *Victory at Valmy. See* Trease, Geoffrey.

PIERS BARBER. English protagonist transplanted to Constantinople (*Istanbul) in *The Emperor's Winding Sheet. See* Paton Walsh, Jill.

PIERS MEDLEY. At eighteen, the English protagonist in *A Cold Wind Blowing,* as the younger brother in *The Eldest Son,* and as a grandfather in *A Flight of Swans. See* Willard, Barbara.

PIRATE ROYAL. See Beatty, John and Patricia.

A PISTOL IN GREENYARDS. See Hunter, Mollie.

PIZARRO, FRANCISCO (1475–1541). After sailing to America and exploring, he returned to Spain and enlisted men to help him on another expedition. After his discovery of Peru, he executed the Inca chieftain *Atahualpa in 1533 when he refused to accept the Christian faith. He marched to Cuzco, captured it, and secured an immense amount of gold. Then he founded the new capital, Lima, in 1535. See *Columbus Sails* by C. Walter *Hodges and *The Amethyst Ring* by Scott *O'Dell.

PLAGUE. This disease is primarily a disease of infected rodents, which they spread on contact with human beings. It has three human clinical forms: bubonic, pneumonic, and septicemic. The first recorded plague appears in the Bible among the Philistines in the eleventh century B.C. Europe was not afflicted with bubonic plague until the sixth century A.D., but that cycle lasted fifty years. Epidemics have occurred since then, but insecticides have helped control outbreaks in modern times. See *Beyond the Weir Bridge* by Hester *Burton; *I, Juan de Pareja* by Elizabeth *de Treviño; *The Writing on the Hearth* by Cynthia *Harnett; *Master Cornhill* by Eloise *McGraw; *A Parcel of Patterns* by Jill *Paton Walsh; *The Road to Miklagard* and *Westward to Vinland* by Henry *Treece; *The Devil on the Road* by Robert Westall; and *A Cold Wind Blowing* and *The Eldest Son* by Barbara *Willard.

PLATO (c. 428–348 B.C.). The disciple of *Socrates and the teacher of Aristotle, he founded his school of philosophy known as the Academy. His extant works are dialogues, each of which utilizes Socrates in a leading role. *See* Trease, Geoffrey, *Web of Traitors*.

POLL. Nine, English protagonist in *The Peppermint Pig*. *See* Bawden, Nina.

POPE, ELIZABETH MARIE (1917–   ). American.

BIBLIOGRAPHY AND BACKGROUND
The Perilous Gard. Illustrated by Richard Cuffari. Boston: Houghton Mifflin, 1974. *The Sherwood Ring*. Illustrated by Evaline Ness. Boston: Houghton Mifflin, 1958.

Elizabeth Marie Pope was honored by the Newbery for *The Perilous Gard*. The American Library Association named *The Sherwood Ring* as a Notable Book in 1958.

WORKS
In **The Perilous Gard**, Queen *Mary, during 1558, relocates Kate Sutton from Hatfield House, where she has been serving Princess *Elizabeth to Sir Geoffrey's Elvenwood Hall, known as the "perilous gard," in Derbyshire. In a castle from which she cannot roam for more than a mile, she finds inhabitants filled with fear of "Those who rule over the Well," the *fairy folk who live in caves. Villagers think that Kate is one of these folk until she saves a little boy during a flash flood. When his mother, Susan, explains the beliefs of the folk, Kate guesses that they have stolen Sir Geoffrey's four-year-old daughter, Cecily. Christopher, Geoffrey's brother, thinks he is responsible for Cecily's death because she disappeared while in his care. Kate's idea seems valid, and he offers himself to the unseen guardian of the well in return for Cecily. Christopher evidently seems a much more powerful *teind* (tax to the gods every seven years so that food and fertility will be abundant), so they accept his offer. Because Kate sees the transfer, the castle custodian, Master John, delivers her to the

queen of the fairy folk. Once underground, Kate refuses the drugs offered her, thus keeping her senses to locate Christopher. After finding him, she tries to tell the queen about the supreme *tiend* (sacrifice), that of Christ, but the queen cannot comprehend that Christ continues to live in Christopher. Kate figures how to escape from the caves during the preparation for the fire on All Hallows' Eve (*All Saints' Day) and sees Christopher as the sacrifice begins. An ancient ballad sung by Randal, the half-witted minstrel, tells that the victim can be claimed by one outside the group before the sacrifice, and Kate states her claim. After Queen Mary dies, Kate is free to marry Christopher.

Although set in contemporary times, the historical fantasy **The Sherwood Ring**, reveals life during the *American Revolution. Peggy Grahame, at seventeen, goes to the Grahame family home, Rest-and-Be-Thankful, in New York state after her father dies in Scotland. She tells her first-person story during encounters with the resident ghosts who lived during the 1770s. As soon as Peggy exits the local train, she meets a girl dressed in a cape on horseback who tells her that she can ride to the house with a man around the curve trying to fix his car. The man, Pat Thorne, recently arrived from England, denies seeing the girl but takes Peggy anyway. They both meet Peggy's Uncle Enos, who denies any knowledge of a family member Pat wants to research and tells Pat to leave immediately. The ghosts who appear to Peggy and reveal the family's past are Barbara Grahame, the girl on horseback whose portrait bears the date 1773; her brother Dick, who spent time trying to capture Peaceable Drummond Sherwood and stop his British spy organization; Eleanor Shipley, the woman whom Dick married; and Peaceable, the man whose uncle bought him an army commission and requested he receive the worst posting in America because he would not marry his uncle's choice. Their stories reveal that Peaceable and his followers almost defeated the Americans, but because of Peaceable's uncle's instructions, his superiors would not acknowledge his talents. When Peaceable met Barbara, he decided immediately to marry her and was further convinced by her ability to outwit him in order to rescue Dick. Peggy is a descendant of Dick Grahame, and Pat, actually named Peaceable, descends from the Sherwoods. When Enos acquires a psychosomatic illness, he admits that he took information from Pat's aunt capable of changing the historical account of the British in the American Revolution. Instead of accusing Enos, Pat asks him to co-author the history. Pat and Peggy supposedly prepare to marry although the romance between them is unmotivated and undeveloped. Parallels between Barbara and Peggy and between Peaceable and Pat are not strong enough to foreshadow a marriage. Regardless, the plot development and the story are intriguing.

STYLE AND THEMES

In neither book do actual historical events integrate with the action. But both books establish a sense of the beliefs during the historical time each presents. In *The Perilous Gard*, Pope brings out the fact that pagan customs survived long after the coming of Christianity. The fairy folk and pagans supposedly hated iron bells because their ringing symbolized an ability to destroy old ways. Although the story sometimes seems implausible with its description of daily life in the fairy folk caves and because of modern diction, its mythological importance and exciting plot make it a unique type of historical fantasy. A different approach in *The Sherwood Ring* creates a similar result. Presumably, one does not confer with ghosts, but Pope entices one to do so since Peggy finds that ghosts do not "rattle chains or flap about wailing in misty sheets." Diction seems accurate here with words like *hob*. Imagery and metaphor create such concepts as a house that "smelled of misery," wine glasses "fragile as bubbles," and a doctor who "darted at Dick like a dragonfly." Throughout the two novels, Pope supplies the characters with strong moral and spiritual beliefs which help them make wise decisions.

PORT ROYAL. Once a port of trade in Jamaica, a violent earthquake destroyed it in 1693. See *Pirate Royal* by John and Patricia *Beatty and *Deadmen's Cave* by Leonard *Wibberley.

PRASUTAGUS (d. 60 A.D.). He was the king of the *Iceni of Britain under the Romans. His wife, *Boudicca, succeeded him. See *Song for a Dark Queen* by Rosemary *Sutcliff and *War Dog* and *The Queen's Brooch* by Henry *Treece.

PROHIBITION. A legal prevention of the manufacture and sale of alcoholic beverages, prohibition became law in the United States when the Eighteenth Amendment was ratified in January 1919. It was repealed by the Twenty-first Amendment in December 1933. See *Shadrach's Crossing* by *Avi and *No Promises in the Wind* by Irene *Hunt.

PURIM. A Jewish semifestival celebrated in February, it commemorates the joyousness of the Jews when Queen Esther interceded with King Ahasuerus for delivering her people from Haman's vengeance. Dressed in costume, child actors in European Jewish communities go from house to house acting out the story and collecting alms for the poor. *See* Lasky, Kathryn, *The Night Journey*.

PURITANS. In the 1560s the term *puritan* showed contempt for all persons within the Church of England who wanted more reform in the church, as well as those who broke away from the church to carry out reforms. The age of Puritanism in England occurred in the century following the Reformation until approximately 1660. In New England, it dates from the first settlement in 1620 to the new Massachusetts charter of 1691. Jonathan Edwards, a theologian, tried to create a resurgence in the 1730s. See *Constance* by Patricia *Clapp and *The Witch of Blackbird Pond* by Elizabeth George *Speare.

PYRENEES. This mountain range extends from the Bay of Biscay to the Mediterranean, generally marking the border between France and Spain. It is approximately 250 miles long and 60 miles in width. *See* Almedingen, E. M., *A Candle at Dusk.*

— Q —

QUAKERS. George Fox founded the Religious Society of Friends in 1650. He said that the society's members were derisively called Quakers because "we bid them tremble at the word of God." These people were severely persecuted because they refused to swear allegiance to anyone or anything other than God, including governments. See *Night Journeys* by *Avi; *Through the Fire, Beyond the Weir Bridge,* and *To Ravensrigg* by Hester *Burton; *Jump Ship to Freedom* by Christopher and James *Collier; *Thee, Hannah!* by Marguerite *de Angeli; *Sarah Bishop* by Scott *O'Dell; and *The Man with the Silver Eyes* by William O. *Steele.

QUETZALCOATL. Named the "Plumed Serpent," he was first worshipped by the Aztecs in central Mexico before 300 A.D. He was the god of the wind and of dawn, identified with the planet Venus, the light, and the color white. He symbolized wisdom and knowledge, as well as other positive attributes. As Kukulcán, he figures in *The Captive* and *The Feathered Serpent* by Scott *O'Dell. Here he is described as being a fair-skinned and bearded king who reigned c. 925–950. He sailed eastward but prophesied his return in the Aztecan year of *One Reed. *See* Baker, Betty, *The Blood of the Brave.*

THE QUEEN ELIZABETH STORY. See Sutcliff, Rosemary.

THE QUEEN'S BROOCH. See Treece, Henry.

THE QUEEN'S OWN GROVE. See Beatty, Patricia.

THE QUEEN'S WIZARD. See Beatty, John and Patricia.

QUINCE HEFFENDORF. Seventeen, American protagonist in *The Dunderhead War. See* Baker, Betty.

— R

RACHE. Thirteen, American Jewish female protagonist in *The Night Journey*. *See* Lasky, Kathryn.

RACHEL AND WILL ELMY. Young English protagonists of *Through the Fire*. *See* Burton, Hester.

RANDAL. English protagonist who matures from ten to twenty-two in *Knight's Fee*. *See* Sutcliff, Rosemary.

RANOFER. Twelve, Egyptian, protagonist of *The Golden Goblet*. *See* McGraw, Eloise.

RANSOM FOR A KNIGHT. *See* Picard, Barbara.

RAVEN'S CRY. *See* Harris, Christie.

THE REBEL. *See* Burton, Hester.

REBELS OF THE HEAVENLY KINGDOM. *See* Paterson, Katherine.

RED PAWNS. *See* Wibberley, Leonard.

RED ROCK OVER THE RIVER. *See* Beatty, Patricia.

THE RED TOWERS OF GRANADA. *See* Trease, Geoffrey.

REED, JOHN (1887–1920). An American journalist and poet, he reached Russia in time to observe the revolution of October 1917. In the United States, he organized and led the Communist Labor party. After he was indicted for sedition, he escaped to Russia and was buried outside the Kremlin walls in

Moscow next to Russian heroes. *See* Trease, Geoffrey, *The White Nights of St. Petersburg*.

REES, DAVID (1936–   ). British.

BIBLIOGRAPHY AND BACKGROUND

The Exeter Blitz. New York: Elsevier Nelson, 1980; London: Hamish Hamilton, 1978. *Landslip*. Illustrated by Gavin Rowe. London: Hamish Hamilton, 1977.

David Rees won the Carnegie Medal in 1979 for *The Exeter Blitz*. He has also won awards for books written in other genres. Rees says he has investigated his Irish heritage: "specifically, the life and times of my great-great-great-grandfather, a military commander in the unsuccessful rebellion of 1798. I was intrigued by the fact that his younger brother, a less important figure, was hanged by the British for his activities, whereas my direct ancestor was merely exiled (to Hamburg, then Paris)." Additionally, he has "interest in the history of the city where I live, Exeter, England, which was founded by the Romans in A.D. 79, and the visible presences of what they, and every successive age, has left in the city." His research time varies according to the amount of material available, and as a "creature of habit," he writes most days of the year from ten until five.

WORKS

In **Landslip**, around 1875, George, twelve, and Josie, eleven, experience the shock of a landslip near England's Shipden and Norfolk. Intense rain causes the soft underground chalk to collapse and engulf several houses. When Josie curiously returns to stare into the hole, the ground around her separates from the mainland, and she finds herself on an island. Her friend, Sarah Collins, runs for help but does not reappear. George sends adults to find Josie, but by evening, Sarah still has not returned. Josie thinks to check her family's partially ruined house, and there they find Sarah with her leg broken by a beam that dropped on her when she looked inside. This natural disaster unites the working class with the landowners for a few hours, but rebuilding requires that George leave school to help his father. Josie's limited omniscient viewpoint shows her enjoying the uniqueness of the disaster, unlike the adults, who lose most of their possessions.

In **The Exeter Blitz**, the omniscient viewpoint of Colin Lockwood's family allows the reader to see each member's concern for the others when the Germans bomb during 1942. No one actually believes that the Germans will consider *Exeter for a raid, but since other cathedral towns have been bombed, Mr. Lockwood thinks the Germans may be staging *Baedecker raids, in which they choose targets by descriptions in the travelogue. He is correct. When the bombing begins, Colin is in the cathedral tower retrieving the coat he left during the afternoon; Mr. Lockwood and Jane, Colin's ten-year-old sister, hide under the stairs at home; Mary Lockwood and her boyfriend, Lars, sit in the movie and escape to a shelter; and Mrs Lockwood and three others are trapped in an elevator between floors in an exclusive store where they have been watching a film about the season's new fashions. The building collapses, and two people in the elevator, Colin's history teacher, Mr. Kitchen, and his wife, die. The fashion consultant loses the use of her legs, but Mrs. Lockwood miraculously escapes serious injury. During the aftermath of the raid, Colin becomes friends with one of the London evacuees, Terry, whom he had previously disliked. He realizes that automatically disliking the evacuees has been a mistake because Terry is entertaining. Jane feels lost with the death of the pleasant old lady on the street and the destruction of almost everything in her house. Mary works nonstop in the hospital, and when Lars leaves to join the army, she feels depressed because he has never said he loved her. Out of the hospital, Mrs. Lockwood adjusts to their temporary lodgings, and Mr. Lockwood helps rebuild his beloved cathedral. Although Colin has constantly condemned Mr. Kitchen, he is the best teacher Colin has had, one who believed that "every stone has a tale to tell," and his death disturbs Colin. That life continues in a normal way after catastrophe occurs and that people often find the best in themselves when tested permeates the novel.

STYLE AND THEMES

The Exeter Blitz exemplifies Rees's writing skills, both syntactically and thematically. Realistic dialogue fleshes out the characters and allows each family member to react as an individual. Rees uses strong imagery to describe the scene, but similes such as "leaf-buds . . . like green dust in the slanting light, pale" sometimes complement. Two other devices that Rees employs in this novel are fragments, mainly to describe the war dead, and many rhetorical questions, especially from Colin's viewpoint. By contrasting flowers that continue to bloom outside a bombed house, Rees emphasizes that nature continues to be unperturbed by human destruction.

RHODES, ORDER OF THE KNIGHTS OF. *See* *St. John of Jerusalem.

RICCA. Italian protagonist who matures from thirteen into young womanhood in *The Road to Damietta*. *See* O'Dell, Scott.

RICHARD I OF ENGLAND (1157–1199). Known as the "Lionheart," this third son of *Henry II succeeded to the throne in 1189. The same year, he started on the Third *Crusade, where he aided in the capture of Acre in 1191 and recaptured Jaffa from Saladin. He was captured in Austria as he returned to Europe in 1192 and ransomed and returned to England in 1194. While fighting Phillip II in France, he was mortally wounded by an arrow near Limoges. See *Lost John* by Barbara *Picard and *Knight Crusader* by Ronald *Welch.

RICHARD III OF ENGLAND (1452–1485). The son of Richard Plantagenet, he helped restore his brother, *Edward IV, to the throne by defeating *Lancastrians at Barnet and Tewkesbury in 1471. At Edward IV's death, he became the protectorate of young *Edward V until Edward V was declared illegitimate. Then Richard III took the crown in 1483. Often he is accused of the murders of Edward V and Edward's younger brother Richard. The first of the *Tudor family, *Henry VII, defeated him at the Battle of Bosworth Field on August 22, 1485. See *The Lark and the Laurel* and *The Sprig of Broom* by Barbara *Willard.

RICHARD CAREY. English young adult protagonist in *Escape from France*. *See* Welch, Ronald.

RICHARD LARKIN. Fifteen, American orphan gone to London as protagonist in *At the Seven Stars*. *See* Beatty, John and Patricia.

RICHTER, HANS (1925–   ). German.

BIBLIOGRAPHY AND BACKGROUND
Friedrich. Trans. Edite Kroll. New York: Holt, Rinehart and Winston, 1970. *I Was There.* Trans. Edite Kroll. New York: Holt, Rinehart and Winston, 1972; London: Longmans, 1972.

Hans Richter has won many awards for his numerous writings, including the Mildred Batchelder Award in 1972 for *Friedrich*.

WORKS
A strong statement about the *Nazi treatment of the Jews occurs in **Friedrich**. An unnamed narrator who is Friedrich Schneider's age and is his good friend gives a compassionate log of the events in a German city from 1925 until 1942. In 1929, the narrator's father has no job, and his grandfather, who hates Jews, helps the family financially while Friedrich's father is doing well. The same year, the narrator's mother refuses to allow him to play with Friedrich and his mother as they frolic in the snow. The narrator visits the Schneiders on a Sabbath and foreshadows the rest of the story by noting that the "sun was going down. Everything [in the room] was dipped in red." In 1931, on the boys' first day of school, the families celebrate together, with Friedrich's father paying for almost everything in order not to embarrass the still-unemployed narrator's father. By 1933, the neighborhood hostility increases, and a *Jungvolk* leader declares to the boys, including Friedrich, that "the Jews are our affliction." Herr Schneider loses his job, and when he receives notice to leave the apartment, he appeals and wins. In 1934, Friedrich has to transfer to a Jewish school. In 1935, the cleaning lady announces that the government will not allow women under twenty-eight to work for Jews. The narrator's father joins the Nazi party and finds work, but when he suggests to the Schneiders that they leave Germany, they refuse. Pogroms begin in 1938, the year that the narrator goes to Friedrich's *bar mitzvah. After the police destroy the Schneider apartment, Friedrich's mother dies. Friedrich and his despondent father survive by mending lamps in 1939. In 1940, Friedrich falls in love with an Aryan girl but decides to sever the relationship because of the harm it will cause her. Friedrich has to don a yellow

star in 1941, just as Jews in the Middle Ages had to wear yellow hats, and he and his father lose their apartment. In 1942, Friedrich reappears at the narrator's door, dirty and hungry. The narrator's mother feeds him and wants to help but knows she cannot. When Friedrich enters the air raid shelter with all the neighbors, the landlord ejects him. After the air raid, the narrator finds Friedrich lying on the steps, killed by shrapnel. The narrator cannot understand why Friedrich, such a good person, has had to suffer and die at the hands of someone who knows only that he is Jewish.

The setting and development in **I Was There** parallel the action in *Friedrich*. The first-person unnamed narrator describes his life in Germany beginning in 1933 when he is eight. His father encourages him to become close friends with the son of a Nazi official, Heinz, and not with the Communist Gunther. But all three become close. When a group of boys decides to taunt Friedrich, a Jew, it is Gunther, and not the narrator, who firmly defends him. Eventually police free Gunther's father from prison for opposing Hitler, and Gunther reluctantly becomes a member of the Hitler Youth. He hates the organization but admires Heinz's leadership. As the boys visit each other's homes, each parent reveals a different attitude toward Hitler. Heinz's father is proud to be German; the narrator's parents feel more affluent than they did before Hitler's rise to power; and Gunther's father is convinced that Hitler is leading the country to war. He is right. After the war starts, Heinz enlists and requests that Gunther replace him as the Hitler Youth leader. Heinz returns wounded and tells the others that he only saw one hero, a man who threw himself on a grenade to save men in his platoon. Eventually Gunther and the narrator enlist and are delighted to be reunited with Heinz. On the night they arrive, Heinz sacrifices himself, as foreshadowed, during an attack to save them.

STYLE AND THEMES

Taut imagery and much dialogue fill Richter's first-person narratives. In addition, the active voice heightens the sense of immediacy in the tightly written novels. He describes one victim of a bombing: ''below the knees smashed legs, feet crushed in a bloody, dust-encrusted mass.'' Such alliteration as ''splinters slit up tree trunks'' also reveals his concern for sound and sense. The content of both novels is unsettling as Richter clearly shows how Nazi horrors adversely affected both Jew and Gentile.

RIDE INTO DANGER. See Treece, Henry,

THE RIDER AND HIS HORSE. See Haugaard, Erik.

RIDERS OF THE STORM. See Burton, Hester.

RIFLES FOR WATIE. See Keith, Harold.

THE RIGHT-HAND MAN. See Peyton, K. M.

RING OUT THE BOW BELLS. See *The Sign of the Green Falcon* by Cynthia *Harnett.

RING THE JUDAS BELL. See Forman, James.

RINKO. Japanese-American female protagonist of eleven in *A Jar of Dreams* and *The Best Bad Thing*, growing to twelve in *The Happiest Ending. See* Uchida, Yoshiko.

RIQUETI, HONORE-GABRIEL [MARQUIS OF MIRABEAU] (1749–1791). He was the most important figure during the first two years of the *French Revolution because of his personality and his oratory. He advocated a constitutional monarchy and broke with both Jacques Necker and *Lafayette. Everyone distrusted him because of his moderate stands; however, they elected him president of the National Assembly in 1791, but he died soon after. *See* Trease, Geoffrey, *Victory at Valmy*.

THE ROAD TO DAMIETTA. See O'Dell, Scott.

THE ROAD TO MIKLAGARD. See Treece, Henry.

ROB MCFARLANE. Fifteen, Scottish protagonist in *Lad with a Whistle. See* Brink, Carol Ryrie.

ROBERT WAKEFIELD. Young English protagonist who meets Shakespeare in *The Wonderful Winter. See* Chute, Marchette.

ROBERT STEWART. Sixteen, orphan, Scottish protagonist in *The Ghosts of Glencoe. See* Hunter, Mollie.

ROBERT MARYON. English adult protagonist in *Zulu Warrior. See* Welch, Ronald.

ROBERT LINNLY. English bond servant in America; major character in *Encounter at Easton* and minor character in *Night Journeys. See* Avi.

ROBESPIERRE (1758–1794). In his political decisions, he demanded the death of the king during the *French Revolution in 1793. He was responsible for much of the Reign of Terror and sent some of his friends to the guillotine in 1794. He was overthrown by the Revolution of Ninth Thermidor on July 27, 1794, and was arrested and guillotined the next day by the Revolutionary Tribunal. His death ended the Reign of Terror. *See* Trease, Geoffrey, *Victory at Valmy*.

ROBIN. English young adult in Spain, protagonist of *The Red Towers of Granada. See* Trease, Geoffrey.

ROBIN. Ten, English protagonist in *The Door in the Wall*. *See* de Angeli, Marguerite.

ROBIN HOOD. This hero of English ballads dates probably from the thirteenth century. His chief opponent was the sheriff of Nottingham, but he rebelled against all other authority and tried to help poor knights, women, and persons of humble status. See *Bows Against the Barons* by Geoffrey *Trease.

ROCHAMBEAU. *See* Jean-B.-D. *Vimeur.

ROGER. English young adult servant, protagonist in *The Dutch Are Coming*. *See* Trease, Geoffrey.

ROGER AND JILLIAN SHELFORD. English young adult protagonists in *The Secret Fiord*. *See* Trease, Geoffrey.

ROGER JOLLAND. Fourteen, English protagonist in *A Flight of Swans*. *See* Willard, Barbara.

ROLL OF THUNDER, HEAR MY CRY. *See* Taylor, Mildred.

ROMAN EMPIRE, EASTERN. The Byzantine or east Roman Empire was the Roman empire in its medieval form. It began in the reign of *Constantine the Great with his adoption of Christianity and foundation of Constantinople (*Istanbul) in 330. In 1453, *Mehmet II (Mohammed II) won the city from Constantine XI and ended the Eastern Roman Empire. *See* Paton Walsh, Jill, *The Emperor's Winding Sheet*.

ROMAN EMPIRE, WESTERN. The official date of the Roman Empire's beginning is 264 B.C. when the first Punic War started, although expansion within Italy had started in 510 B.C. The empire extended north through the British Isles, west to Portugal, south into Africa, and east of the Mediterranean. By 565 A.D., the barbarians had destroyed its power. See *The Conquered* by Naomi *Mitchison; *The Bronze Bow* by Elizabeth *Speare; *The Eagle of the Ninth, Song for a Dark Queen, Outcast, The Mark of the Horse Lord, The Silver Branch, Frontier Wolf,* and *The Lantern Bearers* by Rosemary *Sutcliff; and *War Dog, The Centurion,* and *The Queen's Brooch* by Henry *Treece.

ROSALIND. Twelve, orphan, English protagonist in *Master Rosalind*. *See* Beatty, John and Patricia.

ROSEMARY LEIGH. Seventeen, English protagonist in Mississippi in *The Tamarack Tree*. *See* Clapp, Patricia.

ROUNDHEADS. The *Royalists in the *English Civil War called the *Parliamentarians "roundheads," the nickname used for the unruly, close-cropped London apprentices. See *Witch Dog* by John and Patricia *Beatty and *The Devil on the Road* by Robert *Westall.

THE ROYAL DIRK. *See* Beatty, John and Patricia.

ROYALISTS. Members of this group supported *Charles I in the *English Civil War. See *Beyond the Weir Bridge* by Hester *Burton; *The Witch of Blackbird Pond* by Elizabeth George *Speare; *Simon* by Rosemary *Sutcliff; *When the Drums Beat* by Geoffrey *Trease; *The Devil on the Road* by Robert *Westall; and *Harrow and Harvest* by Barbara *Willard.

RUNOLF. Fifteen, Viking protagonist in *Splintered Sword*. *See* Treece, Henry.

RUPERT, DUKE OF CUMBERLAND (1619–1682). Grandson of *James I of England and nephew of *Charles I, he returned to England from imprisonment after the Thirty Years' War to serve as Charles I's general of horse. He became the dominant figure of the *Royalist forces in the *English Civil War until *Cromwell defeated him at *Marston Moor in 1644. He was exiled from England after the war but returned when *Charles II gained the throne. He introduced mezzotint printmaking in England and experimented with gunpowder production. He invented a brasslike alloy called Prince Rupert's metal or Prince's metal. He became a founder and was the first governor of the *Hudson's Bay Company from 1670 to 1682. *See* Beatty, John and Patricia, *Witch Dog*.

RUSSIAN REVOLUTION. In 1917, factory workers in Russia began unexpectedly to demonstrate against the difficulties of World War I, and the armies of Czar Nicholas II, the last of the Romanovs, refused to shoot. When the police did fire, the revolution began. *Lenin returned to the country, and after the revolution ended in 1921, a Soviet Communist dictatorship controlled much of the former Russian Empire. See *The Wild Children* by Felice *Holman; *The Night Journey* by Kathryn *Lasky; and *The White Nights of St. Petersburg* by Geoffrey *Trease.

RUSTY DICKINSON. Twelve, English protagonist in *Back Home*. *See* Magorian, Michelle.

RUTH, EDEK, AND BRONIA BALICKI. Young protagonists from Poland in *The Silver Sword*. *See* Serrailler, Ian.

SAGUNTUM. When *Hannibal attacked this town in Spain in 219 B.C., Rome complained to Carthage. The Carthaginian council refused to ask Hannibal to surrender, and the second Punic War began here. Roman ruins remain in the modern town of Sagunto. *See* Baumann, Hans, *I Marched with Hannibal*.

ST. ALBANS ABBEY. This abbey twenty miles from London was a stopping place for many nobles from its beginning in 1077 at a spot where *Saxon churches had been built. Here, a famous school of history developed, and the first draft of the Magna Carta was prepared in 1213. Several battles were fought in the area, but the abbey began losing support and was dissolved in 1539. *See* Vining, Elizabeth Gray, *Adam of the Road*.

ST. JOHN OF JERUSALEM, ORDER OF THE HOSPITAL OF. Known as the Hospitallers, this order was one of the first orders of knights. Its members were dubbed at the tomb of Christ, the Holy Sepulchre, from the end of the eleventh century. They were international, with a religious purpose and form. The members pledged celibacy, and their grand master, provincial masters ("pillars"), grand priors, and commanders resembled the hierarchy of the church. They served on Rhodes from 1309 to 1522 and then on Malta from 1530 to 1798. Since 1834, they have been known by this name and have kept the headquarters in Rome. See *The Seas of Morning* by Geoffrey *Trease; *Manwolf* by Gloria *Skurzynski; and *Knight Crusader* by Ronald *Welch.

ST. PAUL'S CATHEDRAL. Aethelbert founded the cathedral in London and installed Mellitus as bishop in 604. It has been rebuilt several times, with the last major construction following Sir Christopher *Wren's design after the *Great Fire of London in 1666. See *At the Seven Stars* by John and Patricia *Beatty; *The Wonderful Winter* by Marchette *Chute; *Master Cornhill* by Eloise *McGraw; and *I Will Adventure* by Elizabeth Gray *Vining.

ST. PETERSBURG. Called *Leningrad since 1917 during the *Russian Revolution, Peter I of Russia started building St. Petersburg in 1703 on the model of European cities. See *Young Mark* by E. M. *Almedingen; *The Wild Children* by Felice *Holman; *Fly Away Home* by Christine *Nostlinger; and *The White Nights of St. Petersburg* by Geoffrey *Trease.

SALAMIS. Off the coast of this Greek island, in the Saronic Gulf east of Athens, the Greeks defeated the Persians in 480 B.C. *See* Paton Walsh, Jill, *Crossing to Salamis*.

SALONIKA. *See* *Thessalonica.

SALTY YEAGER. Thirteen, supposedly orphaned American protagonist in *Far from Home*. *See* Sebestyen, Ouida.

SAM CHICHESTER. English protagonist who grows into manhood in *The Sound of Coaches*. *See* Garfield, Leon.

SAM GOODCHILD. Fifteen, English protagonist in *Thunder in the Sky*. *See* Peyton, K. M.

SAMHAIN [SAMBAIN]. *See* *All Saints' Day.

SAMURAI OF GOLD HILL. *See* Uchida, Yoshiko.

THE SAMURAI'S TALE. *See* Haugaard, Erik.

SANDHURST. This is the site and name of the English Royal Military Academy. At the academy, most of the potential regular officers for the British Army undergo training as officer cadets. See *Tank Commander* and *Zulu Warrior* by Ronald *Welch.

SANDRO. Italian young adult male protagonist in *Horsemen on the Hills*. *See* Trease, Geoffrey.

SANDY MAXWELL. Sixteen, Scottish protagonist in *The Lothian Run*. *See* Hunter, Mollie.

SANTA FE (TRAIL). This wagon trail from Independence, Missouri, to Santa Fe, New Mexico, was an important commercial route from 1821 until 1880 when the transcontinental railroad was completed. Probably *Coronado traveled portions of it around 1541. See *The Dunderhead War* by Betty *Baker, and *The Bad Bell of San Salvador* and *Wait for Me, Watch for Me, Eula Bee* by Patricia *Beatty.

SARA LOUISE BRADSHAW. "Wheez," American protagonist who grows from thirteen to adulthood in *Jacob Have I Loved*. *See* Paterson, Katherine.

SARACENS. Christians called their Muslim enemies, both Arab and Turkish, by this name in the Middle Ages. See *A Candle at Dusk* by E. M. *Almedingen and *Son of Columbus* by Hans *Baumann.

SARAH. Young English protagonist in *The Chocolate Boy*. *See* Trease, Geoffrey.

SARAH BISHOP. Fifteen, American protagonist in *Sarah Bishop*. *See* O'Dell, Scott.

SARAH BISHOP. *See* O'Dell, Scott.

SARAH NOBLE. Eight, American protagonist in *The Courage of Sarah Noble*. *See* Dalgliesh, Alice.

SARAH PLAIN AND TALL. *See* MacLachlan, Patricia.

SARATOGA, BATTLES OF. Two battles in the *American Revolution were fought in Saratoga, New York, September and October 1777. They are often called the turning point of the war. *Burgoyne's men were surrounded and defeated by the combined efforts of General Horatio Gates, Colonel Daniel *Morgan's sharpshooters, and General Benedict *Arnold. *See* Wibberley, Leonard, *Sea Captain from Salem*.

SASHA. Ten, Russian protagonist in *The Sound of Dragon's Feet*. *See* Zei, Aliki.

SATURNALIA GAMES. These Roman games celebrated the feast of Saturn, which resembled a Greek harvest feast near December 17, in celebration of the winter solstice. Social distinction was forgotten, and Saturnalia became associated with all forms of social license. *See* Sutcliff, Rosemary, *The Eagle of the Ninth*.

SAVE THE KHAN. *See* Bartos-Höppner, B.

SAXON. This Germanic people supposedly lived in Schleswig and along the Baltic coast. They pirated Roman ships and settled, although not permanently, on the French coast. They made conquests in Britain and on the Continent until 700. Charlemagne fought them beginning in 772 for thirty-two years in the Saxon wars, which ended with the Saxons' becoming incorporated into the Frankish empire. See *The Namesake* and *The Marsh King* by C. Walter *Hodges, and *The Lantern Bearers, Dawn Wind*, and *The Shield Ring* by Rosemary *Sutcliff.

SCHUSCHNIGG, KURT (1897–1977). When he served Austria as federal chancellor, he tried to prevent Adolf Hitler's takeover of Austria, but the *Nazis imprisoned him from 1938 to 1945. After living in the United States until 1967, he returned to Austria. *See* Orgel, Doris, *The Devil in Vienna*.

SCOTT, WALTER, SIR (1771–1832). He was a Scottish poet, novelist, historian, and biographer. He is perhaps best remembered as the creator of the historical novel. *See* Brink, Carol Ryrie, *Lad with a Whistle*.

SEA CAPTAIN FROM SALEM. *See* Wibberley, Leonard.

SEA FEVER. *See* Peyton, K. M.

THE SEA STRANGER. *See* Crossley-Holland, Kevin.

THE SEAS OF MORNING. *See* Trease, Geoffrey.

SEBESTYEN, OUIDA (1924–). American.

BIBLIOGRAPHY AND BACKGROUND
    Far from Home. Boston: Little, Brown, 1980. *Words by Heart*. Boston: Little, Brown, 1979.
    For *Words by Heart,* Ouida Sebestyen received awards from the American Library Association (1979), the International Reading Association (1980), and the American Book Award in 1982. She says, "I need to know my settings: 30 years in Texas for *Words by Heart* and *Far from Home.*" She chose historical fiction because "I wanted to come fresh and free to a time outside my own experience—but a time brought alive to me by the stories and reminiscences I grew up hearing." She notes, "I sort of hoped I could animate a past that would give readers a vivid sense of their kinship in the human family, pride in their roots, and an awareness of how they've arrived at the present." To do this, she chose characters who would have experienced certain things: a son of slaves who could compare the "hopes of Reconstruction with later disappointments," someone who felt the "innocence" of 1910, and another who had been "gassed in World War I." For research, she reads six or so general books and for specific information, "lots of picture books for the *look*. Old catalogues, local pamphlets, journals for the *feel*. Dictionaries of slang and literature, songs, jokes, etc. of the time for the *sound*—always hoping for a tidbit of human interest, a telling detail." She completes a first draft in longhand, revises, then types, then revises and researches further until satisfied with a finished manuscript.

WORKS

In **Words by Heart**, "Miss Magic Mind," twelve-year-old Lena Sills, shows her mental abilities by beating Winslow Starnes in a public contest reciting Bible verses. Since she is a black female, her victory is unanticipated, but she refuses the prize, a bow tie for a male. Her concern that her father might disapprove of her decision evaporates when he states the book's explicit theme in a comment, "Rewards don't prove you're somebody, Lena. When you're somebody inside yourself, you don't need to be told." On the night that Lena wins the contest, the Haneys, white sharecroppers, kill their dog. The next day, when the old cat bears kittens, Mr. Sills tells Lena, "Something comes to take the place of what you lose." This black family in the Midwest of 1910 tries to retain its dignity in a world controlled by whites, both worthless and worthwhile. When Lena brings a book home from her employer, Mrs. Chism, it awes the family to touch it. Mr. Sills brings home scraps of newspaper for Lena to read since they cannot afford to buy them. Mrs. Chism tells the lazy Haney sharecroppers to leave, planning to replace them with the conscientious Ben Sills. The Haneys retaliate by breaking into the Sills's house. When the son, Tater Haney, tries to kill Ben, Lena's father, Ben saves him from being trampled by a runaway horse. The wounded Ben, however, cannot be saved, but he feels that "God's child," Tater, deserves a chance. Lena takes them both home in the wagon, and on the day of her father's funeral, she spots Mr. Haney helping her family pick its cotton.

In 1929, Salty Yeager, a thirteen-year-old orphan, lives with his great-grand-mother in **Far from Home**. When he concludes that they cannot survive the *Depression in Texas without help, he goes to Buckley Arms, a guest house where his mother, Dovie, had worked before her death, to ask for a job. Tom Buckley and his wife, Babe, help Salty, but they hardly have enough money themselves. Various adult problems become apparent while Salty works for them. Hardy and Rose Ann, a couple living in the house, seem very happy, but when Rose Ann becomes pregnant, Hardy accuses her of using the pregnancy to save their marriage. Salty brings home another woman, also pregnant, who has run away from her rich husband. Then Salty realizes that Tom is his father and that Tom had loved his mother who was mute. When he watches Tom and Babe, he understands why Tom has not acknowledged him as his son. These adult themes float around Salty, who is aware that the adults "spoke with the soft evenness adults used when they switched to the special language they had learned in a country he hadn't been to yet." The importance of knowing one's father, of accepting responsibility, and of understanding the needs of others permeate the novel.

STYLE AND THEMES

Sebestyen's style is unique. She incorporates an unusual device of very short clauses to emphasize certain abstract ideas: "Space," "To hope for. To Try," "Scared," "Misplaced." Dialogue is appropriate, with black dialect apparent in *Words by Heart*. Figurative language describes the "house, frozen on its skinny brick stilts like a fat lady who had seen a mouse'' and its surrounding "field curved out like a giant claw, raking the tarpaper house.'' In *Far from Home,* kittens and trains become symbols of hope for the future during a very bleak time. Sebestyen's implicit primary theme in her writing is that the security of being loved helps people endure by giving them hope.

THE SECRET FIORD. See Trease, Geoffrey.

THE SECRET OF THE HAWK. See Wibberley, Leonard.

SENECA. This Indian tribe of *Iroquoian stock lived in western New York State. Its members expanded their territory westward in the seventeenth century by destroying the Neuter and Erie nations. They never bowed to English or French power and remained the most important and conservative Iroquois tribe. The families were linked maternally and had four clans in the two divisions of the tribe. Persons married outside their clans, and preferably, into the other division (moiety) of the tribe. During the *American Revolution, the Seneca allied with the British. *See* Steele, William O., *Tomahawk Border.*

THE SENTINELS. See Carter, Peter.

THE SERPENT'S CHILDREN. See Yep, Lawrence.

SERRAILLIER, IAN, (1912–   ). British.

BIBLIOGRAPHY AND BACKGROUND
   The Silver Sword. Illustrated by C. Walter Hodges. New York: Criterion, 1959; London: Jonathan Cape, 1956; as *Escape from Warsaw.* New York: Scholastic, 1963.
   For *The Silver Sword,* Ian Serraillier received the Boys' Clubs of America Award (1960) and a Carnegie Commendation (1956). His extensive work in other genres has also won him many accolades. For *The Silver Sword,* he researched backgrounds and case histories of refugees for five years. His interest in children and education has kept him writing books in various genres each morning.

WORK
   In **The Silver Sword**, *Nazis take educator Joseph Balicki from Warsaw, Poland, to prison when his children, Ruth, Edek, and Bronia, are thirteen, eleven, and three, respectively, in 1940. Two years later, he knocks out a guard, takes his uniform, and escapes. He walks to Warsaw, where he discovers his house destroyed and his family missing. In the rubble, he encounters Jan, a young boy who has perfected his pickpocketing. Joseph finds a tiny silver sword near Jan that he had once given his wife. When Joseph offers it to Jan as an honest gift, Jan promises to send the Balicki children to Switzerland after Joseph if he ever

meets them. The omniscient point of view reveals that the children are alive. When Germans arrest Mrs. Balicki, the children escape over the roof tops and find a cellar in which to live. Ruth starts an informal school for some of the orphans using her teaching talents. One day when Edek does not return from foraging, Ruth and Bronia assume he has been captured. During the two years of separation, Ruth negotiates with the Russians, who have by then taken Warsaw, for food, clothing, and school supplies. Jan eventually wanders into her school, but not until the silver sword falls out of his treasure box does he recall meeting Joseph. Ruth sees the sword, and the three begin their 200-mile walk to search for Edek. They find him, but meanwhile, he has contracted tuberculosis. Although Edek's illness slows them, they still travel toward Switzerland, having experiences that include an attempt to send them back to Poland as illegal refugees. Friendly adults help them find their parents, and Jan becomes a member of their household.

STYLE AND THEME

Sometimes the children seem to have information unavailable to the reader. They walk toward Switzerland with no mention until the end of the story that they have grandparents in Basel and that they are heading specifically to a Lake Constance refugee camp. The strong description includes such metaphors as the snow "gave a coating of white fur." Serraillier uses rhetorical questions indicating thought. The point of view shifts from first person to omniscient divide the plot into episodes in which the solutions often seem coincidental. For them to find Edek is amazing. At one spot, the children escape by canoeing, and Ruth loses her paddle. The paddle, however, reappears downstream exactly where she and Bronia can retrieve it. The kind farmer mails the silver sword, left on his mantel, and they receive it. Although the plot development seems implausible, the book reveals a positive picture of children managing to survive by ingenuity and intelligence during terrible times.

SHADOW OF THE HAWK. See Trease, Geoffrey.

SHADRACH FAHERTY. Twelve, American, protagonist of *Shadrach's Crossing. See* Avi.

SHADRACH'S CROSSING. See Avi.

SHAKESPEARE, WILLIAM (1564–1616). Often considered the greatest writer to have ever lived because of his ability to capture the universals of humanity in perfect prose and poetry, he worked in England during the reign of *Elizabeth I. Almost no concrete facts survive to offer insight about his life except that he helped establish the *Globe Theatre and that he spelled his name at least forty different ways. See *Master Rosalind* by John and Patricia *Beatty;

The Wonderful Winter by Marchette *Chute; *Cue for Treason* by Geoffrey
*Trease; and *I Will Adventure* by Elizabeth Gray *Vining.

SHAWNEE. This Algonquian-speaking tribe lived in the central Ohio Valley
until the seventeenth century, when the *Iroquois scattered it. They reunited
after 1725 and formed the principal barrier to westward settlement. Tecumseh
failed to keep them united, and they eventually settled in different parts of
Oklahoma. Long influenced by their association with the *Seneca and *Delaware
Indians, they combined eastern woodland and prairie traits. In summer they lived
in bark-covered houses and in winter moved to hunting camps. Each village had
a large council house used for religious ceremonies such as the ritual purification
of warriors. Other rituals included the spring Bread Dance (field planting), the
Green Corn Dance (crop ripening), and the autumn Bread Dance. The clans
were patrilineal. See *Tomahawks and Trouble* and *Trail through Danger* by
William O. *Steele, and *Red Pawns* by Leonard *Wibberley.

SHAYS, DANIEL (1747?–1825). After fighting in the *American Revolution,
he led an insurrection in western Massachusetts to attack a U.S. government
arsenal in Springfield in 1787. After being repulsed, he was sentenced to death
but pardoned in 1788. *See* Collier, Christopher and James, *The Winter Hero*.

SHEM. American who matures from fourteen into young adulthood as
protagonist in *Brothers of the Heart: A Story of the Old Northwest, 1837–38*.
See Blos, Joan.

THE SHERWOOD RING. *See* Pope, Elizabeth Marie.

THE SHIELD RING. *See* Sutcliff, Rosemary.

A SHIP TO ROME. *See* Trease, Geoffrey.

SHOGUN. This Japanese title first appeared in 720 to signify an emperor's
supreme military commander. Minamoto Yoritomo in 1148 first used the title
as a basis for asserting military and political power over the country. In 1867,
the shogun resigned his title and gave civil and military administration back to
the emperor. See *The Sign of the Chrysanthemum* and *Of Nightingales That
Weep* by Katherine *Paterson; *Samurai of Gold Hill* by Yoshiko *Uchida; and
The Samurai's Tale by Erik *Haugaard.

THE SIGN OF THE BEAVER. *See* Speare, Elizabeth George.

THE SIGN OF THE CHRYSANTHEMUM. *See* Paterson, Katherine.

THE SIGN OF THE GREEN FALCON. *See* Harnett, Cynthia.

THE SILKEN SECRET. *See* Trease, Geoffrey.

THE SILVER BRANCH. *See* Sutcliff, Rosemary.

THE SILVER SWORD. *See* Serraillier, Ian.

SILVESTER. Young protagonist of Constantinople (*Istanbul) in *The Dancing Bear*. *See* Dickinson, Peter.

SIMON. Fourteen, English protagonist who matures in *Simon*. *See* Sutcliff, Rosemary.

SIMON. *See* Sutcliff, Rosemary.

SING DOWN THE MOON. *See* O'Dell, Scott.

SIOUX. Part of the Siouan linguistic family, this tribe is also called Dakota. The members are Plains Indians who once hunted buffalo and lived in tepees. They were nomadic, nonagricultural, and proud of their war exploits. Their greatest ceremony was the Sun Dance. The U.S. government took their valuable land of the Black Hills when gold was discovered. See *The Life and Death of Yellow Bird* by James *Forman and *Cariboo Trail* and *Forbidden Frontier* by Christie *Harris.

SITTING BULL (c. 1831–1890). As a member of the Hunkpapa *Sioux tribe, he was made chief of the entire Sioux nation c. 1867. With Gall and *Crazy Horse at the Battle of Little Big Horn, he helped defeat *Custer in 1876. He retreated across the Canadian border in 1877. After returning to surrender at Fort Buford in 1881, he gained international fame as a member of Buffalo Bill's Wild West Show in 1885. By 1890, he had again become active in Sioux affairs, and when trying to nonviolently aid the Sioux plight, he was shot, along with a group of Sioux, by guards. *See* Forman, James, *The Life and Death of Yellow Bird*.

THE SKIES OF CRETE. See Forman, James.

SKIPPACK SCHOOL See de Angeli, Marguerite.

SKURZYNSKI, GLORIA (1930–   ). American.

BIBLIOGRAPHY AND BACKGROUND

Manwolf. New York: Clarion, 1981. *The Tempering.* New York: Clarion, 1983. *What Happened in Hamelin.* New York: Four Winds Press, 1979.

Gloria Skurzynski has received numerous awards for each of her novels. *What Happened in Hamelin* received the Christopher Award; the Reviewers' Choice, American Library Association (ALA) Booklist; and was on the *Horn Book* Honor List. *Manwolf* and *The Tempering* were listed as Best Books for Young Adults by ALA and in the Books of the Year by the Child Study Association. *Manwolf* was also a Reviewers' Choice, ALA Booklist, and a Notable Children's Trade Book in Social Studies. *The Tempering* won the Golden Kite Award as well as being listed in Best Books of the Year 1983, *School Library Journal,* and on the Choice List of Internationale Jugenbibliothek of UNESCO. She says, ''I wanted to write historical fiction because I'd always loved to read it from the time I received my first reading card to the adult library. I had just passed eighth grade.'' Since experts claimed that young people would not read historical fiction, Skurzynski ''thought the well known legend [of Pied Piper] might attract readers.'' Her second book resulted from extensive research on fourteenth-century Poland and her third on her father's adolescent years. She spends equal time on research and writing, about six months each. During the writing, she revises each novel approximately ten times. Although speaking engagements interrupt her work, they allow her to return to her work ''with a fresh eye.''

WORKS

What Happened in Hamelin relates that the pied piper, Gast (''foreigner''), led the 130 children of Hamelin away on June 26, 1284, to sell them to a resettler for a piece of silver each. As the first person in Hamelin to meet Gast, Geist gives his first-person account. After constant rain and rat infestation, Hamelin townsfolk were ready to accept any remedy. Gast enters the bakery where Geist works and says that he can rid the town of rats for payment. After the town leaders pay him part of his fee, he feeds pieces of pork fat and salt to the rats. With the wells covered, the thirsty rats rush to the river, where the children, becoming increasingly vicious with each whack, beat the rats to death. Gast compliments them by comparing them to the army of children that marched to free the Holy Land from the Infidels (see *Perilous Pilgrimage* by Henry *Treece). When Gast buys new clothes for Geist, Geist loves the clothes but has difficulty reconciling Gast's actions with his eerily attractive foreign flute music. The town leaders refuse to pay the balance of money to Gast so Gast orders Geist to prepare sweet rolls containing grains of purple rye with which Gast rewards the children for their work. The grain keeps them from sleeping and psychologically prepares them to follow Gast. Hilde, Geist's boss's daughter, adores Gast, but when she complains of blindness as the children depart Hamelin (all the parents are inside the church praying for their children to sleep), Gast abandons her. Then Gast admits to Geist that he befriended Geist because he needed an ally in the bakery. Fearful for his life, Geist leaves Hilde near the town gate and returns to the convent where he had previously lived. When the Hamelin priest comes, Geist tells him the story so that he can inform the Hamelin parents. The children are never found, but the blind Hilde comes to the convent and eventually regains her sight.

In **Manwolf**, a Knight of the Cross (*see* *St. John of Jerusalem), Reinmar, requests the services of Pan Lucas's serf, Danusha, to cook for him and his servant, Pan Marek, on their journey from Poland to Vienna in 1382. Danusha's beauty so overcomes Reinmar that, though he has taken vows of celibacy, he makes love to her for three weeks before he remorsefully sends her back. Count Reinmar seems threatening because he wears both a leather mask and gloves at all times, and his long mustache covers his entire mouth, but his kindness wins Danusha's love. After nine months, Danusha bears his child and calls him Adam. When Danusha discovers Adam's pink urine, Kasia, the old serf helping her in the kitchen, tells her not to worry. But when Adam's teeth grow pink, Danusha will not let him leave the kitchen. Pan Lucas makes her marry another serf who repulses her but he dies from pitchfork wounds after she bears a second son, Marcin. When Adam is five, Pan Lucas makes him work in the fields, and the sun ruins his skin. The peasants begin to stone this mother, believing she must have wed the devil to produce such an unsightly offspring. The three survive in a forest home given them by the monks, with Marcin protecting Adam until an understanding man meets and marries Danusha. Adam decides to ask the pregnant Polish queen in Krakow, known for her miracles, to heal him. Instead she faints when she sees him, and she and her child both die soon after its birth. In jail, a cruel guard displays Adam in a cage where he hears the trumpeter's unfinished tune (see *The Trumpeter of Krakow* by Eric *Kelly), but Pan Marek sees him and realizes that he must be Reinmar's son. As soon as Marek notifies Reinmar, he comes, pleased to have an heir even though the son has his same affliction. Reinmar visits Danusha and takes Adam when seventeen to study in preparation for entering the Franciscan order.

In the beginning of **The Tempering**, Karl Kerner walks to work on July 4, 1912, delighted that he has gotten a job in a Canaan, Pennsylvania, steel mill while he is still fifteen. He meets Jame Culley, eighteen, who coerces him to walk on the steel girders under the bridge spanning the Mongohela River instead of paying the two cents toll to walk over the bridge. When Karl develops a terrible fear, Jame "talks" him to the other side. When Jame severs a six-inch handlebar mustache from its owner while the man dozes at lunchtime, the man knocks Jame unconscious, and the foreman fires Karl as well as Jame. Karl hates to have to return to school, but he falls in love with the new teacher, Yulyona Petrov, who is a "Hunky," as the Irish condescendingly call Central European immigrants. She encourages him to use his musical ability to add music to a Shakespearean sonnet. During the autumn, Karl's sister, Kathleen, runs away to marry Jame, though her mother blames Jame's family for killing two of her children by spreading diphtheria. Karl almost decides to stay in school after turning sixteen, but he discovers that Miss Petrov is having an affair. Distressed, he runs away with his friend Andy, who after several weeks tells him that Miss Petrov is secretly married since teachers must be single. Karl returns home and tells "Miss" Petrov that he is going to work, because, influenced by Andy's interest in unions, he wants to learn all about the mills so that he can help the men when the unions start organizing them.

STYLE AND THEMES

Each of Skurzynski's novels has a completely different background. The startling but real disease of Adam in *Manwolf* leads to the historical basis of *What Happened in Hamelin*, which in turn leads to the lives of American and immigrant steelworkers in *The Tempering*. She uses figurative language to emphasize action in *Manwolf* when Danusha's husband goes "after her like a bull in a cow byre" and to emphasize theme in *What Happened in Hamelin* when Geist thinks, "You will find a piece of fruit which looks wholesome enough on the outside, smooth and sun-ripened. But when you bite into it, the inside is full of decay and tastes rotten and moldering." She shows the loveliness of the land in the same novel with "feathery ferns thrust their pointed tongues through the fallen pine needles." And she appropriately personifies in *The Tempering*, when the "mill screeched and roared as it gave birth to a million tons of steel a year." In each novel, the male protagonist experiences a serious setback, but Skurszynski gives him inner strengths of religious faith and character to become more capable and compassionate.

THE SLAVE DANCER. *See* Fox, Paula.

A SLAVE'S TALE. *See* Haugaard, Erik.

SMITH. Twelve, English orphan, protagonist of *Smith*. *See* Garfield, Leon.

SMITH. *See* Garfield, Leon.

SNORRI STURLUSON (1179–1241). Before being involved in political intrigues against King Haakon IV of Norway from 1218 and later assassinated, he was a historian who recorded the Icelandic sagas, the *Heimskringla* and *Younger, or Prose, Edda*. *See* Treece, Henry, *Westward to Vinland*.

THE SNOWBIRD. *See* Calvert, Patricia.

SO ENDS THIS DAY. *See* Forman, James.

SOCRATES (c. 470–399 B.C.). A Greek philosopher, he developed the method of inquiry and instruction where a series of questions was designed to elicit a clear expression of something that all rational beings should know. Accused of various offenses, he refused to change his attitudes, and when condemned, he drank hemlock in prison. He left none of his own writings, but his disciple *Plato recorded his philosophies. *See* Trease, Geoffrey, *Web of Traitors.*

SOMETHING TO SHOUT ABOUT. *See* Beatty, Patricia.

SOMMERFELT, AIMÉE (1892–1975). Norwegian.

BIBLIOGRAPHY AND BACKGROUND
  Miriam. Trans. Pat Shaw Iversen. New York: Criteron, 1963.
  Aimee Sommerfelt has been acclaimed internationally for her writing.

WORK
  In **Miriam**, Hanne Hoygard, sixteen, and her parents move into a furnished home in Oslo, Norway, during 1941. She begins to wonder about Miriam, the sixteen-year-old girl whose family unexpectedly had to leave the house. Hanne eventually understands that German *Nazis arriving and *Goebbels's threat to expel Jews had forced Miriam's family into hiding. When Hanne sees a girl outside looking wistfully at the house, she senses that the girl is Miriam and invites her inside. They become friends and soon start seeing Rolf and Terje, two boys who work underground against the Germans. When several of Miriam's family's friends are arrested, the boys help Miriam and her brother escape, although her father is captured. Miriam and her brother live in Sweden throughout the war without news of their father or older sister and her husband. Rolf visits Miriam in Sweden and shares the information that he, Terje, and Hanne work for the Norwegian underground. When the war ends, Miriam and her brother find that the rest of the family is dead. Her emptiness makes readjustment to life in Oslo very difficult, but Hanne and Rolf support her.

STYLE AND THEME
  The novel contrasts people who helped Jews survive with those who hated Jews with no basis for their prejudice. The narrator intrudes by describing an occupied country rather than showing it in the novel's action. Sommerfelt gives perspective to World War II by presenting people directly involved in the horrors of the war but who never observe them firsthand.

SON OF COLUMBUS. *See* Baumann, Hans.

SONG FOR A DARK QUEEN. *See* Sutcliff, Rosemary.

SONG OF THE TREES. *See* Taylor, Mildred.

SONS OF THE STEPPE. *See* Baumann, Hans.

SOPETE. Eleven, *Wichita protagonist in *A Stranger and Afraid*. *See* Baker, Betty.

A SOUND OF CHARIOTS. *See* Hunter, Mollie.

THE SOUND OF COACHES. *See* Garfield, Leon.

THE SOUND OF DRAGON'S FEET. *See* Zei, Aliki.

SOUNDER. *See* Armstrong, William.

THE SPANISH LETTERS. *See* Hunter, Mollie.

SPEARE, ELIZABETH GEORGE (1908–   ). American.

BIBLIOGRAPHY AND BACKGROUND

The Bronze Bow. Boston: Houghton Mifflin, 1961. *Calico Captive*. Illustrated by W. T. Mars. Boston: Houghton Mifflin, 1957. *The Sign of the Beaver*. Boston: Houghton Mifflin, 1983. *The Witch of Blackbird Pond*. Boston: Houghton Mifflin, 1958.

Elizabeth George Speare won Newbery awards for *The Witch of Blackbird Pond* (1959) and *The Bronze Bow* (1962). *The Sign of the Beaver* in 1984 was honored by the Newbery and won the Scott O'Dell Award. Finding the original narrative of Susanna Johnson's Indian captivity led Speare to her first novel, *Calico Captive,* and the fascinating and challenging genre of "historical recreation." For her three New England stories, true anecdotes from history intrigued Speare and provided framework as well as some of the characters. *The Bronze Bow* responded to the need of children in her Sunday school class to understand the life and the conflicts in ancient Palestine. Speare says, "I always begin with a *person* who becomes increasingly real and alive." After a year or more of research in libraries and at actual locations in order to portray "actual people and events . . . with absolute accuracy," the background, subplots, and character development evolve into a definite story with imaginary characters and conflicts. Each book undergoes three complete rewrites with simultaneous revisions.

WORKS

In her four novels, Speare uses limited omniscient point of view to tell the stories of her protagonists who function without immediate parental influence.

Two, Kit in *The Witch of Blackbird Pond* and Daniel in *The Bronze Bow,* are orphans; the parents of two others, Miriam in *Calico Captive* and Matt in *The Sign of the Beaver,* have duties that take them from home for the duration of the story. All four find themselves in places for which they are not psychologically adjusted, but a stable figure, usually an adult, helps them to accept themselves.

The Bronze Bow, set in Roman-occupied *Palestine, shows eighteen-year-old Daniel bar Jamin wanting vengeance from the Roman conquerors. His hate of the Romans stems from their crucifixion of his father and uncle when they could not pay taxes, the subsequent illness and death of his mother, his sister, Leah's, fear, his own bondage to a vile blacksmith, and the Roman contempt for the conquered. When Daniel unexpectedly meets Joel, a scholar, and Thrace, his sister, on a mountain trail, Daniel learns that the blacksmith from whom he escaped bondage has died. He can return to Ketzah to see his grandmother and Leah. Simon the *Zealot takes him to hear Jesus, whose message that one can love one's enemies, the Romans, baffles Daniel. Yet he knows that the outlaw Rosh in the mountains, whom he has followed for five years, lacks a quality he cannot identify. Simon decides to go with Jesus on his journeys and requests that Daniel keep his forge for him. Daniel does, and while there, forms a band of twenty who live in the area to be ready to help Rosh. The Romans, however, catch Joel gathering information for Rosh, and the band has to rescue Joel. Daniel and Joel are saved by Samson, a mute black brute bonded by love for Daniel because Daniel unshackled him when Samson was stolen from a slave merchant. Daniel keeps going to hear Jesus and sees him as "a vital, radiant face, lighted from within by a burning intensity of spirit." Daniel does not believe the healings and miracles, and Simon comments that the healing requires "something from the person himself, a sort of giving up." When Jesus comes to heal Leah, Daniel realizes that love is stronger than hate and that Jesus's nonviolent way would be the only way he could gain God's strength to "bend a bronze bow."

The first novel chronologically of the three New England stories is **The Witch of Blackbird Pond,** set in 1687. Kit Tyler, orphaned in Barbados, by the death of her grandfather, takes the ship the *Dolphin* to New England to live with her only relative, her mother's sister. On the way, she jumps in the water to retrieve a child's wooden doll, only to find from one of the male passengers that *Puritans consider women who do not sink in the water to be witches. The icy actuality of her baptism into New England waters does not come until Kit enters the sparsely furnished Wood home unannounced where her uncle does not welcome her exuberance or her seven trunks. She overtly adjusts to the stringent life but covertly spends spare moments in the meadow grieving for her past. Hannah Tupper, a *Quaker who lives on the riverbank, finds and befriends her. Nat Eaton, the ship's captain's son whom Kit met during her passage, also visits Hannah. Although the townspeople think Hannah is a witch, they do not try to destroy her until several people die of a fever. Then they burn her home, but Kit saves her as the *Dolphin* plays *deus ex machina* by coming upriver at the

exact moment Kit needs a hideout for Hannah. Instead, the people try Kit herself
for being a witch, and Nat helps save her. He brings Prudence, a little girl, into
the court to read the Bible and write her name to show Kit has been teaching
at Hannah's house rather than engaging in witchcraft. The incredible accusations
of the townspeople as to why Kit is a witch clearly illustrate how vile and
malicious people can be. Entwined into the plot are three love matches with
which Speare skillfully plays.

The second New England novel, at the outset of the *French and Indian War,
Calico Captive, tells the story of Miriam Willard. Late on an August night in
1754, Phineas Whitney tells Miriam that he wants to see her as much as possible
before he leaves Number Four Fort for Harvard; however, in the early morning,
Indians enter the cabin and capture Miriam and her pregnant sister, Susanna, Susanna's husband, James, and their three children. On the trail, Susanna gives birth
to Captive. At the camp, James convinces the Indians to sell them to the French
in Montreal. There, James promises the governor to pay a ransom if allowed to
travel to Boston for the money. After the allotted time, James does not return, but
Miriam's innate dress designing skills help her support Susanna and the children.
Miriam's spirited reactions to certain situations attract Pierre, a wealthy trapper,
and he eventually proposes marriage. But Miriam realizes, after James returns
with a letter from Phineas, that she will endure the rigors of prisoner exchange by
sailing from Montreal to Plymouth, England, and back in order to be with Phineas. Miriam grows from an egotistical young girl into a young woman realizing
that material she covets would make a lovely wedding gown for her friend. When
Miriam gives her the material, "the memory [of Hortense's pleasure and surprise]
was like a precious jewel held concealed in her hand."

In the last New England novel, **The Sign of the Beaver**, Matt Hallowel and
his father leave Quincy, Massachusetts, in 1768 to resettle in Maine. After
building a house and planting, Matt stays to watch the new cabin while his father
returns for the rest of the family. Soon afterward, a man comes to the cabin,
eats Matt's game stew, and steals the good gun while Matt sleeps. Later, Matt's
desire for sweets lures him to take honey from a beehive, but the bees sting him
mercilessly. Nearby Indians see him being stung and hear him yelling. They
save him. He tries to repay them with a book, but Saknis from the family of
the Beaver refuses. Saknis decides that Matt will teach his grandson Attean to
read. Attean, whose parents were killed by white men, scorns Matt but comes
dutifully to the unpromising lessons. In desperation, Matt reads *Robinson Crusoe*
to him, but Attean disapproves of the wild man's becoming Crusoe's slave.
Matt, who has never questioned slavery, begins to perceive life differently and
begins to choose carefully the parts he reads aloud. When Matt reads the flood
story of Noah, Attean notes that he knows a similar story, one of Gluskabe who
made the Indian. After several weeks, Attean becomes the teacher by showing
Matt how to trap, fish, and find his trail in the Indian way. After helping Attean
kill a bear, saving Attean's dog from a white man's trap, and refusing to go
with the Indians because he still hopes his family will come even after more

than seven weeks, Matt finally gains Attean's tacit approval. Matt knows that Attean has found his *manitou,* his spirit, when he calls Matt his "white brother" and gives him his dog. When his parents and sister arrive many weeks later than expected after becoming ill with typhus, Matt realizes that he can never explain the value of his experience.

STYLE AND THEMES

Speare uses fragments for emphasis and many questions to present the conflict within the protagonists. Her syntax includes many similes such as Daniel's "memory . . . glow[ing] like a warm coal in the heart of the forge" and Thacia's appearance "like a brilliant scarlet lily, glowing and proud." To Leah, the "words were like a window through which she could peek out at a world of people she did not dare to meet face to face." Metaphors also grace her stories: "the parched brown fields drank in the moisture." Some of the themes from *The Witch of Blackbird Pond* include the difficulty of enduring the strict life of the Puritans and the conflicts between those with *Royalist ties and *Patriots. Hannah explicitly states the main theme when she says, "There is no escape if love is not there." Speare's protagonists learn that only by giving of themselves can they find contentment.

THE SPIRIT IS WILLING. See Baker, Betty.

SPLINTERED SWORD. See Treece, Henry.

THE SPRIG OF BROOM. See Willard, Barbara.

STANDISH, MYLES (1584–1656). He sailed on the *Mayflower* in 1620 with the Pilgrims to the New World. As a leader, he negotiated in England for land ownership and supplies. When he returned, he and John Alden founded Duxbury, Massachusetts, in 1631. No historical account exists for the tale of Alden's proposal to Priscilla chronicled in Longfellow's *The Courtship of Myles Standish. See* Clapp, Patricia, *Constance.*

STANTON, ELIZABETH CADY (1815–1902). With Lucretia Mott, she organized the first women's rights convention in Seneca Falls, New York, in 1848. She helped Susan B. *Anthony with the movement and became the first president of the National Woman Suffrage Association from 1869–90. *See* Beatty, Patricia, *Hail Columbia.*

STARS OF FORTUNE. See Harnett, Cynthia.

STEELE, WILLIAM O. (1917–1979). American.

BIBLIOGRAPHY AND BACKGROUND

The Buffalo Knife. Illustrated by Paul Galdone. New York: Harcourt Brace, 1952. *The Far Frontier.* Illustrated by Paul Galdone. New York: Harcourt Brace,

1959; London: Macmillan, 1960. *Flaming Arrows*. Illustrated by Paul Galdone. New York: Harcourt Brace, 1958; London: Macmillan, 1958. *The Lone Hunt*. Illustrated by Paul Galdone. New York: Harcourt Brace, 1957; London: Macmillan, 1957. *The Magic Amulet*. New York: Harcourt Brace, 1979. *The Man with the Silver Eyes*. New York: Harcourt Brace, 1976. *The Perilous Road*. Illustrated by Paul Galdone. New York: Harcourt Brace, 1958; London: Macmillan, 1960. *Tomahawk Border*. Illustrated by Vernon Wooten. Williamsburg, Va.: Colonial Williamsburg, 1966. *Tomahawks and Trouble*. Illustrated by Paul Galdone. New York: Harcourt Brace, 1955. *Trail through Danger*. Illustrated by Charles Beck. New York: Harcourt Brace, 1965. *The War Party*. Illustrated by Lorinda Bryan Cauley. New York: Harcourt Brace, 1978. *Wayah of the Real People*. Illustrated by Isa Barnett. Williamsburg, Va.: Colonial Williamsburg, 1964. *Wilderness Journey*. Illustrated by Paul Galdone. New York: Harcourt Brace, 1953. *Winter Danger*. Illustrated by Paul Galdone. New York: Harcourt Brace, 1954; London: Macmillan, 1963. *The Year of the Bloody Sevens*. Illustrated by Charles Beck. New York: Harcourt Brace, 1963.

In addition to other major awards, William O. Steele was honored with the Newbery for *The Perilous Road* in 1959. A desire to recreate the frontier country of early America underscored Steele's choice of subject matter. To him, the people who settled the new areas made the history come alive. His protagonist is always a male, and he tells almost all of his stories from a limited omniscient point of view.

WORKS

Although four of the books present Native American protagonists, one, **The War Party,** shows a young Indian boy finding that war has none of the glory he had so often imagined. In another, **The Magic Amulet**, Steele places his characters in prehistoric times. During the days of mastodons and mammoths, Tragg's family clan abandons him because his wounded leg slows their hunting and gathering. Watching an armadillo defend itself from a wolf inspires him to fend for himself. He meets and joins another band of people who accept him when their foot ghosts indicate that he should not be killed. Eventually he earns his place by leading them to food he discovered earlier. The group thinks that Tragg's amulet led them to the spot. Tragg knows otherwise, but someone steals it from him anyway. At the winter gathering of the clans, Tragg rides a mammoth, a feat that gains respect from all who see him. Unlike his other novels, Steele uses dreams and magic to advance the action.

The book from a third Native American viewpoint is **Wayah of the Real People**. Wayah, at eleven, leaves his *Cherokee home in 1752 and goes to Williamsburg, Virginia, where he studies on scholarship with white students at Brafferton Hall in an attempt to create brotherhood between Cherokee and White. Renamed Adam Wolf by the schoolmaster, he has to learn white customs and words he does not understand. Walking up and down wooden ledges surprises him; he has never seen steps. He hates the bell but decides that the white god must be inside it. He does not know what a garnet is but knows that everyone searches for a lost one. He knows only that he has found a beautiful red stone in the grass and thinks it is an amulet that will protect him from difficulties. When one of the boys, Duncan, invites Wayah home for vacation, the mounds of food at meals shock him. More unexpected is Duncan's mother's hitting the teeth on a black box while she sings. Delighted when the year ends, he returns to his tribe, where he soon finds that he can help his people by translating for them. His year has taught him that whites and Indians often view things differently; by knowing the differences, he can help both groups.

In **The Man with the Silver Eyes**, Talatu, eleven, detests his Uncle Old Coat's command that he leave his home to accompany a pale-eyed man, Shinn, in 1780. Talatu thinks the white man must need him as a guide through Dragging Canoe's hostile Cherokees (the Chickamaugas). Cherokees capture Shinn, and Talatu asks them, in their language, to kill him, but the men respect Old Coat and think he must have a reason for sending the two into enemy territory. Shinn tells Talatu that he needs someone to hunt while he builds a cabin. During the winter with Shinn, Talatu contracts smallpox, and Shinn keeps him alive. Encounters with the townspeople show Talatu that Shinn sticks by his *Quaker beliefs by not fighting, even when one of the people, Tyce, goads him. When the two spy against the British, they discover that Tyce is a traitor. The second time Tyce tries to shoot Shinn, he succeeds. But simultaneously Tyce dies from Shinn's tomahawk, thrown to protect Talatu. As Shinn lies dying, he tells Talatu that he is his father. Talatu then realizes that Shinn had understood him when he asked the Cherokees to kill him. Talatu returns to his people astride his prize, Shinn's horse, but he realizes that the horse can never replace Shinn, whom he misses more than he could ever have imagined.

The only book set in the early eighteenth century, **Tomahawk Border** shows sixteen-year-old Dalk Rogers trying to be a ranger on the Virginia border in 1716. Eventually he stops a *Seneca Indian from crossing the border by hitting him with his leather cap. When he takes the Indian captive to Williamsburg, he returns with a recruit, the former British jockey, Jamie Pigg. Their friendship grows as they find that one of the rangers, Stryker, is betraying the friendly Indians. They expose his treachery and decide to become trading partners after the rangers disband.

Seven novels are set late in the eighteenth century. In 1777, **The Year of the Bloody Sevens**, the Indians supposedly scalped more whites than usual. That year, twelve-year-old Kelsey Bond crosses the Cumberland Gap to join his father in Kentucky. Indians attack Kelsey's traveling companions while he retrieves a piece of metal, and he feels ashamed at being unable to make his legs move toward the fighting. He travels the rest of the way alone, even finding his way out of a thick canebrake. Near his father's fort, he sees Indians again, hides inside a tree, and redeems himself by yelling a warning to a man walking outside. He amazes the men for completing such a difficult journey.

In **Wilderness Journey**, Flan Taylor's family leaves for Kentucky in 1782 while he remains with relatives to recover from an illness. When the family arranges for him to travel with Chapman Green, he feels that being ten, frail, and unable to shoot a gun makes him poor company. But Chap teaches him how to shoot and other survival skills while they follow the trail. They have to escape from attacking Indians, and they save a trader, Mr. Rhea, who gives Flan a silver spoon for his mother in appreciation. Flan rides a raft in a swirling river, and he nurses Chap when he develops a fever. When they arrive in French Lick, Chap has given Flan self-confidence and the realization that anyone can readily survive. Although Flan brags to his family that he shot an Indian, he did it in self-defense.

Another story set in 1782 is **The Buffalo Knife**. Andy Clark's uncle gives him a knife before the family begins their flatboat journey down the Tennessee River to French Lick. Andy promptly loses it, and throughout the trip, he longs for his first knife. The two families on the raft have to survive three hazards: the Shoals, the Suck, and the dreaded Muscle Shoals. In addition, Chickamauga Indians using weapons supplied by the British attack the travelers with flame and flint arrows. Although the omniscient point of view reveals fears of others in the group, nine-year-old Andy's only concern is his lost knife. After forty days of arduous travel, they arrive, and Andy's Uncle Az awaits them with Andy's knife. He found it on the ground where it dropped from Andy's pack before the family left.

In **Tomahawks and Trouble**, Indians capture Laird, Matthew, and Jane while they camp with their fathers and friends at Salt Lick. The three walk with *Shawnee captors toward Ohio until an old Indian, disgusted with the drunken younger ones, frees them. As they try to reach home, Tater Nose, an Indian Jane had bitten on the leg, pursues them. They push a boulder down the hill toward him, and it kills him. When they return to civilization, they find that their parents escaped and are safe. The reports they hear about Indians murdering white settlers by killing them as they walk outside their homes in the snow supports the pioneer attitude that the best Indian is a dead one.

Caje Ames, eleven, in **Winter Danger**, has to accompany his woodsman father across cold mountains into Indian country. Chased by Chickamaugas, they escape by swinging off a cliff down a grapevine. Caje's father senses that the winter will be too cold for Caje, so he takes him to his deceased wife's sister's home and disappears. Caje dislikes eating food for which he cannot pay. When his uncle becomes wounded, Caje decides to leave. Soon after his departure, he sees the breath of a hibernating bear coming out of a cave into the cold air. He shoots the bear and takes the meat back to the family. His gift allows them to survive the difficult winter without having to kill their only cow.

In **Flaming Arrows**, eleven-year-old Chad Rabun begins to understand that the Bible lessons his father has taught him can be transferred to actual situations. The Chickamaugas make their annual fall raid of Cumberland in 1784, and all the area settlers collect in the fort controlled by Amos Thompson. When the Logan family arrives without their father, all but the woodsman Amos and Chad's father want them to leave because Logan has betrayed the whites to the Indians.

Although the Logans stay, the adults blame them for the Indian raid. When young Josiah Logan risks his life to get water for the injured Colonel Boyd, the man who had most vehemently opposed his presence in the fort, Chad realizes that a father and his son may not necessarily have the same values. Chad knows, however, that his own father's values are those he appreciates. Chad shoots an Indian before he can kill Amos and burns his hands trying to stop the fire engulfing Colonel Boyd. For Chad's efforts in defeating the Indians, Amos promises him a rifle.

Three novels show the protagonists and their pleasure in achieving something unexpected. In **Trail through Danger**, around 1775, Lafe Birdwell, eleven, hires himself to Mr. Gibbs to hunt buffalo across the Carolina mountains because his father shamed the family by selling weapons to the Shawnees, which they supposedly used to kill whites. Of the men on the hunt, Lafe dislikes both Tully, who calls him an orphan, and Mr. Brown, an old, almost blind man probably enjoying his last hunt. He likes the silent Rice. Lafe helps Mr. Brown kill a charging buffalo by hamstringing it from behind. When Lafe sees Tully trying to get Mr. Brown to kill Rice, he becomes furious with Rice for leaving instead of retaliating. A hurricane scatters the 385 skins, but Lafe gathers them, and the group turns toward civilization. Cherokees, however, immediately surround them and take everything because Mr. Gibbs has been hunting illegally on Cherokee lands. Rice reappears and advises Lafe to go home and talk to his father. He does, but when Rice eventually arrives and asks him to go hunting in the West, Lafe accepts with delight.

In **The Far Frontier**, Tobe Bledsoe is horrified when his father binds him out for six months to the foolish Mr. Twistletree in 1791. He has seen Mr. Twistletree lie on the ground watching ants and do other strange things. What Tobe discovers on their journey to the West is that Mr. Twistletree's knowledge helps them much more than the illiterate Tobe could imagine. Tobe can hunt, but he has no knowledge of why things happen. When Mr. Twistletree mimics a turkey, the beast comes close enough to grab. He sounds so real, however, that a catamount jumps on him expecting a delicious turkey dinner. One night, they settle inside a cave, which catches fire, and Mr. Twistletree recognizes the coal vein. They finally find the prehistoric fort for which Mr. Twistletree has been searching deep in Indian country. While Tobe recovers from a severe snake bite, Indians come and destroy Mr. Twistletree's copious notes. The Indians capture the two and take them to their camp. An old Indian, Hummingbird, thinks Mr. Twistletree is a white medicine man and comes to visit him. They discover a mutual friend, the naturalist William Bartram from Philadelphia, who had come to camp years before. Because of Twistletree's relationship with Bartram, he and Tobe are freed. When he returns home, Tobe believes that what he has learned, including how to read, is so valuable that he decides to accept Mr. Twistletree's offer to study with him in Philadelphia.

During 1810 in **The Lone Hunt**, eleven-year-old Yance Caywood discovers buffalo tracks in the Cumberland Mountains. Distressed that others have also seen the tracks and plan to hunt the animal, Yance dejectedly accompanies them. The buffalo eludes them, and a bear almost attacks Yance. When the others leave because of the snow, Yance decides that he and his dog, Blue, will find the buffalo. Needing food, Yance tracks a deer and kills it with his knife in order to save his last two gun balls to kill the buffalo. A renegade Cherokee appears and threatens him at gunpoint for food. After Yance feeds the Cherokee, he reveals that the gun is empty. When Yance finally sees the buffalo, he shoots as it starts to cross the river's thin ice. It breaks through and has to swim back to shore, which allows Yance to finish his kill. Blue drowns during the effort, but the Cherokee looks after the buffalo while Yance returns home for help. The loss of Blue almost ruins Yance's pleasure, but a neighbor's gift of a puppy starts his recovery.

The Perilous Road is the only novel set during the *American Civil War. Chris Brabson, eleven, distressed with federal troops for taking all the family's food stored for winter, decides to support the Rebels. His brother Jethro's plan to join the Union (*Yankee) Army in 1863 shocks him. After several rebels burn the family's barn because of Jethro and Chris thinks he has caused a battle by reporting a federal wagon train, Chris realizes that people are valuable no matter what side they support. His fear that Jethro might be in the wagon train that he reported helps him understand that war, under any circumstances, is horrible.

STYLE AND THEMES

Steele fills his novels, generally for younger readers, with exciting action. Humor lightens the suspense generated by pioneer difficulties with settling and with Indians. In *The Buffalo Knife,* hyperbole entertains: "I'm hungry enough to eat a settlement of bears." In *The Perilous Road,* figurative language embellishes the description of Chris who "lay . . . curled up like a drowned grub worm." All of the characters speak with dialects appropriate to the time and place. The implicit theme with which Steele permeates all the novels is that doing what one can to make life better for others allows one to keep one's integrity, as well as other people's respect.

STEPHANIE VENABLE. Thirteen, American, protagonist in *Tree of Freedom. See* Caudill, Rebecca.

STEPHEN. English young adult protagonist in *The Writing on the Hearth. See* Harnett, Cynthia.

STEPHEN DE BEAUVILLE. English protagonist of nine who matures to twenty-seven in *One Is One. See* Picard, Barbara.

STEPHEN PARKIN. English protagonist of twenty in *The Rebel* and of twenty-three in *Riders of the Storm. See* Burton, Hester.

THE STONES. See Hickman, Janet.

STORM OVER THE CAUCASUS. See Bartos-Höppner, B.

THE STRANGE AFFAIR OF ADELAIDE HARRIS. See Garfield, Leon.

A STRANGER AND AFRAID. See Baker, Betty.

THE STRONGHOLD. See Hunter, Mollie.

STUARTS. This Scottish and English royal house began with a follower of *William the Conqueror. It provided the sovereigns of Scotland from 1371 to 1688 and various sovereigns of England. After James II was deposed in 1688, the *Jacobites upheld the *Stuart claim for many years. See *Pirate Royal, At the Seven Stars,* and *Who Comes to King's Mountain?* by John and Patricia *Beatty.

SUETONIUS PAULINUS (12–69?). As governor of the Roman province, Britain, c. 50–61 A.D., he fought *Boudicca and her followers, finally defeating them after London burned in 60 A.D. See *Song for a Dark Queen* by Rosemary *Sutcliff and *The Queen's Brooch* by Henry *Treece.

SUMMER OF MY GERMAN SOLDIER. See Greene, Betty.

SUN HORSE, MOON HORSE. See Sutcliff, Rosemary.

SURU. Spanish boy of twelve, protagonist in *I Marched with Hannibal. See* Baumann, Hans.

THE SURVIVOR. See Forman, James.

SUTCLIFF, ROSEMARY (1920–   ). British.

BIBLIOGRAPHY AND BACKGROUND

   The Armourer's House. Illustrated by C. Walter Hodges. London: Oxford, 1950. *Blood Feud.* Illustrated by Charles Keeping. New York: Dutton, 1977; London: Oxford, 1977. *Bonnie Dundee.* New York: Dutton, 1984. *Brother Dusty-Feet.* Illustrated by C. Walter Hodges. London: Oxford, 1952. *Dawn Wind.* Illustrated by Charles Keeping. New York: Henry Z. Walck, 1962; London: Oxford, 1961. *The Eagle of the Ninth.* Illustrated by C. Walter Hodges. New York: Henry Z. Walck, 1961; London: Oxford, 1954. *Frontier Wolf.* New York: Dutton, 1980. *Knight's Fee.* Illustrated by Charles Keeping. New York: Henry Z. Walck, 1960; London: Oxford, 1960. *The Lantern Bearers.* Illustrated by Charles Keeping. New York: Henry Z. Walck, 1959; London: Oxford, 1959.

The Mark of the Horse Lord. New York: Henry Z. Walck, 1965. *Outcast*. Illustrated by Richard Kennedy. London: Oxford, 1955. *The Queen Elizabeth Story*. London: Oxford, 1950. *The Shield Ring*. Illustrated by C. Walter Hodges. New York: Henry Z. Walck, 1962; London: Oxford, 1956. *The Silver Branch*. Illustrated by Charles Keeping. New York: Henry Z. Walck, 1959; London: Oxford, 1957. *Simon*. Illustrated by Richard Kennedy. London: Oxford, 1953. *Song for a Dark Queen*. New York: Crowell, 1978. *Sun Horse, Moon Horse*. Illustrated by Shirley Felts. New York: Dutton, 1978; London: Bodley Head, 1977. *Warrior Scarlet*. Illustrated by Charles Keeping. London: Oxford, 1958. *The Witch's Brat*. Illustrated by Robert Micklewright. New York: Henry Z. Walck, 1970.

Rosemary Sutcliff appeals to readers of all ages and has won recognition as one of the most accomplished writers of historical fiction. She won the Carnegie Medal for *The Lantern Bearers* (1959) and was commended for *The Eagle of the Ninth* (1954), *The Shield Ring* (1956), *The Silver Branch* (1957), and *Warrior Scarlet* (1958). Other awards include the *New York Herald Tribune* Festival Award, the *Boston Globe–Horn Book* Award, and the Phoenix Award in 1985 for *The Mark of the Horse Lord* as well as the O.B.E. (Officer, Order of the British Empire). Because Sutcliff refused to learn to read until she attended school at nine for the first time, her mother read her Greek myths and epics from various countries. These led her to a love of things classical, which gave direction to her writing. She researches as necessary, and she says,

Most of my sources deal chiefly with the "hard facts"—Roman army rates of pay, *Saxon daily life, etc. And the little illuminating flashes have been picked up over forty years or so of reading. But these flashes, combined with a very strong "gut feeling" of my own, convinced me very early on that though surface patterns of behavior and even of thought, depend on place or period, in the big basic things People Do Not Change. And nor do the important basic values—Love, Hate, honor, loyalty and divided loyalty, friendship, remains the same for all men at all times.

Sutcliff writes usually from mid-morning until supper in longhand, revising as necessary.

WORKS

Sutcliff's first three novels, set in the seventeenth century, bear little resemblance to her other novels; they are fantasies dressed in historical costumes. Published before Sutcliff's plot development and style matured, the books have similar themes and motives. **The Queen Elizabeth Story** presents Perdita, a little girl who dreams of seeing *Elizabeth I. **The Armourer's House** concerns Tamsun, an orphan girl living with London relatives. *Brother Dusty-Feet* traces a year in Hugh Copplestone's life after he runs away from his evil aunt to travel with a group of actors. Perdita not only sees Queen Elizabeth but also talks to her. Although eyeing *Henry VIII is not Tamsun's goal, she watches him and Ann Boleyn sail down the Thames from Greenwich to Westminster. Motifs noted in both *The Queen Elizabeth Story* and *The Armourer's House* include birthdays on Midsummer Night's Eve; an ability to see the good fairies, the Pharisees; a lengthy story within a story; major male and female characters fascinated with the sea and ships; and disabled or orphaned characters.

In **Brother Dusty-Feet,** the weak episodic plot concerns Hugh's desire to attend Oxford as his deceased father had wished. Sutcliff uses both Christian and classical motifs by naming Hugh's dog Argos (the same as Odysseus's dog), other dogs named Roland and Oliver, and a person called Tiggy (for Antigone); by including a wandering pilgrim able to attract animals with his piping; and by telling two stories within the main story, one having Pan leave the Christ Child a gift of music and the other revealing the origin of the English version of Saint George and the dragon. Although not indicative of Sutcliff's talent as a writer, these novels include the seeds of themes that she has developed throughout her work. She begins demonstrating the concept that words reveal beauty, both natural and man-made. Persons begin to risk their lives to help friends and family. A beloved pet faithfully serves the master or mistress. She clearly shows how seemingly insignificant events can influence the lives of many different people. After these three initial novels, Sutcliff began creating the works for which she has won many awards and accolades.

Examining the main body of Sutcliff's historical novels according to chronological sequence rather than publication date reveals her panoramic view of Britain throughout the centuries from the *Bronze Age through the *English Civil War into the 1680s. In the historical note to **Warrior Scarlet**, Sutcliff calls the Bronze Age the Heroic Age of Britain and compares it to Homer's Heroic Age of Greece by noting that Baltic amber and Egyptian blue beads showed that Britain traded widely with other areas of the known world. Drem, the protagonist, anticipates the day when he will become a warrior, able to wear the scarlet cloak signifying manhood in his tribe. Drem, however, has only one good arm, and one day he overhears his grandfather commenting that Drem will never be able to become a warrior. He runs to the woods in distress and while there encounters Talore One-Hand, a warrior who lost a hand in the mouth of a wolf. Talore becomes Drem's role model and teaches him to use the tribe's weapon, a throw spear, which Drem must use to kill a wolf singlehandedly before the tribe will accept him as a warrior. With his trusted dog, Whitethroat, Drem prepares for adulthood in the *Boys' House with the other boys his age. There, he develops a close friendship with Vortrix. At the end of his three years, Drem springs to meet his wolf; he slips on a sharp rock and falls. Although violating a tribal taboo, Vortix saves his life and must be sequestered for nine days while Drem suffers a death in life by being ostracized for his failure. He goes to live with the outcasts who serve as sheepherders. In the winter after his disgrace, Drem saves a fellow outcast by killing three wolves trying to attack him. His singular bravery causes the tribal elders to reassess his ability and to find him worthy of his scarlet cloak. Sutcliff includes the pagan rites of Samhain (*See* *All Saints' Day) and *Beltane and the notion that harpers (perhaps Homer) not naturally blind were blinde to keep them singing.

From the Bronze Age, Sutcliff continues her perceptive look at the people of Britain in **Sun Horse, Moon Horse**, set circa 100 B.C. This work is essentially the story of the *Iceni, an *Iron Age tribe known for breaking and breeding horses. The story centers on Lubrin, the son of the chief. Since the matriarchical tribal lineage declares that Lubrin's sister and her chosen husband will rule, as a young boy Lubrin escapes the pressure associated with inheriting a position of power. He enjoys drawing pictures of the horses and dreaming in his tree hideaway until his mother unexpectedly dies. The tribal elders choose his friend Dara as the husband for Lubrin's sister, and their dreams for the future end. On the wedding night, the *Attribates attack and conquer the tribe. The chief, Cradoc, sees the frustrated slave, Lubrin, drawing on the hearth and requests that Lubrin draw a horse for him on the Downs. Lubrin bargains with Cradoc: his people who have not acquiesced to the conquerors to be freed when the horse is completed. Cradoc agrees, but the unspoken portion of the bargain is the sacrifice of Lubrin on the eye of the horse. Another pagan rite noted here in addition to Samhain and Beltane is *Lammas Eve. Themes that infiltrate Sutcliff's novels about war can be found here. One sees that life is a series of wars, with the conquering peoples imposing their customs on the conquered, only to be conquered in turn; life therefore, is transitory and cyclical. The story especially shows how war can reveal true character. Sutcliff underscores the concept that those without loyalty to their tribes or countries will embrace the conqueror; those with loyalty keep it at any cost.

Another novel about the Iceni set circa 100 A.D., **Song For A Dark Queen**, concerns *Boudicca, queen of the Iceni. Sutcliff tells the story from the beautifully poetic point of view of Boudicca's harper, Cadwan, and also from that of a Roman soldier writing letters home to his mother. To develop the story, Sutcliff uses two overtly sexual symbols, a sword that Boudicca first places between her and her chosen husband at night and a marriage cup, the wedding gift from her husband. The plot follows the growth of Boudicca from childhood until the Romans come to Britain and instruct the Iceni to disarm. When Boudicca's husband unexpectedly dies, the Romans will not honor Boudicca as the tribal leader. Instead they beat her and rape her two daughters. Boudicca gathers tribes friendly to her to fight the Romans, but they lose. However, they first burn London. Boudicca then drinks poison rather than allow Suetonius *Paulinus to conquer her. Through the Roman insensitivity to the Iceni customs, Sutcliff shows that the conqueror who accommodates the local tribal customs can rule and subdue much more effectively than one who does not.

Chronologically, Sutcliff's next novel, **The Eagle of the Ninth,** takes place around 130 A.D. Marcus, the protagonist, commands a post in Britain for the Romans but has to resign when he becomes lame from a leg wound. He moves in with an uncle retired from the legions but remaining in Britain. Shocked by the treatment of gladiators at the *Saturnalia games, Marcus buys one of the gladiators, Esca, and frees him. They become friends and together go to search for the lost Legion of the Ninth in which Marcus's father was a member. The two travel north past *Hadrian's Wall pretending to be an apothecary and his helper. They meet a man who reveals that he had been a member of the Ninth but is masquerading as a British tribesman living with his wife. Marcus learns from him that the legion has been overcome by the Epidaii. His father had been brave, but some of his colleagues had mutinied. They go to the Epidaii when the tribe is celebrating the Feast of the New Spears, the same ritual that Drem loved during the Bronze Age of *Warrior Scarlet*. During this feast, Marcus and Esca see the Epidaii parading the eagle of the Ninth Legion. They steal it from the Place of Life guarded by the Horned One, the tribe's most sacred spirit. Pursued, they safely escape with the eagle and return to their home. In this intriguing book, Sutcliff introduces a symbol for a family's lineage, a dolphin signet ring, which she uses in several other books involving members of this same family.

During the same time period, in **Outcast**, the protagonist, Beric, a Roman orphan raised in a British tribe and then outcast by it during a famine, is lured on to a ship sailing for Rome and sold into slavery but later escapes. The action skips two years while Beric, accused of a crime he did not commit, rows as a galley slave. After a fight on the ship, the overseer throws Beric overboard, and Beric swims toward land. The land is Britain. Beric comes ashore at the spot where a Roman architect, Justinius, is building a sea defense. Coincidentally, in one of Sutcliff's weaker plots, Beric has seen this man at the Roman house in which he was a slave. At the end of the novel, Beric has been pardoned for a crime he never committed, helped Justinius defend the Rhee Wall during a terrible storm, found another dog to replace the beloved pet he left with the British tribe, seen Rhiada, the blind harper whom he had known as a child, and been asked by Justinius to stay with him as a horse breeder. For a person who has endured such an incredibly difficult three years, the ending seems unbelievably positive.

The Mark of the Horse Lord, set in the Highlands during Roman rule, shows a former slave, Phaedrus, pretending to be a king. Midir, the young king of the *Dalriadain, was blinded and thought dead by orders of the queen of the *Caledonians, Liadhan. He survived, but his disfigurement kept him from returning to his tribe because the people thought that ugliness brought them bad luck. Phaedrus, a gladiator freed from slavery by winning in the ring, resembles Midir so remarkably that Midir's advisers entice him to play Midir's role as king. Phaedrus goes to the tribe as the returning Midir and plays the role for which he has been carefully trained by Midir and his friends. The biggest hurdle of acceptance is that of Conory, once Midir's best friend. Recently chosen by Liadhan as her new king, Conory has no time to investigate. He must find a way to escape being the man who must fight the old king—and win—but who will be killed himself after the next seven-year cycle. When Phaedrus helps him, Conory temporarily suppresses his doubt. The Dalriadain revolt at the king making, but Liadhan escapes. Phaedrus as Midir undergoes the rites to become the Horse Lord and as king helps prepare the Dalriadain for the inescapable war that awaits them on Liadhan's return with an army. She returns in the spring, and so does the real Midir. In the battle, Midir and Liadhan die, and Phaedrus begins to believe that he actually is the Horse Lord. The fort commander tells Phaedrus that he will be a hostage until the Dalriadian offer one thousand of their men to fight in the Roman legions. Phaedrus knows the tribe cannot spare so many men, and he knows that his sacrificial death will free the tribe. As a final duty of a king helping his people, Phaedrus stabs himself with the Horse Lord's huge brooch. This novel, perhaps Sutcliff's best, with its mythic depth and strong suspense, continues to evoke strong response from the reader long after the story ends.

Next chronologically comes **The Silver Branch**, set in 300 A.D. Justin, a young man who thinks himself unattractive and unappreciated by his father, comes to Britain to serve as a surgeon in *Carausias's legion. Here he meets Flavius, who recognizes his dolphin insignia and realizes that they are cousins. With the help of a *Brigante, they find that Carausias's finance minister, *Allectus, is dealing with the enemy Sea Wolves. When Allectus discovers that they know about his activities, he banishes them and kills Carausias. During their attempted escape to *Gaul, a man wanting to fight Allectus persuades them to remain and join underground forces planning to serve Constantius (*Constantine I) in his effort to keep Britain safe from the northern invaders. They unexpectedly find the lost eagle in Flavius's aunt's house that Marcus in *The Eagle of the Ninth* had brought back from the Epidaii. This eagle becomes the standard for the motley group of soldiers who finally destroy Allectus and his men. The silver branch symbolizes the beauty of the relationship between Carausias and his jestor, Cullen. Cullen entertains him by ringing silver bells hanging from a bronze branch, and this branch helps Justin to identify and rescue Cullen in a later battle. At the end, Justin gains his father's approval for his brave deeds. In this novel, Sutcliff mentions the infiltration of Christianity into Britain by having Justin notice a man drawing the sign of a fish in the fire ashes and remembering that it has something to do with a man called Christos.

Frontier Wolf is also set in the fourth century. The protagonist, Alexios, takes charge of a Roman outpost known for its unruly British soldiers, the Frontier Wolves. The men suspect that Alexios might not have the ability to lead them. He has to learn how to deal with the local leaders as well as his men. After several mistakes, he gains their support. This novel is one of the least interesting of the novels about the Romans in Britain; the next novel chronologically is one of the best.

By the time of **The Lantern Bearers** in 410 A.D., priests and monks dot the British countryside, but religion is not the main topic in this novel. It shows the protagonist, Aquila, and his transition from a happy young soldier to one who goes "wilful missing" when the Romans leave Britain to an embittered *Saxon thrall to a man willing to sacrifice his life to show loyalty to his leader. After returning from leave, Aquila discovers that the Roman soldiers are withdrawing from Britain. The lost splendor of the Romans reflects the lost splendor of the

Greeks in names such as *Nestor* for Aquila's horse and *Clytemnestra* for the ship returning to Rome without Aquila. Aquila deserts because he has never seen Rome, and his family has always lived in Britain. As soon as the Roman soldiers leave, the Saxons arrive. They murder Aquila's father, capture his sister, and burn his home. They leave him with nothing except servitude as a thrall in the homeland of the Saxons. When his master dies, the grandson brings Aquila back to Britain where he sees his sister in a Saxon settlement with Saxon child and husband. Although she will not leave, she gives him the dolphin ring her husband had kept for her. Aquila finds purpose in his life when he decides to join the forces of *Ambrosius who plan to attack *Vortigern, the murderer of Aquila's father. During one of the battles, Aquila recognizes his sister's son among the enemy. Afterward, he returns to the scene to see if the boy is wounded. He finds him and takes him to be nursed. Before his departure, Aquila gives him the dolphin ring, asking for its return only after the boy safely reaches his mother. Finally, Ambrosius's forces defeat Vortigern. In the end, Aquila arrives home to find a lantern lit by his wife to guide his entrance. The lantern motif is one that Sutcliff uses throughout the novel as a sign of hope for a better life, and Vortigern's defeat does promise peace, at least for a while.

Sutcliff carries the dolphin ring through several more generations in **Dawn Wind,** set circa 500 A.D. The novel begins with the protagonist, Owain, awakening in a battlefield filled with dead bodies. Immediately the theme of the waste of war surfaces in the book as Owain tries to survive in a land in which he is the conquered. A dog saves Owain by keeping him warm as they make the long journey back to Owain's home. He meets several people who help him, as well as one, Regina, whom he must help. Regina needs food and care so Owain sells himself into Saxon thralldom. After eight years, Owain saves his master from drowning, and the man rewards him with freedom. Although he is free, Owain remains to help the family with several problems. During this time, he sees Augustine and remembers the Christian faith of his boyhood. After he leaves, he immediately goes to search for the dolphin ring, which had belonged to his dead father, that he had buried before selling himself. He finds instead a lock of hair, and he knows that Regina, after eleven years, is waiting for him. The hope that Augustine had given him does seem more like the wind of dawn than that of dusk.

Invaders continue to infiltrate Britain in the tenth century, the time of **Blood Feud.** Vikings snatch the protagonist, Jestyn, from the British coast where he is herding cattle and sell him into slavery. In Viking land, he and his owner, Thormod, find that Thormod's father has accidentally killed the father of two of his friends. The former friends are looking for Thormod in order to settle the blood feud. Thormod and Jestyn go to Miklagard (*Istanbul) via Kiev, where they encounter the brothers. The ensuing fight to the death is interrupted after the death of one brother, but it continues later in Miklagard when the other brother kills Thormod. Jestyn takes up the blood feud for a master who had become his best friend. When Jestyn meets Thormod's murderer several years later, Jestyn cannot kill him. He realizes that he prefers to save people in his newly found profession of surgeon rather than slaughter them. Although Jestyn feels that he has failed Thormod, he knows that he has done the right thing for his new life.

Knight's Fee, set in Britain, occurs approximately the same time as *Blood Feud* and also presents men killing to increase their power over others. Supposedly the knight system involved reputedly "civilized" men, but Sutcliff shows otherwise. The novel follows the progression of Randal from ten-year-old dog keeper to twenty-two-year-old knight. More than plot and adventure, Sutcliff emphasizes theme and character in this book. Randal, won in a chess game by the minstrel Herluin, is left by Herluin to live at Dean in the D'Aguillon household. There he makes best friends with Bevis, D'Aguillon's grandson. Together they help foil the plot of another man who wants to own Dean. Both must go to Normandy to fight, where Bevis dies in battle. After his death, Randal is knighted, an honor of which he has never even dreamed. He returns to Dean where he finds a second honor—that he has inherited the land. But the thrill of inheritance is bittersweet because he cannot share it with his dear friend. Throughout the novel, people continue to light fires on All Souls' Eve (Samhain) and to celebrate each *May Day (Beltane). Sutcliff shows that although Christianity has come to the British, the pagan beliefs of centuries past still control their imaginations.

A third novel set in this same period is **The Shield Ring**. The action shifts to the Lake Country where Saxons who have not submitted to the conquering Normans have a hideout, the Jarlstead. The major conflict in the novel concerns Bjorn's fear that he might not have the same strength of character as others before him to keep silent if ever tortured by the enemy. Another character, Frytha, knows Bjorn's fear, as well as almost everything else about him, but she never reveals it to anyone else. In fact, unlike her other novels, Sutcliff shifts the point of view between Bjorn and Frytha in such a way that they are complements to each other—and therefore, together, become co-protagonists. Bjorn becomes a harpist, taught by his foster father, a warrior turned harper. With his talent, he is the only member of the Jarlstead who can infiltrate the Norman camp unsuspected and return with information about their battle plans. One of the Normans, however, recognizes Bjorn's ring from a previous encounter, the dolphin ring that has belonged in his family for centuries. He survives the torture without revealing the Jarlstead plans and escapes when his colleagues distract the Normans. The loyalty of the members of this Jarlstead family to each other is what keeps them alive. The ring in this thoughtful novel cements the continuity of British history for over 1,000 years—Sutcliff's tangible evidence that the past is very much an active part of the present.

Sutcliff's least complicated plot occurs in the work set in the twelfth century, **The Witch's Brat**. Blamed for the death of a cow, Lovel is outcast from his community, as was Beric in *Outcast*. He walks to a monastery, where he stays, and shows an ability to understand herbs. The king's jongleur, Rahere, visits the monastery and meets Lovel. Several years later, Rahere returns and asks Lovel to join him in starting a hospital outside London. The remainder of the story concerns the building of St. Bartholomew's Hospital in London and Lovel's attempt to mend the leg of a man wounded while working on the building. Lovel and Rahere reach for dreams; some escape them, but others become real. Sutcliff emphasizes that if one never dreams, one does not even have the chance to fail. Respect for life—through loyalty, through friendship, through healing—underlies this novel as well.

Chronologically Sutcliff's penultimate novel is the first novel of her mature style. **Simon**, set in seventeenth-century England, finds himself, at fourteen, split from his best friend, Amias, because of the *English Civil War. As one might expect, Simon, the *Parliamentarian, and Amias, the *Royalist, meet as foes on the battlefield, where someone else wounds Simon. Later Simon returns home to tend his father's farm, hears that Amias has been wounded, and goes to find him. Simon summons Amias's doctor-father to look after Amias and is immediately arrested for treason because a jealous soldier reports his actions. Because the commanding officer thinks loyalty to a friend is more admirable than the betrayal of a brother soldier, he absolves Simon. After the war's end, Simon and Amias renew their strong friendship although scars of the war surround them.

Bonnie Dundee, the latest novel, is the last chronologically, covering the years surrounding the Highland march of 1689 in Scotland that Colonel John Graham of Claverhouse led for King James against *William of Orange. An orphan stable boy, son of an artist, tells the story to his grandson in a first-person flashback. Supposedly as the only one who remembers, he writes of the faithfulness and kindness of Claverhouse, misnamed Bloody Claver'se, by the Covenanters against whom he defends the king. In this, one of her finest novels, Sutcliff presents the mystical side of Scottish life in the gypsy "tinklers" and their brooch that saves the protagonist's life, the eye of the artist as he views nature, and the willingness of people (and dogs) to follow those with whom they share values.

STYLE AND THEMES

Sutcliff's stylistic control pervades her novels. Because of her complex sentence structure and abstract thematic concepts, the only novel accessible to readers younger than twelve is *The Witch's Brat*. Her use of metaphor, sound repetition, and symbol enhances content. In *Warrior Scarlet*, "there was red wool on his mother's weaving-rod now, the true burning Warrior Scarlet that was the very colour of courage itself." Imagery abounds in descriptions of setting, such as "the driftwood burned with little snapping, crackling salty flames of blue and green and saffron" *(The Shield Ring)*, and "the light of westering sun was flooding into the cell, splashing like quivering golden water on walls and ceiling" *(The Eagle of the Ninth)*. In *The Mark of the Horse Lord*, one hears "the sweeter woodwind whistle of golden plover . . . who swept on and sank again like a falling cloud of storm-spray.'' These glimpses of the beauty of sound and the depth of sense in Sutcliff's novels clearly illustrate that she deserves the awards and accolades she has received.

SWORDS FROM THE NORTH. *See* Treece, Henry.

— T

TABASCO. This Gulf Coast state of Mexico was first explored by Juan de Grijalva in 1518; in 1519, *Cortés arrived. Francisco de Montejo subdued the constant uprisings by the people in the 1530s and 1540s. *See* Baker, Betty, *The Blood of the Brave*.

TAIPING REBELLION. A Chinese rebellion, 1851–64, condemned as the war of bandits and praised as a national agrarian and proletarian revolution, it inspired many other revolutions in late nineteenth-century China, culminating with Sun Yat-sen's overthrow of the Manchu dynasty in 1911–12. It grew out of the political corruption of the Manchu rule, including the foreign aggression before and after the Opium War of 1839–42, agrarian problems, and severe famines that left many people homeless. *See* Paterson, Katherine, *Rebels of the Heavenly Kingdom*.

THE TAKEN GIRL. *See* Vining, Elizabeth Gray.

TAKIKO. Japanese female who matures from eleven to young adulthood in *Of Nightingales That Weep*. *See* Paterson, Katherine.

TALATU. Eleven, *Cherokee protagonist in *The Man with the Silver Eyes*. *See* Steele, William O.

THE TAMARACK TREE. *See* Clapp, Patricia.

TAMSUN. Orphaned English female, protagonist of *The Armourer's House*. *See* Sutcliff, Rosemary.

TANCY. Sixteen, black American protagonist in *Tancy*. *See* Hurmence, Belinda.

TANCY. *See* Hurmence, Belinda.

TANK COMMANDER. *See* Welch, Ronald.

TARO. Japanese male who matures from fourteen to become a samurai named Murakami Harutomo in *The Samurai's Tale*. *See* Haugaard, Erik.

TARTARS [TATAR]. The ancient name *Tatar* has been attributed to many groups with little or no relationship to the Turkic-speaking people whose main locale is in the Soviet Union east of the Ural Mountains. The name was given to single tribes or to all the nomads of the Asian steppes and deserts, including Mongols and Turks. The term also applied to peoples and states of the Mongol Empire in the thirteenth and fourteenth centuries. *See* Kelly, Eric, *The Trumpeter of Krakow*.

TAYLOR, MILDRED. American.

BIBLIOGRAPHY AND BACKGROUND
Let the Circle Be Unbroken. New York: Dial, 1981; London: Gollancz, 1982.
Roll of Thunder, Hear My Cry. New York: Dial, 1976; London: Gollancz, 1977.
Song of the Trees. Illustrated by Jerry Pinkney. New York: Dial, 1975.

Mildred Taylor won the Newbery Medal in 1977 for *Roll of Thunder, Hear My Cry*. In addition to other awards, she received the Coretta Scott King award in 1982. Her three historical fiction novels coalesce into the loving story of the Logan family told from young Cassie's first-person point of view during the early 1930s.

WORKS
In **Song of the Trees**, Cassie Logan is eight. In 1932, during the *Depression, while her father is working in Louisiana, Mr. Anderson comes to buy some trees on their Mississippi land from Cassie's grandmother. She refuses to sell, but Mr. Anderson cuts them down anyway. Stacey, Cassie's brother, rushes to Louisiana to get their father, and when they return, Mr. Logan threatens to dynamite the whole forest unless Mr. Anderson leaves. He tells Mr. Anderson that he is ready to die for the trees. Not quite certain if Logan is bluffing, Mr. Anderson leaves, but the wind can never again whisper through the trees that Anderson has cut.

By 1933, in **Roll of Thunder, Hear My Cry**, Cassie is nine, and her brothers are Stacey, twelve; Christopher-John, seven; and Little Man, six. Cassie sees a lot that happens but often does not understand the full import of the events. Her grandmother, Big Ma, explains to her that cotton prices are so low that her father has to go to Louisiana to work on the railroad. The family still owes money for half of the land purchased by their grandfather after the *American Civil War.

They have to pay both the mortgage and taxes on the land with the money Cassie's father makes in Louisiana. A persistent white landowner, Mr. Granger, wants their land because it had once belonged to his family, and he continues to plan ways to buy it. As a school board member, Mr. Granger arranges for Mama to be fired from her teaching job, but Uncle Hammer, working in Chicago, borrows money to pay the bills. Keeping dignity is more difficult than keeping money. The family has to endure the white ridicule in this rural environment. The white school bus driver loves to speed by the children and splash mud on them as they walk to school. When Wallace, a store owner, and his friends burn two blacks, the Logan parents organize a boycott of the store until the white landowners threaten to remove sharecroppers from their property. A white man, Mr. Simms, makes Cassie apologize to his daughter, Lillian Jean, when the girl bumps into Cassie on the sidewalk. Cassie cannot understand why Big Ma defers to him. The Logan adults constantly warn the children about becoming friends with whites and ask them to rebuff Jeremy Simms who, differing from the rest of his family, continues to seek their company. When Jeremy's obnoxious brothers, R. W. and Melvin, begin inviting T. J., a young black boy, to go places with them, he thinks they like him. But they are actually using him as a scapegoat for their stealing. After they rob Mr. Barnett's store, the ''night men'' come to lynch T. J., but a mysterious fire in the Logan cotton field, which threatens Mr. Granger's forest, interferes. When Mr. Barnett dies after the Simm's brothers hit him, the sheriff arrests T. J. for the murder. For a look at the life of blacks in the southern United States after 1930, this book presents a poignant, unbiased account of a child who sees and reacts with anger to injustice. Certainly she does not comprehend the crass stories of plantation owners using strong blacks as breeding stock for better slaves. And she cannot understand Big Ma's comment that one has to know what battles to fight in life because not all are worth the pain. The powerful value system of the family permeates their lives. They know that humans have no choice of color, but what they do with their lives makes the difference.

Cassie continues her story of the Logan family in **Let the Circle Be Unbroken**. In 1934, Cassie's father considers marbles a type of gambling and forbids her to play. She disobeys him by continuing to play. And she disobeys him another time when she and Stacey sneak into town on T. J.'s trial day. She watches a white jury convict T. J. of murdering Mr. Barnett when his white lawyer, Mr. Jamison, clearly proves that R. W. and Melvin killed Barnett. In the courthouse, she has her first experience of being denied the use of a water fountain or a toilet because she is black. At home, she hears the adults talk about being taxed for planting too much cotton and receiving money for planting less. She hears them discuss a workers' union to help workers get fair wages. She contracts scarlet fever, and although she does not die, others in the community do. Her cousin Suzella, who has a white mother, comes to stay for several months and upsets the family by pretending to be white in front of several white boys who have already raped and impregnated another black girl. Stacey runs away to get a job cutting cane, and the family spends months searching for him, finally finding him in jail for a crime he did not commit and having received no pay for his backbreaking work. Cassie watches a woman just turned sixty-five with whom she has studied the Mississippi constitution try to register to vote and be removed from her sharecropper shack because she requested nothing more than her right. And she sees the same white boys denigrate Suzella's father by making him remove his clothes in punishment for sleeping with a white woman, his wife. Obviously, Cassie still does not understand the meaning, especially the sexual overtones, of what she reports. But her accurate representation of situations allows the reader to feel the emotional undercurrents.

STYLE AND THEMES

Taylor's novels are powerful statements about the condition of blacks in the 1930s from the point of view of a black child whose loving, strong, and trustworthy parents have to teach her that she cannot do certain things because she is black. Taylor's sense of language in dialogue and description breathes life into characters and setting. To emphasize points, Taylor uses short, simple sentences like "I wondered." Big Ma tells a story, "talking softly in fragile, gentle words that seemed about to break." The road to school throws dust "like gritty red snow." In Cassie's Mississippi forest, "birds . . . called out to invite us to go with them." With Suzella, "around us the world of green trees reaching toward blue skies sang a sad song in the soft breeze, sharing our loneliness." Taylor's refusal to make all blacks good and all whites bad gives her stories strong realism. Those people, regardless of color, who fight injustice through legitimate means are humanity's only hope for true freedom.

THE TEMPERING. See Skurzynski, Gloria.

TEMUCHIN. *See* *Ghengis Khan.

THAT'S ONE ORNERY ORPHAN. See Beatty, Patricia.

THEBES. One of the most famed of ancient cities, Thebes lay on either side of the Nile at the modern site of Luxor and Karnak. The eighteenth-dynasty pharaohs made it their capital, with the height of prosperity arriving in the reign of Amenhotep III around 1400 B.C. Also located here is the temple of *Hatshepsut. *See* McGraw, Eloise, *The Golden Goblet.*

THEE, HANNAH! See de Angeli, Marguerite.

THEODORE TEWKER. Thirteen, English protagonist living in China who travels to Tibet in *Tulku. See* Dickinson, Peter.

THESSALONICA. This town in northern Greece, founded by the brother-in-law of Alexander the Great, was an important city of the *Roman Empire (Western). It was also connected with the early history of Christianity. After World War II, during the Greek civil war following German occupation, it was crowded with refugees from the towns and villages of Macedonia. *See* Holm, Anne, *North to Freedom*.

THEY HAD A HORSE. *See* Edmonds, Walter.

THE THIRD EYE. *See* Hunter, Mollie.

THE 13TH MEMBER. *See* Hunter, Mollie.

THOMAS. Twelve, English orphan protagonist in *The Miller's Boy*. *See* Willard, Barbara.

THOMAS. See *Beyond the Weir Bridge* by Hester *Burton.

THOMAS AND RICHENDA. English young adult protagonists in *Beyond the Weir Bridge*. *See* Burton, Hester.

THOR'S HAMMER. Thor was a deity common to all Germanic peoples represented as a red-bearded, middle-aged warrior having enormous strength. He hated giants but was benevolent toward humanity. *Thor* is the Teutonic word for thunder, and his hammer represents a thunderbolt. The hammer, Mjollnir, frequently depicted on runic stones and funerary steles, had marvelous qualities including returning to the thrower like a boomerang. *See* de Angeli, Marguerite, *Black Fox of Lorne*.

A THOUSAND FOR SICILY. *See* Trease, Geoffrey.

THROUGH THE FIRE. *See* Burton, Hester.

THUNDER AT VALMY. See *Victory at Valmy* by Geoffrey *Trease.

THUNDER IN THE SKY. *See* Peyton, K. M.

THUTMOSE III (d. 1450 B.C.). When he overcame the regency of his stepmother, *Hatshepsut, he became one of the greatest Egyptian kings. Among his conquests were Syria, Mitanni, and other parts of Asia. He enlarged the great temple of Amon at Karnak and had his stories written on its walls. He built or restored many temples in cities such as Memphis and Heliopolis. Of many obelisks erected, two known as Cleopatra's Needles stand in London and New York. *See* McGraw, Eloise, *Mara, Daughter of the Nile*.

TIM. Eleven, English, orphan, protagonist of *The Boy and the Monkey*. *See* Garfield, Leon.

TIME OF TRIAL. *See* Burton, Hester.

TIMMY MEEKER. Twelve, American protagonist in *My Brother Sam Is Dead*. *See* Collier, Christopher and James.

TINOCA AND AIRES. Young Portuguese protagonists in *The Barque of Brothers*. *See* Baumann, Hans.

TITUS. Young Roman protagonist coming from Alexandria in *A Ship to Rome*. *See* Trease, Geoffrey.

TO RAVENSRIGG. *See* Burton, Hester.

TOBE BLEDSOE. Young American protagonist in *The Far Frontier*. *See* Steele, William O.

TOBIAS. Thirteen, American Moravian, protagonist of *The Valley of the Shadow*. *See* Hickman, Janet.

TOLEDO. After the Moors arrived in Spain during 711, they established an extensive kingdom, including the central city of Toledo on the Tagus River, that was not conquered until 1085. With the conquest, the Spanish Castilian kingdom absorbed the cultures of Toledo's large Jewish and Mozarab communities, as well as skilled Muslim artisans and agriculturalists. See *Casilda of the Rising Moon* by Elizabeth *de Treviño and *The Red Towers of Granada* by Geoffrey *Trease.

TOLLY DORKING [BARTHOLOMEW]. Fourteen, English protagonist in *Black Jack*. *See* Garfield, Leon.

TOM BARTON. Sixteen, English protagonist in *The Hawk That Dare Not Fly by Day*. *See* O'Dell, Scott.

TOM DOLAN. Thirteen, American, protagonist of *Bert Breen's Barn*. *See* Edmonds, Walter.

TOM LINCOLN. Nineteen, from Massachusetts Bay Colony, protagonist of *Deadmen's Cave*. *See* Wibberley, Leonard.

TOMAHAWK BORDER. *See* Steele, William O.

TOMAHAWKS AND TROUBLE. *See* Steele, William O.

TORY. Meaning *Loyalist, *Tory* was an Irish name suggesting a papist outlaw and was applied to those who in 1679 supported the hereditary right of James II to succeed to the throne in spite of his Roman Catholic faith. In the American colonies, anyone who favored England during the *American Revolution was called a Tory. See *The Fighting Ground* by *Avi; *The Sentinels* by Peter *Carter; *My Brother Sam Is Dead* by Christopher and James *Collier; *Adam and the Golden Cock* by Alice *Dalgliesh; *Johnny Tremain* by Esther *Forbes; *The Cow Neck Rebels* by James *Forman; *Trumpets in the West* by Geoffrey *Trease; and *Treegate's Raiders* by Leonard *Wibberley.

TOURS, BATTLE OF. This battle in 732 A.D. with Charles *Martel defeating Muslim forces that had crossed the *Pyrenees marked the northernmost point in Europe that Muslims reached. *See* Almedingen, E. M., *A Candle at Dusk.*

TRAFALGAR, BATTLE OF. Fought on October 21, 1805, off Cape Trafalgar, south of *Cadiz, Spain, this battle between the English and *Napoleon's French and Spanish fleet combined helped secure British naval supremacy for the next century, but it cost the life of Admiral *Nelson. *See* Burton, Hester, *Castors Away!*

TRAGG. Young protagonist of prehistoric North America in *The Magic Amulet.* *See* Steele, William O.

TRAIL THROUGH DANGER. *See* Steele, William O.

THE TRAITORS. *See* Forman, James.

TRAJAN (53–117). After serving as a Roman soldier, he was adopted as successor by Nerva and became Roman emperor at Nerva's death in 98. He completed fortifications on the Rhine, made Dacia a Roman province, and erected Trajan's column in 113 to commemorate the event, warred against the Armenians and the Parthians, and improved and constructed buildings, roads, and bridges throughout the empire. He died in Selinus after conquering territory near the Persian Gulf. *See* Trease, Geoffrey, *Message to Hadrian.*

THE TREASURE OF TOPO-EL-BAMPO. See O'Dell, Scott.

THE TRUMPETER OF KRAKOW. See Kelly, Eric.

THE 290. See O'Dell, Scott.

TREASE, GEOFFREY (1909–   ). British.

BIBLIOGRAPHY AND BACKGROUND

The Baron's Hostage. London: Phoenix, 1952; rev. ed. Nashville: T. Nelson, 1975. *Bent Is the Bow.* Illustrated by Charles Keeping. London: Nelson, 1965; Camden, N.J.: Nelson, 1967. *Bows against the Barons.* Illustrated by Michael Boland. London: Lawrence, 1934; New York: International, 1934; rev. ed. New York: Meredith Press, 1967. *The Chocolate Boy.* Illustrated by David Walker. London: Heinemann, 1975. *Cue for Treason.* Illustrated by Beatrice Goldsmith. Oxford: Blackwell, 1941; New York: Vanguard, 1941. *The Dutch Are Coming.* Illustrated by Lynette Hemmant. London: Hamilton, 1967. *Escape to King Alfred.* Illustrated by R. S. Sherriffs and J. L. Stockie. New York: Vanguard, 1958; as *Mist over Athelney.* London: Macmillan, 1958. *Follow My Black Plume.* Illustrated by Brian Wildsmith. London: Macmillan, 1963; New York: Vanguard, 1963. *Horsemen on the Hills.* London: Macmillan, 1971. *Message to Hadrian.* Illustrated by Geoffrey Whittam. New York: Vanguard, 1956; as *Word to Caesar.* London: Macmillan, 1956. *The Red Towers of Granada.* Illustrated by Charles Keeping. London: Macmillan, 1966; New York: Vanguard Press, 1967. *The Seas of Morning.* Illustrated by David Smee. Harmondsworth: Puffin, 1976. *The Secret Fiord.* Illustrated by H. M. Brock. London: Macmillan, 1949; New York: Harcourt Brace, 1950. *Shadow of the Hawk.* Illustrated by Treyer Evans. New York: Harcourt Brace, 1949; as *The Hills of Varna.* London: Macmillan, 1948; rev. ed., Leicester: Knight Books, 1967. *A Ship to Rome.* Illustrated by Leslie Atkinson. London: Heinemann, 1972. *The Silken Secret.* Illustrated by Alan Jessett. Oxford: Blackwell, 1953; New York: Vanguard, 1954. *A Thousand for Sicily.* Illustrated by Brian Wildsmith. London: Macmillan, 1964; New York: Vanguard, 1964. *Trumpets in the West.* Illustrated by Alan Blyth. Oxford: Blackwell, 1947; New York: Harcourt Brace, 1947. *Victory at Valmy.* Illustrated by John S. Goodall. New York: Vanguard, 1960; as *Thunder at Valmy.* London: Macmillan, 1961. *A Voice in the Night.* Illustrated by Sara Silcock. London: Heinemann, 1973. *Web of Traitors.* Illustrated by C. Walter Hodges. New York: Vanguard, 1952; as *The Crown of Violet.* London: Macmillan, 1952. *When the Drums Beat.* Illustrated by Janet Marsh. London: Heinemann, 1976. *The White Nights of St. Petersburg.* Illustrated by William Stobbs. London: Macmillan, 1967; New York: Vanguard, 1967.

In 1979, the Royal Society of Literature elected Trease to its membership for his general literary achievement. Certainly Trease's first historical fiction novels changed the genre from what he calls "costume" novels (contemporary characters dressed in other time periods) to stories actually seeming to happen in a particular past time. Saying that he has to "have a *literate* society," Trease has set novels in his favorite countries—Italy, Russia, Greece, and England. The human issues of these countries and periods have led his characters to undergo "political struggle or oppression, to advance racial toleration, and to explore equal opportunity for both sexes." He says, "An idea may lie in my notebook for several years before I use it. Then I begin a simultaneous programme of specific historical research and literary planning." He completely outlines the plot before writing. On the typewriter he cuts and revises unsatisfactory passages while writing but does not totally rework until finishing the first draft. Working fairly fast during both mornings and afternoons, he can complete a 60,000-word novel in about four months.

WORKS

Various aspects of Trease's novels unite them in several ways. The protagonists, all male, usually act in tandem with a strong female character. As either orphans or exiles (physical or emotional), they function unencumbered by parental influence. In addition, most emphasize the importance of freedom, which the protagonists strive to achieve by various methods. Trease writes most of the novels from the omniscient point of view, thus relieving some of the suspense generated by the action. In others he uses first person, from the protagonists' perspective, with some flashbacks.

Two novels deal with the problem of what constitutes citizenship. **Web of Traitors** reveals an Athenian plot to overthrow the democracy after the death of Pericles around 425 B.C. Alexis, a contemporary of *Socrates and *Plato, so loves the Theater Festival each year that he decides to write a comedy. He names his uncle, Alexis, son of Leon, as the author since he believes that the judges will reject his play, regardless of merit, because of his youth. When his play, *The Gadfly,* wins first prize, Alexis admits his authorship. Alexis becomes friends with Corinna, a resident alien unable to become either a citizen of Athens or to marry an Athenian. Her biological parents, Alexis's play patrons, finally recognize her as the daughter they had traded at birth for a son. Thus Corinna, who helped Alexis with his play, suddenly becomes a socially acceptable friend. Before the play's performance, Alexis discovers that the wealthy, foppish Hippias and the exiled Magnes plan to stage a coup against the democratic government. By changing some of the play's lines, Alexis traps the traitors into revealing themselves when they leave the theater early. Among the skillfully incorporated customs and laws of ancient Athens are the restrictions that women could not watch afternoon performances of the comedies, and at home, they could not remain in a room when their husbands entertained. Alexis's love for both drama and democracy shape his decisions.

In the second "citizenship" novel, **A Ship to Rome** Titus tells his first-person story of trying to save a young Cretan boy, Leontius, from being sold as a slave by a Greek captain sailing from Alexandria, Egypt, to Rome. On the journey, the ship passes one of the Seven Wonders of the Ancient World, the *Pharos Island lighthouse. The captain tries to avoid paying customs' duty on Leontius by dressing him in Titus's toga, but a passenger tells him in front of the customs' officers that anyone who wears a toga, even for a moment, becomes a free Roman citizen. Thus Leontius is free, abetted unwillingly by the captain.

Three novels show a view of Italy during the late fifteenth and early sixteenth centuries. Protagonists in *Shadow of the Hawk* and *The Seas of Morning* leave England and embark from Venice for areas east. In **Horsemen on the Hills** in 1475, Sandro stays in his native Italy and fights for local freedom. Constantly reminded at home that he is a bastard son living with his stepmother and father, Sandro prefers the intellectual stimulation of school. Another attraction at school is Caterina, an excellent student who, in the omniscient view, reveals that she dislikes her own home because her parents converse only about money. They betroth her to a handsome but stupid man and ignore visits of Sandro, who tells them that the brave Federigo plans to recapture their home town from the despot Malatesta and his army. To converse, Caterina and Sandro begin meeting at the church during early morning Communion. When the mercenary Taddeo, a schemer also known in school, kidnaps Caterina, Sandro knows that he must try to free her. When he offers Taddeo money, Taddeo's perversity leads him to hang Sandro in a cage over a castle moat. Caterina's keeper, a sympathetic black slave girl who shares her own heartaches of separation with Caterina, ingeniously frees all three. Because Caterina's kidnapping makes her fiancée seem foolish, he breaks the engagement. Sandro reflects years later that their freedom and subsequent marriage outweighed the risk.

In 1480, Dick Stockton meets Brother Simon, a knight of the Order of *St. John, who intrigues him with his tales of battle in **The Seas of Morning**. Taking responsibility for Dick's increasing desire to become a knight, Brother Simon alleviates Dick's disappointment at finding he must be twenty before acceptance in the order by taking him to Rhodes to see the order's main citadel. On the *Santa Lucia* from Venice, Dick meets Tamsin, a young woman traveling with a chaperone. When the ship leaves Rhodes for Jerusalem, Turks capture it and Tamsin. Concerned about her safety, Dick goes to Constantinople (*Istanbul) and uses his father's contact with a local businessman to find that *Mehmet II, the cruel sultan, has chosen Tamsin to become a palace slave. With the help of a free-born Turk, Dick wanders through underground waterways, likened to the River Styx, that feed a well inside the palace garden. He discovers that the sultan plans to attack Rhodes, and his advance warning allows the knights to be prepared and to win the difficult battle. When Dick realizes that he loves Tamsin, he knows he can never fulfill the order's vows of poverty, chastity, and obedience. By leaving home and helping someone else find freedom, he finds himself.

Another protagonist who leaves England in search of something is Alan Drayton in **Shadow of the Hawk**. A student of *Erasmus at Cambridge around 1509, Alan duels and draws the blood of another student who argues that the world is flat. Since Alan has to escape, Erasmus suggests he go to *Varna to try to retrieve a valuable Greek manuscript. In Venice, Alan contacts a printer who promises to find the location of Varna. Word reaches the duke, and as a collector of rare books, the duke decides to kidnap Alan while his own men go to Varna. Alan pretends to begin burning the duke's only edition of Homer, and the frightened duke frees him. Angela, the printer's niece used to the freedom of Venetian women, stows away on Alan's ship and becomes his partner in the venture. On the Adriatic, they face pirates, and on land, they escape both Turkish fighters and the duke's men. Inside the monastery at Varna, they find the volume, but to leave without suspicion, they have to jump from a window into a lake and swim three miles. The duke's men nevertheless find them, fill them with drugged water, and steal the book. Alan, however, has studied the manuscript enough to remember its entire contents. Angela's uncle prints the manuscript, Alexis's play *The Gadfly* (presented in *Web of Traitors*). The story demonstrates that people who hoard the creations of past philosophers and poets selfishly deny others their beauty and wisdom. Such treasures should be available for everyone.

Revolutions cause such important political changes that Trease sets four novels in three countries during such times. A twentieth-century revolution comes to light in *The White Nights of St. Petersburg*. In the nineteenth century, *Garibaldi aided Italy, and both *Follow My Black Plume* and *A Thousand for Sicily* trace his revolution. The earliest revolution chronologically is the *French Revolution in **Victory at Valmy**. A French peasant in 1784, Pierre escapes starvation by washing brushes and mixing paints for Madame de Vairmont after she sees one of his charcoal drawings on a whitewashed wall outside an inn at Valaire. This woman, who knew Thomas Gainsborough, Sir Joshua Reynolds, Richard Sheridan, Dr. Samuel *Johnson, and Benjamin *Franklin, had rejected a society of powered wigs for natural life in the countryside. Pierre accompanies her to Versailles when Louis XVI calls the first Éstates Général in 175 years. He sees Madame have tea with *Robespierre, *Lafayette, Mirabeau (*Riqueti), and Doctor *Guillotin and finds himself victim of a nobleman's *lettre de cachet* after he overhears a conversation about squelching the commoners. When the Swiss Guard takes him to Paris, the Bastille already has been stormed. Concerned about Pauline, the marquise de Morsac's niece, he saves her just before her estate is burned. They return to Madame in Paris and remain until Pierre marches to fight in Valmy. After the victory, Pierre joins the family at Madame's cottage on New Year's Eve 1792. Although only sixteen and a commoner, he asks Pauline of the nobility to marry him. After *Napoleon's rise, Pierre reflects in the first-person narrative that if they had known the future, they would not have so warmly rejoiced. Fortunately, not knowing the future allows one to find pleasure in the present. Pierre's talent and Madame's humanity help them to overcome social class barriers and enrich lives around them.

Being sent to Italy by his grandmother after writing a love letter in 1849 helps Mark Apperley escape from her influence in **Follow My Black Plume**. With his Oxford-educated priest tutor Bilibin, he meets Pietro and Tessa on shipboard as they return to Italy after ten years in London. In Rome, Mark sees them again at the Colosseum where *Mazzini stirs the people into fighting the king of Naples. When Pietro joins the Student Corps to help Italy gain independence, Mark also joins. Pietro dies fighting the French, and Bilibin accompanies Mark as he follows Garibaldi. Tessa also goes as a companion to Garibaldi's wife, Anita, on the march to fight the Austrians. The small band finds asylum in San Marino, but Garibaldi will not accept the Austrians' truce terms. The Austrian Navy pursues them toward Venice, and the few who reach shore include Garibaldi and his wife, who soon dies from pregnancy complications. Tessa returns to her Verona relatives, while Mark and Bilibin continue to London.

A Thousand for Sicily finds Mark, in 1860, wanting to go to Sicily to report on the continuing fight for Italian independence. His newspaper fires him, but Mac, a friend he had met in Rome, decides that he will pay for and go with Mark. Before they leave, Mac arranges to send dispatches to a London man who will sell them to newspapers. On arrival in Turin, a man tells Mark where Garibaldi lives and then captures him after his visit. As the man begins to torture Mark on board a ship, Mac rescues him. Mac's drawings of the sleazy Scalia, a man working for the king, help others recognize him and tell Mac where he is. Mac and Mark go to Sicily with Garibaldi and fight with him there. They also meet Juliet, a lovely British-Italian girl whose physician father has been imprisoned by the king. Mark visits Juliet's family in Palermo though they live in the middle of the battle zone, and he finds her at home. While watching him leave, she sees Scalia recapture him. She engineers a rescue that allows Mark to rejoin Garibaldi's forces as they continue to Naples. After the victory, Mac returns to England. Later, he sees a newspaper notice announcing Mark and Juliet's marriage. Mark's desire to see freedom become reality aids him personally and professionally.

The beginning of the *Russian Revolution in 1917 takes place in **The White Nights of St. Petersburg**. David Hopkins agrees to deliver a package for a Stockholm man after he reaches *St. Petersburg's Finland station en route from New York. At the Pension Yalta, Trease cleverly explains the complex Russian nomenclature by commenting on it during Dave's initial introductions to the other pensioners. Thinking only that he plans to study the Russian language, David finds himself unwittingly involved in the prerevolutionary tactics when the man to whom Anton, one of the pensioners, directs him for the package delivery is almost immediately arrested by secret police. Later at a gypsy restaurant celebration with Rosalind (a boarder), Anton, and Sonia (the pension owner's granddaughter), David sees Rasputin. Anton tells him about Rasputin's influence on the Tsarina. Soon after, Rasputin is murdered, and Anton is arrested as a suspect. When *Lenin returns to St. Petersburg and the revolution begins, Anton and David see Mr. Zorin (a fourth boarder) in Lenin's presence and assume he is a Bolshevik. However, David overhears Zorin on the telephone ordering the destruction of *Pravda* offices where Anton works and realizes Zorin, as a member of the secret police, knew about David's package delivery. On the night of the storming of the Winter Palace, David follows John *Reed's group inside. Looking for Anton, he finds both Sonia and Anton, and seeing their love, knows he no longer has reason to remain in Russia. The frustration of being denied freedom finally forces the Russian revolutionary leaders to fight the czar.

Trease's books with England as the setting cover aspects of British history from Roman times to the mid-eighteenth century. None extends to the British defeat in the *American Revolution. The novels tend to show hardships imposed upon the common people in their unexpected clashes with nobility. The first novel chronologically, **Message to Hadrian**, starts when the exiled Roman poet Lucius Fabius Severus rescues Paul from the *Caledonians at Ravenglass. Paul finds himself with an unsettled future since his Roman soldier father is recently dead and his own arm is severely wounded. Severus takes him to his friend Veranius's villa in Bath. There Severus tells Paul that the emperor *Trajan banished him because of his verses. The wealthy Calvus, a blackmailer who had "bought" the services of all classes of men, including Severus's trusted copier, had been told of Severus's satiric verses about him. He had made the copier replace them with poorly written words satirizing Trajan. Soon Paul hears news of Trajan's death and of the new emperor, *Hadrian. Paul travels to Rome, not without hardship and peril, to tell Hadrian of the crime against Severus. Hadrian tells Paul he must have evidence of the crime, and with great difficulty, Paul gets it. Hadrian allows Severus to return and then hires Paul. Thus Paul, initially rescued by Severus, pays his debt with brave and intelligent investigation, which in turn liberates Severus while gaining security for himself.

The next literate period in England after the Romans is apparently the time of King *Alfred around 878. In **Escape to King Alfred**, Judith and her brother, Edward, along with Elfwyn find themselves hostages to the Danish king *Guthrum in Gloucester. When Guthrum stakes Edward at dice and loses him to King Hubba after making plans to fight Alfred in Wessex during Christmas, Elfwyn and Judith escape to warn Alfred. They succeed, but the siege lasts several months before Alfred finally wins. He positions himself on the island of Avalon (Athelney) where he can watch the fighters come through the hills at Taunton Deane. After Edward is freed from Hubba and Guthrum is defeated, Alfred makes Guthrum take Christian vows and renames him Athelstan. Alfred influences these young people by helping them realize that life is more than killing in battle.

The Baron's Hostage is set during the reign of *Henry III. When Arlette de la Garde and her companion, Sister Helena, come to the Hardraw's castle in 1263, Sister Helena says Michael Hardraw, sixteen, has a claim to the Grevel barony, which could be inherited through the female side. After going to King Henry and while waiting for the courts to investigate his claim, Michael becomes the page to Prince *Edward "Longshanks," while Edward is a hostage to baron Simon de Montfort. At the same place, Simon's wife keeps the king's ward, Arlette, hostage while waiting to hear that the man who wants to marry and claim Arlette's land is finally divorced. Eventually Edward's friends help Edward escape, and he leads them in the Battle of Evesham, which frees King Henry to govern. When he becomes king, Edward decides to continue the meetings of knights and merchants with the barons as Simon had demanded. Arlette and Michael marry. As an early novel, the weak story has little depth, although Longshanks acts to deserve all the support that he obtains. At this early point in his career, Trease's insertion of historical events into the story is often obtrusive.

The Red Towers of Granada exposes superstitions and prejudices of the people during *Edward I's reign (around 1290). This novel has an intriguing beginning when Robin, the protagonist, reflects, "it is a strange and terrible thing to listen to one's own funeral service." Declared a leper by the English village priest when he sees spots on Robin's hands, Robin has to leave the village dressed distinctively so that he will not contaminate anyone. When he surprises two men robbing a man wearing a pointed yellow cap (a Jew), the robbers see his clothes and clapper and run away. Solomon of Stamford, the man being robbed, is a physician who realizes that Robin only has a skin disorder and gives him an ointment. The priest, however, must declare him cured before he can return to Oxford for his third year, so Robin goes to Solomon's home to continue treatment. Robin's skin soon clears, and he returns to the village, but the priest will not accept the word of a Jew. Robin goes back to Solomon's home to find that Jews must leave England by *All Saints' Day. Before Solomon leaves, he responds to a secret summons. *Eleanor, queen to King Edward, wants to know if Solomon has the formula to the Golden Essence, a medicine sent by her brother, the Spanish king, six years before, to cure her ailment. Since Solomon does not know about it, Eleanor gives him extra money for the search. Robin sails with them so that he can return with the essence if found. On shipboard, the captain uses a lodestone and a needle for direction, although he has no idea why it always points north. After the travelers reach Spain, a surly servant betrays Solomon to another man also looking for an elixir of life. His accomplices capture Robin, and they inadvertently reveal the name of the "good serpent," the one person who knows about the Golden Essence. After Robin's escape, the family travels from *Toledo to Cordova (*Córdoba) and then to *Granada looking for the Muslim "Good Serpent" Ibn al Razi. The villains follow and even break into his home, but Robin and David, Solomon's son, become sole possessors of the secret of the Golden Essence. Robin returns to England with Ibn al Razi's Christian granddaughter for a wife, but the queen has not survived. Robin realizes that although cultural differences separate him from Solomon and his children, they all try to help each other in their needs.

The poor servants of the manors also had great difficulties to overcome. In **Bows against the Barons**, set in 1381, Dickon becomes agitated when the king's deer eat the family's carefully tended garden, their only food, while his father fights the *Crusades for his master, D'Eyncourt. When he kills one hart, he flees into the forest because he could lose his hand or even his life for the crime. An editorial comment notes that in England "the masters were the masters. The peasants must obey and be whipped and work again till death brought time for resting.'' They paid taxes, and they heard the priests say ''Pay your tithe by next week or the church's officers will come to seize it.'' Alan à Dale spots Dickon in the forest and takes him to *Robin Hood. Dickon helps Robin Hood defeat D'Eyncourt and joins the subsequent unsuccessful attempt to overtake Nottingham. Although they fail, the support of other commoners indicates that the barons and priests, interested only in power and money, will one day be overcome. As Trease's first historical fiction novel, the writing lacks distinction; however, the tone of hostility for the haughty nobility and sympathy for the unending hardships of the peasants clearly sounds throughout the story.

Not only did peasants suffer low economic status in medieval England but also children who were suddenly orphaned. When news comes in 1400 that Roger Shelford's stonemason father has died in Bergen, Norway, Roger's uncle, Thomas, divides the family property between Roger and his twin sister, Jillian, in **The Secret Fiord**. Uncle Thomas then hastily arranges a marriage between Jillian and the disgusting Henry Snaith. Roger helps Jillian escape on the morning of the wedding by disguising himself in her gown. After they find transport on a ship going to Norway, a ship from the *Hanseatic League tries to capture them at sea, but gunshots scare it before they dock in a secret fiord. In Bergen, they meet someone who tells them that their father may not be dead. After arduous adventures led by the orphaned Erik, they find their father, who recovers from amnesia as soon as he sees them. They return to England with Erik, in whom Jillian has become very interested. They both thwart Uncle Thomas's greed and are lucky to find their father alive.

A second novel set in 1400 shows Welsh hostility against *Henry IV. In **Bent Is the Bow**, Lord Whitney takes Hugh and his sister, Meg, hostage while their father fights in Scotland when Owen Glendower's men proclaim Glendower king of Wales and chant, ''Bent is the bow'' (the Welsh call to war). While Whitney rides them through the countryside, Meg sees a hidden archer aim at Hugh but miss. She realizes that Whitney wants Hugh dead so that she can become heir and marry his son. The two escape during a battle with the Welsh in which Whitney is killed. This rather simple book is appropriate for younger readers.

Another young person has to escape a lord in 1595 in **Cue for Treason**. Peter Brownrigg throws a rock at Sir Philip while his neighbors tear down Sir Philip's wall. After he runs away to avoid prosecution, he becomes attached to the Desmonds' traveling actors troupe, along with another new member, Kit. When the season ends near London, he finds out that Kit, his competitor for the young women's roles in the plays by the young *Shakespeare, is actually a girl. The two go to London's *Globe Theater with a letter for the actor *Burbage from Mr. Desmond telling about Kit's superb acting abilities. When Sir Philip appears as a spectator on the edge of the Globe stage, Kit refuses to play Juliet at *Romeo and Juliet*'s premier performance. She tells Peter that Sir Philip expects to marry her and add her lands to those he has already taken from Peter's neighbors; she ran away to escape the union. Later, when a man asks to borrow Peter's playbook for *Henry V,* they discover that Sir Philip and other men from Cumberland are plotting to kill Queen *Elizabeth. Peter and Kit help the queen's secret service head, Robert *Cecil, save the queen. In Peter's first-person narrative, he reveals that the story is a flashback to his experiences before he married Kit.

In **When the Drums Beat**, during the turmoil of 1641, Mary finds a secret room in her house. Soon after, her brother, Stephen, decides to join the *Royalist army though his father sides with *Parliament. When the Royalist soldiers come to billet in their home, Mary hides her father in the secret room. Stephen sees her with food one day and realizes what she has done. He loudly tells her that he still loves his father even with their different beliefs. Behind the wall, his father can hear and be reassured that politics will not destroy family loyalty.

The Dutch threaten the British in **The Dutch Are Coming**. The Perryman family hears of their impending arrival and prepares to leave London one day in 1667. Roger, a servant, follows Stokes, their coachman, and hears him plan with the highwayman Captain Shadow to rob the family's coach on their night journey. Roger asks the stable owner, Mr. Jackson, to help him warn the family. They reach the coach just as the highwayman forces the family to the roadway. Roger's quick action saves the Perrymans and their belongings.

In **A Voice in the Night**, Mr. Ogg, an English town caller, becomes sick, and Paul offers to take his place since he can mimic Mr. Ogg's voice convincingly. Lisa, Paul's friend, sneaks out to be with him, and together they discover robbers underneath the silversmith's. The kind Mr. Ogg gets credit for the discovery, which pleases the children.

In **Trumpets in the West**, a final seventeenth-century novel, Jack Norwood decides that he wants to be a musician. When he helps a man escape from King James's soldiers in 1686, the man gives him a letter of introduction to Henry Purcell, the Westminster organist. In the London of Sir Christopher *Wren, Purcell advises Jack to learn to play a new instrument, the violin, and perform with theater orchestras. Jack does but finds that musicians have neither social status nor money. When a *Tory patron offers Jack a position, Jack realizes that, as a *Whig, he cannot sell his mind while selling his music. Instead, Jack helps his friend Jane get messages to *William of Orange. Jane also coerces him to contribute to the Glorious Revolution by playing the organ at *Exeter Cathedral when William arrives in Devon. And when Jack returns to London, he performs the first English opera, *Dido and Aeneas,* with its composer Purcell and receives a Stradivarius violin for his efforts. By living his beliefs, Jack enjoys his career in a positive political environment. Distractions in the novel occur when Trease mentions other historical figures living but not yet famous. Knowing that Jonathan Swift is nineteen adds nothing to the plot or theme.

The orphan Dick Arlington, in **The Silken Secret**, decides to forgo attending Oxford in 1710 in order to work for Dr. O'Flynn. Dick locates him in coffee houses and delivers messages to him from patients. Soon Dick realizes that O'Flynn, a quack, has fabricated the messages and has no real patients. Dick briefly works on a newspaper which becomes defunct after Queen Anne declares a new tax. Before its demise, however, he and the editor meet Mr. Mount and his orphaned American niece, Cecily. They discover that Mr. Mount is in danger because Italian silkmakers have followed him from Piedmont to England to kill him for finding the secret for making silk. The group survives vicious attacks, which lead Mr. Mount to decide that he will share the secret with other English manufacturers so that he will no longer be threatened. Destitute at his mother's death, Dick finds a life of excitement, but he also shows his willingness to work hard and risk himself for the benefit of others.

The last historical time Trease covers in a group of novels is 1766. In another story for younger readers, **The Chocolate Boy**, Sarah visits her snobbish aunt, Mrs. Toplady, in Nottingham. Mrs. Toplady's latest fashion brought from London is a black servant named Sam. Sarah discovers Sam playing a drum in the depths of the ice house and realizes that he is as unhappy as she. She cannot help him escape but suggests that he consider it. The omniscient point of view shows that Sam knows that if he leaves his yellow jacket by the river, people will think he drowned. He will then be able to leave with those entertaining at the Goose Fair without being traced. After his disappearance, Sarah returns home, relieved at his success but feeling totally inadequate for not having been able to help him physically.

STYLE AND THEMES

On the whole, Trease's novels are good stories with the characters becoming involved in intriguing adventures. The characters exist in a specific setting constrained by the particular parameters of the time period. Trease rarely refrains, however, from informing the reader that particular situations or people will be important at later times. In *Follow My Black Plume,* he says of Mark, "If he had known how deeply he himself was fated to be involved with what lay ahead . . .''. Such foreshadowing shows a lack of careful integration and becomes obvious instead of ingenious. On the other hand, Trease's vivid imagery allows descriptions such as ''the road ribboned back, its brown ruts crusty with frost'' *(Trumpets in the West).* He also uses similes with agility. One character says, '' 'Your brain flits about like an intoxicated butterfly.' '' In *Red Towers of Granada,* ''Bright fruit hung like a thousand little suns amid the greenery.'' Since all the protagonists have to contend with powerful personages waiting to destroy them, they all have to use intelligence to succeed. More depth of character such as an understanding of a need to believe in something beyond themselves, a trait Robin exhibits in *The Red Towers of Granada,* would elevate the novels to a status above mere adventure stories.

TREE OF FREEDOM. See Caudill, Rebecca.

TREECE, HENRY (1911–1966). British.

BIBLIOGRAPHY AND BACKGROUND

The Centurion. Illustrated by Mary Russon. New York: Meredith, 1967; as *The Bronze Sword.* London: Hamish Hamilton, 1965. *The Dream-Time.* Illustrated by Charles Keeping. New York: Meredith, 1968; Leicester: Brockhampton, 1967. *The Last Viking*. Illustrated by Charles Keeping. New York: Pantheon, 1966; as *The Last of the Vikings*. Leicester: Brockhampton, 1964. *Man with a Sword*. Illustrated by William Stobbs. New York: Pantheon, 1964; London: Bodley Head, 1962. *Perilous Pilgrimage*. Illustrated by Christine Price. New York: Criterion, 1959; as *The Children's Crusade*. London: Bodley Head, 1958. *The Queen's Brooch*. New York: Putnam, 1967; London: Hamish Hamilton, 1966. *Ride to Danger*. Illustrated by Christine Price. New York: Criterion, 1959; as *The Bombard*. London: Bodley Head, 1959. *The Road to Miklagard*. Illustrated by Christine Price. New York: Criterion, 1967; London: Lane, 1967. *Splintered Sword*. Illustrated by Charles Keeping. New York: Duell, 1966; Leicester: Brockhampton, 1965. *Swords from the North*. Illustrated by Charles Keeping. New York: Pantheon, 1967; London: Faber, 1967. *Viking's Dawn*. Illustrated by Christine Price. New York: Criterion, 1956; London: Lane, 1955. *Viking's Sunset*. Illustrated by Christine Price. New York: Criterion, 1961; London: Bodley Head, 1960. *War Dog*. Illustrated by Roger Payne. New York: Criterion, 1963; Leicester: Brockhampton, 1962. *Westward to Vinland*. Illustrated by William Stobbs. New York: Phillips, 1967; as *Vinland the Good*. London: Bodley Head, 1967.

In addition to other accolades, Henry Treece received a Carnegie commendation for *The Dream-Time* in 1967. In his novels, Treece investigates Romans, Vikings, and Normans. His last novel, *The Dream-Time,* is his only venture into prehistory. His other novels focus on male Roman and Viking protagonists.

WORKS

In **The Dream-Time**, during the England of prehistory, Treece supposes that a boy named Crookleg, lame from a broken leg, forsakes his belligerent tribe with its separate men's and women's languages after his parents die. As he walks toward the habitat of the Fish Folk, Crookleg meets Blackbird. After their arrival, Crookleg cannot tolerate their unclean smell. Blackbird stays, but Crookleg departs and searches for the River People. Crookleg's artistic ability to make beautiful brooch designs earns him leadership in the River People tribe. They believe that pictures have magic and that artists are magical. The matriarch renames Crookleg as Twilight. When someone steals a copper brooch, Twilight discovers that he will fight for his creations. Such strong feelings destroy the tribe's unity, and Twilight leaves. Blackbird, who has left the Fish Folk, reappears, and the two affiliate with the Red Men, apelike beings with no ability for human speech. Twilight and Blackbird raise Linnet, a River People orphan, and Twilight draws cave paintings with the Red Men. When wild animals that the Red Men hunt for food attack and kill the Red Men, the unusual "family" of Twilight, Blackbird, and Linnet begins searching for another group, hoping to find a peaceful one. Throughout the novel, dreams propel the development by creating magical mental pictures.

In **War Dog**, Treece personifies Bran, the war hound of Gwyn, a *Catuvellauni warrior. The *Iceni *Prasutagus, husband of *Boudicca, had requested his minstrel to write a song about the bravery of Bran's mother, Rhianna, after she attacked him in battle. Gwyn's father, Garroch of the Long Sword, gives him Bran so that he can serve the prince Caratacus, son of the king *Cymbeline. When faced with the ritual "Testing of Dogs," Bran defeats a Silurian warrior prisoner. As the warrior departs, the visiting Roman ambassador, Gracchus, asks his tribe's help to encircle the Catuvellauni as soon as the Roman ships arrive (around 43 A.D.). Claudius and his men kill Gwyn, but the *tribune Marcus Titus rescues Bran, who decides he likes Marcus almost as well as Gwyn. Gwyn's sister accompanies Marcus and Bran to Ostia, where she marries Marcus and bears children who play with the elderly, faithful Bran.

In *The Queen's Brooch* and *The Centurion,* the Roman protagonists meet Queen Boudicca after the death of her husband. In **The Queen's Brooch**, Marcus, seven, has come from his mother's home in Spain to join his father, Ostorius, a Roman tribune of the Ninth Legion, in Britain. One day near Venta Icenorum, Marcus disobeys his companion and trespasses on a nearby road. He meets a woman with an eye painted on her forehead. She chastises him but gives him a brooch, telling him that it will protect him from her, Boudicca, as long as he keeps it. Ten years pass and Marcus's kind father, Ostorius, a man who believes that gods and men should never be compared, is killed. Because Marcus has a wealthy grandfather, he becomes the tribune. Investigating the theft of Roman horses, Marcus visits an Iceni friend who informs him that after the death of Boudicca's husband, Prasutagus, the Roman Decianus Catus had publicly whipped Boudicca and her daughters and seized her wealth. After Marcus questions Catus, one of Catus's soldiers captures the Iceni friend's sister, Aranrhod. While pursuing the pair, they meet Boudicca and her followers. She recognizes Marcus and makes him join her band. Eventually Marcus escapes and walks quickly to London to warn the Romans of Boudicca's attack. They ignore him and imprison him as a spy, but a *Saxon girl, Gerd, and foreign merchants rescue him. Marcus and Gerd climb a tree and watch the Romans under *Suetonius Paulinus destroy the Iceni. Knowing that he can no longer support either side, Marcus chooses to leave Britain with Gerd and her cousin.

In **The Centurion**, after long service for the Ninth Legion as a *centurion, Drucus Pollio retires. He claims a plot of land and immediately encounters a tribal chieftain preparing to execute his servants on the spot. Drucus purchases the men by paying the chief one belt buckle so they can help him build his farm. Soon Queen Boudicca's tribes begin to rampage the area. Drucus escapes murder by showing courage and honesty before Boudicca. When she sends her nephew Lydd to free him, Lydd offers Drucus a sword for protection, but he refuses. Later Dio, Drucus's servant, finds Lydd dead, killed by a fleeing Roman. Drucus wishes to have had a son like Lydd, but news that Boudicca has killed his dear friends Calgacus and Vitalis ends his mourning. Drucus goes to *Lindum to rejoin the Ninth, but new gatekeepers suspect him of spying and shoot him in the ankle instead of welcoming him. He returns to the farm, bringing another Ninth reject also wounded by the guards, Falco, a man who detests the British so much that he even rejects Drucus's servants. The *Brigantes nurse Falco's wound until the Iceni threaten to kill them for helping a Roman. Lydd's brother, Mabon, appears, starved and wounded, refusing to accept food from anyone but the master of the house. When Drucus hears that Boudicca's merciless killing has alienated Mabon, Drucus feeds and heals him, understanding that Mabon will fulfill his need for a son. A Roman officer searching for prisoners arrives, and Falco almost reveals Mabon's presence, but Drucus sticks a knife in the officer's back. Falco then realizes that Drucus will kill him if Falco betrays Drucus's true friends, regardless of their heritage. In this novel, the protagonist reverses the Telemachus story by searching for a son, and the only son he can accept is one who refuses to harm other people.

Viking's Dawn, The Road to Miklagard, and *Viking's Sunset* trace Harald's development from novice sailor to respected Viking leader. Around 780, in **Viking's Dawn**, Harald and his father, Sigurd, decide to join the crew of the *Nameless* for its first voyage, although Thorkell Fairhair, its captain, has not yet proved his worth as a seaman. To seal the contract, Thorkell gives Harald knucklebones. As long as Harald keeps the bones, he must serve Thorkell; after Harald returns the bones, he can kill Thorkell if the situation warrants. As the ship prepares to sail, Sigurd breaks his leg, and Harald sails without him. On the voyage, Thorkell wins Harald's admiration by being a good sailor. Thorkell is also a berserk (*berserker), a man who lives to fight. On the Scottish coast, exhaustion from repairing the storm-tossed ship, as well as dust in the air, causes Thorkell to lose his sight temporarily. The other leader, Ragnar, takes treasure from a group of monks and makes one of them, John, come aboard. When Thorkell and John talk, they realize that they dreamed about each other the night before. To Thorkell, such an occurrence signifies the existence of afterlife. Off the coast of Ireland, pirates wreck the *Nameless* and imprison the crew. Four who try to escape are killed. The second four—Thorkell, Wolf, John, and Harald—dig a tunnel but capsize after sailing to sea. Only Harald survives, and a Danish ship rescues him and returns him to his father. The mark of the viking or "sea traveler" afflicts Harald, and he is ready to return to sea as soon as he reaches land.

In **The Road to Miklagard**, Harald begins this segment of his life by revealing his fate, a device to hook the reader into wondering how it happened (also a device in *Viking's Dawn* and *Splintered Sword*). By 785, Harald has buried his father and decides to join Arkil, a prince and poet, on his hunt for the Irish giant Grummoch. Although Arkil dies during the conquest, Harald takes Grummoch prisoner and sails north. The ship, however, sinks in a storm, and Turkish slavers capture Grummoch, Harald, and Haro. When the Turks take them to the slave market in Spain, the slave buyer for Abu Mazur recognizes their worth and buys all three. When Harald saves Abu Mazur's own wealth from his greedy gardener, Abu Mazur makes Harald his chief guard and asks Harald to sail his sick daughter, Marriba, to northern islands for a rest. But Marriba has other plans and commands the men to sail her to Miklagard (*Istanbul) where she plans to wed the fifteen-year-old Constantine. Constantine's mother, Irene, imprisons both Marriba and her son, and Grummoch disappears. Harald and Irene's head guard Kristion become friends, and as the *plague infiltrates Miklagard, Kristion helps Harald rescue Marriba. Haro loves her and takes her home. Grummoch's reappearance cheers Harald, and when the two escape from Miklagard, they go north where they hear that Haro and Marriba have married in Spain.

The last book about Harald, **Viking's Sunset**, takes place in 815 when Harald rushes away from his home to avenge the burning of his village and killing of its men by Haakon Redeye and his eighty berserks. Furious when Redeye wounds his ten- and twelve-year-old sons, Harald leaves his wife, Asa, to chase him. Instead of Harald's catching Redeye, the Innuits catch Harald and his blood brother, Grummoch. Grummoch's power impresses the Innuits, and they travel to the gathering place of the tribes near the Great Lakes. Although the *Beothuk, *Algonkin, and *Oneida tribes pledge peace during the gathering, a lame boy, Heome, kills his own brother, Wawasha. Because Knud, one of Harald's men, helps Heome, Harald kills him. When men bring Wawasha's body home to his chieftain father, Heome blames Harald for Wawasha's death and knocks Harald over a cliff, but Harald pulls Heome with him. Thus Harald dies without seeing his family again. Grummoch places Harald in his long ship and creates a funeral pyre befitting an honest and powerful man.

Banished from Norway and Iceland by 960, in **Westward to Vinland**, Red Eirik creates a home with his wife in Greenland. When his exile ends, he returns to Iceland to persuade others to settle in this new land, but a man says that he has seen other land previously unknown to the Northmen. Eirik's son, Leif the Lucky, goes to search and finds Vinland, with vines so ripe that one of his men becomes ill from eating too many grapes. He also meets a woman in the Hebrides with whom he lives for a time. When returning to Greenland, the sons stop to rescue people from a shipwreck. Many have the *plague, and they take it to Greenland, where Eirik himself dies from it. The others leave and find a new land. Leif's mother and sister, Gudrid, have prayed to the Whitechrist and know that Gudrid should not marry someone Greenland born. She marries a man from the ship, and their son, *Snorri, is born in the new land, becoming the first white American. The family, howerver, returns to Norway after the group's fight with the natives. Leif's own son, whom he did not know existed, arrives from the Hebrides after his mother dies and with his second sight keeps Leif content, refusing to tell him that the Eskimos are taking over their lands as Leif lies dying during the year 1013.

Soon after Leif's death, from 1034 to 1044, Harald Hardrada, the Stern, begins adventures that he chronicles in *Swords from the North, Man with a Sword,* and *The Last Viking.* In **Swords from the North**, Harald serves in the Varangian Guard of Miklagard for Empress Zoe and the emperor. Harald deals honestly with people, and as the future king of Norway, betrothed to King Jaroslav's daughter, Elizabeth, he refuses to be obsequious to Zoe. The guard's general, Georgios Maniakes, despises his attitude and tries to trick him through-out his duty. Not until one of Harald's friends is wounded does he begin to act pompously, but then a vision of his dead half-brother, Olaf, reminds him that people do not appreciate others for bad deeds. Harald goes to Jerusalem to protect the Christians who are rebuilding a church over Christ's grave, but on his return to Miklagard, Maniakes accuses Harald of leaving without permission and imprisons him. The empress's niece, Maria, loves Harald, and in her own vision, Olaf tells her to lower a ladder into the tower so that Harald and his two companions can escape. She does, and they do, but the Greek soldiers have chained the harbor. Harald maneuvers his own long ship over the chain, but the boat behind, carrying his dearest friends, sinks. Maria claims that he should marry her because she saved him, but Harald feels bound to Elizabeth so he sends Maria back to Miklagard.

In 1046, two years after Harald's return from Miklagard, in **Man with a Sword**, he discovers Hereward working on Gytha's farm. While serving Harald, king of Norway, Hereward slowly regains his memory. He finally recalls that five years before, *Harold Godwin had wounded him on the head while he fought for Empress Gunhilda of Germany. Harald and Hereward pledge to avenge Harold Godwin. But during leisure time, when Harald talks about melons, Here-ward becomes so curious that Harald decides to take him to Miklagard to see them. There Hereward meets Euphemia and marries her. When their son, Cnut, arrives, Hereward loses all interest in battles. But Harold Godwin grabs the crown of England after Edward's death, and Hereward must go with Harald to unseat him. Harald Hardrada dies at *York, and the long ships depart without Hereward. King Sweyn of Denmark finally arrives and promises to reunite Hereward with his family if Hereward loots for him. Hereward plunders but feels guilty for his deeds. When a priest overhears him trying to bargain with God, the priest tells him that God controls all but will not listen to men attempting to bargain with him. One night as Hereward fishes, he chats with a man whom he later identifies as *William the Conqueror when he faces William as a prisoner. Since William knows Hereward's story, he gives him a barony instead of sending him to prison, and brings Eugenia and Cnut to England. Soon after they are reunited, Queen *Mathilde asks Eugenia to go to Normandy to work on a tapestry, and William's brother requests Cnut's help. Distressed, Hereward loses interest in everything. After Mathilde and Eugenia die, Hereward and William suffer separation, as well as their sons' disloyalty to them. When William dies in France with Hereward, Hereward alone takes him to Caen where William wanted to be buried. There as Hereward also dies, Cnut finds him and admits he has been a bad son.

The Last Viking overlaps the action in *Swords from the North*. At York in 1066, Harald tries to raise his standard against Harold Godwin, but the wind keeps it down. As Harald stares at his old friend, Styrka, the voice of his dead brother, Olaf, seems to come from Styrka, reminding Harald of the battle at Stiklestad. Harald flashes back to his first battle when fifteen and the year afterward. At Stiklestad, King Sweyn's men had killed Olaf, but Harald and the old Earl Rognvald had escaped. Bolverk the Bonder helped them recover from battle wounds and suggested that they find Arsleif Summerbird, a man as courageous and as interesting as Olaf. Harald refused to believe anyone could be as brave as Olaf so he ignored the advice. As he and Earl sail on a long ship to Finland, an altercation on board leads them to jump overboard and swim toward shore, but an arrow shot from the ship kills Earl. Harald meets Summerbird, and he takes Harald to Novgorod and King Jaroslav, a relative who says that Olaf had wanted Harald to marry Jaroslav's daughter Elizabeth. Elizabeth's feisty manner exasperates Harald so he is happy to leave for Miklagard. On the way, they have problems, and Summerbird sacrifices himself to save Harald and two other men. Olaf tells him in a vision that he will die in York. When Harald returns to his position in battle at York, he faces his death.

In **Splintered Sword**, during 1098, fifteen-year-old Runolf runs from the tyranny of his foster father, Kolbein, when an old berserk claiming to have been with Hardrada at York convinces Runolf that goodness is more valuable than false security. When Runolf sees the old berserk row out to sea and capsize, he tries to save him but fails. The next day, Runolf finds the berserk's sword, named Gudrun Gore, and takes it as protection from Kolbein's thralls who are pursuing him. Gudrun himself flounders in the water, and Gilli, a sheep barge servant, rescues him. For payment, Gilli requests that Runolf find his kinsman, Prince Nial, and ask him to free Gilli. When Runolf finds Nial, he promises to serve him for Gilli's freedom, and Nial agrees. Uncomfortable with the plundering of Nial and his group, Runolf suggests investigating an ancient treasure site in Ireland, and they sail. Just before Nial and Runolf reach the treasure, a cave-in almost smothers them. News arrives that Gilli will meet them on the coast of Wales, where they can fight newly arrived Normans and gain larger treasure. On the Welsh coast, Runolf charges the solid fort of *Hugh of Avranches, as Nial commanded, and is captured. The others disappear, but Runolf acts honorably, and Hugh decides Runolf will be a good soldier for him.

The action in **Perilous Pilgrimage** skips to the thirteenth century when in 1212, Stephen, a shepherd boy of twelve, influences thousands of children to follow him on a *Crusade to overcome the Infidels. During their distress over their father's announced remarriage, a piper who cunningly plays his flute entices Geoffrey and Alys, children of Robert of Beauregard, to join the masses marching to Marseilles. After an arduous journey during which Alys wonders about some of the incidents, Stephen tries to part the sea as he thinks God has told him to but fails. The piper arranges for ships to take the children across the Mediterranean. The Beauregard family monk, Brother Gerard, finds the children in Marseilles and accompanies them on their quest. The piper, however, sends them to the slave market in Algeria. Coincidentally, the man who buys Alys, Geoffrey, and Brother Gerard knows Robert de Beauregard but makes no attempt to contact him. Implausible positive treatment changes to bad when kidnappers grab them and sell them to another man who plans to hang them if they will not confess belief in Islam. But Bertrand de Gisors, a best friend of their father, saves them, having met the children before they left with Stephen. Bertrand's knowledge of the people and the customs allows him to sail them back to France. Although the children's crusade actually occurred, many of the events in the novel are coincidental and seem implausible.

The latest time period of which Treece writes is the fourteenth century. **Ride to Danger** occurs in 1346 while *Edward III, father of the Black Prince (*Edward), is king. Welsh tribal bands and the Norman lord, Fulk de Bossu, besiege David Marlais of Onny and his family. After *Cadwalader's Welsh outlaws shoot an arrow into David's father, Gareth of Llanhedr helps David move him into his house and offers to be a hostage because David's mother is Welsh. Gareth explains that the Welsh of the Marches are ambushing because the English have subjected them to unjust laws. David's family, however, refuses to enforce the right to take taxes from the people on its land and hardly has money to live. When David rides to the king with Gareth requesting royal protection, the king grants it because he wants David to fight King Philip of France for him. David and Gareth fight first at *Crécy where they lose their horses but meet Piers of Gascon with whom they learn about the new weapons, the bombards. By learning how to use them correctly, they win at *Calais. Back at Onny, David uses his knowledge about the bombard to free his sister, Jeannine, from the Bossu castle, Goronwy. Ironically, Brother Robert, who remains on the farm to help David's ailing father, reveals that he built bombards for five years when serving the Turks. He helps, but when David bombards the castle, people falling from the wall to their deaths horrify Brother Robert. He demands that David destroy the weapon, but when David explodes it, a shard kills Brother Robert, and flying pieces of metal break both of David's legs. Simultaneously, the Welsh, summoned by Gareth, rush into the castle and conquer it. Gareth frees Jeannine, while Bossu and his fat son die. Although the death of Brother Robert continues to haunt David, Jeannine and Gareth, the new Welsh leader since the death of Cadwalader, become betrothed.

STYLE AND THEMES

Treece's stories are entertaining and informative. In some, however, the diction damages the sense of time and place because contemporary slang replaces more appropriate language. In *Swords from the North,* phrases such as "forewarned is forearmed" and "after God made him he broke the mold" do not sound like eleventh-century comments. In many of the novels, plot movement relies on cliffhangers, although subtle, at the end of chapters. Personification is more successful. Humor shines through the character's response to hunger in *Splintered Sword:* "My teeth have done no work for three days. They get lazy." In another, Treece's beauty of language appears: "The pine woods sighed, as though overcome by a great and unnameable sadness, the melancholy sound made by all ancient forests." Allusions intensify the stories such as those in *Perilous Pilgrimage,* where castles are "dead as the Great Circle at *Carnac, where the *Druids used to worship'' and the children's comment that their mother's tapestry was better than Queen Matilda's ''silly piece of stitchery at Bayeux.'' Humor lightens the stories, reminding contemporary readers that humans have often survived bleak moments by refusing to take them too seriously. Treece states explicit theme in *The Last Viking* when Harald comments, ''Life is nothing if there are not friends in it to share with.'' Most interesting is Treece's repeated use of dreams as a way of revealing character and foreshadowing future actions. His recognition of the validity of the subconscious helps to deepen his characterizations.

TREEGATE'S RAIDERS. See Wibberley, Leonard.

TRIBUNE. In ancient Rome, this title was given to different types of officers and magistrates. One designation of the title was as an official chosen by the plebs to protect their rights against the patricians. See *War Dog* and *The Queen's Brooch* by Henry *Treece.

TRUDY AND ALBERTA. Young American female protagonists in *The Great Desert Race. See* Baker, Betty.

TRUMPETS IN THE WEST. See Trease, Geoffrey.

TUDORS. Owen Tudor, born in 1400, founded this English house, which occupied the throne of England from 1485 to 1603. See *Caxton's Challenge* by Cynthia *Harnett and *The Sprig of Broom* by Barbara *Willard.

TULKU. See Dickinson, Peter.

TURI. At eight, Slavic immigrant to Italy and protagonist in *Turi's Poppa. See* de Treviño, Elizabeth.

TURI'S POPPA. See de Treviño, Elizabeth.

TURN HOMEWARD, HANNALEE. See Beatty, Patricia.

TYBURN. At this spot was the principal execution place in London from 1388 until 1783, when the hangings moved outside *Newgate Prison. *See* Garfield, Leon, *Black Jack*.

TYNDALE, WILLIAM (c. 1494–1536). As the first English translator of the New Testament and Pentateuch of the Bible, he began printing it in Cologne in 1525 and completed it in Worms in 1526. After a controversy with Sir Thomas More in 1531, he was arrested at Antwerp and condemned for heresy, strangled, and burned at the stake. *See* O'Dell, Scott, *The Hawk That Dare Not Fly by Day*.

TYRE. This ancient seaport of Phoenicia, now in Lebanon, dates from 1500 B.C. Egyptian, Roman, and biblical figures played parts in its history. *See* Haugaard, Erik, *The Rider and His Horse*.

_U_

UCHIDA, YOSHIKO (1921–   ). American.

BIBLIOGRAPHY AND BACKGROUND

The Best Bad Thing. New York: Atheneum, 1983. *The Happiest Ending*. New York: Atheneum, 1985. *A Jar of Dreams*. New York: Atheneum, 1981. *Journey Home*. Illustrated by Charles Robinson. New York: Atheneum, 1978. *Journey to Topaz*. Illustrated by Donald Carrick. New York: Scribner's, 1971; rpt. San Mateo, Calif.: Creative Arts Book Co., 1985. *Samurai of Gold Hill*. Illustrated by Ati Forberg. New York: Scribner's, 1972; rpt. San Mateo, Calif.; Creative Arts Book Co., 1985.

Yoshiko Uchida has received many accolades for her diverse writing skills. *Journey to Topaz* (1972) was an American Library Association Notable Book, and the Commonwealth Club of California Medal honored *Samurai of Gold Hill* (1973) and *A Jar of Dreams* (1982). Her books, as well as her body of writing, have been nominated for numerous other awards. In an attempt to show the strength of first-generation Japanese struggling in the United States, Uchida has chosen the difficult times of World War II as settings for several of her books. She says, "Young Japanese Americans, aware of their ethnicity, began [in the past decade] to search for a sense of self and continuity with their past. I wanted to reinforce their self-esteem and self-knowledge." However, the struggles, she feels, are not only those of the Japanese-Americans but also those of all other humans everywhere. She researches by talking to Japanese-Americans who lived through the period or by finding relevant material. Writing mainly in the morning, she writes at least four drafts with many revisions.

WORKS

During 1869, in **Samurai of Gold Hill**, the emperor's supporters overcome the *Shogun in Japan, and Koichi's samurai father has to leave the country. When twelve, Koichi finds himself on a ship, then on land, and finally in Gold Hill, a place on the U.S. West Coast where his father and his partners plan to start a tea and silk farm. Few people accept the Japanese, and a gold digger,

One-Eye, continually threatens them and almost kills Koichi's friend, Rintaro. An Indian friendly to Rintaro shows him how to fish with a net and how to pan gold. When Koichi and Rintaro watch the Maida Indian ceremony for the dead, they realize that it is similar to their Buddhist ritual, Obon, which they observe on the thirteenth day of the eighth month by using fire to call back spirits of the dead. The farm flounders when silkworms, and then the tea plants, die. One-Eye stops the productivity by damming the only creek during a dry spell. One of the families leaves for Japan, promising to return; none of them do. Koichi and his father realize that the farm can never be a reality. They become employees instead of owners, anticipating better times and possibly another farm. Uchida shows that diligence may not reap visible rewards but that one who works honestly and fairly can always hope for future satisfaction.

In a trilogy—*Jar of Dreams, The Best Bad Thing,* and *The Happiest Ending*— Rinko tells her first-person story of being Japanese in the San Franscisco area during 1935 and 1936. In **A Jar of Dreams**, Rinko, eleven, looks forward to becoming a teacher, but her brother, Cal, studying engineering at the university, tells her that the public schools will not hire Japanese teachers. He wonders if he himself will be able to find a job after graduation. Her father, a barber, dreams of being a mechanic with his own garage. Rinko's mother begins to turn dreams into reality by starting a laundry in her basement when the woman for whom she cleans house says that all her friends need dependable washing services. Threats from nearby Starr laundry, which include slashed tires, stolen laundry bundles, and a dead dog, almost defeat the family, but Aunt Waka arrives from Japan and urges them to face their adversities. She inspires Rinko to accept her Japanese self—to be who she really is rather than what she thinks others expect her to be. Before Waka leaves, Rinko's father starts his garage, Cal decides to finish college, and Rinko gains self-confidence. Although Waka functions as a fairy godmother, she works no miracles other than reminding each individual family member that personal integrity, and dreams, come only with hard work.

The Best Bad Thing begins on the forty-ninth day after Mrs. Hata's husband's death. Rinko's family visits her to celebrate with the customary food. Rinko's mother realizes how much her friend, Mrs. Hata, needs help with her cucumber crop and suggests that Rinko work for a month during the summer. Thinking Mrs. Hata slightly crazy, Rinko dreads the stay, but when Mrs. Hata calls her outside to look at the lovely spider webs floating in the wind, Rinko's attitude changes. During the month, when Mrs. Hata's son, Abu, coerces Rinko to jump on and off a moving freight train, she sprains an ankle. Another train runs over Abu's arm, and while they wait at the hospital, someone steals the family truck. An old man living in the barn makes beautiful kites, and when he gives one to Rinko to fly, it becomes for her, as Old Man says, an extension of the sky. When a welfare department official arrives to question Old Man, an illegal alien trying to make money with which to return to Japan, he decides that going home without money will be acceptable. Mrs. Hata refuses welfare, expecting fully to find a job somewhere. Meeting these diverse people causes Rinko's summer to become the "best bad thing" ever to happen to her.

In **The Happiest Ending**, Rinko is twelve and still trying to understand herself and her Japanese heritage. She admits loving parades and dancing to the radio when no one else is home. She is surprised to find that Mrs. Hata had sent her daughter, Teru, back to Japan, as many other Japanese did, because the family had too little money to raise her. After Mrs. Hata arranges a marriage for Teru with Mr. Kinjo, Teru returns to the United States. The age difference between Teru and Mr. Kinjo horrifies Rinko, so she begins searching for an alternate prospect. At the same time, her Japanese teacher's husband, Mr. Sugino, tries to double the money of one of their boarders, Mr. Higa, and by gambling loses it all. After Teru arrives and Rinko encourages her to sever her tie to Mr. Kinjo, Mr. Kinjo delays the marriage in order to give Mr. Higa money to return to Japan. When Rinko sees Teru's approving look at Mr. Kinjo, she realizes that Mrs. Hata has made an excellent match. Rinko endures typical adolescent problems, but her misunderstanding of her culture compounds the difficulties.

In two poignant novels, Yuki Sakane, an American citizen, describes her family's evacuation to and return from a Japanese relocation camp during World War II. On December 7, 1941, in **Journey to Topaz**, Yuki of Berkeley, California, looks forward to her eleventh Christmas, but the Japanese bombing of Pearl Harbor ruins her plans. FBI (Federal Bureau of Investigation) agents arrive and take Yuki's father to an unknown destination. Not for several days does the family hear about him, and then they hear that he and ninety other men from the area who work for Japanese companies as first-generation Japanese (Issei) will be transported to Missoula, Montana. Not until the following Christmas can the family reunite. During that year, the government evacuates Yuki, her nineteen-year-old brother, Ken, and her mother, with 110,000 other Japanese. Yuki feels completely lost when they have to pack all their belongings and leave the home where she was born a Japanese-American (Nisei) to go to Topaz, Utah. Ken loses interest in life and isolates himself when he has to stop his university education. In Topaz, the needless death of her friend Emi's grandfather, shot by a guard as he bends to retrieve an arrowhead instead of heeding an unheard "Halt," shocks her. Ken's decision to join a Nisei unit to fight for the United States in Europe also distresses her. When agitators in Topaz try to harm her father, the family goes to Salt Lake City where Mr. Sakane finds a menial job far below his capabilities. Eventually the Japanese gain permission to return to California, and Yuki's family returns. By revealing such a devastating event through a child's view, Uchida heightens its impact.

In the beginning of **Journey Home** appears a brief recount of the main action in *Journey to Topaz*. The added facts that Sakane grandfathers were samurai shows that the children, Yuki and Ken, have a legacy of strength and honor. One finds unrevealed sadness in the family when Yuki's mother visits the grave with its cherry tree marker of Yuki's older sister, Hana, who had died at age one. Back home, Yuki finds that people and things have changed, but when Emi and Emi's grandmother join them, she feels much better, even with their news that an old family friend, Mr. Toda, had died before leaving Topaz. They and Mr. Oka, another friend, repurchase the store that Mr. Oka owned before the war. Someone throws a firebomb in the window, but a neighbor, Mr. Olssen, offers his carpentry expertise for rebuilding. Ken returns, wounded not only physically, but also spiritually. The Olssens invite everyone to their home to celebrate Thanksgiving, where they see a portrait of the Olssens' son, killed by Japanese at Iwo Jima. The forgiving attitude of the Olssens helps Uncle Oka and Ken find a new balance in their own lives. They all learn that being home is a state of mind. Yuki learns with difficulty that she must appreciate the present rather than long for the past. To symbolize her decision to accept the present, Yuki starts wearing the ring that her friend, Mrs. Jamieson, had given her before Topaz. "Someday" must one day be "today."

STYLE AND THEMES

Uchida's relatively unadorned style reflects the Japanese concept of beauty in simplicity. The stories of Koichi, Rinko, and Yuki reveal that Japanese-Americans undergo the same maturation process as Americans, but they, like other Americans with strong heritages, have the added difficulty of assimilation without loss of cultural identity. Uchida's refusal to portray all Japanese as moral and all Americans as immoral helps her characters to assess more accurately which practices to accept.

UKRAINE. This republic, currently part of the Soviet Socialist Republic in the southwest, has as its capital Kiev. Through the centuries, it belonged to both Poland and Russia as it gained a national entity. After the *Russian Revolution, it was annexed as part of the Soviet Union. Ukrainians have a reputation of being merry and musical, as well as individualistic. *See* Almedingen, E. M., *Young Mark.*

UNDERGROUND RAILWAY. Before 1861 in the United States, a secret network of citizens, mainly white, cooperated in aiding fugitive slaves. They hid the slaves as they moved north to find freedom and sanctuary in the free states (those not recognizing slavery) and Canada. See *Blue Stars Watching* by Patricia *Beatty; *The Tamarack Tree* by Patricia *Clapp; and *Thee, Hannah!* by Marguerite *de Angeli.

UNION ARMY. *See* *Yankee.

THE UNTOLD TALE. *See* Haugaard, Erik.

URSULA MEDLEY. At eighteen, English character in *The Iron Lily* and as adult protagonist in *A Flight of Swans*. *See* Willard, Barbara.

UTE. This group of Shoshonean-speaking Indians comes from western Colorado and eastern Utah, giving its name to that state. In 1776, the members had no horses and lived in small family clusters surviving on gathered food. In the early nineteenth century, they acquired horses and began to steal livestock from settlers. Some of them are now known as Paiutes. See *The Bad Bell of San Salvador* by Patricia *Beatty and *Komantcia* by Harold *Keith.

V

V-1. The Germans started launching this robot rocket bomb in World War II on June 13, 1944. The rocket flew low over the tops of trees and houses on its way to a target. *See* Pelgrom, Els, *The Winter When Time Was Frozen.*

THE VALLEY OF THE SHADOW. See Hickman, Janet.

VAN DIEMAN'S LAND. In 1642, Anton van Dieman, the governor general of the East Indies, sent a Dutch expedition under Abel Janszoon Tasman to investigate the west and south of Australia. When Tasman reached the western shore of Tasmania, he called it Van Dieman's Land. *See* Burton, Hester, *No Beat of Drum.*

VARNA. This city in northeastern Bulgaria on the Black Sea was founded as Odessos in the sixth century B.C. It gained the name Varna in the first Bulgarian kingdom beginning in 697. See *Shadow of the Hawk* by Geoffrey *Trease and *Kevin O'Connor and the Light Brigade* by Leonard *Wibberley.

VEER SCHUYLER. Fifteen, American orphan, protagonist of *The Taken Girl.* *See* Vining, Elizabeth Gray.

VELAZQUEZ, DIEGO (1599–1660). The Spanish court painter for *Philip IV, he attained fame with religious works and portraits. He used light in a way that anticipated the impressionists of the nineteenth century. *See* de Treviño, Elizabeth, *I, Juan de Pareja.*

VENETI. One use of this term is in referring to a Celtic tribe of the Morbihan district in modern Brittany (France). By the time of Caesar, the people controlled all of the Atlantic trade to Britain. They submitted to Caesar in 57 B.C. but became concerned with his interest in Britain and seized some of his officers in an attempt to gain independence. He defeated them in 56 B.C. Then he executed the tribal elders and sold the rest as slaves. Many ancient peoples and places of Western Europe are also known by this term. (Lake Constance was Lacus Venetus.) The most important people were the inhabitants of northeastern Italy who arrived about 1000 B.C. Their horses were famous in the Greek world, and they had much commerce with other areas. *See* Mitchison, Naomi, *The Conquered*.

VERA CRUZ. *Cortés landed here in this central Gulf area of Mexico on Good Friday in 1519. *See* Baker, Betty, *The Blood of the Brave*.

VICTORIA OF ENGLAND (1819–1901). Her very long and intelligent reign (1837–1901), even after the death of her beloved husband, signified a new idea of British monarchy with reforms which improved the plight of working classes and kept the empire unified. See *A Likely Lad* by Gillian *Avery; *The Huffler* by Jill *Paton Walsh; and *Hetty* by Barbara *Willard.

VICTORY AT VALMY. *See* Trease, Geoffrey.

VIKING'S DAWN. *See* Treece, Henry.

VIKING'S SUNSET. *See* Treece, Henry.

VIMEUR, JEAN-B.-D. (1725–1807). A French soldier known as Rochambeau, he commanded the French force sent to aid General Washington in the *American Revolution in 1781. Their joint forces defeated *Cornwallis at Yorktown, Virginia. He returned to France and commanded the army of the North during the *French Revolution. *See* Dalgliesh, Alice, *Adam and the Golden Cock*.

VINING, ELIZABETH GRAY (1902–   ). American.

BIBLIOGRAPHY AND BACKGROUND
    Adam of the Road. Illustrated by Robert Lawson. New York: Viking, 1942. *I Will Adventure*. Illustrated by Corydon Bell. New York: Viking, 1962; Edinburgh: Oliver and Boyd, 1964. *The Taken Girl*. New York: Viking, 1972.
    For *Adam of the Road*, Elizabeth Janet Gray (Vining) received the Newbery Medal in 1943. She has also been honored with other awards for her writing in several genres. Vining's chief interest in her books is creating the main character, but she notes varied reasons for choosing specific settings. She says, "The 13th century produced three great steps toward freedom—which were threatened at the time I was writing [*Adam of the Road*], in 1941. They were: Magna Carta at the beginning of the century, the establishment of the universities, and at the end of the century, the first parliament of which commoners were elected." She adds, "I have loved history from my early childhood. I began with Eva March Tappan's *Stories from English History* at the age of eight." For her novels, she

usually spends about a year on research and visits the settings. She comments, "When I wrote *Adam* in 1942 I had previously walked over much of the ground covered in the book." She usually writes in the morning, but earlier in her career, she wrote six to seven hours daily. About her work habits, she adds, "I have a period of meditation before beginning to write and I call on the 'deep self' when in difficulty."

WORKS

Adam of the Road begins in 1294 with Adam waiting at the abbey of *St. Alban for his minstrel father, Roger, to return from France. His mother is dead. After Roger's arrival, they start their life on the road, walking from place to place entertaining for pay. Roger's musical abilities and good songs make him a popular addition to festivities. Adam idolizes Roger and listens to his advice, especially when Roger gently chides him about his tendency to boast. When another minstrel, Jankin, steals Adam's faithful dog, Nick, Roger and Adam try to find them by asking everyone they pass on the way to Gile's Fair in Winchester. In the town, Adam spots Jankin and Nick, rushes after them, and loses contact with Roger. Adam searches through towns, looking for and asking about Roger, gaining food and bed by singing and accompanying himself on his harp. Back in Winchester, as Adam watches a morality play, he falls off a wall. When the fall knocks him unconscious and wounds him, a monk nurses him for several months. After recovering, Adam decides to search for Roger in London at Christmas where he should be staying with his regular holiday employer. In London, servants tell Adam that the family is celebrating Christmas in Wales. On one of his journeys, Adam sings the story of the lonely Havelock the Dane to himself, thus augmenting his own feelings. Finally in the spring, Adam returns to St. Alban's and finds Nick, his friend Perkin, and Roger.

In **I Will Adventure**, Andrew Talbot, twelve, leaves his family during 1596 to be a page for his cousin, Sir John, in London. On the way from Canterbury to London, he stops at an inn where players are presenting *Romeo and Juliet*. After the show, he greets the page from the play, expecting him to respond as the character in the play, but the boy rebuffs him. In retaliation, Andrew knocks down Chris Wilson, who hurts his head. Andrew offers to say Chris's lines at the next stop, and *Shakespeare coaches him, but Chris decides he will play even though his head still aches. In London, Andrew finds that Sir John has forgotten his arrival, that he dislikes the steward, and that he does not have enough to do. After several unpleasant situations, Andrew asks Shakespeare to take him as an apprentice, but Shakespeare has no room for an apprentice in his London lodgings. As Andrew prepares to return home, Sir John's doorman warns Sir John, and Sir John retrieves Andrew. The next day, Sir John takes him to see *Love's Labors Lost*. There Andrew spots his brother, returned from fighting for Essex (*Devereux) in *Cadiz, and notices that Horace has been knighted. After the play, they all go to a tavern but do not believe that Andrew knows Shakespeare until Shakespeare greets Andrew by name. Sir John realizes that

Andrew should go to school, and the thought of attending *St. Paul's encourages Andrew to remain in London.

In **The Taken Girl**, Veer Schuyler, fifteen, leaves the home for orphans and half-orphans in New Jersey to work for the Underwoods during 1837. Veer's sailor father had left her at the home after her mother's death. He had sent money for years, but stopped, so Veer knows that he is dead. Her father had also left twenty dollars in gold in her mother's purse, and Miss Moon, the orphanage mistress, gives it to her as she leaves. The Underwoods call her Vera (not her name) and treat her as a servant rather than one of the family. That she cannot control circumstances in her life any more than black slaves like Callie at the orphanage surprises and frustrates her. One day as she vents her anger by throwing china at the kitchen wall, Mrs. Underwood's cousin, Mrs. Healy, enters and suggests that Veer return with her to Philadelphia. Mrs. Healy's husband and their boarders embrace her as one of their family without questions about her past. The omniscient point of view allows the reader to see that Veer has beauty and capability, attributes of which she is totally unaware. One of the boarders, John Greenleaf Whittier, intrigues Veer, and she is delighted to find that he wrote the fourteen-stanza poem about abolition that she had learned at the orphanage from Callie, the free Negro maid. She discovers that all three boarders spend their time outside their working hours fighting for abolition. They have to work secretly for fear of arrest. She begins to help Greenleaf by copying poems and other items for his newspaper. Since the major project of the group is to build a hall where all the liberal factions can speak, including *abolitionists, Veer buys a subscription with her twenty dollars to help finish it. When the first groups meet, angry protestors burn it down. Although the group returns her money, she fully supports the abolitionist cause. She also realizes that she loves Greenleaf. Greenleaf has to leave Philadelphia, however, when his headaches become too frequent to bear, and while mourning his departure, Veer knows his sister can give him better care. Instead of belittling Veer's love for him, Mother Healy notes that Greenleaf could never support a wife with his meager income. She adds that she and Mr. Healy want to adopt Veer and that Veer can get a job teaching school, as she wants. The love and caring in the Healy family clearly contrast with the cold, mercenary Underwoods.

STYLE AND THEMES

Vining varies her style to fit her content. She tells *Adam of the Road* using a minstrel style, talky and rhythmic, but tightly crafted. *I Will Adventure,* loosely written, utilizes more dialogue. And *The Taken Girl* becomes more introspective as Veer matures. Also in *The Taken Girl,* Vining seems to use the names *Healy* and *Underwood* symbolically. The descriptions are concise, and Vining smoothly incorporates information within the action of the plot rather than adding it in asides. Vining's underlying theme for all the novels is that love and support help children mature happily and confidently.

VINLAND THE GOOD. See *Westward to Vinland* by Henry *Treece.

A VOICE IN THE NIGHT. *See* Trease, Geoffrey.

VORTIGERN (c. 450). A British ruler, he is reputed to have invited the *Saxons to Britain in order to repel the Picts and the Scots, as well as to have married Rowena, the daughter of Hengest. See *Hengest's Tale* by Jill *Paton Walsh and *The Lantern Bearers* by Rosemary *Sutcliff.

W

WAIT FOR ME, WATCH FOR ME, EULA BEE. *See* Beatty, Patricia.

WALK THE WORLD'S RIM. *See* Baker, Betty.

THE WALLS OF ATHENS. *See* Paton Walsh, Jill.

WANG LEE. Japanese male of fifteen who matures to twenty-five in *Rebels of the Heavenly Kingdom*. *See* Paterson, Katherine.

WAR COMES TO WILLY FREEMAN. *See,* Collier, Christopher and James.

WAR DOG. *See* Treece, Henry.

THE WAR PARTY. *See* Steele, William O.

WAR WITHOUT FRIENDS. *See* Hartman, Evert.

WARRIOR SCARLET. *See* Sutcliff, Rosemary.

WATIE, STAND (1806–1871). Born near Rome, Georgia, he was an American Indian leader who agreed with the removal of the *Cherokee tribe to Indian territory. He raised a regiment of Cherokee-mounted riflemen to serve with the *Confederates in 1861 and rose to brigadier general in 1864. See *Rifles for Watie* by Harold Keith.

WAYAH. Eleven, Cherokee protagonist in *Wayah of the Real People*. *See* Steele, William O.

WAYAH OF THE REAL PEOPLE. *See* Steele, William O.

WEB OF TRAITORS. *See* Trease, Geoffrey.

WELCH, RONALD (1909–1982). British.

BIBLIOGRAPHY AND BACKGROUND
   Bowman of Crécy. Illustrated by Ian Ribbons. New York: Criterion, 1967; London: Oxford, 1966. *Captain of Dragoons.* Illustrated by William Stobbs. New York: Oxford, 1957; London: Oxford, 1956. *Captain of Foot.* Illustrated by William Stobbs. London: Oxford, 1959. *Escape from France.* Illustrated by William Stobbs. New York: Criterion, 1961; London: Oxford, 1960. *For the King.* Illustrated by William Stobbs. New York: Criterion, 1962; London: Oxford, 1961. *The Gauntlet.* Illustrated by T. R. Freeman. London: Oxford, 1951. *The Hawk.* Illustrated by Gareth Floyd. New York: Criterion, 1969; London: Oxford, 1967. *Knight Crusader.* Illustrated by William Stobbs. New York: Oxford, 1979; London: Oxford, 1954. *Mohawk Valley.* Illustrated by William Stobbs. New York: Criterion and London: Oxford, 1958. *Nicholas Carey.* Illustrated by William Stobbs. New York: Criterion and London: Oxford, 1963. *Tank Commander.* Illustrated by Victor Ambrus. Nashville, Tenn.: Nelson, 1974; London: Oxford, 1972. *Zulu Warrior.* Illustrated by David Harris. Newton Abbot, Devon: David and Charles, 1974.
   Ronald Welch (pseudonym for Ronald Oliver Felton) won the Carnegie Medal for *Knight Crusader* in 1954. In almost all of his historical fiction novels, including *Knight Crusader,* Welch follows the advancements in British military tactics through the exploits of male descendants of the lords d'Aubigny.

WORKS
   The Gauntlet is Welch's least characteristic novel. A historical fantasy time shift from the present to 1326, the novel investigates Peter Staunton's experience of finding a gauntlet (glove) on an isolated path and hearing battle sounds after picking it up. The vicar informs Peter that people descended from participants in a thirteenth-century battle near Llanferon have had experiences such as his. While Peter naps in the Carreg Cennen ruins, he finds himself transported to 1326 as Peter de Blois reunited with his family after a long illness. Peter expects to wake up any moment and discover himself returned to the twentieth century, but he finds that after he becomes used to 1326, he likes it. His servant teaches him about dress, food, hawking, superstitions, leprosy, monastery/hotels, jousting, and the long-bow. He also watches his father fight a battle when his enemy, Maelgwyn, attacks. After rappelling down the steep side of the castle to go for help during the battle, Peter awakens. Anxious to prove that his experience was real, he digs for the dagger he had buried during his days in the castle. He finds an eroded piece of metal exactly where he remembers it from 600 years previously.

In **Knight Crusader**, the first novel mentioning the d'Aubigny family, the protagonist, Philip D'Aubigny, in 1187, has lived in *Outremer all of his life with his father as *Crusader Baron of High Court of the Kingdom of Jerusalem. When Philip meets a Welsh pilgrim and asks about the home of his forefathers, the pilgrim, and later Gilbert d'Assailly from Normandy, assure him that Outremer residents know luxuries, including dry weather, of which northern countries have never dreamed. But after Philip's father, cousin, and uncle die in battle against Saladin, he determines to go there. First, however, he has to escape from Damascus. Since Philip had once saved Jusuf Al-Hafiz from robbers, when Jusuf's ruler Saladin conquered, he gave Philip to Jusuf, and Jusuf took Philip to care for his ninety-year-old father, a scholar. Gilbert is incarcerated near them. The old man senses Philip's restlessness and gives him black pearls so that Philip will be able to sell them when he flees. After four years, one of the Hospitallers (*St. John of Jerusalem) finds Philip and helps him execute the plan for his and Gilbert's escape. As Philip and Gilbert approach Acre, assassins capture them and take them to the legendary Old Man of the Mountains in his Eagle's Nest. He tells them that they have no choice but to serve him when he sends the summons. In Acre, Philip meets and pledges to serve *Richard the Lionheart. When he ignores the Old Man's summons, someone tries to kill him but fails. News arrives that the lord of d'Aubigny has died without an heir, and Richard writes to notify the courts of Philip's claim to the fief. After defeating the Infidels in Acre, Philip travels to England. His jousting fame precedes him to Cardiff, near the d'Aubigny lands, and people request that he demonstrate his abilities as soon as he arrives. He also has to fight deBraose, also claiming to be heir, but men who prefer Philip's integrity to deBraose's trickery help him.

In **Bowman of Crécy**, Hugh fights Walter for leadership in the forest and organizes the outlaws into a cohesive band around 1340. One of the men, a superb bowman, teaches Hugh to shoot the longbow so well that Hugh defeats *Edward III's best bowman. Sir John Carey (Lord d'Aubigny) needs bowmen to fight with him in France. He approaches Hugh and declares that men who fight for him will lose their criminal status. Hugh's men agree to fight. When Carey asks about Hugh's past, Hugh tells him that his parents died of *plague, leaving him beside a road where men in the forest found and raised him. Sir John suggests that Hugh, without knowledge of his past, design a coat of arms for himself. When Hugh and his men prove their valor with a winning strategy at Caen and *Crécy, Edward knights Hugh, and Sir John gives him golden spurs as his first knightly gift.

Since Harry Carey in **The Hawk** speaks Spanish, he deduces from unusual action in the Spanish harbor offices in 1584 that the Spaniards are preparing to capture merchant ships anchored there. He and his captain warn the captain of a sister ship, but he ignores them. Harry's shipmates overwhelm the Spanish guards who try to board their ship and escape, unlike their sister ship. Since the earl d'Aubigny, Harry's father, sits on Queen *Elizabeth's council, he knows that Spain's capture of English ships will cause her to declare war on Spain.

When Harry returns to England, his father hints of war and shows him a galleon he is having built to capture Spanish and French booty in retaliation. Harry and the galleon named the *Hawk* sail to Brazil, where its men capture two Portuguese ships as prizes. But Elizabeth has other problems, too—Queen *Mary's supporters. After Harry returns, the earl's spies decide that he should infiltrate the ring and help save Elizabeth. As Harry makes connections, he discovers that his brother-in-law, Arncliffe, abuses his wife. After Harry confronts him, Arncliffe pays assassins to kill Harry, but the encounter allows Harry to demonstrate his swordplay skill. One of Harry's contacts disguises himself as a beggar, and Harry's servant educates him on the types of beggars. For his efforts infiltrating the spy ring, Harry almost loses his life. Elizabeth, vain but intelligent, commends him. He, however, decides that he prefers sailing instead of spying. The omniscient point of view delays suspense but also allows the reader to feel sympathy for some of the villains.

At Cambridge, in **For the King**, Neil Carey loves the solitude of studying the classics. His peace shatters in 1642 when his brother, Denzil, demands that he declare for King *Charles and his cousin, Francis, demands that he declare for *Parliament. Neil and his father, Lord Aubigny, prefer not to declare for anyone but when forced decide to support the king. In Llanstephan, Aubigny raises a Welsh army which fights valiantly throughout several campaigns. Eventually Denzil and Francis die, and Neil is captured. The court condemns him to death. Word, however, arrives in time to absolve him of the false accusation that he had said he would never fight against Parliament when he had actually refused to make such a statement. Those trying to slander him suffer condemnation, but Neil is exiled from Wales for two years, a short time when he has retained both his life and his honor.

In 1703, Charles Carey, in **Captain of Dragoons**, fights in Cadogan's Regiment of *Dragoons during a European campaign. Recognized as one of the most accomplished swordsmen and pistol shots in Europe, Charles's skill is highly regarded. One night while returning to camp, he discovers someone in a tavern selling secrets to the enemy. Charles tells his cousin, John. The next day, Charles finds papers hidden in his own belongings accusing him of spying, and he immediately suspects his commanding officer, Major Alford. When he reports the papers and his suspicions at headquarters, Hensall, the senior officer, asks him to spy at the French court in the hope of uncovering French summer campaign plans. Charles's fluent French enables him to take the identity of a Lord Carnworth, currently detained in a Dutch prison. Charles communicates with Hensall through a French Huguenot who also teaches him to pick locks to get the plans. In Paris, when a man accuses him of being a turncoat, Charles rashly challenges him to a duel. While fighting, he disguises his skill until he wins using a rare maneuver that surprises several observers. When a man arrives at court with whom Charles has dueled and identifies him, Charles becomes a prisoner in the Bastille. When finally freed with bribes after four months, Charles finds that his uncle has died, and he is earl of Aubigny. He also finds that the spy about whom he told his cousin, John, is not Major Alford but John himself, jealous of Charles's money. This revelation disturbs the kind Charles, who has often paid John's gambling debts and tried to help John overcome his feelings of inferiority.

In 1759, in **Mohawk Valley**, Alan Carey, unjustly blamed for marking cards, is sent down from Cambridge. Although he is a champion boxer and wrestler, he dismays his friends for being unable to shoot his gun in a duel to protect his honor. Alan's father, Charles, unperturbed by his behavior, agrees with his friend Billy (William) Pitt, the statesman, that Alan go to America, the land with enormous possibility. When Alan arrives in Boston, he contracts with Jake, a frontiersman, to take him to his father's property in New York State. Jake teaches Alan about the land, and Alan saves the nonswimmer Jake from drowning. Unhappy with Alan's arrival, the bailiff, Hepburn, lures Alan into the woods so that a hired assassin can kill him, but Jake's teaching helps Alan survive. When Alan finds an injured Indian boy and returns him to his tribe, the chief remarks that Hepburn has promised to give the Indians guns as rewards for Alan's murder. However, Alan's refusal to abandon the boy proves him a friend, and none of the Indians will harm him. Alan dismisses Hepburn and wrestles with one of Hepburn's supporters who resists leaving the farm. The money Hepburn had been embezzling stays on the farm, and the lands become quite profitable for Alan's father. Eventually the British, including Alan's Cambridge friends who accused him of cheating, come to fight in the *French and Indian War. When they encounter Alan and observe his abilities in coping with the wilderness and his swimming feat, which enables them to win Quebec, they realize that they have misjudged him. Alan's accuser, Harry, on his American deathbed, admits that he had marked the cards and that Alan had honorably not exposed him because Harry, with neither title nor money, would have lost all chances for a respectable career. After the war, Lord Aubigny visits. Pleased with Alan's accomplishments and Alan's happiness with his life, he gives him the family's American land. The phrase "he little knew then how familiar it would become" illustrates the rather awkward foreshadowing that Welch uses in several of his novels.

In 1791, in **Escape from France**, Richard's cousin Jeffrey disappears without paying a 5,000 pound gambling debt. Then word arrives in Llanstephan that French citizens have imprisoned a branch of the Carey family, the Assaillys, in Normandy during the *French Revolution. Richard's father calls him home from Cambridge, and Uncle Rupert arranges for smugglers to deliver Richard near the French coast where he can locate the Assailly family home. He arrives and safely leads the mother, daughter, and son to meet the boat on the following night. The son, Armand, refuses to board, and someone ambushes Richard and Armand as they return to the Assailly home. They hide, and de Marillac, a man known for his swordplay, finds them. Richard, also an accomplished swordsman, kills him. Using de Marillac's identification, the two go to Paris to try to free Armand's father from prison. Various intricacies and underground ties, including

Jeffrey's liaison with a baron who operates gambling tables, allows them to retrieve Assailly and escape across the channel to England.

By 1808, in **Captain of Foot**, Chris Carey, grandson of Rupert and grand-nephew of Alan, fights for England's Light Brigade in Spain against *Napoleon. Captured, he escapes en route to prison in Paris when Spanish guerrillas kill his French guard. Remaining with the guerrillas while he recovers from a gun wound, Chris learns Spanish. After a brief respite in England, Chris returns, and the guerilla leader, El Empecinado, asks British military headquarters for Chris's aid. Chris helps, and with them, he again succeeds in foiling the French. A captaincy opens, and Chris's peers suggest he buy it. Although he has the money, he feels sorry for those who have to earn promotion by performance, not having enough money for purchase. Chris's Uncle Richard persuades him by recalling that the army was intended for rich men and others had always entered at their own risk. As captain, Chris tries to defend the bridge at Ponte Mucella. Near the end of the novel, Welch shifts the point of view between Chris and a French soldier, Jules, just before they kill each other at the bridge. The reader learns that both planned to forget soldiering at the end of that campaign.

In 1853, Nicholas Carey, in **Nicholas Carey**, serving in the 110th Foot, decides soldiering bores him. He welcomes a request to search for his cousin, Andrew, known to be working in Paris for the unification of Italy (*Mazzini and *Garibaldi). Nicholas enjoys the advantages of a wealthy man in Paris, but he also risks his life. Twice he saves the emperor from an Italian assassin. Then only Andrew's and Nicholas's ability to speak Welsh, coupled with Nicholas's wrestling ability, enables them to escape from the tenacious Italian fanatics who catch them spying. Eventually the *Crimean War begins, with the French and British fighting together against Russia. The initial lack of action in Nicholas's first war frustrates him, and he detests the inconvenience of camp. He reminds one veteran soldier of his Uncle Chris, who also complained about food and quarters before he died in Spain. Action begins after a doctor arrives in camp whom Nicholas recognizes as his Russian school chum, Alexis, using his perfect English to spy for the enemy. Later Nicholas proves his bravery in an assault, but he is captured. Alexis sees him and casually arranges for his escape. Although injured when he returns, Nicholas is happy that none of his close friends died in the attack. Because of the important contribution of talented men who should command but have no money, Nicholas and the current earl d'Aubigny agree that the purchase system for promotion should be changed.

In **Zulu Warrior**, Robert Maryon describes the 1879 battle between the Zulus and the British. Although educated at *Sandhurst, Robert can no longer buy a commission; he must earn it. He goes to Africa to escape English military rituals and discovers that the Zulus are fearless fighters. They can marry only after bathing their spears in enemy blood, so they search for conflict. Over 20,000 Zulus challenge Robert and 200 other men at Isandhlwana. The few British who survive defeat the Zulus only because they have rifles. Robert learns that strict military orders sometimes have no place in battle when a dispatching officer refuses to distribute gunpowder without proper papers, an act that almost destroys the entire British force. Robert escapes, but barely.

In 1914, in **Tank Commander**, John Carey fights in Europe for the first British campaign since 1815. When the Germans march through Belgium on their way to France, the British must honor an 1830 treaty to protect Belgium's neutrality. John leaves the formality of the officers' mess in Britain where men cannot speak of work, religion, politics, or women. Trained at Sandhurst to lead men, John demonstrates in the battle at Mons that he learned well. In addition, his ability to speak French and German helps him. In France, the sight of his first dead soldier sickens him, and he has to deal with the death of his cousin, a close friend and strong leader. Advancements in warfare include camouflaged uniforms and smokeless gunpowder. But carrier pigeons still transport messages. While at home recovering from a wound, John accompanies his father to a secret demonstration of a strange new weapon, a tank, as progressive for World War I as the long bow was at *Crécy for 1340. The omniscient narrator comments that John could "not know that what he was about to see would change his entire career as a professional soldier." John foresees great possibilities for the tank, and his most exciting war efforts come after its advent when he joins the tank battalion. During the war, John fights at Mons, Le Cateau, Aisne, Ypres, Somme, and Cambrai. He sustains wounds, earns medals, and wins promotions until his last battle at Cambrai, where he has a chance, as a major, to break through the German lines. After he wins the tank battle, his horse, frightened by an enemy blast, throws him, and he breaks his ribs. He leaves the battlefront, however, pleased that his tanks have helped with the Allies.

STYLE AND THEMES

Although loose structure appears in spots, Welch's imagery clarifies both scene and tone. In *Captain of Foot,* the soldiers on the bridge are "tattered bearded men staring down the valley with dull, resentful eyes." Welch skillfully inserts the correct pronunciation of Ypres by letting the soldiers practice saying the word "Eepres." Many allusions and similes liven the language. In *Captain of Foot,* Lord Byron is the "latest toast of London society," and people read Walter Scott and the *Edinburgh Review.* Hamlet appears, as do other literary figures. In *Zulu Warrior,* a soldier watches a battle begin "like a theatre-goer . . . waiting impatiently for the curtain to rise." In *Tank Commander,* the "howl of the shell deepened to a rumbling rattling roar like that of an express train hurtling through a wayside station." Welch's use of omniscient point of view in many of the novels allows dramatic irony because the reader often knows information unavailable to the protagonist. Although Welch could have edited his novels more carefully, they remain an exciting and most interesting source of British military history.

WESLEY, JOHN (1703–1791). He became an English religious leader after an experience at Aldersgate where he began to accept the principle of justification by faith. He also traveled to Georgia where he served as a missionary among colonists and Indian tribes. See *Peter Treegate's War* and *Sea Captain from Salem* by Leonard *Wibberley.

WEST WITH THE WHITE CHIEFS. *See* Harris, Christie.

WESTALL, ROBERT (1929–   ). British.

BIBLIOGRAPHY AND BACKGROUND

The Devil on the Road. New York: Greenwillow, 1979; London: Macmillan, 1978. *Fathom Five.* New york: Greenwillow, 1980; London: Macmillan, 1979. *The Machine-Gunners.* New York: Greenwillow, 1976; London: Macmillan, 1975. *The Wind Eye.* New York: Greenwillow, 1977; London: Macmillan, 1976.

Robert Westall received a Carnegie Medal for *The Machine-Gunners* in 1975. He has also received a second Carnegie and other awards for his writing in another genre. The books that Westall calls time-slips contain more research than his novels fitting the traditional historical fiction definition. He says, "I write about times that have been lifelong hobbies. I write about places I know and have thoroughly researched." Locales of military violence attract him even though he is "very nearly a pacifist." He comments, "I do not glory in war, but find it a useful source of dramatic incident, in which the character of individuals and societies can be analyzed by conflict." However, in his attempt to create a kind of fourth dimension, he allows century to "clash with century, hopefully illuminating the essence of both." He notes, "If I can spot where mankind has been, perhaps I can guess where mankind is going. History has always fascinated me as the relationship and conflicts between ideas, and how they finally manifest themselves in concrete reality. A medieval castle, a sunken ship, a curious and outmoded by-law began as an idea in some man's mind." Such concerns lead to research. For *The Devil on the Road,* he relied upon an accumulation of thirty years of reading. After the background has become second nature, Westall writes during long vacations and revises on the weekends, usually two revisions per book.

WORKS

A historical fantasy, **The Wind Eye** is a time-shift novel into the seventh-century world of *Cuthbertus, a *Lindisfarne monk whose body was believed to work miracles. The family who experiences the time shift consists of the pious Beth; her sister, Sally, whose hand was disfigured on an electric heater when two; their father, Bertrand, a Cambridge don with a scientific answer for everything; their self-assured half-brother, Michael; and their manic stepmother, Madeline. En route to a home on the shore inherited from a recently deceased uncle, they visit *Durham Cathedral, where Madeline deliberately steps on the grave of Cuthbertus, a man known to have hated women and to haunt those who disturb him. At the house, they discover a Viking ship in the shed, and while Bertrand prepares to sail it, a man riding by on his bicycle tells him the boat is *The Wind Eye.* Disregarding the man's inherent warning, all but Madeline climb aboard and sail into a mist that propels them through time and space to Inner Farne, one of the nearby islands. Bertrand decides that they have found a different island and sails back. Sally subsequently sleepwalks trying to return to something that she saw on the island, and Beth and Michael also have unusual experiences. They read about Cuddy (Cuthbert) and discover that people believed he could control the wind, raise storms, and strike them dead from inside his tomb. They begin to believe the legends when they experience time shifts and find themselves suddenly in his presence. Michael no longer dotes on himself, Beth balances her piety, and Sally's hand heals. Bertrand becomes aware of psychic phenomena, and Madeline experiences new depths in her life. Westall's treatment of time present mixed with time past works. By putting modern people in a different time frame, he illustrates that individuals rarely change things very much and that not all controlling circumstances are recorded in history annals.

The Devil on the Road shifts John (Jack) Webster in and out of the seventeenth century. He says he is hooked on the drug of Chance, which leads him from the crowded British highway, the A2, and from his plan to vacation at the shore to a reenactment of a *Roundhead-*Royalist battle. His preference for the Royalists instead of the disgustingly rude Roundheads surprises him. Afterward, he rides his motorcycle down a road where he stops at a barn, somehow becomes involved in a scuffle, and loses his motorcycle helmet. He cannot ride the cycle without a helmet, but the barn's owner, Derek Pooley, asks him to stay to look after the grounds. Since Jack likes the kitten rubbing against his legs, he decides to remain for a few days. Dead animals soon start to appear outside the barn door, and local residents begin to call him "Cunning" when he goes into town. In addition, he finds a black rat, no longer extant, that Derek's wife, Susan, identifies as a carrier of the *plague. He dreams in the seventeenth century, and a cat named Daily News transports him back and forth into 1647 when *Hopkins (Hobekinus) was profiting from accusing and trying witches. When Jack helps Joanna escape hanging in 1647, she enters the twentieth century with him but keeps her seventeenth-century ways. When he sees an inscription inside the barn written by a Cambridge student in 1877, one hundred years before, he knows that Joanna has summoned others into her world. Jack soon understands that he must get away from her or he will never escape this precarious time poisoning. The intricate story wanders back and forth from past to present, revealing conflicts between Derek and Susan and the Pooley family history, as well as those of the defenseless women accused of witchcraft. Jack's thoughts, fragments of ideas, unravel the complex plot.

Two novels trace fourteen-year-old Chas through a portion of World War II. In **The Machine-Gunners**, Chas competes with one of his friends to have the best war souvenir collection. When a bomber crashes near his home in England, Chas stumbles across the wreck in the woods. The pilot rots inside and flies buzz around him. Chas discovers a machine gun that he detaches with a saw and transports home on his friend's wagon. When the police find the plane with its missing gun, they suspect the Irish Republican Army until they notice the messy sawing job. They ask a teacher for names of students whose homes they should search. Chas asks Nick, a wealthy boy with whom few others play, to hide the gun in his unused bomb shelter. Nick agrees, so Chas and three friends,

Cem, Audrey, and Chucker, move the gun. They all meet regularly at the shelter and eventually protect a German pilot who parachutes safely into Nick's yard. When invasion hysteria overcomes the town, Chas rushes to the shelter, and the boys, thinking they see Germans, start shooting. This action reveals their location and loses the gun for them. Chas and his friends are not malicious, only foolhardy.

In **Fathom Five**, Chas McGill, the intelligent protagonist of *The Machine-Gunners,* at sixteen in 1943, still spends his time outside school concerned with the war. When he and Cem find a strange piece of flotsam, an olive oil can holding a cigarette package with a message inside naming an arriving ship, they decide that a spy lurks in Garmouth. They search for threads leading to identity in Low Street, an undesirable area of town peopled with sailors, brothels, and immigrants. At first they suspect the owner of the only store selling that brand of olive oil. They next secretly accuse the pawnbroker. Then they look for other possibilities by pretending to be "lowlife" in the bars with their friends Audrey, a newspaperwoman, and Sheila, a daughter of nobility. When Chas becomes friends with the brothel owner, Nelly Stagg, she says she can find the spy. Later Chas finds Nelly's purse and beloved dog speared on shore and knows that she has been murdered. After almost drowning in pursuit, Chas identifies the spy, a man who vehemently castigates Germans but is a German soldier. Chas's sleuthing keeps the submerged German submarine from destroying a carrier scheduled to enter the harbor that night. His uncle, Robert, a navy captain, acknowledges Chas in front of Garmouth's leaders, but Chas cannot receive official recognition because the situation remains secret. Chas decides he likes Shelia and mopes when her parents send her away to school, but when his father suggests that he read the leftist literature in the house before going to university, Chas realizes that her father is a typical "boss." Chas and Cem continue to risk themselves, perhaps feeling that they can in some way help win the war.

STYLE AND THEMES

Westall's taut prose complements his complex plots. He uses imagery and figurative language appropriate to the period. In *The Devil on the Road,* Jack sees "cow parsley . . . leaving splashes of trickling green blood" in the seventeenth century and "a tin of beef . . . spattered in a dark red fan" in the twentieth. "The blue distances swaddle you like a blanket" gives a sense of time shift. In *Fathom Five,* the title itself an allusion, Westall's humor shows through Dave's metaphorical lament: "Why was life composed of days [when your first serve went in at tennis] and other days when you kept on double faulting?" And in the light of the vicious murder of Nelly, among the flotsam that Dave and Cem observe, the "old boots displayed their nails like sharks." Westall's credible and complicated characters never let the reader feel comfortable about guessing their future conduct or its consequences. Westall's stories create circumstance and chance but never conclusion.

WESTWARD TO VINLAND. See Treece, Henry.

WHAT HAPPENED IN HAMELIN. See Skurzynski, Gloria.

WHEN THE DRUMS BEAT. See Trease, Geoffrey.

WHIG. This term of abuse introduced in 1679 during the heated struggle to keep James II from succession referred to people who wanted to exclude the heir from the throne. Cattle and horse thieves were the original Whigs, but Scottish Presbyterians also gained the name. In the eighteenth century, people who represented the interests of dissenters, and industrialists who desired electorial, parliamentary, and philanthropic reforms were also Whigs. See *The Sentinels* by Peter *Carter; *Johnny Tremain* by Ester *Forbes; and *Trumpets in the West* by Geoffrey *Trease.

WHISTLE FOR THE CROSSING. See de Angeli, Marguerite.

THE WHITE NIGHTS OF ST. PETERSBURG. See Trease, Geoffrey.

WHO COMES TO KING'S MOUNTAIN? See Beatty, John and Patricia.

WHO IS CARRIE? See Collier, Christopher and James.

WIBBERLEY, LEONARD (1915–1985). Irish.

BIBLIOGRAPHY AND BACKGROUND

Attar of the Ice Valley. New York: Farrar, Straus & Giroux, 1968; London: Macdonald, 1969. *Deadmen's Cave.* Illustrated by Tom Leamon. New York: Farrar, Straus & Giroux, 1957; London: Faber, 1957. *John Treegate's Musket.* New York: Farrar, Straus & Giroux, 1959. *Kevin O'Connor and the Light Brigade.* New York: Farrar, Straus & Giroux, 1957; London: Harrap, 1959. *The King's Beard.* Illustrated by Christine Price. New York: Farrar, Straus & Giroux, 1952; London: Faber, 1954. *The Last Battle.* New York: Farrar, Straus & Giroux, 1976. *Leopard's Prey.* New York: Farrar, Straus & Giroux, 1971. *Peter Treegate's War.* New York: Farrar, Straus & Giroux, 1960. *Red Pawns.* New York: Farrar, Straus & Giroux, 1973. *Sea Captain from Salem.* New York: Farrar, Straus & Giroux, 1961. *The Secret of the Hawk.* Illustrated by Christine Price. New York: Farrar, Straus & Giroux, 1953; London: Faber, 1956. *Treegate's Raiders.* New York: Farrar, Straus & Giroux, 1962. *The Wound of Peter Wayne.* New York: Farrar, Straus & Giroux, 1955; London: Faber, 1957.

In 1977, Leonard Wibberley was honored for the Treegate series by the Southern California Committee on Literature for Children and Young People Award.

WORKS

The Treegate series follows the exploits of Peter Treegate, son of the Boston merchant John Treegate, from his eleventh year in 1769 until 1814 when his own achievements become combined with those of his nephews. Only one of the books, *Peter Treegate's War*, is first person; the others give an omniscient point of view, which allows the reader to examine various aspects of the American wars from the enemy's stance, as well as the American. In this male world of the sea and battle, Peter learns that nature reveals secrets unavailable to those who ignore it. Other characters in each book believe in a God who controls all and to whom one should openly be thankful. Throughout, the series retains a balance between the spiritual and the physical, which keeps Peter Treegate from becoming a stereotypical American hero.

In 1769, as John Treegate in **John Treegate's Musket** celebrates the tenth anniversary of England's defeat of the French in 1759, Peter hears one of his father's guests express distress at not being able to ship his merchandise directly to the West Indies but having to ship it to England, pay taxes, and then have England send it forward. Another notes that Boston has become a mob led by Sam Adams, a lawyer and tax collector who refuses to collect taxes. On the following morning, Peter leaves home to become an apprentice to Tom Fielding, a barrel stave maker not allowed by the British to make barrels for his staves. Peter's father leaves for England to petition for the colonies, and Peter's younger brother goes to a Philadelphia relative. Peter discovers the apprentice hierachy when an older apprentice, Blake, and his friends beat him. During the snow in the winter of 1769–70, a soldier blames Peter for throwing a snowball, and a riot ensues causing the deaths of seven men. Soon after, Peter sees Blake kill a man, and to save his life, Peter jumps in a boat. John *Hancock's ship, a free trader leaving Boston in the darkness, rescues him. The ship wrecks, and Peter washes to the South Carolina coast. Maclaren of Spey finds him and carries him one hundred miles into the wilderness. Amnesia prevents Peter from telling Maclaren of his past, and Maclaren teaches Peter the ways of the forest as well as the *blood feuds of the Scottish clans transported to the colonies after *Culloden. When Peter remembers his identity, he and Maclaren go to Boston in 1775 and reunite with John Treegate. Although John and Maclaren distrust each other, they join for the first shots of the *American Revolution at Breed's Hill.

In **Peter Treegate's War**, Maclaren of Spey takes control of a group of men after the Battle of Bunker Hill in 1775. Peter, sixteen, follows him. When they sneak to Roxbury one night to abduct a British soldier, the British capture them instead, but Sir John Pett refuses to hang them when he sees Maclaren's clan tara (brooch). Imprisoned on a British warship, they escape soon after meeting *Peace of God Manly, the best pilot in the area. Their contacts tell Peter that his estranged father is organizing an American navy. When Maclaren, afraid of the water, disappears, Peter replaces him as troop captain and marches with Washington across the Delaware to attack Trenton at Christmas. Peace of God, one of "John *Wesley's underserving poor," throws his Bible at a *Hessian gunner and saves the men. Inside the British captain's deserted quarters, Peter sees a portrait of a British soldier who wears the same tara stone as Maclaren. He knows that he must return to Maclaren because he believes, as Maclaren once told him, that the tara mysteriously appears to call clan heirs when they are needed. But Peter first has to recover from wounds for several months. After he arrives at Maclaren's home, he becomes involved in the blood feud between the Campbells and the Farquesons. When Peter refuses to retaliate as expected in a blood feud for an insult, Maclaren kills a man and his child. Peter leaves and joins *Morgan's Rifle Brigade, a group of men fighting in the wilderness. He forces the surrender of Sir Pett, the man who refused to hang him in Roxbury, and Pett tells him that the portrait in Trenton was of his foster son, the real son of Maclaren whom he had retrieved after Culloden and who had died at Princeton. He gives the brooch to Peter.

In **Sea Captain from Salem**, the action shifts to Peace of God Manly after he reaches Paris in pursuit of Benjamin *Franklin with news from John Treegate of *Burgoyne's surrender at *Saratoga. Franklin encourages him to capture prizes in the English Channel, but Peace of God refuses to attack poor fishermen. Peace of God continues to exhibit his expertise at a ship's helm, as well as his understanding of men by outsmarting and capturing several British ships. Finally, a British spy who had seen him first in France helps to capture him by fitting a fishing boat with a gun. The men on the boat destroy Peace of God's ship, but an Irish fisherman, Reagan, rescues Peace of God and hides him until they can safely cross the channel. On the way, Reagan captures the sloop of war searching for Peace of God and takes it to France as his prize. Peace of God's exploits encourage the French to enter the war on the American side on February 2, 1778. Peace of God returns with the blue ribbons binding the treaty as a gift to his daughter Nancy in Salem.

By 1780, in **Treegate's Raiders**, Peter Treegate, twenty-one, joins his father in company with General George Washington to discuss the progress of the war. News of Benedict *Arnold's treason has upset Washington and made him wonder about the loyalty of other men in his command. Peter tells him that the war will be won on the frontier, not in the cities, as Washington thinks. Peter knows that local *Tories have been using the war as an excuse to burn nonconforming churches, to loot, and to free slaves. Only leaders for the Americans in the frontier, such as Francis *Marion (the Swamp Fox) and Nollichucky Jack Sevier, can help fight the civil war churning underneath the war against the British. The scene shifts to Peter at Peace of God's Salem home, where he meets Nancy for the first time. Foreshadowing indicates that Peter and Nancy will marry after the war ends. But before then, Peter enlists the aid of warring Scottish clans by winning a fight against Thomas McClintock. They go to battle against the British Patrick *Ferguson and his Tory band. A traveling bookman, Paddock, helps Peter locate Ferguson's forces, and after a capture and an exchange, Peter and other frontier forces corner Ferguson on top of King's Mountain on October 6, 1780. After this bloody English defeat, *Cornwallis marches against Daniel

Morgan's forces. Peter's men lose at Cowper's, perhaps because Peter's pride in refusing to apologize to Donald Oge causes them to fight separately rather than together. As Peter waits for hanging, he remembers Nancy. But the cowardly Paddock rescues him, and they march toward Yorktown where they watch the British surrender on October 19, 1781. Peter returns to Nancy at Salem.

Peter and Nancy never have children, but they take the orphaned children of Peter's brother when smallpox kills him. One of the four, Manly Treegate, becomes the protagonist of **Leopard's Prey** when he is thirteen. In 1807, Manly accompanies Peter to Norfolk. Free to enjoy himself for a day, Manly rents a horse and pays Tobias Coffin for a sail in his boat. When the two try to rescue a man pressed into British naval service, a British picket boat captures them and impresses them to service on the *Leopard*. When Peter Treegate discovers what happened to Manly, he enlists the help of the escaped Haitian slave, Theopolius Jones, the one man who can rescue Manly in the Caribbean. Manly, however, escapes by jumping into shark-infested waters, where a free trader (pirate), Gubu, finds him. Mama Amelia, Gubu's mother, nurses Manly back to health, and the two return to Boston and the warmth of Peter and Nancy Treegate's home.

In **Red Pawns**, Manly Treegate, at eighteen, returns to Boston to see his uncle and receives Peter's directions to go to the Great Lakes area where ships will be important for keeping freedom. Peter knows that Indian tribes, under the *Shawnee Tecumseh, will try to keep whites east of the Ohio boundary. He tells Manly that they are "red pawns" in a chess match, only good for use by either side. He meets Zimmerman, a Hessian, who shoes the horse and tells them that the British would have won the American Revolution if they had had religion. Manly discovers that Peter has followed him, and the two continue the journey together. Meanwhile, Peter Treegate, the elder, arrives in London, where he tries to negotiate a peace treaty. When a man challenges his American intelligence, they decide to fight a duel. The opponent's bullet grazes Peter's forehead, and Peter then shoots a hare to show that if he had decided to shoot the man, he would not have missed. On the American frontier, Manly hires the guide, Pouch, to take him to Tippecanoe. Pouch helps Manly realize that listening to nature and understanding the differences between the white and the Native American cultures is more important than bravery. When the Indians capture young Peter, he joins Pouch in the prison, and Pouch tells him how and when to escape. Peter's warning to Harrison and the men helps them to defeat the Shawnee, *Iroquois, *Algonquin, and the *Delaware gathered under the name of The Prophet, Tenskwatawa, Tecumseh's brother. Peter Treegate returns from England with a letter of peace, but by the time he reaches the American shore, war has been declared.

In 1812, in **The Last Battle**, Manly captains a ship, the *Wild Duck*, with Peter serving as midshipman. After capturing a British prize ship in the Caribbean, Peter ignores Manly's command to return to the *Wild Duck*, but Peter finds papers revealing British plans for the war. Manly and Peter begin a silent battle as master and man. When the free trader, Gubu, sees Manly, the two embrace, shocking Manly's subordinates. But Gubu is the son of Mama Amelia, the woman who nursed Manly to health after his escape from the *Leopard* and who lives with the Treegate family in Salem. Gubu helps Manly and Peter capture the British ship, *Warspite* and looks after the wounded Peter, along with his compatriot, the godly Luke, while Manly returns to America with the information found on board. When Peter regains his senses after a head wound, Gubu decides to respond positively to his Brethren leader Jean Lafitte's request that he and his men join in the battle at New Orleans against the British. After the ship arrives, all the men except Luke leave. When he sees the wind blow parts of his Gospel of Saint Luke into the sea, he follows it, never to return. In Spain, British soldiers capture Peter Treegate, the elder. The man who should hang him, Major Bingham, remembers him from the London duel and gives him a horse instead. While riding to the nearest harbor, Treegate asks directions from a woman who is trying to keep several children from starving. He sees her need, purchases food, and departs. The male characters are reunited in New Orleans where on December 22, 1814, the British and the Americans under General Andrew Jackson fight. By January 8, the Americans defeat the British, and Peter the elder sees that the one British soldier to penetrate the American line before his death is Major Bingham, the man who wanted to see the wild horses roaming the American frontier. Back in Salem, Peter reveals that the peace treaty at Ghent had been signed on December 24, making the British slaughter unnecessary. He decides to return to Spain for the starving children and bring them to his land on the frontier for a new life. Thus Peter Treegate's story ends with him continuing to try to serve a greater cause than himself.

Of Wibberley's novels, one is unique. In **Attar of the Ice Valley**, Wibberley tries to recreate the world of the Neanderthals. Attar, a young hunter in approximately 50,000 B.C., lives with his small tribe in an area completely covered with ice. He captures game and wins approval for killing a large animal. When the weather continues to be so harsh that the tribe cannot hunt, its members fear that Attar has insulted the Great Bear, their god, by his kill. Attar leaves and tames another wild animal, a dungo, who begins to hunt with him. Eventually Attar returns to the tribe, and when the new chieftain jeopardizes their relationship with other clans, some of them search for a new hunting ground and home. They find a tribe that speaks much as they do and has pictures inside its sacred cave. When the new tribe invites them to join them, Attar returns to the valley and brings those remaining to the new land.

The remainder of Wibberley's novels, told in first person, trace the journeys of young adult male protagonists. The one American protagonist, Peter Wayne, rides from the southern United States to the western frontier of Denver; the others, all from the British Isles, travel by sea. By the time they return home, they have fought battles and made prudent decisions that gain them the recognition of respectable members of their communities.

The first of these novels chronologically, **The King's Beard**, tells John Forrester's story, begun when he is sixteen in 1587. As an orphan living with his schoolmaster, Mr. Hoxton, in Exeter, England, he goes to market one day and returns with a package given him by a strange Indian who says only "Matagorda." Mr. Hoxton realizes that the Spanish have captured John's father, Sir Guy Forrester, and that they have been keeping him in Matagorda, a prison in *Cadiz, probably trying to get him to tell about El Dorado, the land of gold that he has reputedly found. Soon after John arrives, a man named Benjamin Allardyce appears and asks for the package. When Hoxton does not produce it, Allardyce mortally wounds him. John hides in the attic with the package. Before Hoxton dies, he tells John that he is John Forrester, not Hoxton, and that the attic contains all that John's father left him. He also sends him to Sir Walter Raleigh with the package. Raleigh takes John and the parson's son, Roger, with him to tell *Elizabeth I about the maps and description of Philip's Spanish Armada, which Sir Guy has sent with the Indian. After attempts on their lives, the boys sail with Sir Francis Drake to Cadiz. The Spanish capture John in a sea battle and throw him into a dungeon, where he finds his father. Roger speaks Spanish and helps rescue them but not until they have survived a turn on the rack forced by Tallow Joe, a Spanish spy who believes Sir Guy knows about El Dorado. Eventually Drake cripples the Spanish Armada at Cadiz, obtains its surrender, and liberates the slaves. They return to England knowing that Philip will rebuild the armada but that England will also have time to prepare for war. The queen knights John and Roger for singeing the Spanish king's beard, and John begins his new life with his real father.

In **Deadmen's Cave**, Tom Lincoln, a runaway servant from the Massachusetts Bay Colony in 1670, finds himself alone in a long boat with a murderer, Peters, after his ship, *Daphne*, is dismasted off the coast of *Hispaniola. When Peters tries to drink the remaining fresh water, Tom shoots at him and misses, but Peters falls into the water, where sharks attack him. Tom sails to a nearby island and finds a cave in which to sleep. A sulfuric wind wakes him, and when he escapes from the cave, he realizes that the rocks he had seen the previous night are actually skulls attached to skeletons. He realizes that the twelve men, too drunk to smell the deadly fumes, had died in their sleep. On the volcanic island, he fights wild dogs but tames one and meets pirates led by Cutlass, who make him sail with them to Port Royal. There he meets Big Belize, Cutlass's friend. She reads cards and says that Tom will return but that Cutlass will not. The ship leaves with Tom and the unusual pirate, God Ha' Mercy Bones, a man who left Edinburgh University and has been atoning ever since by reading the Bible to those around him. They join Harry *Morgan's raid on the Spanish garrison in Panama, but the fighting appalls Tom and God Ha' Mercy. When the pirates catch the escaping Tom, God Ha' Mercy starts a fire that allows the two to leave with a girl, Celita Matheus, who has asked for their help. The Spanish king had commissioned her brother to make the jewels for his coronation, but the treasure never arrived in Spain. She knows that her brother was honest and wants to find the treasure so that people will know that pirates took it from him. The three return to the volcanic island, find the treasure, and escape. Cutlass, drunk, dies from the sulfuric fumes. When the three report to the Spanish governor, he imprisons Tom and God Ha' Mercy and tells Celita they have left. When she sees Tom working in the sugar cane fields after God Ha' Mercy dies in prison, she rescues him. Tom returns to Big Belize, who gives him Cutlass's inheritance in payment for his maltreatment.

Peter Millet, in **The Secret of the Hawk**, finds in 1791 that his uncle was one of the owners of the slaver *Hawk,* ruined in London's River Thames. The uncle, dying from leprosy, tells Peter that the slaves on the ship had leprosy, and since he burned them, he was paying with his own life as Imbangi (unknown to Peter) had warned him. His last request to Peter is to find the girl, a request that Peter does not understand. Needing money, Peter joins the crew of an East India ship, *Trades Increase,* routed to sail by the slave coast. A black on board named Jim befriends him. The rumor that the ship carries much gold causes another ship to attack it, and the ship sinks with the gold on board. Peter and Jim escape. Jim tells Peter that he is actually Imbangi and was once the chief of the *Ashanti tribe. *Fanti tribe members had captured him and sold him into slavery. When they reach Jim's village, Peter helps him regain his position by challenging the witch doctor, and the people in turn help him find the girl, Lucy Adams. She has survived her years in Africa after being sold to a chieftain by Peter's uncle, and Peter finds that she is the daughter of the ship owner who helped him get his position on *Trades Increase*. The tribe, so pleased to have Imbangi returned, gives Peter many ivory tusks so that when he and Lucy reach England, Peter has money to last a lifetime.

In **Kevin O'Connor and the Light Brigade**, Kevin O'Connor, at seventeen, digs potatoes in 1853 and remembers that his father and six brothers and a sister died from the potato famine of 1846. A visitor, Tom of the Three Fingers, comes to the hovel at Galway, on the estates of Lord Wedcomb, where Kevin and his mother live, and mentions that the two will be wealthy after Kevin finds the Foggy Dew, a black opal that had belonged to Kevin's ancestor Phelin O'Connor, who disappeared. The legend states that the seventh son of the seventh son will endure hardships, after which the Foggy Dew will find him. Since Kevin fulfills the first part of the legend, Tom thinks that perhaps he may also fulfill the second. After Tom leaves for Dublin, the new Lord Wedcomb evicts Kevin and his mother for not paying the rent on time. Kevin hits the lord and finds himself a fugitive. People help him escape to Dublin via boat, and there, Tom tells him he must assassinate the lord for the Young Irelanders. Kevin refuses and joins the Tenth Hussars instead. The unit receives orders to go to *Varna, where they will fight the Russian *Cossacks. Upon arrival, many die of cholera, and those remaining serve under officers who seem to have no idea about how they are supposed to fight. Kevin becomes part of the charge of the Light Brigade under Lord Cardigan, a misdirected offensive with overwhelming negative odds. Kevin lives, and he saves the life of the despicable Lord Wedcomb before capture by the enemy. As a prisoner, Kevin meets Count Vinarsky, who sends for his father, Prince Paul, to meet Kevin. Prince Paul hears Kevin's story of the charge and establishes that Kevin fulfills the criteria for the Foggy Dew, which the prince's family has kept for 200 years. Kevin has fought a battle impossible to win, is Irish, and has spared the life of an enemy he has hated. With the stone, Kevin returns to Ireland, buys land, and marries.

The Wound of Peter Wayne takes place beginning in 1865 at the end of the *American Civil War. Peter Wayne returns home at the end of the war despising *Lincoln, loving Robert E. *Lee, and finding his mother dead. The family lawyer suggests that he go out West where he can overcome his feelings of hatred toward the North. He takes the advice after asking his friend Winter's mother, and sister Prudence, to care for his land. Big Jim, now a freed slave, goes with him. On the way, they meet Stephen Hauptmann, a musician from Vienna who fought on the northern side. Peter refuses to let him ride with them, but after Stephen saves Peter from a buffalo attack, Peter realizes his foolishness. Cheyenne Indians kill Jim when the three encounter the blacksmith Bill Williams, and Peter continues to Denver with Hauptmann and the wagon train where Bill meets Miss Susan, the one woman he thinks he might like to marry. In Denver, they find that Hauptmann's son Joseph was killed two weeks earlier from the only man in a saloon who would have known the circumstances, his partner. Hauptmann challenges the killer and wins. Thus he and Peter make money from the gold claim. When Peter receives a letter from his Georgia lawyer asking for tax money, Peter returns to Georgia, refuses to keep blacks enslaved, and marries Prud. At times simplistic, at times coincidental, the story serves mainly as a reminder of the hostility of young men who fought in the American Civil War toward their opponents.

STYLE AND THEMES

Although at times a rather careless stylist who repeats phrases from novel to novel and sometimes makes mistakes when relaying information from previous books, Wibberley is a superb storyteller. Coincidence advances many of the plot lines, but the adventures reveal historical perspectives unavailable in other historical fiction. When Wibberley takes time, parallelism and alliteration accent content, as in *Deadmen's Cave* when Tom remembers the "sickening sights that accompanied the sack of the city." Sometimes short sentences enveloped by long ones emphasize concepts. In *Peter Treegate's War,* Wibberley follows a long, complex sentence with a brief one: "He had died of cold." Imagery and figurative language appear in *John Treegate's Musket* when the hurricane is a "dirty rim of black, like a fingernail, appear[ing] on the horizon." In *Peter Treegate's War,* the reader sees the "sun turning the grass to a pale gold," contrasted to the British soldiers who lay "in windrows as if cut down by a scythe." In *Leopard's Prey,* a man's "face . . . [was] furrowed, it seemed, by the winds and waves of all the seas of the world." In *Red Pawns,* a horse "contrived to lose a shoe." In *The Last Battle,* "the sea fog lay as thick as smoke around the brig *Wild Duck,* enveloping it in a cocoon." If one ignores the technical lapses, Wibberley's stories have strong ethical undercurrents asserting spiritual values. The honest and the good survive long enough to help others overcome distress. In each novel, God, whether the Great Bear or the God of the Pentateuch, gives guidance through one of the characters. Wibberley's stories about American battles serve as an important counterpart to Ronald *Welch's novels about British military engagements.

WICHITA. *Coronado encountered this tribe of Indians, which dwelled near the modern Wichita, Kansas, in 1541. They lived in villages of round straw houses and raised maize, beans, and melons. *See* Baker, Betty, *A Stranger and Afraid.*

THE WILD CHILDREN. See Holman, Felice.

WILDCAT UNDER GLASS. See Zei, Aliki.

WILDERNESS CLEARING. See Edmonds, Walter.

WILDERNESS JOURNEY. See Steele, William O.

WILL BEECH. Eight, English orphan evacuated to Wales, protagonist of *Good Night, Mr. Tom. See* Magorian, Michelle.

WILL KINMONT. Thirteen, American, protagonist of *Blue Stars Watching. See* Beatty, Patricia.

WILLARD, BARBARA (1909–   ). British.

BIBLIOGRAPHY AND BACKGROUND

A Cold Wind Blowing. New York: Dutton, 1973; London: Longman, 1972. *The Eldest Son.* London: Kestrel, 1977. *A Flight of Swans.* London: Kestrel, 1980. *Harrow and Harvest.* New York: Dutton, 1975; London: Kestrel, 1974. *Hetty.* Illustrated by Pamela Mara. New York: Harcourt, Brace, & World, 1963. *The Iron Lily.* New York: Dutton, 1974; London: Longman, 1973. *The Lark and the Laurel.* Illustrated by Gareth Floyd. New York: Harcourt, Brace, & World, 1970; London: Longman, 1970. *The Miller's Boy.* Illustrated by Gareth Floyd. New York: Dutton, 1976; London: Kestrel, 1976. *The Sprig of Broom.* Illustrated by Paul Shardlow. New York: Dutton, 1972; London: Longman, 1971.

Barbara Willard has received awards for her writing in several genres. In 1974, she won *The Guardian* Award for *Harrow and Harvest.* Willard explains about her choice of locale: "I became involved in my own part of Sussex [England], and it proved impossible to ignore." She wanted to write about people and notes that "anyone who cries 'If only I'd been in the-whatever-century' always imagines being born into nobility. I prefer to think of the commoner— the thirteenth child, say, of some cowherd's exhausted wife." She has collected an extensive library covering the periods about which she writes. When she began writing about the area, she realized that one generation of people would have known other generations; therefore, the stories have become one story about a place, with characters coming and going, being influenced by externals such as the Wars of the Roses, the Tudor dynasty, the Reformation, and others. About her writing habits, she says, "I used to keep set hours but I find this leads to a lot of stuff needing to be scrapped [the] next day. Now when I stick I go out and walk over the ground itself, which begins precisely at my garden gate."

WORKS

In **The Miller's Boy**, twelve-year-old Thomas in 1478 has to help support himself and his failing miller grandfather. Orlebar, the owner of Ghylls Hatch, encourages him, in his spare time, to befriend Orlebar's nephew and ward, Lewis Mallory, when Lewis moves into the estate manor. After initial difficulties, they rapidly become best friends. When a storm destroys Gospels Mill, Thomas breaks his arm in a vain attempt to save his grandfather. Orlebar invites him to live at Ghylls Hatch. But during the winter, the stable keeper's jealousy continually reminds Thomas that he can never be classed as a gentleman like Lewis. On the day that Orlebar awards Lewis with the papers to and full ownership of the beautiful horse Solitaire, Lewis gives the horse to Thomas. He knows that Thomas needs the horse to work a farm with his sister and that with the horse, Thomas can avoid the ignominy of having to become Lewis's servant instead of remaining his friend.

In **The Lark and the Laurel**, Lewis Mallory's story continues, with his point of view juxtaposed to that of another character, Cecily Jolland. In 1485, the *Yorkist King *Richard lost to the *Lancastrian side, and Cecily's father, who had supported the Yorkists, had to escape to France. Although having little regard for his older sister, he had to leave Cecily with her. When Cecily is sixteen, her aunt dies, and Cecily goes to live with Dame Elizabeth, another aunt, but one whom her father had mistreated by marrying her to an immoral crippled bastard, a *Fitz-edmund. With her, Cecily learns to run a farm raising rabbits for their skins. She also learns to read and write. At the neighboring horse farm, Cecily meets seventeen-year-old Lewis Mallory, still living with his uncle after his father unexpectedly disinherited him. She tells him about life before Dame Elizabeth when her other aunt had kept her so that "I was a dead thing—a bundle of sticks tied with golden thread." Cecily and Lewis fall in love, and when the winter snows part them, Lewis endures the doubts of separation. In the spring, Cecily's father returns from France having found a man for her to marry, but Dame Elizabeth reveals that Cecily has been married since she was five. Cecily vaguely recalls a ceremony but remembers only a crest of lark and laurel. In her attempt to synthesize her past, she realizes that she married Lewis ten years previously. Cecily sees that Dame Elizabeth had carefully nurtured their love. When Cecily's father tries to annul the marriage, Cecily and Lewis refuse.

In the first chapter of **The Sprig of Broom**, Richard at ten leaves his guardian in 1485 and meets his father on the eve of a major battle. The second chapter starts over twenty years later at Mantlemass in 1506 where two boys, Roger Mallory and Medley Plashet, finish their schooling under Sir James, the old priest who had presided at the marriage of Roger's parents, Lewis and Cecily. Medley's father, Dick, does many things well; he is a carpenter, joiner, and a superb guide through the dense forest. He also reads and writes in Latin and English, an unusual ability for a mere worker. The remainder of the novel explores Medley's life after Master Crespin comes to visit his father and gives Medley a sprig of broom, which Medley plants. Soon after, Medley meets Dick riding with three strangers near the forest edge, but Dick ignores Medley as if he had never known him. Afterward the three men return, but Dick vanishes. People in the village stone Medley's mother, Anis, suspecting she is a witch because of her healing abilities with herbs and also because she has lived, unwed, with Dick Plashet for many years. The Mallorys at Mantlemass take Medley into their home and train him to keep the accounts after Lewis Mallory discovers his fine handwriting. Although Medley grows increasingly fond of Catherine Mallory, Roger's sister, he has no inheritance, and thus no expectations of marriage. But Roger, the second son, decides to become a priest and wills his inheritance to Medley. At the time Medley hears of his good fortune, he has gone to search for his father and has found that he, Medley, is King Richard Plantagenet's grandson. This discovery ends the dramatic irony created at the beginning of the novel. He learns that his father's secrecy had been his way to protect both of them from those who wanted to reclaim the throne from the *Tudors. With this knowledge, Medley understands the significance of the sprig of broom; it is the *planta genista* on the Plantagenet emblem, his family crest.

In **A Cold Wind Blowing**, Medley and Catherine Plashet's family, living at Ghylls Hatch, endures the destruction in 1538 of the convents and priories during *Henry VIII's separation from the church. In addition, they hear first rumblings of the *plague. When beckoned secretly to help his Uncle Roger (become the priest Dom Thomas), Piers, the eighteen-year-old son of Medley and the deceased Catherine Mallory, goes. But he inherits the charge to look after a young girl who had asked for his uncle's help moments before an enemy stabbed him to death. Piers is quite distressed with the events. The girl refuses to talk, and he brings her back to Ghylls Hatch. Finally his ten-year-old brother, Richard, coerces her to say that her name is Isabella, but she admits nothing about her past. Eventually Piers marries her, and they conceive a child. Soon after, Piers's former school chum, Robin Halacre, arrives to question Piers's grandmother, Cecily, at Mantlemass about two new tenants. Robin accuses the wife of being a former nun never released from her vow of chastity by King Henry VIII. Fearful that Robin will question her own past, Isabella reveals to Piers that she had been a novitiate and had taken similar although not final vows. To escape Robin's possible inquiries, Isabella and Piers leave Ghylls Hatch, and Piers finds jobs to support them until their daughter is born. After the birth, Isabella feels guilty, runs away, and as she tries to escape from Piers who pursues her, she suddenly dies. Piers returns to Ghylls Hatch leaving his daughter, Catherine Medley, with an interim nurse.

The Eldest Son begins the story of Harry Medley, brother of Piers in *A Cold Wind Blowing,* in his eighteenth year in 1534. He remembers that his deceased mother, Catherine Mallory Medley, compared him to a falcon picking its prey and swooping directly toward it without being diverted. He decides first that he wants to work as an iron master rather than with the horses he expects to inherit from Ghylls Hatch, and second, that he wants to marry Sir John Furnival's daughter. He convinces his father, Piers, to speak to Sir John about Anne even though Sir John faces huges fines for refusing to malign Queen Katherine, the woman Henry VIII is divorcing. Harry and Anne marry three years later, after Piers marries Judith, the woman who served Catherine at Mantlemass and who has cared for his family since Catherine's death at their youngest son, Richard's, birth. When the entourage leaves for Anne's home and the wedding, the Mantlemass servants wear new livery decorated with the Mallory emblem of the lark and the laurel. After the ceremony, the ancient custom of friends undressing the bride and groom in separate rooms and pushing them to the marriage bed embarrasses both Harry and Anne. In 1543, the government jails Anne's father for reading the English Bible to his servants, and Piers helps gain his release by asking for aid from London relatives in favor at Henry's court. After Piers leaves, a stranger comes to Ghylls Hatch leading a "toy" pony, which Harry decides to purchase for his delighted daughter, Cecilia. His brother Piers, who knows horses much better than he, disapproves because no horse breeder allows foreign and unknown stock to contaminate his own herd. Soon the toy, symbolically named Black Lady but called Lady, fulfills the foreboding of both Piers and Anne by giving Cecilia and some of the other horses plague, which kills them. After a long self-imposed quarantine, the foresters demand that the family burn fields, stock, and buildings to keep the disease from spreading. After the family moves to Mantlemass, Harry hears about the death of Anne's uncle, an iron master near the forest of Dean. He decides to fulfill his second goal by helping the widow continue the work. Piers, his father, gives him his inheritance money but refuses to acknowledge him as heir to Ghylls Hatch. Harry and Anne leave with their family and servants to become iron masters, separating from the Mantlemass and Ghylls Hatch people forever.

In **The Iron Lily**, Lilias Rowan is fifteen in 1570. Her mother dead of plague, Lilias runs away from a scheming sister-in-law who says that the deceased Mr. Rowan was not Lilias's father. When she checks the church records, she finds that the priest has crossed out a third name . . . which she reads as "Medley." She goes to work at Penhurst mixing herbs, where five years later, her considerable talent leads her to treat Lady Mary Sidney of Penhurst for her smallpox blotches. Lilias's success in healing Lady Mary makes Lady Mary want to find a husband for Lilias even though she has a crooked shoulder. The book skips a generation to Lilias's daughter, Ursula, who returns home from the village to find that her father has died, crushed by an iron hammer. Of the men who try to buy Froreden, the iron master's home, one is Richard Medley, who with his crooked shoulder feels a kinship with Lilias. Lilias, however, decides to rent Froreden and establish a new home on the site of a ruined monastery. Lilias also decides that Ursula should marry the tenant, young Christy Willard, but Ursula falls in love with Robin, son of Piers Medley. To thwart the romance, Lilias sends Ursula to Penhurst, but Ursula runs away as her mother had done years before. Lilias, thinking that Ursula has left with Robin, goes to Mantlemass with the ring her mother had given her. It displays the same insignia that Lilias has seen on a tapestry in the Mantlemass house. Lilias discovers that Piers is actually her father and that an age difference had kept her mother from marrying him. She also finds that Robin is the son of Piers's old friend Robin Halacre, condemned and dead as a heretic. The last revelation to Lilias comes from Piers when he shows her the Plantagenet dagger and his father's book saying that the last Plantagenet had a crooked shoulder. Upon Ursula and Robin's safe return, they find not only that Piers but also Lilias blesses their marriage.

By 1588, in **A Flight of Swans**, Ursula, married to Robin Medley, Piers's adopted son, lives at Ghylls Hatch, looking after the sons of a London relative, Francis Jolland, whose wife has recently died. Humphrey Jolland, irritated at having to live in the country while his father recuperates, escapes from Robin's guard on a trip selling horses and rides to the coast hoping to see the Spanish fleet fight the English. Humphrey disappears; he was last seen when he left shore in the boat of a man later found drowned, but his brother Roger, fourteen, "sees" that Humphrey has not died. Roger remains at Ghylls Hatch, loving the land and his cousin Ursula. But Ursula also has other problems, which include her unhappy marriage to Robin. Robin continues to exhibit an imbalance of judgment in his business dealings, as illustrated when he depletes the Ghylls Hatch stable by selling too many horses at one time. When Roger's father, Sir Francis Jolland, arrives after Humphrey's disappearance, Ursula and he find each other attractive. Francis leaves Roger to be tutored in the ways of iron forging by Piers's younger brother, Richard, who, because he bears the thick shoulder of his forefathers, has refused to marry. In five years, Richard dies, and Roger becomes the accomplished iron master of Plashets. Soon after, Roger sees a stranger in the area and knows that Humphrey has returned, most likely to obtain guns and supplies for the Spanish. Roger protects Humphrey from the men at Plashets who discover that Humphrey and his cohorts have stolen plans for making guns from Ursula's mother, Lilias. The men consider Roger a traitor and refuse to obey him as their master. But when Ursula tells the manager that Roger protected his brother, he suggests that Lilias become the master and that Roger should return in a few years. Piers, dying of a broken heart over the ruin of Ghylls Hatch, tells Ursula on the night he dies that he is her grandfather and that they are linked to the Plantagenets. She records in the journal about her life at both Ghylls Hatch and Mantlemass, which she writes for her granddaughter, unborn and unknown, that Harry's family is the true heir to Mantlemass. Ursula sees Sir Francis again, after he has remarried, and although they both love each other, they know that, even with Robin dead, they must not consummate the love. They remain like the faithful swans that mate for life that they watch fly over the water in both morning and evening.

In **Harrow and Harvest**, when Edmund Medley is fifteen, *Parliament troopers during the *English Civil War kill his father and burn his home. Honoring his father's last words to get to Mantlemass, Edmund and his brother, Harry, and a trusted servant trudge through England in the 1630s. Cecilia Highwood, living at Mantlemass with her brother, Nicholas, her mother, and her uncle's wife with her two children, knows when unknown Edmund comes that he is the true heir because she has read her grandmother Ursula's journal, hidden in a secret drawer. When Cecilia's cousin Roger returns from the New World soon after Edmund's arrival, she reveals what she knows. The news at first distresses Nicholas, married to Pleasance, but he adjusts. Aunt Dorian, however, does not. She betrays the family's Parliament sympathies to her *Royalist friend Henry Stapley. Stapley shoots Edmund on the night that Parliament troops burn Mantlemass. Nicholas and Pleasance decide to go to the New World with Roger, but Cecilia stays, knowing that she must find if her friend, John Verrall, has survived the battles. While waiting, she sees the little book that Edmund had lost in the forest just before arriving at Mantlemass. In it, she discovers that the family has descended from Richard, the last Plantagenet. When John reappears, she decides to start anew by burning the book.

Hetty, unlike the Mantlemass novels, takes place in 1887, *Victoria's Diamond Jubilee year, when thirteen-year-old Hetty undergoes the stigma of having her family repay the debts of a business partner who embezzled. As a working family in the millinery business, Hetty does not have the class status of her friend Blanche Verrity. In fact, the family's need to cut spending leads Rose, Hetty's sister, to secure employment as Blanche's governess. Hetty feels that Blanche will shun her when Blanche goes to boarding school, but Hetty's fears are never tested because her uncle Joe returns from the sea with a lot of money earned from his voyages. Hetty herself goes to boarding school in France. Although Hetty's story is pleasant, it has little of the power of Willard's Mantlemass books.

STYLE AND THEMES

The intriguing stories in the Mantlemass series present various periods of English history from the time of Richard Plantagenet through that of Oliver Cromwell. Willard's mastery of imagery and figurative language throughout appears in phrases like this example from *The Lark and the Laurel:* the "sun ...plunging a long blade of light through the greenish glass of the deep set window." In another, the swans silhouetted by the cloudy sky in *A Flight of Swans* appear "alabaster against lead." In the forest around Mantlemass, one sees "the spreading fingers of the great birches." In *The Eldest Son*, Henry VIII's commands are a ripple "into the great pool of all England." In the same novel, Willard perfectly understates Harry and Anne's consummation of their marriage with "they recognized one another with astonishment and with delight." The dialect, deftly translated, never intrudes on story and continues to clarify setting. Several symbols, such as the male Plantagenet family dagger and the female ring bearing the lark and laurel crest, deepen the Mantlemass ties. The book that Cecilia finally burns represents the family heritage, as does the little piece of glass engraved with a saint's head that Dick retrieves after Anis's death in *The Sprig of Broom*. The reader's only regret after finishing the Mantlemass books is that Willard has written too few of them.

WILLIAM THE CONQUEROR (c. 1028–1087). As the bastard son of a duke of Normandy, he was accepted by nobles as his father's successor. He probably received a promise from Edward the Confessor of England that he should succeed him, and *Harold, earl of Wessex, supported his claim until Edward died. In 1066, William invaded England, and with Harold's brother Tostig's support, defeated Harold at Senlac. After his crowning at Westminster, he began building the Tower of London. To complete his conquest, he made a land survey which he recorded in the Domesday Book. He then established the feudal system and refused to pay homage to the pope. He died after falling from his horse and was buried in the abbey he had built in Caen. *See* Treece, Henry, *Man with a Sword*.

WILLIAM JONES. Twelve, English protagonist in *Footsteps*. *See* Garfield, Leon.

WILLIAM OF ORANGE AND OF ENGLAND (1650–1702). Through his marriage to Mary, daughter of James II of England, he became king of England in the Glorious Revolution of 1688. Both *Whigs and *Tories asked him to become king, and when he landed in Torbay, Devonshire, with a Dutch army, before any blood was shed, Parliament invited him to accept the throne. He built Kensington Palace and founded the Greenwich Naval Hospital. See *Bonnie Dundee* by Rosemary *Sutcliff and *Trumpets in the West* by Geoffrey *Trease.

WILLIE BANNERMAN. Fourteen, American female protagonist in *The Snowbird*. *See* Calvert, Patricia.

WILLY FREEMAN. Thirteen, black American female protagonist of *War Comes to Willy Freeman* and character in *Who Is Carrie? See* Collier, Christopher and James.

WILLY OVERS. English protagonist who grows from six to eleven in *A Likely Lad*. *See* Avery, Gillian.

THE WIND EYE. *See* Westall, Robert.

WINDFALL. See *Sea Fever* by K. M. *Peyton.

WINTER DANGER. *See* Steele, William O.

THE WINTER HERO. *See* Collier, Christopher and James.

THE WINTER WHEN TIME WAS FROZEN. *See* Pelgrom, Els.

WITCH DOG. *See* Beatty, John and Patricia.

THE WITCH OF BLACKBIRD POND. *See* Speare, Elizabeth George.

WITCHES' CHILDREN. *See* Clapp, Patricia.

THE WITCH'S BRAT. *See* Sutcliff, Rosemary.

THE WONDERFUL WINTER. *See* Chute, Marchette.

THE WOOL-PACK. See *The Merchant's Mark* by Cynthia *Harnett.

WORD TO CAESAR. See *Message to Hadrian* by Geoffrey *Trease.

WORDS BY HEART. *See* Sebyesten, Ouida.

THE WOUND OF PETER WAYNE. *See* Wibberley, Leonard.

WREN, CHRISTOPHER (1632–1723). An English architect, he proposed a plan for rebuilding London after the *Great Fire of 1666. He designed and built fifty-three churches in London and is perhaps best known for his design of the present *St. Paul's Cathedral. See *The Great House* by Cynthia *Harnett and *Trumpets in the West* by Geoffrey *Trease.

THE WRITING ON THE HEARTH. *See* Harnett, Cynthia.

WULF. Protagonist from the British Isles at eleven in *The Sea Stranger* and at twelve in *The Fire-Brother*. *See* Crossley-Holland, Kevin.

— Y

YANCE CAYWOOD. Eleven, American protagonist in *The Lone Hunt*. *See* Steele, William O.

YANKEE. During the *American Civil War, U.S. (Union) soldiers fighting for the North, as well as citizens in the northern states, gained this label. See *A Long Way to Whiskey Creek, Wait for Me, Watch for Me, Eula Bee,* and *Turn Homeward, Hannalee* by Patricia *Beatty; *The Tamarack Tree* by Patricia *Clapp; and *The Perilous Road* by William O. *Steele.

***THE YEAR OF THE BLOODY SEVENS.** See*, Steele, William O.

YELLOW BIRD. *Cherokee protagonist in *The Life and Death of Yellow Bird*. *See* Forman, James.

YELLOW FEVER. An acute infectious disease of tropical and subtropical regions, its virus is transmitted by several species of mosquitos. An outbreak occurred during the times of the Mayans around 1484, and the Spanish explorers reported fatal epidemics of blood vomiting. It can be prevented with modern immunization. *See* Fleischman, Paul, *Path of the Pale Horse*.

YEP, LAURENCE (1948–). American.

BIBLIOGRAPHY AND BACKGROUND
   Dragonwings. New York: Harper, 1975. *The Serpent's Children*. New York: Harper, 1984.
   Laurence Yep has received awards for *Dragonwings*, including the International Reading Association's Children's Book Award in 1976. In both historical fiction novels, Yep tells the story of young Chinese protagonists through their first-person point of view.

WORKS

In **Dragonwings**, Moon Shadow comes from China to join his father, Windrider, in San Francisco during 1903. The two live in the Tang area until Windrider accidentally kills someone trying to attack Moon Shadow. They move into an area where whites live, near Miss Whitlow and Robin. One day, a man's horseless carriage malfunctions, and Windrider repairs it, using his ingenuity. The owner, Mr. Alger, helps him get work. The concept of flying fascinates Windrider, so when he hears of the Wright Brothers, Shadow writes to them, using the English Miss Whitlow has taught him. When the Wright brothers answer, Windrider continues the correspondence. Black Dog, a boy influenced by American hoodlums, robs Shadow and Windrider, and Windrider has to borrow money for his rent and to join the Company, a group of Chinese men who own a laundry and help each other. When the San Francisco *Earthquake occurs in 1906, they rescue people and help them resettle. Windrider makes and very briefly flies his machine, Dragonwings, before the Wrights fly at Kitty Hawk, but he cannot spend any more money on flying because he needs it to bring his wife and mother to America. He eventually collects enough money to return to China and reunite the family.

The Serpent's Children follows Cassia at eight and her family of the Young clan as they try to survive the British ("demons") attempts to sell opium in an invasion of the Middle Kingdom (China). Cassia's father leaves home to fight for the *Manchu government against the British, although he plans to help overthrow it with the group of revolutionaries to which he belongs. After he leaves, Cassia's mother tells the story of the lovely serpent woman in the window lattice carving created by Cassia's grandfather. She tells Cassia and her brother, Foxfire, seven, that she and they are children of the lovely serpent woman. The mother dies in the rice field soon afterward, probably from tuberculosis. The Strangers (people not born in the village), to whom Cassia's mother was friendly, help Cassia and Foxfire escape the mercenary plans of their relatives for binding Cassia's feet and betrothing her for a dowry. Their father eventually returns, wounded, and the children continue to care for the meager fields. Seven years later, during the intense famine, a neighboring clan comes in the fog to take the crops. That same day, rather unrealistically, the father's Brotherhood friend Spider arrives, as well as another village man long away from home. They tell of the Golden Mountain in America, and Foxfire, seemingly unable to please his father and definitely disinterested in the "Work" to overthrow the government, wants to go. When his father disinherits him, he disappears, reaches America, and sends money. They realize that perhaps he belongs in America since his way of saving his family from the drought and of helping loyal friends is more effective than the "Work."

STYLE AND THEMES

Yep's stories help the reader understand problems faced by Chinese immigrants in California, as well as those faced by family members left behind. He verbalizes the difficulties of nineteenth-century China when "demons' opium began to seep through the countryside like poison through the body of a sick giant." Those who kept their respect for family and friends tended to live more happily in both China and America. The description and vocabulary seem too sophisticated for an uneducated writer in the letter Foxfire sends to his family, but Yep exemplifies the love of beauty and the thrill of the intangible in both books. Moon Shadow thinks the kite string is "like a leash" and the kite is "like a hound that I had sent hunting, to flush a sunbeam or stray phoenix out of the clouds." Cassia sees the sunrise "like a piece of amber" and visualizes a "fleet of ships, lean and sleek as hunting hounds." Such understanding of the spirit as this forges the bonds between children and parents.

YERMAK TIMOFEYEVICH (d. 1584). He was a *Cossack leader who led a small army in an expedition to conquer Siberia from 1581 to 1584 and occupied the Tatar capital of Kashlyk in 1582. *See* Bartos-Höppner, B., *The Cossacks.*

YORK. This English royal house, one branch of which was Plantagenet, had as its symbol the red rose in the Wars of Roses with the *Lancasters. Its kings were *Edward IV and V and *Richard III. *See* Willard, Barbara, *The Lark and the Laurel.*

YORK. The Roman city of Eburacum was built for the Ninth Legion. After the Romans left, it regained status around 627 and by the eighth century had become a famous center of learning under Alcuin. Its present name of York dates from 867 when the Danes captured the city and retained it as their capital. Today the beautiful York Cathedral and the Viking remains draw many visitors. See *Witch Dog* by John and Patricia *Beatty; *Madatan* by Peter *Carter; *Ransom for a Knight* by Barbara *Picard; and *Man with a Sword* and *The Last Viking* by Henry *Treece.

YORUBA. Members of this tribe in modern Nigeria were taken as slaves to the Americas. They worshipped a pantheon of gods, including the trickster, and brought this worship to North America. *See* Carter, Peter, *The Sentinels.*

YOUNG MARK. See Almedingen, E. M.

THE YOUNG PRETENDERS. See Picard, Barbara.

YUKI SAKANE. Japanese-American protagonist of eleven and twelve in *Journey to Topaz* and *Journey Home. See* Uchida, Yoshiko.

YUMA. A tribe of Indians living at the lower end of the Colorado River during sixteenth-century Spanish expeditions, the Yumas were primarily agrarians who irrigated their land. They also made excellent pottery. *See* Baker, Betty, *Do Not Annoy the Indians.*

Z

ZEALOTS. This Jewish religious activist sect relentlessly opposed the attempt to bring Judaea under the dominion of idolatrous Rome. Its members regarded themselves as defenders of Jewish law and the national life of the Jewish people. They were first influential in Galilee, and later, Jerusalem from the time of Herod (37–4 B.C.) until the fall of the city. *See* Haugaard, Erik, *The Rider and His Horse*.

ZEI, ALIKI (1928–   ). Greek.

BIBLIOGRAPHY AND BACKGROUND
   Petros' War. Trans. Edward Fenton. New York: Dutton, 1972. *The Sound of Dragon's Feet*. Trans. Edward Fenton. New York: Dutton, 1979. *Wildcat under Glass*.Trans. Edward Fenton. New York: Holt, 1968.
   All three of Aliki Zei's novels were awarded the Mildred Batchelder Award.

WORKS
   In **The Sound of Dragon's Feet,** ten-year-old Sasha, living in Russia in 1894, constantly asks first-person questions, many of which her physician father says he will answer when her braid is longer. One of her questions is how the protagonist in her favorite fairy story can hear the sound of dragon's feet, like a train vibrating the track as it travels many miles away. When Mooney Moonevitch, a medical student convicted of inciting other students and previously exiled to Siberia for three years, becomes her tutor, she begins to like learning and preparing for her school exams. When Sasha asserts that being a lion tamer would be the bravest thing one could do, Mooney helps her understand that a lion tamer could never be a heroine because she does not help others by sticking her head inside a lion's mouth. Although under government surveillance, Mooney still tries to organize beer factory workers into striking for more rights. Soon he has to flee from authorities, but before he goes, he marries a woman whom he had met while in prison when she pretended to be his fiancée to bring him

messages from his friends. Sad that Mooney must leave but happy to hear she will see him and his bride again, she begins adjusting to her likable French tutor.

Melia narrates her first-person view in **Wildcat under Glass** when she and her older sister, Myrto, enjoy stories about the stuffed wildcat with a blue and a black eye sitting in the glass case in their parlor. But Melia hears different kinds of stories in Greece during 1936. After she hears the family adults talk about the king's interest in a dictatorship, the girls' father makes them change their cat's name from Democracy to Demmie. When Niko, a cousin, comes to the island summer home, he tells of the *Black Shirts in Spain. Eventually Niko disappears, and a message directs them to deliver food to a deserted windmill. There Niko hides and says he must remain for several days. When the girls return to town, secret police burn Grandfather's books about the Ancients, as well as those written by the father of Melia's friend Alexis. When authorities imprison Alexis's father, Grandfather loses a lot of his spirit, and Niko leaves for Spain. In school, Myrto enjoys being a leader of the Youth Organization, but she soon realizes that spying on her own family is disloyal. Melia's aunt refuses to acknowledge the horror of the situation, while Melia's father worries about keeping his job. The novel ends indeterminately with no solution in sight for either the Spanish Civil War or for the pre–World War II Greek dictatorship.

In 1940, Petros is nine in **Petros' War** when the Greeks declare war against the Italians. When Petros becomes involved with the underground resistance to the Italians and then to the Germans, the war becomes personal for him. His childhood interests shift from dead animals and turtles to writing slogans on public walls about the lack of food in Athens. His sister Antigone's friend, Michalis, induces him to throw nails on the road for puncturing tires on German ammunition carriers. He watches the black market thrive and the baker gather every valuable in the neighborhood because only he has any flour. His friend Sotiris starts begging on street cars, and Sotiris's family buries the grandmother after dark so that they can keep using her food coupons. Everyone in Petros's family begins resisting the Germans, all independently—his father delivers messages, his mother hides an Italian, his grandfather begs for food, and Antigone distributes leaflets. The Andartes fighting in the mountains, however, are a major force behind Greek survival, and Uncle Angelos fights with them, sending messages to the family via the BBC. Just before the Germans leave Athens, Sotiris publicly belittles a soldier, and the man kills him. By uniting, the Greeks retain their dignity in this senseless war.

STYLE AND THEMES

Zei tells interesting stories about adult situations through a child's viewpoint. She uses allusions to deepen the intrinsic value of her novels—mythology, past battles, *Don Quixote, David Copperfield,* and others. Dreams help foreshadow action. Imagery and figurative language clarify tone. In *Petros' War,* a gang follows Sotiris "like a litter of puppies." When Antigone's hair is "all busy like a cauliflower," the reader can identify a younger brother's description. All of the protagonists are directly connected with people who refuse to accept government terrorism—Sasha with Mooney, Melia with Niko, and Petros with Michalis. Zei demonstrates that these people help freedom survive by risking their lives to thwart those who try to take it away.

ZEPPELIN. Designed by the German Count Ferdinand von Zeppelin, this cigar-shaped aluminum airship powered by gasoline first flew on July 2, 1900. *See* Peyton, K. M., *Thunder in the Sky*.

ZIA. Fourteen, Spanish niece of Karana in *Island of the Blue Dolphins*, protagonist of *Zia*. *See* O'Dell, Scott.

ZIA. *See* O'Dell, Scott.

ZOAR BLUE. *See* Hickman, Janet.

ZULU WARRIOR. *See* Welch, Ronald.

Appendix A
_____ _Setting Dates and Locales_ _____

The works begin in the years listed. They may end several years later.

PREHISTORY

? 50,000 B.C.—Wibberley, Leonard, _Attar of the Ice Valley_ (Europe).

JFIC 11,000 B.C.—Treece, Henry, _The Dream-Time_ (British Isles).

* 10,000 B.C.—Steele, William O., _The Magic Amulet_ (North America).

JFIC 1550 B.C.—McGraw, Eloise, _Mara, Daughter of the Nile_ (Egypt).

JFIC 1400 B.C.—McGraw, Eloise, _The Golden Goblet_ (Egypt).

JFIC 900 B.C.—Sutcliff, Rosemary, _Warrior Scarlet_ (British Isles).

* 480 B.C.—Paton Walsh, Jill, _Crossing to Salamis_ (Greece).

* 472 B.C.—Paton Walsh, Jill, _The Walls of Athens_ (Greece).

* 471 B.C.—Paton Walsh, Jill, _Persian Gold_ (Greece).

JFIC 420 B.C.—Trease, Geoffrey, _Web of Traitors_ (Greece).

ROMAN EMPIRE (c. 200 B.C.–476 A.D.)

JFIC 200 B.C.—Baumann, Hans, _I Marched with Hannibal_ (Spain, Italy).

JFIC 100 B.C.—Sutcliff, Rosemary, _Sun Horse, Moon Horse_ (British Isles).

* 58 B.C.—Mitchison, Naomi, _The Conquered_ (France, Italy).

JFIC 50 B.C.—Hunter, Mollie, _The Stronghold_ (British Isles).

* 1 A.D.—Beatty, John and Patricia, _A Donkey for the King_ (Jerusalem).

IC/JNC 30 A.D.—Speare, Elizabeth George, _The Bronze Bow_ (Jerusalem).

JFIC 40 A.D.—Sutcliff, Rosemary, _Song for a Dark Queen_ (British Isles).

* 43 A.D.—Treece, Henry, _War Dog_ (British Isles).

JFIC 50 A.D.—Treece, Henry, _The Centurion_ (British Isles).

JFIC 55 A.D.—Treece, Henry, _The Queen's Brooch_ (British Isles).

JFIC 70 A.D.—Haugaard, Erik, _The Rider and His Horse_ (Jerusalem).

* 100—Trease, Geoffrey, _A Ship to Rome_ (Egypt).

*117—Trease, Geoffrey, *Message to Hadrian* (British Isles).

JFIC 130—Sutcliff, Rosemary, *The Eagle of the Ninth* (British Isles).

JFIC 150—Sutcliff, Rosemary, *Outcast* (British Isles).

JFIC 200—Sutcliff, Rosemary, *The Mark of the Horse Lord* (British Isles).

JFIC 290—Sutcliff, Rosemary, *The Silver Branch* (British Isles).

JFIC 350—Sutcliff, Rosemary, *Frontier Wolf* (British Isles).

FIC/JFIC 410—Sutcliff, Rosemary, *The Lantern Bearers* (British Isles).

ANGLO-SAXON AND EASTERN EMPIRES (c. 450–1066)

450—Paton Walsh, Jill, *Hengest's Tale* (Germany).

JFIC 500—Sutcliff, Rosemary, *Dawn Wind* (British Isles).

JFIC 558—Dickinson, Peter, *The Dancing Bear* (Constantinople).

J398.0942 655—Crossley-Holland, Kevin, *The Sea Stranger* (British Isles).

J398.0942 657—Crossley-Holland, Kevin, *The Fire-Brother* (British Isles).

FIC/JFIC 675—Westall, Robert, *The Wind Eye* (British Isles).

JFIC 730—Almedingen, E. M., *A Candle at Dusk* (France).

JFIC 780—Treece, Henry, *Viking's Dawn* (Vikings to British Isles).

JFIC 785—Treece, Henry, *The Road to Miklagard* (Vikings to Constantinople).

*790—Carter, Peter, *Madatan* (British Isles).

JFIC 815—Treece, Henry, *Viking's Sunset* (Vikings).

JFIC 870—Hodges, C. Walter, *The Namesake* (England).

JFIC 878—Hodges, C. Walter, *The Marsh King* (England).

JFIC   Trease, Geoffrey, *Escape to King Alfred* (England).

JFIC 950—de Angeli, Marguerite, *Black Fox of Lorne* (Scotland).

JFIC 960—Treece, Henry, *Westward to Vinland* (Vikings to North America).

JFIC 990—Haugaard, Erik, *Hakon of Rogen's Saga* (Vikings).

JFIC 996—Haugaard, Erik, *A Slave's Tale* (Vikings to France).

J398.22 1000—Crossley-Holland, Kevin, *Havelock the Dane* (Denmark to England).

*Sutcliff, Rosemary, *Blood Feud* (Vikings to Constantinople).

JFIC 1034—Treece, Henry, *Swords from the North* (Vikings to Constantinople).

JFIC 1046—de Treviño, Elizabeth, *Casilda of the Rising Moon* (Spain).

JFIC   Treece, Henry, *Man with a Sword* (Vikings to England).

JFIC 1060—Sutcliff, Rosemary, *Knight's Fee* (England).

JFIC 1066—Treece, Henry, *The Last Viking* (England).

JFIC 1070—Sutcliff, Rosemary, *The Shield Ring* (England).

CRUSADES AND THE EAST (1100–1299)

JFIC 1098—Treece, Henry, *Splintered Sword* (England).

JFIC 1100—Sutcliff, Rosemary, *The Witch's Brat* (England).

C/JPB 1170—Paterson, Katherine, *The Sign of the Chrysanthemum* (Japan).

JFIC 1180—Paterson, Katherine, *Of Nightingales that Weep* (Japan).

     *1187—Welch, Ronald, *Knight Crusader* (Jerusalem).

JFIC 1190—Picard, Barbara, *Lost John* (England).

JFIC 1212—Treece, Henry, *Perilous Pilgrimage* (France, Morocco).

JFIC 1225—O'Dell, Scott, *The Road to Damietta* (Italy, Egypt).

     *1250—Baumann, Hans, *Sons of the Steppe* (Mongolia).

JFIC 1265—Trease, Geoffrey, *The Baron's Hostage* (England).

JFIC 1284—Skurzynski, Gloria, *What Happened in Hamelin* (Germany).

JFIC 1290—Trease, Geoffrey, *The Red Towers of Granada* (England, Spain).

JFIC 1294—Vining, Elizabeth Gray, *Adam of the Road* (England).

FOURTEENTH AND FIFTEENTH CENTURIES (1300–1499)

JFIC 1315—Picard, Barbara, *Ransom for a Knight* (England).

JFIC 1318—Picard, Barbara, *One Is One* (England).

JFIC 1326—Welch, Ronald, *The Gauntlet* (England).

JFIC 1327—de Angeli, Marguerite, *The Door in the Wall* (England).

JFIC 1340—Welch, Ronald, *Bowman of Crécy* (England, France).

JFIC 1346—Treece, Henry, *Ride to Danger* (England).

JFIC 1380—Chute, Marchette, *The Innocent Wayfaring* (England).

JFIC 1381—Trease, Geoffrey, *Bows against the Barons* (England).

JFIC 1382—Skurzynski, Gloria, *Manwolf* (Poland).

     *1400—Trease, Geoffrey, *Bent Is the Bow* (England).

     JFIC   Trease, Geoffrey, *The Secret Fiord* (England, Norway).

JFIC 1406—Haugaard, Erik, *Leif the Unlucky* (Greenland).

     *1415—Harnett, Cynthia, *The Sign of the Green Falcon* (England).

FIC 1439—Harnett, Cynthia, *The Writing on the Hearth* (England).

JFIC 1440—Baumann, Hans, *The Barque of Brothers* (Portugal, Africa).

     *1445—Paton Walsh, Jill, *The Emperor's Winding Sheet* (Constantinople).

C/JNC 1461—Kelly, Eric, *The Trumpeter of Krakow* (Poland).

     *1475—Trease, Geoffrey, *Horsemen on the Hills* (Italy).

JFIC 1478—Willard, Barbara, *The Miller's Boy* (England).

JFIC 1482—Harnett, Cynthia, *Caxton's Challenge* (England).

JFIC 1485—Willard, Barbara, *The Lark and the Laurel* (England).

JB 1492—Hodges, C. Walter, *Columbus Sails* (Spain).

     *1493—Harnett, Cynthia, *The Merchant's Mark* (England).

SIXTEENTH CENTURY AND ELIZABETH I OF ENGLAND (1500–1603)

     *1500—Trease, Geoffrey, *The Seas of Morning* (England; Rhodes, Greece).

     *1502—Baumann, Hans, *Son of Columbus* (Spain, New World).

JFIC 1506—O'Dell, Scott, *The Captive* (New World).

JFIC Willard, Barbara, *The Sprig of Broom* (England).

JFIC 1509—Trease, Geoffrey, *Shadow of the Hawk* (England, Italy).

JFIC 1510—O'Dell, Scott, *The Feathered Serpent* (New World).

JFIC 1518—Baker, Betty, *The Blood of the Brave* (New World).

JFIC 1524—O'Dell, Scott, *The Hawk That Dare Not Fly by Day* (England, Belgium).

JFIC 1527—Baker, Betty, *Walk the World's Rim* (New World).

JFIC 1530—O'Dell, Scott, *The Amethyst Ring* (New World).

▪ 1534—Willard, Barbara, *The Eldest Son* (England).

JFIC 1535—Sutcliff, Rosemary, *The Armourer's House* (England).

JFIC 1538—Willard, Barbara, *A Cold Wind Blowing* (England).

▪ 1540—Baker, Betty, *A Stranger and Afraid* (Native Americans).

JFIC 1541—O'Dell, Scott, *The King's Fifth* (New World).

JFIC 1550—Haugaard, Erik, *The Samurai's Tale* (Japan).

JFIC 1555—Harnett, Cynthia, *Stars of Fortune* (England).

JFIC 1558—Pope, Elizabeth Marie, *The Perilous Gard* (England).

JFI C 1570—Willard, Barbara, *The Iron Lily* (England).

JFIC 1580—Bartos-Höppner, B., *The Cossacks* (Russia).

JFIC Sutcliff, Rosemary, *The Queen Elizabeth Story* (England).

JFIC 1584—Welch, Ronald, *The Hawk* (England).

▪ 1587—Wibberley, Leonard, *The King's Beard* (England).

▪ 1588—Willard, Barbara, *A Flight of Swans* (England).

JFIC 1589—Hunter, Mollie, *The Spanish Letters* (Scotland).

▪ 1590—Trease, Geoffrey, *Cue for Treason* (England).

JFIC Hunter, Mollie, *The 13th Member* (Scotland).

JFIC 1595—Sutcliff, Rosemary, *Brother Dusty Feet* (England).

JFIC Beatty, John and Patricia, *Master Rosalind* (England).

JFIC 1596—Chute, Marchette, *The Wonderful Winter* (England).

▪ Vining, Elizabeth Gray, *I Will Adventure* (England).

JFIC 1598—Bartos-Höppner, B., *Save the Khan* (Russia, Mongolia).

JFIC 1599—Beatty, John and Patricia, *The Queen's Wizard* (England).

JFIC 1601—Beatty, John and Patricia, *Holdfast* (England).

EARLY SEVENTEENTH CENTURY (1603–1630)

JFIC 1610—Haugaard, Erik, *The Untold Tale* (Denmark).

JFIC 1620—Clapp, Patricia, *Constance* (American colonies).

JNC/JFIC 1630—de Treviño, Elizabeth, *I, Juan de Pareja* (Spain).

▪ de Treviño, Elizabeth, *Nacar* (New World, Spain).

ENGLISH CIVIL WAR AND CROMWELL (1635–1660)

JFIC 1638—Beatty, John and Patricia, *Witch Dog* (England).

1640—Sutcliff, Rosemary, *Simon* (England).

JFIC Willard, Barbara, *Harrow and Harvest* (England).

JFIC 1641—Haugaard, Erik, *A Messenger for Parliament* (England).

Trease, Geoffrey, *When the Drums Beat* (England).

FIC 1642—Welch, Ronald, *For the King* (England).

JFIC 1643—Haugaard, Erik, *Cromwell's Boy* (England).

JFIC 1646—Burton, Hester, *Kate Ryder* (England).

JFIC 1647—Westall, Robert, *The Devil on the Road* (England).

FIC 1649—Beatty, John and Patricia, *King's Knight's Pawn* (England).

1651—Beatty, John and Patricia, *Campion Towers* (American colonies, England).

FIC 1655—Burton, Hester, *Beyond the Weir Bridge* (England).

LATE SEVENTEENTH CENTURY (1660–1699)

J FIC 1665—Paton Walsh, Jill, *A Parcel of Patterns* (England).

1666—Burton, Hester, *Through the Fire* (England).

JFIC McGraw, Eloise, *Master Cornhill* (England).

JFIC 1667—Beatty, John and Patricia, *Pirate Royal* (American colonies, England).

Trease, Geoffrey, *The Dutch Are Coming* (England).

1670—Wibberley, Leonard, *Deadmen's Cave* (Caribbean).

1682—Carter, Peter, *Children of the Book* (Vienna, Austria).

JFIC 1686—Trease, Geoffrey, *Trumpets in the West* (England).

JFIC 1687—Speare, Elizabeth, *The Witch of Blackbird Pond* (American colonies).

JFIC 1689—Sutcliff, Rosemary, *Bonnie Dundee* (Scotland).

JFIC 1690—Harnett, Cynthia, *The Great House* (England).

JFIC 1692—Clapp, Patricia, *Witches' Children* (American colonies).

JFIC Hunter, Mollie, *The Ghosts of Glencoe* (Scotland).

EARLY EIGHTEENTH CENTURY (1700–1773)

1700—de Angeli, Marguerite, *Skippack School* (American colonies).

Trease, Geoffrey, *A Voice in the Night* (England)

1703—Welch, Ronald, *Captain of Dragoons* (England, France).

JFIC 1707—Dalgliesh, Alice, *The Courage of Sarah Noble* (American colonies).

JFIC 1714—Edmonds, Walter, *They Had a Horse* (American colonies).

JFIC Trease, Geoffrey, *The Silken Secret* (England).

1716—Steele, William O., *Tomahawk Border* (American Frontier).

JFIC 1736—Hunter, Mollie, *The Lothian Run* (Scotland).

1739—Almedingen, E. M., *The Crimson Oak* (Russia).

JFIC 1740—Garfield, Leon, *The Boy and the Monkey* (England).

JFIC 1741—Field, Rachel, *Calico Bush* (American colonies).

JFIC 1742—Almedingen, E. M., *Young Mark* (Russia).

JFIC 1745—Calvert, Patricia, *Hadder MacColl* (Scotland).

• 1746—Beatty, John and Patricia, *The Royal Dirk* (Scotland).

JFIC Picard, Barbara, *The Young Pretenders* (Scotland).

JFIC 1749—Garfield, Leon, *Black Jack* (England).

JFIC 1750—Garfield, Leon, *Devil-in-the-Fog* (England).

JFIC Garfield, Leon, *The Drummer Boy* (France, England).

JFIC Garfield, Leon, *Smith* (England).

JFIC 1752—Beatty, John and Patricia, *At the Seven Stars* (England).

JFIC Steele, William O., *Wayah of the Real People* (Native Americans).

JFIC 1754—Speare, Elizabeth, *Calico Captive* (American colonies, Canada).

JNC/JFIC 1757—Edmonds, Walter, *The Matchlock Gun* (American frontier).

JFIC 1759—Welch, Ronald, *Mohawk Valley* (England, American colonies).

JFIC 1760—Garfield, Leon, *Footsteps* (England).

JFIC Garfield, Leon, *Jack Holburn* (England).

• 1765—Garfield, Leon, *The Confidence Man* (Germany, England, colonies).

• 1766—Trease, Geoffrey, *The Chocolate Boy* (England).

JFIC 1767—Avi, *Night Journeys* (American colonies).

JFIC 1768—Avi, *Encounter at Easton* (American colonies).

JFIC Speare, Elizabeth, *The Sign of the Beaver* (American frontier).

• 1769—Garfield, Leon, *The Sound of Coaches* (England).

JFIC Wibberley, Leonard, *John Treegate's Musket* (American colonies).

JFIC 1772—O'Dell, Scott, *The Treasure of Topó-el-Bampo* (Mexico).

AMERICAN REVOLUTION AND INDEPENDENCE (1774–1781)

Fic/JFic 1774—Forbes, Esther, *Johnny Tremain* (American colonies).

JFIC 1775—Collier, Christopher and James, *My Brother Sam Is Dead* (American colonies).

JFic Forman, James, *The Cow Neck Rebels* (American colonies).

JFic Steele, William O., *Tomahawks and Trouble* (American frontier).

JFic Steele, William O., *Trail through Danger* (American frontier).

JFic Wibberley, Leonard, *Peter Treegate's War* (American colonies).

• 1776—Clapp, Patricia, *I'm Deborah Sampson* (United States).

JFic O'Dell, Scott, *Sarah Bishop* (United States).

JFic 1777—Edmonds, Walter, *Wilderness Clearing* (American frontier).

JFic Steele, William O., *The Year of the Bloody Sevens* (American frontier).

JFic Wibberley, Leonard, *Sea Captain from Salem* (France, England).

Fic 1778—Avi, *The Fighting Ground* (United States).

JFic 1779—Haugaard, Erik, *A Boy's Will* (England).

JFic Pope, Elizabeth Marie, *The Sherwood Ring* (United States).

Fic 1780—Beatty, John and Patricia, *Who Comes to King's Mountain?* (United States).

JFic Caudill, Rebecca, *The Far-off Land* (American frontier).

JFic Caudill, Rebecca, *Tree of Freedom* (American frontier).

JFic Steele, William O., *Winter Danger* (American frontier).

JFic Wibberley, Leonard, *Treegate's Raiders* (United States).

Fic 1781—Collier, Christopher and James, *War Comes to Willy Freeman* (black Americans).

JFic Dalgliesh, Alice, *Adam and the Golden Cock* (United States).

• Hickman, Janet, *The Valley of the Shadow* (American frontier).

LATER EIGHTEENTH CENTURY (1782–1799)

JFic 1782—Collier, Christopher and James, *The Bloody Country* (United States).

JFic Steele, William O., *Buffalo Knife* (American frontier).

JFic Steele, William O., *The Man with the Silver Eyes* (Native Americans).

JFic Steele, William O., *Wilderness Journey* (American frontier).

Fic 1783—Almedingen, E. M., *Anna* (Russia).

⟩ Avi, *Captain Grey* (United States).

Fic 1784—Steele, William O., *Flaming Arrows* (American frontier).

JFic 1785—Collier, Christopher and James, *Who is Carrie?* (black Americans).

JFic Harris, Christie, *Raven's Cry* (Alaska natives).

JFic Paterson, Katherine, *The Master Puppeteer* (Japan).

•1786—Burton, Hester, *To Ravensrigg* (England).

JFic Collier, Christopher and James, *The Winter Hero* (United States).

JFic 1787—Collier, Christopher and James, *Jump Ship to Freedom* (black Americans).

JFic 1788—Burton, Hester, *The Rebel* (England).

JFic 1790—Cameron, Eleanor, *The Court of the Stone Children* (United States, France).

JFic Garfield, Leon, *The Night of the Comet* (England).

JFic Garfield, Leon, *The Strange Affair of Adelaide Harris* (England).

JFic Trease, Geoffrey, *Victory at Valmy* (France).

JFic 1791—Steele, William O., *The Far Frontier* (American frontier).

JFic Welch, Ronald, *Escape from France* (England, France).

JFic Wibberley, Leonard, *The Secret of the Hawk* (England, Africa).

JFic 1793—Burton, Hester, *Riders of the Storm* (England).

Fic/JFic Fleischman, Paul, *Path of the Pale Horse* (United States).

• 1796—Carter, Peter, *The Gates of Paradise* (England).

EARLY NINETEENTH CENTURY (1800–1860)

1801—Burton, Hester, *Time of Trial* (England).

1805—Burton, Hester, *Castors Away!* (England).

1807—Wibberley, Leonard, *Leopard's Prey* (United States).

•1808—Welch, Ronald, *Captain of Foot* (England, Spain).

•1810—Brink, Carol Ryrie, *Lad with a Whistle* (Scotland).

Steele, William O., *The Lone Hunt* (American frontier).

1811—Wibberley, Leonard, *Red Pawns* (American Frontier).

1812—Wibberley, Leonard, *The Last Battle* (United States).

1818—Peyton, K. M., *The Right-Hand Man* (England).

1819—Carter, Peter, *The Black Lamp* (England).

•Dalgliesh, Alice, *The Little Angel* (Brazil).

1829—Burton, Hester, *No Beat of Drum* (England, Australia).

1830—Blos, Joan, *A Gathering of Days* (United States).

•1833—Paton Walsh, Jill, *A Chance Child* (England).

•1834—Bartos-Höppner, B., *Storm over the Caucasus* (Russia).

1835—O'Dell, Scott, *Island of the Blue Dolphins* (Native Americans).

1836—Almedingen, E. M., *Katia* (Russia).

1837—Blos, Joan, *Brothers of the Heart* (Native Americans).

Vining, Elizabeth Gray, *The Taken Girl* (United States).

1837—Blos, Joan, *Brothers of the Heart* (Native Americans).

1839—Yep, Lawrence, *The Serpent's Children* (China).

•1840—Carter, Peter, *The Sentinels* (England, Africa).

Fox, Paula, *The Slave Dancer* (United States, Africa).

1842—Beatty, Patricia, *The Bad Bell of San Salvador* (Native Americans).

1844—McGraw, Eloise, *Moccasin Trail* (American frontier).

1846—Baker, Betty, *The Dunderhead War* (United States).

•Forman, James, *So Ends This Day* (United States).

•O'Dell, Scott, *Carlota* (Mexico).

1849—Lasky, Kathryn, *Beyond the Divide* (American frontier).

Trease, Geoffrey, *Follow My Black Plume* (Italy).

1850—Baker, Betty, *Killer-of-Death* (Native Americans).

de Angeli, Marguerite, *Thee Hannah!* (United States).

MacLachlan, Patricia, *Sarah Plain and Tall* (United States).

Paterson, Katherine, *Rebels of the Heavenly Kingdom* (Japan).

Steele, William O., *The War Party* (Native Americans).

1851—Beatty, Patricia, *Jonathan Down Under* (Australia).

•1852—de Angeli, Marguerite, *Whistle for the Crossing* (United States).

1853—Hurmence, Belinda, *A Girl Called Boy* (black Americans).

Welch, Ronald, *Nicholas Carey* (England, Varna).

Wibberley, Leonard, *Kevin O'Connor and the Light Brigade* (Ireland, Varna).

1854—Harris, Christie, *Forbidden Frontier* (Canadian frontier).

Hunter, Mollie, *A Pistol in Greenyards* (Scotland).

1858—Baker, Betty, *And One Was a Wooden Indian* (Native Americans).

Baker, Betty, *Do Not Annoy the Indians* (American frontier).

1860—Harris, Christie, *Cariboo Trail* (Canadian frontier).

O'Dell, Scott, *The Dark Canoe* (United States).

Trease, Geoffrey, *A Thousand for Sicily* (Italy).

AMERICAN CIVIL WAR (1861–1865)

1861—Beatty, Patricia, *Blue Stars Watching* (United States).

Beatty, Patricia, *Wait for Me, Watch for Me, Eula Bee* (United States).

Hunt, Irene, *Across Five Aprils* (United States).

Keith, Harold, *Rifles for Watie* (United States).

1862—Hickman, Janet, *Zoar Blue* (United States).

O'Dell, Scott, *The 290* (England, the Atlantic).

1863—Clapp, Patricia, *The Tamarack Tree* (United States).

Harris, Christie, *West with the White Chiefs* (Canadian frontier).

Haugaard, Erik, *Orphans of the Wind* (England, United States).

O'Dell, Scott, *Sing Down the Moon* (United States).

Steele, William O., *The Perilous Road* (United States).

1864—Beatty, Patricia, *Turn Homeward, Hannalee* (United States).

Brink, Carol Ryrie, *Caddie Woodlawn* (United States).

Hurmence, Belinda, *Tancy* (black Americans).

1865—Wibberley, Leonard, *The Wound of Peter Wayne* (United States).

LATE NINETEENTH CENTURY (1866–1899)

1866—Peyton, K. M., *The Maplin Bird* (England).

Peyton, K. M., *Sea Fever* (England).

1867—Keith, Harold, *Komantcia* (Native Americans).

1869—Uchida, Yoshiko, *Samurai of Gold Hill* (Japan, United States).

1870—O'Dell, Scott, *Zia* (United States).

1874—Beatty, Patricia, *Just Some Weeds from the Wilderness* (United States).

1875—Avi, *Emily Upham's Revenge* (United States).

Beatty, Patricia, *Something to Shout About* (United States).

Rees, David, *Landslip* (England).

*1876—Forman, James, *The Life and Death of Yellow Bird* (Native Americans).

JFIC 1879—Beatty, Patricia, *A Long Way to Whiskey Creek* (United States).

    *Welch, Ronald, *Zulu Warrior* (England, Africa).

*1880—Peyton, K. M., *Dear Fred* (England).

JFIC 1881—Beatty, Patricia, *How Many Miles to Sundown* (United States).

    JFIC Beatty, Patricia, *Red Rock over the River* (United States).

JFIC 1882—Beatty, Patricia, *By Crumbs, It's Mine!* (United States).

    JFIC Beatty, Patricia, *Me, California Perkins* (United States).

JFIC 1883—Calvert, Patricia, *The Snowbird* (United States).

JFIC 1885—Baker, Betty, *The Spirit is Willing* (United States).

    JFIC Beatty, Patricia, *Bonanza Girl* (United States).

JFIC 1886—Beatty, Patricia, *The Nickel-Plated Beauty* (United States).

JFIC 1887—Beatty, Patricia, *The Queen's own Grove* (United States).

    JFIC Willard, Barbara, *Hetty* (England).

JFIC 1889—Beatty, Patricia, *That's One Ornery Orphan* (United States).

    *1890—Paton Walsh, Jill, *The Huffler* (England).

    *Baker, Betty, *The Night Spider Case* (United States).

JFIC 1891—Burton, Hester, *The Henchmans at Home* (England).

JFIC 1893—Beatty, Patricia, *Hail Columbia* (United States).

    JFIC Beatty, Patricia, *Lacy Makes a Match* (United States).

    JFIC Beatty, Patricia, *Melinda Takes a Hand* (United States).

    JFIC Beatty, Patricia, *O the Red Rose Tree* (United States).

    *Keith, Harold, *The Obstinate Land* (United States).

JFIC 1894—Zei, Aliki, *The Sound of Dragon's Feet* (Russia).

JFIC 1895—Avery, Gillian, *A Likely Lad* (England).

JFIC 1898—de Angeli, Marguerite, *Fiddlestrings* (United States).

JFIC 1899—Hodges, C. Walter, *The Overland Launch* (England).

EARLY TWENTIETH CENTURY, INCLUDING WORLD WAR I (1900–1919)

JFIC 1900—Dickinson, Peter, *Tulku* (China, Tibet, England).

    JFIC Lasky, Kathryn, *The Night Journey* (Russia, United States).

JFIC 1901—Bawden, Nina, *The Peppermint Pig* (England).

    JFIC de Angeli, Marguerite, *The Lion in the Box* (United States).

JFIC/FIC 1903—Yep, Lawrence, *Dragonwings* (United States).

JFIC 1908—Baker, Betty, *The Great Desert Race* (United States).

    JFIC Brink, Carol Ryrie, *Louly* (United States).

    JFIC Peyton, K. M., *Flambards* (England).

JFIC 1910—Bartos-Höppner, B., *Hunters of Siberia* (Russia).

JFIC Edmonds, Walter, *Bert Breen's Barn* (United States).

JFIC Sebestyen, Ouida, *Words by Heart* (black Americans).

JFIC 1912—Peyton, K. M., *The Edge of the Cloud* (England).

JFIC Skurzynski, Gloria, *The Tempering* (United States).

JFIC 1914—Peyton, K. M., *Thunder in the Sky* (England, France).

• Welch, Ronald, *Tank Commander* (England, France).

JFIC 1916—Beatty, Patricia, *Eight Mules from Monterey* (United States).

JFIC Peyton, K. M., *Flambards in Summer* (England).

JFIC Trease, Geoffrey, *The White Nights of St. Petersburg* (Russia).

JFIC 1918—Peyton, K. M., *Flambards Divided* (England).

BETWEEN THE WORLD WARS, INCLUDING THE DEPRESSION (1919–1936)

JFIC 1920—Holman, Felice, *The Wild Children* (Russia).

JFIC Hunter, Mollie, *A Sound of Chariots* (Scotland).

• 1929—Beatty, Patricia, *Billy Bedamned, Long Gone By* (United States).

JFIC Sebestyen, Ouida, *Far from Home* (United States).

JFIC 1932—Avi, *Shadrach's Crossing* (United States).

JFIC Holman, Felice, *The Murderer* (United States).

JFIC Hunt, Irene, *No Promises in the Wind* (United States).

JFIC Taylor, Mildred, *Song of the Trees* (black Americans).

C/JFIC 1933—Armstrong, William, *Sounder* (black Americans).

JNC/JFIC Taylor, Mildred, *Roll of Thunder, Hear My Cry* (black Americans).

JFIC 1934—Taylor, Mildred, *Let the Circle Be Unbroken* (black Americans).

• 1935—Hunter, Mollie, *The Third Eye* (Scotland).

JFIC Uchida, Yoshiko, *The Best Bad Thing* (United States).

JFIC Uchida, Yoshiko, *A Jar of Dreams* (United States).

JFIC 1936—Uchida, Yoshiko, *The Happiest Ending* (United States).

WORLD WAR II AND AFTERWARD (1937–1960)

JFIC 1937—Haugaard, Erik, *Chase Me, Catch Nobody!* (Germany, Denmark).

JFIC Hunter, Mollie, *Hold On to Love* (Scotland).

• Richter, Hans, *I Was There* (Germany).

JFIC Zei, Aliki, *Wildcat under Glass* (Greece).

• 1938—Forman, James, *The Traitors* (Germany).

JFIC Orgel, Doris, *The Devil in Vienna* (Austria).

JFIC 1939—Forman, James, *The Survivor* (Holland, Germany).

FIC/JFIC Magorian, Michelle, *Good Night, Mr. Tom* (England).

JFIC 1940—Bawden, Nina, *Carrie's War* (England).

JFic Burton, Hester, *In Spite of All Terror* (England).

JFic Paton-Walsh, Jill, *The Dolphin Crossing* (England).

JFic Serrailler, Ian, *The Silver Sword* (Poland).

JFic Zei, Aliki, *Petros' War* (Greece).

JFic 1941—Forman, James, *The Skies of Crete* (Greece).

JFic Sommerfelt, Aimée, *Miriam* (Norway).

JFic Uchida, Yoshiko, *Journey to Topaz* (United States).

JFic 1942—Greene, Bette, *Summer of My German Soldier* United States).

JFic Hartman, Evert, *War without Friends* (Germany).

JFic Paton Walsh, Jill, *Fireweed* (England).

Rees, David, *Exeter Blitz* (England).

JFic Richter, Hans, *Friedrich* (Germany).

JFic Westall, Robert, *The Machine Gunners* (England).

1943—Forman, James, *Ceremony of Innocence* (Germany).

JFic Haugaard, Erik, *The Little Fishes* (Italy).

JFic Westall, Robert, *Fathom Five* (England).

JFic 1944—Forman, James, *Horses of Anger* (Germany).

JFic Hickman, Janet, *The Stones* (United States).

JFic Pelgrom, Els, *The Winter When Time Was Frozen* (Holland).

JFic 1945—Forman, James, *My Enemy, My Brother* (Poland, Palestine).

JFic Magorian, Michelle, *Back Home* (England).

JFic Nostlinger, Christine, *Fly Away Home* (Austria).

JNC/JFic Paterson, Katherine, *Jacob Have I Loved* (United States).

JFic Uchida, Yoshiko, *Journey Home* (United States).

JFic 1946—de Treviño, Elizabeth, *Turi's Poppa* (Poland, Italy).

JFic 1947—Forman, James, *Ring the Judas Bell* (Greece).

Fic/JFic 1950—Greene, Bette, *Morning Is a Long Time Coming* (United States, France).

JFic 1952—Holm, Anne, *North to Freedom* (Russia, Europe).

Appendix B
Age Level of Readability

The readability reflects the levels established by the Fry Readability Graph. The ages listed in parentheses after the titles indicate a possible interest level of the content based on a combination of reading interest studies and Lawrence Kohlberg's stages of moral development. Because content appropriate for seventeen-year-olds could appear in a book with a readability level for eight-year-olds, the guide does not suggest upper age levels for either readability or interest. The content of many of the works is quite suitable for and will be of much interest even to adult readers, regardless of the readability level.

READABILITY LEVEL BEGINNING AT SEVEN YEARS

(Beginning interest level in parentheses)

MacLachlan, Patricia, *Sarah Plain and Tall* (8).

Hickman, Janet, *The Stones* (10).

Orgel, Doris, *The Devil in Vienna* (12).

READABILITY LEVEL BEGINNING AT EIGHT YEARS

(Beginning interest level in parentheses)

Dalgiesh, Alice, *Adam and the Golden Cock* (8).

Dalgliesh, Alice, *The Courage of Sarah Noble* (8).

Steele, William O., *The War Party* (8).

Trease, Geoffrey, *The Dutch Are Coming* (9).

de Angeli, Marguerite, *The Lion in the Box* (9).

Steele, William O., *The Lone Hunt* (9).

Baker, Betty, *The Night Spider Case* (9).

Taylor, Mildred, *Song of the Trees* (9).

Trease, Geoffrey, *A Voice in the Night* (9).

Trease, Geoffrey, *When the Drums Beat* (9).

Burton, Hester, *Castors Away* (10).

Garfield, Leon, *Jack Holborn* (10).

Avi, *Shadrach's Crossing* (10).

Zei, Aliki, *The Sound of Dragon's Feet* (10).

Baker, Betty, *The Dunderhead War* (11).

Paton Walsh, Jill, *Fireweed* (11).

Forbes, Esther, *Johnny Tremain* (11).

Haugaard, Erik, *The Little Fishes* (11).

Steele, William O., *The Magic Amulet* (11).

Paterson, Katherine, *The Master Puppeteer* (11).

Hodges, C. Walter, *The Namesake* (11).

Uchida, Yoshiko, *Samurai of Gold Hill* (11).

Edmonds, Walter, *They Had a Horse* (11).

Trease, Geoffrey, *Trumpets in the West* (11).

Forman, James, *Horses of Anger* (12).

Richter, Hans, *I Was There* (12).

Wibberley, Leonard, *The Last Battle* (12).

Westall, Robert, *The Machine Gunners* (12).

Trease, Geoffrey, *The Seas of Morning* (12).

Clapp, Patricia, *The Tamarack Tree* (12).

Sebestyen, Ouida, *Far from Home* (13).

Westall, Robert, *Fathom Five* (13).

Burton, Hester, *Kate Ryder* (13).

Sommerfelt, Aimée, *Miriam* (13).

Peyton, K. M., *Sea Fever* (13).

Burton, Hester, *To Ravensrigg* (13).

Edmonds, Walter, *Wilderness Clearing* (13).

Wibberley, Leonard, *The Wound of Peter Wayne* (13).

O'Dell, Scott, *Sarah Bishop* (14).

READABILITY LEVEL BEGINNING AT NINE YEARS

(Beginning interest level in parentheses)

Steele, William O., *Buffalo Knife* (9).

Trease, Geoffrey, *The Chocolate Boy* (9).

Avi, *Emily Upham's Revenge* (9).

Richter, Hans, *Friedrich* (9).

Beatty, John and Patricia, *Holdfast* (9).

Steele, William O., *The Man with the Silver Eyes* (9).

Beatty, Patricia, *The Nickel-Plated Beauty* (9).

Beatty, Patricia, *That's One Ornery Orphan* (9).

de Angeli, Marguerite, *Thee, Hannah!* (9).

Burton, Hester, *Through the Fire* (9).

de Angeli, Marguerite, *Whistle for the Crossing* (9).

Steele, William O., *Wilderness Journey* (9).

Beatty, Patricia, *Billy Bedamned, Long Gone By* (10).

de Angeli, Marguerite, *Fiddlestrings* (10).

Uchida, Yoshiko, *The Happiest Ending* (10).

Vining, Elizabeth Gray, *I Will Adventure* (10).

Collier, Christopher and James, *My Brother Sam Is Dead* (10).

Speare, Elizabeth George, *The Sign of the Beaver* (10).

Steele, William O., *Tomahawks and Trouble* (10).

Steele, William O., *Trail through Danger* (10).

Trease, Geoffrey, *Victory at Valmy* (10).

Beatty, Patricia, *Wait for Me, Watch for Me, Eula Bee* (10).

Steele, William O., *Wayah of the Real People* (10).

Sebestyen, Ouida, *Words by Heart* (10).

Harris, Christie, *Cariboo Trail* (11).

Collier, Christopher and James, *Carrie's War* (11).

Baker, Betty, *Do Not Annoy the Indians* (11).

Avi, *Encounter at Easton* (11).

Trease, Geoffrey, *Escape to King Alfred* (11).

Avi, *The Fighting Ground* (11).

Crossley-Holland, Kevin, *The Fire-Brother* (11).

Garfield, Leon, *Footsteps* (11).

Welch, Ronald, *The Gauntlet* (11).

Rees, David, *Landslip* (11).

Avery, Gillian, *A Likely Lad* (11).

Garfield, Leon, *The Night of the Comet* (11).

Crossley-Holland, Kevin, *The Sea Stranger* (11).

Serrailler, Ian, *The Silver Sword* (11).

Fox, Paula, *The Slave Dancer* (11).

Hartman, Evert, *War without Friends* (11).

Trease, Geoffrey, *Web of Traitors* (11).

Harris, Christie, *West with the White Chiefs* (11).

Skurzynski, Gloria, *What Happened in Hamelin* (11).

Trease, Geoffrey, *The White Nights of St. Petersburg* (11).

Almedingen, E. M., *Young Mark* (11).

O'Dell, Scott, *Zia* (11).

Almedingen, E.M., *Anna* (12).

Collier, Christopher and James, *The Bloody Country* (12).

Speare, Elizabeth George, *The Bronze Bow* (12).

Garfield, Leon, *The Drummer Boy* (12).

McGraw, Eloise, *The Golden Goblet* (12).

Magorian, Michelle, *Good Night, Mr. Tom* (12).

O'Dell, Scott, *The King's Fifth* (12).

Holman, Felice, *The Murderer* (12).

O'Dell, Scott, *Sing Down the Moon* (12).

Baker, Betty, *Walk the World's Rim* (12).

Collier, Christopher and James, *The Winter Hero* (12).

Hickman, Janet, *Zoar Blue* (12).

Magorian, Michelle, *Back Home* (13).

Sutcliff, Rosemary, *Blood Feud* (13).

Blos, Joan, *Brothers of the Heart* (13).

Welch, Ronald, *Captain of the Dragoons* (13).

Carter, Peter, *The Gates of Paradise* (13).

Baker, Betty, *Killer-of-Death* (13).

Welch, Ronald, *Knight Crusader* (13).

Hodges, C. Walter, *The Marsh King* (13).

Welch, Ronald, *Mohawk Valley* (13).

Hunt, Irene, *No Promises in the Wind* (13).

Fleischman, Paul, *Path of the Pale Horse* (13).

Haugaard, Erik, *The Rider and his Horse* (13).

Baker, Betty, *The Spirit Is Willing* (13).

Burton, Hester, *No Beat of Drum* (14).

Forman, James, *Ring the Judas Bell* (14).

Paterson, Katherine, *The Sign of the Chrysanthemum* (14).

Forman, James, *Ceremony of Innocence* (15).

Carter, Peter, *Children of the Book* (15).

Willard, Barbara, *A Cold Wind Blowing* (15).

Clapp, Patricia, *Constance* (15).

Willard, Barbara, *A Flight of Swans* (15).

Peyton, K.M., *Dear Fred* (17).

READABILITY LEVEL BEGINNING AT TEN YEARS

(Beginning interest level in parentheses)

Trease, Geoffrey, *Bent Is the Bow* (10).

Garfield, Leon, *The Boy and the Monkey* (10).

Steele, William O., *The Far Frontier* (10).

Steele, William O., *Flaming Arrows* (10).

Nostlinger, Christine, *Fly Away Home* (10).

Willard, Barbara, *Hetty* (10).

Beatty, Patricia, *Jonathan Down Under* (10).

Uchida, Yoshiko, *Journey to Topaz* (10).

Beatty, Patricia, *Lacy Makes a Match* (10).

Dalgliesh, Alice, *The Little Angel* (10).

Beatty, Patricia, *A Long Way to Whiskey Creek* (10).

de Treviño, Elizabeth, *Nacar* (10).

Avi, *Night Journeys* (10).

Zei, Aliki, *Petros' War* (10).

Beatty, Patricia, *The Queen's Own Grove* (10).

Trease, Geoffrey, *The Red Towers of Granada* (10).

Trease, Geoffrey, *A Ship to Rome* (10).

de Angeli, Marguerite, *Skippack School* (10).

Armstrong, William, *Sounder* (10).

O'Dell, Scott, *The Treasure of Topo-el-Bampo* (10).

Steele, William O., *Winter Danger* (10).

Steele, William O., *The Year of the Bloody Sevens* (10).

Edmonds, Walter, *Bert Breen's Barn* (11).

Trease, Geoffrey, *Bows against the Barons* (11).

Hodges, C. Walter, *Columbus Sails* (11).

Beatty, John and Patricia, *A Donkey for the King* (11).

Yep, Lawrence, *Dragonwings* (11).

Harnett, Cynthia, *The Great House* (11).

Bartos-Höppner, B., *Hunters of Siberia* (11).

Collier, Christopher and James, *Jump Ship to Freedom* (11).

Brink, Carol Ryrie, *Lad with a Whistle* (11).

Brink, Carol Ryrie, *Louly* (11).

Paton Walsh, Jill, *Persian Gold* (11).

Beatty, John and Patricia, *The Royal Dirk* (11).

Beatty, Patricia, *Something to Shout About* (11).

Paton Walsh, Jill, *The Walls of Athens* (11).

Sutcliff, Rosemary, *Warrior Scarlet* (11).

Beatty, John and Patricia, *Who Comes to King's Mountain?* (11).

Zei, Aliki, *Wildcat under Glass* (11).

de Angeli, Marguerite, *Black Fox of Lorne* (12).

Baker, Betty, *The Blood of the Brave* (12).

Speare, Elizabeth George, *Calico Captive* (12).

Treece, Henry, *The Dream-Time* (12).

Beatty, Patricia, *Eight Mules from Monterey* (12).

Haugaard, Erik, *Hakon of Rogen's Saga* (12).

McGraw, Eloise, *Moccasin Trail* (12).

Burton, Hester, *The Rebel* (12).

Wibberley, Leonard, *Red Pawns* (12).

Harnett, Cynthia, *Stars of Fortune* (12).

Baker, Betty, *A Stranger and Afraid* (12).

O'Dell, Scott, *The 290* (12).

Westall, Robert, *The Wind Eye* (12).

Baker, Betty, *And One Was a Wooden Indian* (13).

Paton Walsh, Jill, *A Chance Child* (13).

Paton Walsh, Jill, *The Dolphin Crossing* (13).

Trease, Geoffrey, *Escape from France* (13).

Caudill, Rebecca, *The Far-off Land* (13).

Trease, Geoffrey, *Follow My Black Plume* (13).

Welch, Ronald, *For the King* (13).

Willard, Barbara, *The Lark and the Laurel* (13).

Taylor, Mildred, *Let the Circle Be Unbroken* (13).

McGraw, Eloise, *Mara, Daughter of the Nile* (13).

Beatty, John and Patricia, *Pirate Royal* (13).

Haugaard, Erik, *A Slave's Tale* (13).

Haugaard, Erik, *The Untold Tale* (13).

Welch, Ronald, *Zulu Warrior* (13).

Beatty, John and Patricia, *Campion Towers* (14).

Peyton, K. M., *Flambards* (14).

Willard, Barbara, *Harrow and Harvest* (14).

O'Dell, Scott, *The Hawk That Dare Not Fly by Day* (14).

Forman, James, *The Life and Death of Yellow Bird* (14).

Picard, Barbara, *Lost John* (14).

Peyton, K. M., *The Maplin Bird* (14).

Forman, James, *The Skies of Crete* (14).

Forman, James, *The Cow Neck Rebels* (15).

Westall, Robert, *The Devil on the Road* (15).

Peyton, K. M., *Flambards Divided* (15).

Keith, Harold, *The Obstinate Land* (15).

Forman, James, *The Survivor* (15).

READABILITY LEVEL BEGINNING AT ELEVEN YEARS

(Beginning interest level in parentheses)

Edmonds, Walter, *The Matchlock Gun* (8).

Bawden, Nina, *The Peppermint Pig* (9).

Uchida, Yoshiko, *The Best Bad Thing* (10).

Brink, Carol Ryrie, *Caddie Woodlawn* (10).

Uchida, Yoshiko, *A Jar of Dreams* (10).

Almedingen, E. M., *Katia* (10).

Beatty, Patricia, *Me, California Perkins* (10).

Vining, Elizabeth Gray, *Adam of the Road* (11).

Wibberley, Leonard, *Attar of the Ice Valley* (11).

Trease, Geoffrey, *The Baron's Hostage* (11).

Beatty, Patricia, *Blue Stars Watching* (11).

Beatty, Patricia, *Bonanza Girl* (11).

Haugaard, Erik, *A Boy's Will* (11).

Beatty, Patricia, *By Crumbs, It's Mine!* (11).

Avi, *Captain Grey* (11).

Paton Walsh, Jill, *Crossing to Salamis* (11).

Trease, Geoffrey, *Cue for Treason* (11).

de Angeli, Marguerite, *The Door in the Wall* (11).

Hurmence, Belinda, *A Girl Called Boy* (11).

Beatty, Patricia, *Hail Columbia* (11).

Burton, Hester, *The Henchmans at Home* (11).

Paton Walsh, Jill, *The Huffler* (11).

Baumann, Hans, *I Marched with Hannibal* (11).

O'Dell, Scott, *Island of the Blue Dolphins* (11).

Uchida, Yoshiko, *Journey Home* (11).

Wibberley, Leonard, *Leopard's Prey* (11).

Harnett, Cynthia, *The Merchant's Mark* (11).

Willard, Barbara, *The Miller's Boy* (11).

Lasky, Kathryn, *The Night Journey* (11).

Beatty, Patricia, *O the Red Rose Tree* (11).

Hodges, C. Walter, *The Overland Launch* (11).

Pope, Elizabeth Marie, *The Perilous Gard* (11).

Steele, William O., *The Perilous Road* (11).

Harnett, Cynthia, *The Sign of the Green Falcon* (11).

Greene, Bette, *Summer of My German Soldier* (11).

Steele, William O., *Tomahawk Border* (11).

Beatty, Patricia, *Turn Homeward, Hannalee* (11).

Collier, Christopher and James, *War Comes to Willy Freeman* (11).

Treece, Henry, *Westward to Vinland* (11).

Collier, Christopher and James, *Who Is Carrie?* (11).

Pelgrom, Els, *The Winter When Time Was Frozen* (11).

Beatty, John and Patricia, *Witch Dog* (11).

Speare, Elizabeth, *The Witch of Blackbird Pond* (11).

Chute, Marchette, *The Wonderful Winter* (11).

Picard, Barbara, *The Young Pretenders* (11).

Burton, Hester, *Beyond the Weir Bridge* (12).

Field, Rachel, *Calico Bush* (12).

Harnett, Cynthia, *Caxton's Challenge* (12).

Haugaard, Erik, *Chase Me, Catch Nobody!* (12).

Garfield, Leon, *Devil-in-the-Fog* (12).

Wibberley, Leonard, *John Treegate's Musket* (12).

Treece, Henry, *The Last Viking* (12).

Beatty, John and Patricia, *Master Rosalind* (12).

Holm, Anne, *North to Freedom* (12).

Treece, Henry, *Ride to Danger* (12).

Taylor, Mildred, *Roll of Thunder, Hear My Cry* (12).

Wibberley, Leonard, *Sea Captain from Salem* (12).

Trease, Geoffrey, *The Secret Fiord* (12).

Trease, Geoffrey, *The Silken Secret* (12).

Garfield, Leon, *Smith* (12).

Baumann, Hans, *Son of Columbus* (12).

Treece, Henry, *Swords from the North* (12).

Hunter, Mollie, *The 13th Member* (12).

Wibberley, Leonard, *Treegate's Raiders* (12).

Kelly, Eric, *The Trumpeter of Krakow* (12).

Treece, Henry, *Viking's Dawn* (12).

Baumann, Hans, *The Barque of Brothers* (13).

Welch, Ronald, *Bowman of Crécy* (13).

Welch, Ronald, *Captain of Foot* (13).

Haugaard, Erik, *Cromwell's Boy* (13).

Rees, David, *Exeter Blitz* (13).

Harris, Christie, *Forbidden Frontier* (13).

Hunter, Mollie, *The Ghosts of Glencoe* (13).

Burton, Hester, *In Spite of All Terror* (13).

Chute, Marchette, *The Innocent Wayfaring* (13).

Treece, Henry, *Man with a Sword* (13).

Haugaard, Erik, *A Messenger for Parliament* (13).

Hunter, Mollie, *A Pistol in Greenyards* (13).

Beatty, John and Patricia, *The Queen's Wizard* (13).

Bartos-Höppner, B., *Save the Khan* (13).

Carter, Peter, *The Sentinels* (13).

Calvert, Patricia, *The Snowbird* (13).

Treece, Henry, *The Splintered Sword* (13).

Treese, Geoffrey, *A Thousand for Sicily* (13).

Peyton, K. M., *Thunder in the Sky* (13).

Holman, Felice, *The Wild Children* (13).

O'Dell, Scott, *The Captive* (14).

Garfield Leon, *The Confidence Man* (14).

Peyton, K. M., *Flambards in Summer* (14).

Keith, Harold, *Komantcia* (14).

Carter, Peter, *Madatan* (14).

Treece, Henry, *The Queen's Brooch* (14).

Haugaard, Erik, *The Samurai's Tale* (14).

Forman, James, *So Ends this Day* (14).

Hunter, Mollie, *The Third Eye* (14).

Dickinson, Peter, *Tulku* (14).

Clapp, Patricia, *Witches' Children* (14).

Carter, Peter, *The Black Lamp* (15).

Treece, Henry, *The Centurion* (15).

Peyton, K. M., *The Edge of the Cloud* (15).

Willard, Barbara, *The Eldest Son* (15).

Sutcliff, Rosemary, *Frontier Wolf* (15).

Willard, Barbara, *The Iron Lily* (15).

Greene, Bette, *Morning Is a Long Time Coming* (15).

Paton Walsh, Jill, *A Parcel of Patterns* (15).

Burton, Hester, *Riders of the Storm* (15).

Peyton, K. M., *The Right-Hand Man* (15).

O'Dell, Scott, *The Road to Damietta* (15).

Baumann, Hans, *Sons of the Steppe* (15).

READABILITY LEVEL BEGINNING AT TWELVE YEARS

(Beginning interest level in parentheses)

Beatty, Patricia, *Red Rock over the River* (11).

de Treviño, Elizabeth, *Turi's Poppa* (11).

Beatty, John and Patricia, *At the Seven Stars* (12).

Almedingen, E. M., *A Candle at Dusk* (12).

Almedingen, E. M., *The Crimson Oak* (12).

Paton Walsh, Jill, *The Emperor's Winding Sheet* (12).

Blos, Joan, *A Gathering of Days* (12).

Baker, Betty, *The Great Desert Race* (12).

Calvert, Patricia, *Hadder MacColl* (12).

Trease, Geoffrey, *Horseman on the Hills* (12).

Beatty, Patricia, *How Many Miles to Sundown* (12).

Beatty, Patricia, *Just Some Weeds from the Wilderness* (12).

Wibberley, Leonard, *Kevin O'Connor and the Light Brigade* (12).

Beatty, John and Patricia, *King's Knight's Pawn* (12).

McGraw, Eloise, *Master Cornhill* (12).

Beatty, Patricia, *Melinda Takes a Hand* (12).

Trease, Geoffrey, *Message to Hadrian* (12).

Haugaard, Erik, *Orphans of the Wind* (12).

Treece, Henry, *Perilous Pilgrimage* (12).

Wibberley, Leonard, *Peter Treegate's War* (12).

Picard, Barbara, *Ransom for a Knight* (12).

Treece, Henry, *The Road to Miklagard* (12).

Trease, Geoffrey, *Shadow of the Hawk* (12).

Sutcliff, Rosemary, *The Shield Ring* (12).

Sutcliff, Rosemary, *Sun Horse, Moon Horse* (12).

Caudill, Rebecca, *Tree of Freedom* (12).

Treece, Henry, *War Dog* (12).

O'Dell, Scott, *Carlota* (13).

Sutcliff, Rosemary, *Dawn Wind* (13).

Welch, Ronald, *The Hawk* (13).

Paton Walsh, Jill, *Hengest's Tale* (13).

Haugaard, Erik, *Leif the Unlucky* (13).

Hunter, Mollie, *The Lothian Run* (13).

Sutcliff, Rosemary, *The Mark of the Horse Lord* (13).

Forman, James, *My Enemy, My Brother* (13).

Picard, Barbara, *One Is One* (13).

Pope, Elizabeth Marie, *The Sherwood Ring* (13).

Hunter, Mollie, *The Spanish Letters* (13).

Welch, Ronald, *Tank Commander* (13).

Skurzynski, Gloria, *The Tempering* (13).

Hickman, Janet, *The Valley of the Shadow* (13).

Harnett, Cynthia, *The Writing on the Hearth* (13).

Baker, Betty, *The Bad Bell of San Salvador* (14).

Bartos-Höppner, B., *The Cossacks* (14).

O'Dell, Scott, *The Dark Canoe* (14).

O'Dell, Scott, *The Feathered Serpent* (14).

Clapp, Patricia, *I'm Deborah Sampson* (14).

Harris, Christie, *Raven's Cry* (14).

Keith, Harold, *Rifles for Watie* (14).

Yep, Lawrence, *The Serpent's Children* (14).

Bartos-Höppner, B., *Storm over the Caucasus* (14).

Hurmence, Belinda, *Tancy* (14).

Burton, Hester, *Time of Trial* (14).

Forman, James, *The Traitors* (14).

O'Dell, Scott, *The Amethyst Ring* (15).

Lasky, Kathryn, *Beyond the Divide* (15).

Mitchison, Naomi, *The Conquered* (15).

Hunter, Mollie, *Hold on to Love* (15).

Paterson, Katherine, *Jacob Have I Loved* (15).

Sutcliff, Rosemary, *The Lantern Bearers* (15).

Skurzynski, Gloria, *Manwolf* (15).

Paterson, Katherine, *Rebels of the Heavenly Kingdom* (15).

Sutcliff, Rosemary, *Song for a Dark Queen* (15).

Garfield, Leon, *The Sound of Coaches* (15).

Willard, Barbara, *The Sprig of Broom* (15).

Hunter, Mollie, *The Stronghold* (15).

READABILITY LEVEL BEGINNING AT THIRTEEN YEARS

(Beginning interest level in parentheses)

Sutcliff, Rosemary, *The Armourer's House* (11).

Sutcliff, Rosemary, *Brother Dusty-Feet* (12).

Sutcliff, Rosemary, *The Witch's Brat* (12).

Hunt, Irene, *Across Five Aprils* (13).

Dickinson, Peter, *The Dancing Bear* (13).

Wibberley, Leonard, *Deadmen's Cave* (13).

Crossley-Holland, Kevin, *Havelock the Dane* (13).

de Treviño, Elizabeth, *I, Juan de Pareja* (13).

Wibberley, Leonard, *The King's Beard* (13).

Welch, Ronald, *Nicholas Carey* (13).

Wibberely, Leonard, *The Secret of the Hawk* (13).

Sutcliff, Rosemary, *Simon* (13).

Hunter, Mollie, *A Sound of Chariots* (13).

Garfield, Leon, *The Strange Affair of Adelaide Harris* (13).

Vining, Elizabeth Gray, *The Taken Girl* (13).

Treece, Henry, *Viking's Sunset* (13).

Paterson, Katherine, *Of Nightingales That Weep* (15).

READABILITY LEVEL BEGINNING AT FOURTEEN YEARS

(Beginning interest level in parentheses)

Sutcliff, Rosemary, *The Queen Elizabeth Story* (11).

Garfield, Leon, *Black Jack* (13).

Sutcliff, Rosemary, *Bonnie Dundee* (14).

de Treviño, Elizabeth, *Casilda of the Rising Moon* (14).

Sutcliff, Rosemary, *The Eagle of the Ninth* (14).

Sutcliff, Rosemary, *Outcast* (14).

Sutcliff, Rosemary, *The Silver Branch* (15).

Appendix C
Bibliography on Writing Historical Novels: Works by __ Authors Included in the Guide ____

Avery, Gillian. *Childhood's Pattern: A Study of Heroes and Heroines in Children's Fiction, 1770–1950*. London: Hodder and Stoughton, 1975.

Beatty, John, and Patricia. "Watch Your Language—You're Writing for Young People!" *Horn Book* (February 1965).

Burton, Hester. "The Writing of Historical Fiction." *Horn Book* (June 1969).

Clapp, Patricia. "Making the Past Come Alive." In Donna Norton, *Through the Eyes of a Child*. 2d ed. Columbus, Ohio: Merrill, 1987.

Collier, Christopher. "Criteria for Historical Fiction." *School Library Journal* (August 1982).

———. "Historical Novels in the Classroom." *Connecticut Humanities Council News* (April 1982).

———. "Johnny and Sam: Old and New Approaches to the American Revolution." *Horn Book* (April 1975).

Harnett, Cynthia. "From the Ground Upwards." *Horn Book* (October 1961).

Haugaard, Erik C. "Before I Was Born: History and the Child." *Horn Book* (October-December 1979).

Hickman, Janet. "The How and Why of Historical Literature." *Bulletin of the Children's Literature Assembly* (Spring 1982).

Hodges, C. Walter. "Children? What Children?" In Edward Blishen, *The Thorny Paradise*. London: Kestrel, 1974.

Hunter, Mollie. "Shoulder in the Sky." *New York Public Library Bulletin* (Winter 1976).

McGraw, Eloise. *Techniques of Fiction Writing*. Boston: Writer, Inc., 1959.

O'Dell, Scott. "David." *Psychology Today* (January 1968).

———. "The Tribulations of a Trilogy." *Horn Book* (April 1982).

Paterson, Katherine. "Do I Dare Disturb the Universe?" *Horn Book* (October 1984).

———. *Gates of Excellence: On Reading and Writing Books for Children*. New York: Elsevier/Nelson Books, 1981.

Sutcliff, Rosemary. "Beginning with Beowulf." *Horn Book* (February 1953).

———. *Blue Remembered Hills*. New York: Morrow, 1984.

———. "Combined Ops." In *Only Connect: Readings on Children's Literature*. 2d ed. Edited by Shelia Egoff. New York: Oxford, 1980.

———. "History Is People." In *Children and Literature: Views and Reviews*. Edited by Virginia Haviland. Glenview, Ill.: Scott, Foresman, 1973.

Trease, Geoffrey. "The Historical Novelist at Work." *Children's Literature in Education*
    (March 1972); rpt. *Writers, Critics, and Children*. New York: Agathon, 1976.
————. "The Historical Story: Is It Revelant Today?" *Horn Book* (February 1977).
————. "Old Writers and Young Readers." In *Essays and Studies 1973*. Edited by John
    Lawlor. London: John Murray, 1973.
————. "Problems of the Historical Storyteller." In *Signposts to Criticism of Children's
    Literature*. Chicago: American Library Association, 1983.

Appendix D
Secondary Bibliography on Writers and Historical Novels __ Included in the Guide_____

WORKS ON INDIVIDUALS

Edmonds, Walter D.
Wyld, Lionel D. *Walter D. Edmonds, Storyteller*. Syracuse, N.Y.: Syracuse University Press, 1982.

O'Dell, Scott
Raymond, Allen. "A Visit with Scott O'Dell, Master Storyteller." *Early Years* (March 1984).

Serrailler, Ian
Crouch, Marcus. *The Nesbit Tradition: The Children's Novel In England 1945–1970*. London: Benn, 1972.

Sutcliff, Rosemary
Brown, M. O. "Rosemary Sutcliff." *Ontario Library Review* (May 1958): 84–86.
Colwell, Eileen H. "Rosemary Sutcliff Lantern Bearers." *Horn Book* (June 1960): 200–5.
Corbett, E. V. "Carnegie Medal Goes to Rosemary Sutcliff." *Library Association Record* (May 1960): 159–60.
Keenan, S. V. "Rosemary Sutcliff." *Wilson Library Bulletin* (September 1960): 75.
MacMurray, Susan E. *Rosemary Sutcliff: A Bibliography*. Johannesburg: Department of Bibliography and Librarianship and Topography, University of Witwatersrand, 1972.
Meek, Margaret. *Rosemary Sutcliff*. New York: Walck Monograph, 1962.
"The Search for Selfhood: The Historical Novels of Rosemary Sutcliff." *Times Literary Supplement* June 17, 1965 p. 489.

COLLECTIVE WORKS

Carpenter, Humphrey, and Mari Prichard. *The Oxford Companion to Children's Literature*. New York: Oxford, 1984.
Crouch, Marcus. *The Nesbit Tradition: The Children's Novel in England, 1945–1970*. London: Benn, 1972.
Egoff, Shelia. *Thursday's Child*. Chicago: American Library Association, 1983.

Eyre, Frank. *British Children's Books in the Twentieth Century*. New York: E. P. Dutton, 1971.

Francis, S., and J. L. Hirst. *Time Past: Historical Fiction for Young People*. Chester, England: Chester County Council Library, 1972.

Jones, Cornelia, and Olivia R. Way. *British Children's Authors: Interviews at Home*. Chicago: American Library Association, 1976.

Kirkpatrick, D. L., ed. *Twentieth Century Children's Writers*. 2d ed. New York: St. Martin's Press, 1984.

Rees, David. *The Marble in the Water: Essays on Contemporary Writers of Fiction for Children and Young People*. Boston: Horn Book, 1980.

———. *Painted Desert, Green Shade*. Boston: Horn Book, 1983.

Townsend, John Rowe. *A Sense of Story: Essays on Contemporary Writers for Children*. Philadelphia: Lippincott, 1971.

———. *Written for Children: An Outline of English Children's Literature*. Rev. ed. New York: Lothrop, Lee and Shepard, 1974.

Weiss, M. Jerry, ed. *From Writers to Students: The Pleasures and Pains of Writing*. Newark, Del.: International Reading Association, 1979.

Wintle, Justin, and Emma Fisher, eds. *The Pied Pipers: Interviews with the Influential Creators of Children's Literature*. New York: Paddington Press, 1974.

Index

Across Five Aprils, 165, 166
Adam and the Golden Cock, 92
Adam of the Road, 329, 330
Almedingen, E. M., 5–8
The Amethyst Ring, 219–20
And One Was a Wooden Indian, 21–22
Anna, 5, 7
The Armourer's House, 286
Armstrong, William, 11–12
At the Seven Stars, 35
Attar of the Ice Valley, 347
Avery, Gillian, 13–14
Avi, 14–18

Back Home, 202
The Bad Bell of San Salvador, 37
Baker, Betty, 19–24
The Baron's Hostage, 307–8
The Barque of Brothers, 28, 29
Bartos-Höppner, B., 24–27
Baumann, Hans, 27–29
Bawden, Nina, 29–31
Beatty, John and Patricia, 31–36
Beatty, Patricia, 36–45
Bent is the Bow, 309
Bert Breen's Barn, 107
The Best Bad Thing, 322–23
Beyond the Divide, 191, 192
Beyond the Weir Bridge, 55–56, 60
Billy Bedamned, Long Gone By, 39
Black Fox of Lorne, 94–95
Black Jack, 128, 130
The Black Lamp, 68–69

Blood Feud, 291–92
The Blood of the Brave, 20
The Bloody Country, 82
Blos, Joan, 47–49
Blue Stars Watching, 39
The Bombard. See *Ride to Danger*
Bonanza Girl, 41
Bonnie Dundee, 293
Bostock and Harris; or, The Night of the Comet. See *The Night of the Comet*
Bowman of Crécy, 335
Bows against the Barons, 308–9
The Boy and the Monkey, 125–26
A Boy's Will, 151
Brink, Carol Ryrie, 51–52
The Bronze Bow, 277
The Bronze Sword. See *The Centurion*
Brother Dusty-Feet, 287
Brothers of the Heart, 48, 49
The Buffalo Knife, 282, 284
Burton, Hester, 53–60
The Butty Boy. See *The Huffler*
By Crumbs, It's Mine!, 44

Caddie Woodlawn, 52
Calico Bush, 112–13
Calico Captive, 278
Calvert, Patricia, 62–63
Cameron, Eleanor, 63–65
Campion Towers, 34, 36
A Candle at Dusk, 5, 6
Captain Grey, 16–17, 18
Captain of Dragoons, 336–337

Captain of Foot, 338, 339
The Captive, 218–19
Cariboo Trail, 144
Carlota, 223
Carrie's War, 30–31
Carter, Peter, 66–70
Casilda of the Rising Moon, 98–99, 100
Castors Away!, 56–57
Caudill, Rebecca, 71–72
Caxton's Challenge, 141–42
The Centurion, 313–14
Ceremony of Innocence, 119–20,
    122
A Chance Child, 236, 238
Chase Me, Catch Nobody!, 152
Children of the Book, 67–68
The Children's Crusade. See *Perilous
    Pilgrimage*
The Chocolate Boy, 311
Chute, Marchette, 75–76
Clapp, Patricia, 76–79
A Cold Wind Blowing, 353–54
Collier, Christopher and James,
    79–83
Columbus Sails, 159, 160
The Confidence Man, 129, 130,
    131
The Conquered, 207–8
Constance, 77
The Cossacks, 25
The Courage of Sarah Noble, 91–92
The Court of the Stone Children,
    64–65
The Cow Neck Rebels, 116–17, 122
The Crimson Oak, 5, 6
Cromwell's Boy, 151
Crossing to Salamis, 233–34, 238
Crossley-Holland, Kevin, 86–88
The Crown of Violet. See *Web of Traitors*
Cue for Treason, 309–10

Dalgliesh, Alice, 91–92
The Dancing Bear, 101–2, 103
The Dark Canoe, 221
The Daughter of Don Saturnino. See
    Carlota
David. See *North to Freedom*
Dawn Wind, 291

de Angeli, Marguerite, 94–97
de Treviño, Elizabeth, 97–100
Deadmen's Cave, 348–49, 350
Dear Fred, 243, 245
Devil-in-the-Fog, 129–30
The Devil in Vienna, 225–26
The Devil on the Road, 341, 342
Dickinson, Peter, 101–3
Do Not Annoy the Indians, 22
The Dolphin Crossing, 237
A Donkey for the King, 31–32, 36
The Door in the Wall, 95, 96–97
The Dragonfly Years. See *Hold on to
    Love*
Dragonwings, 360
The Drawbridge Gate. See *The Sign of
    the Green Falcon*
The Dream-Time, 312
The Drummer Boy, 128–29
The Dunderhead War, 22–23
The Dutch Are Coming, 310

The Eagle of the Ninth, 288–89,
    293
The Edge of the Cloud, 244, 245
Edmonds, Walter D., 105–7
Eight Mules from Monterey, 41–42
The Eldest Son, 354, 356
Emily Upham's Revenge, 15
The Emperor's Winding Sheet,
    234–35
Encounter at Easton, 17
Escape from France, 337
Escape from Warsaw. See *The Silver
    Sword*
Escape to King Alfred, 307
The Exeter Blitz, 256–57

Far from Home, 267, 268
The Far Frontier, 283
The Far-off Land, 71–72
Fathom Five, 342
The Feathered Serpent, 219
Fiddlestrings, 96
Field, Rachel, 112–13
The Fighting Ground, 16
The Fire-Brother, 87
Fireweed, 237

Flambards, 243–44, 245
Flambards Divided, 244–45
Flambards in Summer, 244
Flaming Arrows, 282–83
Fleischman, Paul, 114
A Flight of Swans, 355–56
Fly Away Home, 214–15
Follow My Black Plume, 305–6
Footsteps, 127–28, 130
For the King, 336
Forbes, Esther, 115–16
Forbidden Frontier, 145
Forman, James, 116–22
Fox, Paula, 122–23
Friedrich, 258–59
Frontier Wolf, 290

Garfield, Leon, 125–31
The Gates of Paradise, 68
A Gathering of Days, 47–48, 49
The Gauntlet, 334
The Ghosts of Glencoe, 169
A Girl Called Boy, 173
The Golden Goblet, 198–99
*Good Night, Mister Tom. See Good
   Night, Mr. Tom*
Good Night, Mr. Tom, 201–2
The Great House, 142–43
The Great Desert Race, 23–24
Greene, Bette, 133–35

Hadder MacColl, 62–63
Hail Columbia, 41
Hakon of Rogen's Saga, 148–49
*Hakon's Saga. See Hakon of Rogen's
   Saga*
The Happiest Ending, 323
Harnett, Cynthia, 140–43
Harris, Christie, 143–46
Harrow and Harvest, 356
Hartman, Evert, 146–47
Haugaard, Erik, 147–53
Havelock the Dane, 87–88
The Hawk, 335–36
The Hawk That Dare Not Hunt by Day,
   220–21
The Henchmans at Home, 54–55
Hengest's Tale, 235

Hetty, 356
Hickman, Janet, 155–57
*The Hills of Varna. See Shadow of the
   Hawk*
Hodges, C. Walter, 157–60
Hold On to Love, 171–72
Holdfast, 32–33
Holm, Anne, 160–61
Holman, Felice, 162–63
Horsemen on the Hills, 304
Horses of Anger, 120, 122
How Many Miles to Sundown,
   42–43
The Huffler, 236–37
Hunt, Irene, 165–66
Hunter, Mollie, 166–67
Hunters of Siberia, 26
Hurmence, Belinda, 172–74

I, Juan de Pareja, 99–100
I Marched with Hannibal, 27, 29
I Was There, 259
I Will Adventure, 329–30
I'm Deborah Sampson, 78
In Spite of All Terror, 57
The Innocent Wayfaring, 75
The Iron Lily, 354–55
Island of the Blue Dolphins, 223–24

Jack Holborn, 127, 131
Jacob Have I Loved, 232
A Jar of Dreams, 322
John Diamond. See Footsteps
John Treegate's Musket, 344, 350
Johnny Tremain, 115–16
Jonathan Down Under, 37–38
Journey Home, 323–24
Journey to Topaz, 323
Jump Ship to Freedom, 81–82
Just Some Weeds from the Wilderness,
   43

Kate Rider. See Kate Ryder
Kate Ryder, 56, 60
Katia, 5, 7–8
Keith, Harold, 183–86
Kelly, Eric, 186–87

Kevin O'Connor and the Light Brigade, 349–50
Killer-of-Death, 21
The King's Beard, 347–48
The King's Fifth, 220
King's Knight's Pawn, 33–34
Knight Crusader, 334–35
Knight's Fee, 292
Komantcia, 185, 186

Lacy Makes a Match, 43
Lad with a Whistle, 51
Landslip, 256
The Lantern Bearers, 290–91
The Lark and the Laurel, 352, 356
Lasky, Kathryn, 190–92
The Last Battle, 346–47
The Last of the Vikings. See *The Last Viking*
Leif the Unlucky, 149
Leopard's Prey, 346, 350
Let the Circle Be Unbroken, 297–98
The Life and Death of Yellow Bird, 117–18
A Likely Lad, 14
The Lion in the Box, 96
The Little Angel, 92
The Little Fishes, 152
Little Katia. See *Katia*
The Load of Unicorn. See *Caxton's Challenge*
The Lone Hunt, 283–84
A Long Way to Whiskey Creek, 38
Lost John, 246–47
The Lothian Run, 169–70, 172
Louly, 51

McGraw, Eloise, 197–200
The Machine-Gunners, 341–42
MacLachlan, Patricia, 200–201
Madatan, 67, 70
The Magic Amulet, 280
Magorian, Michelle, 201–2
Man with a Sword, 316
The Man with the Silver Eyes, 281
Manwolf, 273, 274
The Maplin Bird, 242

Mara, Daughter of the Nile, 198, 200
The Mark of the Horse Lord, 289–90, 293
The Marsh King, 158–59, 160
Master Cornhill, 199
The Master Puppeteer, 231
Master Rosalind, 32
The Matchlock Gun, 106
Me, California Perkins, 40–41
Melinda Takes a Hand, 43–44
The Merchant's Mark, 142
Message to Hadrian, 307
A Messenger for Parliament, 150–51, 153
The Miller's Boy, 352
Miriam, 275
Mist over Athelney. See *Escape to King Alfred*
Mitchison, Naomi, 207–8
Moccasin Trail, 199
Mohawk Valley, 337
Morning Is a Long Time Coming, 134
The Murderer, 163
My Brother Sam Is Dead, 80
My Enemy, My Brother, 121–22

Nacar, The White Deer, 99
The Namesake, 158, 160
Nicholas and the Wool-Pack. See *The Merchant's Mark*
Nicholas Carey, 338
The Nickel-Plated Beauty, 43
The Night Journey, 192
Night Journeys, 17
The Night of the Comet, 126, 130–31
The Night Spider Case, 23
No Beat of Drum, 59–60
No Promises in the Wind, 165–66
North to Freedom, 160–61
Nostlinger, Christine, 214–15

O the Red Rose Tree, 43
O'Dell, Scott, 217–25
The Obstinate Land, 185–86

Of Nightingales That Weep, 230, 233

One Is One, 247, 248

Orgel, Doris, 225–26

Orphans of the Wind, 151–52

Outcast, 289

The Overland Launch, 159–60

A Parcel of Patterns, 235–36

Paterson, Katherine, 230–33

Path of the Pale Horse, 114

Paton Walsh, Jill, 233–38

Pelgrom, Els, 239

The Peppermint Pig, 30

The Perilous Gard, 249–50

Perilous Pilgrimage, 317–18

The Perilous Road, 284

Persian Gold, 234

Peter Treegate's War, 344–45, 350

Petros' War, 364

Peyton, K. M., 241–45

Picard, Barbara Leonie, 246–48

Pirate Royal, 34

A Pistol in Greenyards, 170

Pope, Elizabeth Marie, 249–51

The Queen Elizabeth Story, 286

The Queen's Brooch, 313

The Queen's Own Grove, 40

The Queen's Wizard, 32

Ransom for a Knight, 247, 248

Raven's Cry, 144–45, 146

The Rebel, 58

Rebels of the Heavenly Kingdom, 231–32, 233

Red Pawns, 346, 350

Red Rock over the River, 44

The Red Towers of Granada, 308, 311

Rees, David, 256–57

Richter, Hans, 258–59

Ride to Danger, 318

The Rider and His Horse, 148

Riders of the Storm, 58–59

Rifles for Watie, 184–85, 186

The Right-Hand Man, 241–42

Ring Out the Bow Bells. See *The Sign of the Green Falcon*

Ring the Judas Bell, 118–19

The Road to Damietta, 222

The Road to Miklagard, 314–15

Roll of Thunder, Hear My Cry, 296–97

The Royal Dirk, 34–35

Samurai of Gold Hill, 321–22

The Samurai's Tale, 149–50

Sarah Bishop, 222–23

Sarah, Plain and Tall, 200–201

Save the Khan, 25

Sea Captain from Salem, 345

Sea Fever, 242–43

The Sea Stranger, 87

The Seas of Morning, 304

Sebestyen, Ouida, 266–68

The Secret Fiord, 309

The Secret of the Hawk, 349

The Sentinels, 69

The Serpent's Children, 360

Serraillier, Ian, 268–69

Shadow of the Hawk, 304–5

Shadrach's Crossing, 15–16

The Sherwood Ring, 250, 251

The Shield Ring, 292, 293

A Ship to Rome, 303–4

The Sign of the Beaver, 278–79

The Sign of the Chrysanthemum, 231, 233

The Sign of the Green Falcon, 140–41

The Silken Secret, 310–11

The Silver Branch, 290

The Silver Sword, 268–69

Simon, 293

Sing Down the Moon, 224

The Skies of Crete, 118

Skippack School, 95–96

Skurzynski, Gloria, 272–74

The Slave Dancer, 122–23

A Slave's Tale, 149

Smith, 126–27

The Snowbird, 63

So Ends This Day, 117

Something to Shout About, 40

Sommerfelt, Aimée, 275
Son of Columbus, 28–29
Song of the Trees, 296
Song for a Dark Queen, 288
Sons of the Steppe, 27–28, 29
A Sound of Chariots, 171, 172
The Sound of Coaches, 130
The Sound of Dragon's Feet,
    363–64
Sounder, 11–12
The Spanish Letters, 168
Speare, Elizabeth George, 276–79
The Spirit Is Willing, 23
Splintered Sword, 317, 318
The Sprig of Broom, 353, 357
Stars of Fortune, 142
Steele, William O., 279–84
The Stones, 157
Storm Over the Caucasus, 25–26
The Strange Affair of Adelaide Harris,
    126, 131
A Stranger and Afraid, 21
The Stronghold, 167–68
Summer of My German Soldier,
    134
Sun Horse, Moon Horse, 288
The Survivor, 121
Sutcliff, Rosemary, 285–94
Swords from the North, 315–16,
    318

The Taken Girl, 330
The Tamarack Tree, 78–79
Tancy, 173–74
Tank Commander, 339
Taylor, Mildred, 296–98
The Tempering, 273–74
That's One Ornery Orphan, 42
Thee, Hannah!, 96
They Had a Horse, 106
The Third Eye, 170–71
The 13th Member, 168–69
Thomas. See *Beyond the Weir Bridge*
A Thousand for Sicily, 306
Through the Fire, 56
Thunder at Valmy. See *Victory at Valmy*
Thunder in the Sky, 243, 245
Time of Trial, 59

To Ravensrigg, 57–58
Tomahawk Border, 281
Tomahawks and Trouble, 282
Trail Through Danger, 283
The Traitors, 119
Trease, Geoffrey, 302–11
The Treasure of Topo-el-Bampo, 218,
    224–25
Tree of Freedom, 71, 72
Treece, Henry, 311–19
Treegate's Raiders, 345–46
The Trumpeter of Krakow, 186–87
Trumpets in the West, 310, 311
Tulku, 102–3
Turi's Poppa, 98
Turn Homeward, Hannalee, 39
The 290, 221–22

Uchida, Yoshiko, 321–24
The Untold Tale, 150, 153

The Valley of the Shadow, 156
Victory at Valmy, 305
Viking's Dawn, 314
Viking's Sunset, 315
Vining, Elizabeth Gray, 328–30
Vinland the Good. See *Westward to
    Vinland*
A Voice in the Night, 310

Wait for Me, Watch for Me, Eula Bee,
    38–39, 40
Walk the World's Rim, 20
The Walls of Athens, 234
War Comes to Willy Freeman,
    80–81
War Dog, 312–13
The War Party, 280
War without Friends, 146–47
Warrior Scarlet, 287, 293
Wayah of the Real People, 280–81
Web of Traitors, 303
Welch, Ronald, 334–39
West with the White Chiefs, 144
Westall, Robert, 340–42
Westward to Vinland, 315
What Happened in Hamelin, 272–73,
    274

When the Drums Beat, 310
Whistle for the Crossing, 96
The White Nights of St. Petersburg, 306–7
Who Comes to King's Mountain?, 35–36
Who Is Carrie?, 81
Wibberley, Leonard, 343–51
The Wild Children, 162–63
Wildcat under Glass, 364
Wilderness Clearing, 106–7
Wilderness Journey, 281–82
Willard, Barbara, 351–57
The Wind Eye, 340–41
Windfall. See *Sea Fever*
Winter Danger, 282
The Winter Hero, 82–83
The Winter When Time Was Frozen, 239
Witch Dog, 33
The Witch of Blackbird Pond, 277–78, 279

Witches' Children, 77–78
The Witch's Brat, 292–93
The Wonderful Winter, 75–76
The Wool-Pack. See *The Merchant's Mark*
Word to Caesar. See *Message to Hadrian*
Words by Heart, 267–68
The Wound of Peter Wayne, 350
The Writing on the Hearth, 141

The Year of the Bloody Sevens, 281
Yep, Laurence, 359–61
Young Mark: The Story of a Venture, 6, 7, 8
The Young Pretenders, 248

Zei, Aliki, 363–65
Zia, 224
Zoar Blue, 156–57
Zulu Warrior, 338, 339

About the Author

LYNDA G. ADAMSON is Professor of English at Prince George's College,
Maryland. She has contributed articles on various subjects to literary journals.

DISCARD